D1532355

MODERN REAL ESTATE FINANCE

MODERN REAL ESTATE FINANCE

FINANCE

Third Edition

by

William Atteberry

©COPYRIGHT 1972, 1976, 1980, GRID PUBLISHING, INC.
  4666 Indianola Avenue
  Columbus, Ohio 43214
ALL RIGHTS RESERVED. No part of this publication may
be reproduced, stored in a retrieval system, or transmitted, in
any form or by any means, electronic, mechanical, photo-
copying, recording or otherwise, without prior written permission of the copyright holder.
Printed in the United States

1 2 3 4 5 6 ☒ 5 4 3 2 1 0

Library of Congress Cataloging in Publication Data

Atteberry, William.
    Modern real estate finance.

    (Grid series in finance & real estate)
    Includes index.
    1. Real estate business—United States—Finance.   I.
Title.
HD1375.A88 1980   332.7'2'0973   79-24627
ISBN O-88244-212-0

332.72
A883m3

TABLE OF CONTENTS

INTRODUCTION

Real estate finance is one of today's most rapidly changing industries. In fact, the real estate finance expert of the 1950s would have an extremely difficult time understanding today's principals and techniques.

Twenty years ago, condominiums could not be built in most states; real estate investment trusts, as we know them today, were just being established; Federal National Mortgage Association was a government agency, not a private corporation as it is today; Government National Mortgage Association and the Federal Home Loan Mortgage Corporation were not even contemplated; government housing programs were handled by the Housing and Home Finance Agency; the Department of Housing and Urban Development had not yet been formed; government subsidizing of home ownership was unheard of; state housing agencies were practically unknown; life insurance companies were heavily investing in FHA and VA loans; private mortgage insurance was confined to one company and was not universally used; 66 2/3 percent loan-to-value income property loans and 75 percent single family conventional loans were the rule not the exception; mortgage interest rates in excess of 7 percent were rare; and wrap-around mortgages, joint ventures, and sale-leasebacks were virtually untried financing methods.

Not only has real estate financing drastically changed since 1960, but it is playing an even greater role in the life of every American. One need only look around to witness the tremendous impact of real estate financing upon our society. Without our system of real estate financing, there would exist fewer office buildings, shopping centers, and homes. In fact, the success of the nations housing programs for the future is heavily dependent upon maintaining very liberal real estate financing terms.

Today in many foreign countries a family purchasing a home must pay at least half the purchase price in cash and the amount financed must be repaid normally within ten to fifteen years. In the United States, however, a low to middle-income family can purchase a home with zero to $200.00 cash, and most homes of $50,000 and under can be purchased by the majority of Americans with as little as $2,000 to $2,500 cash.

Keeping pace with and learning the particulars of all these spectacular developments and financing innovations has been a great task for those involved day-to-day with real estate finance. Thus, the confusion of the students and laymen who are only on occasion concerned with the subject is understandable.

This text is written with the purpose of providing the reader with a fundamental knowledge of real estate instruments and financial institutions.

Throughout the text, words such as "primarily," "frequently," "occasionally," and the like are used. This is due to the fact that real estate finance cannot in any way be considered an exact science, for exceptions to the rule always seem to be present. State laws vary and are ever changing. Lender techniques vary with the passage of time. New methods of finance are constantly being promulgated and the federal government is frequently and dramatically making itself felt in the field. Thus, the text is compiled and presented in a manner which notes the more common methods, laws, and techniques while using words and phrases that will alert the reader to the fact that variations of a real estate financing transaction are possible. Essentially, the reader should acquire a basic knowledge of the "tools of the trade" but while doing so should give thought to (a) what new methods and techniques can be developed, (b) how many different ways financing for a specific project can be arranged, and (c) what financing alternatives can be made available to a borrower desiring to enter into a real estate transaction.

In presenting the subject material, the text begins with a discussion of the basic legal aspects and finance techniques of real estate lending. Such a background is fundamental to a complete understanding of the most elementary types of real estate financing. Next, the mortgage market, fund flows, and lender decision-making processes are discussed in order to provide the reader with the hows and whys of mortgage investment policies. Then the major lenders (originators of mortgage loans) and investors (purchasers of mortgage loans originated by others) in the field of real estate finance are identified and discussed with emphasis on their method of operation, the mortgage loans favored by each, how their lending and/or investing is regulated, and loan terms and conditions demanded.

The latter part of the next text deals with government involvement and participation in mortgage financing. Here the many recent and significant changes in this area are detailed and their impact stressed.

The final chapter deals with private mortgage insurance companies and their purpose and impact upon real estate financing.

MAJOR INSTRUMENTS OF REAL ESTATE FINANCING

The instruments used in financing real estate are primarily the following: (1) the *note* or bond evidencing the obligation of the borrower to repay the lender, and (2) the *mortgage* or other security instrument subjecting the real estate to the payment of the indebtedness.

MORTGAGES

A real estate mortgage is defined as "a pledge or security of property or an interest therein, created by formal written agreement, for the repayment of a money debt or the performance of some other act."

Interests which can be secured by a mortgage includes any interest in real estate such as rental income, dower interest, estate for years, or leaseholds, in addition to fee ownership. Mortgages can also be used to protect obligations such as a bank line of credit or performance of a contract.

LIEN AND TITLE THEORIES

Mortgages can vest in the mortgagee (lender) title to property, or constitute a lien on property, depending on state law. The difference in viewpoint between these theories is of greatest importance with respect to the mortgagee's right to possession and rents of the mortgaged property, particularly in the event of default.

In title theory states the mortgagee on signing of the mortgage acquires the right to take possession and collect rents. In lien theory states the mortgagee obtains the right to acquire property through foreclosure of the mortgage with the mortgagor (borrower) retaining title to the property and the right to possession and rents until the foreclosure deed has been issued to the mortgagee. The lien theory is the more modern view and prevails in all the western states as well as many others.

A few states, such as Ohio, take an intermediate position and provide for mortgagee possession only upon default.

It is important to note that possession in all cases does not mean ownership. Foreclosure is always required for the mortgagee to take ownership.

Chart 3-1 in Chapter 3 lists all states and the theories that prevail in them.

Different legal results arise from the consideration of a mortgage as a lien or conveyance of title. These results arise only when the mortgage instrument itself does not contain an answer to a specific problem. When the problem is answered by the mortgage instrument, the mortgage provision giving the answer is controlling as long as it does not violate public policy.

For example, A borrows money from B to construct an apartment complex. A gives a mortgage to B. If the mortgage does not recite who has the rights to rents from the property, then how is the right to rents resolved? If the mortgage is made in a title theory state, then B has the rights to rents as that right accrues to the mortgagee upon execution of the mortgage. In lien theory states, A would retain rights to the rents until a default occurred and foreclosure ensured.

In intermediate theory states, legislation or court decision give answers to some problems not covered in the mortgage as though the mortgage was a conveyance in others as though it was a lien.

MORTGAGE REQUIREMENTS

In Ohio, California, Florida, and several other states, laws have been passed permitting the recording of an instrument (a master mortgage) containing a form or forms of covenants, conditions, obligations, powers, and other clauses normally contained in a mortgage. The provisions of the master mortgage may be incorporated by reference in any subsequent mortgage of real property located in the county where the master mortgage is recorded by stating in the subsequent mortgage the recording data of the master mortgage and the parts of the master mortgage which are to be included in the subsequent mortgage. A copy of the master mortgage is furnished to the borrower. This method saves on recording costs, particularly when income property mortgages are concerned.

Minimum mortgage requirements:

1. All mortgages should be in writing.
2. All parties thereto must have contractual capacity; for example, they must be mentally competent and of legal age.
3. The interest in the property being mortgaged should be specified; for example, leasehold, fee, rental income, etc.
4. A description of the note or obligation secured should appear in the mortgage. Most mortgagees prefer to make reference to a "note of even date" and omit the specific terms of the note, particularly any mention as to interest rate. The omission of the interest rate has the purpose of preventing the practice of "raiding." When mortgage interest rates fall, mortgage solicitors may search the mortgage records to find those which are likely candidates for refinancing. The solicitor will then contact the mortgagor and try to arrange a new mortgage at a lower interest rate. Thus

one lender's mortgage portfolio could easily be depleted and another's filled.

5. Words of grant or a granting clause must be contained in the mortgage even though such a clause will be tailored to reflect the lien or title nature of the mortgage; for example, "Mortgagor hereby mortgages and warrants to Mortgagee the following described real property," or "Grantor hereby grants, bargains, sells and conveys to Grantee, its successors and assigns, forever, the following described real estate."

6. A legal description of the mortgaged property is essential, and must be included in the mortgage.

7. Any covenants and contractual agreements must be included. In many instances a reference to the note is sufficient to include all terms and contractual agreements recited in the note in the mortgage. If the mortgage secures the performance under a building loan agreement, that fact should be noted in the mortgage and such is the requirement in many states in order to establish lien priority over mechanic liens.

8. The mortgage must be signed by the mortgagor and, if the mortgagor is an individual, the mortgagor's spouse.

9. The mortgage must be acknowledged, delivered to the mortgagee and recorded.

Other mortgage requirements are:

1. *Seal*—In some states seals are still required as to individuals and corporations. In such states the signatures of individuals should have "L.S." or "seal" beside their names. Similar corporate executions should be made with the corporate seal affixed to the instrument.

2. *Witnesses*—Some states (e.g., California) require no witnesses to a mortgage instrument, while other states (e.g., Ohio) require as many as two. State requirements for witnesses, and in fact for all formal mortgage requirements are to be strictly adhered to.

3. *Mortgage Recordation Tax*—Where required, a recordation tax, in some cases both local and state, must be paid at time of recordation. In some states where such a tax is required, it must be paid before the mortgage is valid.

4. *Time of Recordation*—In general, the first mortgage required has priority over all other subsequently recorded mortgages. In the case of simultaneously recorded mortgages neither mortgage can claim advantage unless one of the instruments contains a provision or designation that makes it subject to the other.

5. *Local Provisions*—As alluded to above, state and local provisions should be reviewed for specific requirements. In some states an affidavit as to consideration must be filed with the mortgage; in some an affidavit that the instrument has been prepared by an attorney admitted to practice in state must appear on the instrument; and, in others, the residence address of the mortgagor must appear on the instrument.

MORTGAGE CLAUSES

Some common mortgage clauses used in addition to the minimum requirements are worthy of discussion.

ACCELERATION

The acceleration clause, which usually appears only in the note instrument, not in the mortgage instrument securing payment of the note, allows the holder of the note, the lender, to accelerate the maturity of the obligation upon a default by the maker of the note, the borrower. In the absence of this provision, the lender's only recourses in the event of a default are to sue on the note or foreclose. In either case, the lender may claim only that portion of the debt presently due, rather than the outstanding balance of the debt. Thus, the lender would be faced with a multiplicity of suits rather than a single and final action.

If default be made in the payment of any installment of principal and/or interest when due under this Note or in the performance of any of the terms, covenants, conditions or warranties contained in the Mortgage securing payment hereof, at the option of the holder of this Note, the entire principal sum evidenced hereby and secured by said Mortgage together with interest accrued thereon, without notice, shall immediately become due and payable. Failure to exercise this option shall not constitute a waiver of the right to exercise same in the event of any subsequent default.

INTEREST ESCALATION

Two types of interest escalation are quite common in notes. The first relates to notes in general and provides for the rate of interest to increase upon default to the highest legal rate allowable in the jurisdiction in which the note was executed. For example, if the legal rate is 8 percent and the note bears interest at 7 percent, a one percent escalation would be possible upon default. In cases where the maker of the note is not subject to the legal interest limitation, the escalation may be to a definite rate in excess of the legal rate. The purpose of such an escalation provision is to penalize the maker for defaulting. However, the practical aspect is that a borrower who cannot meet the note payments and save his equity in property is not likely to be swayed by the possibility of an increase in interest rate.

In the event of any such default and upon acceleration of the entire indebtedness aforesaid, interest thereon shall accrue thereafter at the rate set forth herein or at the legal rate, whichever is higher.

Another type of escalation is utilized in short term land, land development, and construction loans. Commercial banks, savings and loan associations, mortgage companies, mortgage investment trusts and other suppliers of mortgage funds must pay for the funds they loan. Commercial banks and savings and loan associations pay interest on savings accounts, mortgage companies pay interest on commercial paper or establish compensating balances and pay interest on bank warehouse lines, and mortgage investment trusts must pay dividends to their beneficial interest holders. The yield (profit) to these lenders on any loan is determined by the spread (differential) between their acquisition cost of funds and the interest rate for which these funds are loaned to others. To maintain the spread or differential between acquisition costs and loan charge during the term of the loan, an escalation of interest rate tied to a standard, usually the "prime rate" (that interest rate charged by commercial banks to their most preferred borrowers) is used. The "prime rate" does not always affect the acquisition cost of funds, but it is an accepted indicator of the cost of money. It is important to note that escalation clauses such as the one below provide for increases in the interest rate, but not for decreases.

> The rate of interest expressed herein shall not be decreased, but at the option of the holder hereof shall increase in relation to the "Prime Rate." Therefore, if the prime rate advances over its present level of 8-1/2%, the rate of interest provided for herein shall advance in the same amount. The prime rate shall be the rate so announced by any one of the following: First National City Bank, Irving Trust, Chase Manhattan or Chemical Bank (all of New York City), the highest such rate in effect at any one time by any of said banks to be deemed controlling.

PREPAYMENT

Unless specifically set forth in the note instrument, the borrower has no right to pre-pay the indebtedness, but must make the installment payments as set forth in the note for the term stated. Therefore, certain prepayment privileges will be provided in mortgage notes on long-term loans. The prepayment provision will most likely meet halfway the lender's desire to have its funds invested for a fixed period of time, in order to avoid an unanticipated reinvestment problem, at a determined rate, and the borrower's desire to be able to prepay the obligation at any time. Certainly, when interest rates are high, lenders want to prevent the borrower from prepaying (or at least extract from them a significant charge in such event) in order to forestall refinancing when interest rates drop. When interest rates are low and a rise anticipated, lenders are inclined to be more favorable toward prepayment and the charge extracted from borrowers for prepayment.

The first sample provision below does not allow the borrower an out through foreclosure. The second allows partial prepayment during the first ten years and thereafter full privilege, but with a penalty.

> In the event of default hereunder, a tender of payment of the amount necessary to satisfy the entire indebtedness evidenced hereby, made at any time prior to sale under foreclosure of the Mortgage securing this Note, will constitute an evasion of the prepayment provisions hereunder and such payment will, therefore, to the extent permitted by law, include the premium required under the prepayment privilege or if at that time there is no privilege of prepayment, then such payment will, to the extent permitted by law, include a premium of five (5%) percent of the then principal balance.
>
> The privilege is reserved to make, on any installment payment due, additional principal payment in an amount which is in accordance with the plan of amortization of this indebtedness, the total thus paid in any calendar year not to exceed five (5%) percent of the face amount of this note; to pay the loan in full on any installment payment date on or after ten (10) years from the date that required amortization begins, on sixty (60) days' written notice and on payment of three per centum (3%) of

such balance as a prepayment fee; each year thereafter such prepayment fee will be reduced at the rate of one-half per centum (1/2%) per year.

LATE PAYMENT

In order to encourage prompt payment of loan installments when due and save the lender accounting and collection problems, a late charge is usually assessed for delinquent payments. A clause stating this penalty is usually inserted in the note.

In the event that any installment shall become overdue for a period in excess of fifteen days, a "late charge" of Five Per Cent of the amount overdue may be charged by the holder hereof for the purpose of defraying the expense incident to handling such delinquent payment.

COGNOVIT

The cognovit or confessed judgment provision when contained in a note allows the lender upon a default to obtain judgment on a speedy basis (and a lien against *all* real property owned by the borrower) by simply filing an affidavit that default has taken place. The borrower, in order to set aside the judgment, must come into court and prove that there was no default or present a valid defense. Without the cognovit provision the borrower will have his day in court before a judgment is granted.

In some states this provision is ineffective and in others its presence will make the note unenforceable.

The undersigned, and if there be more than one, each of the undersigned, authorizes any attorney at law to appear in any court of record in the United States, after the indebtedness becomes due, whether by lapse of time, acceleration, or otherwise, and waive the issuance and service of process and confess judgment against any one or more or all of the undersigned in favor of the holder hereof for the amount then appearing due hereunder, together with interest at the rate herein mentioned, costs of suit, and thereupon, to waive and release all errors in the judgment so confessed, all right and benefit of appeal, and all proceedings to set aside, vacate, open, or stay any such judgment, or any execution issued thereon.

EQUITY PARTICIPATION

Rapid inflation and the excessively long periods of "tight money" experienced during the latter half of the 1960s gave birth to long-term lenders' participation in the cash flow from income-producing properties, notably apartment developments and shopping centers. By such participation, lenders feel they can obtain a hedge against inflation and increase their total yield on the loan.

Two major types of participation are in vogue. The most common one, shown below, provides for participation in gross rents over a fixed base (usually 85 to 90 percent of project gross rental potential). The problem which arises with this type of provision is that rentals may be increased only to keep pace with rising property taxes and operating expenses as opposed to an increase reflecting a greater demand for rental units. Thus, the increases for taxes and operating expenses will at some point trigger participation by the lender and thereby decrease the return to the borrower. If this situation perpetuates itself, the borrower will eventually have his return reduced substantially. Therefore, care should be taken to insure that the lender's participation, if such a provision is contained in the note and mortgage, covers only increases in rent due to market conditions and not increases in rent due to adjustments to meet higher operating costs and taxes.

The other common type of participation provides for from one to three percent, usually two percent, participation in gross rents, and is thereby immediately effective.

> The undersigned agree to deliver to the holder, on or before the first day of April, 1976, and on or before the first day of April in each year thereafter, a statement certified to by an independent Certified Public Accountant showing the gross receipts for the preceding calendar year, and promise to pay to the holder as additional interest, on or before the due date for delivery of each such statement, Ten per centum (10%) of the amount by which the gross receipts for the preceding calendar year exceed the sum of Two Hundred Eighty-five Thousand Dollars ($285,000.00). For the purposes of this paragraph, the term "gross receipt" shall mean the gross amount of payments made as rent, fees, charges or otherwise for the use or occupancy of any part of the property conveyed or encumbered as security for the payment of this Note or for any services, equipment or furnishings provided in connection with such use or occupancy, whether such payments are to be made to the undersigned or to any other person or entity whatsoever, excepting payments made to a sublessor unrelated to and unaffiliated with the undersigned and who leased from the undersigned a portion of said property for the purpose of occupying the same. Neither the obligation to pay additional interest nor the manner herein prescribed for the computation of the amount of such additional interest shall constitute the holder and the undersigned as partners or joint adventurers, and the term "payments" shall include cash and the cash value of any property or other consideration given in lieu of and in addition to cash. The obligation of the undersigned to make the payment of the additional interest as provided in this paragraph is expressly limited so that the aggregate amount of all interest on this note charged to the undersigned or accruing hereunder for any year shall never exceed the rate of Eighteen per centum (18%).

SUBORDINATION

When a builder purchases a large tract of land for development he will frequently attempt to convert a portion of the seller's equity to his advantage when seeking financing for land development and construction. The builder accomplishes this by giving a purchase money mortgage with a subordination right contained therein. For example, a tract is purchased for a price of $100,000 with $10,000 down and a $90,000 purchase money mortgage. The builder then obtains financing of $500,000 for development and construction. The lender requires a first lien position for its $500,000 and the builder provides this by enacting the purchase money mortgage "subordination" provision and having it placed in a subordinated or second lien position. To the lender, the builder has $100,000 equity in the property. Thus, the builder has used the seller's equity to his advantage.

Normally, the seller would charge a premium for subordination or request that additional principal payments be made by the builder at time of subordination. Nevertheless a seller with a tract of land often cannot find a buyer and/or the price desired for it unless he makes the deal attractive. Subordination is one way to make the property saleable. With a substantial builder the method is reasonably safe and usually produces, for the seller, a sale at an attractive price and, for the builder, a building situation wherein little front money is required.

Under these circumstances principal due on the construction loan and purchase money mortgage would be reduced, and in time paid off, as houses are built and sold.

Mortgagee shall, upon written request from Mortgagor, subordinate the lien of this Mortgage on any lot or lots created by the subdivision of the premises to the lien of any Mortgage given with respect to such lot or lots to secure a bona fide construction loan or loans from a recognized lending institution approved by Mortgagee (which approval shall not be unreasonably withheld).

RELEASE

After execution of a mortgage, the borrower may subdivide his property and/or be required to dedicate a portion thereof to the city or state. In addition, and most frequently in the development of a tract of land, easements must be granted for utility installation purposes. Therefore, provisions should be made in cases of mortgages on undeveloped property for the release of the mortgage lien as to such dedications or grants of easements.

Mortgagee shall, upon written request from Mortgagor, execute and join in the granting of any easements, rights of way and dedications as may be necessary and/or required by local, county, state or federal authorities or public utility companies for the purpose of acquiring and obtaining public utilities, sanitary and/or storm sewer, water, gas, electric and telephone facilities, upon, over and under the premises, and shall execute and join in any plats of subdivision so long as said subdivision meets the requirements of the county or applicable governing authorities.

DEFEASANCE

The mortgage instrument used in title theory states should always contain a "defeasance clause" giving the borrower the right to redeem his property provided payment is made in full of the obligation to the lender.

In some jurisdictions the defeasance provision may be contained in a separate instrument. If this is the case, the separate instrument should be recorded with the mortgage.

NOW, THEREFORE, if Grantors shall pay to Grantee the said sums of money described in the note secured hereby and the interest thereon, in the manner and at the times mentioned in said note, and any and all other sums which may become payable by Grantors hereunder, and shall fully keep and perform the terms, covenants, conditions, and agreements hereof by Grantors to be kept and performed, then this mortgage and the eatate hereby granted shall cease, determine, and be void, and said mortgage shall thereupon be released by the Grantee at the cost and expense of Grantors (all claims for statutory penalties, in case of Grantee's failure to release, being hereby waived); otherwise, this mortgage shall remain in full force and effect.

DUE-ON-SALE

A popular mortgagee requirement is one that restricts the mortgagor from selling his property unless the mortgage is paid in full. This provision has two main purposes:

a) It allows the mortgagee an opportunity to approve the credit of any new purchaser.

b) It gives the mortgagee the right to force refinancing or increase the interest rate on the mortgage, thereby upgrading the rate of return on the mortgagee mortgage portfolio.

A due-on-sale provision may read as follows:

If all or any part of the Property or an interest therein is sold or transferred by Borrower without Lender's prior written consent, excluding (a) the creation of a lien or encumbrance subordinate to this mortgage, (b) the creation of a purchase money security interest for household appliances, (c) a transfer by devise, descent or by operation of law upon the death of a joint tenant or (d) the grant of any leasehold interest of three years or less not containing an option to purchase, Lender may, at Lender's option, declare all the sums secured by this mortgage to be immediately due and payable. Lender shall have waived such option to accelerate if, prior to the sale or transfer, Lender and the person to whom the Property is to be sold or transferred reach agreement in writing that the credit of such person is satisfactory to Lender and that the interest payable on the sums secured by this mortage shall be at such rate as Lender shall request. If Lender has waived the option to accelerate provided in this paragraph and if Borrower's successor in interest has executed a written assumption agreement accepted in writing by Lender, Lender shall release Borrower from all obligations under this mortgage and the Note.

As might be anticipated, restrictions of this nature have been the subject of much ongoing legal controversy and in some states the validity of the provision has been questioned.

A due-on-sale clause is usually found in conventional mortgage loan instruments such as the FNMA-FHLMC standard mortgage forms. The clause, however, is not found in FHA and VA mortgage loan instruments.

CLASSIFICATION OF MORTGAGES

Mortgages vary with respect to both type of security and provision for repayment. One type of mortgage gives the lender a first claim on the security while another allows for only a secondary claim. A mortgage may secure the repayment of funds advanced to build improvements or may be given to secure repayment of monies lent to purchase real estate. Regarding repayment, provision may be made for a lump sum repayment by a specific date or repayment in installments. The more common mortgages, classified as to security and repayment are discussed below.

DEED OF TRUST

Several states, particularly those where the lien theory prevails, use what is called a deed of trust. Whereas a mortgage is a two-party agreement, a deed of trust is a tri-party agreement. Under a deed of trust, the borrower conveys title to a trustee who holds title for the benefit of the borrower and lender. The trust deed contains the terms of the trust agreement and sets forth the trustee's powers.

The main advantage of the deed of trust is the power given to the trustee in the event of default to foreclose the borrower's equity by a sale of the property at public auction, after proper advertisement, rather than taking a formal court action.

Deeds of trust have a distinct disadvantage in that the trustee, or as in some states trustees, must execute a reconveyance once the debt has been paid. This can present problems in locating individual trustees and having to produce the cancelled original note in order to obtain a reconveyance.

FIRST MORTGAGE

This mortgage constitutes the first lien on a property. The holder of this mortgage must have his claims satisfied before the claims of all other junior mortgages.

JUNIOR MORTGAGE

Whenever a prior mortgage lien exists on a property, and the owner desires more financing to bridge the gap between the amount of money required to purchase a property in excess of what the first mortgage provides, the owner sometimes gives an additional mortgage or mortgages to make up the difference. These are called *junior mortgages*. Other uses include cases where the prior mortgages have been paid down and the owner's equity has increased and the owner desires additional funds and gives an additional mortgage or mortgages.

Since prior mortgages have priority as to payment, the risk of default by the mortgagor on the junior mortgage is generally increased; and, hence, the junior mortgage holder will demand a higher rate of interest.

CONSTRUCTION LOAN MORTGAGE

This type of mortgage secures a loan made to a developer or builder in installments as portions of the project are completed. These completed portions then become subject to the terms of the mortgage. Initially the only collateral for a construction loan is land, but as construction progresses the collateral is increased in the form of structures built upon the land.

Disbursements on construction loans for commercial projects are usually not staged, but are made monthly on the basis of percentage of work in place and complete.

The theory of construction loan mortgages is that the lender disburses funds at such time or times when his security has been increased and made subject to the mortgage.

PURCHASE MONEY MORTGAGE

This mortgage is given by the purchaser to the seller for all or part of the purchase price of the land.

This is an alternative means of financing between two individuals which excludes a possible third party, usually a financial institution. It might be used to enable a purchaser with less equity funds available than required by a financial institution to still purchase the property.

The importance of a purchase money mortgage is that, when it is executed and recorded simultaneously with the deed conveying title, it takes precedence over all debts and judgments against the purchaser and other mortgages on the same property previously given by the purchaser.

OPEN END MORTGAGE

An open end mortgage contains a provision which allows the mortgagor to borrow additional funds under the terms of the original mortgage or as stipulated in the mortgage agreement.

Under this plan the mortgagor can obtain additional funds for property improvements or for other uses. Repayment of the additional borrowing can then be amortized by a relatively small addition, if any, to the monthly payments required under the mortgage.

The problem encountered with open end mortgages is the securing of future advances without running the risk of making such advances junior to intervening liens. In the majority of states an obligatory future advance under an open end mortgage will prime intervening liens.

The prevailing theory seems to turn on the obligatory or non-obligatory nature of the future advance. If non-obligatory, the consensus is that the mortgagee must search the title to the property to insure that there are no junior liens; otherwise, newly created junior liens will intervene. A few states go so far as to require a title search prior to an obligatory advance in order to secure the priority of the advance, while others give priority to non-obligatory future advances made in face of junior liens.

PARTICIPATING MORTGAGE

This is a method whereby many investors pool funds to lend on real estate. In return, they receive certificates of beneficial interest evidencing the extent of participation in the mortgage.

This type of mortgage is gaining prominence today particularly in view of recent legislation authorizing the Government National Mortgage Association to guarantee the prompt payment of principal and interest on securities issued against pools of FHA-insured and VA-guaranteed mortgages. The GNMA-mortgage-backed security is discussed in detail in a later chapter.

PACKAGE MORTGAGE

A package mortgage is special in that it represents not only a lien on real property, but also on certain fixtures which are attached to the property. Examples of the fixtures are rugs, ranges, dishwashers and air conditioning equipment.

The advantage of this mortgage type to the mortgagor is that he can finance these fixtures over the life of the mortgage instead of resorting to an installment sales arrangement for a shorter period. This may enable him to purchase a home and furnishings that he might not have been able to finance had he tried to finance them separately.

The advantage to the builder is that it should stimulate sales.

This method of financing has been used to a great extent in income property loans where carpets, dishwashers, ranges, refrigerators are normally considered part of the security.

VARIABLE RATE MORTGAGE

Due to the desire on the part of lending institutions to maintain a spread between their borrowing cost (cost of attracting savings) and their lending cost, particularly in view of continuing inflation and periods of extremely tight money, recent years have seen a movement toward a mortgage instrument that would allow the interest rate to vary, usually between a set high and low interest figure. Such a mortgage instrument is termed a "variable rate mortgage", and has met with great success in Great Britain while only recently being contemplated for wide use in the United States. The rate on the mortgage usually varies according to some index such as passbook interest rates, cost of living index, or the prime lending rate of the mortgagee. These mortgages make lending more palatable for savings institutions that traditionally borrow short and lend long, but the concept has yet to be fully accepted by a public that has been conditioned to fixed rate mortgage borrowing.

GRADUATED PAYMENT MORTGAGE

Graduated Payment Mortgages (GPM) provide for lower initial monthly payments in the early years of a loan with payments rising gradually for a set period of years before leveling out to a constant amount for the remaining term of the mortgage.

BLANKET MORTGAGE

A blanket mortgage is a form of financing which usually applies to a situation where many parcels of land are secured by one mortgage.

ROLLOVER MORTGAGE

Also known as a Canadian Rollover, this mortgage is written for a specific period of time (normally five years). At the end of the time period, the loan secured by the rollover mortgage is rewritten at current interest rates. Like a variable rate mortgage, the rollover mortgage is used to reduce the period of time that the lender is locked into a fixed rate of interest.

REVERSE ANNUITY MORTGAGE

This mortgage is an outgrowth of the inflationary experience of the late 1970's. It is a method whereby the homeowner can take out fixed monthly payments for life, i.e., borrow against the increasing value of the real estate. Upon the death of the homeowner or the sale of the property, the lender recaptures the equity paid out during the mortgage term.

WRAP-AROUND MORTGAGE

This mortgage has been used in Canada quite successfully and is now coming into vogue in the United States. It is thoroughly discussed in Chapter 4.

Mortgages can also be classed as to repayment provisions:

STRAIGHT TERM MORTGAGE
1. Is of short duration, usually three to five years.
2. Has no provision for amortization of principal.
3. Requires interest payments at stated intervals; usually monthly or quarterly.
4. Provides for all unpaid principal and accrued interest to be paid at maturity.

Sometimes another term mortgage is by necessity negotiated upon maturity of the straight term mortgage.

PARTIALLY AMORTIZED MORTGAGE
1. Provides for periodic installments of interest to be paid.
2. Requires partial amortization of principal with a balloon payment (large sum) due at maturity.

Sometimes another mortgage may be negotiated at maturity covering the unamortized principal balance outstanding.

AMORTIZED MORTGAGE
1. Is most frequently used in residential loans.
2. Has two typical amortization patterns:
   a. Direct reduction of principal wherein constant payment of principal is made plus interest on the declining principal balance.

b. level annunity or self-liquidating requiring constant payments of principal and interest. Each installment is applied first to the payment of accrued interest and then to the reduction of principal.

MORTGAGES TERMED GUARANTEED OR CONVENTIONAL

A *guaranteed* mortgage is one which is insured or guaranteed as to payment by an agency of the federal government; principally the Federal Housing Administration (FHA) or the Veterans Administration (VA). All other mortgages are classified as *conventional*. Some conventional mortgages are insured by private mortgage insurance companies. Nevertheless, privately insured mortgages are still deemed conventional mortgages.

Both FHA and VA insure or guarantee approved lenders against losses arising out of the failure of a borrower to repay the principal borrowed and secured by a mortgage. Under the FHA program a premium is paid by the borrower for the insurance. No premium is charged for the VA guaranty. The insurance or guaranty given provides an incentive to the lender to make a loan for a longer term, with less down payment, and for a lower interest rate than that the lender would normally make without the insurance or guaranty. Both FHA and VA require that the borrower be capable of repaying the loan and that the property secured meet certain minimum standards.

IMPORTANT ASPECTS OF MORTGAGE DEBT

The nature of the mortgagor and mortgagee's respective interests and their rights to possession of the mortgaged property and collection of rents were discussed earlier in this chapter under the heading "Lien and Title Theories". In this section, other important aspects of the mortgage transaction will be covered.

EFFECT OF LEASES

When a lease is entered into prior to the mortgage, the *mortgagee,* if entitled to possession of the mortgaged premises, may demand the rent. The *lessee,* after notice from the mortgagee is liable to the mortgagee for all unpaid rent, and for all rent to become due. The rights of the lessee to possession under a lease prior to the mortgage cannot be upset, unless the lease contains a provision that subjects it to all mortgages on the land.

Once a mortgage is executed and recorded, the mortgagor may not make a lease which will give the lessee greater rights than he, the mortgagor, possesses. A tenant under a lease made subsequent to a mortgage may lose his rights to possession after the mortgagor defaults. The tenant may, however, avoid eviction by "attorning" to the mortgagee. That is, by recognizing the mortgagee as landlord. Attornment establishes a new tenancy and acts as a defense against the mortgagor's claim for rent. In any event, such creation of a new tenancy terminates the existing lease and the lessee becomes a month-to-month tenant of the mortgagee. Hence a lease made subsequent to a mortgage is in the same position as a junior lien and may be cancelled by foreclosure (see Mortgagor's and Mortgagee's Rights in the Event of Default, Chapter 3, supra). Thus the mortgagee whose mortgage is prior to a lease may decide to either keep or cancel the tenancy. It is possible, however, for an attornment agreement to be entered into at the outside whereby the mortgagee agrees from the onset to honor the lease arrangement in the event a subsequent mortgagor default and the tenant also agree to attorn to the mortgagee if an event of default occurs.

REPAIRS AND IMPROVEMENTS

If the mortgagee comes into possession of the mortgaged property he may expend and recover in a foreclosure action all costs of necessary repairs made by him. Expenditures for improvements, however, may be recovered only if they are necessary for the proper enjoyment of the premises, not if they are merely to make the property more enjoyable.

INSURANCE

The mortgagor has an insurable interest in property mortgaged by him and this interest continues until his right to redeem the property after foreclosure is barred. Insurance may be obtained for the full value of the property irrespective of the mortgage amount. If the insurance is taken out in compliance with a mortgage provision to that effect, then the mortgagee has an equitable lien on insurance proceeds to the extent of his lien. But, if the mortgagor takes out insurance for his own account, without any agreement with the mortgagee, then the mortgagee can exercise no claim on insurance proceeds. Hence, the mortgagor should always require the mortgagor to keep the property insured with policies naming the mortgagee in the loss payable clause.

The mortgagee also has an insurable interest in the property and may insure the full value of the property. Where there is no provision requiring the mortgagor to insure, insurance obtained by the mortgagee is for his own account. In the event of a loss the mortgagee is entitled to the insurance proceeds, but must apply them to the mortgage debt. The mortgagee is not allowed to collect both the insurance proceeds and the mortgage debt.

PRIORITY OF LIEN

When a number of liens are placed against a property the general rule is that the first lien in time is the first in right. For example, mortgage lien A is recorded against Blackacre in 1974, then mortgage lien B is recorded in 1975 and subsequently judgment lien C in 1976. Priority of these liens would be A, then B and finally C. Hence, the lien created by A must be discharged in full before B, and B must be discharged in full before C. In the event of foreclosure of lien A, liens B and C may be completely extinguished. (Priority of liens with regard to foreclosure is discussed further in Chapter 3).

FUTURE ADVANCES

In some instances a mortgage will provide for advances under the mortgage at times subsequent to recordation. Most common is the construction loan mortgage which is disbursed in increments as construction work progresses. The question that arises in future advanced situations is the priority of the advances over other liens which may attach to the property before all advances are made. Generally, the rights of junior lien holders center around the obligatory or non-obligatory nature of the advances and the state in which the mortgage is recorded.

Generally, a mortgage which provides for obligatory advances of mortgage funds by the mortgagee is a first lien to the extent of the total mortgage obligation irrespective of when it is disbursed and regardless of the mortgagee's knowledge of subsequent liens on the property. For example, A agrees to lend B the sum of $500,000 to be disbursed in five equal draws as construction of a building progresses. A's loan is secured by a mortgage on B's property. After $200,000 is disbursed, a judgment lien attaches to the mortgage property. The question now is whether or not the judgment lien has priority over the $300,000 yet to be disbursed or not. The answer is that since A's agreement was to lend a total of $500,000 and since A is obligated to disburse that sum, then A has a first lien for $500,000 regardless of when the judgment lien is recorded.

Exceptions to the above related theory exist in several states with regard to their mechanics lien laws and the priority of mechanics liens.

As to non-obligatory advances, the question of priority arises usually in connection with open-end mortgages. Such a mortgage secures not only a specific debt, but advances which the mortgagee may elect to make to the mortgagor in the future. Hence, if the mortgagor requests additional funds at a later date to expand his property, the mortgagee, if agreeable, can disburse those funds under the open-end mortgage without recording a new mortgage. In most states the amount of future advances under an open-end mortgage is limited to a specific dollar amount. Hence, the question of lien priority can best be expressed in the following example: A lends to B the sum of $100,000 under an open-end mortgage, which mortgage provides than an additional $100,000 may be advanced under certain circumstances and at A's sole option. B subsequently gives a second mortgage on the same property to C for $10,000. Then B requests and A agrees to advance an additional $100,000 under the open-end mortgage. Does A now have a first lien for $200,000 or a first lien for $100,000 and a third lien for $100,000? In Alabama, California, Colorado, Florida, Georgia, Indiana, Iowa, Kentucky, Louisiana, Maine, Minnesota, Mississippi, Missouri, Montana, Nebraska, Nevada, New Hampshire, New Jersey, New York, Oregon, South Carolina, Texas, Vermont, Virginia, Washington, West Virginia and Wisconsin (the majority of states), A will have a first lien for $200,000 unless he had actual knowledge of C's mortgage at the time the second advance was made.

In Illinois, Michigan, Ohio and Pennsylvania A would have had a first and third lien for $100,000 each, since the laws of these states hold that record notice of intervening liens is sufficient to give such liens priority over future optional advances.

MULTIPLE NOTES

From time to time, one mortgage may secure the payment of several notes. For example, A, B and C sell Blackacre to D for $500,000 payable $200,000 in cash and $300,000 deferred note secured by a mortgage. A, B and C each desire separate notes for $100,000 maturing so as to give A his part of the sales price first, then B his and finally C his. Hence, three notes are issued and all are secured by one mortgage. To prevent any problems as to preference of lien by reason of maturity (or for any other reason) the mortgage instrument should contain a clause to the effect that all notes shall enjoy equal security under the mortgage. Under this parity clause or preference and priority clause, all three notes will enjoy equal lien rights. Failure of the mortgage to contain such a clause may, depending upon the state involved, cause A to have a first lien for his $100,000, B a second lien for his $100,000 and C a third lien for the remainder. Hence, when multiple notes are involved in a mortgage transaction, care is to be taken to make sure that a priority position is not given when one is not intended.

USURY

A problem quite prevalent in the area of real estate finance is that of usury. Defined, usury is a charge extracted for the use of money in excess of that allowed by law.

Modern-day inflation and rising interest rates due to competition for money has led to the demand for interest rates which, if charged, will exceed state usury laws. Hence, rising interest rates have caused a diversion of funds from states with low usury ceilings to those with higher ones. For example, an investor seeking an 11 percent return on a conventional loan would not be able to invest in loans secured by Missouri real estate, since Missouri has a 10 percent ceiling on conventional loans, but could find that yield legally available in Colorado, a state that has a 12 percent usury ceiling (see Chart 1-1). It could be concluded then that mortgage funds would be diverted from Missouri and states with similar low usury ceilings such as Colorado where a higher ceiling prevails at such times as interest charges due to market conditions exceed those states statutory maximum interest rates.

Usury laws date back to biblical times and are virtually universal. In the United States such laws are statutory and vary state by state. However, they share certain general characteristics as noted below:

1. *FHA/VA exemption*—Many states exempt FHA and VA loans from their usury laws in order to insure a constant flow of funds into their states for investment into these type loans.
2. *Corporate exemption*—The majority of states exempt corporations from usury on the theory that such entities are sophisticated in business matters and do not need the protection of law as to the rate they pay for borrowings. Some states that do not exempt corporations do go so far as to raise the interest allowed to be charged to corporations over that ceiling set for individuals.
3. *Business entity exemption*—For the same reason that corporations are usually exempt from state usury laws, business entities such as partnerships and joint ventures are in many states also exempt from usury laws.
4. *Penalties*—The penalties for violation of usury laws vary considerably, from loss of interest to loss of principal and interest plus, in some states, a prison sentence.
5. *Loans in excess of a certain sum*—As with corporation and business entities, loans in excess of a high amount in a few states are usury exempt.
6. *Fees and charges computed in determining usury*—There is a wide diversity

among the states as to what constitutes interest. The face or coupon rate on a mortgage is only one factor. Loan fees, discounts, and other charges in connection with a loan may or may not be included with the loan coupon rate in determining legal compliance with usury laws.

7. *Specific lender*—In some states local institutions are exempt from the states usury laws while outside institutions are not. Also, within a state some institutions may be usury exempt while others are not.

Usury laws have a definite affect upon mortgage money availability on a state by state basis. These laws vary as to state, but do have some very similar aspects and characteristics.

The immediate delivery multi-family purchase program is mandatory within sixty days of offer acceptance by FHLMC. Offers to sell multi-family conventional loans at FHLMC's a maximum $5,000,000 per contract. FHLMC's net required yield, as with home mortgages, is exclusive of servicing. To this net required yield must be added the fee that the servicing fee allowed on loans of $750,000 or less is .25%. On loans over $750,000 it is .125%. Hence, if FHLMC requires a net yield of 10% for a purchase of a multi-family loan, a $1,000,000 would have a bear a 10.125% it would have to be sold to FHLMC at a discount that would provide a 10.125% yield. If the coupon is greater than 10.125% FHLMC will still only purchase the loan at par, but the excess over 10.125% is retained by the Seller as an additional loan servicing fee. Similar net yield requirements apply to have mortgages sold to FHLMC.

Multi-family mortgages eligible for sale to FHLMC may have loan to values as high as 80% and original mortgage terms of up to 30 years (10 years minimum). At time of sale the multi-family project must have 80% occupancy or a higher percentage as is necessary to carry all expenses and mortgage debt. Maximum mortgage amounts per unit are established by FHLMC and cannot be exceeded.

Under the prior approval multi-family loan purchase program, FHLMC contracts with the loan Seller to purchase a conventional multi-family mortgage on a specific project in advance of the closing of the mortgage. The minimum offer amount under this program is $250,000 and the maximum is $5,000,000. Once approved, all provisions of FHLMC's immediate delivery multi-family loan program applies. The benefit of the prior approval procedure is that the Seller can obtain FHLMC's commitment that the specific mortgage will be purchased. Under the immediate delivery program, FHLMC may accept or reject any loans offered for purchase.

CHART 1-1
Usury Laws For First Mortgage Real Estate Loans in Brief

STATE	BASIC RATE	EXEMPTION	REMARKS
Alabama	8%	yes*	For individuals the rate is unlimited on loans over $100,000. For corporations, the maximum rate is 15% with no ceiling above $100,000.
Alaska	6%	no	Maximum allowable rate is established at 5% above the Federal Reserve rediscount rate

STATE	BASIC RATE	EXEMPTION	REMARKS
			at the 12th District Bank. Loans in excess of $100,000 are exempt from usury.
Arizona	12%	yes	Basic rate applies to individuals and partnerships. Corporate ceilings for loans over $5,000 is 1-1/2% per month.
Arkansas	10%	yes	Corporations are not exempt. The ceiling is set by constitution.
California	10%	yes	Corporations are not exempt. The ceiling is set by constitution. California domiciled banks and savings and loan associations are exempt as are companies qualifying under the Industrial Loan Act.
Colorado	12%	no	Maximum rate varies under the Consumer credit code effective in Colorado as of 10/1/71.
Connecticut	12%	yes	Ceiling of 18% on loans to commercial, industrial, and manufacturing corporations. Real estate mortgages above $5,000 are exempt.
Delaware	9%	yes	Corporations exempt. Maximum allowable rate established at 4% plus Federal Reserve discount rate.
District of Columbia	11%	yes	Corporations exempt.
Florida	18%	yes*	Ceiling is 18% for non-corporate loans of under $500,000 and 25% for corporate loans and loans of $500,000 and above. Savings and loans are exempt.
Georgia	9%	yes	No ceiling on loans over $3,000 to corporations and on loans above $100,000 to individuals. Maximum allowable rate established monthly at 2.5% over index of long-term U.S. government bond yields.
Hawaii	12%	yes	No ceiling on loans of $750,000 and higher to corporations.
Idaho	13%	no	
Illinois	9.5%	yes	No ceiling for corporations and business loans. Maximum allowable rate established

STATE	BASIC RATE	EXEMPTION	REMARKS
			monthly at 2.5% over index of long-term U.S. government bond yields.
Indiana	18%	no	Partnerships and corporations are exempt. Uniform consumer credit code applies to loans above 10%. FHA/VA loans closed by a trust company, savings and loan, or an insurance company are exempt.
Iowa	9%	yes	Corporations exempt. Maximum rate 2% over index of 10 year U.S. government notes and bonds.
Kansas	11%	no	Corporations exempt. Uniform consumer credit code applies to loans over 10%.
Kentucky	8.5%	yes	Any rate may be charged on loans over $15,000.
Louisiana	10%	yes	Corporations exempt.
Maine	12.25%	—	All business loans are exempt. Maine consumer credit code effective as of January 1, 1975.

STATE	BASIC RATE	EXEMPTION	REMARKS
Maryland	None	yes*	No limit, but points/discounts are allowable on FHA/VA loans and loans sold to FNMA/GNMA, FHLMC, or FMHA. No prepayment penalty allowed.
Massachusetts	20%	no	Limit on mortgages over $15,000 secured by dwelling with 6 or fewer households and with an assessed value of not over $40,000 is 1-1/2% per month.
Michigan	11%	yes	Regulated lenders and corporations exempt.
Minnesota	8%	yes*	Corporations exempt. Maximum rate 2% over index of long-term U.S. government bonds.
Mississippi	10%	yes*	Corporations may pay up to 15% on loans over $2,500. Partnerships may pay up to 15% on non-agricultural loans of $250,000 or more.
Missouri	10%	no	Corporations exempt as are real estate loans other than agricultural and residential.
Montana	10%	no	Corporations not exempt.

STATE	BASIC RATE	EXEMPTION	REMARKS
			Maximum rate 4% to 5% over 9th Federal Reserve District 90-day discount rate. Loans over $300,000 are exempt.
Nebraska	11%	yes*	Corporations exempt. Loans over $100,000 exempt.
Nevada	12%	yes	Corporations exempt. Loans over $100,000 exempt.
New Hampshire	none		
New Jersey	9.5%	yes	Corporations exempt.
New Mexico	10%	yes	Corporations exempt.
New York	9.5%	yes	Corporation ceiling is generally 25%. Maximum rate 2% over rate on 10-year constant maturity U.S. government notes and bonds.

STATE	BASIC RATE	EXEMPTION	REMARKS
N. Carolina	12%	yes*	Banks, savings and loans, credit unions, and federally-insured mortgagees are exempt. No limit on loans over $25,000.
N. Dakota	12%	yes	Corporation and business loans over $25,000 are exempt. Maximum rate 5.5% over the maximum interest rate payable on 30-month certificates of deposit.
Ohio	none	no	Corporations are exempt as well as loans to individuals above $100,000. Savings and loan associations are exempt. Maximum rate is 3% over 90-day discount rate of 4th Federal Reserve District.
Oklahoma	10% to 18%	yes	10% is constitutional ceiling, but uniform consumer credit code allows 18% to supervised lenders and 10% to others lending to consumers.
Oregon	12%	yes	Corporate ceiling is 12%. Loans in excess of $50,000 are exempt.
Pennsylvania	6%	yes	Corporations exempt as are loans above $50,000. Maximum rate is 2.5% plus monthly index of U.S. government bond yields.
Puerto Rico	10.5%	yes	Corporations exempt.
Rhode Island	21%	no	Corporations are not exempt.
S. Carolina	none	yes*	No limit on first mortgage loans, but loans under $100,000 must

be at fixed rate of interest and allow full prepayment without penalty. Corporations without $40,000 worth of stock issued are exempt.

STATE	BASIC RATE	EXEMPTION	REMARKS
S. Dakota	10%	yes	Corporations exempt.
Tennessee	10%	yes	Corporations are not exempt. Maximum rate 2% over FNMA Conventional Auction rate.
Texas	12%	no	Corporation loans above $5,000 have a 1% per month ceiling, except charitable and religious corporations which have a 10% ceiling. Individuals may agree to loans at the corporate rate as to all loans of $500,000 or more. Maximum rate is 2% plus monthly index of government bond rate up to 12%.
Utah	18%	FHA loans only	Utah uniform consumer credit code governs loans above 10%.
Vermont	None	yes	Ceiling on income property and second home loans is 12%. Business and corporate loans are exempt. Maximum residential mortgage rate is 1.25% above selected U.S. government and corporate bond rate.
Virginia	None	yes	Ceiling removed on all first mortgage loans.
Virgin Islands	9%	—	
Washington	12%	no	Above $100,000 loans to corporations and to individuals in the real estate business are exempt.
West Virginia	None	yes	Corporate loans are exempt. Maximum rate 1.5% plus average yield on long-term U.S. government bonds.
Wisconsin	12%	yes	Corporate loans and loans over $150,000 on 1-4 family residential property are exempt.
Wyoming	18%	—	Corporate loans and most business loans are exempt. The Uniform Consumer Credit Code applies to loans above 12% if for less than $25,000.

In view of the complexity and changing nature of state usury laws, this chart should not be relied upon as a definite source of information.

*Conventional loans sold fo FNMA/FHLMC also exempt.

Historically, usury laws have been passed to prevent unscrupulous lenders from extracting too high an interest charge from unsophisticated borrowers. In these modern times, however, particularly with respect to first mortgage loans, market conditions universally dictate interest levels. Hence, usury laws today as far as mortgage lending is concerned generally act to prevent individuals from obtaining mortgage loans much more often than they protect an unsuspecting borrower from paying too high an interest charge. The trend today is to legislate National exemptions to local usury laws in order to stimulate money availability, particularly in times of money shortages, on the theory that funds at some price are many times better than no funds at all.

QUESTIONS FOR THOUGHT AND DISCUSSION

1. What is your opinion as to variable interest rate mortgages?
   a. Do you think borrowers would accept such clauses in mortgages if the initial rate were lower, but escalation was included as the lender's hedge against inflation?
   b. Recently a bank in Hawaii, after interest fell from an abnormal high, unilaterally agreed to reduce the interest rate on mortgages made during the peak interest period with the reservation to increase the rate up to the rate stated in mortgage as and when interest rates begin to climb. Do you feel that such benevolent action is wise and would justify later adoption of variable interest rate mortgages which would work in an opposite manner?
   c. Do you feel that the universal use of variable rate mortgages would cause more funds to be available for mortgage investments? Explain.
2. a. Do you feel that packaged mortgages as applied to home purchasers will find acceptability to borrower and lender alike?
   b. What do you feel is the biggest lender deterrent to such an arrangement?
3. a. Consider, the term and partial amortization mortgages. What rate of interest (high or low) and required downpayment might you expect in using these types of mortgages as compared to an amortized mortgage?
   b. Can you name at least one situation in which the partial amortized mortgage is used or could be beneficially used?
4. Under what circumstances is a blanket mortgage used? Can you think of any instances other than the one contained in the text?
5. Do you feel that state usury laws should or should not be abolished as to first mortgage loans as has been done in several states? Explain your reasons pro or con.
6. What age group would most benefit from: (a) a graduated payment mortgage; (b) a reserve annuity mortgage?

2

LAND CONTRACTS

A land contract is a contractual arrangement whereby the Seller of property gives up possession to the Buyer, but retains legal title to the property. In essence, a land contract is an agreement to deliver a deed at a definite time provided certain conditions, as set forth in the contract, are met.

VESTING OF EQUITABLE TITLE

Upon the execution by Seller and Buyer of a valid land contract, the courts hold that equitable title to the premises passes from the Seller to the Buyer. Thus, legal and equitable title to the premises are divided between Seller and Buyer. The Seller, however, holds the legal title to the premises in trust for the Buyer and the Buyer is the trustee of the unpaid purchase money due to the Seller.

LAND CONTRACT IN GENERAL

The Buyer under a land contract makes payments to the Seller with the proviso, as prearranged and set forth in the land contract, that the Seller will convey legal title to the property when all payments have been made.

The Seller will usually retain the right to mortgage his interest and to sell and assign his rights in the property subject to the land contract.

Land contracts are frequently used when a Buyer doesn't desire to rent a home, farm, or vacant land but can't buy because of insufficient cash or credit. In such an instance, the Seller should provide for the property to be purchased within a set period of time or upon the Buyer improving his cash, credit, or property equity situation, whichever happens first. Long-term land contracts can create many problems for Sellers. In a few states, after the passage of certain periods of time or the acquisition of sufficient equity in the property by the Buyer, foreclosure becomes the only method for repossessing property under land contract upon the purchaser's default. When used for home sales in some states, land contracts are considered as an intermediate financing device which allows the Buyer time to find a mortgage loan, not as a permanent mortgage substitute.

When houses are poorly located or in a deteriorating area the land contract is sometimes the only vehicle available for sale of that type property.

In states where land contracts are *not* in favor, Sellers will take back a note and mortgage providing for refinancing at a certain date. The problem here is the immediate requirement to foreclosure in the event a default occurs. The states in which this method is used over a land contract usually have power of sale foreclosure laws which can put a Seller in title almost as quickly as eviction proceedings on a defaulted land contract.

RIGHTS AND OBLIGATIONS OF THE BUYER

Since the property under a land contract is equitably owned by the Buyer, the Buyer, absence any fault on the part of the Seller, must assume a risk for loss of property in the event of fire, or other hazard. Thus, a Buyer in possession must take precautions to secure the property from risk of loss.

LAND CONTRACT AND PROPERTY RIGHTS

A land contract is an agreement which may be specifically enforced by a court of law. It is unlike an option to purchase land which does not give rise to specific performance until the option is exercised. Hence, a land contract is of the nature that once entered into, converts the interest of the Seller into personal property of money receivable. If the Seller dies prior to conveyance of title to the Buyer, then the Seller's interest passes to his personal representative, not to his heirs. His personal representative is then entitled to collection of the purchase money. Conversely, the interest of the Buyer in a land contract is considered realty and will pass to his heirs, upon his death, subject to the fulfillment of the conditions of the land contract.

Property under a land contract is considered sold upon the entering of the contract, not when the property is, at some future date, deeded from Seller to Buyer. The completion of installment payments and the transfer of title by deed are concurrent conditions.

LAND CONTRACTS AND LOT SALES

A very important and frequent use of land contracts is in connection with lot sales where the Buyer does not anticipate building for several years and the Seller doesn't want to give up title or pay off an existing mortgage until the Buyer pays a substantial portion or all of the sales price.

In at least one area known to the author, builders buy developed lots on a blanket land contract as a matter of course. Construction financing is obtained from a local bank on a line of credit basis and homes are built with little cash investment on the builder's part. The land contract is obtained with a nominal down payment and interest only is paid on the line of credit. When a house is sold, the lot is released from the land contract and the line of credit repaid. Since deeds to all lots are placed in escrow with a title company at the execution of the land contract, no delays or problems are incurred in obtaining title once payment has been made.

PROBLEMS OF LAND CONTRACTS

The fact that the buyer under a land contract can usually make only a small down payment indicates some risk of default is present. Factors tending to increase this risk are small monthly contract payments, poor credit ratings of buyers, and possibilities of property value declines.

Some other problems which are commonly experienced in land contract transactions are:

1. The refusal or inability of the Seller to convey title once the Buyer has paid in full. This failure can be caused by refusal of a wife to release dower, or the tying up of the property in an estate settlement.

2. If a money judgment is obtained against the Seller it becomes a lien on all real property owned by the Seller. Therefore, a title search prior to execution of the land contract is a wise move on the Buyer's part. Judgment against the Seller after the contract is entered into would in most instances be subject to the Buyer's right to possession. However, it is a good idea to record the land contract in order to give constructive notice to the world of Buyer's interest. Many Sellers will object to recordation due to the legal ramifications of clearing title in the event of a default by the Buyer.

3. Mechanics and materialmen in most jurisdictions have from thirty days to six months to file their liens. Therefore, a prudent land contract Buyer will carefully inspect the premises to determine if any repairs or improvements have been accomplished in the last six months. If so, affidavits of payment or similar proof should be obtained from all mechanics and materialmen involved. A provision should be included in the land contract to the end that the Buyer may discharge any liens placed against the property and deduct the cost of same from payments due under the land contract. Work performed at the request of the Buyer after execution of the land contract does not give rise to a valid lien against the property, but becomes a personal obligation of the Buyer.

4. It is advisable to include a clause which prohibits assignment of the land contract, unless approved by the Seller.

5. It is also wise to incorporate an acceleration clause, making the debt due and payable on any default by the Buyer. In fairness to the Buyer, a grace period may be provided before the debt can be accelerated in a foreclosure action.

ADVANTAGES OF THE LAND CONTRACT

The sources of investment return on land contracts include not only the nominal interest on the declining balance, but also the sales price premium or, if the land contract is purchased, the discount from par at which it is bought.

By mortgaging his legal title, the Seller under a land contract reduces his own dollar investment, and can make use of the principle of leverage.

In the event of the Buyer's default, the Seller is usually able, under a land contract, to secure quicker repossession than he would under mortgage foreclosure.

The Buyer is benefited under a land contract, because it enables him to purchase real property otherwise not available to him because of his financing problems. Land contracts are used more frequently with older properties than with new. Older properties may not be able to qualify for mortgage loans.

FORM OF LAND CONTRACT

Chart 2-1 represents a form of land contract used by an Ohio mortgage banking company. The important provisions of the contract, which distinguish it from a mortgage or purchase agreement are:

1. Payments as collected are deemed interest until semi-annual adjustments are made to determine what portion of the payments received for the previous six months are to be credited to principal. This is in contrast to the standard mortgage method of calculating principal and interest application on a monthly basis. Figured semi-annually the seller obtains a dollar advantage. (see paragraph (2) of the form contract)

2. Upon default the Buyer stands to lose all previous payments as well as any security deposits or additional guarantees of performance that are given. This penalty can be quite severe on contracts which have been in existence for long periods of time and has precipitated legislation in some states requiring foreclosure on certain land contracts. In Ohio, for example, a contract which is five years old or in which the Buyer has a 20 percent equity, must be foreclosed rather than cancelled by eviction of the Buyer. Foreclosure allows the defaulting Buyer to at least have an opportunity of retaining some of his equity. (see paragraphs (7) and (14) of the form contract).

3. As previously stated, the Seller is usually permitted to mortgage the property, provided the mortgage balance doesn't exceed the land contract balance. (see paragraph (11) of the form contract)

4. Also, as previously mentioned, it is a good idea for the Seller to provide for the Buyer's refinancing of the property in order to terminate the land contract. This is a normal provision when the contract has been made solely because the Buyer did not have sufficient cash or credit to purchase the property. (see paragraph (13) of the form contract)

In general every land contract should contain at least the following provisions:

a. The full names and addresses of the parties to the contract.
b. The date when signed by each party.
c. A legal description of the property conveyed.
d. The contract price of the property conveyed.
e. The amount of the vendee's down payment.
f. The principal balance owed (contract price less down payment).
g. The amount and due date of each contract installment.
h. The interest rate on the unpaid balance and the method of computing the rate.

CHART 2-1

L A N D   C O N T R A C T

THIS AGREEMENT made at _____ , this _____ day of

_____ , 19 ___ , between _____ ,

an Ohio corporation, hereinafter called SELLER, and _____

_____ , hereinafter called BUYER, WITNESSETH:

(1) SELLER agrees to sell to BUYER, and BUYER agrees to purchase from
SELLER, the following described premises:

    Situated in the State of _____ , County of
    _____ , and _____ of _____
    _____ , and

    Being Lot Number _____
    of _____ ,
    as the same is numbered and delineated upon the recorded
    plat thereof, of record in Plat Book _____ , Page _____ ,
    Recorder's Office , _____ County, _____ ,

    Also known as _____ ,
    _____ .

subject to use restrictions, zoning restrictions, easements, if any, and any other
laws, regulations or ordinances of any governmental authority, and including all
screens, awnings, storm windows, storm doors and other fixtures.

(2) The total purchase price which BUYER agrees to pay is _____
                                                             DOLLARS
($), the sum of _____
DOLLARS ($) upon the execution hereof, receipt of which is hereby
acknowledged, and the balance of said purchase price, namely, _____
_____ DOLLARS ($), shall
be paid in installments of not less than _____
DOLLARS ($) per month including principal and interest on the first
(1st) day of each month beginning _____ until the purchase price
has been paid in full. The rate of interest on this contract shall be _____
_____ per cent (%) per annum, adjusted semi-annually. On the last
day of each six (6) months' period (beginning six (6) months from the date of the
first monthly payment due herein), the amount in excess of the interest due for
said period, paid by BUYER (during said period), shall be deducted from the existing principal, and the balance shall be the new principal for the succeeding six
(6) months' period. In the event of any default, interest shall be at the rate
of eight per cent (8%) per annum. BUYER will pay to SELLER, together with and in
addition to, such payments of principal and interest, the following:

(A) A sum equal to 1/12th of the annual taxes and assessments.

(B) A sum equal to 1/12th of the annual premium for the fire and hazard insurance protection.

(C) Upon written request by SELLER, BUYER will pay to SELLER together with and in addition to the payments aforesaid, the following:

   (1) Such additional amounts as may be necessary to pay taxes due or insurance preminums due in excess of the amounts paid with the monthly payment, if the rates for said items shall increase.

   (2) A "Late Charge" of Eight Dollars ($8.00) for each monthly payment or any part thereof, which is received by SELLER more than fifteen (15) days after due (1st of each and every month). Said late charge is hereby agreed upon as reasonable in amount, and is understood to be paid for the purpose of reimbursing SELLER for the additional expenses incurred by SELLER for collection and handling the delinquent account.

   (3) Upon receipt of the balance of the purchase price in full, together with interest, SELLER shall convey the said real estate to BUYER by good and sufficient deed of general warranty, excepting only those items hereinbefore mentioned, taxes and assessments as hereinafter provided, and any lien and/or encumbrance which might have been caused and/or created by BUYER.

   (4) SELLER agrees that he will provide for the payment of all municipal charges, taxes and current installments of special assessments that shall have become a lien upon the premises at the time of the execution of this contract, except such portion thereof as shall accrue after the date of execution, which subsequent portion of such charges, taxes and installments of special assessments the BUYER shall assume and agree to pay.

   (5) Possession shall be delivered to BUYER on _____, 19____ .

   (6) BUYER agrees to pay for insurance coverage against loss by hazard and/or fire and extended coverage, on the buildings now existing and to be built on the subject premises in a sum not less than the amount of the purchase price specified herein, which said insurance coverage shall extend to SELLER, and BUYER, and a mortgagee, if any, as their respective interests in the subject premises shall appear. BUYER agrees that SELLER shall procure said insurance coverage and shall advise BUYER of the premium. SELLER shall be responsible for having obtained said insurance coverage to the extent herein provided, and if BUYER desires additional coverage, BUYER shall obtain and pay for such additional coverage.

   (7) If BUYER shall fail to pay one of said installments of purchase money or interest, or one of the installments for insurance on the premises, or one of the installments for real estate taxes, or the late charge as provided herein, when the same becomes due, or within fifteen (15) days thereafter, or shall fail to comply with any of the terms and conditions hereof, then all of the installments and amounts remaining unpaid shall immediately become due and payable, and SELLER may, at his option, terminate this agreement without demand on or notice to BUYER; on such termination all payments made by BUYER hereunder may be retained by SELLER as fixed and liquidated damages for non-performance by BUYER of this agreement, and as rent and compensation for the use and occupancy of the premises, and this agreement shall be void; and all the right, title and interest, claim and demand of the BUYER in and to the premises shall cease and determine. On such termination, it shall be lawful for SELLER to enter upon said real estate and again have, repossess and enjoy the same as if this agreement had not been made, and until such entry BUYER shall be deemed and regarded as a tenant at will. The commencement of a proceeding in forcible detainer or in ejectment or otherwise, after such termination, shall be equivalent in every respect to actual entry by SELLER. Failure or delay of SELLER to terminate this agreement because of any default shall not operate as a waiver by SELLER of the right to terminate this agreement in the event of any subsequent or other default of BUYER; upon default aforesaid, a court of competent jurisdiction, upon application at any time and without notice, may appoint a receiver to take possession of, manage and control

said real estate, collect the rents and profits thereof, and apply the net proceeds to the payment of taxes, assessments, and insurance premiums against the
premises, or any of them, or in the reduction of BUYER'S debt, as SELLER may
elect. Upon default aforesaid, BUYER agrees to pay SELLER reasonable rent on a
per diem basis for the period BUYER is in possession of said premises after said
default.

   If a receiver' is appointed for BUYER, or if BUYER becomes bankrupt,
or makes an assignment for the benefit of creditors, or should any action, instrument for the purpose of causing a lien, or proceeding be filed in any court house
record, to enforce any lien on, claim against, or interest in the premises seeking to reach the interest of BUYER therein, the unpaid balance of this contract,
together with interest and other charges thereon, shall at once become due and
payable at the option of SELLER without notice to BUYER.

   SELLER'S remedies provided herein are not exclusive and SELLER at his
election may pursue all other available remedies, whether legal or equitable.

   (8) Should BUYER default in the performance of his obligations of this
contract, at any time before twenty-five per cent or more of the purchase price
under this contract has been paid to SELLER, BUYER does hereby appoint the SELLER
or any officer thereof as his agent (for the exclusive purpose herein mentioned)
and true and lawful attorney in fact and hereby expressly authorizes SELLER or
any officer thereof to execute in the BUYER'S name, place and stead, and to place
of record in the Recorder's Office in which a copy of this contract may be recorded a cancellation of this contract for and on behalf of BUYER, such cancellation executed as authorized herein being hereby confirmed and ratified as
if said cancellation had been made by BUYER personally.

   (9) BUYER shall keep the buildings on said premises in good repair, shall
commit no waste, shall not use the same for any unlawful purpose, and shall abide
by all applicable laws and regulations of all duly constituted authorities.
BUYER shall not remove any portion of the buildings on said premises or make any
structural changes therein without the prior written consent of the SELLER.

   (10) BUYER shall not assign this contract without the prior written consent
of SELLER.

   (11) SELLER may mortgage and/or maintain a first mortgage lien upon the
real property in any amount SELLER so desires, provided, however, that such
amount does not exceed the balance then due and owing from the BUYER under this
contract and so long as said mortgage lien can be paid off within the remaining
time for payment in full of this contract. The consent of the BUYER shall not
be required in order for the SELLER to place such a mortgage lien on said real
property. In the event that SELLER fails to pay the installment on such mortgage
when due or within sixty (60) days after the same shall become due, and it shall
become necessary for the said BUYER to make said mortgage installments to protect
his interest in this contract, then BUYER is authorized to make such payment or
payments and any such payment so made by BUYER shall be credited to his account
in such amount as though payments had been directly made to the SELLER as provided herein.

   (12) BUYER, and each of them, hereby agree and by these presents, do hereby subordinate any and all interest which they or each of them have in the subject
premises (arising pursuant to this land contract) to any first mortgage loan or
loans which are or may be obtained by SELLER, subsequent to the date of the execution of this agreement.

   (13) If first mortgage financing in an amount not less than the balance
due hereunder shall, at any time, become available to BUYER on terms, including
monthly payment and interest rate, not less favorable than those provided herein
and with loan charges usual and customary in _____ County, _____,
the BUYER shall: (1) make application to the first mortgage lender for said loan;
and (2) upon obtaining said loan, apply the proceeds thereof in full payment of
the balance of principal and all accrued interest then due hereunder. Within
thirty (30) days after having received actual notice from SELLER of the availability to BUYER of said mortgage loan financing on the terms provided herein,
should BUYER fail or refuse to cooperate in obtaining said loan, then SELLER may
at its option declare the entire balance on said Land Contract, and all installments, due and payable immediately without notice and/or demand therefor.

(14) As a further inducement for SELLER to enter into this agreement, BUYER agrees and has, in fact, executed a promissory note of even date payable on demand to SELLER, in the sum of _____
DOLLARS ($). Said note is executed and delivered to SELLER as an additional guarantee that BUYER will comply with the terms of this agreement, pertaining to BUYER, for at least the period of thirty (30) months from the date hereof. Should BUYER within thirty (30) months from the date hereof, default in the terms of this contract, judgment shall be taken on said note against BUYER. However, should BUYER perform the terms of this contract pertaining to BUYER, for at least thirty (30) months from the date hereof, said promissory note shall be returned forthwith to BUYER upon BUYER'S written request therefor to SELLER.

(15) SELLER shall have the right to make periodic inspections of said real property and all the buildings thereon at any reasonable times and at any reasonable intervals.

(16) This agreement shall inure to the benefit of and be binding upon the heirs, executors, administrators, devisees and legatees of the parties hereto. As used herein the singular shall include the plural and the masculine shall include the feminine, except as the context may otherwise require. This instrument comprehends the full agreement of the parties and shall be interpreted and construed by and under the laws of the State of _____.

(17) Notices and payments to SELLER shall be given and made at 30 Warder Street, Springfield, Ohio, or at such other address as may be specified by SELLER in writing.

Notices to BUYER shall be given at the mailing address of the premises described in this contract, or at such other mailing address as may be specified by BUYER in writing.

IN WITNESS WHEREOF, the parties have hereunto set their hands to duplicate originals hereof the day and year above written.

Signed and delivered in
the presence of:

_____

_____

By _____

By _____

"SELLER"

_____

_____

_____

"BUYER"

STATE OF   )
) SS:
COUNTY OF   )

BE IT REMEMBERED, that on this _____ day of _____, in the year of our Lord one thousand nine hundred and _____ (19), before me, the subscriber, a Notary Public in and for said County, personally appeared _____
_____, by _____, its _____,
and _____, its _____, they being duly authorized officers of said corporation, who acknowledged the signing thereof to be their voluntary act and deed for and on behalf of said corporation.

IN TESTIMONY WHEREOF, I have hereunto subscribed my name and affixed my Notarial Seal on the day and year last aforesaid.

_____
Notary Public

```
STATE OF            )
                    ) SS:
COUNTY OF           )
```

BE IT REMEMBERED, that on this _____ day of _____ , in the year
of our Lord one thousand nine hundred and _____ (19), before me, the
subscriber, a Notary Public in and for said County, personally appeared _____
_____ , _____ , and _____
_____ , BUYER, who acknowledged the signing thereof to be their
voluntary act and deed.

IN TESTIMONY WHEREOF, I have hereunto subscribed my name and affixed my
Notarial Seal on the day and year last aforesaid.

_____

Notary Public

Source: An Ohio Mortgage Banking company.

  i. A statement of any encumbrances against the property.
  j. A statement requiring the vendor to deliver a deed of general warranty on completion of the contract, or such other deed as is available when the vendor is legally unable to deliver a deed of general warranty.
  k. A provision that the vendor provide evidence of title in accordance with the prevailing custom in the area where the property is located.

Other provisions recommended for protection of both parties, in particular the vendee and that should be included are:

  a. A provision that if the vendor defaults on any mortgage on the property, the vendee can pay on said mortgage and receive credit on the contract.
  b. A provision requiring recordation of the contract.
  c. A provision as to who shall be responsible for payment of taxes, assessments and other charges against the property. (Usually the vendee is responsible for these charges).
  d. A provision preventing the vendor from placing a mortgage on the property that is in excess of the balance due under the contract.

CONCLUSION

Land contracts are a method of finance used in special instances where the normal deeding and mortgaging of property is not feasible. Hence, the reader should become aware of when and how a land contract is to be used.

QUESTIONS FOR THOUGHT AND DISCUSSION

1. List all the circumstances you can think of in which land contracts are used or could be used.
2. What advantages would be gained by escrowing the deed to property under a land contract?
3. What are some common problems that are involved in land contract transactions?

MORTGAGOR'S AND MORTGAGEE'S RIGHTS IN THE EVENT OF DEFAULT

DEFAULT AND ITS CONSEQUENCES

The general public believes that a default on a mortgage obligation means the failure of the borrower to remit a required installment or installments of principal and interest or the consistent and frequent delinquency of the borrower in making such payments. These, however, are only two instances of default, while admittedly the most common. A default can occur by failure to pay property taxes, assessments, or hazard insurance premiums when due, or through the breach of any of the many covenants and conditions contained in the mortgage instrument.

The fact that a default has occurred does not mean that foreclosure will ensue. In fact, most lenders will take great efforts to prevent foreclosure, even when foreclosure would be to their distinct monetary advantage. Thus, it is a default combined with the lender's decision to terminate the mortgage arrangement that gives rise to a foreclosure action.

HISTORY

The "Magna Carta" of mortgagor rights as against the mortgagee can be said to have been adopted by the courts of the fourteenth century. Historically, the mortgagor was required to make payment of his mortgage indebtedness on what was called *law day*. If payment were made at that time, the mortgage debt was cancelled. However, if the mortgagor failed to pay, the courts extinguished all the mortgagor's rights and interest in the property. Foreclosure was not necessary, as it did not exist.

EQUITY OF REDEMPTION

Mortgagors finally became wise and questioned the existing procedure that could instantly deprive them of the equity that they had in mortgaged property. The only recourse available to them was to seek assistance from the king, for the king was the last and final authority and could make laws and rulings as well as change them. But, many times the king delegated his decision-making power to someone else. Thus, the mortgage problem came to bear upon the lord chancellor who was the supreme legal authority in the land. The chancellor in hearing cases, particularly those concerning mortgage hardship, acted as a court of equity rather than one of law and when circumstances demanded, he ruled on the merits rather than legalities of a case. Therefore, a system soon developed where, for justifiable reasons, a mortgagor who did not make payment as required by the mortgage instrument was given a further opportunity to pay his

CHART 3-1
Summary Chart
(Selected aspects of foreclosure operations in the various states)

State	Nature of mortgage	Customary instrument	Predominant method	Statutory redemption period	Posession during redemption	Average time involved[a]
Alabama	Title	Mortgage	Power of sale	2 years	Purchaser	4-6 weeks
Alaska	Lien	Trust deed	Court action	1 year		4 months
Arizona	Lien	Mortgage	Court action	6 months	Mortgagor	3 months
Arkansas	Intermediate	Mortgage	Court action	2 years		2 months
California	Lien	Trust deed	Power of sale	None		5 months
Colorado	Lien	Trust deed	Power of sale	6 months	Mortgagor	4-6 weeks
Connecticut	Intermediate	Mortgage	Strict foreclosure	None		4 months
Delaware	Intermediate	Mortgage	Court action	None		7 months
Dist. of Columbia	Intermediate	Trust deed	Power of sale	None		4-6 weeks
Florida	Lien	Mortgage	Court action	None		45 days
Georgia-	Title	Security deed	Power of sale	None		1 month
Hawaii	Lien	Mortgage	Court action	None		1 month
Idaho[d]	Lien	Trust deed	Power of sale	None		3 months
Illinois	Intermediate	Mortgage	Court action	1 year[e]		3 months
Indiana	Lien	Mortgage	Court action	6 months	Mortgagor	3 months
Iowa	Lien	Mortgage	Court action	1 year	Mortgagor	4-6 weeks
Kansas	Lien	Mortgage	Court action	18 months[f]	Mortgagor	3 months
Kentucky	Lien	Mortgage	Court action	1 year[g]	Mortgagor	3 months
Louisiana	Lien	Mortgage	Court action	None		3 months
Maine	Title	Mortgage	Public notice	1 year	Mortgagor	4-6 weeks
Maryland	Title	Mortgage	Power of sale[h]	None		4-6 weeks
Massachusetts	Intermediate	Mortgage	Power of sale	None		3 months
Michigan	Lien	Mortgage	Power of Sale	1 year	Mortgagor	13 weeks
Minnesota	Lien	Mortgage	Power of sale	1 year	Mortgagor	6 weeks
Mississippi	Intermediate	Trust deed	Power of sale	None		4 weeks
Missouri	Intermediate	Trust deed	Power of sale	1 year[i]	Mortgagor	4-6 weeks
Montana	Lien	Mortgage	Court action	1 year	Mortgagor	3 months
Nebraska	Lien	Mortgage	Court action	6 months[c]	Mortgagor	90 days
Nevada	Lien	Mortgage	Court action	1 year	Mortgagor	3 months
New Hampshire	Title	Mortgage	Power of sale	None		4-6 weeks
New Jersey	Intermediate	Mortgage	Court action	None[j]		4 months
New Mexico	Lien	Mortgage	Court action	9 months[k]	Purchaser	4 months
New York	Lien	Mortgage	Court action	None		5 months
North Carolina	Intermediate	Trust deed	Power of sale	None		4-6 weeks
North Dakota	Lien	Mortgage	Court action	1 year	Mortgagor	3 months

State	Nature mortgage	Customary instrument	Predominant method	Statutory redemption period	Posession during redemption	Average time involved[a]
Ohio	Intermediate	Mortgage	Court action	None		4 months
Oklahoma	Lien	Mortgage	Court action	6 months[e]	Mortgagor	3 months
Oregon	Lien	Mortgage	Court action	1 year	Purchaser	3 months
Pennsylvania	Title	Mortgage	Court action	None		3 months
Rhode Island	Title	Mortgage	Power of sale	None		4-6 weeks
South Carolina	Lien	Mortgage	Court action	None		3 months
South Dakota	Lien	Mortgage	Power of sale	1 year	Mortgagor	6 weeks
Tennessee	Title	Trust deed	Power of sale	None[b]		4-6 weeks
Texas	Lien	Trust deed	Power of sale	None		4-6 weeks
Utah	Lien	Mortgage	Court action	6 months	Mortgagor	3 months
Vermont	Intermediate	Mortgage	Strict foreclosure	1 year	Mortgagor	3 months
Virginia	Intermediate	Trust deed	Power of sale	None		6-8 weeks
Washington	Lien	Mortgage	Power of sale	6 months	Purchaser	6 months
West Virginia	Intermediate	Trust deed	Power of sale	None		2 months
Wisconsin[d]	Lien	Mortgage	Court action	6 months	Mortgagor	4-6 weeks
Wyoming	Lien	Mortgage	Power of sale	6 months	Mortgagor	6-8 weeks

[a]Time computed is for completion of foreclosure.

[b]Provided redemption rights have been waived expressly in the security instrument.

[e]The redemption period *precedes* sale in Indiana, Nebraska (court stays sale on borrower's request), and Wisconsin.

[d]Listings for Idaho and Wisconsin contemplate certain mortgages on properties of 3 acres or less.

[e]Redemption period may be shortened under certain conditions. Receiver may be had for rents if authorized by security instrument.

[f]Redemption period is six months in cases of (1) abandoned property, (2) purchase money mortgages with less than one-third paid down.

[g]However, if sale brings two-thirds or more of appraised value (court appraiser), there is no redemption after sale.

[h]Except in Baltimore, where decree of equity court orders sale.

[i]Provided mortgagor has within ten days of sale given notice of intent to redeem, together with security for payment of taxes, interest, etc.; otherwise, no redemption.

[j]Provided no suit is instituted for deficiency.

[k]Nine months maximum, one month minimum, as court directs.

Sources: Russell and Bridewell, "Mortgage Law and Mortgage Lending," *Journal of Land and Public Utility Economics,* Vol. XIV, No. 3, August, 1938; Guiliani, "Some Legal Considerations—Methods of Foreclosure," *U.S. Investor,* Vol. 61, 1950 pp. 846, 849; Jones, *Mortgages,* Vol. 1, pp. 18-69, 1928; Russell, *Home Owners' Loan Corporation, Survey of Foreclosure Operations,* 1937; Sherman, *Mortgage and Real Estate Investment Guide,* 1957; and a private study of foreclosure costs and time elements by Melvin F. Lanphar and Co., mortgage bankers, published in 1954.

debt and cure his default. If payment in full was made and the default cured, the mortgagor's property would be restored to him. This important right became known as the mortgagor's *equity of redemption.*

FORECLOSURE

Now the mortgagee was at a disadvantage since he did not know for certain whether or not property acquired through mortgage default would have to be returned by court order to the mortgagor. To remedy this situation a new practice developed whereby the mortgagee upon default would file a petition in court requesting the judge to enter an order or decree, allowing the mortgagor only a fixed period of time to pay the debt and reacquire his property. If the decree was entered the mortgagor was requested to pay in the time stated, and if he did not his equity of redemption was barred and forever *foreclosed* This action as it developed was termed a foreclosure suit, a suit to bar or terminate the mortgagor's equitable right of redemption.

The particular method of foreclosure just described is known as *strict foreclosure* and is still used today in the states of Connecticut and Vermont. (See Chart 3-1.) Under this method the mortgagor has a set time, three to four months, in which to redeem his property or lose all his equity in it to the mortgagee.

PUBLIC SALE

Strict foreclosure was soon deemed inequitable since the mortgagor was still deprived of all his interest in the property if he did not make payment in full during the equity of redemption period. Courts and the people felt it would be more just to offer the foreclosed property for sale at a public auction because, if at such sale the property sold for more than the debt, the mortgagor would at least save a part if not all of his equity. This method of *public sale* is the predominant method of foreclosure utilized in the United States today.

STATUTORY REDEMPTION

In some states the citizens were still dissatisfied and felt that mortgagees had too many rights. Therefore, they convinced their state legislators to pass laws giving the mortgagor one last chance to get his property back. These laws, enacted during the last century, provide for a period of time, usually a year after the foreclosure sale, in which the mortgagor can, by paying the amount of the debt plus interest, reacquire his property from the auction sale purchaser. In most states where this *statutory right of redemption* exists the mortgagor has the further right of full possession of the property during the statutory redemption period.

Thus, a mortgagee in order to exercise his rights may have to (1) declare a default; (2) institute foreclosure proceedings; (3) bid at a public sale of the property and (4) wait up to one year before he is able to close his files on the matter.

JUNIOR LIENS

When an action to foreclose is begun, all junior lien holders as well as any other persons having an interest in the premises are joined in the suit. This puts all those joined on notice of the impending foreclosure. Upon completion of the action all liens and interest in the property which are inferior, in priority to the mortgage foreclosed, lose all their rights in the property. If, after payment the first lien, sale proceeds remain for distribution they are paid over to satisfy the next lien in priority and so forth down the line of line holders until no funds remain. In the event all liens are paid from sale proceeds any remaining balance goes to the mortgagor. Junior lien holders will often bid the property in at the foreclosure sale in order to save their position or will negotiate with the senior lien holder to assume the obligation rather than lose their interest in the property. Therefore, at a foreclosure sale, regardless of the number of liens against the property, the purchaser at the sale takes the property free and clear of the lien which was foreclosed and all those junior to it. A second mortgagee's foreclosure of his lien will not disturb the first mortgage lien but will wipe out all liens inferior to the second mortgage.

All is not lost for the junior lien holders, however, for if they elect not to assume the foreclosed lien or bid for the property, they always can pursue the mortgagor on the note which the mortgage secured.

One major exception to the priority of mortgage liens is the lien of unpaid real property taxes. Such lien is in essence a first mortgage in favor of the taxing jurisdiction and primes (comes ahead of) all other existing mortgages on the property. Either the taxes have to be paid from foreclosure sale proceeds or the property passes to the purchaser at foreclosure sale, subject to all unpaid tax liens.

DEFICIENCY JUDGMENT

A mortgagee's rights are not necessarily limited to foreclosure nor does the mortgagee have to look only to the proceeds of the foreclosure sale for payment of his debt. The mortgage debt is evidenced by a note which is secured by a mortgage on the debtor's property. The mortgagee upon the mortgagor's default can either exercise his rights against the property or attempt collection against the signatories to the note, or can do both. A suit and subsequent judgment against the signers of the note will act as a lien on all property owned by the signers. This method is rarely resorted to, but can be advantageous when the property is over-financed (mortgaged for more than it is worth) and the signers of the note have substantial assets against which a judgment can be collected. If the mortgagee forecloses and does not realize the amount of his debt out of the proceeds of the foreclosure sale, he can obtain what is termed a *deficiency* judgment against the signatories to the note and attempt collection of the balance of the debt against their personal assets.

Deficiency judgments, however, are not always available. Some states prohibit such actions, other limit them, while many have liberal laws which, for example, allow purchase at foreclosure sale for two-thirds of a property's market value while also establishing a right in the mortgage to claim as a deficiency the difference between the two-thirds figure and the original indebtedness. The mortgagee sometimes, especially with income property loans, will agree with the mortgagor that an *exculpatory* clause be put in the note and mortgage. An exculpatory clause limits the mortgagee, in the event of a default, in the exercise of his rights against the property securing the debt. Due to the possibility of losing all lien rights on the property secured in the event of foreclosure of a senior lien, it is not wise to include an exculpatory clause in a second or junior mortgage.

POWER OF SALE

Deeds of trust vest in the trustee a *power of sale.* Under such power a speedy and non-judicial sale of the mortgaged premises can be made. Many states limit the mortgagee's right to a deficiency judgment where the exercise of the power of sale is used. In California the use of the power of sale cuts off the mortgagee's right to a deficiency judgment. The power of sale has its advantage in California since it can be concluded in five months as opposed to over a year in the case of judicial foreclosure. The power of sale is not limited to deeds of trust, since many states now provide for such a power to be included in mortgages. The method of sale is to give notice to the mortgagor of the default, allow the required time for equitable right of redemption, advertise for the public sale of the property and then hold the sale.

SOLDIERS AND SAILORS CIVIL RELIEF ACT

The Soldiers and Sailors Civil Act affects mortgages in several important ways.

The court in which an action to foreclose a mortgage appears has the power to stay or postpone the proceedings where a civilian mortgagor now in the military service is unable to comply with the terms of his obligation because of such military service. However, the inability to meet the mortgage obligation must have been caused by the mortgagor's induction into the military service and a reduction in the mortgagor's income occasioned by such induction.

A power of sale foreclosure is void if the mortgagor is in the military service or was in the military service anytime within three months preceding the sale. The only exception to this is a prior court order authorizing a power of sale foreclosure. This is just another disadvantage of the power of sale method.

In statutory redemption states the period of military service is not included in computing the redemption period, thus indefinitely prolonging the foreclosure.

The toughest provision of the act, particularly when interest rates are high, is that the mortgagee can collect no more than 6 percent interest during the period of the military service, unless the mortgagor's ability to pay is not affected by his military status.

MORTGAGE ADJUSTMENTS

As an alternative to foreclosure or suit on the obligation there may be a voluntary transfer of the property by the mortgagor to the mortgagee. When a *deed in lieu of foreclosure* is given, the mortgagee steps into the mortgagor's place and is subject to junior liens, whereas foreclosure removes all junior liens. The big problem surrounding deeds in lieu of foreclosure, at least from a mortgagee's standpoint, is the question of consideration given for the transfer. If the transfer takes undue advantage of the mortgagor, the possibility exists that the mortgagor can at some future time sue on the basis of mortgagee fraud or duress and recover his property. The obvious advantage to the mortgagee is the savings of time, attorney fees and court costs involved in a foreclosing.

ASSUMPTION OF MORTGAGE

When mortgaged property is sold, the Grantee can take title either *subject* to the mortgage or by *assumption.*

If the Grantee takes title subject to the existing mortgage, he does not obligate himself to its payment. If he or a subsequent grantee defaults, the grantee taking subject to the mortgage cannot be held personally liable for the obligation or for any deficiency judgment. If he defaults, he, of course, stands to lose the mortgaged property and his equity in it.

A Grantee who takes title and assumes the obligation to pay a mortgage debt is personally liable for it and for any deficiency judgment. His assumption of the debt does not release the mortgagor or any subsequent assumer of the debt from liability. In the absence of any release of liability by the mortgagee the original mortgagor and all subsequent grantees, assuming the mortgage under him whether or not they are in possession of the property, are liable to the mortgagee for a deficiency judgment. A prior grantee who is called on to pay a deficiency judgment is subrogated to the rights that the mortgagee has against the original mortgagor and all subsequent grantees. The mortgagee, however, is required to exhaust his rights first against the defaulting grantee.

The above discussion, of course, presupposes the absence of an exculpatory clause in the mortgage instrument.

A transfer of title subject to or by assumption of the mortgage cannot always be done without the mortgagee's consent. Mortgagees desiring a responsible party to be in possession of the mortgaged premises will at times insert in the mortgage a provision that a transfer of the property without consent constitutes a default and accelerates the debt to maturity. In times of rising interest rates, mortgagee consent to a transfer of title is very rare. However, recent court decisions in several states have had an important impact on the mortgage lending industry by declaring such a provision limiting transfer unenforceable.

ASSIGNMENT OF MORTGAGE

Since a mortgage is considered to be an asset owned by its holder, it can be disposed of by the holder by *assignment.* An assignment by the mortgagee does not require the consent of the mortgagor, unless the parties have otherwise agreed. The party taking the assignment must assure himself of two things:

1. That, he succeeds to the rights of the original mortgagee. This can be done by a search of the record and immediate recordation of the assignment to assure priority over any prior unrecorded assignment.

2. Secondly, in order to verify the mortgage balance and discover an offset or defense, if any, which the mortgagor may impose, an *estoppel certificate* should be obtained from the mortgagor showing the unpaid balance as of the date of assignment and listing all defenses or claims the mortgagor may have against the mortgagee.

EXTENSION OF MORTGAGE

Occasionally a mortgagor cannot make a payment when the obligation matures and therefore requests an extension of the debt for a period of time in order to raise funds to discharge the debt. This is a common occurrence in construction lending when the houses covered by the loan have not sold, due to construction or marketing problems, and the builder needs more time to find buyers. Mortgage extensions, however, cause several problems for the mortgagee. One specific problem relates to guarantors and previous grantees. An extension of a debt or a recasting of a debt releases them from liability unless they agree in writing to the extension or recasting. Guarantors and prior grantees have in essence agreed to act as sureties on the obligation as originally made. Therefore, any change in the terms of the original obligation constitutes a change in the guarantors' and prior grantees' surety agreement, thereby releasing them from liability. To avoid the releasing of such grantees and guarantors and to avoid foreclosure, many mortgagees in this situation carry the obligation past due. This allows the mortgagee to declare a default at any time and commence foreclosure proceedings while also keeping the sureties intact.

EFFECT ON MORTGAGE FUND AVAILABILITY

Mortgagees place a great significance on their rights in the event of a mortgagor's default. When a default occurs mortgagees want to quickly act upon their security and receive payment for all unpaid principal and accrued interest on the defaulted obligation. For this reason a mortgagee, before making a mortgage investment, analyzes the security he will receive from the standpoint of his rights and of the laws affecting any action that may be taken to liquidate the security.

Hence, a mortgagee is less likely to invest funds in mortgages on properties in states with statutory redemption periods than he is to channel mortgage funds into states with favorable foreclosure laws. Similarly, a mortgagee will prefer a mortgage which provides for a deficiency judgment and power of sale foreclosure over one that does not contain those provisions.

It may then be said that the geographical availability of mortgage funds is greatly influenced by state foreclosure laws and that the willingness of investors to place funds in mortgages is directly related to the respective rights of mortgagor and mortgagee. The greater the balance is of foreclosure laws and mortgagee rights in favor of the mortgagee the more willing investors will be to make a mortgage investment.

QUESTIONS FOR THOUGHT AND DISCUSSION

1. California has adopted what is termed the "one action rule." Under this rule if the mortgagee uses the power of sale foreclosure method he cannot go against the borrowers personally.
   a. Do you feel that such a method of foreclosure should be adopted nationwide, whereby a speedy method of foreclosure is available to a mortgagee on a "one action rule" basis?
   b. If you held a second trust on a California property in a time of declining real estate values, what would you do in the event of a default on your trust and the one superior to it?
2. What is the advantage of appointing a receiver in the event of default by the borrower on a mortgage loan?
3. If you were the mortgagee on a defaulted loan and the mortgagor not wishing to litigate the matter offered to give you a deed in lieu of foreclosure, would you take it? Why or why not?
4. Do you feel that deficiency judgments should be abolished?
5. A mortgages Blackacre to B, a mortgage lender. C buys Blackacre from A subject to the mortgage and subsequently sells to D who assumes the existing mortgage. The title to Blackacre later passes to E, then to F and finally to G, all of whom take subject to the mortgage. G defaults on the mortgage and B forecloses obtaining a deficiency judgment.
   a. Against whom can mortgagee B collect his deficiency judgment?
   b. If one of those liable for the deficiency pays, what are his rights against others?
   c. If the mortgage indebtedness had been increased prior to the transfer from F to G would your first answer be the same? Why?
6. What effect, if any, do you feel laws like statutory redemption have upon the availability of mortgage funds to the citizens of the states where such laws prevail?
   a. Are citizens served or harmed by such legislation?
   b. Is your thinking the same with regard to strict foreclosure?

4

JUNIOR LIENS

Junior liens play a significant part in real estate financing. Such liens are by definition subject and subordinate to liens enjoying a first or prior claim to real estate security. The most popular form of junior lien is the second mortgage. However, subordinated debentures and ground rents are also important modern forms of junior liens. Some may take exception to the classification of ground rents as junior liens for, in essence, they are first in priority. Ground rents can be thought of either as substitutes for second mortgages or as leaseholds. Nevertheless, they are appropriately discussed along with other types of junior liens. In addition, mechanics liens which may at times be first liens, are best covered in this chapter.

It is important to know where mortgage funds for junior liens can be found and what type of junior lien investments are favored by various lenders. These facts will also be covered in this chapter.

SECOND MORTGAGES

Because of their inferior lien position on real estate, second mortgages are considered a speculative investment. From a security standpoint, should a default occur in the first mortgage and a foreclosure take place, the second mortgage holder stands to lose all his rights against the real estate security. The second mortgage holder has a junior claim on all income from the real estate secured since the income earned is applied first to the debt service on the first mortgage, then to payment of the second. Thus, second mortgages carry higher interest rates and are made for shorter terms. Nevertheless, there is a strong demand and need for secondary financing and many individuals and lenders are willing to invest in such loans.

EXAMPLES OF SECONDARY FINANCING

The most common examples of secondary financing situations with usual rates and terms are as follows:

1. *Home builders* who desire a fast market for their product and are willing to offer prospective purchasers 90 percent or better loan-to-value financing by using a conventional 80 percent first mortgage and taking back a 10 percent second. This combination is not available using FHA-insured mortgages, since most FHA form mortgages prohibit secondary liens. Rates are usually one to two percent higher than the conventional first-mortgage rate and are for terms of five to ten years with monthly payments of principal and interest equal to $10 per $1,000 of mortgage amount. In such cases balloon payments are common.

   The builder making such loans frequently markets them in quantity and at discount to commercial finance companies, thereby obtaining capital for future housing projects.

2. *Individuals* who, in order to sell their homes with the existing mortgage being assumed by the purchaser (thereby passing on to the purchaser a favorable first-mortgage rate) or for that matter on a straight-sale basis, will take back a second mortgage to ease the initial cash requirements of the purchaser. These mortgages are made at rates and upon terms similar, but frequently lower, than those mentioned in the above case. In this and the above example usury laws (laws placing a legal ceiling on interest rates charged by lenders to borrowers) have a limiting effect upon the interest rate charged.

3. *Business or personal loans* for which collateral security is required. Here the rate and terms are related to the credit transaction rather than to the real estate security.

4. *Improvements to existing property,* both home and commercial. These loans were the source of much notoriety and a major cause of Truth-in-Lending legislation. Improvement mortgages are somewhat safer than most second mortgages since they are made against a percentage of the value of additions to property and are usually junior to first mortgages which have been paid down. Accordingly, rates are only slightly above the going conventional first-mortgage rate and can run for terms up to twenty years. Under FHA's Title I program, home modernization loans up to $12,000 are obtainable by private homeowners for repairs or remodeling at the current FHA maximum interest rate plus discounts of up to eight points (one point is equivalent to one percent of mortgage amount) and for seven-year-32-day terms. The Title I program is primarily for credit loans, but second mortgages are usually taken as additional collateral.

5. *Interim financing* in the form of land purchase mortgages subordinated to a construction loan. Builders and developers, when purchasing large tracts of unimproved land for development into housing or income projects, will attempt to negotiate a subordination clause into their purchase money mortgages. Such a clause will provide for subordination of the purchase money mortgage to a bona fide first-mortgage loan obtained for developing the tract and construction improvements thereon. The seller, by agreeing to such a provision, finds he can more easily market his property. The builder-developer with subordination advantage can use the value of

the land as equity when obtaining his development and/or construction loan and can lessen his cash requirement.

Most subordination clauses do not become effective until the mortgagee (seller) has been paid a predetermined sum. When instituted, the interest rate on the mortgage usually increases by as much as one percent to three percent during the subordination period. At a certain point in time or upon closing of a permanent loan, the subordinated mortgage must be released in full or at least with regard to a portion of property it secures. Interest rates before subordination are usually equal to conventional mortgage rates but can vary greatly.

6. *Owners* seeking to raise equity for an apartment, shopping center, or similar income-producing project, and in need of secondary financing. Since many institutional investors are limited to 66-2/3 percent to 75 percent loan-to-value ratio mortgages, sufficient equity remains that can be mortgaged. Similarly, enough cash flow should be left after payment of the first mortgage debt service to discharge the debt service on the second mortgage. Of significance to the mortgage lender in this instance is the fact that, in the event of a default, the property can be taken over subject to the first mortgage and be readily marketed. Income properties are more easily sold subject to large existing mortgages than other types of properties. Terms from three to five years, and occasionally up to ten years, are obtainable at interest rates generally from 12 to 18 percent with one to two points due at time the loan is closed. Loans which cannot be made at these terms and rates are probably too risky to even be considered.

7. *Gap financing* brought about by recent institutional lending techniques on income-producing properties, primarily apartments. Institutional permanent loan commitments may be conditioned upon a specific rent and/or occupancy achievement. For example, a commitment may provide that $2,300,000 will be advanced at the permanent loan closing if a specific rental and/or occupancy requirement is met. If it is not met, then only $2,000,000 will be advanced. The problem created is that the borrower usually needs and obtains a construction loan for the higher amount. To insure payment in full at the permanent loan closing the construction lender will require the borrower to cover the $300,000 differential, or "gap", with a letter of credit or a $300,000 second mortgage loan commitment. The commitment alone usually costs about 5 percent of the second mortgage amount, or in this example $15,000. If the gap second mortgage is closed, the rate will range from 13 to 18 percent. The great risk here is evident. If the rental and/or occupancy achievement cannot be met within the time allotted, the market for the units must be deemed poor and the availability of sufficient cash flow to meet the second mortgage debt service is unlikely, or at most, questionable. Needless to say, most lenders issuing such a commitment as well as the borrower anticipate and firmly hope that the second mortgage loan will never be made. If made, the term will be very short, six months to one year or even upon demand.

8. *The subordinated land sale leaseback* is a form of junior lien. In this situation the land under a commercial building, such as the land under an office building, is sold by the owner and then leased-back by him (sale-

leaseback transactions are discussed in detail in Chapter 7, supra). The lease for the land is then made subordinate to any claim against the property (land and building) that may be made by the holder of the first mortgage on the improvements. The subordinated land lease then maintains a junior lien position with respect to the property.

9. The wrap-around mortgage is another recent development in secondary mortgage financing. This type of mortgage has been used quite successfully in Canada and is now coming into vogue in the United States. A wrap-around mortgage usually involves an existing property where financing either cannot be readily prepaid due to an unfavorable prepayment provision or where the interest rate on the present first mortgage is so low as to make prepayment impractical. However, due to amortization of the first mortgage, and/or increased property value, and/or improvements or additions, and/or better leasing income, there is justification for refinancing with a larger mortgage.

The borrower receives a new mortgage based on the current value of the property. The lender advances to the borrower the difference between the principal amount of the new mortgage loan and the existing financing. The lender then agrees to meet the debt service of existing mortgage. He does so by collecting principal and interest payments on the combined liens, paying the debt service on the existing mortgage, and retaining the difference.

This arrangement, while it does not actually put the new lender in a first lien position, does technically give him that advantage. However, a wrap-around mortgage must be considered a second mortgage. The advantage of this financing arrangement to the lender is the increased yield due to the differential in interest rates on the existing and new mortgages.

In the case of the borrower, he usually receives his additional financing at a lower rate than a straight refinancing due to the interest differential received by the new lender.

Accordingly, interest rates on the wrap-around are below prevailing second mortgage rates. The terms are usually longer, ranging up to twenty-five years.

A specific example of a wrap-around mortgage is as follows:

Existing first:	$2,000,000 @ 6% for 25 years
Remaining approximate principal balance:	$1,500,000
Present value of property:	$4,000,000
Additional financing requested:	$1,500,000
Wrap-around mortgage terms and rate:	$3,000,000 @ 8% for 25 years

The wrap-around lender disburses $1,500,000 collects the debt service on the $3,000,000 mortgage ($278,000) and pays the debt service on the existing $2,000,000 mortgage ($154,800). He retains the differential which represents his yield plus principal amortization on the $1,500,000 loaned ($124,000). Note that after the original $2,000,000 mortgage is repaid, the wrap-around lender will collect 8 percent on $3,000,000 for ten years against a $1,500,000 disbursement.

LOAN SOURCES FOR JUNIOR LIENS

The second mortgage market is made up of a variety of lenders desirous of obtaining a high yield on relatively short-term paper. The more important participants in the second mortgage market and their reason for investing in these mortgages are set forth below:

1. *Life insurance companies and mutual savings banks* which usually are prohibited from investing in second mortgages. However, under the "basket" or "leeway" provisions of the insurance company investment regulations and the regulatory acts governing most mutual savings banks, a small percentage of total assets (usually 3 to 5 percent) may be placed in otherwise illegal investments. Life insurance companies are the best sources for wraparound type second mortgages when they can "basket" them until the first mortgage loan is completely paid off.

2. *Individuals,* who as previously noted, invest in various ways in second mortgages.

3. *Commercial financing companies* who obtain their funds by borrowing from commercial banks and who then re-lend the money at high yields.

4. *Real estate finance companies* which operate similarly to commercial finance companies, but are primarily interested in real estate lending.

5. *Material suppliers* who, usually through subsidiaries, extend credit in order to encourage use of their products.

6. *Small business investment companies* created by the Small Business Investment Act of 1958 in order to stimulate and supplement the flow of private capital to beginning and small business organizations in general.

7. *Real estate holding companies and industrial corporations* who desire to invest their surplus funds on a high yield and fairly secure basis.

8. *The Small Business Administration.*

9. *State and local development authorities* which, in order to attract industrial development, will make low-interest rate second mortgages.

10. *Foreign nationals* seeking to invest their funds abroad at a high rate of return.

11. *Mortgage investment trusts* which favor the high yields produced by gap commitments, wrap-around mortgages and second mortgages.

Noticeably absent from the above list are two major financial institutions: *savings and loan associations* and *commercial banks,* which are either prohibited or severely restricted by law from directly making second mortgage loans. These institutions can normally only take second mortgages as additional security for other loans made by them.

EVALUATION OF THE RISK

Because of the greater risks confronting second mortgage lenders, the evaluation of a second mortgage opportunity is usually more carefully made than when considering a first lien investment. Particular attention is given to location, property income, soundness of the first mortgage financing, ability of the property management, and the credit of the borrower.

PARTICULAR LENDER REQUIREMENTS

In order to sufficiently protect their position, most second mortgage lenders will impose certain requirements on borrowers in the form of special mortgage provision. Some of the more noteworthy provisions which may be imposed are listed below:

1. Cross default, or a default in the first mortgage which will trigger a default in the second mortgage.

2. The right of the second mortgagee to pay taxes, insurance, and similar charges upon failure of the mortgagor to do so. Such payments will be added to the mortgage debt.

3. The right to require the mortgagor to escrow funds for future payment of taxes, insurance and even the first mortgage debt service.

4. Provision that the mortgagor will not amend the first mortgage covenants and conditions nor any leases, grant rent concessions or accept more than one month's advance rental.

5. Provision that the mortgagee shall have the right to cure any default in first mortgage.

6. Personal guaranty of the borrower. (First mortgages on income-producing properties, particularly apartments, usually do not require individual liability.)

SUBORDINATED DEBENTURES

An instrument of finance used quite extensively today, particularly by large corporations, is the subordinated debenture.

A debenture is an obligation secured primarily by the financial integrity of the issuer and at times by a mortgage or mortgages.

The debenture is simply the issuer's contract for repayment and security. Normally the issuer executes an indenture with a trustee, such as a bank. The indenture will state the denomination, interest rate, maturity date and special features (such as convertibility, call ability, etc.) of the debenture bonds which the trustee will issue. It will also restrict the extent of the issuer's future indebtedness.

Since non-subordinated debentures restrict the issuer's future borrowing capacity, many issuers have turned to subordinated debentures which specifically provide that they are inferior to present and future indebtedness, including mortgages on the issuer's property, and share only in priority with general creditors. Naturally, this flexibility requires the payment of a greater return to bond purchasers than do non-subordinated debentures. Nevertheless, many real estate development companies find subordinated debentures a very satisfactory route to raising capital since nearly 100 percent financing of real estate can be obtained by this method with credit flexibility still maintained.

Such non-subordinated debentures give the bond holders priority over most creditors and, in many instances, over subsequently recorded liens on the issuer's property. Therefore, a non-subordinated debenture many times acts as a mortgage substitute and, in fact, is frequently used by chain stores, drug stores, discount houses, and other similar companies to raise capital to purchase properties.

RATES AND TERMS

Subordinated debentures are marketed in the same way as common stocks and bonds and bear rates determined by the credit rating of the issuer, particular features of the debenture, and restrictions, if any, on future indebtedness of the issuer. In general, the interest rates are higher than the average prevailing bond rates, but lower than second mortgage rates. In fact, debentures bearing rates in excess of 11 percent are extremely difficult to market. (As to issuer, it is important to note that brokerage fees of up to 15 percent must be paid, thereby reducing the net to the issuer and the cost of such borrowing.) Maturity dates on issues vary from five to thirty years and average twenty years. In essence, a company with a sound financial condition can raise large sums of capital with subordinated debentures at terms and rates much more favorable than the second mortgage method.

SPECIAL FEATURES

Many debentures are issued with special features which affect their marketability. Some of the more important features are as follows:

Call Ability is a provision that permits the issuer to redeem the debentures prior to maturity. This feature is unfavorable from a marketing standpoint, since debenture investors seek investment of their funds for a definite and known period of time. Early redemption causes the problem of reinvestment of funds. This fact is particularly significant when the debentures are issued during peak interest rate periods, since redemption will take place normally when rates fall and the investor will not likely be able to reinvest his funds at interest rates that are as favorable.

Sinking Fund debentures require a certain percentage of the principal amount of the debt to be escrowed annually to insure availability of funds for redemption at maturity.

Convertible deventures allow the holder to exchange his bonds for stock in the issuing corporation at a pre-determined exchange rate. This provision is extremely favorable when the issuer's shares are rapidly increasing in value, since an increase in market value of issuer's stock will directly affect the market value of the convertible debentures. The opposite is also true, but in lesser proportion.

GROUND RENTS

Ground rents are a system of financing real estate by the granting of a perpetual lease on vacant land to be used for building purposes. The system has been used quite extensively in the city of Baltimore and areas of Pennsylvania since colonial times and is today gaining new popularity, especially in the west.

Under the original Maryland ground rent system land was leased by the leessor to the lessee for 99 years with the lease renewable forever. These early ground leases contained no provisions whereby the lessee could acquire the fee. The only method of fee title acquisition and ground lease cancellation was to bargain the title from the lessor. In the late nineteenth century, due to vociferous public opinion, the legislature declared irredeemable ground rents undesirable and, through a succession of laws, determined that all subsequent residential ground leases for as long as fifteen years should be redeemable after five years for a price equal to the capitalization of the ground rent at 6 percent.

Therefore, the ground lease system is firmly established in Maryland and, for that matter, in various other jurisdictions to the extent that mortgagees have been accustomed for many years to financing the construction of buildings on leased ground. A mortgage made for such purposes is really a leasehold mortgage second in priority to the ground rent and, for most purposes, is identical to the leasehold mortgages discussed in Chapter 6. However, in a ground rent situation the redeemable feature is frequently present (since the late nineteenth century in both Maryland and Pennsylvania it is always present as to residential property); and, in the event of foreclosure, the mortgagee can accede to the position of the mortgagor-ground lessee and thereby protect his position.

Since the creation of a ground rent allows the lessee to build and own a house for less initial cash, it is many times considered a second mortgage substitute. For example, a home valued at $40,000 and mortgaged conventionally for $32,000 (80 percent of value) would normally require a downpayment of $8,000. Using the ground rent method with an established land value of $6,000, a mortgage of $27,200 (80 percent of improvement value) would be obtainable and would reduce the cash requirement to $6,800 with a $30 per month ground rent payment. The result is a deferment of a required equity of $1,200 by using a ground rent instead of a second mortgage.

The obvious advantages of the ground rent over a second mortgage are a much longer term, in perpetuity if the redemption option is available and is not exercised, and lower rates which combine to ease the monthly cash payment effect. As to ground rent rates, they most commonly run 6 percent per annum of the value of the property, but can be more, particularly in times of higher interest rates. Also, in some areas renegotiation clauses in ground leases are common as are provisions for increased rent tied to a price index.

Until recently the ground rent system never caught on outside the states of Maryland and Pennsylvania. Today, however, due to high land costs, ground rents have become very popular in Hawaii and parts of California. Because of land covenants the development of the 88,000-acre Irvine Ranch located in Orange County, California, one of the fastest-growing counties in the United States, is being accomplished on a strictly leasehold basis. Such a system has not hindered, but rather aided, the development of the Irvine Ranch, and houses located there are easily sold for up to $300,000 subject to a long-term ground lease without financing problems.

Leaseholds are eligible for FHA mortgage insurance if the unexpired term of the lease is at least fifty years, or if the lease is for ninety-nine years and renewable. The Veterans Administration will guarantee a leasehold mortgage if the primary term of the lease is at least fifteen years beyond the maturity date of the mortgage.

Individuals and pension funds are the best sources for ground leases. Leasehold financing, when insured by FHA or guaranteed by VA, is available from most institutional sources. As to conventional leaseholds on residences subject to ground rents, the sources are governed by the local situation as to acceptability and legal lending requirements of the institution. Normally, residential leaseholds subject to ground rents can be financed as if the ground rent did not exist.

MECHANICS LIENS

Mechanics liens are not a method of real estate finance as are the other junior liens previously discussed. However, mechanics liens play an important role in real estate financing.

Mechanics lien laws were passed to protect those persons whose labor and materials enhanced the value of real estate on the theory that they should have a preferred lien on the improvements they created in order to insure payment for their labor and materials. The lien created is similar to a mortgage lien and in most jurisdictions may be foreclosed as such.

THOSE PROTECTED

Some older statutes on mechanics liens protected only those who furnished labor or materials to a project other than by direct contract with the property owner. Today, however, a labor or materialman is protected whether or not his contract is with the landowner, general contractor (other than landowner and under contract directly to the landowner) or even with a subcontractor (one who has contracted with the general contractor).

As to subcontractors, their liens are obtained either directly (Pennsylvania System) or by reference to the general contractor's lien (New York System). With regard to the latter, the subcontractor is subrogated to the rights of the general contractor and cannot claim a sum greater than that claimable by the general contractor. Due to the subrogation, a subcontractor can claim no lien when the general contractor defaults under his contract with the owner, causing cancellation of that contract and no additional funds due and owning. The Pennsylvania System of direct subcontractor lien obligates the landowner to see to the payment of those with whom he has no contract (the landowner contracts with general contractors who in turn employ under contract, subcontractors). Under this system the landowner must have the general contractor identify the subcontractors and must withold sufficient funds from the general contractor to insure payment of all subcontractors.

In certain states, materialmen are dealt with separately as to lien rights, whereas in others, materialman men are regarded as either contractors or subcontractors.

OWNER'S CONSENT

The consent of the owner is an important incident to creation of the mechanics lien. The labor and materials must have been furnished by reason of contract or agreement by the landowner. Some states require that the claimant show he was hired directly by the owner or his agent, whereas others simply require that the lien claimant prove that the landowner gave his consent to the doing of the work or furnishing of the materials, even though the work or materials were ordered by other than the landowner.

As between landlord and tenant, work ordered by the tenant does not automatically bind the landlord. There must be consent on the part of the landlord, either by express and specific wording in a lease requiring the tenant to make certain improvements or by the landlord's direct consent to the work. Few states allow a lien to be created if the landowner simply knows that the construction work is being done and fails to protest. These states and others have what are termed "consent statutes". In most of these states, the property owner is deemed to have consented to those improvements ordered by a tenant or others unless within a specific time after learning about the work, the property owner conspicuously posts a notice of nonresponsibility for the work in question. The notice must be posted on the premises and within three to ten days, depending upon the state, after finding out about the work.

PRIORITY OF MECHANICS LIEN

The priority of mechanics liens vary from state to state. The variances and hence the priority of the lien are generally affected by the time of attachment of the mechanics lien.

The majority of the states hold that a mortgage recorded prior to the commencement of any work on the property will prime any future recorded mechanics liens. Among these states, however, three different interpretations exist:

1. In a few of the states, the mechanics lien attaches when the specific mechanic commences work. Hence, the time of attachment of lien and the time of recordation of a mortgage or other lien have to be first determined in order to find out which lien has priority. In these jurisdictions it would be possible for some mechanics liens to prime a mortgage and for others not to, depending upon the timing of attachment and recordation.
2. In other states, the mechanics lien is always a prior lien as to the improvements for which the lien is created, but not as to a mortgage or other lien on the land and pre-existing improvements.
3. In other jurisdictions, mechanics liens attach from the date of the first work. Hence, if work commenced prior to the date of a mortgage, then *all* mechanics liens for work performed will be prior to the mortgage.

A few states give mechanics liens priority from the date of the first contract for improvements. Thus, if an owner enters into a general contract for construction of a building on his property and then obtains a mortgage, any mechanics liens arising out of the transaction will be prior to the mortgage.

These states are the ones most protective of labors and materialmen. The lien created is a secret one since it is not required to be filed of record. For this reason a mortgagee is fully at a disadvantage, not knowing whether or not his lien may be primed by an already created mechanics lien.

In few jurisdictions, it is the filing of a notice of record that gives rise to the time of attachment of the mechanics lien. Hence, a mortgage recorded before a notice is filed will enjoy a superior lien right over that mechanics lien and all future filed mechanics liens. The laws in these jurisdiction strongly favor the mortgagee.

ENFORCEMENT OF MECHANICS LIENS

The attachment of a mechanics lien or the right to file a lien does not give rise to automatic enforcement of the lien. Many state statutes provide that the person seeking to enforce the lien must notify the landowner particularly when the person is seeking to claim his lien through another party, such as a subcontractor or material supplier who has not been paid by a general contractor. Besides notification to the landowner, the person seeking to assert a mechanics lien must in many states timely file his lien of record. The filing requirements vary from state to state, but in general the claimant must give an affidavit as to work done, amount claimed, and the property against which the claim is made. Some jurisdictions require the claim to state the time of the last work or furnishing of materials due to the timely filing requirements of the statutes.

COLLECTION OF MECHANICS LIEN

To collect on a mechanics lien, the claimant must take court action to sell the property liened. Such action is similar to the foreclosure of a mortgage lien.

WAIVER OR RELEASE OF MECHANICS LIENS

In order to protect against a future mechanics lien claim it is wise to obtain a waiver or release of liens as money is disbursed for labor and materials furnished to a construction project. For example, if construction disbursements are made monthly, as work progresses, the owner is wise to require the general contractor to list each subcontractor and materialman furnishing work or materials covered by the billing period and the dollar amount of such work or materials so provided. Then as payment is made the general contractor, subcontractors, and materialmen can be required to execute a release or waiver of lien statement to the extent of the payments received. This is not a foolproof system, but it does provide for proper application of funds and some insurance against improperly filed liens.

Many times landowners obtain a release or waiver of lien prior to payment of any funds. Most jurisdictions hold that such waivers or releases are not binding if indeed they were obtained without payment of consideration. Some further hold that execution of waivers or releases without payment is invalid as being against public policy and in contravention of mechanics liens laws.

If a mechanics lien has been filed of record and is then discharged by the owner or builder, the execution of a normal release or waiver of mechanics liens will not release the lien of record. A particular recordable form of release of mechanics liens as required by statute must be formally executed and properly recorded in order to discharge the lien from record. In many states a recorded mechanics lien may be removed from a particular property by the obtaining and filing of a surety bond. This particular method is resorted to in those instances where the owner has a valid dispute with the lien claimant, but wants to transfer property free and clear of the mechanics liens prior to settling the dispute.

DOUBLE PAYMENT

The major problem faced by the mortgagee and mortgagor in relation to mechanics liens is double payment. The mortgagee through the mortgage will make payment to the general cotractor who in turn is to pay his sub-contractors. When the contractor defaults in his obligations to the sub-contractors, the mortgagor becomes liable to them when a mechanics lien is filed. Thus, the mortgagor and many times the mortgagee are faced with a double payment situation due to a defaulting general contractor.

QUESTIONS FOR THOUGHT AND DISCUSSION

1. Explain the difference between a claim secured by a cognovit note and one secured by a lien.
2. Who gets paid first in the event of liquidation—a subordinated debenture holder or a common stockholder?
3. List several instances in which secondary financing may be required.
4. What is gap financing?
5. Many first mortgage lenders write a provision into their mortgage making a further encumbering of the property secured an event of default. What is their reasoning?
6. a. List as many factors as come to mind which could have an effect on a decision to make a second mortgage loan.
   b. Would you add or delete any factors with respect to a first mortgage loan decision? Explain.

5

COOPERATIVES AND CONDOMINIUMS

COOPERATIVES

Cooperative ownership of real property, as we know it today, had its beginning in the nineteenth century. The concept gained favor in the years immediately following World War I, but floundered during the depression. After World War II there was a resurgence of interest in cooperatives, with a mild boom taking place in the 1960s due to the passage of several government subsidized cooperative programs.

Some of the first major cooperative projects were built in New York City as a means of avoiding rent control. In the post World War II era, New York City set the pattern and has been an early pioneer in rent control laws directed toward preventing excessive rental charges in periods of housing shortages. Cooperative developments are a method of producing rental-type housing without rent control and hence led to the post World War II boom in cooperative development.

The cooperative pattern of financing has been used both primarily and successfully with large apartment complexes in major metropolitan areas, but has also been applied to single family community development. Greenbelt, Maryland, a large suburban Washington, D.C. town, began as a cooperative community and is possibly the largest single family cooperative development in existence today.

FORM OF ORGANIZATION

Cooperatives predominately take the corporate form. The first step is to organize the cooperative corporation. That entity then purchases an existing housing development to convert over to a cooperative or will sponsor the construction of a new housing development. Through the sale of stock, capital is raised to purchase the existing land and structures or to acquire land for construction. The stock subscriptions plus a large mortgage enable the corporation to accomplish its purposes. Once ownership by the corporation is established each apartment or single family unit, as the case may be, is assigned a rental price dependent upon the arrangement, location, size of the unit, and such other factors which effect the value of one unit over another.

The corporation then leases all of the units it has purchased or built to those persons who are shareholders of the corporation. Such occupants, called *tenant-shareholders*, execute what is termed a *proprietary lease*. A tenant-shareholder acquires the right to use and occupy his unit so long as he meets all his obligations to the corporation. As a prerequisite the tenant-shareholder has purchased stock in the corporation and is required to retain said stock for as long as he occupies the apartment unit. Naturally, the stock is priced to cover the difference between the mortgage financing secured and the cost of purchase or construction with contingencies included.

Title to the cooperative real estate is always vested in the corporation with the tenant-shareholder paying what amounts to rent. The rent, however, is applied to the mortgage debt service, upkeep of the property, and payment of operating expenses. Thus, the tenant-shareholder's rent, in part, accrues to his benefit through an increase in the cooperative corporation's equity in the residential development. This equity increase is passed on to the tenant-shareholder in proportion to his stock ownership.

Cooperatives are not always organized as corporations. They can take the form of trust with legal title vested in a trustee such as a bank, or the individual can take title to the unit he uses as a tenant-in-common.

Advantages

The major advantages of the cooperative form of ownership are:
1. The opportunity to enjoy the benefits that normally come from the ownership of property, and which, in the absence of the cooperative form, would be nothing more than a straight rental situation.
2. Of particular importance today, the ability to provide for adequate security by being able to hire staff as is necessary and install safety devices as agreed upon by the tenant-shareholder as opposed to a landlord who has a right of refusal.
3. The stabilization of rents. Under the cooperative form, increases are only made to meet additional taxes and operating expenses, not to obtain a higher rate of return for a landlord.
4. The tax advantages to the tenant-shareholder of being able to deduct his share of real estate taxes and mortgage interest from his personal income. Such deductions are not available to tenants under a normal rental contract.

Disadvantages

Some of the more important disadvantages of cooperatives are:

1. The high initial promotion cost must be borne by the tenant-shareholders.
2. The liability of each tenant-shareholder for the solvency of the cooperative. Since the cooperative corporation or entity must carry the total project through rentals obtained from tenant-shareholders, a decrease in occupancy will directly affect its ability to meet debt service and operating expenses. The cost of carrying the vacancies is therefore passed on to the remaining tenant-shareholders who must either invest additional funds or lose their investments. Therefore, each tenant-shareholder is dependent upon solvency of the entire project. If the cooperative mortgage is defaulted and foreclosed, the tenant-shareholders can be dispossessed and they will retain only a right to receive whatever is left over after liquidation of the cooperative's assets.
a. *Escape Provision*—In order to provide relief from future assessments, some cooperative charters contain "escape" provisions allowing the tenant-shareholders to surrender their units in return for a release of all future liability.

SALE OF STOCK

With the consent of the cooperative corporation, a tenant-shareholder may sell his stock and assign his lease. A prudent purchaser will assure himself that they are free from assessments and sub-leases and that no defaults have occurred in the mortgage of the cooperative corporation.

FHA INSURED COOPERATIVE MORTGAGES

The Federal Housing Administration has five major mortgage insurance programs for cooperative projects. The programs encompass construction, rehabilitation, or acquisition of five or more units of single family or multifamily housing for occupancy by tenant-shareholders of a nonprofit cooperative corporation.

Section 213 of the National Housing Act is the primary cooperative program. Cooperatives eligible for mortgage insurance under this section can either be *management-type,* where permanent occupancy of the project is restricted to tenant-shareholders, or *sales-type,* which is organized for the purpose of constructing homes for its tenant-shareholders.

Sales-type projects must involve new construction. The procedure is for FHA to insure a blanket mortgage for construction of single family homes by a cooperative for sale to its members. Upon completion of construction individual FHA insured mortgages are made to home purchases and the loan proceeds used to discharge the blanket mortgage. Financing of the individual mortgage loans is accomplished at terms similar to the standard, Section 203b, FHA home ownership program. After all loans are made, the cooperative retains ownership only of the common areas (green spaces) and facilities, such as tennis courts and swimming pools.

Mortgages insurable under the management-type program are $25,000,000 for a public mortgagor and $20,000,000 otherwise, (no limit for unsubsidized cooperative multifamily housing projects) with a maximum term of forty years or three-quarters of the remaining economic life, whichever is less. Under the sales-type program the maximum mortgage is $12,500,000 or the sum of the individual insurable mortgages, whichever is less, with a thirty-five year or three-quarters of remaining economic life term. Interest rates for both are limited to the prevailing FHA maximum rate plus 1/2 of 1 percent mortgage insurance premium.

Mortgage insurance for cooperative projects built for low income families is available under Sections 221 and 236 of the National Housing Act. Such insurance commitments provide for subsidy payments by FHA to assist the tenant-shareholders in meeting their rental obligations. Existing Section 236 rental projects may be converted to cooperatives at any time the owners and tenants elect to do so. The Section 236 insurance program and subsidies available thereunder are discussed in detail in the chapter on the Federal Housing Administration.

CONDOMINIUMS

The condominium is a new concept in property ownership and real estate finance in the United States. European countries, since the Middle Ages have experimented with condominium ownership. It was not until after World War II, however, that the concept gained strong favor in Europe. The reason for the post World War II rise in condominiums was the formulation of rules and regulations of condominium ownership and the high demand for apartment units. Condominiums drew special favoritism in France, particularly in Paris where it has become the most popular form of apartment occupancy. Condominiums have long been a favorite form of ownership in South America.

In the United States, prior to the late 1950s, a number of projects were attempted under the condominium form. In fact, one project located in New York City, became a reality in the late 1940s in spite of numerous legal problems.

In 1958 a condominium law was passed in Puerto Rico providing for FHA insurance of condominium units. This law prompted the passage by Congress of Public Law 87-70 (The Housing Act of 1961) which in part authorized the Federal Housing Administration to insure loans for condominium development, thus giving birth to the condominium concept as we know it today.

The new Section 234 of the National Housing Act spurred many states into legislation providing for the creation of fee-simple title to individual units in a multi-unit project, coupled with an undivided interest in all elements owned in common (such as the land on which the project is built and in most instances the stairways, corridors and recreational facilities). Without this legislation it would not be possible to convey title to many condominium type units. Prior to such legislation several states, notably Florida, did allow conveyance of units in condominium-type projects under a tenancy-in-common system. Such a system, however, was not as complete and applicable as the specific condominium, frequently called property regime, statutes existing in all states and the District of Columbia today.

A condominium, then, can be defined as a statutory estate combining one person ownership in severalty with ownership in common. While the concept is applied most frequently to high rise apartments, it is also applicable to single family developments, office buildings, shopping centers and industrial complexes.

CREATION

The statutory creation of a condominium requires four basic items of legal documentation:

1. The *Declaration* by which the property is brought within the respective condominium statute and divided into what are termed either apartments or units. As a general practice, the declaration of condominium ownership is signed and recorded by the property owner prior to the sale of any units. The declaration usually contains the following information:

   a. A description of the property and improvements.

   b. A description of the common elements and facilities and the rights, privileges, and percentage of ownership that each unit owner will have in them.

   c. The number of units in the project and a description of each, including size, number of rooms, and location with respect to other units.

   d. A description of which units are to be used for residential purposes and which, if any, will be used for commercial purposes.

   e. The creation of an owner's association comprised of all unit owners and the rules and regulations governing the operation of the association.

   f. Provisions relating to the enforcement of liens for defaults by a unit owner in making its pro rata payment of the costs for upkeep of the common areas and facilities.

   g. Provision that each unit owner maintain the interior of his unit, with the exterior maintained by the owner's association.

   h. Amendment provisions.

2. The *plot plan* or floor plan which is an architect's schematic drawing that shows how each floor in the condominium project is divided into units or apartments. In the case of a condominium townhouse or detached single family housing project, the plot plan would designate the respective building lots and common areas. The plot plan, particularly with respect to a high rise building will permit the conveyance of a unit by its number as shown on the plot plan. Of course, the plot plan must be recorded in the land records of the county where the project is located to establish a legal basis for conveyance of the units by number and reference to a plat.

3. The *By-Laws* that set forth the rules and regulations by which the association of unit owners will be organized and governed. The declaration creates the association and by-laws govern its operations.

4. The *Deed* to the unit or apartment by which the unit or apartment and an interest in the common areas are conveyed to purchasers.

   The legal description in the deed will refer to the recorded plot plan and is usually divided into two parts. First, a description of the specific unit being conveyed and then a description of the common areas and the percentage of interest in them, that is being conveyed. The percentage of common ownership of each unit purchaser is determined by statute either by:

a. The value that his unit bears to the value of the total project, or
b. The ratio of square footage of his unit to the square footage of the entire project.

The deed should also contain a clause conveying those rights, benefits and easements which are set forth in the declaration and which run with the title to the condominium units.

In a high rise condominium where the unit conveyed is but a delineated area of space, provision in the deed should be made that title to the air space should survive destruction of the building.

Several reasons can be advanced for the necessity of statutory creation of a condominium, these are:

1. To legally provide for conveyance of title to a unit independent of the property of which it is a part, as was previously stated. This conveyance problem is quite apparent when thought of in relation to an apartment unit which is a part of a high rise building. The unit taken alone is suspended in space and is not attached to real estate. It is only attached to a building which is affixed to realty.
2. To provide a legal basis for separate taxation of each unit.
3. To be able to mortgage each unit separate of the total project. The declaration may state that each owner holds his unit subject to the right of first refusal in his co-owners, if he should choose to sell. Such a statement, however, is not as common in present times, as it was in the past, for it has become suspected as an attempt to restrict membership.

LEASEHOLD CONDOMINIUMS

Today, particularly in Hawaii, condominium projects are being constructed on a leasehold basis. As will be pointed out in the next chapter, leaseholds provide a non-debt method of financing all or a portion of the value of real estate. In this instance, the non-debt financing applies to land.

A leasehold condominium may be accomplished in one of several ways:

1. By an *original lease* between the land owner and project developer, after construction is completed, individual unit leases are substituted for the original lease. The new leases run from the land owners to the unit purchasers and in reality are ground rent situations.
2. By the creation of *separate leases* at the outset. The separate leases run from the land owner to the developer and are assumed by unit purchasers.
3. By allowing the original lease to remain in force and making *partial assignments* from it as units are purchased. This method, however, calls for a rent apportionment formula to be established.
4. By *subleasing* from the original lease instead of pursuing the partial assignment method.

Leasehold condominiums create many problems for lenders. The more important problems are identical to the leasehold problems outlined in the next chapter. As to the project, the leasehold can present a separate unit taxation problem. Tax assessors in some jurisdictions, such as California, are not obligated to separate the tax billings on a leasehold condominium. Thus, specific agreements with the assessors may be necessary or at a minimum the requirements of the respective condominium statutes will have to be reviewed and adhered to.

OWNERS' ASSOCIATIONS

An important part of a condominium project is the owners' association. This association is created by Declaration, and its authority and scope of operation are set forth in the By-Laws. In general, the association is composed of all unit owners as is the legal entity for ownership and operation of the common areas. Its operations are supported by assessments levied against each unit owner. Assessments which are levied and not paid become junior liens of the unit owners title. The By-Laws usually empower the association to take such legal action as is necessary to collect the assessment, including foreclosure. Many associations also have the right to force unit owners to properly maintain their units by assessing fines against those who fail to do so or by having the maintenance work performed and charged to the unit owner. It may be provided in the Declaration that the lien for non-payment of assessment takes precedence over any mortgages on the condominium unit. In view, however, of the problem this creates for mortgage lenders, such a provision may cause financing difficulties.

The powers and obligations of the association usually include:

- The maintenance, management, repair, replacement, and opera tion of the condominium and the common element.
- The levy and enforcement of collection of general and specific as sessments for common condominium expenses.
- The right of access to each unit when necessary for maintenance, repair, or replacement of common elements, or for the making of emergency repairs.
- The acquisition, holding, leasing, mortgaging, and conveying of units in the condominium.
- The obtaining and maintaining of adequate insurance coverage for the condominium.
- The authority to modify or move any easement for ingress, egress, or utilities for the benefit of the unit owners.
- The establishment and maintaining of an adequate fund for the periodic maintenance, repair, and replacement of the consumer elements.
- The establishment of a working capital fund during the initial months of the condominium operations equivalent to at least two months estimated common area charges for each unit.

Owners' Associations are managed either by the unit owners themselves or, usually, by professional management hired by the association. Initially the developer is retained as the manager, since the developer often has the staff and expertise to handle the day-to-day maintenance and operational problems associated with the condominium complex. In fact, many times the developer attempts to perpetuate his income and continued involvement in the condominium project by retaining ownership of the common areas and leasing them back to the owners. This reduces the owners' association's responsibility for management and operation of the common areas, but could well, and normally does, increase the cost to each of the unit owners. This very problem has been the subject of legal actions and much debate in the state of Florida to the end that legislation has been passed to eliminate the leasing of the common areas, particularly, the recreational facilities by the developer to the unit owners.

In general, the Owners' Association selects the management agent or performs the management themselves by hiring and supervising a work force or by subcontracting the various maintenance responsibilities.

PLANNED UNIT DEVELOPMENTS

Condominiums are often thought of as vertical properties. They, however, also apply to horizontal property developments usually termed "Planned Unit Developments", or, referred to as "cluster housing" or "Home Owner's Association". In essence, the horizontal condominium is a development which groups the housing units into clusters surrounded by common or green areas. The housing units composing the development can be and many times are a mix of detached houses, townhouses, quadrominiums, and even apartments. Amenities, such as tennis courts, swimming pools, lakes and riding trails may be located in the common areas.

Under this system a unit purchaser gains fee title to his unit and an undivided ownership of the common areas. Many advantages are gained by this development.

Some of these advantages are:
1. The aesthetic value of clustering the housing unit around green areas and common facilities as opposed to the standard, usually unaesthetic, grid-type subdivision development.
2. The freedom from normal home ownership maintenance for all unit exterior repairs and renovations as well as lawn mowing and maintenance of the common areas as performed by the Home Owner's Association.
3. The built-in amenities which are not a part of most standard subdivisions.
4. The absence of backyard neighbors, since the units are frequently backed up against the green areas.

Weighed against the advantages are the higher unit cost necessitated to underwrite the common area costs and the recurrent association dues.

The Home Owner's Association or predecessor to today's Planned Unit Development (PUD) existed prior to the statutory creation of condominiums. This concept is now being applied to new town developments such as Reston, Virginia and Columbia, Maryland, as well as to much small housing developments. Most professional land planners heartily endorse the PUD concept. The future progress of the PUD is directly related to how quickly local planning and zoning codes can be revised and updated to meet the PUD demand. The Federal Housing Administration has established a Planned Unit Development loan insurance program which is presently providing impetus for a number of new PUDs. The FHA-PUD program is quite similar to and has many of the advantages of the Section 234 insurance plan which will be discussed later.

RESORT CONDOMINIUMS

Of recent vintage are the numerous resort and second-home condominiums. The tax benefits of condominium ownership combined with the increasing amount of leisure time have caused a surge in the number of resort condominiums planned and constructed in recent years.

The biggest problem with many resort condominium developments is the violation of the Securities Act of 1933. It has been the practice in many resort areas to create what are termed "rent pools." Under the rent pool arrangement, a condominium unit purchaser occupies the unit for a portion of the year and contracts for the rental of his unit for the balance of the year. Each unit available for rent is placed in a pool and offered for rent by an individual or company retained as a property manager. Each year the rent received from the units, less management fees, is pooled and distributed equally to the unit owners, without regard to an individual unit occupancy or vacancy during the rental period. While this procedure can be very advantageous to each unit owner, care must be taken to comply with the Securities Act of 1933 as well as most state securities laws. Compliance in the case of rent-pool condominiums is similar to compliance required in the sale of any security.

Arrangements for year-round usage of resort homes can also be disadvantageous to the owner from the standpoint that short-term transients have a tendency to cause greater wear and tear on a facility than the owner occupant. Thus, a greater incident of repair and maintenance and the cost associated with same may result.

BUSINESS CONDOMINIUMS

Another recent trend in the condominium area is that of the business condominium. This concept is particularly effective with professional office complexes since it allows the occupant-owner to have an additional tax deduction for his space costs in the form of depreciation. (Business office space lease payments are deductible in full as a business expense as would be the total mortgage interest payments on a business condominium). Of less acceptability is multitenant condominium office space and shopping center space. The business condominium has been little tried and mildly accepted by prospective purchasers and lenders due largely to the fact that what is being sold is space tailored to a specific users needs. Hence, resale of the space poses a difficult problem. In a rental situation, a user will adapt himself to a space usage, particularly when a short term tenancy is involved. A purchaser, becomes much more selective and less adaptable.

TIME-SHARING CONDOMINIUMS

A relatively new condominium concept is time-sharing. Under this concept, units in a condominium project, normally one located in a resort area, are sold to multiple purchasers who have use of the one unit only for a given time period during the year. For example, Unit 205 in an ocean front condomimium would be sold to Mr. A for use in the month of April only, to Mr. B for use in May only, and so forth. Naturally, the purchase price of the unit would be about one-twelfth of the market value of the unit, with the more favorable months of usage commanding a higher purchase price than those of less favorable occupancy months. This arrangement allows for a minimum investment on the part of a purchaser who only needs the use of a unit for one month out of a year. However, while the concept has meritorious advantages from a marketing standpoint, it is extremely difficult, if not impossible, to finance and prospective time-sharing purchasers normally pay cash.

CONDOMINIUM CONVERSIONS

Primarily in many large metropolitan areas, but also in other areas to a lesser extent, apartment owners are converting their projects to condominium ownership. Several major reasons for this are:

1. Rising operation and maintenance costs, which have made it difficult for apartment owners to show a positive cash flow.
2. The profits available from the conversion of an apartment complex to condominium units, particularly when depreciation write-offs have been fully utilized. Such profits are normally ten to twenty percent more than the profits that would be realized through a sale of the same project at an apartment complex.
3. Proposed federal tax reforms which will reduce the incentive for investment in apartment projects.
4. The availability of high-ratio/low down payment financing for condominium unit purchasers.

A number of legal problems arise in a conversion case, the major of which are:

1. The delineation of common areas and individual units.
2. The normal condominium documentation.
3. The treatment of tenants who may not all be in favor of moving or buying their unit. (Many states are seeking legislation to prevent conversion of apartments where less than 50 percent of the tenants are in favor of the conversion.)
4. The release of individual units from under the existing mortgage.

Most of the obvious problems of conversion can be overcome with good real estate professional and legal guidance. This conversion phenomenon has become very popular and seems to be an ever-growing method of constituting condominium ownership.

FHA INSURED CONDOMINIUMS

Ironically, practically all the units built under the FHA-inspired state condominium laws have been conventionally financed. In fact, between 1961 and 1969 an average of slightly more than 160 units per year were constructed under the Section 234 federally insured program.

Certainly FHA red tape and the availability of conventional funds during the early sixties kept many builders and developers from pursuing the federally insured route. However, certain recent changes in the Section 234 program such as the Housing Act of 1968, accelerated FHA multifamily processing, conventional lenders' desires for participations, and the many years of short supply of conventional financing have all combined to make Section 234 financing worthy of consideration by property owners and developers. In addition, 80 percent to 90 percent construction financing and up to 98.5 percent permanent financing is available under the Section 234 insured loan program.

By FHAs definition, a condominium project may consist of one building containing five units or more, a group of elevator buildings, a group of low-rise buildings, townhouse units, detached single-family units, or a combination of these types. The program provides for insured mortgages to finance the construction or rehabilitation of multifamily projects intended for use as a condominium. After construction or rehabilitation the individual units may be released from the blanket mortgage and sold for cash or financed by conventional or FHA-insured permanent loans.

The Federal Housing Administration's Section 234 commitment to insure may cover construction financing under a blanket mortgage. The mortgage to be insured may be as high as 90 percent of the project replacement value or the sum of the proposed unit sale prices. Eighty percent of all units, based on value, must be pre-sold to FHA-approved buyers at time of initial FHA endorsement (closing of the construction loan) or the mortgage will be for 80 percent of value only. The latter case usually prevails. Thus, when construction is complete, an insured blanket permanent loan is closed. The sponsor-owner then has two years after the permanent closing to pre-sell 80 percent of the value of all units to FHA-approved and other buyers. As each sale is closed individual unit mortgages are "spun-off" (released) from the blanket mortgage, all without pre-payment penalty. If the sponsor-owner is unable to meet the pre-sale requirements, then he has an apartment rental-type project with a forty year term mortgage. Federal National Mortgage Association's cooperation is of great assistance. Delivery of multifamily loans upon which FNMA has committed is usually mandatory. However, FNMA will, in the case of Section 234 insured loans, release from the blanket mortgage units sold on a condominium basis and conventionally financed, FHA insured loan financed, or sold for cash. It is noteworthy that FHA in its Section 234 commitment agrees to insure not only blanket construction loans, but also all loans made to purchasers of the individual condominium units. Downpayment, maximum insurable mortgages, and other terms on the permanent loans are the same as for the FHA standard (Section 203b) single-family insured loans or Section 235 where applicable. Blanket construction loans are insurable up to any dollar limit approved by FHA and may include commercial and community facilities to serve the people who live in the project. Up to four units may be purchased by one person under an insured loan. However, as to a mortgage on a unit not lived in by the owner, the amount cannot exceed 85 percent of the maximum mortgage amount computed for an owner-occupant.

A major change in the Section 234 program was brought about by the Housing Act of 1968 with the establishment of the Section 235 low-income home ownership program. This program which provides for $200 cash down including closing costs and monthly payments as low as 20 percent of adjusted family income, can be used in conjunction with the Section 234 program thereby bringing subsidy funds to condominiums and condominiums to low-income families. (The Section 235 program is discussed in detail in the chapter on the Federal Housing Administration.)

Another change in the Section 234 program as a result of the Housing Act of 1968 was the authorization of Section 234 insurance for individual units in a condominium project with two to eleven dwelling units without requiring prior FHA project insurance. This allows smaller developments to be constructed without FHA processing delays and expenses.

Buildings originally constructed under any FHA multifamily residential insured loan program except Section 213 management-type cooperatives may be converted into condominium form and FHA mortgage insurance made available to lenders when the units involved in the conversion are offered for sale.

Blanket leaseholds and subleases are not eligible for FHA insurance; leaseholds must be on the individual units only. By statute, leasehold condominiums are not permitted in New York, Illinois and many other states.

The continued national emphasis on apartment developments, the desire for homeownership, the tax advantages of owning as opposed to renting, and the increasing favor of cluster or planned-unit developments as opposed to the unaesthetic grid·system should all contributed to the boom in condominium development in the 1970s. Federal Housing Administration insured financing has played a much greater part in the condominium developments of the 1970s than it did in the 1960s. The case for FHA insured financing for condominiums is supported by the following reasoning:

1. FHA-insured financing offers an 80 percent to 90 percent construction mortgage as opposed to 60 percent to 75 percent under conventional terms.
2. There is no lender equity participation under the FHA program.
3. With an FHA insured commitment, financing is practically always available, whereas the availability of conventional funds fluctuates.
4. Conventional construction lenders usually demand a certain percentage of the end (permanent) loans, whereas FNMA, the largest purchaser of FHA-insured project loans, makes no such demand.
5. The FHA Section 234 program allows two years after construction and permanent loan closing for making the necessary sales for establishment of a condominium, whereas conventional lenders usually want a certain percentage of presales prior to advancement of construction funds with sufficient sales at the end of construction to pay off the interim loan.
6. A project constructed under Section 234 may fail as a condominium, but still can be carried on as a rental project. This feature is not readily available under conventional financing; when it is, it is usually in the form of a costly stand-by commitment.
7. Accelerated FHA processing and the recent trend of many mortgage companies and financial institutions toward development of an expertise in FHA-insured multifamily financing greatly reduces the time required in obtaining an FHA-insured commitment.
8. Unless the project was originally constructed under an FHA commitment or contains less than twelve units, FHA-insured permanent loans on individual units are not available.

RESTRAINTS ON ALIENATION

One problem of particular importance with condominiums is the restraints placed on resale of the units. For instance, many condominium declarations provide for owners' association approval of prospective purchasers or establish criteria for occupancy. Such a restraint is justified on the basis that it serves to insure a continued homogeneous ownership group. Some Florida condominium developments, for example, limit occupancy to persons fifty years of age or older. A restraint of this nature can obviously cause severe resale problems. Complicating the problem is the fact that most condominiums are not blessed with the "escape" provisions found in many cooperatives.

A more palatable restraint found in some declarations calls for the association's right of first refusal to purchase a unit offered for sale.

CONVENTIONAL FINANCING OF THE CONDOMINIUM

Financing in general comes in two stages:
1. Financing of the project.
2. Financing of each unit through permanent loan take-outs.

Since many condominium statutes provide that a unit or apartment cannot be sold subject to a construction or project loan, the burden is placed on the developer to pre-sell a number of units or apartments sufficient to pay off the construction loan. This is, of course, in contrast to FHA's 80 percent pre-sale requirement.

Coincidental to this problem are lender requirements that
1. The permanent loans be placed with them as an additional consideration for having made the construction loan.
2. The developer retain the option to "call-off" the condominium plan if sufficient units are not sold or if it appears that the required sales will not take place. If "call-off" occurs the project will most likely revert to unit rental situation.
3. The developers voting rights under the declaration be transferred to the lender, thereby allowing the lender to participate in major owners' association decisions. Added to this provision is the frequent requirement that the developer maintain control of the owners' association until all or a substantial portion of the units are sold.

Lender acceptance of condominium loans has been spotty due to several factors, such as:
1. Whether or not the condominium to be financed will be successful as a condominium. This fear has led many prospective lenders to require that 50 to 70 percent of the condominium units in a project be pre-sold prior to any loan closings.
2. The common area charges that each unit owner has to pay monthly in addition to his regular monthly mortgage payment. These charges and the anticipated from time to time increases in them are a burden upon the borrower. They are a factor not present in a single family detached subdivision which the lender must evaluate and which he must live with as an encumbrance upon the borrower's ability to meet his mortgage payment. Accordingly, many lenders restrict their lending to those projects where the common area charges are nominal, i.e., $55 per month or less.
3. In a true condominium the purchaser is buying air space not fee title. Hence the mortgagee acquires a mortgage on air space and not on fee property. This departure from traditional single family mortgage lending

has kept many conservative lenders out of the condominium loan market. Then too, many of those that have ventured into condominium lending have restricted themselves to loans on townhouse condominiums or PUDs where fee ownership of the unit can be conveyed.

4. A secondary market for condominium loans. Since these type loans are not yet as universally fully acceptable as single family detached residential loans, the market for resale is not as strong. Thus a lender making condominium permanent loans must take into consideration the fact that he may not be able to sell these loans in the secondary market at a time when he is in need of doing so in order to gain liquidity.

5. The most intangible factor is that of value. It is as easy to build a 100 unit building and rent it as an apartment as it is to build the same building and sell the units as a condominium. The difference is that the condominium project will, if successful as a condominium, have a value in excess of that of the same building as an apartment project. Two similar reasons are given for this phenomonon:

   a) The owner of an apartment building buys or builds same to obtain a yearly "cash flow" income plus depreciation. The sponsor of a condominium project, however, builds it to receive an immediate profit. The comparative tax and income differences of the two situations produce the major price differences.

   b) More easily seen are the tax differences from the renter-purchaser standpoint that create the price differences. A unit that normally rents for $200 per month in an apartment building could feasibly be sold for $25,000 if the building were sold as condominium as opposed to being rented as an apartment. A purchaser paying $2,000 down and obtaining a $23,000 mortgage at 9 percent interest would have monthly mortgage payments of about $185 plus an estimated common area charge of say $25 per month and real estate taxes of $30 per month for a total monthly payment of $240. However, the purchaser would gain a tax advantage since annual interest of $2,070 (first year) and taxes of about $60 per month in income taxes by being a homeowner, hence, his effective monthly cost of housing is $180 as compared to $200 (no tax benefit on a lease payment) if he were a renter.

The unit as an apartment would be worth about $20,000. Thus, by selling the unit as a condominium, the purchaser gains by reducing his effective shelter cost while the seller obtains a net of about $3,000 (after marketing costs, interest, and closing costs) over what he would receive if the unit was sold as a rental.

The lender then realizes that he may make a $23,000 mortgage on a unit and if the project in which the unit is located becomes unmarketable for some reason as a condominium, its value upon conversion of the project to a rental will be only $20,000, or $2,000 less than the mortgage loan.

While most of the lender objections to condominium loans will be cured by the passage of time and more universal acceptance of this growing concept, the above problems exist today and will continue to exist in the near future.

COOPERATIVES VERSUS CONDOMINIUMS

Following is a comparison of the relative advantages and disadvantages of the cooperative and condominium forms of ownership.

1. In a condominium there is normally fee ownership whereas in a cooperative there is stock ownership and rental type occupancy. This is the theory of *economic interdependence.* Each condominium unit owner is liable for his own mortgage, but cooperative tenant-shareholders are collectively liable for the entire mortgage debt.
2. A cooperative tenant-shareholder has no way to refinance the increased value of his unit on a sale whereas a condominium owner can, thus making it easier and more advantageous to sell a condominium unit as opposed to a cooperative unit.
3. Generally a cooperative tenant-shareholder has more selectivity as to his neighbors.
4. In a condominium, unit-owners are separately taxed on their individual units whereas cooperative tenant-shareholders pay their share of taxes of the whole project.
5. Condominium unit owners are liable for the mortgage and taxes on their units only, whereas cooperative tenant-shareholders must bear the burden of the entire project and thus are dependent upon its solvency.

STATISTICS

The growth and acceptance of the cooperative and condominium concepts are reflected in figures published by the Department of Housing and Urban Development. During 1970, one out of every eight apartment units constructed that year were in either a condominium or cooperative project. In 1969, only one out of every thirteen new apartment units was contained in a cooperative or condominium development. Led by Florida, the South is presently the major geographical area of cooperative and condominium project concentration. Approximately 70 percent of the apartments built in the South during 1970 were classed as cooperatives or condominiums. Condominiums now seem to have eclipsed cooperatives in public favor. The increasing cost and scarcity of urban land combined with the problems involved in rental units should all give impetus to the ever increasing popularity of condominium ownership.

EXHIBITS

The following exhibits are standard FHA forms which very adequately set forth some standard and basic cooperative and condominium agreements. The specific exhibits (Chart 5-1, 5-2, and 5-3) are:

1. FHA Form No. 3245—Model Form of By-Laws for a cooperative.
2. FHA Form No. 3237—Model Form of Occupancy Agreement for a cooperative.
3. FHA Form No. 3277—Standard Form By-Laws for a condominium.

CHART 5-1

FHA FORM NO. 3245
Revised June, 1970

U. S. DEPARTMENT OF HOUSING AND URBAN DEVELOPMENT
FEDERAL HOUSING ADMINISTRATION

MODEL FORM OF BY-LAWS

*(For use by Cooperatives in Sections 213,
221 and 236 cases)*

ARTICLE   I.   NAME AND LOCATION OF CORPORATION

ARTICLE II.   PURPOSE

ARTICLE III.   MEMBERSHIP

> Section 1. Eligibility
> Section 2. Application for Membership
> Section 3. Subscription Funds
> Section 4. Members
> Section 5. Membership Certificates
> Section 6. Lost Certificates
> Section 7. Lien
> Section 8. Transfer of Membership
> > (a) Death of Member
> > (b) Option of Corporation to Purchase
> > (c) Procedure Where Corporation Does
> > > Not Exercise Option
> > (d) Transfer Value
> Section 9. Termination of Membership for Cause
> Section 10. Sales Price

ARTICLE IV.   MEETINGS OF MEMBERS

> Section 1. Place of Meetings
> Section 2. Annual Meetings
> Section 3. Special Meetings
> Section 4. Notice of Meetings
> Section 5. Quorum
> Section 6. Adjourned Meetings
> Section 7. Voting
> Section 8. Proxies
> Section 9. Order of Business

ARTICLE V.   DIRECTORS

> Section 1. Number and Qualification
> Section 2. Powers and Duties
> Section 3. Election and Term of Office
> Section 4. Vacancies
> Section 5. Removal of Directors
> Section 6. Compensation
> Section 7. Organization Meeting
> Section 8. Regular Meetings
> Section 9. Special Meetings
> Section 10. Waiver of Notice
> Section 11. Quorum
> Section 12. Fidelity Bonds
> Section 13. Safeguarding Subscription Funds

ARTICLE VI. OFFICERS

> Section 1. Designation
> Section 2. Election of Officers
> Section 3. Removal of Officers
> Section 4. President
> Section 5. Vice-President
> Section 6. Secretary
> Section 7. Treasurer

ARTICLE I

NAME AND LOCATION OF CORPORATION

Section 1. The name of this Corporation is _____
_____ . Its principal office is located at _____
_____

ARTICLE II

PURPOSE

Section 1. The purpose of this Corporation is to provide its members* with housing and community facilities, if any, on a nonprofit basis consonant with the provisions set forth in its Certificate of Incorporation.

ARTICLE III

MEMBERSHIP

Section 1. Eligibility. Any natural person approved by the Board of Directors shall be eligible for membership, provided that he or she executes a Subscription Agreement and Occupancy Agreement in the usual form employed by the Corporation covering a specific unit in the housing project.**

Section 2. Application for Membership. Application for membership shall be presented in person on a form prescribed by the Board of Directors, and all such applications shall be acted upon promptly by the Board of Directors.

Section 3. Subscription Funds. *** All subscription funds (except funds required for credit reports) received from applicants prior to the endorsement of the mortgage note by the Federal Housing Administration (hereinafter sometimes referred to as the ''Administration'') shall be deposited promptly without deduction in a special account or accounts of the Corporation as escrowee or trustee for the Subscribers to Membership, which monies shall not be corporate funds, but shall be held solely for the benefit of the Subscribers until transferred to the account of the Corporation as hereinafter provided. Such special account or accounts shall be established with _____
_____ (name of institution) located at _____
_____ , whose deposits are insured by an agency of the Federal Government. Such account or accounts may be interest bearing, with the interest earned to be retained and owned by the Corporation. Such funds shall be subject to withdrawal, or transfer to the account of the Corporation

or disbursed in a manner directed by the Corporation only upon certification by the President and Secretary of the Corporation to the above-named institution or institutions that:

(a) The Subscription Agreement of a named applicant has been terminated pursuant to its terms and such withdrawal is required to repay the amount paid by him under such agreement; or

---

* In corporations organized on a stock basis, change the word "members" to "stockholders" and add thereafter the following parenthetical clause: "(hereinafter referred to as 'members')."
** In corporations organized on a stock basis, change the word "membership" to "stock ownership" and add thereafter the following parenthetical clause: "(hereinafter referred to as 'membership')."
*** In view of the fact that certain sponsoring groups such as labor unions, veterans' organizations, church groups, cooperative sponsoring organizations, may wish to use some other method of handling subscriptions or subscriptions funds, this section may be altered, subject to prior approval of the Administration.

(b) Applicants for _____ * dwelling units have not been procured within the effective period of the FHA Commitment, or any extension thereof, and such withdrawal is required to repay to the applicants the amounts paid by them; or

(c) Applicants for _____ * dwelling units (or such lesser number as may be approved by the Administration) have signed Subscription Agreements, have been approved as to their credit by the Administration, and have paid the subscription price in full. If these requirements have been met and the mortgage loan has been scheduled for closing with the approval of the Administration, the entire amount of the funds in the subscription escrow account may be transferred to the corporation, at which time the corporation shall issue and deliver membership certificates to all members.

If more than one mortgage is to be executed by the corporation, this section shall be deemed to be applicable to the specific subscription fund received from applicants with respect to the specific dwelling units to be covered by each mortgage and to require the creation of separate and specific escrow accounts with respect to each mortgage.

Section 4. Members. The members shall consist of the incorporators and such subscribers as have been approved for membership by the Board of Directors and who have paid for their membership and received membership certificates. The status of the incorporators as members shall terminate at the first annual meeting of members unless they have executed Subscription Agreements and, where required by the Administration, Occupancy Agreements. The authorized membership of the Corporation shall consist of _____ regular memberships. **

Section 5. Membership Certificates. Each membership certificate shall state that the Corporation is organized under the laws of the State of _____ , the name of the registered holder of the membership represented thereby, the Corporation lien rights as against such membership as set forth this Article, and the preferences and restrictions applicable thereto, and shall be in such form as shall be approved by the Board of Directors. Membership certificates shall be consecutively numbered, bound in one or more books, and shall be issued therefrom upon certification as to full payment. Every membership certificate shall be signed by the President or Vice President, and the Secretary, and shall be sealed with the corporate seal.

Section 6. Lost Certificates. The Board of Directors may direct a new certificate or certificates to be issued in place of any certificate or certificates previously issued by the Corporation and alleged to have been destroyed or lost, upon the making of an affidavit of that fact by the person claiming the share certificate to be lost or destroyed. When authorizing such issuance of a new certificate or certificates, the Board of Directors may, in its discretion, and as a condition precedent to the issuance thereof, require the registered owner of such lost or destroyed certificate or certificates, or his legal representative, to advertise the same in such manner as the Board of Directors shall require and to give the Corporation a bond in such sum as the Board of Directors may require as indemnity against any claim that may be made against the Corporation.

Section 7. Lien. The Corporation shall have a lien on the outstanding regular memberships in order to secure payment of any sums which shall be due or become due from the holders thereof for any reason whatsoever, including any sums due under any occupancy agreements.

Section 8. Transfer of Membership. Except as provided herein, membership shall not be transferable and, in any event, no transfer of membership shall be made upon the books of the Corporation within ten (10) days next preceding the annual meeting of the members. In all transfers of membership the Corporation shall be entitled to a fee it deems appropriate to compensate it for the processing of the transfer.

---

* Insert number required by the applicable FHA Commitment.
** In cases where FHA control is via ownership of preferred stock, add "and _____ preferred memberships."

(a) <u>Death of Member.</u> If, upon death of a member, his membership in the Corporation passes by will or intestate distribution to a member of his immediate family, such legatee or distributee may, by assuming in writing the terms of the Subscription Agreement and Occupancy Agreement, where required by the Administration, within sixty (60) days after member's death, and paying all amounts due thereunder, become a member of the Corporation. If member dies and an obligation is not assumed in accordance with the foregoing, then the Corporation shall have an option to purchase the membership from the deceased member's estate in the manner provided in paragraph (b) of this Section, written notice of the death being equivalent to notice of intention to withdraw. If the Corporation does not exercise such option, the provisions of paragraph (c) of this Section shall be applicable, the references to "member" therein to be construed as references to the legal representative of the deceased member.

(b) <u>Option of Corporation to Purchase.</u> If the member desires to leave the project, he shall notify the Corporation in writing of such intention and the Corporation shall have an option for a period of thirty (30) days commencing the first day of the month following the giving of such notice, but not the obligation, to purchase the membership, together with all of the member's rights with respect to the dwelling unit, at an amount to be determined by the Corporation as representing the transfer value thereof, less any amounts due by the member to the Corporation under the Occupancy Agreement, and less the cost or estimated cost of all deferred maintenance, including painting, redecorating, floor finishing, and such repairs and replacements as are deemed necessary by the Corporation to place the dwelling unit in suitable condition for another occupant. The purchase by the Corporation of the membership will immediately terminate the member's rights and the member shall forthwith vacate the premises.

(c) <u>Procedure Where Corporation Does Not Exercise Option.</u> If the Corporation waives in writing its right to purchase the membership under the foregoing option, or if the Corporation fails to exercise such option within the thirty (30) day period, the member may sell his membership to any person who has been duly approved by the Corporation as a member and occupant.

If the Corporation agrees, at the request of the member, to assist the member in finding a purchaser, the Corporation shall be entitled to charge the member a fee it deems reasonable for this service. When the transferee has been approved for membership and has executed the prescribed Occupancy Agreement, the retiring member shall be released of his obligations under his Occupancy Agreement, provided he has paid all amounts due the Corporation to date.

(d) <u>Transfer Value.</u>* Whenever the Board of Directors elects to purchase a membership, the term "transfer value" shall mean the sum of the following:

(1) The consideration (i.e. down payment) paid for the membership by the first occupant of the unit involved as shown on the books of the Corporation;

(2) The value, as determined by the Directors, of any improvements installed at the expense of the member with the prior approval of the Directors, under a valuation formula which does not provide for reimbursement in an amount in excess of the typical initial cost of the improvements; and

(3) The amount of principal amortized by the Corporation on its mortgage indebtedness and attributable to the dwelling unit involved as paid by the member involved and previous holders of the same membership.** However, the amount of principal paid by the Corporation for a period of three (3) years after the Corporation has made its first principal payment on the mortgage shall not be included in this computation.

---

* If desired, a provision may be added to the effect that the transfer value otherwise applicable may be increased and decreased pursuant to fluctuations in the economy as evidenced by a Cost of Living Index or a Construction Cost Index. The language of such provision must be cleared with the FHA.

** In Section 221 below market interest rate cases and in Section 236 cases the sentence following the asterisks should be added. (A limitation which further restricts the amount payable to the retiring member in such cases may be imposed subject to the approval of FHA.)

* Whenever a member who has received rent supplement assistance sells his membership, the amount of such assistance shall be deducted from the transfer value to which such member would otherwise be entitled as follows:

(i) A portion of that amount of principal amortized as determined in (d) (3), above, will not be made available to the member. The amount so withheld shall be determined by multiplying the amortized principal attributable to the unit by the quotient of the total rent supplement assistance to the member divided by the total monthly carrying charges the member was obligated to pay under his occupancy agreement and would have paid if he had not received rent supplement assistance.

(ii) In the event the corporation exercises its option to purchase the membership pursuant to paragraph (b), above, an amount computed in accordance with (i), above, shall be withheld from the proceeds of such sale and retained by the Corporation.

(iii) In the event the member sells his membership pursuant to paragraph (c), above, the selling member and the purchaser who purchases from such member shall jointly certify to the Corporation as to the sales price of the membership in such manner and in such form as may be required by the Corporation. An amount equal to the amount computed in accordance with (i), above, shall be paid to the Corporation prior to the Corporation's release of such member's obligation under his occupancy agreement and the transfer of his membership to the new owner; provided, however, that in the event the sales price does not exceed the total paragraphs d(1) and d(2), above, then the selling member shall be entitled to receive the full amount of the sales price.

(iv) All funds received by the Corporation representing withheld amortized principal attributable to Rent Supplement Payments shall be deposited in a special account by the Corporation and disbursed as directed by the Federal Housing Administration.

Section 9. Termination of Membership for Cause. In the event the Corporation has terminated the rights of a member under the Occupancy Agreement, the member shall be required to deliver promptly to the Corporation his membership certificate and his Occupancy Agreement, both endorsed in such manner as may be required by the Corporation. The Corporation shall thereupon at its election either (1) repurchase said membership at its transfer value (as hereinabove defined) or the amount the retiring member originally paid for the acquisition of his membership certificate, whichever is the lesser, or (2) proceed with reasonable diligence to effect a sale of the membership to a purchaser and at a sales price acceptable to the Corporation. The retiring member shall be entitled to receive the amount so determined, less the following amounts (the determination of such amounts by the Corporation to be conclusive)

(a) any amounts due to the Corporation from the member under the Occupancy Agreement;

(b) the cost or estimated cost of all deferred maintenance, including painting, redecorating, floor finishing, and such repairs and replacements as are deemed necessary by the Corporation to place the dwelling unit in suitable condition for another occupant; and

(c) legal and other expenses incurred by the Corporation in connection with the default of such member and the resale of his membership. In the event the retiring member for any reason should fail for a period of 10 days after demand to deliver to the Corporation his endorsed membership certificate, said membership certificate shall forthwith be deemed to be cancelled and may be reissued by the Corporation to a new purchaser.

** Section 10. Sales Price. Memberships may be sold by the Corporation or the member only to a person approved by the Board of Directors in accordance with the requirements of the Regulatory Agreement, and the sales price shall not exceed the transfer value as provided in this Article, except that in sales effected by the Corporation a service charge not in excess of $100 may be charged by the Corporation. Where the sale is accomplished by a member, a certificate in form approved by the FHA as to the price paid shall be executed by the seller and purchaser and delivered to the Corporation.

---

* Include this paragraph only in projects where rent supplements are contemplated.
** Omit in Section 213 cases and market interest rate cases under Section 221(d) (3).

ARTICLE IV

MEETINGS OF MEMBERS

Section 1. Place of Meetings. Meetings of the membership shall be held at the principal office or place of business of the Corporation or at such other suitable place convenient to the membership as may be designated by the Board of Directors.

Section 2. Annual Meetings. The first annual meeting of the Corporation shall be held on _____ . (Date) Thereafter, the annual meetings of the Corporation shall be held on the _____ (1st, 2nd, 3rd, 4th) _____ (Monday, Tuesday, Wednesday, etc.) of _____ (Month) each succeeding year. At such meeting there shall be elected by ballot of the members a Board of Directors in accordance with the requirements of Section 3 of Article V of these By-Laws. The members may also transact such other business of the Corporation as may properly come before them.

Section 3. Special Meetings. It shall be the duty of the President to call a special meeting of the members as directed by resolution of the Board of Directors or upon a petition signed by twenty (20) percent of the members having been presented to the Secretary, or at the request of the Federal Housing Commissioner or his duly authorized representative. The notice of any special meeting shall state the time and place of such meeting and the purpose thereof. No business shall be transacted at a special meeting except as stated in the notice unless by consent of four-fifths of the members present, either in person or by proxy.

Section 4. Notice of Meetings. It shall be the duty of the Secretary to mail a notice of each annual or special meeting, stating the purpose thereof as well as the time and place where it is to be held, to each member of record, at his address as it appears on the membership book of the Corporation, or if no such address appears, at his last known place of address, at least _____ but not more than _____ days prior to such meeting (the number of days notice to comply with state statute). Service may also be accomplished by the delivery of any such notice to the member at his dwelling unit or last known address. Notice by either such method shall be considered as notice served. Notices of all meetings shall be mailed to the Director of the local insuring office of the Federal Housing Administration.

Section 5. Quorum. The presence, either in person or by proxy, of at least _____ * percent of the members of record of the Corporation shall be requisite for, and shall constitute a quorum for the transaction of business at all meetings of members. If the number of members at a meeting drops below the quorum and the question of a lack of quorum is raised, no business may thereafter be transacted.

Section 6. Adjourned Meetings. If any meeting of members cannot be organized because a quorum has not attended, the members who are present, either in person or by proxy, may, except as otherwise provided by law, adjourn the meeting to a time not less than forty-eight (48) hours from the time the original meeting was called, at which subsequent meeting the quorum requirement shall be _____ * percent.

Section 7. Voting. ** At every meeting of the regular members, each member present, either in person or by proxy, shall have the right to cast one vote on each question and never more than one vote. (Note - If desired, a provision may be included to the effect that where a husband and wife are joint members, each shall be entitled to cast a one-half vote.) The vote of the majority of those present, in person or by proxy, shall decide any question brought before such meeting, unless the question is one upon which, by express provision of statute or of the Certificate of Incorporation or of these By-Laws, a different vote is required, in which case such express provision shall govern and control. No member shall be eligible to vote or to be elected to the Board of Directors who is shown on the books or management accounts of the Corporation to be more than 30 days delinquent in payments due the Corporation under his Occupancy Agreement.

Section 8. Proxies. A member may appoint as his proxy only a member of his immediate family (as defined by the Board of Directors) except that an unmarried member may appoint any other member as his proxy. In no case may a member cast more than one vote by proxy in addition to his own vote. Any proxy must be filed with the Secretary before the appointed time of each meeting.

Section 9. Order of Business. The order of business at all regularly scheduled meetings of the regular members shall be as follows:

(a) Roll Call.
(b) Proof of notice of meeting or waiver of notice.
(c) Reading of minutes of preceding meeting.
(d) Reports of officers.
(e) Report of committees.
(f) Election of inspectors of election.
(g) Election of directors.
(h) Unfinished business.
(i) New business.

In the case of special meetings, items (a) through (d) shall be applicable and thereafter the agenda shall consist of the items specified in the notice of meeting.

If present, a representative of the Administration will be given an opportunity to address any regular or special meeting.

---

* The figure to be inserted will vary with the size of the cooperative, as follows:

Number of Memberships	Quorum percentage to be inserted in Article IV, Sec. 5	Quorum percentage applicable to adjourned meetings to be inserted in Article IV, Sec. 6
20 or less	50	25
21 - 150	25	15
151 - 300	20	10
301 - 500	15	10
501 or more	10	5

** There will be no objection to including a provision permitting voting by mail, and this may be desirable in the larger cooperatives.

ARTICLE V

DIRECTORS

Section 1. Number and Qualification. The affairs of the Corporation shall be governed by a Board of Directors composed of _____ persons*, a majority of whom shall be members of the Corporation.

Section 2. Powers and Duties. The Board of Directors shall have all the powers and duties necessary for the administration of the affairs of the Corporation and may do all such acts and things as are not by law or by these By-Laws directed to be exercised and done by the members. The powers of the Board of Directors shall include but not be limited:

    (a) To accept or reject all applications for membership and admission to occupancy of a dwelling unit in the cooperative housing project, either directly or through an authorized representative;

    (b) Subject to the approval of the Administration, to establish monthly carrying charges as provided for in the Occupancy Agreement, based on an operating budget formally adopted by such Board;

    (c) Subject to the approval of the Administration, to engage an agent or employees for the management of the project under such terms as the Board may determine;

    (d) To authorize in their discretion patronage refunds from residual receipts when and as reflected in the annual report;*

    (e) To terminate membership and occupancy rights for cause;

    (f) To promulgate such rules and regulations pertaining to use and occupancy of the premises as may be deemed proper and which are consistent with these By-Laws and the Certificate of Incorporation;** and

    (g) ***Pursuant to a plan approved by the Administration, to prescribe additional monthly carrying charges to be paid by families whose incomes exceed the limitations for continuing occupancy established from time to time by the Administration; or, at the Board's option, to terminate the membership and occupancy of such families.

Section 3. Election and Term of Office. The term of the Directors named in the Certificate of Incorporation shall expire when their successors have been elected at the first annual meeting or any special meeting called for that purpose. At the first annual meeting of the members the term of office of two Directors shall be fixed for three (3) years. The term of office of two Directors shall be fixed at two (2) years, and the term of office of one Director shall be fixed at one (1) year. At the expiration of the initial term of office of each respective Director, his successor shall be elected to serve a term of three (3) years. The Directors shall hold office until their successors have been elected and hold their first meeting. (If a larger Board of Directors is contemplated, the terms of office should be established in a similar manner so that they will expire in different years.)

Section 4. Vacancies. Vacancies in the Board of Directors caused by any reason other than the removal of a Director by a vote of the membership or by the vote of the preferred members **** shall be filled by vote of the majority of the remaining Directors, even though they may constitute less than a quorum; and each person so elected shall be a Director until a successor is elected by the members at the next annual meeting to serve out the unexpired portion of the term.

Section 5. Removal of Directors. At any regular or special meeting duly called, any Director may be removed with or without cause by the affirmative vote of the majority of the entire regular membership of record and a successor may then and there be elected to fill the vacancy thus created. Any Director whose removal has been proposed by the members shall be given an opportunity to be heard at the meeting. The term of any Director who becomes more than 30 days delinquent in payment of his carrying charges shall be automatically terminated and the remaining Directors shall appoint his successor as provided in Section 4, above.

Section 6. Compensation. No compensation shall be paid to Directors for their services as Directors. No remuneration shall be paid to a Director for services performed by him for the Corporation in any other capacity, unless a resolution authorizing such remuneration shall have been unanimously adopted by the Board of Directors before the services are undertaken. No remuneration or compensation shall in any case be paid to a Director without the approval of the Administration. A Director may not be an employee of the Corporation.

---

* Any convenient number of Directors (not less than three nor more than nine) may be provided.

Section 7. <u>Organization Meeting</u>. The first meeting of a newly elected Board of Directors shall be held within ten (10) days of election at such place as shall be fixed by the Directors at the meeting at which such Directors were elected, and no notice shall be necessary tp the newly elected Directors in order legally to constitute such meeting, providing a majority of the whole Board shall be present.

Section 8. <u>Regular Meetings</u>. Regular meetings of the Board of Directors may be held at such time and place as shall be determined, from time to time, by a majority of the Directors, but at least four such meetings shall be held during each fiscal year. Notice of regular meetings of the Board of Directors shall be given to each Director, personally or by mail, telephone or telegraph, at least three (3) days prior to the day named for such meeting.

Section 9. <u>Special Meetings</u>. Special meetings of the Board of Directors may be called by the President on three days notice to each Director, given personally or by mail, telephone or telegraph, which notice shall state the time, place (as hereinabove provided) and purpose of the meeting. Special meetings of the Board of Directors shall be called by the President or Secretary in like manner and on like notice on the written request of at least three Directors.

Section 10. <u>Waiver of Notice</u>. Before or at any meeting of the Board of Directors, any Director may, in writing, waive notice of such meeting and such waiver shall be deemed equivalent to the giving of such notice. Attendance by a Director at any meeting of the Board shall be a waiver of notice by him of the time and place thereof. If all the Directors are present at any meeting of the Board, no notice shall be required and any business may be transacted at such meeting.

Section 11. <u>Quorum</u>. At all meetings of the Board of Directors, a majority of the Directors shall constitute a quorum for the transaction of business, and the acts of the majority of the Directors present at a meeting at which a quorum is present shall be the acts of the Board of Directors. If, at any meeting of the Board of Directors, there be less than a quorum present, the majority of those present may adjourn the meeting from time to time. At any such adjourned meeting, any business which might have been transacted at the meeting as originally called may be transacted without further notice.

Section 12. <u>Fidelity Bonds</u>. The Board of Directors shall require that all officers and employees of the Corporation handling or responsible for corporate or trust funds shall furnish adequate fidelity bonds. The premiums on such bonds shall be paid by the Corporation.

Section 13. <u>Safeguarding Subscription Funds</u>. It shall be the duty of the Board of Directors to see to it that all sums received in connection with membership subscriptions prior to the closing of the mortgage transaction covering the housing project of the Corporation, are deposited and withdrawn only in the manner provided for in Article III, Section 3 of these By-Laws.

ARTICLE VI

OFFICERS

Section 1. <u>Designation</u>. The principal officers of the Corporation shall be a President, a Vice President, a Secretary, and a Treasurer, all of whom shall be elected by and from the Board of Directors. The Directors may appoint an assistant treasurer, and an assistant secretary, and such other officers as in their judgment may be necessary. (In the case of a corporation of one hundred members or less the offices of Treasurer and Secretary may be filled by the same person).

Section 2. <u>Election of Officers</u>. The officers of the Corporation shall be elected annually by the Board of Directors at the organization meeting of each new Board and shall hold office at the pleasure of the Board.

Section 3. <u>Removal of Officers</u>. Upon an affirmative vote of a majority of the members of the Board of Directors, any officer may be removed, either with or without cause, and his successor elected at any regular meeting of the Board of Directors, or at any special meeting of the Board called for such purpose.

Section 4. <u>President</u>. The President shall be the chief executive officer of the Corporation. He shall preside at all meetings of the members and of the Board of Directors. He shall have all of the general powers and duties which are usually vested in the office of president of a corporation, including but not limited to the power to appoint committees from among the membership from time to time as he may in his discretion decide is appropriate to assist in the conduct of the affairs of the Corporation.

---

* Delete in Section 236 cases.
** Add " and the Regulatory Agreement" where Regulatory Agreement is executed by the Corporation .
*** Include this provision only in Section 221 below market rate cases.
**** Delete ''or by a vote of the preferred members'' where Corporation has executed Regulatory Agreement.

Section 5. **Vice President.** The Vice President shall take the place of the President and perform his duties whenever the President shall be absent or unable to act. If neither the President nor the Vice President is able to act, the Board of Directors shall appoint some other member of the Board to so do on an interim basis. The Vice President shall also perform such other duties as shall from time to time be imposed upon him by the Board of Directors.

Section 6. **Secretary.** The Secretary shall keep the minutes of all meetings of the Board of Directors and the minutes of all meetings of the members of the Corporation; he shall have the custody of the seal of the Corporation; he shall have charge of the stock transfer books and of such other books and papers as the Board of Directors may direct; and he shall, in general, perform all the duties incident to the office of Secretary.

Section 7. **Treasurer.** The Treasurer shall have responsibility for corporate funds and securities and shall be responsible for keeping full and accurate accounts of all receipts and disbursements in books belonging to the Corporation. He shall be responsible for the deposit of all moneys and other valuable effects in the name, and to the credit, of the Corporation in such depositaries as may from time to time be designated by the Board of Directors.

ARTICLE VII

RIGHTS OF FEDERAL HOUSING ADMINISTRATION

Section 1.* The management, operation and control of the affairs of the Corporation shall be subject to the rights, powers, and privileges of the Federal Housing Administration pursuant to a Regulatory Agreement between the Corporation and the Federal Housing Administration. The Corporation is bound by the provisions of the Regulatory Agreement which is a condition precedent to the insurance of a mortgage of the Corporation on the project.

ARTICLE VIII

AMENDMENTS

Section 1. These By-Laws may be amended by the affirmative vote of the majority of the entire regular membership of record at any regular or special meeting, provided that no amendment shall become effective unless and until it has received the written approval of the Administration. Amendments may be proposed by the Board of Directors or by petition signed by at least twenty (20) percent of the members. A description of any proposed amendment shall accompany the notice of any regular or special meeting at which such proposed amendment is to be voted upon.

ARTICLE IX

CORPORATE SEAL

Section 1. **Seal.** The Board of Directors shall provide a suitable corporate seal containing the name of the Corporation, which seal shall be in charge of the Secretary. If so directed by the Board of Directors, a duplicate of the seal may be kept and used by the Treasurer or any assistant secretary or assistant treasurer.

---

* Delete the language of this Section where FHA regulation is exercised through ownership of preferred stock rather than by Regulatory Agreement and substitute the following:

"Section 1. Rights of Federal Housing Administration. The rights and privileges of the regular memberships of the Corporation and the management, operation and control of the affairs of the Corporation shall be subject to the rights, powers and privileges of the preferred memberships of the Corporation registered in the name of the Federal Housing Administration as provided in the Certificate of Incorporation."

ARTICLE X

FISCAL MANAGEMENT

Section 1. **Fiscal Year.** The fiscal year of the Corporation shall begin on the _____ day of _____ every year, except that the first fiscal year of the Corporation shall begin at the date of incorporation. The commencement date of the fiscal year herein established shall be subject to change by the Board of Directors should corporate practice subsequently dictate, but not without the prior written approval of the Administration.

Section 2. **Books and Accounts.** Books and accounts of the Corporation shall be kept under the direction of the Treasurer and in accordance with the Uniform System of Accounts prescribed by the FHA Commissioner. That amount of the carrying charges required for payment on the principal of the mortgage of the Corporation or any other capital expenditures shall be credited upon the books of the Corporation to the "Paid-In Surplus" account as a capital contribution by the members.

Section 3. Auditing. At the closing of each fiscal year, the books and records of the Corporation shall be audited by a Certified Public Accountant or other person acceptable to the Administration, whose report will be prepared and certified in accordance with the requirements of the Administration. Based on such reports, the Corporation will furnish its members with an annual financial statement including the income and disbursements of the Corporation. The Corporation will also supply the members, as soon as practicable after the end of each calendar year, with a statement showing each member's pro rata share of the real estate taxes and mortgage interest paid by the Corporation during the preceding calendar year.

Section 4. Inspection of Books. Financial reports such as are required to be furnished to the Administration and the membership records of the Corporation shall be available at the principal office of the Corporation for inspection at reasonable times by any members.

Section 5. Execution of Corporate Documents. With the prior authorization of the Board of Directors, all notes and contracts, including Occupancy Agreements, shall be executed on behalf of the Corporation by either the President or the Vice President, and all checks shall be executed on behalf of the Corporation by (1) either the President or the Vice President, and countersigned (2) by either the Secretary or Treasurer.

ARTICLE XI*

COMMUNITY FACILITY PROVISIONS

Section 1. Applicable Provisions. Notwithstanding any provision herein to the contrary, upon the payment in full of each FHA-insured mortgage executed by the Corporation and the release of the dwelling units included therein to the respective members, the following provisions of these By-Laws shall not be applicable to such members:

(a) Article III; and

(b) Sections 2 and 13 of Article V; and

in lieu thereof the following provisions shall apply to such members, and to all members upon payment in full of all FHA-insured mortgages executed by the Corporation:

Section 2. Membership.

(a) **Members.** Members shall consist of the owners of the dwelling units listed in Appendix B of the Articles of Incorporation, a copy of which is attached hereto, who have been approved for membership by the Board of Directors, and who have paid for their membership and received membership certificates, and such other persons to whom memberships have been transferred as provided herein.

(b) **Transfer of Membership.** Except as herein provided, memberships are not transferable or assignable:

1. The Board of Directors shall determine the membership value (hereinafter called the "Membership Fee") at which same may be transferred.

2. Subject to the prior approval of the Board of Directors, memberships may be permanently transferred by members to any of the following, in the order listed:

a. To the purchaser or lessee of the member's home if same is listed in Appendix B of the Articles of Incorporation.

b. To the owner or lessee of any of the other houses listed in Appendix B of the Articles of Incorporation who does not already own a membership.

c. To the applicant for membership at the top of a waiting list maintained by the Board of Directors, who is a resident of the area, the confines of which shall be as determined by the Board of Directors.

d. To a non-resident of the area.

(c) **Temporary Transfers.** Subject to the prior approval of the Board of Directors, a member may temporarily assign his membership to his lessee for a designated period of time provided, however, that the member making the temporary assignment remains obligated to the Corporation for the payment of all assessments and other charges approved by the membership, and for the payment of the lessee's dues. Any delinquency in payment of dues, assessment and such other charges shall be subject to the provisions of paragraph (d) hereof.

---

* This Article to be included only in Sales Type projects where community facilities are to be owned by the Corporation.

(d) Termination of Membership. Any member failing to pay annual dues, assessments or other charges duly approved by the Board of Directors within thirty (30) days after notification of delinquency has been mailed to him at the address appearing on the records of the Corporation shall be suspended by the Board of Directors. Any person thus suspended shall be notified promptly in writing by the Secretary of his suspension, and if the amounts due and payable are not paid within fifteen (15) days after the sending of such notice he shall cease to be a member of the Corporation and shall not be entitled to the privileges accorded to members. The Corporation shall be obligated, after reassignment and sale of said membership to return the Membership Fee less amounts due. (The Board of Directors, in its discretion, may reinstate any member upon request and payment of all amounts in arrearage.) The Board of Directors, at its discretion, may cancel the membership of any member upon the return of the Membership Fee provided, however, that the member may be reinstated upon appeal and approval of reinstatement by the majority of the members present at a regular or special meeting. The Corporation shall not be obligated to refund any membership fee to any member except as provided herein.

Section 3. Directors. The Board of Directors shall have the powers and duties necessary for the administration of the affairs of the Corporation and may do all such acts and things as are not by law or by these By-Laws directed to be exercised and done by the members. The powers of the Board of Directors shall include but not be limited:

(a) To promulgate such rules and regulations pertaining to the use and operation of the community facilities which are consistent with these By-Laws and the Certificate of Incorporation.

(b) To establish the annual dues, assessments and charges for the operation and maintenance of the community facilities and any other property, real or personal, owned by the Corporation.

GP O 8 9 6 - 36 3

CHART 5-2

FHA FORM NO. 3237
Revised February 1969
(For use by Sec. 213,
Sec. 221 and Sec. 236
Cooperatives composed
of one mortgage parcel.
(Multi-Section coopera-
tive should use FHA
Form 3237-B.)

U. S. DEPARTMENT OF HOUSING AND URBAN DEVELOPMENT
FEDERAL HOUSING ADMINISTRATION

MODEL FORM OF OCCUPANCY AGREEMENT

THIS AGREEMENT, made and entered into this _____ day of _____ , 19 ___ , by and between _____ (hereinafter referred to as the Corporation), a corporation having its principal office and place of business at _____ , and _____ (hereinafter referred to as Member);

WHEREAS, the Corporation has been formed for the purpose of acquiring, owning and operating a cooperative housing project to be located at _____ , with the intent that its members ⌈in stock corporations change "members" to "stockholders" and add the following parenthetical clause "(hereinafter called members)"⌉ shall have the right to occupy the dwelling units thereof under the terms and conditions hereinafter set forth; and

WHEREAS, the Member is the owner and holder of a certificate of membership ⌈or _____ shares of common capital stock⌉ of the Corporation and has a bona fide intention to reside in the project;

*WHEREAS, the Member has certified to the accuracy of the statements made in his application and family income survey and agrees and understands that family income, family composition and other eligibility requirements are substantial and material requirements of his initial and of his continuing occupancy.

NOW, THEREFORE, in consideration of One Dollar ($1.00) to each of the parties paid by the other party, the receipt of which is hereby acknowledged, and in further consideration of the mutual promises contained herein, the Corporation hereby lets to the Member, and the Member hereby hires and takes from the Corporation, dwelling unit number _____ , located at _____ ;

TO HAVE AND TO HOLD said dwelling unit unto the Member, his executors, administrators and authorized assigns, on the terms and conditions set forth herein and in the corporate Charter and By-laws of the Corporation and any rules and regulations of the Corporation now or hereafter adopted pursuant thereto, from the date of this agreement, for a term terminating on 19 ___ , **renewable thereafter for successive three-year periods under the conditions provided for herein.

ARTICLE 1. MONTHLY CARRYING CHARGES

Commencing at the time indicated in ARTICLE 2 hereof, the Member agrees to pay to the Corporation a monthly sum referred to herein as "Carrying Charges", equal to one-twelfth of the Member's proportionate share of the sum required by the Corporation, as estimated by its Board of Directors to meet its annual expenses, including but not limited to the following items:

(a) The cost of all operating expenses of the project and services furnished.
(b) The cost of necessary management and administration.
(c) The amount of all taxes and assessments levied against the project of the Corporation or which it is required to pay, and ground rent, if any.
(d) The cost of fire and extended coverage insurance on the project and such other insurance as the Corporation may effect or as may be required by any mortgage on the project.
(e) The cost of furnishing water, electricity, heat, air conditioning, gas, garbage and trash collection and other utilities, if furnished by the Corporation.
(f) All reserves set up by the Board of Directors, including the general operating reserve and the reserve for replacements.
(g) The estimated cost of repairs, maintenance and replacements of the project property to be made by the Corporation.
(h) The amount of principal, interest, mortgage insurance premiums, if any, and other required payments on the hereinafter-mentioned insured mortgage.
(i) Any other expenses of the Corporation approved by the Board of Directors, including operating deficiencies, if any, for prior periods.

The Board of Directors shall determine the amount of the Carrying Charges annually, but may do so at more frequent intervals, should circumstances so require. No member shall be charged with more than his proportionate share thereof as determined by the Board of Directors. That amount of the Carrying Charges required for payment on the principal of the mortgage of the Corporation or any other capital expenditures shall be credited upon the books of the Corporation to the "Paid-In Surplus" account as a capital contribution by the members.

***Notwithstanding the above provisions it is understood and agreed by the Member and the Corporation that where the annual family income of the Member is such that he is entitled to the benefit of the interest reduction payment made by the FHA to the mortgagee, the monthly Carrying Charges for the member shall be reduced to the extent required by the FHA as set forth in the Regulatory Agreement.

Until further notice from the Corporation the Monthly Carrying Charges for the abovementioned dwelling unit shall be $ _____
_____ .

***It is understood and agreed that if the annual family income of the Member is hereafter increased, his monthly Carrying Charges will be increased to the extent required by the FHA as set forth in the Regulatory Agreement.

---

* Required only in Sec. 236 cases and in Sec. 221(d)(3) below market interest rate cases.
** The termination date to be inserted should be three years from the date of the Occupancy Agreement.
*** Required only in Section 236 cases.

84

*The Member agrees, however, that if during the term of this agreement the total income of his family exceeds the limitations for occupancy which may be established from time to time by the Federal Housing Administration, he will pay to the Corporation, at the option of the Corporation and upon 60 days' written notice, additional Monthly Carrying Charges in an amount commensuate with the amount of his family income in excess of the FHA income limitations, pursuant to a plan previously developed by the Corporation and approved by the Federal Housing Administration. In no event shall the total Monthly Carrying Charge, including such additional charges for excess income, exceed that which would have been applicable had the mortgage of the Corporation borne interest at the rate of 6 percent per annum and a mortgage insurance premium of ½ of 1 percent been required.

**The Member agrees that his family income, family composition and other eligiblity requirements are substantial and material conditions with respect to the amount of monthly carrying charges he will be obligated to pay and with respect to his continuing right of occupancy. The Member agrees to make a recertification of his income to the Corporation at least every two years from the date of this Agreement so long as he is receiving the benefit of interest reduction payments made by the FHA to the mortgagee. The Member further agrees that the monthly carrying charges are subject to adjustment by the Corporation to reflect income changes which are disclosed on any of the Member's recertifications, as required by the Regulatory Agreement. Immediately upon making such adjustment, the Corporation agrees to give 30 days written notice to the Member stating the new amount the Member will be required to pay, which, until further notice shall then be the Member's monthly carrying charge.

ARTICLE 2. WHEN PAYMENT OF CARRYING CHARGES TO COMMENCE.

After thirty days' notice by the Corporation to the effect that the dwelling unit is or will be available for occupancy, or upon acceptance of occupancy, whichever is earlier, the Member shall make a payment for Carrying Charges covering the unexpired balance of the month. Thereafter, the Member shall pay Carrying Charges in advance on the first day of each month.

ARTICLE 3. PATRONAGE REFUNDS.***

The Corporation agrees on its part that it will refund or credit to the Member within ninety (90) days after the end of each fiscal year, his proportionate share of such sums as have been collected in anticipation of expenses which are in excess of the amount needed for expenses of all kinds, including reserves, in the discretion of the Board of Directors.

ARTICLE 4. MEMBER'S OPTION FOR AUTOMATIC RENEWAL.

It is covenanted and agreed that the term herein granted shall be extended and renewed from time to time by and against the parties hereto for further periods of three years each from the expiration of the term herein granted, upon the same covenants and agreements as herein contained unless; (1) notice of the Member's election not to renew shall have been given to the Corporation in writing at least four months prior to the expiration of the then current term, and (2) the Member shall have on or before the expiration of said term (a) endorsed all his (stock) (membership certificate) for transfer in blank and deposited same with the Corporation, and (b) met all his obligations and paid all amounts due under this Agreement up to the time of said expiration, and (c) vacated the premises, leaving same in good state of repair. Upon compliance with provisions (1) and (2) of this Article, the Member shall have no further liability under this agreement and shall be entitled to no payment from the Corporation.

ARTICLE 5. PREMISES TO BE USED FOR RESIDENTIAL PURPOSES ONLY.

The Member shall occupy the dwelling unit covered by this agreement as a private dwelling unit for himself and/or his immediate family and for no other purpose, and may enjoy the use in common with other members of the corporation of all community property and facilities of the project so long as he continues to own a [membership certificate] [share of common stock] of the Corporation, occupies his dwelling unit, and abides by the terms of this agreement. Any sublessee of the Member, if approved pursuant to Article 7 hereof, may enjoy the rights to which the Member is entitled under this Article 5.

The Member shall not permit or suffer anything to be done or kept upon said premises which will increase the rate of insurance on the building, or on the contents thereof, or which will obstruct or interfere with the rights of other occupants, or annoy them by unreasonable noises or otherwise, nor will he commit or permit any nuisance on the premises or commit or suffer any immoral or illegal act to be committed thereon. The Member shall comply with all of the requirements of the Board of Health and of all other governmental authorities with respect to the said premises. If by reason of the occupancy or use of said premises by the Member the rate of insurance on the building shall be increased, the Member shall become personally liable for the additional insurance premiums.

ARTICLE 6. MEMBER'S RIGHT TO PEACEABLE POSSESSION.

In return for the Member's continued fulfillment of the terms and conditions of this agreement, the Corporation covenants that the Member may at all times while this agreement remains in effect, have and enjoy for his sole use and benefit the dwelling unit hereinabove described, after obtaining occupancy, and may enjoy in common with all other members of the Corporation the use of all community property and facilities of the project.

ARTICLE 7. NO SUBLETTING WITHOUT CONSENT OF CORPORATION.

The Member hereby agrees not to assign this agreement nor to sublet his dwelling unit without the written consent of the Corporation on a form approved by the Federal Housing Administration. The liability of the Member under this Occupancy Agreement shall continue notwithstanding the fact that he may have sublet the dwelling unit with the approval of the Corporation and the Member shall be responsible to the Corporation for the conduct of his sublessee. Any unauthorized subleasing shall, at the option of the Corporation, result in the termination and forfeiture of the member's rights under this Occupancy Agreement. Non-paying guest of the Member may occupy Member's unit under such conditions as may be prescribed by the Board of Directors in the rules and regulations.

ARTICLE 8. TRANSFERS.

Neither this agreement nor the Member's right of occupancy shall be transferrable or assignable except in the same manner as may now or hereafter be provided for the transfer of memberships in the By-Laws of the Corporation.

---

* Required only in Sec. 221 below market interest rate cases.
** Required only in Section 236 cases.
*** Omit this paragraph in Section 236 cases.

ARTICLE 9. MANAGEMENT, TAXES AND INSURANCE.

The Corporation shall provide necessary management, operation and administration of the project; pay or provide for the payment of all taxes or assessments levied against the project; procure and pay or provide for the payment of fire insurance and extended coverage, and other insurance as required by any mortgage on property in the project, and such other insurance as the Corporation may deem advisable on the property in the project. The Corporation will not, however, provide insurance on the Member's interest in the dwelling unit or on his personal property.

ARTICLE 10. UTILITIES.

The Corporation shall provide water, electricity, gas, heat and air conditioning in amounts which it deems reasonable. (Strike out any of the foregoing items in this Article which are not applicable.) The Member shall pay directly to the supplier for all other utilities.

ARTICLE 11. REPAIRS.

(a) By Member. The Member agrees to repair and maintain his dwelling unit at his own expense as follows:

   (1) Any repairs or maintenance necessitated by his own negligence or misuse;
   (2) Any redecoration of his own dwelling unit; and
   (3) Any repairs, maintenance or replacements required on the following items:

        (Insert the items desired, subject to FHA approval.)

(b) By Corporation. The Corporation shall provide and pay for all necessary repairs, maintenance and replacements, except as specified in clause (a) of this Article. The officers and employees of the Corporation shall have the right to enter the dwelling unit of the Member in order to effect necessary repairs, maintenance, and replacements, and to authorize entrance for such purposes by employees of any contractor, utility company, municipal agency, or others, at any reasonable hour of the day and in the event of emergency at any time.

(c) Right of Corporation to Make Repairs at Member's Expense. In case the Member shall fail to effect the repairs, maintenance or replacements specified in clause (a) of this Article in a manner satisfactory to the Corporation and pay for same, the latter may do so and add the cost thereof to the Member's next month's Carrying Charge payment.

ARTICLE 12. ALTERATIONS AND ADDITIONS.

The Member shall not, without the written consent of the Corporation, make any structural alterations in the premises or in the water, gas or steampipes, electrical conduits, plumbing or other fixtures connected therewith, or remove any additions, improvements, or fixtures from the premises.

If the Member for any reason shall cease to be an occupant of the premises, he shall surrender to the Corporation possession thereof, including any alterations, additions, fixtures and improvements.

The Member shall not, without the prior written consent of the Corporation, install or use in his dwelling unit any air conditioning equipment, washing machine, clothes dryer, electric heater, or power tools. (Strike out any of the foregoing items which are not applicable.) The Member agrees that the Corporation may require the prompt removal of any such equipment at any time, and that his failure to remove such equipment upon request shall constitute a default within the meaning of Article 13 of this agreement.

ARTICLE 13. DEFINITION OF DEFAULT BY MEMBER AND EFFECT THEREOF.

It is mutually agreed as follows: At any time after the happening of any of the events specified in clauses (a) to (i)* of this Article the Corporation may at its option give to the Member a notice that this agreement will expire at a date not less than ten (10) days thereafter. If the Corporation so proceeds all of the Member's rights under this agreement will expire on the date so fixed in such notice, unless in the meantime the default has been cured in a manner deemed satisfactory to the Corporation, it being the intention of the parties hereto to create hereby conditional limitations, and it shall thereupon be lawful for the Corporation to re-enter the dwelling unit and to remove all persons and personal property therefrom, either by summary dispossess proceedings or by suitable action or proceeding, at law or in equity or by any other proceedings which may apply to the eviction of tenants or by force or otherwise, and to repossess the dwelling unit in its former state as if this agreement had not been made:

   (a) In case at any time during the term of this agreement the Member shall cease to be the owner and legal holder of a membership [or share of the stock] of the Corporation.
   (b) In case the Member attempts to transfer or assign this agreement in a manner inconsistent with the provisions of the By-Laws.
   (c) In case at any time during the continuance of this agreement the Member shall be declared a bankrupt under the laws of the United States.
   (d) In case at any time during the continuance of this agreement a receiver of the Member's property shall be appointed under any of the laws of the United States or of any State.
   (e) In case at any time during the continuance of this agreement the Member shall make a general assignment for the benefit of creditors.
   (f) In case at any time during the continuance of this agreement any of the stock or membership of the Corporation owned by the Member shall be duly levied upon and sold under the process of any Court.
   (g) In case the Member fails to effect and/or pay for repairs and maintenance as provided for in Article 11 hereof.
   (h) In case the Member shall fail to pay any sum due pursuant to the provisions of Article 1 or Article 10 hereof.
   (i) In case the Member shall default in the performance of any of his obligations under this agreement.
 **(j) In case at any time during the term of this agreement the limitations for occupancy which may be established from time to time by the Federal Housing Administration are exceeded.
 **(k) In case at any time during the term of this agreement, the Member fails to comply promptly with all requests by the Corporation or the Federal Housing Commissioner for information and certifications concerning the income of the Member and his family, the composition of the Member's family and other eligibility requirements for occupancy in the project.

The Member hereby expressly waives any and all right of redemption in case he shall be dispossessed by judgment or warrant of any Court or judge; the words "enter", "re-enter", and "re-entry", as used in this agreement are not restricted to their technical legal meaning, and in the event of a breach or threatened breach by the Member of any of the covenants or provisions hereof, the Corporation shall have the right of injunction and the right to invoke any remedy allowed at law or in equity, as if re-entry, summary proceedings, and other remedies were not herein provided for.

The Member expressly agrees that there exists under this Occupancy Agreement a landlord-tenant relationship and that in the event of a breach or threatened breach by the Member of any covenant or provision of this Agreement, there shall be available to the Corporation such legal remedy or remedies as are available to a landlord for the breach or threatened breach under the law*** by a tenant of any provision of a lease or rental agreement.

---

* Change "(i)" to "(k)" in Section 236 cases and in Section 221 below market interest rate cases.
** Required only in Section 236 cases and in Section 221 below market interest rate cases.
*** In some States it may be desirable to include reference to a particular State statute on this subject.

The failure on the part of the Corporation to avail itself of any of the remedies given under this agreement shall not waive nor destroy the right of the Corporation to avail itself of such remedies for similar or other breaches on the part of the Member.

ARTICLE 14. MEMBER TO COMPLY WITH ALL CORPORATE REGULATIONS.

The Member covenants that he will preserve and promote the cooperative ownership principals on which the Corporation has been founded, abide by the Charter, By-Laws, rules and regulations of the Corporation and any amendments thereto, and by his acts of cooperation with its other members bring about for himself and his co-members a high standard in home and community conditions. The Corporation agrees to make its rules and regulations known to the Member by delivery of same to him or by promulgating them in such other manner as to constitute adequate notice.

ARTICLE 15. EFFECT OF FIRE LOSS ON INTERESTS OF MEMBER.

In the event of loss or damage by fire or other casualty to the above-mentioned dwelling unit without the fault or negligence of the Member, the Corporation shall determine whether to restore the damaged premises and shall further determine, in the event such premises shall not be restored, the amount which shall be paid to the Member to redeem the (membership) (common stock) of the Member and to reimburse him for such loss as he may have sustained.

If, under such circumstances, the Corporation determines to restore the premises, Carrying Charges shall abate wholly or partially as determined by the Corporation until the premises have been restored. If on the other hand the Corporation determines not to restore the premises, the Carrying Charges shall cease from the date of such loss or damage.

ARTICLE 16. INSPECTION OF DWELLING UNIT.

The Member agrees that the representatives of any mortgagee holding a mortgage on the property of the Corporation, the offices and employees of the Corporation, and with the approval of the Corporation the employees of any contractor, utility company, municipal agency or others, shall have the right to enter the dwelling unit of the Member and make inspections thereof at any reasonable hour of the day and at any time in the event of emergency.

ARTICLE 17. SUBORDINATION CLAUSE.

The project, of which the above-mentioned dwelling unit is a part, was or is to be constructed or purchased by the Corporation with the assistance of a mortgage loan advanced to the Corporation by a private lending institution with the understanding between the Corporation and the lender that the latter would apply for mortgage insurance under the provisions of the National Housing Act. Therefore, it is specifically understood and agreed by the parties hereto that this agreement and all rights, privileges and benefits hereunder are and shall be at all times subject to and subordinate to the lien of a first mortgage and the accompanying documents executed by the Corporation under date of _____, (or to be executed by the Corporation) payable to _____ in the principal sum of $ _____ with interest at _____ per centum, and insured or to be insured under the provisions of the National Housing Act, and to any and all modifications, extensions and renewals thereof and to any mortgage or deed of trust made in replacement thereof and to any mortgage or deed of trust which may at any time hereafter be placed on the property of the Corporation or any part thereof. The Member hereby agrees to execute, at the Corporation's request and expense, any instrument which the Corporation or any lender may deem necessary or desirable to effect the subordination of this agreement to any such mortgage, or deed of trust, and the Member hereby appoints the Corporation and each and every officer thereof, and any future officer, his irrevocable attorney-in-fact during the term hereof to execute any such instrument on behalf of the Member. The Member does hereby expressly waive any and all notices of default and notices of foreclosure of said mortgage which may be required by law.

In the event a waiver of such notices is not legally valid, the Member does hereby constitute the Corporation his agent to receive and accept such notices on the Member's behalf.

ARTICLE 18. LATE CHARGES AND OTHER COSTS IN CASE OF DEFAULT.

The Member covenants and agrees that, in addition to the other sums that have become or will become due, pursuant to the terms of this Agreement, the Member shall pay to the Corporation a late charge in an amount to be determined from time to time by the Board of Directors for each payment of Carrying Charges, or part thereof, more than 10 days in arrears.

If a Member defaults in making a payment of Carrying Charges or in the performance or observance of any provision of this Agreement, and the Corporation has obtained the services of any attorney with respect to the defaults involved, the Member covenants and agrees to pay to the Corporation any costs or fees involved, including reasonable attorney's fees, notwithstanding the fact that a suit has not yet been instituted. In case a suit is instituted, the Member shall also pay the costs of the suit, in addition to other aforesaid costs and fees.

ARTICLE 19. NOTICES.

Whenever the provisions of law or the By-Laws of the Corporation or this agreement require notice to be given to either party hereto, any notice by the Corporation to the Member shall be deemed to have been duly given, and any demand by the Corporation upon the Member shall be deemed to have been duly made if the same is delivered to the Member at his unit or to the Member's last known address; and any notice or demand by the Member to the Corporation shall be deemed to have been duly given if delivered to an officer of the Corporation. Such notice may also be given by depositing same in the United States mails addressed to the Member as shown in the books of the Corporation, or to the President of the Cooperative, as the case may be, and the time of mailing shall be deemed to be the time of giving of such notice.

ARTICLE 20. ORAL REPRESENTATION NOT BINDING.

No representations other than those contained in this agreement, the Charter and the By-Laws of the Corporation shall be binding upon the Corporation.

IN WITNESS WHEREOF, the parties hereto have caused this agreement to be signed and sealed the day and year first above written.

_____
Corporation

By _____(SEAL)

_____

_____
Member and Stockholder

TO BE DULY ACKNOWLEDGED

HUD-Wash., D. C.

CHART 5-3

FHA FORM NO. 3277
(For use by Condominiums
in Section 234)

U. S. DEPARTMENT OF HOUSING AND URBAN DEVELOPMENT
FEDERAL HOUSING ADMINISTRATION

BY-LAWS OF _____ CONDOMINIUM

ARTICLE I

PLAN OF APARTMENT OWNERSHIP

Section 1. Apartment Ownership. The project located at _____

Street, City of _____ , State of _____ , known

as '' _____ Condominium'' is submitted to the provisions of *

_____ .

Section 2. By-Laws Applicability. The provisions of these By-Laws are applicable to the project. (The term
"project" as used herein shall include the land.)

Section 3. Personal Application. All present or future owners, tenants, future tenants, or their employees, or any
other person that might use the facilities of the project in any manner, are subject to the regulations set forth in
these By-Laws and to the Regulatory Agreement, attached as Exhibit "C" to the recorded Plan of Apartment Ownership.

The mere acquisition or rental of any of the family units (hereinafter referred to as "units") of the project or the
mere act of occupancy of any of said units will signify that these By-Laws and the provisions of the Regulatory
Agreement are accepted, ratified, and will be complied with.

ARTICLE II

VOTING, MAJORITY OF OWNERS, QUORUM, PROXIES

Section 1. Voting. Voting shall be on a percentage basis and the percentage of the vote to which the owner is entitled is the percentage assigned to the family unit or units in the Master Deed.

Section 2. Majority of Owners. As used in these By-Laws the term "majority of owners" shall mean those owners
holding 51% of the votes in accordance with the percentages assigned in the Master Deed.

Section 3. Quorum. Except as otherwise provided in these By-Laws, the presence in person or by proxy of a "majority of owners" as defined in Section 2 of this Article shall constitute a quorum.

Section 4. Proxies. Votes may be cast in person or by proxy. Proxies must be filed with the Secretary before the
appointed time of each meeting.

ARTICLE III

ADMINISTRATION

Section 1. Association Responsibilities. The owners of the units will constitute the Association of Owners (hereinafter referred to as "Association") who will have the responsibility of administering the project, approving the

* Identify state law establishing apartment ownership.

annual budget, establishing and collecting monthly assessments and arranging for the management of the project pursuant to an agreement, containing provisions relating to the duties, obligations, removal and compensation of the management agent. Except as otherwise provided, decisions and resolutions of the Association shall require approval by a majority of owners.

Section 2. Place of Meetings. Meetings of the Association shall be held at the principal office of the project or such other suitable place convenient to the owners as may be designated by the Board of Directors.

Section 3. Annual Meetings. The first annual meeting of the Association shall be held on _____ (Date)*. Thereafter, the annual meetings of the Association shall be held on the _____ (1st, 2nd, 3rd, 4th)_____ (Monday, Tuesday, Wednesday, etc.) of _____ (month) each succeeding year. At such meetings there shall be elected by ballot of the owners a Board of Directors in accordance with the requirements of Section 5 of Article IV of these By-Laws. The owners may also transact such other business of the Association as may properly come before them.

Section 4. Special Meetings. It shall be the duty of the President to call a special meeting of the owners as directed by resolution of the Board of Directors or upon a petition signed by a majority of the owners and having been presented to the Secretary, or at the request of the Federal Housing Commissioner or his duly authorized representative. The notice of any special meeting shall state the time and place of such meeting and the purpose thereof. No business shall be transacted at a special meeting except as stated in the notice unless by consent of four-fifths of the owners present, either in person or by proxy.

Section 5. Notice of Meetings. It shall be the duty of the Secretary to mail a notice of each annual or special meeting, stating the purpose thereof as well as the time and place where it is to be held, to each owner of record, at least 5 but not more than 10 days prior to such meeting. The mailing of a notice in the manner provided in this Section shall be considered notice served. Notices of all meetings shall be mailed to the Director of the local insuring office of the Federal Housing Administration.

Section 6. Adjourned Meetings. If any meeting of owners cannot be organized because a quorum has not attended, the owners who are present, either in person or by proxy, may adjourn the meeting to a time not less than forty-eight (48) hours from the time the original meeting was called.

Section 7. Order of Business. The order of business at all meetings of the owners of units shall be as follows:

(a) Roll call.
(b) Proof of notice of meeting or waiver of notice.
(c) Reading of minutes of preceding meeting.
(d) Reports of officers.
(e) Report of Federal Housing Administration representative, if present.
(f) Report of committees.
(g) Election of inspectors of election.
(h) Election of directors.
(i) Unfinished business.
(j) New business.

ARTICLE IV

BOARD OF DIRECTORS

Section 1. Number and Qualification. The affairs of the Association shall be governed by a Board of Directors composed of _____ persons,** all of whom must be owners of units in the project.

Section 2. Powers and Duties. The Board of Directors shall have the powers and duties necessary for the administration of the affairs of the Association and may do all such acts and things as are not by law or by these By-Laws directed to be exercised and done by the owners.

---

* This date must be approved by the FHA Insuring Office.
** The number should be an odd number not less than five.

Section 3. <u>Other Duties</u>. In addition to duties imposed by these By-Laws or by resolutions of the Association, the Board of Directors shall be responsible for the following:

    (a) Care, upkeep and surveillance of the project and the common areas and facilities and the restricted common areas and facilities.

    (b) Collection of monthly assessments from the owners.

    (c) Designation and dismissal of the personnel necessary for the maintenance and operation of the project, the common areas and facilities and the restricted common areas and facilities.

Section 4. <u>Management Agent</u>. The Board of Directors may employ for the Association a management agent at a compensation established by the Board to perform such duties and services as the Board shall authorize including, but not limited to, the duties listed in Section 3 of this Article.

Section 5. <u>Election and Term of Office</u>. At the first annual meeting of the Association the term of office of two Directors shall be fixed for three (3) years. The term of office of two Directors shall be fixed at two (2) years, and the term of office of one Director shall be fixed at one (1) year. At the expiration of the initial term of office of each respective Director, his successor shall be elected to serve a term of three (3) years. The Directors shall hold office until their successors have been elected and hold their first meeting. (If a larger Board of Directors is contemplated, the terms of office should be established in a similar manner so that they will expire in different years.)

Section 6. <u>Vacancies</u>. Vacancies in the Board of Directors caused by any reason other than the removal of a Director by a vote of the Association shall be filled by vote of the majority of the remaining Directors, even though they may constitute less than a quorum; and each person so elected shall be a Director until a successor is elected at the next annual meeting of the Association.

Section 7. <u>Removal of Directors</u>. At any regular or special meeting duly called, any one or more of the Directors may be removed with or without cause by a majority of the owners and a successor may then and there be elected to fill the vacancy thus created. Any Director whose removal has been proposed by the owners shall be given an opportunity to be heard at the meeting.

Section 8. <u>Organization Meeting</u>. The first meeting of a newly elected Board of Directors shall be held within ten (10) days of election at such place as shall be fixed by the Directors at the meeting at which such Directors were elected, and no notice shall be necessary to the newly elected Directors in order legally to constitute such meeting, providing a majority of the whole Board shall be present.

Section 9. <u>Regular Meetings</u>. Regular meetings of the Board of Directors may be held at such time and place as shall be determined, from time to time, by a majority of the Directors, but at least two such meetings shall be held during each fiscal year. Notice of regular meetings of the Board of Directors shall be given to each Director, personally or by mail, telephone or telegraph, at least three(3) days prior to the day named for such meeting.

Section 10. <u>Special Meetings</u>. Special meetings of the Board of Directors may be called by the President on three days notice to each Director, given personally or by mail, telephone or telegraph, which notice shall state the time, place (as hereinabove provided) and purpose of the meeting. Special meetings of the Board of Directors shall be called by the President or Secretary in like manner and on like notice on the written request of at least three Directors.

Section 11. <u>Waiver of Notice</u>. Before or at any meeting of the Board of Directors, any Director may, in writing, waive notice of such meeting and such waiver shall be deemed equivalent to the giving of such notice. Attendance by a Director at any meeting of the Board shall be a waiver of notice by him of the time and place thereof. If all the Directors are present at any meeting of the Board, no notice shall be required and any business may be transacted at such meeting.

Section 12. <u>Board of Director's Quorum</u>. At all meetings of the Board of Directors, a majority of the Directors shall constitute a quorum for the transaction of business, and the acts of the majority of the Directors present at a meeting at which a quorum is present shall be the acts of the Board of Directors. If, at any meeting of the Board affect the project in its entirety or in a part belonging to other owners, being expressly responsible for the damages and liabilities that his failure to do so may engender.

(b) All the repairs of internal installations of the unit such as water, light, gas, power, sewage, telephones, air conditioners, sanitary installations, doors, windows, lamps and all other accessories belonging to the unit area shall be at the owner's expense.

(c) An owner shall reimburse the Association for any expenditures incurred in repairing or replacing any common area and facility damaged through his fault.

Section 3. Use of Family Units - Internal Changes.

(a) All units shall be utilized for residential purposes only.

(b) An owner shall not make structural modifications or alterations in his unit or installations located therein without previously notifying the Association in writing, through the Management Agent, if any, or through the President of the Board of Directors, if no management agent is employed. The Association shall have the obligation to answer within _____ days and failure to do so within the stipulated time shall mean that there is no objection to the proposed modification or alteration.

Section 4. Use of Common Areas and Facilities and Restricted Common Areas and Facilities.

(a) An owner shall not place or cause to be placed in the lobbies, vestibules, stairways, elevators and other project areas and facilities of a similar nature both common and restricted, any furniture, packages or objects of any kind. Such areas shall be used for no other purpose than for normal transit through them.

(b) The project shall have _____ elevators, _____ devoted to the transportation of the owners and their guests and _____ for freight service, or auxiliary purposes. Owners and tradesmen are expressly required to utilize exclusively a freight or service elevator for transporting packages, merchandise or any other object that may affect the comfort or well-being of the passengers of the elevator dedicated to the transportation of owners, residents and guests.

Section 5. Right of Entry.

(a) An owner shall grant the right of entry to the management agent or to any other person authorized by the Board of Directors or the Association in case of any emergency originating in or threatening his unit, whether the owner is present at the time or not.

(b) An owner shall permit other owners, or their representatives, when so required, to enter his unit for the purpose of performing installations, alterations or repairs to the mechanical or electrical services, provided that requests for entry are made in advance and that such entry is at a time convenient to the owner. In case of an emergency, such right of entry shall be immediate.

Section 6. Rules of Conduct.

(a) No resident of the project shall post any advertisements, or posters of any kind in or on the project except as authorized by the Association.

(b) Residents shall exercise extreme care about making noises or the use of musical instruments, radios, television and amplifiers that may disturb other residents. Keeping domestic animals will abide by the Municipal Sanitary Regulations.

(c) It is prohibited to hang garments, rugs, etc., from the windows or from any of the facades of the project.

(d) It is prohibited to dust rugs, etc., from the windows, or to clean rugs, etc., by beating on the exterior part of the project.

(e) It is prohibited to throw garbage or trash outside the disposal installations provided for such purposes in the service areas.

of Directors, there be less than a quorum present, the majority of those present may adjourn the meeting from time to time. At any such adjourned meeting, any business which might have been transacted at the meeting as originally called may be transacted without further notice.

Section 13. Fidelity Bonds. The Board of Directors shall require that all officers and employees of the Association handling or responsible for Association funds shall furnish adequate fidelity bonds. The premiums on such bonds shall be paid by the Association.

ARTICLE V

OFFICERS

Section 1. Designation. The principal officers of the Association shall be a President, a Vice President, a Secretary, and a Treasurer, all of whom shall be elected by and from the Board of Directors. The Directors may appoint an assistant treasurer, and an assistant secretary, and such other officers as in their judgment may be necessary. (In the case of an Association of one hundred owners or less the offices of Treasurer and Secretary may be filled by the same person.)

Section 2. Election of Officers. The officers of the Association shall be elected annually by the Board of Directors at the organization meeting of each new Board and shall hold office at the pleasure of the Board.

Section 3. Removal of Officers. Upon an affirmative vote of a majority of the members of the Board of Directors, any officer may be removed, either with or without cause, and his successor elected at any regular meeting of the Board of Directors, or at any special meeting of the Board called for such purpose.

Section 4. President. The President shall be the chief executive officer of the Association. He shall preside at all meetings of the Association and of the Board of Directors. He shall have all of the general powers and duties which are usually vested in the office of president of an Association, including but not limited to the power to appoint committees from among the owners from time to time as he may in his discretion decide is appropriate to assist in the conduct of the affairs of the Association.

Section 5. Vice President. The Vice President shall take the place of the President and perform his duties whenever the President shall be absent or unable to act. If neither the President nor the Vice President is able to act, the Board of Directors shall appoint some other member of the Board to so do on an interim basis. The Vice President shall also perform such other duties as shall from time to time be imposed upon him by the Board of Directors.

Section 6. Secretary. The Secretary shall keep the minutes of all meetings of the Board of Directors and the minutes of all meetings of the Association; he shall have charge of such books and papers as the Board of Directors may direct; and he shall, in general, perform all the duties incident to the office of Secretary.

Section 7. Treasurer. The Treasurer shall have responsibility for Association funds and securities and shall be responsible for keeping full and accurate accounts of all receipts and disbursements in books belonging to the Association. He shall be responsible for the deposit of all moneys and other valuable effects in the name, and to the credit, of the Association in such depositaries as may from time to time be designated by the Board of Directors.

ARTICLE VI

OBLIGATIONS OF THE OWNERS

Section 1. Assessments. All owners are obligated to pay monthly assessments imposed by the Association to meet all project communal expenses, which may include a liability insurance policy premium and an insurance premium for a policy to cover repair and reconstruction work in case of hurricane, fire, earthquake or other hazard. The assessments shall be made pro rata according to the value of the unit owned, as stipulated in the Master Deed. Such assessments shall include monthly payments to a General Operating Reserve and a Reserve Fund for Replacements as required in the Regulatory Agreement attached as Exhibit "C" to the Plan of Apartment Ownership.

Section 2. Maintenance and Repair.
(a) Every owner must perform promptly all maintenance and repair work within his own unit, which if omitted would

(f) No owner, resident or lessee shall install wiring for electrical or telephone installation, television antennae, machines or air conditioning units, etc., on the exterior of the project or that protrude through the walls or the roof of the project except as authorized by the Association.

ARTICLE VII

AMENDMENTS TO PLAN OF APARTMENT OWNERSHIP

Section 1. By-Laws. These By-Laws may be amended by the Association in a duly constituted meeting for such purpose and no amendment shall take effect unless approved by owners representing at least 75% of the total value of all units in the project as shown in the Master Deed.

ARTICLE VIII

MORTGAGEES

Section 1. Notice to Association. An owner who mortgages his unit, shall notify the Association through the Management Agent, if any, or the President of the Board of Directors in the event there is no Management Agent, the name and address of his mortgagee; and the Association shall maintain such information in a book entitled "Mortgagees of Units."

Section 2. Notice of Unpaid Assessments. The Association shall at the request of a mortgagee of a unit report any unpaid assessments due from the owner of such unit.

ARTICLE IX

COMPLIANCE

These By-Laws are set forth to comply with the requirements of*

In case any of these By-Laws conflict with the provisions of said statute, it is hereby agreed and accepted that the provisions of the statute will apply.

* Identify state law establishing apartment ownership.

QUESTIONS FOR THOUGHT AND DISCUSSION

1. What is a cooperative? A condominium?
2. Compare the cooperative and condominium forms of ownership.
3. Discuss the FHA insured programs for cooperatives and condominiums and point out the advantages and disadvantages of each.
4. What are the four statutory requirements for establishment of a condominium?
5. If a condominium apartment building was located in a planned unit development would you need two owners' associations (one for the apartment building and one for the PUD) or would one suffice? Explain your answer.
6. What problems are involved in financing a condominium, whether FHA or conventional?
7. If a condominium development is established and it is subsequently discovered that for some reason it was not legally constituted, what problems, if any, would likely arise?

6

LONG—TERM LEASES
AND THEIR FINANCING

By definition a *lease* is an agreement whereby the right to possession and enjoyment of real estate is transferred for a definite period of time. The person transferring the right of possession is called the "lessor" and the person obtaining possession is called the "lessee". The lessor owns the fee subject to possession by the lessee for a fixed term. The lessee owns what is termed a "leasehold estate" or an "estate for years." The lessor is often referred to as the "reversionary owner" since possession will sometime revert to him and he will at that time own the property in fee and free from another party's right of possession.

CLASSIFICATION OF LEASES

Leases may be classed as to term or payment provisions. As to term, in real estate financing a short-term lease is considered to be one made for less than twenty-one years and a long-term lease to be one made for at least twenty-one years. This derives from the insurance and banking laws which regulate most leasehold financing institutions and provide that these institutions can lend only on leases with unexpired terms of not less than twenty-one years from the date the loan is closed.

Leases classed as to payment provisions are of several types:

1. A *net* lease is one in which the tenant pays all or a substantial part of the operation and maintenance costs. In the real estate industry a net lease can mean one where the lessee pays for all expenses except taxes, insurance and exterior repairs. In such a case, the term "net-net," "absolutely net," or "100 percent net" is used to refer to a situation where the tenant pays all costs of operation and maintenance. As used herein, the term "net lease" will mean the lessee pays for everything. The net lease is used primarily with free standing single tenant buildings where the Lessor desires to make the Lessee responsible for all cost relating to

95

occupancy and in those situations where the Lessor wants to maintain set net rental income.

2. A *flat* lease is one calling for a fixed periodic payment for the use of the property over the term of the lease. Such a lease is usually made for a short period of time since inflation can easily erode the buying power of a set rental figure.

3. A *step-up* lease provides for the fixed payments to be adjusted periodically. The adjustment can be made either by new rentals taking effect after the passage of certain periods of time or by periodically adjusting the rent in accordance with a predetermined formula. The purpose of a step-up lease is to cover inflation, hence the term of this type lease is normally longer than that of the flat lease. Coverage includes both appreciation of the property and increases in costs of insurance, taxes and maintenance which in step-up leases are usually the lessor's responsibility. The cost of living index published by the federal government is most often used as a basis for determining rental increases under the step-up lease.

4. In a *percentage* lease, the lessee is required to pay a fixed basic rent plus a designated percentage of sales volume. Food store leases, shopping center leases, and most other commercial business leases provide for percentage payments. As with the step-up lease, the percentage factor acts as an inflation hedge as well as a means of keeping rentals in line with market conditions related to a specific location.

5. *Escalator* leases call for increases in taxes, insurance, and operating costs to be paid for by the lessee. This is a type of step-up lease, but such a clause is contained in most leases with terms of five years or more.

6. The *sandwich* lease refers to a multiple lease situation in which the lessee in turn subleases the property to a sub-lessee for a higher sum than what is paid to the original lessor and the sub-lessee further subleases at a profit. For example, A, the original lessor leases to B; B executes a sublease with C; and C then subleases to D. B is the sandwich lessor and C the sandwich lessee.

LONG-TERM LEASES

For the purpose of real estate financing, long-term leases have the greatest significance as opposed to short-term leases. Long-term leases can be for use of unimproved property upon which the lessee desires to construct improvements or for improved property where the lessee contemplates long-term use of existing structures. The ground rent situations, which were discussed in a previous chapter, are an example of the former type of leases.

The latter situation of leasing improved property has grown in favor since World War II due primarily to income tax considerations. Lease payments are fully deductible whereas construction of a building requires an initial equity investment. Annual mortgage payments are deductible only to the extent of the interest portion of the payment. In this chapter, the initial discussion will concern long-term leases, and then in the next chapter long-term improved property leases will be viewed from a sale-leaseback standpoint.

The lessee in a long-term *ground* lease usually falls into one of four basic categories:

1. A principal desiring to construct a building for subleasing to a large commercial or mercantile corporation.
2. A principal desiring to construct a building for subleasing to a number of tenants; for example, a principal who develops office buildings or shopping centers.
3. A user building for his own exclusive use and occupancy. Typical of this category would be a large commercial or industrial organization constructing a factory, home-office or combined factory-home office building on leased land.
4. A user desiring to occupy a portion of a building and to sublet part to one or several individual tenants. This category may contain a commercial organization constructing an office building on leased land for its own occupancy but also seeking additional space for rental to outside tenants either as a space inventory for future company expansion or as a means of reducing the company's over-all cost of occupancy.

RESPECTIVE LESSOR—LESSEE FINANCING RIGHTS

Unless the ground lease provides otherwise, the lessor is unrestricted in his right to mortgage the fee and the lessee has the right to finance his leasehold improvements.

As a general rule the lessor's fee should not be subject to mortgages which are prior to the lease nor should the lessor be allowed to subsequently execute a mortgage with priority to the lease. If this were allowed, the leasehold estate would be in a third lien position with the lessor's fee and the mortgage on the fee coming ahead of it. In the event the lessor defaults on his mortgage, the lessee would be at the mercy of the mortgagee. Where a high credit tenant is involved, some mortgagees will execute a non-disturbance agreement with the lessee, providing that in the event of a default by the lessor, the mortgagee will not foreclose the tenant out of lease position. Therefore, it can be said that the landlord should retain the right to mortgage his reversion and his present interest in the leasehold rents so long as he does not impair the tenant's right to mortgage his leasehold estate.

In real estate financing a fee mortgage superior to a leasehold is rare. This is because the leasehold tenant will invariably want to mortgage his leasehold improvements. The three major lenders in leasehold financing are life insurance companies, large mutual savings banks, and large commercial banks. These institutions are respectively regulated by state insurance laws and state banking laws both of which prohibit leasehold loans made on leases which are subordinate to an outstanding and prior fee mortgage (unless the loans are "basketed"—made under the provisions of such laws which allow a percentage of assets to be placed in otherwise unauthorized investments). This is because such loans are considered no better security than a second mortgage. For example, consider the blocks in the diagrams below as liens on real estate from a priority standpoint. In diagram A, the fee mortgage is in first position, the lessor's fee is in a second position and the lessee's lease rights (the leasehold) in a third position. In the event of a foreclosure of the fee mortgage the fee mortgagee would accede to the lessor's fee position (diagram B). Thus it can be seen in diagram C that a mortgage of the leasehold would be in a third lien position.

Diagram A presupposes a non-disturbance agreement between the fee mortgagee and the lessee; otherwise, the lessee would have lost all rights in the property upon foreclosure. Recall that all liens junior to a foreclosed mortgage are removed by the foreclosure action.

A	B	C
Fee Mortgage	Fee Mortgage	Fee Mortgage
Lessor's Fee		Lessor's Fee
Leasehold	Leasehold	Leasehold Mortgage

Mortgages of long-term leaseholds can be made either with the lessor's fee subordinate to or prior to the leasehold mortgage.

Leasehold mortgages with the reversionary interest in a prior lien position are usually only made to high credit tenants. The reason for this is the obviously greater risk to the lender. In such a case, failure of the tenant-lessee to pay rent puts the mortgagee in the position of having to take over the lease - a protection, incidentally, that all prudent lenders require. Therefore, the mortgagee is faced with a situation wherein the lessee-mortgagor must be financially able not only to meet his mortgage payments, but also to meet his lease payments.

One of the biggest boons to financing a leasehold where the reversion remains in a superior position was the original FHA regulations which made provision for insurance of mortgages where houses were constructed on leased land. (the ground rent situation previously discussed). The regulation provided that mortgages would be insured on "property held in fee simple or under renewable lease for not less than ninety-nine years or under lease with terms of not less than fifty years from date of mortgage." But, the regulation did not limit this leasehold provision to the states for which it was specifically intended.

Because of this regulation the post World War II period found many an astute entrepreneur engaged in the development of large-scale rental projects. These entrepreneurs would buy land in one company controlled by them and lease it to another company also under their control. The latter company would then arrange an insured FHA mortgage, usually covering full cost of construction. The fee owner, who was in reality, through the controlled corporation set-up, both lessor and lessee under different legal entities, made an investment that took priority over the government insured mortgage. The ownership of the fee would survive a default and subsequent foreclosure of the FHA mortgage, with the new leasehold owner, possibly FHA, required to make the lease payments. This situation is diagramed below:

Fee Owner
FHA Insured Mortgage
Leasehold

SUBORDINATED FEE MORTGAGE

In those instances where there is a mortgage on the fee at the time of execution of the lease, the fee mortgagee will, many times, be asked to subordinate his mortgage to the lease in order to permit the leasehold tenant to obtain leasehold financing. Any fee mortgage so subordinated (and, for that matter, any fee mortgages executed and recorded after the lease is made) will remain a first lien on the fee in most jurisdictions, subject, however, to superior encumbrances such as the lease. Thus, a foreclosure of the subordinated fee mortgage will not affect the lien of leasehold mortgage. Upon foreclosure, the leasehold tenant will normally remain liable for the payment of rent reserved in the lease and the performance of all other covenants and conditions of the lease, all for the benefit of the foreclosure sale purchaser. Once subordination is agreed to, the fee mortgagee must look for his security to (1) the payment of the leasehold rent, (2) the ground lessor's reversionary interest, and (3) whatever equity the leasehold tenant has or will have in the proposed improvements.

As a condition of subordination, the fee mortgagee will usually require that:
1. There be no amendment to the ground lease, without the consent of the mortgagee, where the effect of such amendment would be to decrease the rent or increase the ground lessor's liability.
2. The rent, which is the fee mortgagee's main source of payment shall not be prepaid more than one month in advance.
3. In the event of default by the ground lessor, notice be given by the tenant to the fee mortgagee and the fee mortgagee be allowed a reasonable time in which to cure such default.

SUBORDINATED FEE

In most cases of leasehold financing the ground lessor will be called upon to subordinate his unencumbered fee title. Most ground lessors will acquiesce to such a request and subordinate their fee title to a leasehold mortgage provided the leasehold tenant contemplates non-speculative and logical real estate improvements. Subordination here is quite similar to a first mortgagee's subordination of his lien priority to a bona fide construction loan mortgage as was discussed in a previous chapter.

The advantages gained by the leasehold tenant when the fee is subordinated are listed below:
1. The obtaining of a greater amount of financing, which can approximate 100 percent loan-to-value. As with the case of a first mortgage subordinated to a construction loan, the increased financing is a result of the leasehold tenant's ability to borrow against the ground lessor's (first lienor's) interest in the land and allows for a reduction in the leasehold tenant's equity capital requirements.
2. The obtaining of a greater amount of financing, which reduces the leasehold tenant's equity capital requirements.
3. The leasehold tenant's tax position, which is greatly improved under this arrangement from two standpoints:
   a. First, the ground rent is tax-deductible, whereas capital tied up in

non-depreciable land provides no tax benefits.

b. Secondly, the greater amount of financing will increase the leasehold tenant's interest liability, thereby increasing his tax deduction for interest paid.

4. The availability of financing, which is increased by having the fee subordinated, since most major lenders as previously noted cannot lend, or are limited in lending on a leasehold subject to a prior interest. With the fee subordinated from the outset, a subsequent fee mortgage will not affect the leasehold mortgage.

Advantages occurring to the leasehold mortgagee are as follows:

1. The value of the mortgage security can be considered equal to the value of the fee, due to the subordination.
2. The mortgagee has, in effect, an additional security by being able to exercise his lien against the fee.

To the ground-lessor, there are both advantages and disadvantages from subordinating his fee interest:

1. On the advantage side (presuming the leasing situation would not arise unless the fee is subordinated) the ground lessor:

   a. Can obtain a higher rental due to the increased risk of losing his fee ownership in the event of the leasehold tenant's default on the mortgage and a subsequent successful foreclosure by the mortgagee.

   b. Enjoys the tax advantages of leasing as opposed to selling, since a sale could trigger a capital gain tax whereas leasing does not.

   c. Receives the benefit of having improvements built on his land. The improvements will accrue to his benefit and be owned by him upon expiration of the ground lease. While this is of no immediate consequence, the future benefits can be of great value depending upon the length of the lease term and the condition of the improvements at lease expiration.

   d. Receives an annual return on his invested capital or value of his land while at the same time holds onto an asset that will usually increase in value. Upon expiration of the ground lease the increased value of the land due to appreciation and the value of improvements made by the leasehold tenant will accrue to the ground lessor's benefit.

   e. May alleviate the problem of being taxed as a dealer in real estate. (Those who frequently sell real estate are deemed dealers as opposed to investors and their profit from such sales is taxed as ordinary income not as capital gain. There are no set guidelines as to how many sales in any one year or over a period of time will cause a change from investor to dealer status in the eyes of Internal Revenue. Most accountants therefore will advise their clients to keep the number of sales down and will draw a line at a prudently determined point). In such dealer possibility cases, the land owner is better off leasing his land and mortgaging the fee than risking the penalties of an outright sale. The amount realized in immediate cash may be less by leasing and mortgaging, but as an end result, the cash benefits may be greater. It is worth noting that once a transaction puts the seller into dealer status, all previous sales are subject to question and loss of capital gains tax treatment.

2. As to disadvantages, the ground lessor stands to lose his equity in his fee in

the event of a default on the leasehold mortgage, and subsequent success-ful foreclosure thereof; otherwise in order to protect his equity he will have to make the leasehold tenant's mortgage payments. Therefore, unless a financially strong tenant is involved, the ground lessor would demand and receive a higher rental or a percentage rental feature of some type. Certainly a 1 percent to 2 percent additional rental or participation rental is small consideration for the high risk the ground lessor takes in subordinating his fee.

Subordination of the fee by the ground lessor may be accomplished by provision in the lease itself or by separate recorded instrument. However, it is most frequently done by having the ground lessor join in the leasehold mortgage for the purpose of subjecting the fee to the mortgage so executed.

MORTGAGE PROVISIONS

A mortgage given in cases of subordinated fees will usually include as a minimum the following:

1. A description of both the fee and leasehold with provision for separate foreclosure. For example, a foreclosure of the leasehold would allow the ground lease to remain intact. Such proviso is many times demanded by ground-lessors who will subordinate their fee only upon the mortgagee's agreement that in the event of a default he will realize his security first against the leasehold and then against fee; the latter action would be taken only if foreclosure sale proceeds were inadequate.

2. Approval by the mortgagee of any and all proposed lease modifications in order to insure no changes to the detriment of the mortgagee or his security.

3. A requirement that the mortgage provisions and the ground lease provisions conform particularly with respect to distribution of proceeds from condemnation or hazard loss.

4. A provision that any condemnation award be assigned to the mortgagee to be applied in partial payment of monies due under the mortgage or to be used to repair damages from a partial taking. Any balance remaining after repairs is to be applied to the mortgage balance. Here the specific wording will be determined by contest between the ground-lessor and the mort-gagee, with the ground-lessor seeking to obtain compensation for the portion of his fee that is taken and the mortgagee looking for as much of the proceeds as possible to apply against the mortgage. It must be realized that the ground-lessor is not going to passively stand by and watch a portion or all of his fee ownership be lost through condemnation with the proceeds applied to reduce the leasehold tenant's debt. Thus, a definite agreement for sharing of condemnation proceeds is needed.

5. A requirement that any hazard loss proceeds be used, if possible, to repair all damage and destruction or in the event repair is not feasible to be applied in reduction of the mortgage debt. It is noteworthy that here as well as with the condemnation situation any structural damage which is not repaired will cause a serious problem as regards the leasehold tenant's ability to meet his debt service and ground lease rental requirements. Thus, an application of proceeds to the reduction of the mortgage debt without

a corresponding diminution in debt service (and in the case of condemnation, ground lease rental) not only will work a hardship on the leasehold tenant, but also could create a foreclosure situation. For example, an apartment community of five buildings on leased land produces a cash flow of $100,000 (or $20,000 per building) after expenses but before an annual debt service of $75,000 and a yearly ground lease rental of $10,000. If one building is condemned for highway right-of-way purposes and the proceeds split between the mortgagee and ground lessor without any debt service or ground lease rental changes there will remain a cash flow of only $80,000 with which to discharge $85,000 of combined debt service and rental.

6. A provision that the ground lessor notify the mortgagee of any default in the ground lease and allow sufficient time for curative action by the mortgagee.

The ground lessor as a condition to his agreement to subordinate will usually require that the mortgage include certain provisions favorable to him. Some frequently demanded provisions are:

1. That the mortgagee specifically agree to waive all his rights to a deficiency judgment against the ground lessor. This requirement is important only when the ground lessor has joined in the mortgage and the mortgage contains no general exculpatory clause (provision against holding the mortgagor personally liable for the debt).

2. That the mortgagee advise the ground lessor of any default in the mortgage by the leasehold tenant and allow sufficient time for curative action by the ground lessor.

3. That the mortgagee is required to foreclose the leasehold first or pursue the leasehold tenant's other assets before attempting to collect the defaulted debt against the fee.

4. That there be a partial subordination only. There is an increasing tendency on the part of ground lessors to partially subordinate their fee estate, to the end that all ground lease rent payments will cease until the mortgagee, by taking control of the leasehold, has through rent free occupancy received enough money to cancel the debt. Partial subordination allows the ground lessor at some point in time to recover his fee, but causes the mortgagee to wait much longer for receipt of payment in full of his debt. Nevertheless, this compromise has been used with increasing frequency in recent years.

5. That adequate protection by way of completion bond, cash escrow or other satisfactory completion assurance be given with respect to proposed leasehold improvements.

GROUND LEASE PROVISIONS

When leasehold financing is to be secured the ground lease should contain provisions which will probably be demanded by a prospective mortgagee. Putting in proper provisions in the ground lease from the start will insure quicker action on the part of a mortgagee and will prevent a time-consuming amendment procedure. Leasehold tenants who find they have an unmortgagable lease may also find it costly to negotiate amendments required by the mortgagee with an avaricious ground lessor.

Minimum ground lease requirements are as follows:

1. The ground lease should be for a term of at least twenty-one years, due to statutory requirements of most major institutional investors. Also, the term of the lease should be for at least one year longer than that of the proposed mortgage to allow time for foreclosure.

2. It should grant to the tenant the right to encumber the leasehold by obtaining mortgage financing and define whatever rights the tenant is to have with respect to encumbering the fee (subordination). As to the latter most ground lessors will seek to establish a dollar limitation on the leasehold mortgage to be obtained.

3. The ground lease should allow assignment of any purchase or renewal options. If the ground lease contains any purchase or renewal options they should be assignable to the mortgagee who can then exercise them on behalf of the leasehold tenant.

4. It should provide for any refunded security deposit to be paid over to the mortgagee. When the leasehold tenant has been required to put up a security deposit, the mortgagee will want the right to it upon refunding as additional security.

5. There should be liberal subletting rights in order to allow a leasehold tenant the flexibility of movement and to keep the leasehold improvements fully occupied.

6. There should be provision for a periodic estoppel certificate to be executed between the ground lessor, leasehold tenant, and mortgagee. This is important in order to establish that there is no default in the lease or mortgage and to set forth the exact amount due and owing under them.

7. A curative action clause for default similar to previously mentioned mortgage provisions should be included.

8. Insurance and condemnation clauses taking into consideration the same problems discussed with respect to similar mortgage provisions are necessary and should be included in ground leases.

9. The ground lease should provide for the substitution of the mortgagee as tenant in the event of a tenant default and dispossession. The substitution may be accomplished by a new lease between the ground lessor and mortgagee or by assignment. In any event, the terms and conditions should be the same as in the original lease.

As to leasehold mortgage loans insured by FHA, a default, foreclosure, and subsequent acquisition by FHA or assignment to FHA in lieu of foreclosure will enact a requirement that FHA have a twelve-month option to purchase the ground lessor's fee.

QUESTIONS FOR THOUGHT AND DISCUSSION

1. How could a combination percentage and escalator lease be used to the lessor's advantage?
2. Give an example of how a long-term ground lease can be used advantageously.
3. a. Why would a credit tenant want the leasehold mortgagee to agree to a

    non-disturbance mortgage provision?
    b. Why would a mortgagee agree or not agree to such a provision?
4. a. What provisions should a prudent lender require in his mortgage on a leasehold?
    b. Should he review the provisions of the ground lease? If so,
    c. What should he look for in the ground lease?
5. Why is a loan made on a leasehold, subject to a mortgaged ground lease, a poor investment?

7

SALE-LEASEBACK AND OTHER MODERN REAL ESTATE FINANCING TECHNIQUES

The sale-leaseback is not a new financing innovation. However, it has been used extensively in recent years and is considered a modern real estate financing technique. It is a transaction involving the simultaneous sale of real property at either cost or other established market value and the leasing back of the property to the seller by the purchaser for a long term of years, frequently with renewal options, at an annual rental rate computed as a certain percentage of the sale price. The sale-leaseback transaction is not a loan transaction even though under certain circumstances, as will be discussed later, it may be deemed a loan.

SALE-LEASEBACK

The sale-leaseback technique can be traced back to the early 1940s. It became popular for two main reasons. First, since institutional investors were limited by state regulatory laws to loan-to-value ratios of 66-2/3 percent to 75 percent, a method was sought which would be legal and would increase the amount of money that could be loaned against real estate security. Secondly, corporations had large sums of money tied up in real estate assets and were anxious to put those funds to work in a more advantageous and active way.

Thus, the sale-leaseback technique appeared as an alternative to the mortgage and as a means of increasing the amount of financing available for any single real estate transaction. It also presented a feasible and workable method of exchanging ownership, but not possession for cash. The sale-leaseback method is in fact the way to 100 percent financing. It also presents an opportunity for institutional investors who have exceeded their out-of-state lending ratios to continue to make out-of-state investments. For example, an institutional investor in a small, capital plentiful, New England state may find that in-state investments are scarce and that out-of-state loans are the only way to invest surplus cash. If the institution is limited by state law to investing only 60 percent of its assets in out-of-state loans and is at that ceiling, the sale-leaseback technique presents a way around the asset ratio requirement, an opportunity to continue out-of-state investments, and a chance for high yield investment.

THE TRANSACTION

A sale-leaseback transaction at its inception simulates a real estate purchase. The seller agrees to sell and the purchaser agrees to buy, but from that point the resemblance to a real estate transaction is lost and the incidents of a sale-lease-back appear.

The main differences between a sale-leaseback transaction and a real estate purchase are given below:

1. The purchaser does not put up a good faith deposit or even agree to a downpayment. In fact, it is the purchaser who often asks the seller to put up a deposit to insure that the transaction is completed.
2. There is no need to apportion rents, taxes, assessments or the like, for the seller will either pay these items as tenant or will collect rent and pay the taxes, assessments, and other similar charges.
3. The occupancy of the premises remains the same after the sale-leaseback as before the transaction.
4. The documentation of the transaction is complex and transfer of title is simultaneous with the exception of a lease agreement.
5. The care and maintenance of the property almost always remain the responsibility of the seller.

TERM OF LEASE AND REPURCHASE OPTION

The rental, which the seller-lessee will pay, is customarily calculated at a rate which will pay out the investment over the initial lease term and will produce a satisfactory interest rate to the purchaser-lessor. For example, in New York an insurance company investor is required to amortize the cost of a real estate property purchase at not less than 2 percent annually and all income over 4 percent must be used to amortize the cost of the property. Therefore, the rent on a lease in a sale-leaseback transaction made for 8 percent of the sale price annually may be distributed on the basis of 4 percent for interest and 4 percent for amortization. Most investors will attempt to amortize the sale price over the term of the lease. This can be advantageous, for at some point in time their accounting records will reflect ownership of unencumbered real estate with a zero investment.

The sale price as previously stated will be at cost or other established market value. If the transaction involves a new building, the purchaser-lessor may require that all costs of construction be audited and the price determined on the basis of audited costs. The purchaser-lessor also frequently may require that the purchase price be supported by an independent appraisal by a member of the appraisal institute (MAI).

TERM OF LEASE AND REPURCHASE OPTION

Sale-leaseback transactions have been made for many different initial terms, but in the majority of transactions the initial term has been for twenty or twenty-five years when the tenant's credit has been prime. In instances where the tenant's credit has been satisfactory but not prime, the common range of initial term has been ten to twenty years.

Many of the earlier sale-leaseback transactions contained provisions giving the seller an option to repurchase the property at the owner's book value (or at some equivalent figure) after a predetermined period of time. For example, assume the purchaser-lessor's investment in a property which sold for $600,000 is reduced to $350,000 after ten years, after distributing the rental between amortization and interest. Under the purchase-option, the seller-lessee would have the option to repurchase the property at the end of ten years for $350,000.

This purchase-option method was effectively used until Internal Revenue declared transactions of this type strictly mortgages and not bona fide sale-leaseback transactions. The result was a disallowance for the seller-lessee for tax purposes of that portion of the rental attributed to amortization. Since under a standard lease situation rental payments for business purposes occupancy are deductible, the loss of a substantial portion of that deduction can have serious tax consequences for a seller-lessee. On the other hand, a purchaser-lessor in most jurisdictions can terminate a lease and evict a defaulting tenant more easily than he can foreclose a mortgage. Thus, an unfavorable effect occurs to the purchaser-lessor when a determination is made that a sale-leaseback transaction is in reality a mortgage. Herein lies a serious problem which is best resolved by making certain from the outset that any repurchase option price contained in a lease under a sale-leaseback bears no relationship to the purchaser-lessor's book value at the time the option is exercised.

TYPES OF TRANSACTIONS

Sale-leasebacks can be classified into two major types of transactions:

1. *Prime credit* transaction in which the tenant is a large and prominent corporation and in the past has probably conducted a number of sale-leaseback transactions. An example of this type would be a gas station sale-leaseback with a major oil company seller-lessee. In prime credit transaction 100 percent financing is usually available since the purchaser-lessor investor is entering the transaction on the basis of the seller-lessee's credit standing as opposed to the value of the real estate. The form of lease used in such a situation of a rental to a very high credit rated tenant with a demonstrated history of earnings over a period of years is usually termed a "bond-type" lease. The "bond-type" lease is one that is also non-cancellable, 100 percent net, long term, and provides for a rental sufficient to amortize any mortgage on the property during the lease term.

2. *Realty* transactions in which the purchaser-lessor is investing on the basis of the property without too great a regard for the seller-lessee's credit status. Therefore, realty transactions involve buildings which have a general purpose use. Examples are office buildings, warehouses, and shopping centers where the key factor is the rentability of the building. When the investor is entering the deal on the basis of the real estate security, the

purchase price is quite commonly 80 percent to 90 percent of the property value rather than 100 percent as with prime credit tenants.

In recent years there has been a noticeable increase in sale-leaseback transactions involving investment builders. For example, an investment builder will construct an apartment complex and obtain a permanent loan from an institutional investor. The investment builder manages the property for several years, establishing a constant cash flow and taking advantage of double declining depreciation. He then sells it to a real estate investment trust, an institutional investor, or one of several large apartment purchasers at value and leases the project back. In such a transaction the builder frees up equity to use in putting together several other similar deals and retains management control of the apartments. He therefore has a management profit and usually a small return from the cash flow left after his lease payment. The investor gains a fixed return and has the local, experienced management to protect his investment. Many times the standard deal provides for an assumption by the purchaser-lessor of the existing institutional mortgage, thus reducing the purchaser's cash outlay. Of course, such transactions are realty type in that they are made on the basis of cash generated by the realty.

INVESTOR SOURCES

Since sale-leaseback transactions are generally illegal investments for savings and loan associations and commercial banks, the biggest sources of capital for these transactions have been life insurance companies, pension funds and tax exempt institutions such as universities and religious investment funds. Real estate investment trusts and mutual savings banks are also becoming extensively involved in a sale-leaseback transactions.

The majority of the investors just named would not have become involved in sale-leaseback transactions if it were not for the fact that they are either tax exempt or virtually tax exempt. For example, income in the form of mortgage payments is taxable as income regardless of the fact that on his books the investor apportions the lease payment part to rent and part to amortization. With a tax-exempt investor, however, the source of funds has no particular meaning.

It should be noted that the tax exempt status is lost to the extent that borrowed funds are used in the transaction; in such a case the income is classed by Internal Revenue as "unrelated business income" and is taxable. The theory is that an exempt investor should not be allowed to make tax-free income from borrowings. Life insurance companies are classified in the exempt category since their income is taxable at very low rates.

Investor interest in sale-leaseback transactions is enhanced by the bond-type nature of the investment. Mortgage principal is usually repaid in small increments over the term of the loan, whereas bonds return interest periodically and principal only at maturity. Pension funds and other investors with a steady flow of income are interested primarily in investments which return interest only. They have enough of an investment problem without having to try to re-invest principal as it is returned on a mortgage. The sale-leaseback, like a bond, pays a periodic return and the principal investment is secured until repurchase or lease termination and subsequent sale. Unlike a bond, the principal investment may appreciate and thus provide a bonus return.

Life insurance companies pioneered the sale-leaseback transaction and are still the most important source of funds for this financing technique. According to the Institute of Life Insurance 1978 Fact Book, at the end of 1977, life insurance companies had $11.1 billion invested in real estate. Of that sum, 65 percent, or $7.2 billion, was invested in commercial and residential properties. Figures on how many dollars life insurance companies have invested in sale-leaseback transactions are not readily available. It can be surmised, however, that a substantial portion of the 65 percent is invested in sale-leaseback transactions.

ADVANTAGES

The advantages to purchaser and seller in a sale-leaseback transaction are as follows:

To the Purchaser-Lessor

1. The investor-purchaser's freedom from the early repayment exposure present in most mortgages. However, an exception is the right of the seller to repurchase at any time or after a fixed period prior to lease expiration.
2. The opportunity to invest usually large sums in seasoned property with real estate as security and quite often additional security in the form of a prime credit tenant.
3. The income tax advantage to non-tax-exempt purchasers of being able to depreciate the non-land portion of the investment.
4. The flexibility obtained in the event of a default. It is easier to act against a defaulting tenant than to foreclose a mortgage.
5. The residual value which accrues to the purchaser-lessor after expiration of the lease or in the event of exercise of a purchase option, the premium charged therefore.
6. The ability to obtain a greater dollar return on investment than is possible under a mortgage arrangement. The difference in return gains greater significance in states where usury laws limit the amount of interest that a mortgage lender is allowed to charge. A sale-leaseback is an investment in realty and is not governed by usury laws.

To the Seller-Lessee

1. The ability to free up capital which is presently frozen in the form of real estate equity.
2. An opportunity to obtain better than mortgage ratio financing while approaching 100 percent financing or gain possession with little or no capital investment.
3. The appreciation in the value of the realty due to inflation. This appreciation may be converted into cash by subleasing or mortgaging the leasehold, if allowable under the terms of the lease. This seller-lessee advantage would of course be a disadvantage to the purchaser-lessor.
4. A means of retaining management control over property while receiving full sale value for it.
5. The tax advantage of being able to deduct all lease payments.

LAND ONLY TRANSACTIONS

While sale-leasebacks are usually thought of as applicable to improved property only, the technique is used many times in connection with a vacant parcel of land. The principles are the same as in the standard sale-leaseback transactions, but the relative advantages to the parties are slightly different.

To the Seller-Lessee

1. He is able to free up a large capital investment in presently unusable land. This is quite important to builder-developers who need to land-bank property for future development but do not desire to tie up their usually sparse capital.
2. He obtains a tax deduction. Land is not depreciable and provides no tax advantage to the owner as does a lease situation where the rents are deductible.

To the Purchaser-Lessor

1. He has the ability to tie up future rights to financing improvements to the land.
2. He obtains the opportunity to gain leverage and thereby a greater return by mortgaging the fee.
3. He benefits from a residual value which should be proportionately greater, since over the years land has enjoyed much faster appreciation than buildings.

APPLYING THE SALE-LEASEBACK TECHNIQUE

The following is an example of effective use of the sale-leaseback technique:
A builder enters into a long-term lease on a certain parcel of real property upon which he constructs a building costing $5,500,000. The building is fully leased and produces an annual cash flow of $495,000 or 9 percent after payment of the ground rent and all expenses.

Interim financing for the building was obtained from a large commercial bank. After construction the leasehold was sold to an institutional investor for $4,200,000 and leased back for $315,000 (7.5 percent). Thus, the institutional investor became the leasehold lessee and the builder the sub-lessee. Since the sublease was showing a net cash flow of $180,000 ($495,000 less the $315,000 lease payment) the builder was able to sell it to an investor for $1,300,000 and lease back the building for $143,000 or 11 percent. The new investor now becomes the sub-lessee and the builder the sub-sub-lessee. To express it another way, the new investor is a sandwich lessor and the builder a sandwich lessee.

The result of this fractionalization of leases is that the builder has a gross income of $495,000 from which he has to pay lease payments of $315,000 and $143,000 ($458,000 total), leaving him an annual return of $37,000 with no equity investment.

Many life insurance companies as well as other similarly regulated investors are able to use the sale-leaseback method as a means of providing higher than allowable loan-to-value ratio financing while at the same time providing the builder-developer with a near 100 percent mortgage loan.

For example, a life insurance company wanted to finance a $2,000,000 proposed shopping center. Its mortgage lending by statute was limited to a 75 percent loan-to-value ratio or in this case, $1,500,000. However, the builder-developer wanted $1,750,000, which equalled his land plus actual construction cost. A solution was reached by the insurance company agreeing to purchase and lease-back the land valued at $400,000 and mortgage the land and improvements for $1,350,000. The loan-to-value ratio with the ground lease subordinated now becomes 67-1/2 percent, well within the statutory limitation. With a land purchase commitment, the builder-developer should easily be able to obtain $300,000 from a local bank until the sale-leaseback becomes effective, thus providing front money for the project.

SALE-CONTRACT-BACK

The sale-contract-back technique of real estate financing involves the purchase of property by an investor and a simultaneous resale back to the seller on a long term land contract. The sale price and resale usually ranges between 80 and 90 percent of the market value of the property. The investor retains the title to the property, but the developer (original seller) has an equitable interest in the title and retains the right to take depreciation deductions.

Under the sale-contract-back method a term of ten years of more in excess of that obtainable on a mortgage basis is usual. Land contract payments are computed so as to liquidate the sale price investment over a normal mortgage term using an interest rate which is slightly below existing mortgage rates.

For example, if the land contract payment is computed as 8.5 percent of the purchase price and the contract term is thirty-six years, the investor-vendor can amortize his investment in less than twenty-nine years at a 7.5 percent yield and continue to receive an additional seven years of contract payments at an 8.5 percent yield. In other words, during the first twenty-nine years the investor-vendor distributes the 8.5 percent constant payment on the basis of a 7.5 percent interest rate return on investment and the balance as a return of invested capital or principal amortization.

In many cases the investor will also require a contingent payment in the form of a percentage of net income generated from the property less the contract payment.

However, there are disadvantages. The investor-vendor has more of a problem in realizing on his security under the sale-contract-back than under the sale-lease-back. The latter method usually involves only a dispossession action whereas the former, as stated in the discussion on land contracts in Chapter 1, may involve foreclosure. In fact, in California, the vendor under a land contract may find himself in a less favorable position than a mortgagee when it comes to expeditious enforcement of rights in the event of default.

This financing technique, which is readily applicable to leasehold, air rights, and condominium situations, has not found too much favor. Presently, life insurance companies are the main investors in sale-contract-back transactions, with other institutional investors and many life insurance companies not yet convinced of the worthiness of this method of real estate financing.

FRONT MONEY DEALS

Historically, real estate developers have sought to invest as little money as possible in a project while retaining a substantial equity. On the other hand, lenders have tried to secure themselves by providing low ratio loan-to-value financing and at the same time obtaining high yields on their investments.

Possibly the best technique for satisfying both the developer's and the lender's desires is the "front money deal."

This new real estate financing technique, which has found increasing favor with life insurance companies and mutual savings banks, calls for the investor to put up or arrange for up to 100 percent of the cash equity investment required for development of a project. The developer for his part contributes his time and entrepreneurship to the undertaking.

As an example of a front money deal, a developer who owns or has an option on land which is to be used for the proposed project will sell a one-half interest in the land to the investor for a price which gives the developer enough cash to contribute to his part of the transaction. The investor and developer then form a joint venture or some other form of ownership-entity, such as a corporation or a limited partnership, in which the ownership interest usually is apportioned equally between the investor and developer. While in some states usury laws make the corporation form mandatory, the undertaking most frequently will be accomplished through a joint venture or limited partnership in order to make depreciation readily available as an offset to ordinary income. The division of ownership and profits between investor and developer is negotiated. In many instances, when the investor is putting up all of the cash, provision is made for him to receive all of his capital contribution (sometimes plus interest) back out of cash flow available for distribution prior to any division of cash flow between investor and developer. Generally, the investor will be called upon to provide whatever mortgage financing is required or at least to provide a back-up "umbrella" commitment to enable the development entity to secure the required construction and permanent financing for preparation of the site and construction of improvements.

Life insurance companies and mutual savings banks usually form subsidiary companies for purposes of ownership of real estate equities instead of conducting front money deals through their parent companies. A new subsidiary of a major life company created in 1968, issued a policy statement that "in selected situations it would enter into joint ventures with corporations or individuals equipped both financially and professionally to carry out real estate ventures, mainly in the field of office buildings." The policy statement went further to state that transactions should be $5 million or over and that they were looking for a 15 percent return on capital invested plus depreciation. Another large life insurance company, through a subsidiary, has gone strongly into the joint venture area. It has a considerable investment in a new town located between Washington and Baltimore, and has recently entered into a joint venture involving a large residential project to be constructed near Columbus, Ohio.

Both life insurance companies and mutual savings banks are limited to investing only a small percentage of their total assets in joint-venture transactions.

The future should witness a large number of front money deals with developers finding a way to zero equity investment and institutional investors desiring a hedge against inflation as well as a greater return on their investments.

STAGED SALE-LEASEBACK

The staged sale-leaseback technique is applicable where a builder-developer desires to develop a large tract of land in sections over an extended period of time. The procedure is for the builder-developer to build one section and then sell the improvements plus the total tract to an investor who leases the same back to the builder-developer. Under this arrangement the builder-developer will retain the right to free from the transaction the unused portion of the tract for future development. Thus when an additional section is planned the portion of the tract involved is either repurchased or separately leased. Usually the original investor will provide construction mortgage financing for the new section under a pre-arranged right of first refusal.

All the advantages of a sale-leaseback are present with the additional advantage to the developer of land-banking real estate for future development without tieing up equity capital. This technique is readily applicable to the development of large apartment communities, regional shopping centers, and industrial parks.

COMBINATION FINANCING

Combination financing is simply the application of two or more forms of financing to a specific real estate financing situation. An easy example is the sale-leaseback of ground only with a mortgage obtained for construction of leasehold improvements. The improvements then can be sold to an investor on a sale-contract-back subject to the ground lease and leasehold mortgage. Thus, three types of financing techniques would be used.

A more complex example is the joint venturing of the development of a twelve story office building, which after completion is sold to the institutional investor from whom a mortgage on the building has been previously obtained, and then leased back. At this point we have a joint venture, mortgage and sale-leaseback subject to a mortgage. Now the air rights or space above the building can be separated and mortgaged for the purpose of constructing a twenty story apartment building on the office building base. Irrespective of legal ramifications, combination financing of this type has been accomplished and opens up many opportunities for imaginative and creative real estate financing concepts.

SALE-CONDOBACK

The sale-condoback is a new variant to the sale-leaseback concept. In the sale-condoback transaction, the owner of real property agrees to sell it on the condition that a part of the property be deeded back to him in the form of a condominium unit. For example the owner of a ten story office building may contract to sell it contingent upon the buyer reselling the third floor back to him. This would allow the original owner-seller to retain office space required by him in ownership form as opposed to lease form.

Advantages of this financing technique are generally:

1. The seller in a sale-condoback situation has the *flexibility* of retaining space for his own use even if he must rent some of it for a period of time

pending expansion. If expansion doesn't take place, the excess condominium units may be sold.

2. The lessee in a sale-leaseback situation loses his *mobility* since the agreement "ab initio" usually depends upon the long term credit dependability of the lessee where the lessee enters the transaction to knowingly remain in occupancy of property. In the sale-condoback situation, the original owner-seller can vacate or sell his premises without permission of the person to whom the total property was sold.

3. Ownership by virtue of sale-condoback allow the occupant (original owner-seller) to benefit from *appreciation,* while in a sale-leaseback transaction appreciation normally accrues to the seller-lessee.

CONCLUSION

When contemplating the use of any or a combination of financing techniques it must be remembered that several pitfalls are present, any of which may have serious consequences. Some of these are given below:

1. There is a great tendency toward over-financing and therefore under-securing an investment in real estate. Succumbing to an attractive and innovative financing situation and proceeding to over-finance will cause the total concept to fail when the burden of heavy debt service or lease payments is felt. Thus serious consideration should always be given to the economics of any proposed financing transaction, however attractive or novel, to insure that the financing technique or techniques to be used will accomplish the job while leaving a margin for error or unexpectancies.

2. As previously implied, the legal cost involved in pursuing these new types of financing can be great. One must question whether or not the time and costs involved in undertaking a sale-leaseback, sale-contract-back, or other modern forms of financing are necessary or sufficiently rewarding.

3. The problem of foreclosure versus easy eviction must be explored and the method and timing of repossessing the realty in event of default weighed in arriving at a lending decision.

QUESTIONS FOR THOUGHT AND DISCUSSION

1. List several examples of how the sale-leaseback technique is applicable to real estate financing situations.
2. What are the advantages of a sale-leaseback over a mortgage as regards the developer? The investor?
3. Do you feel that use of the modern forms of real estate financing discussed in this chapter can benefit the consumer through better rental terms (apartment, office building, or shopping center tenant)? Why or why not?
4. a. What legal limitations are placed upon life insurance company participation in sale-leaseback transactions?
   b. In joint ventures?
5. a. What tax advantages are available from a sale-leaseback transaction?
   b. Who benefits from these advantages?
6. Do you feel the sale-contract-back technique has any future? Explain.
7. a. Do you think it wise for life insurance companies and mutual savings banks to be allowed to participate in joint ventures?
   b. Should the right be extended to commercial banks and savings and loan associations?
   c. Should an asset investment limitation be placed on joint venture participation by institutional investors?

8

MORTGAGE MARKET AND FUND FLOWS

Real estate financing is only one of many uses to which funds available for investment may be put. Corporate bonds, government bonds, and obligations, common stocks, commercial loans, and promissory notes are among the more prominent competitors for credit. Thus mortgages as well as other real estate financing forms must compete along with other types of assets for available dollars. Certainly the extent of competition and the demand of mortgages compared to the demand of all its competitors for funds can affect the price of mortgage money at any one point in time.

For the purposes of this chapter, the term *mortgages* will include all forms of real estate financing such as sale-leaseback, joint ventures, and the like.

SUPPLY

The amount of funds which are at any time available for mortgage investment will rest primarily upon the total supply of funds, but will be affected by the amount of funds which are used to satiate competitive demands.

Sources of lendable funds can be classified into three main categories:
1. Savings
2. Insurance premiums
3. Repayments on existing loans.

Savings include those by businesses, individuals, or governments and as a group have the greatest single impact upon the availability or supply of lendable funds. Savings in banks as well as in pension funds are a part of this category. Added to savings in general are the reserves of commercial banks and action taken by the Federal Reserve to increase or decrease the supply of funds. Insurance premiums are those paid primarily on life insurance policies but also include premiums on fire and casualty policies. Repayments on existing loans are those received from loan installments and from prepayments.

The supply of funds increases most dramatically when individuals, businesses, or governments save more, when borrowers speed up their rate of loan repayment, and when the Federal Reserve acts so as to create money. When businesses, governments, and individuals increase their savings, it allows the financial institutions in which their funds are placed to increase their lending, including mortgage loans. An increase in savings, as will be pointed out later, most often comes from a reduction in spending by businesses, governments, and individuals. Additionally, loan repayments combine with savings to produce more loanable funds.

When the Federal Reserve acts to lower discount rates and raise reserve ratios, it sharply increases the flow of money into the various lending activities including mortgages. Federal Reserve actions and their effect will be discussed later on in this chapter.

On the other hand, the supply of funds may decrease. Institutions pay interest for the use of savings from all sectors. When institutional interest rates do not favorably compare to bond yields or when other investment opportunities become more attractive, savings are diverted into those other investment areas. Hence, the amount of savings which can be used for institutional lending purposes declines and directly affects mortgage lending, which relies greatly upon institutional savings deposits.

When the number of loan defaults increases, repayments are affected and add to the decline in money supply. Further reduction in supply may be caused by the Federal Reserve lowering reserve ratio requirements and increasing the discount rate.

As all these supply reducing factors come into play, the amount of funds available to fulfill all demands naturally slackens and the forces of competition come to bear. Mortgages in short supply of money periods must compete more vociferously for what funds are available, but nevertheless will suffer to some degree along with most or all of its competitors.

THE EFFECT OF DISINTERMEDIATION

Financial institutions act as intermediaries between savers and borrowers, funneling the savings of individuals into mortgages or other forms of credit. The ability of financial institutions to maintain or increase their level of investment depends directly upon the flow of savings into these institutions. The process of individuals placing their savings with banks, savings and loan associations, and similar institutions for investment by these institutions is termed "intermediation." Thus, the greater the intermediation, the more funds there are available for mortgages and similar investments.

However, when individuals decide not to place their funds with financial institutions, but to invest them directly, the opposite process, known as "disintermediation" occurs. By-passing of financial institutions, or disintermediation, occurs when proportionately higher yields are available on secure investments such as high grade corporate bonds and government securities than can be obtained on savings deposits. In 1966, 1969, and 1974 disintermediation was extremely pronounced as a result of the quick acceleration of interest rates during those years. Disintermediation, however, only adds to existing scarce money problems. When interest rates are rising, it is usually because of increased demand and decreased supply. Therefore, if savings are diverted from financial institutions without a marked decrease in demand, interest rates must continue to rise.

The effect of disintermediation is felt most in the mortgage sector, since diverted savings rarely find their way into mortgages. Such divergence of savings usually goes to meet corporate and governmental capital needs, thus providing no increase in the supply of mortgage funds.

Disintermediation is a relatively new phenomenon and should be watched closely during times of increasing interest rates to determine the effect it may have on a further acceleration of rates, particularly in the mortgage sector.

DEMAND

As supply fluctuates, so the demand for money has its ups and downs. When businesses decide to finance their own investments instead of borrowing funds, the demand for money has a tendency to decrease. Accordingly, an increase in demand may take place when corporate treasurers decide to go into the bond market to borrow for plant expansion, new facilities, or the like. During times when governments have surpluses, the demand for money drops. But when governments run deficits, demand builds. The amount of new house construction also has its effect. When housing starts are many, the demand for mortgage funds acts to increase the general demand for credit. In periods of light new construction the demand for mortgage funds decreases as usually does the general demand. Naturally, it is a combination of all these factors which interact to cause a lessening or an increase in the demand for loanable funds.

Thus, it can be seen that the following events can affect the demand for money and, consequently, interest rates:

1. War—increase in government surpluses.
2. Formation of newer households—increase in new construction.
3. Number of housing units becoming unusable or obsolescent—increase in new construction.
4. Decline in business profits—decrease in corporate expansion.

More recently, inflation has played a major role in the demand for credit. When the typical demand forces are coupled with rapid inflation, the demand for credit will accelerate to abnormal highs, as was reflected in the interest rates of 1974-75 and 1978-79. Inflation causes governments to have to borrow more to meet current debts, business to borrow more to meet costs of operations (let alone expansion) and individuals to borrow more to pay for the higher cost of goods and services. An easy example of the part inflation plays is the comparison of demand in normal times and in times of extreme inflation. If normally the demand for credit in any one year was $10 billion, then with an inflation rate of 12 percent instead of the normal 6 percent, the demand for credit would accelerate to $11.2 billion. Thus, above normal inflation alone would have caused a $600 million increase in the demand for funds.

The movement in money supply and demand directly affects the level of interest rates and generally plays a most important part in mortgage fund availability and cost. In other words, mortgages are most susceptible to being influenced by variations in supply and demand for credit.

MORTGAGE MARKETS AND COST OF MONEY

There is no single organized market for funds, such as the New York and American exchanges for stocks. Instead there are thousands of submarkets in cities and towns throughout the United States where a variety of items such as bills, mortgages, notes, and bonds are traded. Funds flow from each of these submarkets to other submarkets. When an eastern lender decides to invest its funds in California mortgages, it may become difficult to find mortgage money in the Midwest. In other words, mortgage funds flow from areas of heavy supply to areas of low supply. Thus, the mortgage market is affected and can be analyzed by the interrelationships of the various submarkets.

As has been stated previously, the basic sources of funds for investment are the excess amounts received by individuals, businesses, and governments over what they spend for current consumption. This excess is available for lending directly to others who may want to borrow or it may be placed in the form of savings with financial intermediaries (commercial banks, savings and loans, etc.) which in turn lend the funds to others.

Governments save when they run a surplus. Such funds, which are either deposited in financial institutions or used to pay off debts, are available in either case to the loan market. But as has been the case in recent years when governments as a whole run a deficit, they must borrow funds in the market.

Over the past two decades both individual and business savings have increased, with business savings causing the greatest expansion in total savings. Government savings, on the other hand, have been erratic, and their fluctuation has caused major shifts in the supply of and demand for funds. Therefore, in times when businesses are not experiencing profits, unemployment is high, and governments are running deficits, the supply of money will be low. When all these factors are present in the economy, as they have been in recent years, "tight money" conditions usually prevail.

Added to the short supply of money is a large demand. Federal government deficits caused in part by the Vietnam War have made a huge demand on the supply of funds. Businesses with small profits borrow to meet payrolls or withhold payments to creditors causing these creditors in turn to have to borrow operating capital. People on unemployment borrow to cover living expenses. Therefore, with a short supply and high demand, the price of money increases.

The mortgage market must compete in terms of yield, risk, and profitability with all other potential uses of funds. Mortgages must maintain a strong competitive position since they are by far the main use for all investments. Net investments in mortgages usually approximate 50 percent of total available lendable funds. In fact, in recent years the volume of mortgage loans has been as large as total personal savings.

Also, in recent years variations in the amount of savings deposits in financial institutions and the changing demand from other users of credit have caused the amount of money available in the mortgage market to be drastically compressed. Such shifts in the market have translated themselves into jumps in interest rates, loan fees and mortgage discounts. (Discounts come into play when interest rates are held constant and loan yields increase. The yields are increased by charging points or a percentage of the loan amount, payable in cash at the time of making the loan. For example, one point on a $20,000 loan would be $200 and is payable in cash when the loan is funded or is discounted by funding only $19,800.) These shifts have also brought about sharp changes in standard lending practices and interrelationships among lenders.

SECURITY

The supply and demand of funds may be quite different for one user of credit as opposed to another. Mortgage funds may be scarce, but AAA-rated corporate bonds may be readily sold. Thus, in addition to the general supply and demand of funds the factor of security must be considered.

An investor will place his funds in those investments which not only produce a satisfactory yield, but secure his investment. Given the same maturity and yield to maturity, a government backed security is certainly a safer investment than a B-rated corporate bond and an AAA-rated corporate bond is usually more secure than an A-rated corporate bond. Thus if an investor can receive approximately the same yield on a government security as an AAA-rated bond he will most likely choose the former because of the security.

Mortgages in the past have been rated a much more speculative investment than the best corporate bonds because of the problems with principal recovery and the prime security being in the form of unliquid real estate as opposed to the credit of a financially responsible corporation. Hence, where yields are relatively the same, investment funds will flow to bonds as opposed to mortgages.

The same investment flow principal holds true for government securities when the relative yield spread between government securities and mortgages becomes so narrow that security is the governing factor. Lately the security question has been quite evident in the case of common stocks. Due to a heavy fall-off in the stock market, funds which would have been invested in common stocks have gone into mortgages. The reasoning here is that mortgages are more secure even though the return may be less.

With some investors, however, security does not affect the flow of funds into mortgages. Savings and loan associations are organized for the purpose of mortgage investment and by law are prohibited from investing in corporate bonds.

It can therefore be said that the security of any investment is of importance in fund flow determination.

YIELD

Yield is quite possibly more important to an investor than security. If one form of credit use returns a higher income in the form of interest than another, even though the former is less secure, it may attract funds due to yield. Hence, mortgages may pull funds away from corporate bonds because of yield. Said another way, mortgages must present a better yield in order to attract funds away from a more secure investment.

In the case of disintermediation, yield also plays an important part. For example, when government securities yield more than insured savings accounts, funds flow out of the savings institutions into government securities.

DEMAND BY SECTORS

The demand for mortgage funds comes from many mortgage demand sectors. While most of the demand comes from the single-family residential sector, other sectors include commercial, industrial, multi-family units, farms, mobile home parks, hotels, and special purpose uses.

Estimating the demand for new construction in any one of these sectors is very difficult, but it is necessary for planning future mortgage money needs.

Some determinants of demand for residential units, correspondingly translated into mortgage loans in a given area at a given time, are listed below:

1. The rate of population growth.
2. The rate of formation of new households.
3. The number of existing housing vacancies.
4. The number of living units demolished.
5. The number of immigrants arriving in the area who will ultimately be employed and thus will demand housing.
6. The economic base of the area, which is indicative of the level of new and existing industry and the amount of population that this activity will support.
7. The rate of emigration.
8. The level of income and employment.
9. Planned new industry and other new sources of employment.

While these factors determine to a large extent the demand for mortgages in newly constructed dwellings, it must be remembered that the same factors operate to turn over existing properties with mortgage loans outstanding. When these older properties are bought and sold, new mortgages are created in the majority of cases. The extent of the increase in the new mortgage over the existing mortgage constitutes a net demand for funds required in order to complete the purchase.

The determinants of demand for the other categories of mortgages besides residential property include many of the same factors as previously mentioned, but are more influenced by the state of the economy in general. The level of business and specifically the level of demand for the goods and services provided by these sectors determine whether or not investments for expansion of industrial plants or land acquisition, which might be mortgaged, will occur. The demand for these services and goods are, in turn, related to the level of income and employment in the economy.

ROLE OF THE FEDERAL RESERVE

One item already mentioned that needs to be expanded is the role the Federal Reserve plays in any determination of the availability of money. The Federal Reserve has three methods or economic weapons which it uses to expand and contract the amount of money and credit.

1. By its open-market operations the Federal Reserve sells securities when it wants to tighten credit. The securities buyer pays for his purchase with a check drawn on a commercial bank. When the check is presented, the member bank's reserve balances at the Federal Reserve are debited for the

amount of the check. The open-market sale, therefore, has the effect of simultaneously cutting the Federal Reserve's assets of bonds and its liabilities to commercial banks. Since these liabilities or deposits of the commercial banks serve as their reserves, the amount of reserves now available falls as a result of the open-market operations. This method represents the primary tool used by the Federal Reserve to change the availability of lendable funds.

2. By raising reserve ratios the Federal Reserve creates money. For example, if the reserve requirements is 16-2/3 percent then each bank must have $1.00 in reserve for every $6.00 in demand deposits. If a bank acquires an additional $1.00 in reserves, it may make loans up to a total of $5.00. The bank is not required to make additional loans, but usually does so because it is profitable. If the Federal Reserve increases the reserve ratio, say to $1.00 for every $7.00 in demand deposits, banks can increase their lending with the lendable funds thus created. But if the Federal Reserve reduces the reserve ratio, banks must sell loans and securities in their portfolio in order to re-establish their reserve ratio, thus reducing the supply of money.

3. The third method of affecting the supply of money, and probably the least effective method, is for the Federal Reserve to change the discount rate. The discount rate is the amount charged to member banks for funds lent to them. An increase in the rate raises the member banks' costs and lowers the desirability of borrowing. Since banks pay off their discounts by adjusting their assets, the volume of discounting by member banks (or the opposite, the amount of free reserves they hold which could be used as a base for expanded credit) is a primary indicator of the degree of tightness or ease in the banking system.

It can thus be seen that many forces—supply, demand, yield, security, Federal Reserve, and others—have a direct effect upon the availability and cost of money, particularly mortgage money. A constant view of all these forces is required to determine how the mortgage market will react or is reacting. Similarly, trends such as decreasing supply or increasing demand must be measured and determinations made as to when they will bottom-out or top-out. But, whatever is said, it remains quite evident that many forces and factors are at work influencing the mortgage market and the flow of funds into that market.

QUESTIONS FOR THOUGHT AND DISCUSSION

1. Name the primary sources of lendable funds.
2. How does unemployment affect the availability of mortgage funds?
3. What effect on the availability of funds would numerous industrial plant expansions throughout the United States have? What effect would large government deficits have?
4. What is disintermediation and how does it affect the mortgage market?
5. What factors combine to produce periods of "tight money" and high interest rates?
6. How does inflation affect the demand for credit?
7. In what ways can the Federal Reserve act affect money and credit?
8. What effects do the factors of security and yield have upon the flow of funds into mortgage investments?

9

SAVINGS AND LOAN ASSOCIATIONS

Savings and loan associations, sometimes called homestead associations, building and loan associations, or cooperative banks, were first organized in the United States in 1831 and had as their principal purposes *thrift* and *home ownership*.

EARLY ASSOCIATIONS

It was hoped that members of these early associations could pool their funds and make them available to those members who needed assistance in financing the purchase of homes.

During this early period the typical association had small amounts of money. Therefore, it did not need the services of full-time management or full-time office space in which to pursue its lending activities. What small amount of business there was to transact could be accomplished in the homes of members, in local meeting halls, or in back rooms of store buildings. It was the purpose of these early association meetings to receive whatever savings the members had to contribute and, if any loan applications had been submitted, to discuss their approval with respect to available funds. Thus, these first associations were managed and operated like today's local civic clubs or investment groups.

In these first associations members would buy shares and pay dues; when sufficient funds accumulated, they were loaned to members. The choice of which member or members were entitled to borrow the accumulated funds was made in different ways: one method was to auction off the funds as a certain amount was accumulated. The bidder willing to pay the highest discount was the one who received the funds. Other methods were members drawing lots or funds being lent on the basis of time of filing of loan applications.

In order to encourage and compel thrift while providing for a constant input and availability of funds, members were required to pay fines if they missed dues payment dates; in some cases they paid fines and forfeited their membership. Similarly, penalties were imposed upon share withdrawals in the form of dividend forfeitures.

It should be remembered that the theory of the majority of early associations, which has to some extent carried over to modern times, was that borrowed funds were repaid as to principal by share subscriptions equal to the face amount of the obligation. When the total shares subscribed for were purchased, the debt was cancelled out by an exchange of the obligation for the shares.

For example, if shares were $200 each, a borrowing of $20,000 would be reflected by a subscription for 100 shares. In these early associations, monthly subscription payments were one percent or $200, including interest.

Lending decisions of the earlier associations, and for that matter some of today's associations, were made on the basis of the applicant's financial ability and standing in the local community as opposed to the security of the property for which the loan was sought.

These early associations were divided into two classes: *terminating* and *serial.*

The *terminating* associations had a fixed group of members and terminated when the association's purpose was fulfilled (when every member had acquired a home and had paid for it).

Serial associations admitted members in groups, each group constituting an independent series of shares that paid no accumulations (premium on admission to make a new member's contribution equal to the accounts of existing members) and had its own maturity date. In essence, these associations were a series of terminating associations.

To meet the needs of those interested in thrift but not necessarily homeownership and to continue servicing the needs of those who desired to save toward homeownership, the modern associations emerged. They are *permanent* and permit members to join at any time.

MODERN ASSOCIATIONS

It can therefore be said that today's savings and loan associations accomplish two basic purposes:

1. They encourage thrift by agreeing to pay favorable rates of interest on savings accounts, irrespective of the individual depositor's purpose for savings accumulations.
2. They make the savings of their depositors available for financing the purchase and improvement of homes of their depositors and others.

In addition to accomplishing these primary purposes, savings and loan associations provide commercial bank-type services such as selling United States savings bonds, money orders and travelers' checks. Many savings and loans have adopted Christmas and vacation club programs as well as payroll and school savings plans. Some even engage in safety-deposit box rentals. Since the passage of the Housing and Urban Development Act of 1968, savings and loans are also now issuing certificates of deposit, debentures, and bonds.

Today savings and loan associations are the largest and most prominent source of conventional mortgage funds for one to four-unit residences in the United States. Savings and loan associations also invest in FHA, VA, construction, business, and special purpose loans. Throughout most of the 1960s only about 5 percent of the loans made by savings and loan associations were FHA or VA loans. In recent years, however, the FHA/VA loan holdings of associations have slowly increased. At the end of 1977, FHA/VA loans constituted 9.6 percent (30.1 billion) of association loan holdings while conventional and other loans accounted for 85.4 percent and construction loans for 5.0 percent of the entire savings and loan industry's mortgage portfolio. In total assets, savings and loan associations in 1977 ranked second behind commercial banks and had more than three times the total assets of the fourth-ranked mutual savings banks. (See Charts 9-1, 9-2, and 9-3.)

Modern savings and loan associations follow one of two methods of organization. They are either mutual associations or permanent capital stock associations.

The permanent capital stock associations are similar to corporations. Each savings and loan association shareholder owns a part of the association and receives dividends on his investment.

Most savings and loan associations, however, are mutually owned; that is, they are owned by their members. This is true of practically all federal associations. Members of a mutual association are considered part owners and therefore participate directly in the association's earnings. Gross income, after deduction of operating expenses and establishment of a set-aside reserve, is distributed to association members on a pro rata basis. However, the Federal Home Loan Bank Board sets ceilings on member association dividend rates thereby limiting the amount of distribution of earnings to association members. As a sound business move, most savings and loan associations will accumulate their earnings for use in times of small earnings so that their dividends can be maintained at constant and "as advertised" rates. The early associations usually made no provision for reserves. Thus, gains and losses as they occurred were added or subtracted from members' accounts. Members could expect high dividends because of this method, but also stood the risk of heavy losses. Evolution of legislation requiring the establishment of reserves put an end to early methods and brought about the constant dividend system.

WITHDRAWALS

Most associations, both federal and state, have liberal withdrawal policies and allow savings of depositors to be withdrawn upon request. All associations, however, reserve the right to require thirty to sixty days or more notice prior to withdrawal.

This right is seldom enforced since enforcement could give rise to depositor fear about the association's ability to return savings and thus create a run on savings withdrawals. Association-issued savings account passbooks state the association's policies and regulations including the withdrawal procedure and any special circumstances under which additional notice may be required.

REGULATION

The early savings and loan associations were relatively free from public regulation. Those regulations that did exist were imposed by the individual states. Savings and loan associations suffered along with commercial banks and other sectors of the economy during the Great Depression of the 1930s. Thus, during the "New Deal" era, three major laws were passed affecting savings and loan associations:

1. The Home Loan Bank Act (1932) which created the Federal Home Loan Bank System.
2. The Home Owners' Loan Act (1933) providing for the chartering of

CHART 9-1

Mortgage Portfolio of All Savings Associations

Year-End	Total Portfolio†			Type of Loan (Millions of Dollars)		
	Amount (Millions)	Number of Loans	Avg. Loan Balance	Conventional	VA-Guaranteed	FHA-Insured
1950	$ 13,749	3,763,000	$ 3,654	$ 9,928	$ 2,973	$ 848
1955	31,466	5,859,000	5,371	24,179	5,883	1,404
1960	60,070	8,069,000	7,445	49,324	7,222	3,524
1965	110,306	10,930,000	10,092	98,763	6,398	5,145
1970	150,331	10,970,000	13,704	131,659	8,494	10,178
1971	174,250	11,490,000	15,177	149,952	10,623	13,675
1972	206,182	12,230,000	16,875	177,308	13,474	15,400
1973	231,733	12,550,000	18,465	201,995	$29,738	
1974*	249,306	‡	‡	219,486	29,820	

*Preliminary.
†Beginning with 1970, includes (1) junior liens; (2) real estate sold on contract; and (3) collateral loans secured by assignment of first mortgage loans; beginning with 1973, excludes participation certificates guaranteed by FHLMC, loans and notes insured by the Farmers Home Administration, and certain other government-insured mortgage-type investments.
‡Not available.
Sources: Federal Home Loan Bank Board; United States League of Savings Associations.

federal savings and loan associations. Under this act existing associations and any association organized after the passage of the act could apply for a federal charter. By becoming federal associations, savings and loan associations can enjoy the benefits of borrowing from home loan banks. However, federal associations have the obligation of joining the Federal Home Loan Bank System and the Federal Savings and Loan Insurance Corporation. Membership in these two federal bodies is open to state chartered associations.
3. The National Housing Act of 1934 under which the Federal Savings and Loan Insurance Corporation was created. Each individual savings account in FSLIC member associations is insured today up to a maximum limit of $40,000.

The purpose and effect of the above laws were to instill public confidence in savings and loan associations as depositories of individual savings while encouraging the opening of new accounts and an increase in gross savings.

As long as it complies with its charter, state statutes, and the rules and regulations of the FHLBB and the FSLIC, an association is free to pursue its own policies and formulate its own methods of operation. Due to the importance of savings and loan associations in the mortgage market and the effect

CHART 9-2

Mortgage Portfolio of All Associations, by Type of Property

Year-End	Loans Outstanding (Millions of Dollars)†			Percentage Distribution		
	One- to Four-Family Homes	Other Properties	Total	One- to Four-Family Homes	Other Properties	Total
1950	$ 13,116	$ 633	$ 13,749	95.4%	4.6%	100.0%
1955	30,001	1,465	31,466	95.3	4.7	100.0
1960	55,386	4,684	60,070	92.2	7.8	100.0
1965	94,225	16,081	110,306	85.4	14.6	100.0
1970	124,970	25,361	150,331	83.1	16.9	100.0
1971	142,275	31,975	174,250	81.6	18.4	100.0
1972	167,049	39,133	206,182	81.0	19.0	100.0
1973	187,750	43,983	231,733	81.0	19.0	100.0
1974*	201,986	47,320	249,306	81.0	19.0	100.0

*Preliminary.
†Beginning with 1970, includes (1) junior liens; (2) real estate sold on contract; and (3) collateral loans secured by assignment of first mortgage loans; beginning with 1973, excludes participation certificates guaranteed by FHLMC, loans and notes insured by the Farmers Home Administration, and certain other government-insured mortgage-type investments.
Sources: Federal Home Loan Bank Board; Federal Reserve Board.

CHART 9-3

Total Assets of Financial Intermediaries at Year-End
(Billions of Dollars)

Financial Intermediary	1950	1955	1960	1965	1970	1974*
Commercial Banks	$168.9	$210.7	$257.6	$377.3	$ 576.2	$ 916.3
Savings and Loan Associations	16.9	37.7	71.5	129.6	176.2	295.6
Life Insurance Companies	64.0	90.4	119.6	158.9	207.3	263.8
Mutual Savings Banks	22.4	31.3	40.6	58.2	79.0	109.6
Finance Companies	9.3	18.3	26.9	44.8	62.5	92.4
Investment Companies	3.3	7.8	17.0	35.2	47.6	35.8
Credit Unions	1.0	2.7	5.7	10.6	17.8	31.8
Private Pension Funds	6.7	18.3	38.2	73.6	110.8	144.4
State and Local Pension Funds	4.9	10.8	19.6	33.2	58.1	93.5
Total	$297.4	$428.0	$596.7	$921.4	$1,335.5	$1,983.2

*Preliminary.
Sources: CUNA International, Inc.; Federal Home Loan Bank Board; Federal Reserve Board; Institute of Life Insurance; National Association of Mutual Savings Banks; U. S. League of Savings Associations.

that regulation by the Federal Home Loan Bank and Federal Savings and Loan Insurance Corporation has upon savings and loan associations, these two regulatory agencies will be discussed at length in a later chapter.

CLASSIFICATION

Savings and loan associations are divided into several classifications for the purpose of study and with respect to regulation:

State-charted uninsured associations are generally those which are not members of either the Federal Home Loan Bank System or the Federal Savings and Loan Insurance Corporation. Therefore, all associations within this classification are state-chartered associations and are subject to such public control as is prescribed by state statutes and such changes and amendments to those statutes as are from time to time made by the respective state legislatures.

Over the last several years state statutes regulating and supervising the creation and operation of savings and loan associations have changed in order to bring state laws more in line with federal savings and loan statutes. In most states, supervision of savings and loan associations is accomplished under a state banking department or other agency of the state government, while all states directly employ examiners to make regular audits of state-chartered savings and loan associations operations to insure compliance with governing laws and adoption of sound operating practices. In addition to audits by state employees, independent accounting firms may be brought in to make annual examinations of state-chartered associations' books and records.

Also included in this classification are state-chartered associations which are members of the Federal Home Loan Bank system. Hence, these associations are not only subject to state supervision, but must comply with the rules, regulations, and standards of operation promulgated by the Federal Home Loan Bank Board. The major requirements imposed by the FHLBB on its member institutions are listed below:

1. The interest rates charged on mortgage loans must be reasonable and not exorbitant.
2. An association's mortgage loan policies must be economically sound.
3. A portion of an association's assets must be liquid (in the form of cash or United States Government Securities). Liquidity is necessary to insure prompt response to deposit withdrawal request. By law the FHLBB can vary the liquity ratio between 4 percent and 10 percent. In general the liquity ratio is reduced to increase the funds available for mortgage lending in times of savings inflow declines and is increased when lendable funds are more abundant.

State-chartered insured associations are members of and have deposits insured by the Federal Savings and Loan Insurance Corporation. Membership in the Federal Savings and Loan Insurance Corporation requires Federal Home Loan Bank System membership. Hence, state-chartered insured associations are subject to supervision by the FHLBB and to annual federal examinations by auditors of the FSLIC.

FSLIC supervision covers every activity of member associations, particularly with regard to savings solicitation methods, mortgage and other investments, and general account handling.

Federal associations are by nature members of the Federal Home Loan Bank System and the Federal Savings and Loan Insurance Corporation. They receive their charters from the Federal Home Loan Bank Board under the terms of the Home Owners Loan Act of 1933, pursuant to rules and regulations issued by the FHLBB.

By charter, federal savings and loan associations have the right to accept savings and the power to invest these savings primarily in mortgage loans and, to a much lesser extent, in United States government securities.

Supervision of federal associations is conducted by both the FSLIC and the FHLBB. Yearly audits are mandatory. Should they uncover any violations of FSLIC or FHLBB rules and regulations, expeditious corrective action is taken.

DUAL SYSTEM

The dual state and federal charter system for savings and loan associations has fostered healthy competition with a balance between federal and state chartered associations being fairly well maintained during the last decade. Charts 9-4 and 9-5 reflect the distribution and the assets of savings associations by type of charter and classification. Preliminary 1977 figures reflect 2,758 state-chartered associations versus 2,012 federal associations with assets divided $197.4 billion to $261.9 billion respectively. Also readily noticeable from these charts is a steady decrease in the number of state-chartered and federal associations.

CHART 9-4

Assets of Savings Associations, by Type of Charter
(Millions of Dollars)

Year-End	Federally Chartered†	State-Chartered Total	FSLIC-Insured	Noninsured‡	Grand Total
1950	$ 8,457	$ 8,436	$ 5,234	$3,202	$ 16,893
1955	20,035	17,621	14,163	3,458	37,656
1960	38,511	32,965	28,919	4,046	71,476
1965	66,715	62,865	57,861	5,004	129,580
1970	96,259	79,924	74,386	5,538	176,183
1971	114,229	91,794	85,755	6,039	206,023
1972	135,925	107,202	100,424	6,778	243,127
1973	152,240	119,665	112,557	7,108	271,905
1974*	167,671	127,945	120,552	7,393	295,616

*Preliminary.
†All federally chartered associations are insured by the Federal Savings and Loan Insurance Corporation.
‡Includes the assets of institutions insured by the Co-operative Central Bank of Massachusetts, the Maryland Savings-Share Insurance Corporation, the North Carolina Savings Guaranty Corporation and the Ohio Deposit Guarantee Fund.
Sources: Federal Home Loan Bank Board; United States League of Savings Associations.

CHART 9-5

Distribution of Savings Associations, by Type of Charter

Year-End	Federally Chartered†	State-Chartered Total	FSLIC-Insured	Noninsured‡	Grand Total
1950	1,526	4,466	1,334	3,132	5,992
1955	1,683	4,388	1,861	2,527	6,071
1960	1,873	4,447	2,225	2,222	6,320
1965	2,011	4,174	2,497	1,677	6,185
1970	2,067	3,602	2,298	1,304	5,669
1971	2,049	3,425	2,222	1,203	5,474
1972	2,044	3,254	2,147	1,107	5,298
1973	2,040	3,130	2,123	1,007	5,170
1974*	2,060	3,042	2,081	961	5,102

*Preliminary.
†All federally chartered associations are insured by the Federal Savings and Loan Insurance Corporation.
‡Includes institutions insured by the Co-operative Central Bank of Massachusetts, the Maryland Savings-Share Insurance Corporation, the North Carolina Savings Guaranty Corporation and the Ohio Deposit Guarantee Fund.
Sources: Federal Home Loan Bank Board; United States League of Savings Associations.

STATE ACCOUNT INSURERS

Several states have established insuring agencies that are similar to and have the same purposes as the FSLIC. The Ohio Deposit Guarantee Fund insures accounts in approximately 100 state savings and loan associations. The North Carolina Savings Guaranty Corporation presently insures the accounts of seventeen associations while the Maryland Savings-Share Insurance Corporation serves about 154 savings and loan associations in that state. The oldest state insuring organization, the cooperative Central Bank of Massachusetts cover over 140 cooperative banks (the term used for savings and loan type organizations in the state of Massachusetts).

CHART 9-6

Savings Flows at Savings Associations
(Dollar Amounts in Millions)

					Pct. of Savings at Start of Year		
Year	Gross Savings Receipts	With-drawals	Net Savings Receipts	With-drawal Ratio	Gross Receipts Ratio	Turn-over Ratio	Net Receipts Ratio
1950	$ 5,307	$ 3,820	$ 1,487	72.0%	42.6%	30.6%	11.9%
1955	13,481	8,590	4,891	63.7	49.5	31.5	17.9
1960	24,413	16,854	7,559	69.0	44.7	30.9	13.8
1965	39,218	30,705	8,513	78.3	38.5	30.1	8.4
1970	63,957	52,939	11,018	82.8	47.2	39.1	8.1
1971	77,888	49,914	27,974	64.1	53.2	34.1	19.1
1972	95,884	63,221	32,663	65.9	55.0	36.3	18.8
1973	113,212	92,975	20,237	82.1	54.8	45.0	9.8
1974*	125,855	109,847	16,008	87.3	55.5	48.4	7.1

*Preliminary.
Source: Federal Home Loan Bank Board.

SAVINGS FLOWS

Since savings and loan associations invest a large percentage of their assets in mortgage loans, the amount of net savings (receipts over withdrawals) is an important indicator for any determination of the amount of money available for mortgage loan investment. Chart 9-6 very adequately reflects this fact. Notice that in the plentiful money years of 1955, 1960, 1971 and 1972, the withdrawal ratio was under 70 percent. Possibly the most important thing to consider in that chart is that the volume of savings (gross receipts) is not an important factor; net savings receipts are the most significant indicator of interest rate levels and mortgage money availability.

LENDING DECISIONS

Lending decisions of most savings and loan associations are reached through loan committee deliberations. Board of directors or executive committee approval is reserved for the larger, more complex lending decisions. Loan committees meet periodically, sometimes daily, and not only approve the borrower and property, but also make determinations as to interest rate.

In the long run, interest rates are established according to market conditions and savings and loan association committees always must be cognizant of prevailing rates at other local thrift institutions. In addition to interest rate determinations, the amount of loan, the time of maturity, and security are prime matters to be considered by loan committees. Guidelines are established by state statutes as to state chartered associations and by FHLBB regulations as to federal associations. Because FHLBB regulations are used as a basis for state statutes concerning state chartered association operations and are national in scope, a study of the more important mortgage lending regulations and restrictions imposed upon federal savings and loan associations is significant.

LENDING POWERS OF FEDERAL ASSOCIATIONS

One-to-four family home loans constitute the largest single area of savings and loan association asset investment. In 1977, approximately $308.4 billion or 80.9 percent of assets of savings and loan associations taken as a whole (both state-chartered and federal) were invested in one-to-four family home mortgage loans. Chart 9-2 reflects this fact. These loans, which can include a combination of residential and business units, are allowably made on either a "straight-term" or an "amortized" basis.

Straight-term loans repayable in thirty-six months may be made up to 80 percent of appraised value provided interest payments are made on a semi-annual basis. Also allowable are 50 percent of appraised value loans for up to five year terms and 60 percent of appraised value loans for up to three year terms.

Amortized conventional loans at up to 80 percent loan-to-value ratio may run for a term of up to thirty years with the amount of mortgage limited to $60,000 per single family residence (mortgages in excess of $60,000 are allowable, but are charged against the associations 20 percent of assets allowance for non-home mortgage investments). Amortized conventional loans are permissible on single-family residences in excess of 80 percent but not exceeding 95 percent if the loan is for $75,000 or less as to 80 percent to and including 90 percent loans and $60,000 or less as to those in ex-

CHART 9-7

**Mortgage Portfolio of All Savings Associations,
by Type of Property and Type of Mortgage, Year-End 1974**

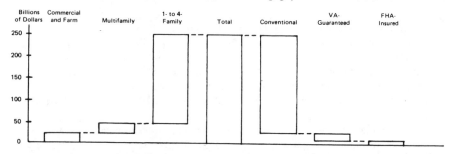

Sources: Federal Home Loan Bank Board; Federal Reserve Board.

cess of 90 percent of value. The amount of loan in excess of 90 percent of property value must be insured by a private mortgage insurance) or the savings and loan association making the loan must hold in reserve an amount equal to 1 percent of the unpaid loan balance of the mortgage until that unpaid balance is no more than 90 percent of the value of the property secured.

On the higher ratio loans (over 80 percent of value), escrows must be established for real estate taxes and hazard insurance premiums, and affidavits obtained that no secondary financing will be obtained and that the borrower is or intends to occupy the property as his established residence.

Only 50 percent of a savings and loan's assets may be invested in loans of over 80 percent loan-to-value and only 25 percent in loans of over 90 percent loan-to-value.

In 1977, the average maturity of conventional loans made all savings and loan associations on new single family homes was 28.60 years with an average 76.3 percent loan-to-value ratio. Both criteria were in excess of those allowed by commercial banks, mutual savings banks and life insurance companies. In 1977, the average purchase price of a new single family home financed by a savings and loan association was $58,000, up from $34,700 in 1971.

In 1977, multifamily loans (loans on properties containing five or more dwelling units) constituted 8.5 percent of the dollar volume of all mortgage loans held by insured associations, according to the United States Savings and Loan League 1978 Fact Book. At the end of 1977, savings and loan associations were the largest holders of multifamily loans of any of the major financial institutions. Savings associations held $33.3 billion in multifamily loans as compared to 18.9 billion for life companies and 15.3 billion for mutual savings banks. Loan terms on multifamily mortgages cannot exceed thirty years nor can they be made in excess of 80 percent of a property's appraised value.

A limitation of 20 percent of assets is placed on loans secured on multifamily or commercial-income properties. Multifamily loans are further limited by a 20 percent-of-assets regulation. Such asset limitation, however, applies only to the amount of loan per unit in excess of FHA Sec. 207 (c)(3) per unit allowable loan amounts. An exception to these limits and to the 80 percent-of-value, 30-year rule are multifamily loans insured by the Federal Housing Administration. Included in this category are loans on high rise condominium units which are allowable at up to 90 percent loan-to-value ratio with term and maximum limit identical to the one-to-four family residential loans.

Multifamily loans are favored by savings and loan associations because they provide a more attractive mortgage yield than single family mortgage loans do.

Commercial income property loans are permissible when amortized monthly and made for no longer than twenty-five year terms and for no greater than 75 percent of appraised value. When made on a straight-term basis they are allowable with up to five year maturities at 50 percent or less loan-to-value ratio with interest payable semi-annually.

In calculating the loan-to-value ratio no consideration can be given to installed equipment or "goodwill" The property appraisal must be made solely on the value of the real estate which the mortgage will secure.

Land loans made for the purposes of acquiring and developing real estate (by grading, engineering, and installing roads and utilities) are permissible, usually on a straight-term basis with short maturities.

A loan on an improved lot is now allowable for the purpose of assisting an individual with limited income to build up equity for a future home. The improved lot must, however, be intended for use as a permanent home site—not for a vacation or seasonal home. The loans can be for a maximum 75 percent of appraised value with maturities of up to five years, provided 40 percent of the principal obligation is amortized during the five year term. Builders are also eligible for loans on improved lots where their intention is to build single family homes.

Unsecured loans are loans for property alteration or improvement, both FHA-insured and conventional, and may be made for up to $10,000 to finance equipment that will be placed in homes or to finance the construction of vacation homes, with no more than a five year maturity. These loans need not be secured by a mortgage and are usually made on a loan-discounted basis (the interest for the term is deducted from the loan amount in advance and the net amount distributed to the borrower). The gross amount of the loan is then repaid over the established term. An unsecured loan at least 20 percent of which is guaranteed by VA may have a maturity of eight years provided the loan does not exceed $10,000 and is amortized. No more than 20 percent of an association's assets may be invested in unsecured loans.

Leasehold mortgage loans are permissible on leaseholds which extend for only ten years beyond the term of the mortgage.

Construction loans are now allowed to be made for up to 80 percent of appraised value and for three years. Savings and loan associations and commercial banks dominate the construction loan market. However, savings and loan associations since the mid-1950s have had a rapidly decreasing percentage of their assets invested in construction loan.

Property acquisition by associations is now permissible. In order to prod savings and loan associations to invest in low income neighborhoods, the FHLBB has approved regulations allowing the acquisition by savings and loan associations of existing homes where the acquiring associations plan "remodeling, rehabilitation, modernization, renovation, or demolition, and re-building" for sale.

Mobile home loans are a new investment opportunity for savings and loan associations. The Housing and Urban Development Act of 1968 authorized the FHLBB to issue regulations for the making of mobile home loans by savings and loan associations. The regulations subsequently issued by the FHLBB currently permit savings and loan associations to invest up to 20 percent of their assets in loans for consumer purchase of new or used mobile homes units and for mobile home dealer inventory financing. Maturities permitted are for up to twenty years with up to 90 percent of the buyer's total cost financed.

These loans are not real estate secured but in reality are chattel loans and are included in the savings associations consumer loan category. However, with one family moving into a mobile home for every two families that move into a single family residence, the impact of mobile homes on the construction industry and mortgage lending is generally quite significant and any strong moves toward mobile home lending by savings and loan associations and other institutional investors will reduce the amount of funds available for mortgage financing. In 1977 mobile home loans by savings and loan associations increased by $231 million to a total of $2.54 billion outstanding in such loans.

Non-home mortgage investments are generally limited to 20 percent of an association's assets. Mortgage loan investments which may be made and are included in the 20 percent of asset limitation are shown on Chart 9-7.

CHART 9-7

Loans Subject to General 20%-of-Assets Category

(Affects only conventional and FHA loans; any VA loan at least 20% of which is guaranteed is excluded.)

Real Estate Loans[1] Within The Regular Lending Area
    Conventional[2] Home Loans
        Excess Over $60,000 on single family dwellings
        Excess Over 207(c)(3) on two-to-four family units
    Apartment Loans Excess Over 207(c)(3)
    Commercial and Income Property Loans not in a
        Special Category
    Developed Building Lot & Site Loans
Loans Subject to Nationwide Lending and Which are
    Outside the Regular Lending Area[3] including
    originated FHA apartments
Real Estate Owned Applicable to Above Categories

---

[1] Participations in conventional loans on residential properties may be classified in the same manner as whole loans or, alternatively, classified in the participation 20 percent-of-assets category. Participations in non-residential loans must be classified in the same manner as a whole loan.
[2] FHA loans are subject to the same limitations.
[3] Exclude loans classified in the special 5 percent urban renewal category.

CHART 9-8

Loans and Investments Subject to Percentage Limitations Under Federal and FSLIC Regulations

CATEGORY	MAXIMUM % OF ASSET LIMITATION
FEDERAL	
Real Estate Loans:	
General 20 percent	20
Conventional Participations Beyond Regular Lending Area	20
Over 80 percent	50
Over 90 percent	25 (a)
Flexible Payment Loans	5 (b)
Developed Building Lots	5
Acquisition and Development of Land	5 (c)
Housing for the Aging	5

Urban Renewal
    (a) Loans and Obligations   5
    (b) Ownership Interests   2 (d)
Trade-in   5
Foreign Loans   1
Spillover Loans   2 (f)

Non-Real Estate Loans:
Business Development Credit Corporation   (f)
Mobile Home Loans   20
Unsecured Loans   20
Equipment Loans   5 (g)
Unsecured "line of credit" Loan   2 (e)
Educational Loans   5
Unrated Tax Exempt Securities   1
Service Corporations   1
National Corporations for Housing Partnerships   1
    (a) Equity Interest   ¼
    (b) Loans and Loan Commitments   5 (h)

FSLIC
Real Estate Loans Beyond 50-mile radius
   but Within State   20 (i)
Nationwide Loans   15
Conventional Participations Beyond Normal
   Lending Territory   40
State House Corporations
    (a) Equity Interests   ¼
    (b) Loans and Loan Commitments   5 (h)

(a) Included in 50 percent limitation for over 80 percent loans.
(b) Included in 50 percent limitation for over 80 percent loans and 25 percent limitation for over 90 percent loans if such loans are over 80 percent or 90 percent.
(c) Of savings rather than assets.
(d) Included in 5 percent urban renewal limitation.
(e) Up to a maximum of 5 percent as based on "good" reserves.
(f) The lesser of: (1) 0.5 percent of association's outstanding loans; (2) $250,000; (3) limit for state associations.
(g) Included in the 20 percent limitation for unsecured loans.
(h) Of net worth rather than assets.
(i) When association's normal lending territory is reduced to 50 miles because scheduled items exceed 4 percent.
(j) Including real estate owned.

Loan participations between savings and loan associations and other lenders are permitted, provided the lenders participating are FDIC-insured banks, members of the FSLIC, or FHA approved mortgagees, including mortgage brokers and mortgage companies. Participations can also be entered into with instrumentalities of the federal government. Presently, participations are limited to residential property loans, but steps are underway by the FHLBB to permit participations on any real estate which a federal savings and loan association can legally accept as security.

Loans and investments subject to asset limitations are set forth on Chart 9-9.

LENDING AREA

A savings and loan association's general lending area includes the state in which its home office is located and that area within 100 miles of its home office, but this is subject to a 20 percent-of-assets limitation for loans over fifty miles unless the amount of an associations "scheduled items" is less than 4 percent of its "specified assets." ("Specified assets" means the total assets of the institution, including its mortgage portfolio, less those assets involving a minimal risk. "Scheduled items" means loans having poor repayment record as well as certain real estate owned or sold on substandard terms.) In order to enable savings and loan associations in areas of capital surplus to offer their funds to areas which are capital poor, savings and loan associations can invest 15 percent of their assets nationwide, provided they have a local loan servicing agent such as a mortgage company or another savings and loan association.

CHART 9-9
• Total Assets of All Savings and Loan Associations
(Millions of Dollars)

Year-End	Mortgage Loans[1,2]	Cash and Investment Securities[3]	Real Estate Owned	FHLB Stock	Other Assets[2,3]	Total Assets
1950	$ 13,657	$ 2,456	$ 21	$ 177	$ 582	$ 16,893
1955	31,408	4,549	33	507	1,159	37,656
1960	60,070	7,888	158	978	2,382	71,476
1965	110,306	12,123	1,065	1,236	4,850	129,580
1966	114,427	12,049	1,271	1,313	4,873	133,933
1967	121,805	13,941	1,353	1,327	5,108	143,534
1968	130,802	14,078	1,026	1,328	5,656	152,890
1969	140,232	13,311	822	1,424	6,360	162,149
1970	150,331	16,526	746	1,539	7,041	176,183
1971	174,250	21,042	775	1,550	8,406	206,023
1972	206,182	24,355	776	1,675	10,139	243,127
1973	231,733	21,055	910	2,075	16,132	271,905
1974	249,301	23,251	1,211	2,575	19,207	295,545
1975	278,590	30,853	1,662	2,600	24,528	338,233
1976	323,005	35,724	1,930	2,800	28,448	391,907
1977*	381,216	39,197	1,850	3,200	33,819	459,282

*Preliminary
[1]Beginning with 1966, includes (1) junior liens; (2) real estate sold on contract; and (3) collateral loans secured by the assignment of first mortgage loans.
[2]Beginning in 1973, participation certificates guaranteed by FHLMC, loans and notes insured by the Farmers Home Administration, and certain other government-insured mortgage-type investments, previously included in mortgage loans, are included in other assets.
[3]Beginning in 1973, GNMA-guaranteed mortgage-backed securities of the pass-through type, previously included in cash and investment securities, are included in other assets.
Sources: Federal Home Loan Bank Board; United States League of Savings Associations.

PURCHASE AND SALE OF MORTGAGES

Associations which find they have excess funds that cannot be advantageously invested in loans directly originated, resort to mortgage loan purchases. Purchases are made from mortgage brokers, mortgage companies, and even the

Federal National Mortgage Association. Savings and loan associations have been the largest institutional purchasers of Government National Mortgage Association guaranteed-mortgage-backed securities.

Sales of mortgages enable associations to free-up their assets for use in originating additional mortgage loans. The Federal National Mortgage Association and the Federal Home Loan Mortgage Corporation have been important purchasers of savings and loan association originated mortgages. FHLMC, or Freddie Mac as it is often called, was established by the Emergency Home Finance Act of 1970 to create a secondary market for residential mortgages held by any Federal Home Loan Bank member, any Federal Home Loan Bank, the Federal Savings and Loan Insurance Corporation, any commercial bank, or any other financial institution whose deposits are insured by an agency of the United States. FNMA and FHLMC are fully discussed in subsequent chapters.

The creation of a secondary market is accomplished by providing for the purchase of mortgages originated by others. Mortgages so purchased are held and resold as market conditions allow. The purpose of a strong secondary market is to provide more funds for mortgages during "tight money" periods through heavy mortgage purchases and to provide mortgage investments during "easy money" times by the sale of mortgages. Funds for secondary market mortgage purchases are acquired primarily by sale of stock, through bond issues, or from the sale of mortgage backed securities.

Federal Home Loan Banks are also active purchasers of mortgages from savings and loan associations and several $100 million Government National Mortgage Association guaranteed mortgage-backed securities have been marketed by FHLB's using FHA and VA mortgages purchased from member associations.

MORTGAGE-BACKED BONDS

The newest and most important loan sale vehicle for savings and loan associations is the issuance of mortgage-backed bonds. These securities which are similar to GNMA securities are backed by pools of FHA, VA and conventional loans owned by the issuing association. Generally, a savings and loan association may issue mortgage-backed bonds in an amount equal to 5 percent of its savings deposits. Mortgage-backed bonds are direct obligations of the issuing association, but unlike GNMA securities, carry no federal guaranty.

The investor in a mortgage-backed bond acquires a first claim to the specified loans in the collateral pool in the event the issuing association defaults. During the life of the bond, interest is paid semi-annually and principal is repaid at designated intervals.

Several advantages are derived by savings and loan associations through issuing mortgage-backed bonds. They are:

(a) It allows an association to utilize many of its old, low rate loans to raise new funds without having to sell these loans at a loss.

(b) The maturities on the mortgage-backed bonds closely match the maturities on the underlying collateral, thereby providing the association with a good asset versus liability maturity. Under its regular lending activities, an association is using short term deposits to make long-term loans and, in times of negative deposit flows, this presents a very serious problem.

The first mortgage-backed bonds issued after the May, 1975 FHLBB approval of the concept contained a high portion of FHA and VA loans in order to secure a Standard and Poor's AAA bond rating. However, the acceptability of mortgage-backed bonds has been such that issuers are now pooling only conventional loans.

As of year-end 1979, savings and loan associations had issued over $2 billion in mortgage-backed bonds.

APPRAISALS

Regulations require that associations obtain at least one appraisal for each loan made. When FHA and VA loans are involved, appraisals made by those respective government agencies are acceptable. Most savings and loan associations have their own staff of appraisers or employ independent fee appraisers, but some still have their officers or directors make appraisals as required. Appraisal practices of member associations are subject to periodic review by their federal home loan bank.

The above lending limitations and requirements are simply permissible limitations. Each association is free to formulate its own policies and adopt its own regulations within the confines of the above specified limitations.

HOLDING COMPANIES

Specialized management has been made possible by the establishment of savings and loan holding companies, primarily in the capital-scarce states of California and Texas. Under the holding company theory, several savings and loan associations are grouped together with stock control vested in the holding company. Great Western Financial Corporation and First Charter Financial are two of the larger holding companies. Common shares of both companies are traded on the New York Stock Exchange.

The appearance and growth of savings and loan associations holding companies in California and Texas probably is due in part to the high concentration of savings and loan associations in those states. Over 17 percent of total associations' assets are located in California, representing more than double the assets of the next leading savings and loan association state.

ASSETS

Chart 9-9 reflects the total assets of savings and loan associations by type of investment and by year, demonstrating a tremendous growth in mortgage loan portfolios (an average of approximately $20 billion per year during the period 1970 through 1974 and an average of $43 billion per year during the period 1975 through 1977.) Chart 9-10 is a listing of the 100 largest savings and loan associations by savings capital and total assets. It is noteworthy that eight of the top ten associations are located in California.

SERVICE CORPORATIONS

Over the past few years the Federal Home Loan Bank Board has pressed Congress for passage of legislation to expand savings and loan association operations into other areas of real estate finance and development. In addition to lobbying for legislation, the board has itself promulgated a number of liberal and operationally expansive regulations for savings and loan associations.

Perhaps the most expansive and revolutionary authority handed down by the Federal Home Loan Bank Board was the regulation established in mid-1970 for the expansion of savings and loan association service corporations' activities. Under these new regulations, federal savings and loan associations may invest in the capital stock of any service corporation, the home office of which is located in the same state as the investing association. One or more federal associations may also bind together to form a service corporation in which they will own all the capital stock.

Specifically the two types of service corporations are allowable:

A *type A* corporation is statewide and may be invested in by all eligible associations in the state.

A *type B* corporation, however, may be owned only by a limited number of associations. Type B corporations are further divided into two categories: Those owned by five or more associations and those owned by less than five associations.

The most preferred type of service corporation has been the type B corporation with fewer than five association owners. This type in 1977 accounted for 97 percent of all service corporations.

Some important operational areas of the service corporation include the following:

1. The origination, sale, purchase and servicing of loans and loan participations secured by first liens upon real eatate and mobile homes.
2. The brokerage and warehousing of first lien real estate and mobile home loans.
3. The investment in obligations fully guaranteed as to principal and interest by the United States, GNMA guaranteed mortgage-backed securities, Federal Home Loan Bank stock, and FNMA stock.
4. The performance of clerical, accounting, data processing, credit information, appraisal, property inspection, research, and advertisement services for savings and loan associations with home offices in the same state.
5. The acquisition of unimproved real estate lots and other unimproved real estate for immediate subdivision and development, principally for construction of housing units or for resale to others for housing construction, or for use as mobile home sites.
6. The acquisition of improved residential properties and mobile homes for rental purposes.
7. The acquisition of improved residential property for remodeling, rehabilitation, modernization, renovation, or demolition and rebuilding all for the purpose of subsequent resale or rental.
8. The maintenance and management of rental properties acquired or constructed, including rental properties owned by its shareholders.
9. The participation in loans and development activities with other savings and loan association service corporations.

CHART 9-10

FIRST 100 LARGEST SAVINGS & LOAN ASSOCIATIONS IN U. S.

In order of Deposits June 30, 1974, compared with June 30, 1973 and Dec. 31, 1973

Compiled by AMERICAN BANKER—*Copyright 1974*

Rank 6/30/74	(.000 Omitted in Dollar Amounts)	Total Deposits 6/30/74 $	Total Deposits 6/30/73 $	Rank 6/30/73	Gain	Total Deposits 12/31/73 $	Rank 12/31/73	Gain	Interest Rate ‡ 6/30/74 %	Interest Rate ‡ 12/31/73 %
1	**Home Savings & Loan Assn., Los Angeles**	4,331,997	4,204,904	1		4,209,612	1		5¼–7½	5¼–7½
2	**Great Western Savings & Loan Assn., Beverly Hills, Calif.**	3,572,431	3,576,339	2		3,554,991	2		5¼–7½	5¼–7
3	**American Savings & Loan Assn., Beverly Hills, Calif.**	3,401,437	3,243,674	3		3,293,629	3		5¼–7½	5¼–7½
4	**California Federal Savings & Loan Assn., Los Angeles**	1,928,312	1,886,087	4		1,850,265	4		5¼–7½	5¼–7½
5	**Glendale Federal Savings & Loan Assn., Calif.**	1,525,200	1,431,600	5		1,406,362	5		5½–7½	5½–7½
6	**First Federal Savings & Loan Assn., Detroit**	1,310,929	1,211,913	6		1,248,085	6		5¼–7½	5¼–7
7	**Gibraltar Savings & Loan Assn., Beverly Hills, Calif.**	1,228,405	1,121,972	7		1,149,588	7		5¼–7½	5¼–7½
8	**Twin City Federal Savings & Loan Assn., Minneapolis**	1,138,966	1,041,873	9	+ 1	1,081,395	8		5¼–7½	5¼–8
9	**Citizens Savings & Loan Assn., San Francisco**	1,115,570	1,067,363	8		1,076,654	9		5¼–7½	5¼–9
10	**Farm & Home Savings Assn., Nevada, Mo.**	1,104,815	1,018,504	10		1,075,458	10		5¼–7½	5¼–7½
11	Coast Federal Savings & Loan Assn., Los Angeles	1,073,778	971,654	12	+ 1	970,848	12	+ 1	5¼–7½	5¼–8½
12	First Federal Savings & Loan Assn., Chicago	1,035,690	1,007,505	11		993,782	11		5¼–7½	5¼–7½
13	Home Federal Savings & Loan Assn., San Diego, Calif.	1,027,938	844,633	16	+ 3	911,688	16	+ 3	5¼–7½	5¼–9
14	Talman Federal Savings & Loan Assn., Chicago	1,012,059	950,380	13		960,453	13		5¼–7½	5¼–7½
15	Standard Federal Savings & Loan Assn., Troy, Mich.	992,189	874,604	15		924,212	15		5¼–7½	5¼–7
16	First Federal Savings & Loan Assn., Miami	984,350	907,370	14		939,124	14		5¼–7½	5¼–7½
17	Midwest Federal Savings & Loan Assn., Minneapolis	811,172	683,970	21	+ 4	691,168	20	+ 3	5¼–7½	5¼–8¼
18	Bell Federal Savings & Loan Assn., Chicago	804,562	781,375	17		753,466	17		5¼–7½	5¼–7½
19	First Federal S & L Assn. of Broward Cty., Fort Lauderdale, Fla.	761,824	705,705	19		730,948	18		5¼–7½	5¼–7
20	Florida Federal Savings & Loan Assn., St. Petersburg, Fla.	736,534	634,120	24	+ 4	678,741	21	+ 1	5¼–7½	5¼–7½
21	**Pacific First Federal Savings & Loan Assn., Tacoma, Wash.**	711,552	700,439	20		709,694	19		5¼–7½	5¼–7½
22	**First Federal Savings & Loan Assn., Phoenix**	696,986	551,401	34	+ 12	617,884	26	+ 4	5¼–7½	5¼–9¾
23	**Community Federal Savings & Loan Assn., St. Louis**	690,920	636,489	23		657,972	23		5¼–7½	5¼–7½
24	**Atlanta Federal Savings & Loan Assn.**	680,224	621,047	25	+ 1	646,373	24		5¼–7½	5¼–7½
25	**Western Savings & Loan Assn., Phoenix**	667,029	523,769	38	+ 13	576,358	33	+ 8	5¼–7½	5¼–10½
26	**City Federal Savings & Loan Assn., Elizabeth, N. J.**	657,698	554,998	33	+ 7	601,553	28	+ 2	5¼–7½	5¾–7½
27	**Golden West Savings & Loan Assn., Oakland, Calif.**	644,709	595,251	27		611,515	27		5¼–7½	5¼–7½
28	**San Diego Federal Savings & Loan Assn., Calif.**	643,161	561,140	29	+ 1	598,390	29	+ 1	5¼–7½	5¼–7½
29	**West Side Federal Savings & Loan Assn., New York**	642,139	713,630	18		663,273	22		5¼–7½	5¼–7½
30	**Perpetual Building Assn., Washington, D. C.**	626,025	657,069	22		619,831	25		5¼	5¼
31	Imperial Savings & Loan Assn. of the North, San Francisco (a)	616,246	372,548	69	+ 38	588,730	31		5¼–7½	5¼–7½
32	Capitol Federal Savings & Loan Assn., Topeka, Kan.	611,564	559,798	31		585,282	32		5¼–7½	5¼–7½
33	Imperial Savings & Loan Assn., San Diego, Calif.	602,448	606,540	26		595,211	30		5¼–7½	5¼–7½
34	Northern California Savings & Loan Assn., Palo Alto	595,158	567,267	28		576,308	34		5¼–7½	5¼–7
35	County Federal Savings & Loan Assn., Rockville Centre, N. Y.	592,023	558,390	32		558,597	36	+ 1	5¼–7½	5¼–7½
36	Dallas Federal Savings & Loan Assn.	576,468	535,455	36		546,693	38	+ 2	5¼–7½	5¼–7½
37	Dade Federal Savings & Loan Assn., Miami	575,381	517,901	39	+ 2	550,286	37		5¼–7½	5¼–7½
38	Loyola Federal Savings & Loan Assn., Baltimore	575,294	560,581	30		571,650	35		5¼–7½	5¼–9¼
39	Security Savings & Loan Assn., San Francisco	563,436	523,947	37		537,465	39		5¼–7½	5¼–7½
40	Fidelity Savings & Loan Assn., San Francisco	561,513	535,928	35		533,555	40		5¼–7½	5¼–7½
41	**First Federal Savings & Loan Assn., Rochester, N. Y.**	560,846	444,235	52	+ 11	469,694	50	+ 9	5¼–7½	5¼–8
42	**Equitable Savings & Loan Assn., Portland, Ore.**	545,042	493,064	44	+ 2	519,982	41		5¼–7	5¼–7
43	**Chase Federal Savings & Loan Assn., Miami Beach, Fla.**	541,808	502,360	41		510,878	45	+ 2	5¼–7½	5¼–7½
44	**Minnesota Federal Savings & Loan Assn., St. Paul**	527,239	511,614	40		511,592	43		5¼–7½	5¼–7½

45	Coral Gables Federal Savings & Loan Assn., Fla.	525,614	499,256	43		511,498	44		5¼–7½	5¼–8½
46	Benjamin Franklin Federal Savings & Loan Assn., Portland, Ore.	510,737	466,171	48	+2	503,146	46		5¼–7½	5¼–7
47	Financial Federal Savings & Loan Assn., Miami Beach, Fla.	510,307	499,677	42		516,581	42		5¼–7½	5¼–10
48	Western Federal Savings & Loan Assn., Denver	507,122	480,927	45		494,596	47		5¼–7½	5¼–7½
49	Broadview Savings & Loan Co., Cleveland	489,575	462,259	50	+1	468,401	51	+2	5¼–7½	5¼–7½
50	Astoria Federal Savings & Loan Assn., Queens, New York	488,096	462,553	49		472,855	49		5¼–7½	5¼–7½
51	Baltimore Federal Savings & Loan Assn.	483,017	475,919	46		478,710	48		5–7½	5¼–7½
52	First Federal Savings & Loan Assn., Tampa, Fla.	471,534	416,999	59	+7	445,922	54	+2	5¼–7½	5¼–7½
53	Decatur Federal Savings & Loan Assn., Ga.	467,153	427,863	56	+3	437,058	56	+3	5¼–7½	5¼–7½
54	Gem City Savings Assn., Dayton, Ohio	458,987	433,064	54		440,790	55	+1	5–7½	5–7½
55	First Federal Savings & Loan Assn., Milwaukee	458,469	433,580	53		447,398	53		5¼–7½	5¼–7½
56	Carteret Savings & Loan Assn., Newark, N. J.	455,622	432,559	55		423,129	60	+4	5¼–7½	5¼–7½
57	Home Federal Savings & Loan Assn., Chicago	454,583	472,000	47		453,928	52		5¼–7½	5¼–7½
58	Gibraltar Savings Assn., Houston	447,891	417,136	58		429,000	58		5¼–7½	5¼–7½
59	Hollywood Federal Savings & Loan Assn., Fla.	444,290	410,120	60	+1	428,322	59		5¼–7½	5¼–7½
60	Atlantic Federal Savings & Loan Assn., Fort Lauderdale, Fla.	441,279	394,923	64	+4	409,583	62	+2	5¼–7½	4–7½
61	Fidelity Federal Savings & Loan Assn., Glendale, Calif.	438,059	453,784	51		435,281	57		5¼–7½	5¼–7½
62	St. Paul Federal Savings & Loan Assn., Chicago	432,715	391,142	65	+3	410,011	61		5¼–7½	5¼–7½
63	Fulton Federal Savings & Loan Assn., Atlanta	431,636	400,058	63		403,704	66	+3	5¼–7½	5¼–9⅛
64	Leader Federal Savings & Loan Assn., Memphis	429,812	407,097	62		404,644	64		5¼–7½	5¼–7½
65	Far West Federal Savings & Loan Assn., Portland, Ore.	426,084	377,908	67	+2	404,091	65		5¼–7½	5¼–7½
66	Suffolk County Federal Savings & Loan Assn., Babylon, N. Y.	410,960	376,440	68	+2	387,082	68	+2	5¼–7½	5¼–7½
67	Sooner Federal Savings & Loan Assn., Tulsa, Okla.	408,665	354,914	76	+9	367,353	76	+9	5¼–7½	5¼–9
68	World Savings & Loan Assn., Lynwood, Calif.	403,256	351,490	79	+11	387,756	67		5¼–7½	5¼–7½
69	Fresno Guarantee Savings & Loan Assn., Calif.	400,649	356,258	75	+6	375,068	71	+2	5¼–7½	5¼–7½
70	Franklin Society Federal Savings & Loan Assn., New York	399,125	417,922	57		405,385	63		5¼–7½	5¼–7½
71	Washington Federal Savings & Loan Assn., Miami Beach, Fla.	398,234	347,482	80	+9	365,928	77	+6	5¼–7½	5¼–9
72	Cardinal Federal Savings & Loan Assn., Cleveland	395,755	......	..		386,452	69		5¼–7½	5¼–7½
73	Home Federal Savings & Loan Assn., St. Petersburg, Fla.	392,073	334,734	87	+14	354,124	83	+10	5¼–7½	5¼–7½
74	San Francisco Federal Savings & Loan Assn.	391,625	367,052	71		369,435	74		5¼–7½	5¼–8
75	State Mutual Savings & Loan Assn., Los Angeles	390,330	408,978	61		386,022	70		5¼–7½	5¼–7½
76	Bay View Federal Savings & Loan Assn., San Francisco	388,829	365,712	72		374,412	72		5¼–7½	5¼–7½
77	Third Federal Savings & Loan Assn., Cleveland	385,336	340,844	84	+7	362,628	79	+2	5¼–7½	5¼–7½
78	Commercial Federal Savings & Loan Assn., Omaha, Neb.	382,262	340,569	85	+7	356,453	82	+4	5¼–7½	5¼–7½
79	Columbia Banking Saving & Loan Assn., Rochester, N. Y.	381,499	342,429	83	+4	353,433	84	+5	5¼–7½	5¾–8¼
80	Columbia Savings & Loan Assn., Denver	376,105	331,674	89	+9	357,181	81	+1	5¼–7½	5¼–10
81	National Permanent Federal S & L Assn., Washington, D. C.	375,215	381,718	66		372,708	73		5¼–7½	5¼–7½
82	Washington Federal Savings & Loan Assn., New York	373,052	363,702	74		363,238	78		5½–7½	5¼–7
83	First Federal Savings & Loan Assn., Toledo, Ohio	370,521	352,253	78		357,895	80		5¼–7½	5¼–8
84	First Federal Savings & Loan Assn., New York	367,836	346,893	81		336,967	90	+6	5¼–7½	5¼–7½
85	Old Colony Co-operative Bank, Providence, R. I.	364,703	372,077	70		367,879	75		4½–7½	4½–7¼
86	San Antonio Savings Assn., Tex.	362,320	334,905	86		342,112	88	+2	5¼–7½	5¼–8¾
87	Cleveland Federal S & L Assn. of Cuyahoga Cty., Cleveland	361,856	354,774	77		350,759	85		5¼–7½	5¼–8¾
88	Detroit & Northern Savings & Loan Assn., Hancock, Mich.	359,602	323,759	91	+3	337,200	89	+1	5¼–7½	5¼–7
89	Akron Savings & Loan Co., Ohio	358,868	346,171	82		343,470	87		5¼–7½	5¼–7½
90	Buckeye Federal Savings & Loan Assn., Columbus, Ohio	358,147	323,961	90		335,827	91	+1	5¼–7½	5¼–9¼
91	First Federal Savings & Loan Assn., Lincoln, Neb.	350,722	312,833	97	+6	327,863	94	+3	5¼–7½	5¼–8
92	Eureka Federal Savings & Loan Assn., San Francisco	343,912	317,712	93	+1	328,046	93	+1	5¼–7½	5¼–7
93	Mutual Savings & Loan Assn., Pasadena, Calif.	343,197	363,822	73		345,971	86		5¼–7½	5¼–7½
94	Oak Cliff Savings & Loan Assn., Dallas	340,819	303,737	100	+6	315,736	96	+2	5¼–7½	5¼–7½
95	American Savings Assn., Southfield, Mich.	333,747	299,763	101	+6	306,152	103	+8	5¼–7½	5¼–7½
96	First Federal Savings & Loan Assn., Sarasota, Fla.	333,330	292,879	103	+7	315,957	95		5¼–7½	5¼–7½
97	Clearwater Federal Savings & Loan Assn., Fla.	332,965	280,533	111	+14	304,458	104	+7	5¼–7½	5¼–7½
98	Santa Barbara Savings & Loan Assn., Calif.	332,214	322,921	92		328,802	92		5¼–7½	5¼–7½
99	Majestic Savings & Loan Assn., Denver	330,343	304,369	99		315,334	98		5¼–7½	3½–7½
100	Pomona First Federal Savings & Loan Assn., Calif.	330,300	306,725	98		313,197	99		5¼–7½	5¼–7½

‡—Range of rates offered on all types of new accounts. On a negotiated basis, many S & Ls pay more than the highest rate indicated for time deposits of $100,000 or more. §—Based on revised data. Rank that S & L would have had if revised data had been available. †—Rate on regular accounts only. (a)—Changed name to Imperial S & L Assn., July 1, 1974.

10. The joint venturing of real estate development projects or engagement in other activities all as may be approved by the FHLBB.

At the end of 1977, savings associations had 0.3 percent of their assets in service corporations or approximately $1.5 billion. A maximum of 1 percent of an association's assets may be invested in a service corporation.

RECENT TRENDS

Most recently, the Federal Home Loan Bank Board has allowed conversion of a few federal associations to capital stock companies. Federal associations are predominately mutually owned and must look solely to after-tax income for growth of their equity base (net worth). Stock associations, however, may utilize both after tax income and proceeds from the issuance of stock in order to increase their equity base. This distinction is of great importance in times of rapid savings growth when regulations usually require large additions to net worth to keep pace with the savings growth.

The conversion subject is very controversial and the FHLBB has only occasionally allowed conversions. However, the trend is toward stock companies and the benefits that stock ownership has for dynamic growth in saving and loan assets.

Mortgage-backed bonds, discussed earlier in this chapter, are also a recent trend that is certain to rapidly expand and produce added assets for savings and loan investment into mortgage loans.

QUESTIONS FOR THOUGHT AND DISCUSSION

1. Compare modern savings and loan associations to their predecessors with respect to:
   a. Purchase
   b. Method of lending
   c. Management
   d. Reserves against losses
   e. Dividend policies.
2. What are the various classifications of associations?
3. Do you feel all associations should be required to become FSLIC and FHLBS members? Why or why not?
4. Give your opinion why asset investment limitations are established for certain types of loans which associations can make.
5. Detail savings and loan association limitation on one-to-four family loans.
6. What do you feel is the purpose of the local servicing requirement for loans purchased outside a savings and loan association's lending area?
7. What advantages do savings and loan associations gain from participation in service corporations? Do you feel that the advantages are the same for a large savings association as they are for a smaller association?

10

MUTUAL SAVINGS BANKS AND COMMERCIAL BANKS

MUTUAL SAVINGS BANKS

Like savings and loan associations, mutual savings banks were organized as thrift institutions. Savings and loan associations had the specific purpose of savings for home ownership; mutual savings banks were established strictly to encourage savings, but for no set purpose. As stated in the charter of one of the larger savings banks, its purpose is to provide "a safe and profitable mode of enabling persons of all descriptions to invest such parts of their earnings or property, as they can conveniently spare, in a manner which will afford them both profit and security."

Savings banks began several years before savings and loan associations were organized in the United States. The first to start business was Philadelphia Savings Fund Society which began operations in 1816. Like Philadelphia Savings Fund Society, most savings banks were organized in the industrialized areas of the East, primarily to encourage savings by factory workers and other persons of moderate means.

All savings banks are state-chartered and, as their title implies, they are mutual organizations, owned and operated solely for the benefit of their depositors. But, while the depositors own the savings banks, they do not run them. Management is vested in a board of self-perpetuating trustees. The first board of trustees was elected when the savings bank was originally organized; and, when vacancies occurred, they were filled by vote of the remaining members. So the practice of self-perpetuating boards remains today.

Approximately three-fourths of the total assets of mutual savings banks are located in New York and Massachusetts. However, savings banks are found in fifteen other states and Puerto Rico.

DEPOSITS AND DIVIDENDS

Savings deposits are not the only service performed by mutual savings banks. Customers are also offerred savings bank life insurance, Christmas clubs, travelers' checks, school savings, credit savings bonds, checking accounts, bill paying, retirement programs, payroll deductions, term savings certificates, tellers' checks, money orders, consumer loans, home loans and safe deposit boxes. Recently mutual savings banks have begun providing typical commercial bank services such as 24-hour cost dispensing services and automated teller facilities. Negotiable orders of withdrawal (interest-paying checking accounts) in Massachusetts and New Hampshire and non-interest bearing negotiable payment orders in New York are a move toward allowing mutual savings banks to better compete with commercial banks.

Like savings and loan associations, savings banks distribute earnings to their depositors in the form of interest on accounts. These distributions are made only after operating expenses and taxes are deducted and adequate reserves are set aside in order to insure the ability to pay dividends (interest).

MORTGAGE INVESTMENTS

Historically, mortgages have been considered prime investments by mutual savings banks, although other types of loans, such as home improvement, personal, educational, passbook, and consumer loans are made. In fact, mortgage investments have commanded a substantial share of savings bank assets. According to figures published by the National Association of Mutual Savings Banks, total savings bank assets in mortgage investments on December 31, 1949, were $6,075 million or about 32 percent of total assets, compared to $24,769 million or 71 percent of total assets on December 31, 1959. Nineteen years later the figure was $96.5 billion or 66 percent of total assets.

The major reasons for the growth and significant increase in mortgage investments between 1949 and 1959 were the changes in mutual savings bank investment policies, their portfolio composition, and a desire for the higher yields available through mortgage investments.

Prior to World War II, mortgage loans constituted the largest single asset of savings banks. Then a change in policy took place; savings bank assets were plowed into United States government securities, and mortgage loans began to lose favor. Patriotism was not as big a reason for their policy changes as was the unfavorable experiences of the depression era. The foreclosures, which were rampant during those crisis years, took their toll on savings bank mortgage portfolios and changed the thinking of savings bank trustees and senior management with respect to mortgages as sound investments. Another factor which moved savings banks out of the mortgage loan area was competition. Other institutions were adopting new methods of lending while savings banks continued their conservative policies, again in reaction to the depression shock. Savings bank management would not move to the direct-reduction method of mortgage loan repayment, but held to the old straight-term demand mortgage method. Similarly, they would not take advantage of the new FHA-insured high loan-to-value ratio mortgage lending practices.

After the war many important changes took place which convinced the professional management of mutual savings banks that policy changes were necessary for growth. Some of the major post-war changes are listed below:

1. The post-World War II heavy sell-off of government securities and the resultant decrease in the market for these investments.
2. The housing boom of the late 1940s and the concurrent demand for mortgage credit.
3. The banking law changes in most savings bank states (at least the states of greatest savings bank concentration) which allowed for the first time the acquisition of out-of-state mortgage loans. This was the most important change.
4. The wide acceptance of FHA and VA loans.
5. The adoption and favoring of amortization on mortgage loans.
6. The yields available on mortgage loans.

Thus it was a combination of forces which spurred savings banks to look again with favor on mortgage loans and to rapidly increase the amount of their assets invested in such loans to the 70 percent level.

MORTGAGE HOLDINGS

While there is variation among savings banks and between savings bank states as to the importance of mortgage investments, it is evident from a comparison of the assets of all savings banks to the amount of mortgages held by them that such investments constitute the most important investment for these banks.

As mentioned, New York and Massachusetts have the highest concentration of savings banks. According to statistics reported by the National Association of Mutual Savings Banks, as of December 31, 1977, New York savings banks had assets of a little more than $79.8 billion with about $51.4 billion of mortgage holdings; and Massachusetts savings banks had assets of $21.4 billion with $14.4 billion of mortgage holdings. Total assets and mortgage holdings of these banks as compared to all savings banks is shown below:

	Assets*	Mortgage Holdings**
New York and Massachusetts savings banks	$101.2	65.9
All savings banks	147.3	96.5

*as of December 13, 1977 in billions
**(includes GNMA Security investments)

The overall investment policies of mutual savings banks will determine the future importance of mortgage loans relative to other investment opportunities. As with other institutional lenders, the following criteria, or a combination of them, will play the greatest part in such policy determination:

1. Yield—the return received on mortgage investments as opposed to return available through other investment media.
2. Liquidity—the need for a certain percentage of assets to be placed in investments readily convertible into cash in order to meet withdrawal demands or to pay scheduled dividends.
3. Safety—the security offered by mortgages as an investment compared to the relative security of other investments such as federal government securities.
4. Portfolio composition—the need to diversify investments in order to maximize

yields while providing for a secure investment. For example, an over-investment in mortgages may well cause problems in periods of high frequency of foreclosures.

5. Statutory requirements—the compliance with state laws that govern the type of investments and the amount of assets which can be placed in them.

Recent changes in banking laws, particularly in New York now allow savings banks to invest in land and to be joint venture participants. However, such actions are limited to a small percentage of assets, similar to the "basket" provisions of the insurance laws (a basket or leeway provision of regulatory laws allows a certain percentage of investments, otherwise unauthorized, to be made). Nevertheless, this new provision should step up income property lending by savings banks.

TYPES OF MORTGAGE INVESTMENTS AND OUT-OF-STATE LENDING

Prior to the passage of the National Housing Act of 1934, mutual savings bank mortgage portfolios consisted solely of conventional loans. After the National Housing Act of 1934, FHA insured loans began to creep into these mortgage portfolios. Even though FHA insured lending expanded mortgage investment opportunities, savings banks did not take full advantage of the program. Mortgage investments subsided during the early 1940s and then increased after World War II. During the late 1940s FHA insured loans and the new VA guaranteed loans (Servicemen's Readjustment Act of 1944) gained favor with savings banks. This favor rapidly increased with the passage of out-of-state mortgage lending authority, since that authorization was particularly slated toward FHA and VA lending.

Prior to 1950 (and the out-of-state lending laws) mutual savings banks were local or, at most, regional lenders. However, with the heavy concentration of savings banks and other large institutional lenders in the eastern and New England areas, those areas soon became capital-abundant. Thus with the housing boom of the post-war era a huge demand was created for capital beyond these areas. The out-of-state lending authority and the FHA and VA mortgage investment opportunities combined to change the status of savings banks from local to national lenders. The result is that over the past twenty-five years savings banks have become an increasingly dominant factor in the national mortgage market.

This national involvement by savings banks has been an important factor in bringing mortgage funds to the capital-deficient regions of the South, Southwest, and Mid-west and West. It is in these geographical areas that construction of housing over the last thirty years has rapidly expanded, producing a heavy demand for mortgage funds and an attractive investment situation for the excess funds held by eastern savings banks.

As mentioned, FHA and VA mortgage loans dominate out-of-state lending activities, even though conventional home loans and income property loans also are purchased out-of-state. This out-of-state policy reflects the facts that, in most savings banks states, statutes limit the volume of conventional loans which savings banks may maintain in their portfolios, and that legal requirements generally confine conventional lending to the state in which the savings bank is located. The increased emphasis on mortgage lending by savings banks, particularly in the FHA and VA area is best expressed by the fact that in 1946 savings banks were the smallest investors in VA loans, but by 1959 they were the largest investors in VA loans, holding nearly three times the volume of commercial banks and considerably more than the volume held by either life insurance companies or savings and loan associations. Today savings banks are still one of the largest investors in and holders of FHA and VA loans. Recently savings and loan associations have moved ahead of mutual savings banks as the largest holder of federally insured or guaranteed loans. According to figures released by the National Association of Mutual Savings Banks, these banks in 1977 held $26.1 billion of FHA/VA loans compared to $30.2 billion for savings and loan associations. Nevertheless, federally underwritten loans account for 30 percent of total savings bank mortgage holdings as compared to 10 percent for savings and loan associations and 11 percent for life companies. (See Chart 10-1.)

Recently, reduced investment opportunities in FHA/VA markets have stimulated a rise in conventional loan activity and a corresponding decrease in saving banks' share of FHA/VA mortgages. In 1977, federally underwritten loans accounted for only 15 percent of total savings bank mortgage acquisitions, down from 20 percent in 1976 and 40 percent in 1967. Factors such as the availability of private mortgage insurance have changed mutual savings bank lending activity and during the past few years conventional loans (both one-to-four family and income property) have dominated out-of-state loan purchases with FHA/VA loans being acquired primarily in the form of GNMA securities.

In making out-of-state mortgage loan investments, savings banks pursue two

CHART 10-1

Holdings of Federally-Underwritten Mortgage Debt by Main Types of Financial Institutions, 1953-1973

(In millions of dollars)

End of year	Total federally-underwritten			FHA				VA			
	All holders	Mutual savings banks	Savings bank holdings as per cent of total	Mutual savings banks	Commercial banks	Life insurance companies	Savings and loan associations	Mutual savings banks	Commercial banks	Life insurance companies	Savings and loan associations
1953	32,118	6,542	20.4	3,489	3,912	6,012	1,048	3,053	3,061	3,560	3,979
1954	36,190	8,062	22.3	3,800	4,106	6,116	1,170	4,262	3,350	4,643	4,709
1955	42,931	9,923	23.1	4,150	4,560	6,395	1,404	5,773	3,711	6,074	5,883
1956	47,843	11,548	24.1	4,409	4,803	6,627	1,486	7,139	3,902	7,304	6,643
1957	51,600	12,459	24.1	4,669	4,823	6,751	1,643	7,790	3,589	7,721	7,011
1958	55,100	13,862	25.2	5,501	5,476	7,443	2,206	8,361	3,335	7,433	7,077
1959	59,200	14,865	25.1	6,276	6,122	8,273	2,995	8,589	3,161	7,086	7,186
1960	62,300	16,060	25.8	7,074	5,851	9,032	3,524	8,986	2,859	6,901	7,222
1961	65,500	17,312	26.4	8,045	5,975	9,665	4,167	9,267	2,627	6,553	7,152
1962	69,400	19,025	27.4	9,238	6,520	10,176	4,476	9,787	2,654	6,395	7,010
1963	73,400	21,174	28.8	10,684	7,105	10,756	4,696	10,490	2,862	6,401	6,960
1964	77,200	23,408	30.3	12,287	7,315	11,484	4,894	11,121	2,742	6,403	6,683
1965	81,200	25,199	31.0	13,791	7,702	12,068	5,145	11,408	2,688	6,286	6,398
1966	84,100	25,971	30.9	14,500	7,544	12,351	5,269	11,471	2,599	6,201	6,157
1967	88,200	26,869	30.5	15,074	7,709	12,161	5,791	11,795	2,696	6,122	6,351
1968	92,800	27,602	29.7	15,569	7,926	11,961	6,658	12,033	2,708	5,954	7,012
1969	100,200	28,028	28.0	15,862	7,960	11,715	7,917	12,166	2,663	5,701	7,658
1970	109,200	28,095	25.7	16,087	7,919	11,419	10,200	12,008	2,589	5,394	8,500
1971	120,700	28,215	23.4	16,141	8,310	10,767	13,700	12,074	2,980	5,004	10,600
1972	131,000	28,635	21.9	16,013	8,495	10,000	15,400	12,622	3,203	4,700	13,500
1973 p	135,000	28,400	21.0	15,500	7,900	9,200	15,000	12,900	3,300	4,400	14,000

p preliminary
SOURCE: Board of Governors of the Federal Reserve System and National Association of Mutual Savings Banks.

methods, either individually or in combination. These methods are the *forward commitment and immediate delivery.*

The **forward commitment** technique is used to insure adequate investment opportunities in the form of mortgages for funds expected to be available. By this method commitments to purchase loans in blocks of usually $500,000 to $3,000,000 are made for delivery at a future date or dates as specified in the commitment. To use this method successfully a savings bank must be able to predict with fair certainty the volume of funds which it will have available for the future. Thus it is a method which favors the larger savings banks that have a relatively substantial amount of savings inflows.

The **immediate delivery** technique, meaning up to ninety days, eliminates the uncertainty of the future, mortgage delivery delays, commitment cancellations, and other problems associated with the commitment program. Because of the irregularity and unpredictability of savings deposit inflows, many of the smaller savings banks find it difficult to plan their mortgage acquisition programs more than a few months in advance and therefore favor this method of purchase. This arrangement, sometimes referred to as an "on the shelf" purchase, permits the acquisition of mortgages in accordance with current net gains in savings deposit inflows and mortgage loan repayments.

The immediate delivery technique is favored by the New England savings banks. Other savings banks, including those in the Middle Atlantic states, prefer the forward commitment. Operations in general are conducted on the basis of commitments, either forward or immediate, issued usually to mortgage companies which predominately originate FHA and VA loans for sale to savings banks and other institutional investors. Loans so purchased are serviced (primarily by collection of monthly installments and payment of hazard insurance and taxes) by the selling mortgage company. By maintaining a purchase and servicing relationship with mortgage companies, savings banks insure themselves of a continuing source of mortgage investments.

Out-of-state lending, therefore, has had an important and progressive effect upon mutual savings banking, their investment policies, and the mortgage market in general. The result of the changes brought about by out-of-state lending may be summarized into several categories:

1. The lending role of savings banks have been more effectively invested with a higher yield due to their ability to seek out areas of great demand.
3. Savings banks have made available substantial funds for FHA/VA lending.
4. A portion of savings bank assets have been attracted to capital-scarce regions from capital-abundant areas of the nation.

At the end of 1977, out-of-state mortgage holdings of savings banks exceeded $27.4 billion.

LENDING LIMITATIONS AND AUTHORITY

Mutual savings banks are state-chartered institutions and hence are regulated by the states in which they are located.

General lending limitations on various type loans are noted below:

1. One-to-four family, owner-occupied, conventional loans are made up to 95 percent of appraised value. During the mid-1970s, loan-to-value ratios on new home loans averaged around 70 percent, and on existing homes around 74.5 percent (see Chart 10-2). Individual loan amounts are generally limited to those set by FNMA, GNMA, FHA and VA. Maturities are usually twenty to thirty years or three-fourths of the remaining economic life of the property concerned, with the loan made on an amortized basis. Conventional single

family residential lending is usually limited to a savings bank's home state or surrounding states. However, no territorial lending limitations are imposed upon savings banks located in Maryland, Pennsylvania, Rhode Island, Delaware, Vermont and Washington.

2. *FHA and VA loans* are made according to the terms and rates established by the Federal Housing Administration and the Veterans Administration. No geographical or territorial limitations are imposed upon FHA and VA mortgage investments.

3. *Multifamily and income property loans* are made at 66-2/3 percent to 80 percent (generally 75 percent) of appraised value for terms of up to thirty years. Loans in this category usually are pursued only by the larger savings banks whose savings deposits are being generated at such a level that they must seek means of investing large amounts of money at one time.

4. *Asset limitations* are imposed upon mortgage investments in general to the extent that from 65 percent to 70 percent of assets is the average permissible limit for conventional loans. In some states, such as New York, FHA and VA loans are free from the asset ceiling while others only allow up to an additional 15 percent of assets to be put into FHA and VA loans.

Property Inspections and Appraisals are required on mortgage loans made by mutual savings banks. In many instances two or more persons appointed by the

CHART 10-2

Average Interest Rate and Other Terms on Conventional First Mortgage Loans on Single Family Homes Originated by Major Lenders, 1972 and 1973

Type of home purchased and institution	Contract interest rate (per cent)		Fees and charges (per cent)		Effective interest rate (per cent)		Maturity (years)		Loan to price ratio (per cent)	
	1972	1973	1972	1973	1972	1973	1972	1973	1972	1973
New home purchase										
All institutions	7.45	7.78	.88	1.11	7.60	7.95	27.2	26.3	76.8	77.3
Mutual savings banks	7.23	7.66	.18	.24	7.26	7.70	25.8	25.4	70.2	71.7
Commercial banks	7.30	7.77	.40	.63	7.37	7.88	24.6	22.7	68.9	70.9
Savings and loan associations	7.46	7.76	1.05	1.29	7.63	7.96	27.6	27.1	78.6	78.8
Mortgage companies	7.84	8.03	.90	1.50	7.99	8.26	28.5	29.0	82.5	84.7
Existing home purchase										
All institutions	7.38	7.86	.81	.94	7.51	8.01	25.7	23.2	76.0	75.2
Mutual savings banks	7.28	7.72	.19	.28	7.31	7.76	24.7	24.3	71.0	70.7
Commercial banks	7.24	7.81	.41	.50	7.31	7.89	22.8	19.7	69.2	69.6
Savings and loan associations	7.44	7.89	1.02	1.23	7.60	8.09	26.2	24.3	78.6	77.6
Mortgage companies	n.a.	8.19	n.a.	1.58	n.a.	8.44	n.a.	29.0	n.a.	88.3

n.a. - not available

NOTE   Data are unweighted averages of monthly loan terms approved during 1972 and 1973 by the four major types of mortgage lenders. Coverage is confined to loans originated directly and excludes loans acquired through correspondents. Fees and charges refer to discounts and initial payments that provide income to the lender and are expressed as per cent of the principal amount of the mortgage. Effective interest rate includes, in addition to the contract interest rate, fees and charges amortized over a ten year period. Loan to price ratio is the amount of mortgage credit extended as per cent of the purchase price of the home.
SOURCE   Federal Home Loan Bank Board and National Association of Mutual Savings Banks

bank examine the real estate security and certify in writing that in their best judgment the security is adequate for investment.

Leasehold and construction loans are permissible investments for savings banks within the limitations established by state laws. In New York, for example, leasehold loans are allowable when the initial lease term is for at least twenty-one years and the leasehold mortgage provides for at least annual amortization of an amount sufficient to pay off the loan within a period of time equal to four-fifths of the unexpired term of the lease measured from mortgage execution. Massachusetts savings banks may make construction loans for any type of real estate improvements for which they are authorized to make a permanent loan. Amortization on such construction loans must commence within one year from the making of the loan.

TAX INCENTIVES

Residential lending activities of mutual savings banks are encouraged by the federal government through income tax legislation which provides income tax credit to those mutual savings banks investing a large (75 to 80 percent) percentage of their assets in residential real estate.

DEPOSIT LIMITS

One factor affecting the growth of savings deposits in some savings bank states, and thus indirectly affecting the amount of funds available for mortgage lending, is the imposition of deposit limitations. Illustrating this fact, the following maximums are placed on amounts which may be deposited in any one account:

State	Individual account Maximum Deposit
Massachusetts	$ 90,000
Connecticut	$150,000
New Jersey	$150,000

Thirteen states have no limitations; six do. Those with limitations, however, are among the states of largest savings bank asset concentration.

SAVINGS BANK ORGANIZATIONS

The savings banks of the largest savings bank states, New York and Massachusetts, have organized member-owned companies to assist in the acquisition and direct servicing of mortgage loans and to perform other real estate and mortgage loan advisory services. The New York company is called Institutional Securities Corporation, the other is the Massachusetts Purchasing Group.

Both states also have savings bank owned organizations to provide secondary liquidity to member institutions, such as the FHLBB does for savings and loan institutions. The two organizations are the Mutual Savings Central Fund, Inc. of Massachusetts and the Savings Bank Trust Company of New York. The former also provides account insurance similar to the FSLIC and FDIC.

LARGEST SAVINGS BANKS

Chart 10-3 is a reprint of a listing reflecting the nation's 100 largest mutual savings banks and the deposits and assets of each. The 100 largest of these banks have total deposits of almost $100 billion as compared to $134 billion for all mutual savings banks.

COMMERCIAL BANKS

Unlike mutual savings banks and savings and loan associations, commercial banks are not mutual in character, but are stock companies. Furthermore, they are relative newcomers into the savings and real estate lending areas.

There are two categories into which commercial banks can be classified. *National* banks are those chartered and supervised by the Comptroller of the Currency. They must use the word "national" in their title and are deemed "instrumentalities" of the federal government. *State banks* receive their charters

CHART 10-3

One Hundred Largest Mutual Savings Banks; Ranked by Deposits, December 31, 1977

Bank	Deposits (in thousands of dollars)	Bank	Deposits (in thousands of dollars)
Bowery Savings Bank, New York	$3,432,487	Syracuse Savings Bank, N.Y.	466,971
Dime Savings Bank of New York	3,042,352	Hamburgh Savings Bank, Brooklyn	466,029
Philadelphia Saving Fund Society, Pa.	3,024,831	Wilmington Savings Fund Society, Del.	449,447
New York Bank for Savings, New York	2,614,158	Roosevelt Savings Bank, Brooklyn	424,668
Emigrant Savings Bank, New York	1,912,731	New Haven Savings Bank, Conn.	417,917
Dollar Savings Bank, New York	1,861,427	Springfield Institution for Savings, Mass.	410,780
Greenwich Savings Bank, New York	1,604,284	Provident Savings Bank, Baltimore, Md.	405,132
Williamsburg Savings Bank, Brooklyn	1,535,621	American Savings Bank, New York	380,634
Lincoln Savings Bank, Brooklyn	1,482,528	United States Savings Bank, Newark	379,512
Buffalo Savings Bank, N.Y.	1,363,581	Provident Savings Bank, Jersey City	378,452
Seamen's Bank for Savings, New York	1,333,573	Connecticut Savings Bank, New Haven	375,742
Dry Dock Savings Bank, New York	1,272,168	Hudson City Savings Bank, Jersey City	374,158
Howard Savings Bank, Newark	1,263,182	North Side Savings Bank, New York	366,362
Greater New York Savings Bank, Brooklyn	1,188,931	Dime Savings Bank of Williamsburgh,	
Washington Mutual Savings Bank, Seattle	1,164,461	Brooklyn	362,602
Jamaica Savings Bank, New York	1,129,082	Richmond Hill Savings Bank, New York	360,274
Western Saving Fund Society, Philadelphia	1,121,359	Newton Savings Bank, Mass.	349,539
Union Dime Savings Bank, New York	1,079,724	The Banking Center, Waterbury, Conn.	348,068
Franklin Savings Bank, New York	1,066,537	Roslyn Savings Bank, N.Y.	338,933
East River Savings Bank, New York	1,059,014	Home Savings Bank, Boston	333,211
Erie County Savings Bank, Buffalo	1,038,977	Savings Bank of Utica, N.Y.	329,604
Manhattan Savings Bank, New York	989,159	Fidelity Mutual Savings Bank, Spokane,	
Society for Savings, Hartford	916,382	Wash.	329,223
People's Savings Bank — Bridgeport, Conn.	904,026	Fulton Savings Bank Kings County,	
Brooklyn Savings Bank, New York	861,331	Brooklyn	326,330
Anchor Savings Bank, Brooklyn	846,087	Morris County Savings Bank, Morristown,	
Provident Institution for Savings, Boston	793,412	N.J.	325,698
Farmers and Mechanics Savings Bank,		Citizens Savings Bank, Providence, R.I.	324,258
Minneapolis	784,451	Eastchester Savings Bank, Mount Vernon,	
East New York Savings Bank, Brooklyn	779,525	N.Y.	316,170
Long Island Savings Bank, New York	755,214	Monroe Savings Bank, Rochester, N.Y.	306,607
Boston Five Cents Savings Bank, Mass.	753,249	Binghamton Savings Bank, N.Y.	300,618
Metropolitan Savings Bank, Brooklyn	735,472	Worcester County Institution for Savings,	
Community Savings Bank, Rochester, N.Y.	703,658	Mass.	299,230
Central Savings Bank, New York	701,442	Yonkers Savings Bank, N.Y.	295,687
Green Point Savings Bank, Brooklyn	672,567	Peoples Savings Bank, Yonkers, N.Y.	285,642
United Mutual Savings Bank, New York	660,174	Union Warren Savings Bank, Boston	278,363
Beneficial Mutual Savings Bank, Philadelphia	657,286	Poughkeepsie Savings Bank, N.Y.	275,212
Ridgewood Savings Bank, New York	647,456	Staten Island Savings Bank, Stapleton, N.Y.	274,638
Dollar Savings Bank, Pittsburgh	644,400	Bloomfield Savings Bank, N.J.	266,111
Eastern Savings Bank, New York	643,827	Peoples Savings Bank, Worcester, Mass.	265,422
Harlem Savings Bank, New York	636,032	Cambridge Savings Bank, Mass.	264,347
Old Stone Savings Bank, Providence, R.I.	620,425	Community Savings Bank, Holyoke, Mass.	264,056
Charlestown Savings Bank, Boston	606,175	Amoskeag Savings Bank, Manchester, N.H.	250,580
Germantown Savings Bank, Philadelphia	598,320	Mechanics and Farmers Savings Bank,	
South Brooklyn Savings Bank, Brooklyn	588,852	Bridgeport	247,601
Prudential Savings Bank, New York	566,746	South Boston Savings Bank, Mass.	247,240
Rochester Savings Bank, N.Y.	537,670	Troy Savings Bank, N.Y.	239,685
Schenectady Savings Bank, N.Y.	533,502	Mechanics Savings Bank, Hartford, Conn.	233,580
Onondaga Savings Bank, Syracuse	526,579	Home Savings Bank, White Plains, N.Y.	233,330
V'estern New York Savings Bank, Buffalo	523,770	Maine Savings Bank, Portland	230,967
Empire Savings Bank, New York	516,031	Dorchester Savings Bank, Boston	227,013
Albany Savings Bank, N.Y.	515,368		
Queens County Savings Bank, Flushing, N.Y.	513,298	Total deposits, one hundred largest	$71,939,737
Savings Bank of Baltimore, Md.	501,488		
Suffolk Franklin Savings Bank, Boston	489,712	Total deposits, all mutual savings banks	$96,495,859

SOURCE National Association of Mutual Savings Banks

from the state in which they are located. Supervision of state banks is performed by the state banking department or similar state agency.

Until the early 1920s, national banks were not permitted to directly lend on real estate security, but could accept a mortgage as additional security for loans made against another form or forms of collateral. State chartered banks, however, had the power to make real estate mortgage loans, and for the most part freely exercised that power.

The Federal Reserve Act of 1913 contained provisions for mortgage lending by national banks; subsequent amendments to that legislation have liberalized the mortgage lending ability of these banks.

Demand for mortgage funds, a desire to keep pace with state chartered banks and other competition, and the call to serve the real estate financing needs of their local communities all combined to bring commercial banks strongly into the real estate finance field.

Commercial bank deposits are either *demand* or *time* deposits. Checking accounts are the most popular form of demand deposits and savings accounts the most familiar type of time deposits. By banking regulations only the time deposits of national banks are allowed to be used for real estate finance. However, it was after the turn of this century when national banks were authorized to accept time savings deposits.

FUNDS FOR MORTGAGE LOANS

A large portion of time deposits of commercial banks are represented by *certificates of deposit.* They come in many denominations and have varying maturities. The small denomination, non-negotiable certificates usually carry higher interest rates than regular savings accounts. These certificates can usually be redeemed before maturity without interest. The negotiable certificates are made in large denominations and, while usually irredeemable, can be readily negotiated. Certainly the creation of the certificate of deposit in the early 1960s gave rise to increased time deposits in commercial banks and correspondingly made more funds available for investment in real estate mortgages.

Bank savings accounts are the other source of funds for mortgage investments. However, federal regulations have allowed savings and loan associations to pay 0.25 of 1 percent more for savings deposits in the form of interest rates than is permitted for commercial banks. Hence, commercial banks do not attract anywhere near the volume of savings that flows to savings and loan associations.

An auxiliary source of mortgage funds for most commercial banks emanates from their trust operations. Individuals and estates with large financial holdings and available cash usually appoint a commercial bank as trustee to manage and invest their funds. Bank trust departments must act in accordance with the trustors' wishes and make investments as directed. Many of these directed investments are in real estate mortgages. Where no directions are given, it is up to the trust officer to select the best investment for the trust corpus (funds in the trust); in such cases mortgages compete with stocks, bonds, and other forms of investment for trust funds.

LENDING POLICIES

The majority of banks prefer to invest in short-term loans to businesses and individual consumers, and therefore lend on long-term mortgages only as a service to regular customers. This is not the case with all banks, since many of the larger ones actively compete for real estate lending opportunities. But lending preferences and the great pressure to maintain liquidity, especially with national banks, keep commercial banks from investing any great portion of their assets in long-term mortgage loans. In fact, only about one-eighth of the total assets and one-half of the time deposits of commercial banks find their way into mortgage loans.

Because of their attitude toward long-term lending, banks tend to be the most conservative of institutional lenders, particularly in regard to loan-to-value ratios and maturity dates (recent years averages have been 69 percent and twenty-two years respectively). In prior years Federal Reserve-dictated conventional loan terms were less favorable than those for most institutions, particularly savings and loans, and thereby enhanced commercial banks' conservative mortgage-lending attitudes. Lately, liberalization of lending regulations has been promulgated in order to pump more mortgage money into a sagging mortgage market. However, only time will tell whether or not recent liberalization will be much of an impetus to commercial banks to step up mortgage lending. Government pressures toward meeting the mortgage fund demand have caused an upturn in mortgage lending by commercial banks, at least during the 1970s. When the mortgage market settles down, commercial banks will most likely return to their practice of supporting their communities' short-term loan needs.

However, only time will tell whether or not recent liberalization will be much of an impetus to commercial banks to step up mortgage lending. Government pressures toward meeting the mortgage fund demand have caused an upturn in mortgage lending by commercial banks, at least during the first part of the 1970s. When the mortgage market settles down, commercial banks will most likely return to their practice of supporting their communities' short-term loan needs.

Mortgage loan policies of national banks are further dictated by a limitation on real estate financing. They cannot lend more than the greater of 70 percent of time deposit or 100 percent of invested capital against real estate security.

Some of the more important lending regulations for national banks are as follows:

1. All mortgage loans must generally be secured by a mortgage or a deed of trust cons'ituting a first lien on the property secured. It is interesting to note that state banks such as those chartered in New York are more liberally regulated. For example, New York banks can make mortgage loans without regard to kind of lien, provided certain appraisal limits are adhered to. Since 1974 commercial banks are allowed to invest a small portion of their assets in real estate mortgage without a first lien.

2. Straight term conventional loans may be made for up to 50 percent of appraised property value with five year maximum maturity.

3. Mortgage loans of up to 95 percent of appraised property value are permissible if the term does not exceed thirty years, the loan is fully amortized within the term, and private mortgage insurance is obtained on all conventional loans of over 80 percent loan to value.

4. Construction loans on industrial and income producing properties with up to thirty-six months maturities may be made by national banks provided a

binding and valid permanent loan takeout commitment is issued by a financially responsible lender. This commitment will insure payoff of the bank's' loan upon completion of all building in compliance with the permanent lender's commitment.

   a. Loans for financing the construction of residential or farm building may be made with up to thirty-six month maturities without existing permanent loan takeout commitments.

   b. The aggregate amount of all construction loans so made cannot exceed 100 percent of the bank's capital and surplus.

5. Land loans up to 66 2/3 percent of value or up to 75 percent on land plus off site improvements. Investment by banks in land loans, is, however, very limited.

6. First lien leasehold mortgage loans are permissible provided the remaining lease term extends for at least ten years beyond the maturity date of the mortgage.

7. FHA insured, VA guaranteed loans and any loans fully guaranteed or insured by a state or state authority may be made in accordance with the regulations of these government agencies then prevailing. VA loans are not included in the 70 percent of time deposit—100 percent of invested capital limitations, but FHA and other insured or guaranteed loans are.

LENDING OPERATIONS

Within the attitude and lending policy of commercial banks, three major lending operations are performed which pump needed funds into the mortgage market. These three operations are not the only ways in which commercial banks participate in the mortgage market, but are the most significant. Commercial banks do make a large dollar volume of home mortgages for their own account, although the percentage of total assets invested in mortgage loans is very low. The three important commercial bank lending operations are as follows:

1. The origination of mortgage loans, primarily single family residential ones, for sale to other investors with servicing retained. This method provides banks with the necessary liquidity while maintaining the goodwill of its customers. The secondary mortgage market for the purchase of mortgage loans by the Federal National Mortgage Association and the Federal Home Loan Mortgage Corporation is of great assistance to commercial banking's mortgage loan origination and sale operations.

2. The making of construction loans. Commercial banks engage in much more construction-loan activity than savings and loan associations, primarily because by law they can lend on more liberal terms. In addition, savings and loan associations are predominantly single family residential construction loan lenders, while commercial banks, in particular the larger ones, are income and industrial property construction lenders. As previously stated, these loans when made on the basis of a firm takeout are not classified as real estate loans, thereby allowing more flexibility in commercial bank lending policies. Without a doubt, commercial banks are the major sources of construction funds for commercial and industrial development in the United States. In fact, the combination of commercial banks and life insurance companies on an interim-permanent loan basis,

accounts for over 60 percent of the commercial and industrial property building loans in North America.

3. Commercial banks provide a tremendous volume of "warehousing" loans to mortgage banking companies, and bank lines to real estate investment trusts thereby indirectly affecting the availability of funds to the mortgage market. Warehousing loan funds are used by mortgage companies to originate loans for resale to institutional and other investors. Since an average of sixty days may elapse between loan origination and sale, a great amount of capital is needed for a volume operation. Thus, mortgage companies borrow from commercial banks on the security of originated but not yet sold loans. Bank line funds are borrowed by real estate investment trust to use in their day to day lending activities. These funds are normally borrowed on the REITs credit without specific collateral. Such leverage of assets is beneficial to the REITs but has proven risky to the commercial banks.

COMMUNITY FACTORS

It must be remembered that the underlying factor in a commercial bank's lending program is a strong concern for the needs of its depositors and, in a greater sense, the welfare of the local community. Hence, if the mortgage needs of its depositors and the community are not being met by other local financial institutions, then the commercial banks will step up their mortgage lending to meet that need. But, when mortgage funds are readily available elsewhere, commercial banks will, as a rule, funnel their assets into short-term loans.

VARIABLE INTEREST RATE MORTGAGES

Lately, in the field of real estate finance there has been much discussion concerning variable interest rates for single family mortgages. These mortgages would contain a provision for the rate of interest to fluctuate with a cost of money indicator such as the prime rate. With the current ups and downs of interest rates and the accompanying availability of mortgage funds, it is anticipated that the variable interest rate concept will provide a continuity in the supply of mortgage funds and will bring about a stabilization of interest rates.

One major factor which has influenced commercial banks' single family real estate lending activities is their favoring of short-term loans over long-term ones. Variable interest rate mortgages may change this attitude at least to the extent of the risks involved in long-term loans at fixed interest rates. Variable interest rate mortgages will also enable commercial banks to better serve their communities by providing mortgage loans at the best possible current rate of interest.

Only a few commercial banks have used variable interest rate mortgages, but many banks are considering them. As an example, one midwestern bank has used a variable interest rate mortgage program which offers borrowers an initial rate of 0.25 percent below the current rate for fixed interest rate mortgages. Semiannually the interest rate is adjusted to 1.5 percent over the then existing prime rate. The mortgages are made at up to 75 percent of property value and are amortized over twenty years. Another method is to establish a maximum fixed rate of interest, but to lower the rate in accordance with a drop in the prime rate or other cost of money indicator. Any increase in the prime rate or cost of money after a lowering of the interest rate would result in an increase in the rate up to the fixed maximum.

ASSETS

Today's assets of commercial banks approximate $1300 billion. Therefore, an increase of just 1 percent in the assets-to-mortgage investment ratio will put an additional $13 billion into the mortgage market. For this reason the role of commercial banks in real estate financing must be studied and watched. The 100 largest banks in the United States ranked according to assets are shown in Chart 10-4. A cursory review of the chart will show that the nation's largest commercial banks measured by assets are found predominantly in California and New York.

RECENT TRENDS

Recently proposed legislation and the Hunt Commission Report (the report in late 1972 by the Presidential Commission on Financial Structure and Regulation) both point toward laws that in the near future will reshape the structure of U.S. financial institutions, particularly banks, to achieve a freer and more competitive market for all financial institutions. Such legislation or changes, if and when made, could well do away with the difference between mutual savings banks and commercial banks by allowing the former wider checking account authority and the latter parity savings account authority. In addition the use of tax credits as an inducement to mortgage lending may well become more widespread. It is also conceivable that future money shortages will cause congress to legislate credit allocation, requiring financial institutions to allocate their funds to specific types of loans and borrowers. In any event mortgage lending appears to be one of the areas that will benefit greatly from the changes and new directions that are proposed.

QUESTIONS FOR THOUGHT AND DISCUSSION

1. Compare mutual savings banks and savings and loan associations with regard to:
   a. Reason for creation,
   b. Organization, and
   c. Investment philosophy.
2. Discuss the impact of out-of-state lending upon mutual savings banking and the availability of mortgage funds.
3. What are forward and immediate delivery commitments and what factors determine the use of each?
4. a. Give your reasons for the imposition of asset and territorial limitations on conventional mortgage loans by mutual savings banks.
   b. Why should FHA and VA loans be treated differently?
   c. What is loan servicing and why is it important?
5. Contrast mutual savings banks and commercial banks as to purpose and lending philosophy.
6. List the three major lending operations of commercial banks and explain the significance of each.

CHART 10-4

The 100 Largest Commercial Banks in U.S.

In Order of Deposits June 30, 1974, Compared with June 30, 1973, and Dec. 31, 1973

Compiled and Copyright by the **American Banker** in Co-operation with Polk's Bank Directory

Rank 6/30/74		June 30, 1974 Deposits (a)	June 30, 1973 Deposits (a)	Rank and Gain from 6/30/73	Dec. 31, 1973 Deposits (a)	Rank and Gain from 12/31/73
1	Bank of America NT&SA, San Francisco	$47,377,582,000	$36,861,723,000	1	$41,844,380,000	1
2	First National City Bank, New York	41,438,901,000	29,551,669,000	2	34,950,857,000	2
3	Chase Manhattan Bank NA, New York	35,156,257,552	26,175,776,664	3	29,818,496,976	3
4	Manufacturers Hanover Trust, New York	21,739,868,322	15,072,333,225	4	16,977,018,954	4
5	Morgan Guaranty Trust Co., New York	18,309,055,276	13,140,262,197	5	15,367,277,651	5
6	Bankers Trust Co., New York	17,215,410,730	12,212,133,000	7 + 1	14,022,424,000	7 + 1
7	Chemical Bank, New York	16,523,626,000	12,868,844,000	6	14,225,653,633	6
8	First National Bank, Chicago	14,419,643,751	10,725,514,219	10 + 2	12,083,748,860	9 + 1
9	Continental Illinois NB&T Co., Chicago	13,585,714,941	11,203,108,131	9	12,366,800,000	8
10	Security Pacific Nat'l Bk., Los Angeles	12,571,391,873	11,304,686,261	8	11,403,764,491	10
11	Wells Fargo Bank NA, San Francisco	8,884,276,270	8,317,071,000	11	9,034,328,215	11
12	Irving Trust Co., New York	8,499,164,193	6,637,579,751	12	6,970,013,624	14 + 2
13	Crocker National Bank, San Francisco	8,327,169,615	6,532,087,124	14 + 1	8,016,015,774	12
14	United California Bank, Los Angeles	7,523,303,479	6,386,378,836	15 + 1	6,855,024,724	15 + 1
15	Marine Midland Bank—New York	7,473,771,000	5,871,799,000	16 + 1	6,655,445,000	16 + 1
16	Mellon Bank NA, Pittsburgh	7,430,681,000	6,553,202,000	13	7,350,839,000	13
17	First National Bank, Boston	7,122,379,749	5,221,311,400	18 + 1	6,103,307,600	17
18	National Bank of Detroit	6,298,853,119	5,397,184,003	17	5,423,351,722	18
19	First Pennsylvania Bank NA, Philadelphia	3,894,483,000	3,428,869,000	19	3,926,227,000	19
20	Union Bank, Los Angeles	3,312,176,000	2,930,064,000	22 + 2	3,615,915,000	21 + 1
21	Northern Trust Co., Chicago	3,263,691,274	2,265,367,774	32 + 11	2,766,052,072	29 + 8
22	Philadelphia National Bank	3,242,259,770	2,560,488,799	25 + 3	2,857,514,095	28 + 6
23	Harris Trust & Savings Bank, Chicago	3,141,234,348	2,959,843,974	21	2,981,704,746	23
24	Seattle-First National Bank	3,135,621,000	2,625,612,048	23	2,919,718,631	26 + 2
25	First National Bank, Dallas	3,088,656,525	2,441,369,000	29 + 4	3,094,460,000	22
26	Republic National Bank, Dallas	3,087,097,425	2,596,078,738	24	2,968,647,762	24
27	Cleveland Trust Co.	2,812,194,679	2,512,604,715	27	2,872,057,544	27
28	Girard Bank, Philadelphia	2,811,046,000	2,470,295,107	28	2,743,812,000	30 + 2
29	North Carolina National Bank, Charlotte	2,785,425,907	2,516,535,691	26	2,960,917,900	25
30	Wachovia B&T NA, Winston-Salem, N. C.	2,634,962,483	2,400,145,457	30	2,729,942,748	31 + 1
31	National Bank of No. America, New York	2,430,987,860	2,256,196,983	33 + 2	2,484,804,203	32 + 1
32	Detroit Bank & Trust Co.	2,410,795,917	2,293,842,031	31	2,340,716,127	36 + 4
33	Manufacturers National Bank, Detroit	2,395,395,000	2,207,487,000	35 + 2	2,354,731,000	35 + 2
34	Bank of California NA, San Francisco	2,373,078,000	2,108,302,000	37 + 3	2,398,328,000	33
35	Valley National Bank, Phoenix, Ariz.	2,342,891,143	2,249,002,538	34	2,362,653,586	34
36	First Wisconsin National Bank, Milwaukee	2,215,924,160	1,853,694,836	40 + 4	1,992,934,982	42 + 6
37	Citizens & Southern NB, Atlanta, Ga.	2,126,345,933	2,152,400,039	36	1,988,890,612	43 + 6
38	First City National Bank, Houston, Tex.	2,097,710,150	1,801,824,281	42 + 4	2,009,943,556	41 + 3
39	Fidelity Bank, Philadelphia	2,092,716,050	1,847,530,579	41 + 2	2,103,992,490	38
40	First National Bank of Oregon, Portland	2,088,343,193	2,106,061,575	38	2,230,742,928	37
41	Bank of New York	2,085,666,248	1,690,926,691	45 + 4	1,952,971,587	44 + 3
42	Franklin National Bank, New York	2,085,336,059	3,408,244,319	20	3,732,241,332	20
43	United States NB of Oregon, Portland	2,052,913,345	1,942,619,259	39	2,066,925,483	40
44	Pittsburgh National Bank	2,046,467,989	1,756,142,095	43	2,075,235,915	39
45	National Bank of Commerce, Seattle	1,978,312,283	1,687,580,297	46 + 1	1,935,740,667	45
46	Marine Midl'd Bk.—West'n, Buffalo, N. Y.	1,879,618,382	1,743,350,275	44	1,851,965,484	46
47	Texas Commerce Bank NA, Houston	1,855,242,096	1,380,982,915	50 + 3	1,756,189,979	47
48	First National Bank of Arizona, Phoenix	1,544,457,402	1,492,758,065	48	1,519,097,687	50 + 2
49	National City Bank, Cleveland	1,522,679,000	1,411,005,000	49	1,755,157,662	48
50	Maryland National Bank, Baltimore	1,499,379,000	1,326,090,555	54 + 4	1,347,991,501	61 + 11
51	First Union NB of No. Car., Charlotte	1,492,724,759	1,311,921,039	57 + 6	1,498,019,138	52 + 1
52	Equibank NA, Pittsburgh	1,484,364,620	1,238,380,581	61 + 9	1,394,392,680	57 + 5
53	Industrial NB of Rhode Island, Providence	1,455,418,000	1,346,712,000	52	1,452,004,000	55 + 2
54	Central National Bank, Cleveland	1,443,750,885	1,317,226,861	55 + 1	1,348,090,079	60 + 6
55	Security National Bank, Hempstead, N. Y.	1,431,956,000	1,595,517,000	47	1,496,522,000	53
56	Hartford National Bank & Trust Co., Conn.	1,418,768,000	1,337,482,000	53	1,523,816,622	49
57	Indiana National Bank, Indianapolis	1,414,496,202	1,167,712,317	63 + 6	1,440,085,850	56
58	American Fletcher NB&T Co., Ind'polis	1,406,092,877	1,315,927,425	56	1,474,754,859	54
59	Bank of Tokyo Trust Co., New York	1,398,633,732	967,016,341	78 + 19	1,256,125,157	64 + 5
60	Virginia National Bank, Norfolk	1,394,027,644	1,248,460,421	59	1,366,969,354	58
61	Connecticut Bank & Trust Co., Hartford	1,393,193,821	1,356,173,200	51	1,504,570,418	51
62	First National Bank, Atlanta, Ga.	1,376,006,247	1,039,124,008	71 + 9	1,288,659,568	62
63	First National Bank, Miami, Fla.	1,302,065,589	1,019,125,196	74 + 11	1,200,714,154	69 + 6
64	Michigan National Bank, Lansing	1,281,073,850	1,294,085,855	58	1,257,084,712	63
65	Provident National Bank, Philadelphia	1,245,434,733	1,128,242,993	66 + 1	1,353,148,826	59
66	Trust Co. of Georgia, Atlanta	1,216,290,000	1,142,767,897	64	1,229,525,976	67 + 1
67	Riggs National Bank, Washington, D. C.	1,209,898,892	1,077,285,258	68 + 1	1,194,974,277	70 + 3
68	Union Commerce Bank, Cleveland	1,203,219,550	1,023,229,555	73 + 5	1,112,278,655	78 + 10
69	Manuf. & Traders Trust Co., Buffalo, N. Y.	1,185,361,037	1,106,763,648	67	1,137,696,558	75 + 6
70	Mercantile Trust Co. NA, St. Louis, Mo.	1,184,341,262	917,440,529	84 + 14	1,159,103,859	74 + 4
71	National Shawmut Bank, Boston	1,173,681,000	1,171,151,000	62	1,240,306,075	65
72	First National Bank, St. Louis, Mo.	1,163,296,514	791,890,201	101 + 29	1,130,608,885	77 + 5
73	First National Bank, Minneapolis, Minn.	1,141,860,752	1,011,452,432	75 + 2	1,165,314,351	72
74	Northwestern National Bank, Minneapolis	1,140,811,732	1,043,783,294	70	1,225,843,867	68
75	American National B&T Co., Chicago	1,108,567,739	1,242,595,741	60	1,230,419,746	66
76	First Western B&T Co., Los Angeles	1,104,056,875	1,138,666,000	65	1,132,561,155	76

Rank 6/30/74		June 30, 1974 Deposits (a)	June 30, 1973 Deposits (a)	Rank and Gain from 6/30/73	Dec. 31, 1973 Deposits (a)	Rank and Gain from 12/31/73
77	State Street Bank & Trust Co., Boston	1,094,815,161	1,037,115,941	72	1,161,477,912	73
78	First National Bank, St. Paul, Minn.	1,054,989,554	833,125,000	94 + 16	978,365,799	86 + 8
79	Lincoln First Bank, Rochester, N. Y.	1,030,651,456	950,013,727	79	1,014,175,725	84 + 5
80	New England Merchants NB, Boston	1,013,367,329	944,239,632	81 + 1	1,039,209,351	80
81	First & Merchants NB, Richmond, Va.	987,872,714	871,631,083	88 + 7	926,150,451	93 + 12
82	First National State Bank of N. J., Newark	983,074,000	943,036,168	82	1,077,120,846	79
83	Bank of Hawaii, Honolulu	979,391,516	909,173,634	85 + 2	920,258,950	94 + 11
84	Society National Bank, Cleveland	978,481,105	842,857,054	92 + 8	957,884,070	88 + 4
85	County Trust Co., White Plains, N. Y.	976,566,126	972,200,945	77	1,017,232,927	83
86	First-Citizens B&T Co., Raleigh, N. C.	970,262,053	858,990,393	90 + 4	1,009,167,721	85
87	First National Bank, Memphis, Tenn.	965,769,173	1,059,957,432	69	1,170,953,145	71
88	Ohio National Bank, Columbus	958,315,639	945,989,838	80	1,024,173,322	82
89	Nat'l Commercial B&T Co., Albany, N. Y.	947,335,827	798,829,314	100 + 11	796,159,390	112 + 23
90	American Sec'y & Tr., Washington, D. C.	935,940,447	877,004,967	87	955,805,667	90
91	Continental Bank, Norristown, Pa.	926,058,575	769,249,422	106 + 15	933,975,502	92 + 1
92	First American Nat'l Bk., Nashville, Tenn.	916,406,778	785,799,483	103 + 11	917,082,666	95 + 3
93	Equitable Trust Co., Baltimore, Md.	915,390,975	846,177,503	91	881,131,468	98 + 5
94	Peoples Trust of New Jersey, Hackensack	913,290,952	906,713,000	86	957,268,000	89
95	Union Planters Nat'l Bk., Memphis, Tenn.	894,954,294	973,573,418	76	1,034,340,235	81
96	First National Bank, Birmingham, Ala.	892,336,473	807,272,826	97 + 1	881,903,995	97 + 1
97	American Bank & Trust Co., Reading, Pa.	888,581,880	745,186,000	111 + 14	836,016,000	105 + 8
98	Michigan National Bank of Detroit	881,476,024	823,273,680	96	882,920,604	96
99	Northwestern Bk, North Wilkesboro, N. C.	877,444,048	790,829,134	102 + 3	880,468,950	99
100	Bank of the Commonwealth, Detroit	875,083,560	859,736,655	89	877,925,873	100

7. a. What reasons can you give for laws limiting commercial banks' mortgage lending to a percentage of time deposits?

b. Why not 50 percent of combined time and demand deposits?

8. Mexico's central bank requires that 30 percent of the assets of Mexican commercial banks be invested in loans for housing low to moderate income groups. Do you feel that the Federal Reserve Board should require a similar regulation for commercial banks in this country? Why or why not?

11

LIFE INSURANCE COMPANIES

Historically life insurance companies have played a prominent role in the mortgage market, but the degree of their importance has changed in recent years due to (1) the great competition from savings and loan associations, particularly with respect to single family home loans and (2) the higher returns available on alternative investment.

BACKGROUND

Life insurance companies were not organized primarily for the purpose of financing homes. Therefore, they have no basic commitment to mortgage investments. Principally their investment pattern is based on *need* and *return*.

As to need, in recent years mortgage investments have been favored as an efficient means of disposing of large amounts of cash and as a solution to the tremendous investment problems facing life companies. Premium income from policies in force is quite steady and not as susceptible to fluctuation as savings deposit inflows. Therefore, life companies have a continuing investment requirement and must always be seeking the best and fastest means of putting their premium income to work. Chart 11-1 gives a very clear picture of this problem. In 1977, life companies had over $72.6 billion in premium income to invest.

Mortgage investments must compete with all other investments for life insurance company funds. When mortgages yield more than corporate and government bonds and stock investments, they are favored for investment. But a lessening yield on mortgages in relation to stocks and bonds can cause a reversal of the flow of premium income into mortgage investments.

Chart 11-2 shows the distribution of assets of life companies and reflects both the diversity of investment and favoring of bond-type investments over mortgages.

159

CHART 11-1

Growth of Life Insurance in United States

Including Canadian Companies operating in U. S.; figures for Written, In Force, Assets before 1928 are percentage approximations. Life premiums include ordinary, industrial, group, annuities, disability, double indemnity, dividends and surrender values applied. Prior to 1932 they are based on total premiums and total insurance of all companies licensed in Michigan, pro rated to our figure of total insurance.

In Millions

Dec. 31st.	Total Premium Income*	Life Insurance Written†	Life Insurance in Force.	Admitted Assets.
1880	$53	$269	$1,642	$479
1890	184	1,086	4,212	815
1900	338	2,037	8,904	1,842
1910	621	2,821	17,061	4,098
1920	1,537	11,149	43,976	7,740
1923	1,987	13,316	59,081	9,998
1924	2,231	14,557	66,336	10,991
1925	2,494	17,071	74,562	12,200
1926	2,742	18,161	82,836	13,683
1927	2,732	18,905	90,510	15,218
1928	3,330	20,746	99,283	16,947
1929	3,233	21,078	108,081	18,610
1930	3,776	21,689	114,375	20,234
1931	3,582	18,992	115,064	21,569
1932	3,741	15,914	109,073	22,155
1933	3,549	15,151	103,228	22,172
1934	3,747	15,716	104,639	23,319
1935	3,890	15,439	106,619	24,842
1936	3,883	16,172	111,107	26,642
1937	3,943	17,075	115,546	27,950
1938	4,173	14,765	118,133	29,579
1939	4,010	14,751	120,460	31,182
1940	4,104	14,719	123,692	32,689
1941	4,306	17,980	131,338	34,769
1942	4,337	18,457	137,447	37,082
1943	4,571	21,188	147,654	40,081
1944	5,040	21,742	157,392	43,626
1945	5,430	21,910	164,134	47,561
1946	5,943	33,959	183,251	51,109
1947	6,432	34,759	202,176	55,111
1948	6,850	36,190	216,132	58,997
1949	7,119	34,682	232,679	63,401
1950	7,607	38,800	255,262	68,100
1951	7,821	38,634	275,227	72,189
1952	8,670	44,244	296,193	77,038
1953	9,407	54,430	331,004	82,499
1954	10,069	61,885	370,934	90,005
1955	10,690	72,510	407,034	95,290
1956	14,043	83,729	455,436	101,926
1957	15,002	96,792	504,295	106,715
1958	15,891	95,242	546,951	113,569
1959	17,020	107,233	598,340	119,838
1960	17,810	112,901	648,712	126,145
1961	18,793	118,083	702,681	134,434
1962	20,062	124,114	752,767	141,166
1963	21,941	144,701	832,466	152,131
1964	23,372	166,483	910,905	161,113
1965	25,182	210,229	1,026,077	171,586
1966	27,072	207,087	1,127,160	180,626
1967	29,872	225,723	1,236,676	191,773
1968	32,265	245,460	1,357,593	203,549
1969	35,115	267,750	1,482,280	213,257
1970	39,520	†243,191	1,624,920	225,944
1971	42,416	252,650	1,747,079	240,627
1972	46,475	287,338	1,905,749	259,671
1973	49,432	310,704	2,020,200	266,753

* Accrual basis since 1951. Previous years are on cash basis. † Life insurance written includes revivals and increases plus reinsurance assumed prior to 1970. New issues only since 1970.

ORGANIZATION AND SUPERVISION

Life insurance companies are in number predominantly stock corporations, however the mutual life companies control over 75 percent of all life insurance company assets.

All life companies, whether corporate or mutual, are chartered under state laws and are regulated by both the state of charter and all states in which they do business. For example, a New York chartered life insurance company selling insurance and making investments in Ohio is governed both by New York and Ohio insurance.

Since they are state regulated, life insurance companies are governed by the laws passed by state legislatures and enforced by the state insurance commission or a similar authority.

CHART 11-2

DISTRIBUTION OF ASSETS OF UNITED STATES LIFE INSURANCE COMPANIES
(000,000 omitted)

	1953 Amount	%	1963 Amount	%	1972 Amount	%	1973 Amount	%
Government Securities	$12,537	15.9	$ 12,630	8.9	$ 11,372	4.8	$ 11,403	4.5
Corporate Securities:								
Bonds	31,865	40.6	53,453	37.9	86,140	35.9	91,796	36.4
Common Stock	1,042	1.3	4,820	3.4	21,793	9.1	19,606	7.8
Preferred Stock	1,531	2.0	2,315	1.6	5,052	2.1	6,313	2.5
Total Corp. Securities	$34,438	43.9	$ 60,588	42.9	$112,985	47.1	$117,715	46.7
Mortgages	$23,322	29.7	$ 50,544	35.8	$ 76,948	32.1	$ 81,369	32.2
Real Estate	2,020	2.6	4,319	3.1	7,295	3.0	7,693	3.0
Policy Loans	2,914	3.7	6,655	4.7	18,003	7.5	20,199	8.0
Cash	1,215	1.5	1,466	1.1	1,981	0.8	2,071	0.8
All Other	2,087	2.7	4,919	3.5	11,146	4.7	11,986	4.8
Total Admitted Assets	$78,533	100.0	$141,121	100.0	$239,730	100.0	$252,436	100.0

Note: All data is shown at convention statement values.
Source: Institute of Life Insurance.

Over the years a large number of bills have been introduced in various state legislatures in an attempt to pass a law requiring investment of a certain amount of life insurance company assets in their state as a prerequisite for permission to do business in the state. So far only one state, Texas, has passed such legislation. The "Robertson Law" enacted in 1907 requires, as a condition of licensing of a life insurance company, that 75 percent of the reserves on policies written in the state of Texas be invested in Texas securities.

Primarily state regulations govern the investment policies of life insurance companies which are either chartered in the state or do business in the state. Such regulations place limitations and standards on the following:

1. Real estate investments.
2. Mortgage loan investments.
3. Purchases of common and preferred stock.
4. Purchases of corporate bonds.
5. Unsecured loans made to unincorporated small business.
6. Investments in foreign securities.
7. Investments of out-of-state life companies.

Other areas of investment and company operations are governed as well.

FUNDS

The basic business operation of life insurance companies is the sale of insurance policies which produce income in the form of premiums collected plus reinvested dividends paid to policy holders. Reducing this income flow are benefit claims as they arise and policy loans. The excess income flow after claims and loans is then available for investment in selected areas, such as mortgage loans.

The daily inflow of funds to life companies is both steady and sizable, while the outflow for claims is also steady, but relatively small and quite accurately estimated due to proven actuarial methods. In fact the only disturbing fluctuation in net income has been the demand for policy loans. These loans are available at usually low interest rates in amounts equal to policy value. In times of relatively low interest rates the incidence of policy loans is small. In recent years, however, high interest rates have prevailed causing a run on policy loans and a diminution in investable funds. Additional investment funds are made available from amortization and prepayment of loans held in portfolio. Thus, it is a generally accepted fact that life insurance companies can accurately predict the net inflow of funds. Hence, liquidity is of much lesser importance to life insurance companies than it is to the thrift institutions.

INVESTMENT PATTERNS

The predictability of availability of funds for investment has allowed life insurance companies to plan their investment program for several years in advance with only slight modifications needed to meet periodic market changes. Therefore, lending patterns of life insurance companies generally take the form of forward commitments for bulk purchases of single family mortgages and for permanent income property loans.

MORTGAGE INVESTMENTS

As to *single family* (one to four family non-farm homes) lending after World War II, life insurance companies favored FHA and VA loans and invested heavily in them to the detriment of conventional loans. In the last decade their interest in FHA and VA loans has waned and conventional loans have been more favored. Nevertheless, FHA and VA loans attract more life insurance funds than do single family conventional loans, the ratio of FHA and VA to conventional loans being approximately seven to four. The single family lending of life companies is conducted primarily by bulk purchases from mortgage banking companies. The advent of the GNMA guaranteed-mortgage-backed security could step up life insurance company investments in single family loans, particularly due to the removal of the necessity for inspection of loan documents. Nevertheless, the pattern of life insurance companies over the last decade has been to reduce single family mortgage loans investments and aggressively seek income property mortgage loans. The impetus for this policy is the higher returns available from income property loans, increasing competition for single family mortgage loans, particularly by savings and loan associations, and the efficiency of investing in large loans which is not generally possible with single family loan investments unless they are pooled through a GNMA security

An indication of the lessening impact of single family investments in life insurance companies is the fact that these mortgage holdings have decreased an average of $1.2 billion per year since 1967, while savings and loan association single family loan holdings have increased an average of $20 billion annually during the same period.

During the period of 1967 to 1977 the single family mortgage loan holdings of all major lenders, except life insurance companies, increased. Over the past ten years, the single family mortgage holdings of life insurance companies have decreased by over $15 billion. Today their single family mortgage holdings, compared percentage-wise to all other lenders, represent less than one-sixth of what they did during the early 1950s. (See Chart 11-3)

INCOME PROPERTY LOANS

Because large loans and large blocks of loans have always been favored by life insurance companies as means of rapid investment of funds, it follows that conventional income property loans constitute a large portion of mortgage lending by these companies. The recent shifts from single family mortgages and the higher yields available from income property mortgage loans have made such loans quite popular among life insurance companies.

CHART 11-3

Mortgage Loans Outstanding on Multifamily Residential Properties, by Type of Lender
(Billions of Dollars)

Year-End	Savings Associations	Mutual Savings Banks	Commercial Banks	Life Insurance Companies	All Others	Total
1950	$ 0.2	$ 2.7	$1.0	$ 2.6	$ 3.6	$10.1
1955	0.6	4.5	0.8	3.6	4.8	14.3
1960	2.2	5.9	1.1	3.9	7.2	20.3
1965	8.1	10.0	2.0	8.9	8.2	37.2
1970	13.8	12.6	3.3	16.1	12.2	58.0
1971	17.4	14.4	4.0	16.8	14.2	66.8
1972	20.8	15.5	5.8	17.2	18.0	77.3
1973	22.5	16.8	6.9	18.4	21.2	85.8
1974*	23.8	17.3	7.4	20.0	24.9	93.4
Annual Change						
1950	†	$0.1	$0.2	$0.3	$ 0.9	$ 1.5
1955	$0.1	0.3	†	0.1	0.3	0.8
1960	0.5	0.3	†	0.2	0.7	1.7
1965	1.0	0.9	0.3	1.7	−0.3	3.6
1970	2.0	0.4	0.1	2.0	1.3	5.8
1971	3.6	1.8	0.7	0.7	2.0	8.8
1972	3.4	1.1	1.8	0.4	3.8	10.5
1973	1.7	1.3	1.1	1.2	3.2	8.5
1974*	1.3	0.5	0.5	1.6	3.7	7.6

*Preliminary.
†Less than $50 million.
Sources: Federal Home Loan Bank Board; Federal Reserve Board.

In the 1960s life companies became more involved in multifamily housing mortgages in response to an increasing demand for these loans. Holdings of multifamily mortgages accounted for 9 percent of insurance company held mortgages in 1960. These holdings increased to 21 percent in 1970 and a high of 23 percent in the early 1970s. Growth in multifamily mortgages has slowed since 1974 due to the general decrease in construction of conventional multifamily properties.

According to figures released by the Federal Reserve Board, life insurance companies continue to be the second largest holder of multifamily residential mortgage debt. See comparative figures in Chart 11-4.

CHART 11-4

• Multifamily Mortgage Loans Outstanding, by Type of Lender

(Billions of Dollars)

Year-End	Savings Associations	Mutual Savings Banks	Commercial Banks	Life Insurance Companies	All Others	Total
1950	$ 0.2	$ 2.7	$1.0	$ 2.6	$ 2.8	$ 9.3
1955	0.6	3.7	0.8	3.6	4.8	13.5
1960	2.2	3.7	1.1	3.9	9.9	20.8
1965	8.1	6.3	2.0	8.8	13.0	38.2
1966	8.6	6.6	2.1	10.3	13.7	41.3
1967	9.5	7.0	2.4	11.7	14.2	44.8
1968	10,5	7.3	2.7	12.8	15.0	48.3
1969	11.7	7.6	3.2	14.2	16.5	53.2
1970	13.8	7.8	3.3	16.0	19.2	60.1
1971	17.6	9.6	4.0	16.7	22.2	70.1
1972	21.1	10.9	5.8	17.3	27.7	82.8
1973	22.8	12.3	6.9	18.5	32.6	93.1
1974	23.8	12.9	7.6	19.6	36.1	100.0
1975	25.5	13.8	5.9	19.6	35.8	100.6
1976	28.4	14.2	8.1	19.2	34.4	104.3
1977*	33.3	15.3	8.7	18.9	35.0	111.2

*Preliminary.
Source: Federal Reserve Board.

LOAN ACQUISITION METHODS

Three principal methods are utilized by life insurance companies in their acquisition of income property loans (and for that matter single family bulk loan purchases). These are the *correspondent, branch office,* and *home office* methods.

Under the favored correspondent system, a life insurance company selects and appoints a mortgage company or broker in local areas to originate loans for the life company's portfolio. The area correspondency is frequently exclusive for the insurance company, but the mortgage company or broker is free to deal with other insurance companies on any loans. Generally the correspondent originates a loan application and presents it along with a completely documented package to the life insurance company for approval. Once approved, a commitment is written to the borrower or correspondent. The loan is then closed, either directly with the life insurance company or by the correspondent with subsequent sale to the life insurance company. For its efforts the correspondent receives a fee at the time of execution of the commitment, usually from the borrower, and may receive an additional fee from the life insurance company when the loan is closed. Most often the correspondent will service the loan for the life insurance company (collect interest and amortization, pay real estate taxes and insurance, and inspect the property periodically) and receive a monthly fee depending upon the size and nature of the loan. For example, a $500,000 apartment loan may earn 0.25 percent per year servicing fee on the unpaid principal balance, whereas a $3,000,000 mortgage may be serviced for as low as 0.1

percent per year. This method is also used to a great extent for the purchase of blocks of FHA, VA, and Conventional single family home loan mortgages.

The branch office method of loan origination allows for closer control and supervision over the lending situation than does the correspondent method. Under this arrangement, a life insurance company will establish branch offices throughout the country expressly for the origination of mortgage loans. Personnel in these branch offices are all company employees, usually salaried with no commission or finders fees. Operations are conducted much like those of a correspondent; loan applications are taken and processed on a local basis. It is not rare to find life insurance companies using a mix of branch and correspondent methods particularly to serve areas of lesser population.

The smaller life companies prefer to originate loans out of their home office as opposed to using the correspondent or branch method. However, this method is sometimes used in conjunction with the correspondent system.

LENDING POWERS

Life insurance companies are practically unlimited as to their range of real estate financing opportunities. They can purchase real estate and make leasehold and land contract loans, as well as invest in single family, income property, and farm loans. Thus they are an excellent source of funds for the more modern real estate financing arrangements such as sale-leasebacks, leasehold mortgages, sale-contract-backs, joint ventures, and for special purpose property loans including motels, hotels, nursing homes, and hospitals.

State laws place limitations on loan-to-value ratios, type of loans, and asset investment limitations singly and in aggregate. Since the majority of life insurance companies are either located in New York state or do business in that state, the laws of that state are a good indicator of statutory lending powers of life insurance companies.

In New York, a life insurance company cannot invest more than $30,000 or 2 percent of assets in a single mortgage loan, whichever is greater. Also, no more than 50 percent of assets may be invested in all real estate mortgages (both fee and leasehold) held at one time.

Loan-to-value ratios vary nationally from 66-2/3 percent to 80 percent with 75 percent loan to value ratios being the norm. Many states impose further restrictions to the extent that a life insurance company cannot make a loan out-of-state on a more favorable basis than permissible in its state of charter.

In New York, the loan-to-value ratio, not the lien position, is important. Thus, a life company in that state, where 75 percent loan-to-value ratio mortgage loans are permissible, can legally make a $100,000 mortgage loan on a property appraised for $1,000,000 already subject to a $650,000 mortgage, without having the loan fall under the basket or leeway provisions of the insurance laws. The basket provisions of state insurance laws, as stated in a prior chapter, generally allow from two percent to five percent of assets to be invested in forms of investments not otherwise authorized under other sections of the state's insurance laws.

Loans insured by FHA and guaranteed by VA are universally exempt from loan-to-value requirements and are permissible investments if made in accordance with the regulations of FHA and VA.

Asset limitations imposed upon holdings of income-producing real estate, including sale-leaseback, sale-contract-back, and joint ventures, generally range from 5 percent to 10 percent nationwide.

Leasehold mortgage loans in New York are limited to the leasehold having an unexpired term of at least twenty-one years and are required to be fully amortized within the lesser of thirty-five years or the unexpired leasehold term. Permissible loan-to-value ratios for leaseholds are generally similar to those for fee mortgages. Ohio and Minnesota are notable exceptions with 60 percent and 50 percent respective maximums on leasehold mortgage loan-to-value ratios.

State laws are reasonably liberal with regard to amortization (except on high ratio loans) and maturity dates on mortgage loans. However, most life companies impose their own restrictions and generally require amortization on long term permanent loans and average maximum maturities of twenty-five years. Since the mid-1960s, the trend has been toward twenty-five year amortizations on income property loans with 15-year maturities. The reasoning behind such an arrangement is to create a faster turnover of funds and to prevent a lengthy commitment by life insurance companies to a fixed rate of interest.

Chart 11-4 reflects the statutory provisions of nineteen representative states regulating mortgage investments by life insurance companies.

RECENT TRENDS IN REAL ESTATE OWNERSHIP

Recent years have evidenced a slow increase in real estate ownership by life insurance companies prompted by a favoring of sale-leaseback and joint venture transactions. Life insurance companies, in fact, pioneered the construction of large apartment complexes under their ownership. Real estate ownership offers several advantages:

1. Direct control can be exercised over assets.
2. Higher yield through ownership is obtainable.
3. Investments can be amortized over a period of years while at the end of the amortized period there still remains a residual benefit. Balancing these benefits is the risk involved in real estate ownership. Prime examples of real estate ownership, both individually and through joint ventures and limited partnership, are:
a. The John Hancock Building in Chicago.
b. Connecticut General Life Insurance Company's joint ownership with the Rouse Co. of the new town of Columbia, Maryland.

In 1977, real estate owned by life insurance companies increased by almost $600 million. At the end of 1977, real estate owned amounted to 3.2 percent of total life insurance assets or approximately $11.06 billion.

RECENT TRENDS IN MORTGAGE INVESTMENTS

Several important facts are noteworthy with respect to recent developments regarding life insurance company mortgage investments. They are:

1. Mortgage loans at the end of 1977 amounted to over $96.8 billion or 27.5 percent of assets, down from 38 percent ten years earlier. Mortgage loans for the

CHART 11-5

PRINCIPAL STATUTORY PROVISIONS IN 19 REPRESENTATIVE STATES REGULATING CONVENTIONAL REAL ESTATE MORTGAGE INVESTMENTS BY LIFE INSURANCE COMPANIES

(Capital and Deposit Provisions Not Included)

State	Type of Property	Situs of Property	Loan to Value Ratio [1] (Percent)	Aggregate Limit	Single Parcel Limit	Limit on Mortgages of One Mortgagor— % of Assets	Miscellaneous, Notes, etc.
California	Fee		75[a]				a. Of loan plus public bond, assessment, or tax liens.
	Leasehold		75[b] 66 2/3[c]				b. If loan for not over 30 years and on one-family residence with monthly amortization.
							c. Loan not on one-family residence and not for over 30 years, with amortization.
Connecticut	Fee		75				
	Leasehold		75				
Illinois	Fee	Any state of U.S.	75 }	60% of assets [2]		2% of assets [2]	a. Having term 1/3 longer than term of obligation or unexpired term of at least 20 years and amortized within term of leasehold.
	Leasehold[a]	Same	75 }				Loans on producing oil or gas properties, and participating loans, permitted as prescribed.
Indiana	Fee	U.S., U.S. possessions, or Canada	75				
	Leasehold[a]	Same	75				a. Having unexpired term of at least 50 years.

State	Type of Property	Situs of Property	Loan to Value Ratio 1/ (Percent)	Aggregate Limit	Single Parcel Limit	Limit on Mortgages of One Mortgagor— % of Assets	Miscellaneous, Notes, etc.
Iowa	Fee	U.S., U.S. possessions, or Canada	75				a. Having unexpired term of at least 50 years.
	Leasehold[a]	Same	75				b. Under lease or purchase contract to certain government bodies or corporations.
	Leasehold[b]	Same		15% of legal reserve			
Massachusetts	Fee	Any state of U.S. D.C., or Puerto Rico; Canada[c]	75[a]	Aggregate Canadian loans not to exceed 3% of reserve liability[c]			a. Commissioner may establish minimum amortization schedule required on loans over 60% of value. Participating loans permitted, as prescribed.
	Leasehold[b]	Same	75[a]	Same			b. Having unexpired term of at least twenty-one years. Loan to be amortized within four-fifths of unexpired term.
	Leasehold[d]						c. Not exceeding premiums from insurance on Canadian lives and amounts from authorized Canadian investments.
							d. First lien on lessor's interest required as additional security for bonds, etc., secured by certain leases.
Minnesota	Fee	U.S.	75[b] 66 2/3[b]				a. If approved by Commissioner-- to have unexpired term of at least 40 years.
	Leasehold[a]		50				b. If amortized within thirty years; otherwise, 66-2/3%.

State	Type of Property	Situs of Property	Loan to Value Ratio[1] (Percent)	Aggregate Limit	Single Parcel Limit	Limit on Mortgages of One Mortgagor— % of Assets	Miscellaneous, Notes, etc.
Missouri	Fee	U.S. or U.S. territory or possession	75, 100[b]		Greater of 1% of assets or 10% of capital and surplus		a. Having unexpired term of at least twenty-five years. b. If loan made to corporation which qualifies for investment in its bonds, etc., under subdivision (5), or lease assigned to lender by such corporation, as prescribed. c. Loan to be amortized within four-fifths of unexpired term, but in no event exceeding thirty years.
	Leasehold[a]	Same	75[c], 100[b]	3% of assets	Same		
Nebraska	Fee	Any state or territory of U.S. or D.C., or province of Canada	75				a. Loan to be fully amortized within unexpired term. b. First lien on lessor's interest required as additional security for bonds, etc., secured by certain leases. Participating loans permitted, as prescribed.
	Leasehold[a]	Same	75				
	Leasehold[b]		75				
New Jersey	Fee	States, D.C., Puerto Rico, or Canada	80[b]	50% of assets[2]	2% of assets		a. Loan to be fully amortized within nine-tenths of unexpired term of leasehold. b. Excess of loan over 66-2/3% of value required to be amortized during term of loan. 80 percent limit may be exceeded if loan also secured by aggregate rentals sufficient to repay 90 percent of loan and interest during initial term and payable by certain governmental units or institutions, as prescribed. Participating loans permitted, as prescribed.
	Leasehold[a]	Same	80[b]		Same		

State	Type of Property	Situs of Property	Loan to Value Ratio[1] (Percent)	Aggregate Limit	Single Parcel Limit	Limit on Mortgages of One Mortgagor— % of Assets	Miscellaneous, Notes, etc.
New York	Fee	U.S.	75[a] 66 2/3	50% of assets[2]	Greater of $30,000 or 2% of assets	103[3]	a. If loan fully amortized in thirty years. b. Having unexpired term of at least twenty-one years. Loan to be fully amortized within lesser of four-fifths period of leasehold or thirty-five years.
	Leasehold[b]	Same	75[a] 66 2/3		Same	103[3]	Participation permitted, as prescribed.
North Carolina	Fee	Any state, territory or possession of U.S., or D.C.	75				a. Having unexpired term of at least 30 years. Loan to mature at least 20 years before lease expires.
	Leasehold[a]	Same	75				
Ohio	Fee	Any state, D.C., or Canada	80[b] 75[c] 66 2/3				a. For not less than ninety-nine years, renewable forever. b. Investment in 80 percent loans not to exceed 25 percent of assets. c. If loan not over $30,000, on one-family dwelling, and fully amortized within thirty years. d. Ceiling on loan plus rent capitalized at 5 percent. e. First lien on lessor's interest required as additional security for bonds, etc., secured by certain leases.
	Leasehold[a]		60[d]				
	Leasehold[e]						
Pennsylvania	Fee	Any state, district or territory of U.S.	75[a] 66 2/3[b]		Greater of $10,000 or 2% of assets		a. If loan on improved real estate and fully amortized within 30 years. b. Mortgages on certain corporate or business trust leases excepted. c. Loan to be fully amortized within unexpired term of leasehold.
	Leasehold[c]	Same	75[a] 66 2/3[b]		Same		

State	Type of Property	Situs of Property	Loan to Value Ratio 1/ (Percent)	Aggregate Limit	Single Parcel Limit	Limit on Mortgages of One Mortgagor-- % of Assets	Miscellaneous, Notes, etc.
Tennessee	Real Property	U.S.	75^a				a. If a loan on improved real property and repayable in thirty years. Excess over 75 percent may be deemed to be made under leeway clause.
	Leasehold^b	Same	75^a				b. Loan to be fully amortized two years before end of term.
	Leasehold^c						c. First lien on lessor's interest required as additional security for bonds, etc., secured by certain leases.
Texas	Fee		75				a. Duration and amortization of loan not to exceed four-fifths unexpired term of leasehold, latter term to extend at least ten years beyond term of loan. loan.
	Leasehold^a						
Vermont	Real Estate	State or territory of U.S., or D.C.	90^a 80^b 75^c 66 2/3^d 50^e Same				a. If loan fully amortized within thirty years and on one or two-family dwelling in Vermont.
							b. If loan fully amortized within thirty years and on one or two-family dwelling outside Vermont.
	Leasehold^f	Same	Same				c. If loan fully amortized within thirty years.
							d. If no provision for full amortization in thirty years—loan payable on demand or within two years.
							e. If loan on timberlands, mines, or quarries, with 5-year maturity.
							f. Principal to be fully amortized within four-fifths period of leasehold, which must have unexpired term of not less than twenty-one years.

State	Type of Property	Situs of Property	Loan to Value Ratio [1] (Percent)	Aggregate Limit	Single Parcel Limit	Limit on Mortgages of One Mortgagor— % of Assets	Miscellaneous, Notes, etc.
Vermont (cont.)	Leasehold[g]						g. First lien on lessor's interest required as additional security for bonds, etc., secured by certain leases.
Virginia	Real Property	U.S. or Canada	75[a]			5 [4]	a. Loan on single-family residence to be fully amortized within twenty-five years.
	Leasehold[b]	U.S.	66 2/3[b]			5 [4]	b. For unexpired term of at least 30 years.
Wisconsin	Real Property	U.S. or Canada	75[a]			10 [3]	a. Excess over 75 percent may be deemed to be made under leeway clause.
	Leasehold	Same	75[a]				

1/ Mortgages guaranteed or insured under the National Housing Act or the Servicemen's Readjustment Act of 1944 are exempted, as prescribed, from the ratio requirements listed in this chart.
2/ Limit on aggregate of fee and leasehold mortgages.
3/ Limit on all investments in securities of one corporation.
4/ Limit on all investments in, or loans on, property, securities, etc., of one person or corporation.

Source: Institute of Life Insurance, New York, New York

seventh consecutive year, however, ranked second to corporate debt issues in importance. From 1965 through 1970 mortgage loans had represented the largest asset investment category.

2. For the first time in 1974, mortgages held on non-residential properties exceeded residential loans in the mortgage portfolios of life insurance companies. This trend has continued as dramatically shown on Chart 11-6.

3. Mortgage holdings of life insurance companies as a percentage of assets increased in only one year since 1966 and then only slightly. That increase was in 1974 and was simply a reflection of the closing of loans committed on in the real estate boom years of 1972 and 1973.

The most important of the above facts is that nonresidential lending is taking the forefront with life companies and should continue to be the future trend of life companys' mortgage investments.

CHART 11-6
Distribution of Mortgages by Type in the United States
U.S. Life Insurance Companies

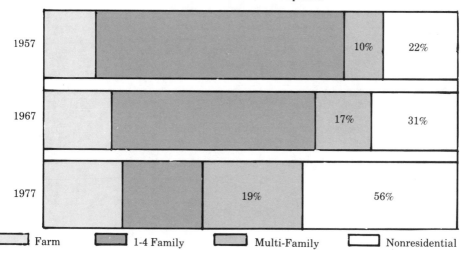

QUESTIONS FOR THOUGHT AND DISCUSSION

1. a. In what respect do life insurance company investment policies differ from those of other financial institutions?
   b. How do their business operations influence such policies?
2. In your opinion, what factors have influenced life insurance companies to move from single-family to income property (multifamily and non-residential loan mortgage investments?
3. What are the economies of the branch system of mortgage loan acquisition over the correspondent method?
4. Should more states pass laws similar to Texas' "Robertson Law"? Why or why not?

12

MORTGAGE COMPANIES PENSION FUNDS AND CREDIT UNIONS

Mortgage banking began in this country in the early 1900s as a mortgage brokerage operation. Real estate brokers, lawyers, individuals, and promoters would act as go-between to arrange a mortgage loan for a homeowner or builder. In other words, mortgage brokers would bring together those persons in need of mortgage financing and those who were suppliers of mortgage funds. For arranging the mortgage financing, the mortgage broker would receive a fee, usually from the borrower. As time passed the mortgage brokers discovered they could successfully devote their efforts full time to arranging loans and thus become specialists in performing such functions. Out of this system came mortgage companies and the correspondent representation of life insurance companies and other national investors.

MORTGAGE COMPANIES

Modern mortgage companies are organized under the corporation laws of a particular state and are usually privately-owned companies. The recent trend, however, has been toward affiliation with a financial institution, particularly through merger with or purchase by a commercial bank, culminating in a one-bank holding company.

Supervision of mortgage companies by state and federal authorities has been minimal, but lately states have adopted mortgage company and mortgage company personnel licensing laws in order to establish professional standards of operation.

The principal function of these companies is to originate FHA, VA and Conventional loans for sale to institutional investors. Corporate capital, commercial paper and funds borrowed from commercial banks through warehousing loans are used to support the loan originations and to keep the mortgage company liquid during the period between loan closing and loan delivery and sale to an investor. Ancillary to loan origination is the servicing of the mortgage loans that have been sold to investors. The servicing function involves the collection of all principal and interest payments; the remittance of these payments to the investor, after deduction of servicing fees; payment of all hazard insurance premiums and property taxes from monies escrowed by borrowers; inspection of properties; supervision of repairs to damaged structures; and foreclosure if necessary.

It is the loan servicing function that primarily separates mortgage banking companies from mortgage brokers. A mortgage broker simply brings the borrower and lender together and earns a fee for that service. A mortgage banker originates loans with his own funds and then sells the loan to an investor usually with servicing retained, thereby maintaining an involvement in the loan he has helped create.

The extraordinary growth of mortgage companies has been one of the most striking developments in real estate financing during the post-World War II period. Basically, this rapid expansion and growth has been directly related to the introduction and tremendous reception of the FHA and VA loan programs. Mortgage companies have been the catalysts in bringing the funds of life insurance companies, mutual savings banks, and savings and loan associations into areas in need of mortgage capital, primarily for FHA and VA insured and guaranteed mortgages, but also for conventional mortgages.

PURPOSE AND OPERATIONS

A mortgage company's basic and primary purpose is to serve as a bridge or financial intermediary uniting the primary and secondary mortgage markets and channeling the flow of mortgage funds from highly developed and capital-abundant areas to undeveloped and capital-short regions of the country. This purpose is served by their FHA, VA, and Conventional loan operations and other loan activities.

The mortgage company's success in the movement of funds is related to it's being part of a nationwide "correspondent" system. The "correspondent" system is made up of this country's major institutional investors and the mortgage companies that operate as their correspondent's recommending to them sound real estate mortgage loan opportunities. The institutions in turn rely on the mortgage companies' specialized knowledge of the local real estate market and their ability to originate in their local areas good loans into which their funds can be channelled.

The typical mortgage company negotiates commitments from these institutional investors such as life insurance companies, mutual savings banks, and savings and loan associations for the sale and purchase of large blocks of FHA insured and VA guaranteed loans and, frequently, for conventional loans.

Commitments for loan deliveries may be one of three major types:

1. **Allocation commitments** are those in which the investor states that it has allocated a certain amount of money for purchase of loans from the mortgage company during a certain period of time. These commitments usually do not obligate the mortgage company to deliver sufficient loans to use up the allocated funds. Failure to deliver under an allocation commitment will not prejudice the mortgage company's reputation with the investor, even though it may well influence the amount of future

allocations.

2. Under a **direct commitment** the mortgage company is obligated to deliver loans to the full amount and in accordance with the terms of the commitment. Failure to deliver usually results in a loss of all or a portion of a prepaid commitment fee and a loss of prestige with the investor. When direct commitments are made by investors, they consider the funds invested; failure to have sufficient loans delivered under the commitment causes re-investment problems.

3. **A Stand-By Commitment** is one in which the investor receives a commitment fee and gives the mortgage company the option to deliver under the commitment or not deliver as it so desires.

Additional commitments may be classed according to delivery, either for immediate or future delivery.

Today, one of the biggest investors in mortgage-company-originated loans is the Federal National Mortgage Association. A complete discussion of FNMAs role in mortgage lending is contained in Chapter 17. Also of great influence upon, and importance to, mortgage company operations are the various GNMA special assistance programs and the FNMA-backed mortgage security programs. These programs are also discussed in a subsequent chapter.

Loans for origination and delivery are solicited by home and branch office operations from real estate brokers or builders.

While serving as an outlet for surplus institutional funds, the mortgage company also performs services as follows:

1. Loan origination (including solicitation, borrower qualification, FHA/VA and investor loan approval, and loan closing).
2. Document inspection.
3. Loan Servicing.

The performance of these duties takes the burden off institutional investors and allows them a means for easy investment of large sums without the usual companion problems.

COMPENSATION

For its efforts in the basic FHA, VA, and Conventional loan origination and sale, the mortgage company receives as compensation:

1. A one to one and one half percent origination fee from the borrower. This fee very seldom compensates for the cost of loan origination, unless a heavy volume of loans is experienced.
2. A 1/4 of one percent (usually as to conventional loans) to 3/8 of one percent (primarily as to FHA and VA loans) servicing fee on those loans sold with servicing retained (the backbone of a mortgage company's financial picture.)
3. Sometimes, a profit from the sale of mortgages at a price better than the origination price. Playing the mortgage market is required here and losses can be as great as anticipated profits.
4. Indirect compensation resulting from the large escrow deposits maintained by mortgage companies with regard to loans serviced. These escrows can

be used as compensating balances for bank lines, thereby obtaining credit for the mortgage banker at a reduced cost. In one-bank holding companies, escrow funds may be deposited with the bank and the funds used by that bank in its normal operations.

5. Commitment fees, averaging one percent of the amount committed on commitments issued to builders or others reserving funds sometimes at a firm interest rate or discount.

ORGANIZATION

The organizational makeup of a mortgage company varies according to its size. Typical divisional operations are explained below. In some smaller companies several of these operations will be performed by one person; in the larger companies the functions will be departmentalized with several persons staffing the departments. Operations and hence organizational structure vary according to the emphasis placed on types of business. For example, FHA and VA loan origination may create the biggest volume for some companies whereas others will have large income property loan operations with little or no FHA and VA business. In general, the major organizational structure of mortgage companies is as follows:

1. The *servicing division* (sometimes called loan administration) maintains all loan records and administers the servicing contracts which have been entered into with the mortgage company's investors and loan correspondents (mortgage money sources). This division receives all payments on mortgage loans serviced, including principal, interest, taxes, and insurance. Principal and interest payments are forwarded to the respective investors monthly, less the mortgage company's servicing fee. Tax and insurance payments are escrowed and used to pay real estate taxes and hazard insurance premiums as they become due. The division performs somewhat like a collection agency with regard to delinquent loans. When foreclosure is recommended and approved the servicing division will usually arrange for a local attorney to handle the action and will coordinate and follow-up on the proceeding. Naturally, the particular investor owning the loan will make the final decision to foreclose and may also select the attorney to be used. Servicing division personnel also periodically inspect all properties securing the mortgages serviced and make reports to the respective investors regarding property condition. If repairs are deemed necessary the servicing division will make arrangement for and supervise them.

2. The *marketing or loan sales division* has the dual responsibility of reviewing all documentation with respect to loans closed by the company and then delivering these loans to an investor. Such responsibility includes the follow-up gathering of all documentation which may be missing from the closing package; for example, the recorded mortgage which may take several weeks to come back from the recorder's office. The FHA Mortgage Insurance Certificate (MIC) and the VA Loan Guaranty are of particular importance. Without these documents an FHA or VA loan becomes a mere conventional loan and, due to the high loan-to-value ratio, would be extremely difficult to market except at a large loss. Once documentation is

complete this division delivers the loan package to an investor for purchase. Once delivered and purchased the servicing division takes over.

3. *Loan Production* is the most important division, for without originated mortgage loans the company would not be able to function. This division is often composed of several branch offices spread throughout a state, region, or the nation depending upon the size of the mortgage company. Through its local branch offices this division solicits and closes mortgage loans. Their product is then forwarded to the marketing (loan sales) division for inspection and delivery to an investor.

The responsibility for finding and maintaining investor contacts usually falls within the purview of the company president or executive vice president. However, larger companies have a separate division staffed by one or more people who spend their time cultivating present investor sources and seeking new ones in order to maintain and hopefully increase the availability of mortgage money.

Accounting and office management functions are needed by every mortgage company, developing in relation to the needs of the operational areas noted above. The larger mortgage companies have found a pressing need for computerization, particularly with regard to the loan servicing operation. Many larger companies now have separate computer or data processing departments, usually as a part of the accounting division.

As companies grow or expand their services, additional divisions may be added. Many of the additional and sideline activities noted below are performed by a separate division in most mortgage companies.

ADDITIONAL AND SIDELINE ACTIVITIES

Mortgage companies usually conduct companion activities other than the normal single family home loan originations. Some of these additional or sideline activities are as follows:

1. **Land purchase, development and construction loans** are made primarily to secure permanent loans. Such activities produce additional loan fee income. Additionally, by tieing the developer into closing the permanent loans with the mortgage company, the standard loan origination and servicing fees are earned. With both tract or single family construction loans and with income property construction loans, a penalty from one percent to 2 percent of the loan amount is charged to the borrower if the permanent loan or loans are not delivered to the mortgage company.

2. **Stand-by commitments** for closing of permanent single family or for the closing of income loans are also issued from time to time by many mortgage companies. With a stand-by commitment a builder can obtain a construction loan from a commercial bank. When construction is completed the standby loan is either closed or, most frequently, another less expensive permanent mortgage is obtained.

3. **Income property loans** both conventional and FHA insured, constitute a large activity for many companies particularly those mortgage companies located in metropolitan areas. The FHA multifamily insured loan area is expanding rapidly and is a high profit opportunity for mortgage com-

panies. Involvement consists of project development, application submission and the arrangement of mortgage financing.

4. **Building leasing and property management** are valuable sideline activities for some mortgage companies with large income loan departments, who desire to offer a complete line of services to their clients.
5. **Land development** is undertaken by mortgage companies in some major metropolitan areas. Such companies purchase large tracts of land and develop them into lots for sale to builders, using their development activities to attract and generate permanent loan business.
6. Other companies like the Rouse Company with its city of Columbia project have gone heavily into land development by spearheading the development of *new cities.* And, like the Rouse Company, a few mortgage bankers are extremely active in **building commercial properties** for their own account.
7. **Insurance companies** are a favored sideline of mortgage companies due to the large number of leads generated by loan closings. Borrowers are prime prospects for hazard or homeowner's insurance and for mortgage redemption life coverage, in addition to the many other types of coverage.
8. **Real estate brokerage** operations are good sidelines for mortgage companies. Many, like The Kissell Company, began as, or were an outgrowth of, real estate brokerage operations.
9. **Real estate investment funds** have been organized by several mortgage companies, notably Lomas and Nettleton and Sutro Mortgage Company. On the opposite side of the coin, many large builders, such as U.S. Home, Ryan Homes and Kaufman and Broad, have established their own mortgage companies to supply funds and close loans on homes built and sold by their construction operations.

REGULATION

Unlike other institutions in the mortgage market, mortgage companies are subject to little direct supervision or regulation. However, they do undergo two types of regulation. One applies only to incorporated companies, which are regulated by the corporation laws of the states of incorporation and the laws of the states in which they do business. The second type of regulation is far more important. It is the regulation by FHA.

All mortgage companies active in FHA loan originations must be FHA-approved mortgagees. This approval must be obtained to originate and service FHA-insured loans and must be obtained not only by the company, but also by each and every branch office.

Each FHA-approved mortgagee is subject to periodic examination and audit by FHA. The examination consists principally of an audit of financial statements filed annually with FHA (primarily to make sure a net worth of $100,000 required for FHA mortgagee approval is maintained) and an irregular sight inspection of company records and loan closing procedures by FHA auditors.

It should be noted that VA makes no special requirements of mortgage companies originating VA-guaranteed mortgage loans. Such originators are probably FHA-approved mortgagees anyhow.

To sell loans to FNMA and GNMA a mortgage company must also be a FNMA-and GNMA-approved seller-servicer. This approval is easily obtained once FHA mortgagee status is attained. FNMA, GNMA and many institutional investors do make periodic audits of the loan administration operations of mortgage companies servicing loans for them.

GROWTH TRENDS

As mentioned, the post World War II period evidenced a spectacular growth in the number and assets of mortgage companies. Today there are approximately 750 mortgage companies with an estimated dollar volume of servicing of over $165 billion or almost 16 percent of the total mortgage debt in the United States. The top 100 mortgage companies in the country rated by volume of mortgage servicing are shown on Chart 12-1.

Several factors have influenced and will continue to influence the future of mortgage companies. The pressing need for huge amounts of capital to originate and hold loans for future sale and to finance sideline activities has forced many of the smaller companies to submit to purchase by larger ones and many of the larger ones to consolidate with or seek purchase by commercial banks, other financial institutions or by large industrial companies. Commercial banks have been very willing and major purchasers of mortgage companies due to the reliance of mortgage companies on commercial banks and particularly due to servicing profits and income available to the banks from use of escrow deposits. Unless laws are passed severely restricting bank holding companies, the pursuit of mortgage bankers by commercial banks will continue.

PENSION FUNDS

The tremendous growth of pension funds, mainly over the last fifty years, is one of the phenomena of this century. Motivated by labor's demand for security and more benefits, employers have reacted by establishing pension and retirement programs. These programs are not one-sided; they also reap benefits for employers by reducing employee turnover and encouraging longevity of service.

The American Express Agency established the first pension plan for employees in 1875. Other plans, created by several railroads and utility companies, followed shortly after the turn of this century. Then the manufacturing industries, prompted by labor unions, began to establish pension programs. By 1920 the Federal Government was thinking in terms of fulfilling worker retirement needs and acted by establishing the Civil Service Retirement System. The first public pension program appeared in the early 1930s when Congress created the Old Age and Survivors Disability Insurance System (social security program).

The Social Security Act of 1935 in essence marked the beginning of the fabulous growth period for both public and private pension funds, both as to total assets and number of funds. However, many of the subsequent programs were planned as supplements to the federal government social security program.

During World War II wage and price controls were established. The only inducements available for use this period in attracting and retaining employees

CHART 12-1

Copyright by American Banker, 1974, New York, N. Y.

THE FIRST 100 LARGEST MORTGAGE COMPANIES

Rank 6/30/74	Name of Firm & Headquarters City	Dollar Volume of Mortgages Serviced 6/30/74	6/30/73	Rank 6/30/73	Gain in Rank	No. of Mortgages Serviced 6/30/74	No. of Investors 6/30/74	Year Established
1	LOMAS & NETTLETON FINANCIAL CORP., DALLAS	$4,406,375,660	$4,204,111,000	1		321,458	691	1894
2	UNIONAMERICA, INC., LOS ANGELES (b)	2,310,882,000	2,126,290,000	2		92,949	200	1972
3	ASSOCIATED MORTGAGE COS., INC., WASHINGTON, D. C.	2,043,754,387	1,832,203,548 #	3		117,200	327	1962
4	COLONIAL MORTGAGE SERVICE CO., PHILADELPHIA	2,021,000,000	1,607,000,000	6	+ 2	91,296	275	1968
5	ADVANCE MORTGAGE CORP., SOUTHFIELD, MICH.	1,980,504,856	1,783,131,000	4		118,152	345	1939
6	JAMES T. BARNES & CO., DETROIT	1,790,852,000	1,725,059,000	5		75,984	177	1946
7	CAMERON-BROWN CO., RALEIGH, N. C.	1,656,393,011	1,485,655,383	8	+ 1	91,900	379	1946
8	NATIONAL HOMES ACCEPTANCE CORP., LAFAYETTE, IND.	1,603,000,000	1,537,879,000	7		130,122	827	1947
9	KISSELL CO., SPRINGFIELD, OHIO	1,501,058,713	1,238,596,779	10	+ 1	97,123	683	1884
10	COLWELL CO., LOS ANGELES	1,418,073,491	1,390,071,039	9		77,753	260	1947
11	STOCKTON, WHATLEY, DAVIN & CO., JACKSONVILLE FLA.	1,336,316,000	1,167,835,397	11		67,819	220	1884
12	WEYERHAEUSER MORTGAGE CO., LOS ANGELES	1,175,658,939	1,035,378,883	12		62,203	160	1955
13	KASSLER & CO., DENVER	1,100,000,000	956,000,000	15	+ 2	60,000	300	1924
14	MASON-McDUFFIE CO., BERKELEY, CALIF.	1,090,331,000	935,003,527	16	+ 2	45,057	152	1887
15	MORTGAGE ASSOCIATES, INC., MILWAUKEE	1,019,740,711	970,571,793	14		68,721	615	1921
16	CHASE MANHATTAN REALTY CAPITAL CORP., NEW YORK	1,009,538,887	1,000,450,015	13		49,201	142	1973
17	BANKERS MORTGAGE CO. OF CALIFORNIA, SAN FRANCISCO	985,194,883	887,870,563	19	+ 2	51,573	118	1954
18	JAMES W. ROUSE & CO., INC., COLUMBIA, MD.	973,707,671	933,243,757	17		12,223	84	1939
19	MORTGAGE & TRUST, INC., HOUSTON	968,472,861	895,329,005	18		56,653	160	1946
20	FIRST MORTGAGE CO. OF TEXAS, INC., HOUSTON	933,155,000	720,030,056	28	+ 8	31,979	171	1961
21	BOWEST MORTGAGE CORP., LOS ANGELES	930,209,007				56,463	125	1970
22	WELLS FARGO MORTGAGE CO., SAN FRANCISCO	912,003,000				46,042	227	1973
23	AMFAC FINANCIAL, INC., LOS ANGELES	891,471,000 ¶	710,833,000 ¶	31	+ 8	45,037	173	1973
24	COLDWELL BANKER MANAGEMENT CORP., LOS ANGELES	857,000,000	713,585,000	30	+ 6	13,840	9	1972
25	AMERICAN FLETCHER MORTGAGE CO., INDIANAPOLIS	846,470,210	715,357,294	29	+ 4	31,915	149	1953
26	PALOMAR FINANCIAL, SAN DIEGO, CALIF.	837,941,772	805,233,199	21		59,953	146	1950
27	FIRST MORTGAGE CORP., RICHMOND, VA.	825,200,871	689,409,000	33	+ 6	28,191	158	1934
28	VNB MORTGAGE CORP., RICHMOND, VA.	809,408,180	749,496,334	25		48,419	118	1946
29	COBBS, ALLEN & HALL MORTGAGE CO., INC., BIRMINGHAM, ALA.	789,304,126	775,248,243	22		47,199	187	1946
30	SOUTHEAST MORTGAGE CO., MIAMI	771,072,522	741,218,000	26		27,854	157	1970
31	CITIZENS MORTGAGE CORP., SOUTHFIELD, MICH.	770,000,000	750,769,000	24		48,000	154	1946
32	WACHOVIA MORTGAGE CO., WINSTON-SALEM, N. C.	768,441,248	676,542,000	34	+ 2	28,137	140	1968
33	PERCY WILSON MORTGAGE & FINANCE CORP., CHICAGO	767,761,470	662,600,824	36	+ 3	41,544	345	1926
34	WEAVER BROS., INC., WASHINGTON, D. C.	757,394,832	740,947,000	27		23,047	30	1888
35	BANCO MORTGAGE CO., MINNEAPOLIS	756,550,000	594,000,000	41	+ 6	32,400	57	1910
36	NORTHLAND MORTGAGE CO., ST. PAUL, MINN.	751,682,174	647,235,482	38	+ 2	24,269	135	1940
37	J. I. KISLAK MORTGAGE CORP., MIAMI	746,550,329	751,509,997	23		50,527	218	1953
38	AMERICAN GENERAL INVESTMENT CORP., HOUSTON	719,029,122	658,048,717	37		30,580	33	1939
39	RALPH C. SUTRO CO., LOS ANGELES	694,759,000	708,956,000	32		25,278	111	1910
40	IDS MORTGAGE CORP., MINNEAPOLIS	671,768,829	626,325,660	391		32,632	122	1894
41	COAST MORTGAGE CO., SEATTLE	671,194,852	667,270,637	35		38,779	50	1948
42	CITIZENS & SOUTHERN MORTGAGE CO., ATLANTA	629,462,402				19,272	164	1887
43	GLENN JUSTICE MORTGAGE CO., INC., DALLAS	626,206,347	608,025,485	39		32,513	124	1953
44	NCNB MORTGAGE CORP., CHARLOTTE, N.C.	619,800,000	315,255,668	81	+ 37	28,064	65	1969
45	COLONIAL MORTGAGE CO. OF INDIANA, INC., FORT WAYNE	614,625,470	523,350,207	45		32,784	70	1951
46	SOUTHERN TRUST & MORTGAGE CO., DALLAS	605,000,000	568,000,000	43		34,000	100	1924
47	JERSEY MORTGAGE CO., ELIZABETH, N. J.	588,835,846	569,957,005	42		19,409	77	1937
48	LATIMER & BUCK MORTGAGE CO., PHILADELPHIA	578,701,461	594,932,805	40		41,635	78	1971
49	FIDELITY BOND & MORTGAGE CO., PHILADELPHIA	573,092,039	502,287,496	49		25,861	86	1940
50	ZENITH MORTGAGE CO., BEVERLY HILLS, CALIF.	557,220,812	555,877,039	44		25,527	120	1969
51	NEW YORK URBAN SERVICING CO., INC., NEW YORK	546,700,000	510,500,000	47		564	7	1936
52	MELLON NATIONAL MORTGAGE CO. OF OHIO, CLEVELAND	544,496,610	509,436,310	48		19,174	51	1945
53	COLLATERAL INVESTMENT CO., BIRMINGHAM, ALA.	521,000,692	485,104,627	51		36,584	150	1933
54	GALBREATH MORTGAGE CO., COLUMBUS, OHIO	520,974,218	463,102,000	54		21,529	125	1946
55	WESTERN PACIFIC FINANCIAL CORP., SAN BERNARDINO, CALIF.	520,000,000	436,207,000	55		29,831	87	1924
56	FIRSTBANK MORTGAGE CORP., SEATTLE	519,763,000	520,764,000	46		29,728	104	1945
57	RYAN MORTGAGE CO., ARLINGTON, TEX.	516,434,646	500,134,852	50		35,181	245	1919
58	MERCANTILE MORTGAGE CO., ST. LOUIS, MO.	447,686,316	409,053,909	57		24,090	80	1947
59	THARPE & BROOKS, INC., ATLANTA	443,099,499	412,078,782	56		6,303	29	1971
60	UNITED JERSEY MORTGAGE CO., HACKENSACK, N. J.	442,082,930	337,366,627	69	+ 9			
61	ATICO MORTGAGE CORP., MIAMI	442,000,000	464,772,800	53		28,870	117	1941
62	FORT WORTH MORTGAGE CORP., ARLINGTON, TEX.	438,710,603	328,146,849	76	+ 14	22,104	128	1952
63	INDIANA MORTGAGE CORP., INDIANAPOLIS	438,431,784	360,631,494	65	+ 2	11,724	65	1954
64	CHARLES F. CURRY & CO., KANSAS CITY, MO.	436,993,000	385,756,844	61		31,387	110	1928
65	NATIONAL MORTGAGE CO., MEMPHIS	435,438,305	316,232,083	78	+ 13	32,298	74	1951
66	MIDLAND MORTGAGE CO., OKLAHOMA CITY	430,173,408	331,085,413	74	+ 8	25,417	122	1950
67	ALISON COMPANY, NEWPORT BEACH, CALIF.	420,146,110	261,838,174	101	+ 34	2,745	8	1934
68	MIDLANTIC MORTGAGE CORP., NEWARK, N. J.	414,792,022	361,128,596	63		32,900	89	1939
69	GULF COAST INVESTMENT CORP., HOUSTON	403,000,000	387,318,688	60		17,132	97	1927
70	UNITED VIRGINIA MORTGAGE CORP., RICHMOND	393,612,875	295,931,603	86	+ 16			
71	LUMBERMEN'S INVESTMENT CORP., AUSTIN, TEX.	390,384,585	361,080,175	64		28,512	107	1954
72	FIRST DENVER MORTGAGE CO., DENVER	388,468,645	342,361,905	67		17,489	71	1953
73	AMERICAN MORTGAGE CO., HOUSTON	385,319,476				23,366	95	1915
74	DETROIT MORTGAGE & REALTY CO.	384,862,273	384,286,168	62		18,850	16	1908
75	PEOPLES MORTGAGE CO., SEATTLE	369,675,150	333,330,818	72		19,747	64	1908
76	FIRST CONTINENTAL MORTGAGE CO., HOUSTON	367,831,778	336,523,968	71		22,174	91	1940
77	GUARANTY MORTGAGE CO., NASHVILLE, TENN	360,000,000	332,417,479	73		27,724	60	1922
78	COMMERCE MORTGAGE CO., PORTLAND, ORE.	356,900,000	357,850,000	66		24,049	50	1955
79	MORTGAGE SECURITIES, INC., CLEVELAND	351,360,581	336,673,080	70		2,115	7	1927
80	WALLACE MOIR CO., BEVERLY HILLS CALIF.	350,291,910	298,656,578	85	+ 5			
81	MODERN AMERICAN MORTGAGE CORP., LITTLE ROCK, ARK.	348,386,177	294,644,366	87	+ 6	18,663	97	1967
82	DRAPER & KRAMER, INC., CHICAGO	343,269,555	315,901,903	80		7,605	70	1893
83	SCHUMACHER MORTGAGE CO., INC., MEMPHIS	342,932,591	315,194,519	82		23,222	126	1933
84	MOLTON, ALLEN & WILLIAMS, INC., BIRMINGHAM, ALA.	342,923,000	224,232,866	125	+ 41	16,230	114	1886
85	HOLLAND MORTGAGE & INVESTMENT CORP., HOUSTON	341,231,000	315,927,811	79		14,487	144	1948
86	ENGEL MORTGAGE CO., INC., BIRMINGHAM, ALA.	338,157,596	301,148,275	83		17,641	73	1946
87	LATIMER & BUCK, INC., PHILADELPHIA	335,396,267	342,042,220	68		1,516	12	1949
88	HONOLULU MORTGAGE CO., LTD.	328,419,000	323,654,304	77		20,621	88	1950
89	INVESTOR'S MORTGAGE SERVICE CO., LOS ANGELES	327,090,700	330,377,767	75		8,634	45	1954
90	STANDARD MORTGAGE CORP., NEW ORLEANS, LA.	326,750,000	275,004,000	93	+ 3	13,742	20	1964
91	STOCKTON, WHITE & CO., RALEIGH, N. C.	322,067,895	247,748,701	106	+ 15	11,464	45	1945
92	BOGLEY, HARTING, MAHONEY & LEBLING, INC., ROCKVILLE, MD.	319,025,686	273,536,037	94	+ 2	17,485	54	1950
93	UNITED FIRST MORTGAGE CORP., SAN DIEGO, CALIF.	317,467,194	279,899,573	90		20,393	35	1972
94	C. DOUGLAS WILSON & CO., GREENVILLE, S.C.	317,000,000	276,724,296	92		20,000	40	1928
95	WATERFIELD MORTGAGE CO. INC., FORT WAYNE, IND.	316,500,000	269,500,000	99	+ 4	19,343	107	1932
96	SHERWOOD & ROBERTS, INC., SEATTLE	316,093,448	285,273,809	88		21,528	66	1920
97	MORTGAGE INVESTMENT CO. OF EL PASO, TEX.	315,828,000	280,217,000	89		15,158	54	1950
98	KENTUCKY MORTGAGE CO., INC., LEXINGTON	313,284,000	269,794,130	98		15,780	70	1966
99	COLONIAL MORTGAGE CORP., MONTGOMERY, ALA.	312,370,993	265,649,889	100	+ 1	1,361	30	1922
100	REPUBLIC REALTY MORTGAGE CORP., CHICAGO	304,342,435	243,013,375	109	+ 9			

(a)—Excluding loans owned by mortgage companies. (b)—Servicing is by Western Mortgage Corp., a division, and by Scott Hudgens Realty & Mortgage, Inc., a subsidiary, both of which are part of Unionamerica Mortgage Banking & Real Estate Group, a division of company. ‡—Based on revised data. Rank that company would have had if revised data had been available. #—Revised. ¶—A major part of servicing is by a subsidiary, Amfac Mortgage Corp., Los Angeles.

were fringe benefits, such as pension plans. Thus, labor unions bargained for and employers preferred pension plans as a means of indirect employee compensation. Pension funds continued as a prime fringe benefit in the post war era particularly after a 1949 court decision upholding the National Labor Relations Board finding that pension plans were an appropriate subject for collective bargaining. In late 1974 the passage of the Employee Retirement Income Security Act of 1974 completely overhauled the entire private pension system, created a set of standards for pension funds and provided for greater employee pension benefit protection. Chart 12-2 and Chart 12-3 reflect the continuation of that growth in recent years.

CLASSIFICATION

Pension Funds can be divided into four major classifications:
1. **Insured funds,** which are administered by life insurance companies, their assets being administered together with the other resources of life insurance companies.
2. **Federal pension funds** including the assets of old age and survivors insurance, civil service retirement, railroad retirement, and disability insurance. (For potential mortgage investment purposes, however, only the following two classifications need be considered).
3. State and local government employees' retirement systems which at the end of 1977 had total assets of approximately $132 billion.
4. Noninsured corporate pension funds which had total assets of over $184 billion at the end of 1977.

STATE AND LOCAL GOVERNMENT PENSION FUNDS

In the past these funds have concentrated their assets in corporate bonds, treasury obligations, and state and local government obligations. Mortgages make up about 11 percent of total investments and a substantial portion of these mortgage holdings consists of FHA Title VIII "Capehart" mortgages on military housing, which are both insured by FHA and guaranteed by the federal government and, therefore, are comparable to obligations of the federal government.

These pension funds try to limit their mortgage investments to their own states. Most of the state and local government retirement systems have stayed out of the mortgage investment field due to the lack of trustees' knowledge about mortgage investments and their desire for simple, no-management problem investments. Those which have ventured into the mortgage market have favored VA-guaranteed mortgages and FHA-insured single and multi-family mortgages.

The eleven percent of assets invested in mortgages by state and local government pension funds is over three times the percentage of mortgages to assets of the noninsured corporate pension funds. Two factors are presently at work motivating these funds into mortgage investments: the need to meet actuarial requirements of their funds, which in past years have required supplementary appropriations from the general revenues of governmental bodies; and the trend away from and current liquidation of holdings of state and local governmental obligations. These holdings return low yields and their tax-exempt features are of no advantage to these funds. The monies thus freed from these investments must be put into higher yielding securities such as mortgages.

NONINSURED CORPORATE PENSION FUNDS

These private funds constitute the largest and fastest growing class of pension funds and represent the greatest untapped source of new mortgage funds in the United States.

Administration of these funds is accomplished by selected or elected employees of the individual corporation. The management and investment responsibility is separate from that of administration and is placed in the hand of trustees. The trustees derive their power from a trust indenture which creates the

CHART 12-2

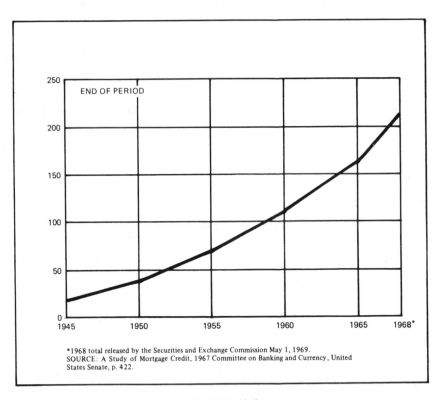

*1968 total released by the Securities and Exchange Commission May 1, 1969.
SOURCE: A Study of Mortgage Credit, 1967 Committee on Banking and Currency, United States Senate, p. 422.

CHART 12-3
Actual and Projected Pension Fund Growth
(Billions(

	1961	1971	1981 a
Insured Funds	$21.6	$ 44.5	$ 91.8
Non-Insured Funds	41.9	128.4	214.2
State & Local Government Systems	24.2	64.8	180.0
Total	$87.7	$237.7	$486.0

a) Estimated Assets

Source: National Bureau of Economic Research

trust and sets up the mechanics of fund receipts, investments, and benefit payouts.

Trustees of these plans are either investment counselors, individuals, or commercial banks.

Investment counselors administer no great number of pension funds. But, in addition to acting as trustees on some funds, they serve as advisors to many funds which are individually managed, thus exerting a considerable amount of influence over these funds.

Those funds which are handled by individuals as trustees, usually officers of the particular corporation, are termed "self-administered." The pension funds of several of the country's largest private corporations are of the self-administered type. However, the total assets of such funds represent only a minor fraction of total noninsured corporate pension funds even though the number of such funds is quite high.

The greatest part of noninsured corporate pension fund assets are managed under commercial bank trusteeships. About 40 percent of this proportion of the total is under the trusteeship of seven banks with two banks, Morgan Guaranty Trust and Bankers Trust Company, accounting for almost 25 percent of the commercial bank trusteeship accounts. This concentration therefore makes a few commercial banks the major investors of private pension funds.

INVESTMENTS

In 1958 corporate bonds accounted for the greatest share of corporate pension fund assets. Now the most significant pension fund investment is common stocks. Chart 12-4, obtained from the Securities and Exchange Commission, reflects the distribution of private noninsured corporate pension fund assets during 1958 and 1969; and Chart 12-5 reflects the recent distribution of pension fund assets. Note that mortgages now account for slightly more than 10 percent of all assets. Pension funds are totally exempt from income and capital gain taxation. This permits their trustees to make investment decisions entirely on the basis of investment judgment.

CHART 12-4
DISTRIBUTION OF ASSETS

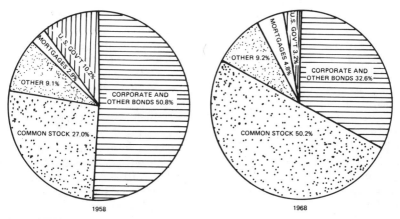

1958   1968

Source: United States Securities and Exchange Commission.

CHART 12-5
Distribution of Pension Assets,
December 31, 1973 ($ billions)

	Life Insurance Companies		Private Non-insured Pension Funds		State and Local Retirement Funds		Total	
Corporate shares	$ 4.8	9.5%	$ 89.2	67.4%	$18.6	17.3	$112.6	45.4%
Corporate and foreign bonds	18.6	37.0	29.8	22.6	49.4	55.9	97.8	33.4
Home mortgages	5.8	11.5	2.7	2.9	—	—	8.5	3.4
Mortgages other than on homes	12.0	23.9	—	—	6.7	11.0	18.7	6.8
U.S. government securities	.9	1.8	4.3	2.1	4.6	9.3	9.8	4.0
Loans, not elsewhere classified	4.7	9.3	—	—	—	—	4.7	1.5
State and local government securities	.8	1.6	—	—	1.4	2.9	2.2	1.1
Cash	.4	0.8	2.3	1.2	1.0	.8	3.7	1.0
Miscellaneous	2.3	4.6	4.9	3.7	—	3.1	7.2	3.6
Total	50.4	100.0	133.3	100.0	81.6	100.0	265.3	100.0

Sources: Federal Reserve Bulletin 60 (October 1974): A59-15; Institute of Life Insurance, Life Insurance Fact Book 1974 (New York: Institute of Life Insurance, 1974), pp. 67-69.

Note: Pension assets of life insurance companies are estimated, based upon the Federal Reserve statements of assets by type, distributed in accordance with total life insurance liabilities (including reserves) and surplus.

BONDS VERSUS MORTGAGES

The problem of bond versus mortgage yields is an interesting one and it probably contains the answer to increased pension fund investment in mortgages. Over the last decade FHA-insured and VA-guaranteed mortgage yields have ranged from 1/2 to one percent over AAA rated corporate bonds and 1 1/4 percent to 2 1/2 percent over municipal and United States government long-term bonds. Mortgages return interest monthly whereas bond interest is paid semi-annually. Thus the yield on mortgages must be increased by the time of payment factor. In addition the safety of FHA and VA mortgages has been assured by the property, the borrower's credit, and the governmental agency insurance or guarantee. Why then have bonds been favored over FHA and VA mortgages as investments? The primary reason appears to be the fact that bonds have long maturities and do not return principal in small monthly amounts, causing reinvestment problems. Speaking to this problem, pension funds, unlike other institutional lenders, generally do not need a return on investment capital to meet benefit needs. They usually serve employee retirement needs by paying monthly benefits. These benefit requirements are easily met by investment yields. Thus, the monthly return of investment capital in the form of mortgage principal repayment creates an added management and investment problem.

There are two other reasons for favoring bonds over mortgages. Mortgage investments require a special knowledge and expertise or at least a fundamental understanding of real estate finance, while bond investments can safely be accomplished by laymen; and mortgage investment requires inspection of all legal documentation by the trustees of the fund or their agent or attorney to insure acquisition of a valid security. No such requirement is placed upon bond investments.

The answer therefore lies in converting a mortgage investment into a bond type investment. Recently this has been partially accomplished by the introduction in the late 1960s of the GNMA mortgage-backed security. An investment in a GNMA security removes the special knowledge and documentation inspection factors and adds the full guarantee of the federal government to the transaction. Thus the GNMA mortgage-backed security is as easy an investment as a bond and certainly safer. Its appearance has drawn more pension fund dollars into the mortgage market and should continue to do so. (At the end of 1978, twelve percent of outstanding GNMA securities were held by pension funds.) However, it retains one salient feature of a mortgage which makes the GNMA security less attractive than a bond. That feature is the repayment of principal in monthly installments. Some steps have been taken to cure this problem, but until a true bond-type government-backed security appears that may be marketed in issues of $10 million or less, mortgages will have an uphill fight to compete equally with bonds for pension fund credits (bond-type GNMA guaranteed mortgage-backed securities may now be issued but the total issue must be $100 million or larger).

OTHER MORTGAGE INVESTMENTS

Besides the FHA and VA mortgages and GNMA-mortgage-backed securities, pension funds participate in a variety of other real estate financing areas. Some of these are as follows:

1. FHA insured multifamily project mortgages loans are a means of quick investment of large sums of money, usually for relatively long periods of time (up to forty years), but have several drawbacks. They usually yield less than single family FHA-insured loans and, in the event of foreclosure, only 99 percent of the unpaid principal is returned or low-yielding debentures are given in place of cash. These latter two problems are curable by a GNMA multifamily mortgage-backed security, but using the GNMA approach further lowers the yield on the mortgage under the security.
2. Sale-leasebacks are a pension fund favorite since the yield on investment is high and the security usually good when the proper selection of deals has been made. Where there are no repurchase options the residual value of the property adds to the investment potential of these transactions.
3. Office building, shopping center, and industrial property loans are made by pension funds with real estate oriented personnel, but are not a normal mortgage investment for the unsophisticated pension fund trustee.

When pension funds obtain the facilities and staff for mortgage portfolio administration, they will place greater emphasis on mortgage investments of the types listed directly above. But, present staff and facilities severely limit the mortgage investments of pension funds to the single family insured and guaranteed mortgage loan area.

REGULATION

Pension funds are state organized and therefore are governed by the laws of the state in which they are established. The trust indenture is the creating instrument and the trustees elected thereunder are bound to invest the monies from the fund according to state statutes governing the investment of trust funds by trustees and according to the specific provisions of the trust indenture.

In practically all states the general standard established for pension trust investments by their trustees is the "prudent man rule." This rule of law states that "in investing, reinvesting, purchasing, acquiring, exchanging, selling and managing property for the benefit of another, a trustee shall exercise the judgment and care, under the circumstances then prevailing, which men of prudence, discretion and intelligence exercise in the management of their own affairs, not in regard to speculation, but in regard to the permanent disposition of their funds, considering the probable income, as well as the probable safety of their capital." State laws do in many instances give a list of legal investments. However, investments so listed are authorized but not mandatory.

IMPACT

The rapid expansion of pension funds and their growing acceptance of mortgages as an appropriate investment medium point to an increasingly important role for these funds in the mortgage market. Recently pension funds have been under pressure from the federal government to step up mortgage investments. This pressure in the form of threatened removal of tax benefits is a definite stimulus to mortgage investment. However, it seems most likely that the mortgage investments of pension funds in the near future will be as large in proportion to their assets as those of the other major groups of institutional investors; nor is it logical to assume that the commitment to the mortgage market of the pension funds, with almost the entire spectrum of investments at their disposal, will be very substantial.

CREDIT UNIONS

Due to recent legislation and growth, credit unions are new potential sources for substantial mortgage credit funds.

HISTORY

Credit Union's trace their beginnings to the depression ridden Southern Germany of 1849. Friedrick Raiffeisen, Mayor of a small German town put forth the concept of having poor farmers and workers pool their resources which could then be re-lent to themselves at low interest rates for productive purposes. This concept, Raiffeisen felt, would allow the workers and farmers to gain financial independence and avoid commercial borrowing sources.

This successful concept came to North America in 1900 with the founding of a credit union in Quebec by Alphonse Desjardins. Desjardins helped to organize 150 credit unions prior to his death. One of those credit unions was the St. Mary's Parish Credit Union, founded in 1909 in New Hampshire as the first credit union in the United States.

The credit union movement in the United States was recognized and assisted in 1934 by the passage of the Federal Credit Union Act which gave power to credit union organizations anywhere in the United States and its territories.

At the end of 1978 credit unions in the United States had grown to over $62 billion in assets and nearly 22,000 separate credit unions.

COMMON BOND

Credit unions exist to serve members with a common bond, not the general public. The predominate common bond is occupational, (members working for the same or closely associated employer), accounting for about 79 percent of the nearly 40 million credit union members. The common bond of association membership, such as church professional groups or labor unions accounts for 17 percent of all members. The 4 percent balance of credit union membership enjoys a residential or community common bond.

FEDERAL VS STATE

A further distinction in credit unions is that they are either state chartered or Federal. Federal credit unions serve all the various employees of the federal government and are by far the largest and group. At the end of 1978 there were 12,500 Federal credit unions with over $34 billion assets, while state chartered credit unions totaled 9,500 and had assets of $28 billion.

LENDING POWERS

In general, credit unions may make the following types of loans to their members.
1. Loans up to 12 years for any purpose, secured or unsecured, (primarily auto loans which account for 30 percent of all loans).
2. Members home loans with mortgages up to 30 years.
3. Mobile home loans up to 15 years.
4. Home improvement loans for periods up to 15 years.
5. State or Federal government insured or guaranteed loans on such terms and provisions as set forth in the specific loan program.
6. Credit card or other line-of-credit loans.
7. Participation loans with other credit unions in authorized loans.

ORGANIZATION

Credit unions are controlled by their members who are generally prohibited from giving proxy voting authority to management. Each member is allowed one vote regardless of the amount of his deposit account and is encouraged to take an active role in decision making.

Since credit unions are primarily volunteer organizations their officers and directors with few exceptions, serve without pay.

MORTGAGE LENDING

Credit unions specialize in consumer lending. However, legislation introduced in 1977 which now allows for 30 year home mortgages, 15 year home improvement loans and mobile home loans will in the future expand the real estate lending activities of credit unions.

As to home mortgages, the 40 million credit union members represent a substantial captive group of home buyers. If credit unions as a total organization are able to establish a secondary market for home loans originated by them, they will become not only mortgage loan investors but originators as well.

Thus the future impact of credit unions in the real estate market will in the areas of (a) the amount of credit union assets which are invested in home mortgages (at the end of 1978 this amounted to just over $4.4 billion or 7 percent of total assets) and (b) their ability to become a source of home loans for their substantial membership.

QUESTIONS FOR THOUGHT AND DISCUSSION

1. What has accounted for the rapid growth of mortgage companies in the post-World War II era?
2. How does a mortgage company function?
3. a. What sideline activities do mortgage companies engage in?
   b. Can you think of any activity other than those listed in this chapter which would be good for a mortgage company to pursue?
4. What is the mortgage company's obligation as to loans serviced for its investors?
5. Account for the phenomenal growth of pension funds in the United States.
6. a. Why do pension funds favor bonds over mortgages as investments?
   b. How would you structure the GNMA mortgage backed security in order to make it bond-like in character, particularly with regard to automatic reinvestment of principal or delay of principal repayment without affecting the mortgage backing the security?
7. Why do you feel common stocks are a good investment for pension funds?
8. What potential impact upon the mortgage market do credit unions have?

13

INVESTMENT TRUSTS

The real estate and mortgage investment trusts, commonly referred to as REITs and MITs respectively, are the creatures of tax legislation. Today's investment trusts are new, but the idea is quite similar to the so-called "Massachusetts trust" or "business trust" that originated more than 100 years ago.

BACKGROUND

The Massachusetts trust was a result of the Massachusetts laws prohibiting the ownership of real estate by a corporate entity other than property incidental to its business operation, such as a building owned by a corporation for use as its own office and/or factory. Thus, the Massachusetts trust form, providing for property ownership vested in a trustee and the issuance by the trustee of transferable shares of beneficial ownership in the trust and trust property, was devised. Originally, these trusts were composed of a small number of beneficial shareholders and their investments were limited to quality center city properties. Once they became successful, the trusts sought out additional share subscriptions from the general public.

Their success flourished and Massachusetts trusts became the medium for participation in large commercial real estate properties by the small investor who otherwise would be unable to enjoy such ownership. As time passed, more trusts were formed, thereby creating a vehicle for the transfer of investment capital from its point of concentration in the East to the then-booming areas of the Midwest and West.

The beginning of the end for these trusts resulted from the post-Great-Depression United States Supreme Court decision holding that a Massachusetts trust with transferable shares was taxable as a corporation. This decision helped sour existing and potential investors who were seeking cash flow and tax advantages, not tax disadvantages. During World War II a heavy corporation tax period obtained, and resulted in an almost complete diminution of interest by investors in purchasing shares of real estate trusts. Investors could find many other sources for their funds and did not need or want the burden of "double taxation" (one tax payable on the trust income at corporate rates, the second payable on the distributions to the investors at individual rates.)

In the postwar years, the trustees of those existing and then-suffering trusts formed a lobby on Capital Hill and sought legislation that would gain for their trusts the same income pass-through benefits that had been given to mutual funds by the Investment Company Acts of 1938 and 1940.

PRESENT TRUSTS LEGISLATION

The results of their long and laborious lobbying was the passage by Congress in the fall of 1960 of Public Law 86-779 adding three new sections to the Internal Revenue Code of 1954, Sections 856, 857, and 858, which make available to real estate and mortgage investment trusts the special tax benefits that had already been given to regulated investment companies. Thus, under present law, real estate or mortgage investment trusts or associations which distribute 90 percent or more of their ordinary income are taxed at corporate rates only on their retained earnings with the beneficial shareholders paying only the tax on the distributions of the trust. To qualify for this special tax treatment the trusts must meet a number of other requirements which are set forth in the law and in regulations issued by the Internal Revenue Service:

1. To be eligible under the statute, a real estate investment company must:
   b. Be organized under state law as an unincorporated trust or association managed by one or more trustees;
   b. Have transferable shares or certificates of beneficial interest;
   c. Be a type of organization which would be taxes as an ordinary domestic corporation in the absence of the provision of these Sections of the Internal Revenue Code.
2. The beneficial ownership of qualifying real estate investment trusts must be held by 100 or more persons with not less than six individuals directly or indirectly owning more than 50 percent of the trust.
3. The real estate investment trust must elect to be treated as such and may not hold any property primarily for sale to customers in the ordinary course of trade or business. This provision, together with certain other provisions restricting trusts from providing services to tenants except through an independent contractor, are designed to make sure that the trust operates as a conduit strictly for investment income.
4. Income requirements are divided into the three following categories, all three of which must be met by a trust in order to qualify:
   a. Ninety percent or more of a trust's gross income must be obtained from dividends, interest, the rents from real property, gains from the sales of securities and real property, and abatements and refunds of taxes on real property.

b. Seventy-five percent of the trust income must be derived from real property. Another 15 percent must be derived from either real property or from sources from which a regulated investment company may derive 90 percent of its income. The remaining 10 percent is not limited as to source.

The difference in the 90 percent and 75 percent tests is that for the 90 percent test, the additional items which may qualify as investment income are dividends, interest on any obligations, and gain from the sale or other disposition of stock or securities.

c. Not more than 30 percent of the trust's gross income may be obtained from sales of securities held for less than six months or from sales of real property held for less than four years apart from involuntary conversions. This test relates to the requirement that the trust not hold property for sale to customers in the ordinary course of business.

d. At the close of each quarter at least 75 percent of the trust's assets must be in real estate assets, cash and cash items, and government securities. The remaining 25 percent may be in other investments, but the trust may not invest more than 5 percent of total assets in the securities of any one issuer nor hold more than 10 percent of the voting securities of any insurer. When it has bought the wrong kind of property or securities, the trust has thirty days after the close of the quarter to meet the tests.

TODAY'S TRUSTS

The intention of the Public Law 86-779 was to afford an opportunity for investment in real estate by the small investor. While this intention has become a reality, it is important to note that the country's large financial institutions, not the smaller investors, have been the prime movers of these trusts. Nevertheless, through investment diversifications and capable management, today's trusts have offered the small investor a means of investing in real estate. The future of these trusts and the security of an investment in them is in question today. This subject will be discussed later in this chapter.

Equity trusts are engaged primarily in the ownership of real property which may or may not be subject to mortgages or other encumbrances. Their investments may be in commercial, residential or industrial real estate, vacant land, or leaseholds.

The primary source of income for equity trusts is rental income. The trusts benefit from inflation increasing the value of their properties, but are particularly sensitive to population shifts, serious recessions, and any other factors that influence real estate ownership.

Perhaps the greatest advantage of equity trusts is the depreciation of their real estate holding. This depreciation, to the extent of trust income, is passed through to the beneficial shareholders and acts as a tax shelter on taxable trust dividends. Thus, a shareholder receiving a dividend of $10 per share may be subject to individual income tax on $2 and be able to retain the balance free of any tax due to depreciation. However, the tax shelter will reduce the purchase price tax base per share and create a capital gains tax situation upon a subsequent sale of shares. On the disadvantage side, their assets are relatively fixed and not as liquid as those of the mortgage trusts.

A review of the prospectus of one of the first equity trusts to be created after the 1960 law reflects that its purpose is "to provide investors with an opportunity to own, through transferable shares, an interest in the Trust which, in turn, will own diversified real estate."

The property investment policy of this same trust, in part, is as follows:

> "The Trust will acquire real estate of such types as office buildings, apartment houses, hotel or motel properties, shopping centers, hospitals, industrial and commercial buildings, and special purpose buildings. The Trust may also acquire unimproved properties and undeveloped acreage for development by others into income-producing properties and undeveloped acreage for development by others into income-producing properties. The Trust will maintain a desirable degree of diversification. However, there is no policy with regard to the percentage of its assets which may be invested in a specific type of real estate. The Trust will seek to acquire real estate interests whenever a desirable investment opportunity is presented. The Trust has no policy with regard to geographic location of its investments.
>
> "Among the main points considered in an investment are location, gross and net rentals, term of tenancies, financial and business position of tenants, operating expenses, fixed charges, physical condition, residual value and future potential, and long-range investment and economic potential.
>
> "The investment policy of the Trust is to acquire properties primarily for cash yields, but with prospects for appreciation in value. The Trust may also invest in mortgages, in other non-equity interests in real estate, and may also invest in securities of real estate corporations and real estate investment trusts, and other securities generally, and in other real estate ventures including joint ventures, partnerships, and syndicates engaged in investing in income-producing properties. The Trust may also invest in interest-bearing obligations of federal, state and local governments to provide liquid reserves for contingencies and future investments. The Trust will not make loans to other persons unless secured by real estate mortgages, nor underwrite securities of other issuers, nor purchase securities of other issuers to exercise control."

As to cash generated by depreciation, its policy is "to use a portion of the funds generated by depreciation for distribution while making the balance available for capital expenditures and working capital."

The early Massachusetts trusts were primarily equity trusts and it was with the equity trusts in mind that Congress enacted the tax legislation which brought about their rebirth. Ironically, it has been the mortgage trusts, not the equity trusts which have captured the favor of investors and which have enjoyed the greatest growth and success over the last decade.

Mortgage trusts have as their goal the investment of assets in mortgages or other liens against real property. In the beginning, mortgage trusts were extremely conservative. They divided their investments between short-term and high-risk land acquisition, land development, and construction loans on the one hand and long-term, primarily FHA-insured and VA-guaranteed loans on the other. A great degree of attention was given to the latter.

The beginning of the tight money period of the mid-1960s saw FHA and VA loan originations declining rapidly, their yields doing likewise, and commercial banks withdrawing from mortgage lending in order to apply what funds they had to commercial loans. Therefore, mortgage trusts began to revise their investment policies. The FHA and VA long-term mortgages were relegated to a minor position, with the higher-yielding short-term mortgages being the backbone of the industry. Thus, in 1968, a new generation of mortgage trusts is said to have been born. Those trusts marketed in 1968 and subsequent years have espoused investment policies of placing trust assets "primarily in construction or development short-term first mortgage loans and to a lesser extent in certain FHA-insured or VA-guaranteed first mortgage loans."

These second generation trusts can also be distinguished from their predecessors by the fact that many have been created by large commercial banks (Chase Manhattan and Philadelphia National Bank), mortgage companies (Lomas and Nettleton Financial Corporation and Galbreath Mortgage Company), and large insurance companies (Mutual of New York and Connecticut General Life Insurance Company). The bank and insurance company involvement in mortgage trusts has drawn congressional attention and comment calling for steps to stop present and future ownership of mortgage trusts by these institutions.

Besides the short-term and long-term lending previously noted, mortgage trusts are involved in other related real estate financing areas, such as:

1. Warehousing loans to mortgage bankers, which are secured by the pledge of mortgages.
2. Standby commitments to make at future dates first mortgage long-term loans. This type of commitment is obtained by builders to satisfy the takeout requirements of construction loans obtained from others, usually commercial banks. It is a commitment that they have paid for and can use if needed. Frequently, however, the builder will go elsewhere for his permanent financing at better terms and rates. Fees derived from Standby commitments are not included in the permitted classes of income in applying both the 75 percent and the 90 percent tests and are therefore infrequently issued.
3. Gap commitments.
4. Wrap-around mortgages.
5. Second mortgages.
6. Sale-leasebacks and sale-contract-backs.
7. Home improvement mortgage loans.
8. Vacation and second home mortgages.
9. FHA-insured multifamily loans.

Chart 13-1 reflects a breakdown of trust investments in properties and mortgage loans as of mid-1977.

Obviously mortgage trusts derive their income chiefly from interest earned and discounts received during the terms of mortgage loans made by them. Therefore, their success hinges on the continuance of demand for land and construction loans at high yields. A change in the economy which acts to decrease construction will hurt these trusts. Additionally, should a recession occur, the incident of failure of construction projects will rise and create foreclosure situations for the trusts.

The loan investment policy of a mortgage trust organized during the mid-1960s is:

"As provided in the Declaration of Trust, the Trust's policy is to invest primarily in (1) first mortgage land acquisition and development loans, (2) first mortgage construction loans, and (3) first mortgage permanent loans (more fully described below).

"To the extent permitted under the tax law and the regulations thereunder, the Trust may invest in warehousing loans (interim financing of mortgages being assembled for permanent financing as a package) secured by the pledge of any of the types of mortgages with other investors, it is primarily engaged in the business of purchasing or otherwise acquiring

CHART 13-1

REIT INDUSTRY BALANCE SHEET (a)

	Most Recent	1st Q 1977	2nd Q 1976
ASSETS	—(in millions of dollars)—		
FIRST MORTGAGES:			
Land & Development	$ 1,592.0	$ 1,733.9	$ 2,246.7
Construction	2,300.8	2,360.7	3,949.3
Completed Properties:			
0-10 years	968.8	996.5	1,328.2
10+ years	1,925.9	1,965.6	1,969.9
JUNIOR MORTGAGES	947.1	975.3	1,231.6
LOAN LOSS RESERVES	(2,158.9)	(2,214.4)	(2,205.5)
PROPERTY OWNED	9,142.6	9,159.3	8,428.2
CASH AND OTHER ASSETS	898.9	894.7	1,009.7
	$15,617.2	$15,871.6	$17,958.1
LIABILITIES			
COMMERCIAL PAPER	$ 543.7	$ 513.6	$ 606.9
BANK LOANS	7,688.4	7,958.2	9,609.9
SENIOR NON-CV. DEBT	342.2	326.6	376.5
SUB NON-CV DEBT	924.9	941.7	1,015.7
CONVERTIBLE DEBT	636.7	624.4	608.6
MTGES ON PROP. OWNED	2,419.5	2,436.5	2,177.3
OTHER LIABILITIES	357.7	361.8	444.5
SHAREHOLDERS' EQUITY	2,704.1	2,708.8	3,118.7
	$15,617.2	$15,871.6	$17,958.1

(a)—From National Association of Real Estate Investment Trusts.

mortgages and liens on or interests in real estate other than participations in mortgage loans.

"It is the policy of the Trust to apportion its mortgage investments as follows: (1) At least 35 percent in first mortgages guaranteed or insured by the FHA, VA or other agency of the Federal or State government, and (2) the balance in acquisition, development, construction, and permanent conventional first mortgage loans not insured or guaranteed by any governmental agency.

"The primary area of investment is in the State of Ohio and Midwest region of the United States; however, the Trust may invest in any area of the United States where favorable yields prevail.

"Generally, the Trust does not originate or service its mortgage invest- ments; however, the Trustees have the right to alter such policies as they see fit. In the case of first mortgage loans involving the FHA or VA, capital is in many instances presently obtained by developers, builders and owners through FHA and VA approved local mortgage banking firms. Local mortgage banking firms, in turn, rely on a variety of sources of capital for the loans which such firms originate. The Trust affords the selected FHA or VA approved local mortgage banking firms with which it deals an opportunity to obtain each type of mortgage capital from a single source."

MIXED TRUSTS

During the last few years, several trusts were created for the purpose of making equity purchased and short-term construction loans. The equity-mort- gage combination offered by these trusts affords the investor the advantage that all depreciation can be utilized and offset against mortgage income.

SPECIALTY TRUSTS

Another recent innovation in the field is the creation of trusts to provide low-cost capital for another corporation. Examples are:
1. Stadium Realty Trust organized to raise funds for construction of the New England Patriots Football Stadium.
2. Marriott Inn Participating Investors—organized to loan exclusively to Mar- riott Inn Franchisees.

ADVANTAGES

Investment trusts offer several economic advantages to investors, as follows:
1. They bring together or *pool* the funds of many small investors for investment in real estate equities and mortgages.
2. They can reduce an investor's risk through *diversification* of investment. This is in comparison to partnership syndications and joint ventures which offer investment opportunities in only one or two properties.
3. They offer a fair degree of *liquidity,* since the shares of most investment trusts are registered and traded on a stock exchange.

TRUST-BORROWING ABILITY AND EARNING

Investment trusts, particularly the mortgage trusts, do not rely solely on sales of beneficial interest shares for acquiring investment capital. Once operational a trust often obtains additional funds for investment through such means as:
1. Bank borrowings.
2. The sale of commercial paper (short-term debt).
3. Additional public offerings or private placements of shares of beneficial interest or subordinated debt.

All of the above serve to create leverage and thereby produce greater returns for the trusts' beneficial intereat holders.

For example, a mortgage trust earning 13 percent net on its mortgage loans, say

4.5 percent over an existing "prime rate" of 8.5 percent, can borrow at 1.5 percent over the prime rate (taking into consideration the establishment of a compensating balance equal to a percentage of funds borrowed from the lending bank). With these borrowed funds the trust can now earn an additional 3 percent return. This leverage through borrowing and the high yields available from land and construction mortgage lending have caused the shares of mortgage trusts to register large gains. Thus, mortgage trusts during the early 1970s outperformed equity trusts, while investment trusts in general consistently did much better than Dow Jones industrials.

Another example of the same leverage technique, which shows the effect on the trusts' earnings per share, follows:

Presume a trust raises its initial investment capital by sales of shares at $20 each. Presume further that it earns 10 percent on its investments after payment of overhead and expenses. Its earnings per share therefore are $2. If it borrows $10 per share and earns at net of 2 percent on these borrowed funds, its total earnings per share will be $2.20 or 10 percent greater through the use of borrowed funds.

It is the ability to perform in excellent economic climates as in the above example that produced an inundation of the market with new trusts in the early seventies.

From the above example, however, it is evident that a decrease in yields on loans made by mortgage trusts will have a serious effect upon their per share earnings. A 10 percent net when the prime rate is at 8 percent may be reduced to 7 percent when the prime drops, assuming other forms of lending will eventually follow a drop in the prime rate. Thus, the per share earning using the above example will fall from $2.00 to $1.40 or 30 percent. In such an instance, the leverage produced by borrowing remains constant since the borrowing rate is usually tied to the prime rate,

The drop in interest rates has the opposite effect upon equity trusts since they can refinance existing mortgages and thereby increase their cash flow or can obtain better mortgage terms for new projects and may translate these more favorable terms into greater profits.

Chart 13-2 is a list of the top 100 trusts in the nation as of 1977.

ADVISORY COMPANIES

The law requires that investment trusts act merely as a conduit to pipe profits from their operations directly to the investors. The trust must be a passive entity. The law further provides that income derived from property, where the trust furnishes services to the tenants or manages or operates the property, is not to be counted in the percentage of income formulas nor can it be regarded as "rents from real property." Therefore, investment trusts must be managed by an independent advisory or management company. Usually the company creating the trust or a company established by the trust originators acts as the trust advisor.

The advisory company makes investments or mortgage loans using trust monies and otherwise administers the affairs of the trust. For this the advisory company receives annually from one to 1.5 percent of the trust's assets and many times an additional sum based upon earnings of the trust.

CHART 13-2

40 LARGEST REAL ESTATE INVESTMENT TRUSTS IN THE NATION IN 1974

Based on Latest Data for Total Assets

Compiled by AMERICAN BANKER — Copyright 1974

1977 Asset Rank	Name of Real Estate Investment Trust	Date of Figs(a)	Total Assets 1977(b) (Thousands of $)	Total Assets 1976(b)	Rank & Gain 1976	Total Loans & inv. (c)	Total Loans(d)	Reserve for Loss(e)	Total Debt(f)	Short-Term Debt(g)	Share Equity(h)
1	CHASE MANHATTAN MTGE. & REALTY TRUST, HYANNIS, MASS. Adviser: Chase Manhattan Bank NA, New York	May 31	424,597	718,686	1	421,374	142,527	150,000	419,518*	0	(6,803)
2	EQUITABLE LIFE MTGE. & REALTY INVESTORS, BOSTON Adviser: Equitable Life Assurance Society of the U. S., New York	July 31	394,364	398,720	5 + 3	389,494	348,259	2,225	253,779*	247,796	133,891
3	FIRST MORTGAGE INVESTORS, MIAMI BEACH, FLA. Adviser: A self-administered REIT	Apr. 30	351,315	454,856	3	449,050	186,338	135,716	333,524*	263,264	8,625
4	CONNECTICUT GEN. MTGE. & REALTY INV., SPRINGFIELD, MASS. Adviser: Congon Realty Advisory Co., Hartford, a subsidiary of Connecticut General Insurance Corp., Hartford, Conn.	June 30	328,431	384,844	6 + 2	319,298	206,129	5,654	213,099*	24,250	110,999
5	CITIZENS & SOUTHERN REALTY INVESTORS, ATLANTA Adviser: Citizens & Southern National Bank, Atlanta	Mar. 31	292,238	442,430	4	356,329	156,943	80,000	310,727	0	(22,255)
6	B. F. SAUL REIT, CHEVY CHASE, MD. Adviser: B. F. Saul Advisory Co., a subsidiary of B. F. Saul Co., Chevy Chase, a Mtge. Co.	June 30	290,650	328,619	10 + 4	285,651	43,875	3,204	246,869*	5,800	36,475
7	GREAT AMERICAN MANAGEMENT & INVESTMENT, ATLANTA (i) Adviser: A self-administered REIT	Apr. 30	278,934	330,747	9 + 2	335,256	60,912	69,099	319,576*	N.A.	(52,770)
8	GENERAL GROWTH PROPERTIES, DES MOINES, IOWA Adviser: General Growth Advisors, Des Moines, a subsidiary of General Growth Cos.	June 30	274,589	243,824	20 +12	260,049	0	0	224,742	0	39,348
9	BUILDERS INVESTMENT GROUP, VALLEY FORGE, PA. Adviser: A self-administered REIT	June 30¶	246,516	379,713	8	308,600	118,302	75,000	245,804	25,091	(5,997)
10	NORTHWESTERN MUTUAL LIFE MTGE. & REALTY INV., MILWAUKEE Adviser: Northwestern Mutual Life Insurance Co., Milwaukee	June 30	245,286	271,544	14 + 4	235,670	178,660	3,300	152,152*	86,667	90,467
11	C. I. MORTGAGE GROUP, BOSTON Adviser: C. I. Planning Corp., New York, a subsidiary of City Investing Co., New York	Apr. 30	231,800	289,200	13 + 2	292,300	130,900	64,000	222,000	37,300	(2,900)
12	IDS REALTY TRUST, MINNEAPOLIS Adviser: IDS Mortgage Corp., Minneapolis, a subsidiary of Investors Diversified Services, Inc., Minneapolis	Apr. 30	224,500	294,187	12	271,000	125,000	65,100	263,100	90,800	(38,600)
13	LOMAS & NETTLETON MORTGAGE INVESTORS, DALLAS Adviser: L & N Management, Inc., a subsidiary of Lomas & Nettleton Financial Corp., Dallas	June 30	224,374	244,628	19 + 6	226,848	170,903	17,686	118,684	25,434	102,456
14	DIVERSIFIED MORTGAGE INVESTORS, BURLINGTON, MASS. Adviser: A self-administered REIT	Mar. 31¶	221,258	314,271	11	277,890	191,275	68,859	154,689*	0	40,343
15	GUARDIAN MORTGAGE INVESTORS, JACKSONVILLE, FLA. Adviser: A self-administered REIT	May 31	218,380	382,989	7	267,446	151,373	57,011	248,394*	214,098	(32,526)
16	BANKAMERICA REALTY INVESTORS, SAN FRANCISCO Adviser: BankAmerica Realty Services, Inc., a subsidiary of BankAmerica Corp., San Francisco	June 30¶	213,720	254,102	16	218,368	102,096	13,200	155,491*	82,497	54,179
17	WELLS FARGO MORTGAGE INVESTORS, SAN FRANCISCO Adviser: Wells Fargo Realty Advisors, a subsidiary of Wells Fargo and Co., Los Angeles, BHC	June 30	212,000	198,492	24 + 7	196,000	133,000	6,900	139,000	128,000	68,000
18	MONY MORTGAGE INVESTORS, NEW YORK Adviser: Mutual Life Insurance Co. of New York	June 30¶	208,249	245,826	18	198,338	172,798	1,200	117,097*	76,935	86,898

#	Company / Adviser	Date										
19	CONTINENTAL ILLINOIS REALTY, SANTA MONICA, CALIF., a subsidiary of Continental Illinois Corp., Chicago, BHC. Adviser: Continental Illinois Realty Advisers, Inc., Los Angeles, a subsidiary of Continental Illinois Corp., Chicago, BHC	June 30	204,445	252,768	17		241,719	153,391	40,348	200,105	169,700	460
20	BAY COLONY PROPERTY CO., BOSTON. Adviser: A self-administered REIT	May 31§	203,893	196,712	25	+ 5	223,356	67,866	26,000	179,151*	115,150	21,411
21	CONTINENTAL ILLINOIS PROPERTIES, LOS ANGELES. Adviser: Continental Illinois Properties, Inc., Los Angeles, a subsidiary of Continental Illinois Corp., Chicago, BHC	Apr. 30	199,227	199,436	23	+ 2	186,167	26,534	820	94,322	11,500	100,025
22	MASSMUTUAL MORTGAGE & REALTY INV., SPRINGFIELD, MASS. Adviser: Massachusetts Mutual Life Insurance Co., Springfield	June 30§	198,573	211,500	21		195,198	166,521	2,400	104,832*	33,175	91,327
23	FIRST UNION REAL ESTATE INVESTMENTS, CLEVELAND. Adviser: A self-administered REIT	Apr. 30	173,286	165,867	33	+10	167,476	9,874	0	124,297*	13,800	46,471
24	COUSINS MORTGAGE & EQUITY INVESTMENTS, ATLANTA. Adviser: A self-administered REIT	May 31	166,464	255,935	15		209,636	113,697	49,750	159,669	129,669	4,079
25	FIRST NEWPORT REALTY INVESTORS, NEWPORT BEACH, CALIF. Adviser: A self-administered REIT	Apr. 30	161,215	177,169	29	+ 4	191,242	49,555	36,300	150,295*	0	8,726
26	FIRST PENNSYLVANIA MORTGAGE TRUST, BOSTON. Adviser: Associated Advisers, Inc., Cherry Hill, N. J., a subsidiary of First Pennsylvania Corp., Philadelphia, BHC	Apr. 30	150,999	169,645	31	+ 5	177,600	65,173	29,000	125,330*	118,000	17,396
27	NORTH AMERICAN MORTGAGE INVESTORS, BOSTON. Adviser: Hampton Advisory Corp., a subsidiary of Sonnenblick-Goldman Corp., New York.	June 30	147,083	170,999	30	+ 3	147,263	63,921	11,884	99,810	55,653	46,015
28	SECURITY MORTGAGE INVESTORS, BOSTON. Adviser: Semorco Inc., a subsidiary of Smith Barney Harris Upham Co., Inc., New York.	June 30	144,170	189,691	26		147,833	102,762	15,405	102,383*	48,799	42,801
29	COLWELL MORTGAGE TRUST, LOS ANGELES. Adviser: Colwell Management Co., a subsidiary of Colwell Co., Los Angeles, a mortgage Co.	June 30	139,836	168,987	32	+ 3	154,083	85,390	24,350	139,763*	29,634	(3,248)
30	HEITMAN MORTGAGE INVESTORS, CHICAGO. Adviser: HMI Management Co., Chicago, a subsidiary of the Heitman Group, Chicago	June 30	138,842	179,698	27		153,071	153,071	16,450	126,957*	89,785	10,617
31	FIRST WISCONSIN MORTGAGE TRUST, MILWAUKEE. Adviser: First Wisconsin Mortgage Co., Milwaukee, a subsidiary of First Wisconsin Corp., Milwaukee, MBH	June 30	136,025	161,148	35	+ 4	156,263	34,125	26,454	116,570	124	11,011
32	FIDELITY MORTGAGE INVESTORS, JACKSONVILLE, FLA. [1]. Adviser: A self-administered REIT	Apr. 30	135,800	138,204	39	+ 7	175,109	68,684	69,039	185,512*	N.A.	(55,523)
33	INSTITUTIONAL INVESTORS TRUST, BOSTON. Adviser: A self-administered REIT	Apr. 30	135,721	163,644	34	+ 1	149,733	82,281	16,830	101,915	71,180	31,151
34	CAMERON-BROWN INVESTMENT GROUP, RALEIGH, N. C. Adviser: Cameron-Brown Co., Raleigh, a mortgage Co. owned by First Union Corp., Charlotte, BHC	June 30	135,247	135,908	43	+ 9	140,864	41,046	16,851	109,385	106,088	15,690
35	REALTY REFUND TRUST, CLEVELAND. Adviser: ReaFund Advisors, Inc., Cleveland	Apr. 30§	134,920	138,819	38	+ 3	133,657	133,657	0	32,200	0	19,430
36	CONSOLIDATED CAPITAL REALTY INVESTORS, OAKLAND, CALIF. Adviser: Consolidated Capital Realty Services, Inc., Oakland, a subsidiary of Consolidated Capital Corp.	May 31	134,844	101,876	61	+25	128,643	0	0	93,383	0	38,206
37	PNB MORTGAGE & REALTY INVESTORS, MELROSE PARK, PA. Adviser: Colonial Advisers Inc., a subsidiary of Colonial Mortgage Service Co., Melrose Park	June 30	128,702	126,008	47	+10	122,910	86,351	2,040	81,810	35,323	45,448

(a)—Figures are for 1977 unless otherwise noted. (b)—Total assets are after reserves for possible losses. (c)—Total real estate loans and investments before reserve for possible losses but after depreciation and unamortized or unamortized discount. (d)—Before reserve for possible losses but after unearned discount. (e)—Reserve for possible losses on both real estate loans and investments. (f)—Total borrowings. (g)—All borrowing and sinking funds due in one year or less. (h)—Shareholders' equity. [1]—Has filed for an arrangement under Chapter XI of Bankruptcy Act. *—REIT has convertible debt which is included in total. ‡—Different date than previous year's figures. ‡—Latest figures are for 1976 and are for a different date than previous year's figures. §—Latest figures are for 1976. ( )—Deficit. N.A.—Not Available.

1977 Asset Rank	Name of Real Estate Investment Trust	Date of Fig(a)	Total Assets 1977(b) (Thousands of $)	Total Assets 1976(b)	Rank & Gain 1976	Total Loans & inv.(c)	Total Loans(d) (1977 Data)	Reserve for Loss(e)	Total Debt(f)	Short-Term Debt(g) (in Thousands of Dollars)	Share Equity(h)
38	BT MORTGAGE INVESTORS, BOSTON. Adviser: BT Advisers, Inc., a subsidiary of Bankers Trust New York Corp., MBH	June 30	128,327	137,108	40 + 2	150,329	102,929	23,218	131,584	112,210	(4,730)
39	MORTGAGE TRUST OF AMERICA, SAN FRANCISCO. Adviser: Transamerica Mortgage Advisors, Inc., a subsidiary of Transamerica Corp. San Francisco	May 31	124,482	136,748	41 + 2	129,787	90,687	18,162	76,267	66,017	46,535
40	UMET TRUST, BEVERLY HILLS, CALIF. Adviser: A self-administered REIT	May 31	124,263	120,107	51 +11	139,301	30,565	19,543	116,814	N.A.	4,804
41	ATICO MORTGAGE INVESTORS, MIAMI. Adviser: Atico Advisory Corp., Miami, a subsidiary of Pan American Banc-shares, Inc., Miami, MBH	June 30	124,219	151,201	36	139,495	42,272	18,200	97,205*	78,461	17,402
42	FIDELCO GROWTH INVESTORS, ROSEMONT, PA. Adviser: Latimer & Buck Advisors, Inc., Philadelphia, a subsidiary of Fidelcor, Inc., Philadelphia, BHC	May 31	123,465	128,412	45 + 3	135,270	66,022	18,400	97,347	96,600	14,285
43	BARNETT MORTGAGE TRUST, JACKSONVILLE, FLA. Adviser: Barnett Mortgage Advisors, Inc., Jacksonville, Fla., a subsidiary of Barnett-Winston Co., Jacksonville	June 30	122,909	135,968	42	145,255	37,208	37,790	127,182*	0	(14,423)
44	C. I. REALTY INVESTORS, BOSTON. Adviser: C. I. Planning Corp., New York, a subsidiary of City Investing Co., New York	May 31	121,179	178,826	28	113,527	16,436	4,580	73,944	16,100	43,904
45	FIRST OF DENVER MORTGAGE INVESTORS, DENVER. Adviser: First National Advisors, Inc., a subsidiary of First National Bancorp., Inc., Denver, MBH	June 30	113,924	107,152	58 +13	109,482	55,176	16,735	94,096	88,305	1,227
46	LMI INVESTORS, BEVERLY HILLS, CALIF. Adviser: CNA Investment Advisors, Inc., Beverly Hills, a subsidiary of CNA Financial Corp., Chicago	Mar. 31	113,660	141,894	37	135,069	70,663	23,500	100,380	0	7,463
47	AMERICAN CENTURY MORTGAGE INVESTORS, JACKSONVILLE, FLA. Adviser: American Century Advisors, Inc., Jacksonville, a subsidiary of American Heritage Life Investment Corp., Jacksonville	Mar. 31	111,292	132,751	44	127,673	35,964	18,304	93,544*	160	16,225
48	TRI-SOUTH MORTGAGE INVESTORS, ATLANTA. Adviser: Tri-South Management Associates, which is owned equally by three bank holding companies: First National Holding Corp., Atlanta, First & Merchants Corp., Richmond, & NCNB Corp., Charlotte	June 30	106,708	205,274	22	132,634	58,565	33,000	91,522*	54,876	8,027
49	INDEPENDENCE MORTGAGE TRUST, ATLANTA. Adviser: Provident Realty, Inc., a subsidiary of Provident National Bank, Philadelphia	Mar. 31	103,502	121,188	50 + 1	147,161	55,657	45,839	98,530	88,530	(10,036)
50	WACHOVIA REALTY INVESTMENTS, WINSTON-SALEM, N. C. Adviser: Wachovia Mortgage Co., a subsidiary of Wachovia Corp., Winston-Salem, BHC	May 31	103,481	121,899	49	119,053	60,657	17,621	66,430	0	35,803
51	U. S. REALTY INVESTMENTS, CLEVELAND. Adviser: Mascom Co., Cleveland	June 30	99,825	126,431	46	101,332	44,352	6,777	84,771*	0	13,690
52	CLEVETRUST REALTY INVESTORS, CLEVELAND. Adviser: CleveTrust Advisers, Cleveland a subsidiary of Cleveland Trust Co.	June 30	98,282	110,656	54 + 2	104,739	33,246	8,907	68,664	3,000	26,551
53	STATE MUTUAL INVESTORS, WORCESTER, MASS. Adviser: America Group Management Corp., a subsidiary of State Mutual Life Assurance Co. of America, Worcester	Mar. 31	94,076	114,995	53	107,810	54,189	20,105	90,415*	59,000	(4,203)
54	BARNES MORTGAGE INVESTMENT TRUST, BOSTON. Adviser: Barnes Mortgage Advisors, Inc., a subsidiary of James T. Barnes & Co., Detroit, a mortgage Co.	June 30¶	91,940	102,056	59 + 5	92,845	53,042	2,362	66,651	66,651	23,546
55	HUBBARD REAL ESTATE INVESTMENTS, BOSTON. Adviser: Merrill Lynch, Hubbard Inc., a subsidiary of Merrill Lynch, Pierce, Fenner & Smith, Inc., New York	Apr. 30	91,620	90,787	63 + 8	84,602	294	4,265	2,536	39	88,239
56	GMR PROPERTIES, BOSTON. Adviser: GULFCO Capital Management Inc., a subsidiary of Gulf United Corp., Jacksonville, Fla.	May 31	89,829	117,956	52	108,478	44,722	21,159	72,946	52,946	8,302
57	REALTY & MORTGAGE INV. OF THE PACIFIC, SAN FRANCISCO. Adviser: Bankoh Advisory Corp., a subsidiary of Bank of Hawaii, Honolulu	May 31¶	86,884	89,511	65 + 8	85,503	58,173	845	51,884*	31,500	34,459
58	ICM REALTY, NEW YORK. Adviser: Investors Central Management Corp., New York	May 31	86,245	108,645	56	99,896	26,233	16,249	42,710	21,600	42,680
59	HOTEL INVESTORS, KENSINGTON, MD. Adviser: A self-administered REIT	May 31	84,386	84,712	68 + 9	81,658	34,988	2,319	55,444*	4,750	27,832
60	HAMILTON INVESTMENT TRUST, ELIZABETH, N. J. Adviser: A self-administered REIT	June 30	83,261	108,968	55	97,704	65,002	16,139	62,946	0	11,377

#	Name / Adviser	Date										
61	MORTGAGE INVESTORS OF WASHINGTON, BETHESDA, MD. — Adviser: MIW Advisors, Inc., Bethesda	June 30	82,873	102,028	60		05,172	48,746	6,720	66,579*	49,250	12,840
62	HNC MORTGAGE & REALTY INVESTORS, WESTPORT, CONN. — Adviser: HNC Realty Advisors, Inc., Westport, Conn., a subsidiary of Hartford National Corp., Conn., BHC	Apr. 30¶	81,290	100,897	62		103,149	54,951	23,876	69,728*	64,981	9,857
63	REALTY INCOME TRUST, PROVIDENCE, R. I. — Adviser: A self-administered REIT	Apr. 30	80,430	88,570	66	+3	74,199	28,091	1,886	59,030*	11,100	19,595
64	REALTY GROWTH INVESTORS, TOWSON, MD. — Adviser: Mortgage & Equity Consultants, Inc., an affiliate of Equitable Bancorp, Baltimore, an MBH	Apr. 30¶	79,021	84,629	69	+5	76,234	45,715	6,090	59,302	56,427	12,921
65	BARNETT-WINSTON INVESMENT TRUST, JACKSONVILLE, FLA. — Adviser: Barnett-Winston Investment Counselors, Inc., Jacksonville, Fla., a subsidiary of Barnett-Winston Co., Jacksonville	June 30¶	77,815	88,090	67	+2	38,395	24,984	15,726	73,726*	23,033	(1,429)
66	PENNSYLVANIA REAL ESTATE INVESTMENT TRUST, WYNCOTE, PA. — Adviser: A self-administered REIT	May 31	77,799	73,519	78	+12	70,849	2,409	151	56,760*	1,818	77,799
67	UNITED REALTY TRUST, BEVERLY HILLS, CALIF. — Adviser: CNA Investment Managers, Beverly Hills, a subsidiary of CNA Financial Corp., Chicago	May 31	75,691	84,229	71	+4	61,999	36,633	4,615	11,482	9,758	63,520
68	BROOKS HARVEY REALTY INVESTORS, NEW YORK — Adviser: Brooks Harvey Advisors, Inc., a subsidiary of Brooks, Harvey & Co., Inc., New York, mortgage broker	July 31	74,947	74,167	77	+9	N.A.	N.A.	N.A.	N.A.	N.A.	N.A.
69	PROPERTY CAPITAL TRUST, BOSTON — Adviser: Property Capital Advisors, Inc., Boston	July 31	72,291	76,085	75	+6	46,839	22,021	915	42,966	15,600	28,235
70	FIRST VIRGINIA MORTGAGE & REIT, FALLS CHURCH, VA. — Adviser: A self-administered REIT	June 30¶	71,683	79,418	74	+4	83,491	40,341	13,376	67,271	13,271	3,464
71	AMERICAN EQUITY INVESTMENT TRUST, CEDAR RAPIDS, IOWA — Adviser: A self-administered REIT	June 30	71,258	82,481	72	+1	66,873	10,381	364	52,363	991	157¶R
72	INDIANA MORTGAGE & REALTY INVESTORS, BALTIMORE — Adviser: Indiana Realty Advisors, Inc., Indianapolis, a subsidiary of Indiana National Corp., Indianapolis, BHC	June 30¶	68,955	84,565	70		75,687	32,695	7,883	57,715	0	9,716
73	MIDLAND MORTGAGE INVESTORS TRUST, OKLAHOMA CITY, OKLA — Adviser: Midland Advisory Co., Oklahoma City	June 30	67,844	108,358	57		77,193	33,048	12,000	65,493*	41,561	972
74	CAPITAL MORTGAGE INVESTMENTS, CHEVY CHASE, MD. — Adviser: Capital Managers. Inc., Chevy Chase, Md.	June 30¶	67,600	125,499	48		77,000	40,300	15,900	65,200*	48,900	1,000
75	FIRST MEMPHIS REALTY TRUST, MEMPHIS — Adviser: First Tennessee Advisory Corp., a subsidiary of First Tennessee National Corp., Memphis, MBH	May 31	66,434	74,321	76	+1	72,501	20,596	8,197	60,413	48,738	4,488
76	SUTRO MORTGAGE INVESTMENT TRUST, LOS ANGELES — Adviser: Ralph C. Sutro Co., Los Angeles, a mortgage Co.	June 30	64,049	80,048	73		66,542	41,066	4,597	26,522*	6,917	36,747
77	CITIZENS MORTGAGE INVESTMENT TRUST, SOUTHFIELD, MICH. — Adviser: Citizens Mortgage Corp., Southfield, a mortgage Co., subsidiary of Manufacturers Hanover Corp., New York, MBH	June 30	61,875	68,328	81	+4	76,089	23,200	22,950	76,017	54,037	(19,767)
78	INVESTORS REALTY TRUST, ATLANTA — Adviser: Thomson McKinnon Advisory Corp., Atlanta, a subsidiary of Thomson McKinnon Inc., New York	July 31¶	60,216	59,769	85	+7	55,518	7,631	664	42,079	11,300	16,478
79	AMERICAN FLETCHER MORTGAGE INVESTORS, BOSTON — Adviser: American Fletcher Mortgage Co., Inc., Indianapolis, a subsidiary of American Fletcher Corp., Indianapolis, BHC	Apr. 30	59,177	71,880	79		84,107	26,386	25,450	56,100	56,100	(666)
80	FRASER MORTGAGE INVESTMENTS, CLEVELAND — Adviser: Fraser Mortgage Co., Cleveland	Feb. 28	57,462	53,806	89	+9	50,658	44,811	422	40,143	40,143	17,009
81	U. S. BANCORP REALTY & MORTGAGE TRUST, PORTLAND, ORE. — Adviser: Bancorp Management Advisers, Inc., a subsidiary of U. S. Bancorp, Portland, BHC	June 30¶	54,111	64,883	84	+3	55,513	26,274	2,570	39,287*	25,192	14,010
82	SAN FRANCISCO REAL ESTATE INVESTORS, SAN FRANCISCO — Adviser: A self-administered REIT	June 30	52,629	68,002	82		54,725	6,876	3,397	24,297	1,425	27,459

(a)—Figures are for 1977 unless otherwise noted. (b)—Total assets are after reserve for possible losses. (c)—Total real estate loans and investments before reserve for possible losses but after depreciation and unamortized or unearned discount. (d)—Before reserve for possible losses but after unearned discount. (e)—Reserve for possible losses on both real estate loans and investments. (f)—Total borrowings. (g)—All borrowing and sinking funds due in one year or less. (h)—Shareholders' equity. (i)—Has filed for an arrangement under Chapter XI of Bankruptcy Act. *—REIT has convertible debt which is included in total. ¶—Different date than previous year's figures. ‡—Latest figures are for 1976 and are for a different date than previous year's figures. §—Latest figures are for 1976. ( )—Deficit. N.A.—Not Available.

1977 Asset Rank	Name of Real Estate Investment Trust	Date of Figs (a)	Total Assets 1977(b)	1976(b) (Thousands of $)	Rank & Gain 1976	Total Loans & inv. (c)	Total Loans(d)	Reserve for Loss(e)	Total Debt(f)	Short-Term Debt(g)	Share Equity(h)
							(1977 Data — in Thousands of Dollars)				
83	BENEFICIAL STANDARD MORTGAGE INVESTORS, GLENDALE, CALIF. Adviser: Beneficial Standard Advisers, Inc., Los Angeles, a subsidiary of Beneficial Standard Corp., Los Angeles	Apr. 30	51,541	66,111	83	62,432	30,995	12,554	46,915*	5,818	1,906
84	NATIONWIDE REAL ESTATE INVESTORS, COLUMBUS, OHIO. Adviser: Nationwide Real Estate Services, Inc. a subsidiary of Nationwide Corp., Columbus, a financial holding Co.	June 30	51,265	46,865	97 +13	46,693	33,470	1,245	24,746	18,684	25,941
85	TIERCO, OKLAHOMA CITY. Adviser: A self-administered REIT	June 30	50,373	55,074	88 + 3	54,393	15,829	6,200	43,818	41,530	5,057
86	REPUBLIC MORTGAGE INVESTORS, BOSTON. Adviser: Mortgage Investment Services, Inc., Miami, Fla.	June 30	49,759	56,770	86	59,866	10,905	13,925	35,968*	29,725	10,407
87	FIRST CONTINENTAL REIT, HOUSTON. Adviser: First Continental Mortgage Advisers, Inc., Houston, a subsidiary of First Continental Corp., Houston, a mortgage Co.	May 31	49,158	51,819	91 + 4	42,828	40,060	910	27,020	27,020	21,623
88	PRUDENT REAL ESTATE TRUST, GREAT NECK, N.Y. Adviser: A self-administered REIT	May 31	49,155	51,156	93 + 5	45,722	0	0	36,662*	N.A.	9,193
89	DENVER REAL ESTATE INVESTMENT ASSN. Adviser: Swanson Properties, Ltd., Denver	June 30	48,849	47,332	95 + 6	48,063	3,678	0	38,574	1,596	9,027
90	API TRUST, NEW YORK. Adviser: A self-administered REIT	June 30	48,808	53,703	90	49,841	13,271	3,547	39,849	16,849	8,169
91	SUMMIT PROPERTIES, AKRON, OHIO. Adviser: A self-administered REIT	June 30	48,665	51,216	92 + 1	48,270	2,398	1,100	36,799	6,357	10,837
92	REAL ESTATE INVESTMENT TRUST OF AMERICA, BOSTON, MASS. Adviser: A self-administered REIT	May 31	48,204	45,766	99 + 7	45,065	693	0	12,895	925	34,399
93	WALTER REALTY INVESTORS, TAMPA, FLA. Adviser: Jim Walter Advisers, Inc., a subsidiary of Jim Walter Corp., Tampa	Apr. 30	44,231	56,217	87	47,063	18,282	6,367	32,565	0	10,769
94	NJB PRIME INVESTORS, CLIFTON, N. J. Adviser: A self-administered REIT	May 31	43,705	89,733	64	72,635	29,058	30,547	48,420*	38,365	(6,685)
95	M & T MORTGAGE INVESTORS, HOUSTON. Adviser: M & T Management Co., Houston, a subsidiary of Mortgage & Trust, Inc., Houston, a mortgage Co.	May 31	43,638	41,789	106 +11	40,694	39,807	325	27,854	27,854	15,204
96	MORTGAGE GROWTH INVESTORS, BOSTON. Adviser: Manchester Advisory Corp.	May 31¶	42,251	39,266	108 +12	39,494	6,190	1,155	12,660*	0	28,567
97	AMERICAN REALTY TRUST, ARLINGTON, VA. Adviser: A self-administered REIT	June 30¶	41,300	42,463	104 + 7	40,360	5,268	330	31,964*	15,764	6,146
98	GOULD INVESTORS TRUST, GREAT NECK, N.Y. Adviser: REIT Management Co., Great Neck, N.Y.	June 30	41,145	46,780	98	30,947	7,067	639	30,740	N.A.	8,118
99	NORTHWESTERN FINANCIAL INVESTORS, CHARLOTTE, N.C. Adviser: Northwestern Advisory Corp, a subsidiary of Northwestern Financial Corp., Wilkesboro, N. C., BHC	June 30	40,194	45,413	100 + 1	45,392	24,850	6,132	17,903	17,534	21,599
100	CHURCH LOANS & INVESTMENTS TRUST, AMARILLO, TEX. Adviser: Affiliated Managers, Inc., Amarillo, Tex.	June 30¶	39,724	36,361	115 +15	38,917	37,019	0	19,783	8,447	19,476

(a)—Figures are for 1977 unless otherwise noted. (b)—Total assets are after reserves for possible losses. (c)—Total real estate loans and investments before reserve for possible losses but after depreciation and unamortized or unearned discount. (d)—Before reserve for possible losses but after unearned discount. (e)—Reserve for possible losses on both real estate loans and investments. (f)—Total borrowings. (g)—All borrowing and sinking funds due in one year or less. (h)—Shareholders' equity. (i)—Has filed for an arrangement under Chapter XI of Bankruptcy Act. *—REIT has convertible debt which is included in total. ‡—Different date than previous year's figures. †—Latest figures are for 1976 and are for a different date than previous year's figures. §—Latest figures are for 1976. ( )—Deficit. N.A.—Not Available.

No person or persons owning 35 percent or more of the trust's shares may hold more than 35 percent of the stock or voting power in a corporate advisory company or interest in the assets and profits of a non-corporate advisory company.

Following is an excerpt from the prospectus of an investment trust which relates to advisory company compensations:

"In order to reward the advisory company for causing the profits to exceed those reasonably to be expected or penalize it if they do not do so and to permit the trustees to change Advisors promptly if the performance of the Advisor proves unsatisfactory, an incentive provision is included in the Advisor's agreement. In general, it regards or penalizes the Advisor by 1/10th of the amount by which net profit exceeds or is less than 8.4/12 of one percent of the average net worth above or below the preceeding month. The agreement may be termined and a new Advisor secured if the rate of net profit falls below a 5 percent return on net worth."

SUBORDINATED DEBENTURES

A favored means of raising additional capital for an investment trust is by subordinated debentures. Many recent issues of trust shares have been in units including debentures. For example, a unit may include five shares valued at $20 each plus a $100 debenture together marketed for a price of $200 per unit. Debentures offer increased leverage since they usually bear a coupon rate below that which would be charged by a bank for a line of credit. In addition, debentures constitute long-term borrowing as opposed to short-term bank loans, and if converted into trust shares repayment never occurs. The issuance of debentures can be disadvantageous if they are sold when interest rates are at their highest point. When rates fall, the trust may be hard pressed to earn enough to meet the face interest rate or at least it will lose the leverage advantage of the debentures.

INVESTMENT TECHNIQUES

Below is an example of investment techniques used by investment trusts to gain high rates of return.

A, a substantial corporation, owns five acres commercial property worth $100,000.

A desires to build an office building costing $300,000 exclusive of land, and rent same to D for a sum which will produce $30,000 net cash flow. A construction/permanent loan for $300,000 is available at 10 percent and 5 points (15,000).

A interests B, a real estate investment trust, in the project and together they decide upon the following deal:

B pays A $100,000 for the property and leases same to C, a limited partnership consisting of A as general partner and B as limited partner. C agrees to pay B a ground rent of $11,500/annum and B agrees to subordinate its lease to a combined construction/permanent loan. B further agrees to arrange the combined construction/permanent loan and pay all fees for same. As additional consideration for the lease, **B** receives a 50 percent limited partnership interest in the venture.

Result:

A receives $9,250 per annum with no investment except its builder's profit. Estimating a builder's profit of $30,000, the yearly return to **A** is approximately 31 percent.

B receives $20,750 on an investment of $115,000 for a return of 18 + percent.

RECENT TRENDS

The year 1974 was the beginning of the end for many real estate investment trusts. Several factors combined in that year to produce disasterous results for trusts. The two most significant factors were:

1. Inflation, which drove interest costs to record levels and real estate investment trust borrowing costs along with it.
2. Recession, which brought to an abrupt end the real estate boom of the early 1970s and with it a high level of real estate project failures.

Hence the trusts found themselves with many projects that they had to take over or that were not paying interest to the trust, with excessive borrowing cost—some of which they were unable to pass on borrowers, and with their credit lines being rapidly decreased. The combined affect was a tremendous loss of income (projects that are taken over cease to produce interest income and those that are in the process of foreclosure don't accrue interest) and an inability on the trusts' part to maintain or even to continue payment of dividends their beneficial interest holders. To date several trust have sought relief in the bankruptcy courts while others have given up their tax status and become development or construction companies.

In 1972, REITs had 20 percent of their assets in property owned and 80 percent in mortgages. As shown in Chart 13-1 that ratio in 1977 had changed to 60 percent of assets in property owned and 40 percent in mortgages. Since 1974, trusts' assets have eroded yearly. This trend has continued with a 6.6 percent drop in assets of the 100 largest trusts in 1975, 13.1 percent in 1976 and 19.1 percent in 1977.

Hardest hit have been the mortgage trusts, but equity trusts have also felt the impact of the combined recession-inflation though admittedly to a lesser extent than mortgage trusts.

Real estate trusts have used various methods to overcome their large burden of debt and interest payments, including:

(a) Sale of properties owned to liquidate debt on the properties and raise capital.

(b) Trading of properties in exchange for debt cancellation.

(c) Entering into creditor arrangements to reduce or waive interest payments.

Based on the condition of the REIT industry and the individual companies, it has been virtually impossible for the majority of companies to raise new capital by means of stock or bond issues or to establish new credit lines. Thus, the above methods have been the only recourse for this ailing industry.

It is now evident that those trusts which do survive the current turmoil will operate much more conservatively than in the past. Investors will no longer pursue as aggressively the purchase of shares or beneficial interest and those who previously extended credit to the trusts will proceed more cautiously in the future.

CONCLUSION

In conclusion, equity and mortgage investment trusts are new financing vehicles which were originally created as a means of providing the small investor with an investment opportunity. Ironically investment trusts have had a profound effect upon real estate financing, diverting into that sector much needed mortgage and equity funds.

The mortgage trusts, the newest and most spectacular type of investment trust, has had its greatest effect in the areas of land, land development, and construction loans on residential and income-producing property.

The heyday of real estate investment trusts is, however, probably passed, due to the economic reversals of 1974. The industry in the next few years will be in a state of retrenchment. It will emerge as a source of funds for real estate finance, but to what degree and on what basis will not be known for some time.

The heyday of real estate investment trusts is, however, probably passed due to the economic reversals of 1975-1975. The industry in the next few years will be in a state of continued retrenchment. It will emerge as a source of funds for real estate finance, but to what degree and on what basis will not be known for some time.

QUESTIONS FOR THOUGHT AND DISCUSSION

1. What was the purpose of Public Law 86-779 and how has that purpose been carried out or not been carried out?
2. a. What is the purpose of an equity trust? Of a mortgage trust?
   b. Under normal circumstances which would you prefer as an investor and why?
3. a. How do bank credit and debenture issues affect mortgage trust earnings?
   b. To what extent should each be used in conjunction with the others to produce maximum profits and minimum exposure to loss?
4. What are the 90 percent and 75 percent rules as applied to investment trusts?
5. What is the purpose of an advisory company?
6. How should mixed trusts regulate their investments for best results?
7. How did the factors of "recession" and "inflation" effect investment trusts?

14

THE FEDERAL HOME LOAN BANK SYSTEM AND THE FEDERAL SAVINGS AND LOAN INSURANCE CORPORATION

FEDERAL HOME LOAN BANK SYSTEM (FHLBS)

Many of the institutional regulatory agencies of today were created as a result of the Great Depression. Out of that critical time in American history came many beneficial changes which have had an important impact on the American life and economy.

Prior to the early 1930s, savings and loan associations and the other thrift institutions were solely dependent upon their own assets to meet the needs of their customers. Similarly, the demand for mortgage money and the meeting of that demand was local in nature. There was no system for the shifting of capital from areas of excess to areas of need.

The depression brought with it an increase in the rate of real estate fore-closures while at the same time savings and loan association depositors were making their heaviest demands for withdrawals. With the majority of their assets frozen in either long-term mortgages or real estate obtained through fore-closures, many savings and loan associations were unable to meet the demands of depositors. Disaster for these institutions and their depositors mounted.

To relieve this troubled situation President Hoover signed into law on July 22, 1932, the Home Loan Bank Act creating the Federal Home Loan Bank System (FHLBS), thereby establishing a nationwide system for providing credit to mortgage-lending institutions.

PURPOSE OF THE FHLBS

The FHLBS has as its primary purpose the supplying of credit to its member institutions to strengthen and supplement their resources.

In accomplishing this purpose the FHLBS performs several major functions:

1. It acts as a lender of funds to its member institutions thereby providing them with *secondary liquidity* to meet seasonal and other heavy or unusual demands for withdrawals. Thus, member institutions no longer have to be solely dependent upon their own assets, but can fall back on the FHLBS to obtain assistance during crisis periods.
2. It establishes specific guidelines for its members to follow. Such guidelines directly influence the type of mortgage loans made by savings and loan associations, the interest rates charged on these loans, loan-to-value ratios, and other mortgage security factors.
3. Its operations assist in moving mortgage funds from capital-surplus areas to capital-deficient areas, producing an even national distribution of these funds.
4. Its sale of *consolidated obligations* brings to the mortgage market capital, which normally would not find its way into mortgage investments. The issuance of consolidated obligations helps to maintain a constant flow of funds into the mortgage market by distribution of proceeds from sales of these securities to the regional banks for use by member institutions. When deposits are down and the demand for mortgage funds heavy, savings and loan associations are able to obtain lendable funds from the system. The system in turn covers the advances made to member institutions by going to the capital market with consolidated obligation issues. Investors purchasing consolidated obligations of the FHLBS include trusts, pension funds, and in most jurisdictions mutual savings banks and life insurance companies.

ADMINISTRATION

The FHLBS is governed and regulated by a three-man board, whose members are appointed by the President of the United States with the consent of the Senate.

The board, located in Washington, D.C., is one of the independent agencies in the executive branch of the federal government. As such its operations are subject to review by Congress.

In addition to administering the FHLBS, the board issues all charters for federal savings and loan associations and supervises the operations of the Federal Savings and Loan Insurance Corporation and the Federal Home Loan Mortgage Corporation.

HOME LOAN BANKS

The major operations of the FHLBS are performed by its regional banks. The country is divided into twelve home loan bank districts each containing one regional bank. Chart 14-1 is a map showing the bank districts with regional banks located in Boston, New York, Pittsburgh, Atlanta, Cincinnati, Indianapolis, Chicago, Des Moines, Little Rock, Topeka, San Francisco and Seattle.

Each regional bank is separately incorporated and issues its own share of stock. Management of each bank is vested in a board of directors, some of whom are appointed by the FHLBB with the balance elected by member institutions. All regional banks are expected to be self-supporting and are free to make their own rules and regulations within guidelines established by the FHLBB.

Regional banks obtain their funds in several ways:

1. From the required purchase and retention by each member institution of FHLB stock equal to one percent of the unpaid principal balance of all its mortgage loans. Prior to January 1, 1962, the stock purchase requirement was 2 percent of all mortgage loans. When the requirement was reduced no withdrawal of stock was allowed, but no new purchases of stock had to be made until total stock holdings fell below one percent of total outstanding loans.

CHART 14-1

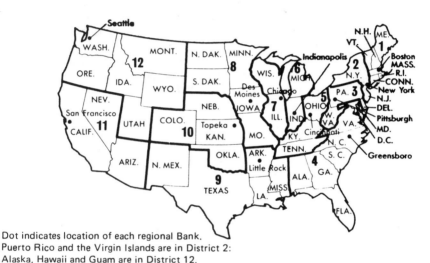

Dot indicates location of each regional Bank.
Puerto Rico and the Virgin Islands are in District 2:
Alaska, Hawaii and Guam are in District 12.

Source: Federal Home Loan Bank Board.

When the amounts borrowed by a member institution from its regional bank equals or exceeds 12 percent of its total mortgage loan portfolio, additional stock must then be purchased equivalent to one-twelfth of the principal balance of all loans owed to the regional bank.

Total capital stock owned by FHLB members as of the end of 1977 amounted to $3.3 billion. Stock dividends are usually low, hence stock is held by member institutions more for the advantages offered by the FHLBS than for appreciation and return.

2. From the deposits of member institutions which represent excesses over funds needed to meet current credit demands. These deposits are available as credit to other regional banks and member institutions, hence contributing to the movement of funds from capital-surplus to capital-deficient areas. Member deposits may be in the form of time or demand deposit. Time deposits are usually escrows received on mortgage loans held in portfolios while demand deposits are used as needed to meet daily

operational requirements. Member deposits at the end of 1977 totaled $4.1 billion.

3. From the deposits of other regional banks used to move funds from areas of surplus to areas of need.

4. From the sale of consolidated obligations. Due to the heavy demand and short supply of funds during 1969, the amount of consolidated obligations of all regional banks outstanding on December 31, 1969, was $8.4 billion; up $3.7 billion from 1969. This "tight money" crisis prompted the passage by Congress of the Rate Control Act of 1969 authorizing the Secretary of the Treasury to purchase at his discretion up to $4 billion of FHLBB obligations whenever the ability of the FHLBS to sell its obligations is seriously endangered. Again in 1974 and in 1979, demand for funds by member institutions soared and so did the FHLBB's sale of consolidated obligations, which reached the record level of $19.4 billion outstanding at the end of 1974. Issuance of consolidated obligations by regional banks is limited by FHLBB regulation to: The sum of regional banks' secured advances to member institutions; cash on hand; and guaranteed obligations of the United States held in portfolio; or twelve times the combined capital and reverses of all regional banks. Chart 14-2 is the consolidated balance sheet of all FHLB's for the period of 1976-1977.

CHART 14-2

FHLB Combined Statement of Condition, 1973-1974
(Thousands of Dollars)

Item	December 31, 1974	December 31, 1973
ASSETS:		
Cash	$ 144,392	$ 156,659
Investments	3,097,415	3,437,495
Advances	21,804,462	15,147,143
Other assets	452,481	324,757
Total Assets	$25,498,750	$19,066,054
LIABILITIES:		
Members' time deposits	$ 1,820,241	$ 1,215,095
Members' demand deposits	573,291	528,637
Total Deposits	$ 2,393,532	$ 1,743,732
Consolidated obligations	19,445,218	14,449,280
Other liabilities	496,662	376,738
Total Liabilities	$22,335,412	$16,569,750
CAPITAL:		
Capital stock—all member-owned	$ 2,624,306	$ 2,122,334
Legal reserve	304,619	244,071
Undivided profits	234,413	129,899
Total Capital	$ 3,163,338	$ 2,496,304
TOTAL LIABILITIES AND CAPITAL	$25,498,750	$19,066,054

Note: Components may not add to totals due to rounding.
Source: Federal Home Loan Bank Board.

MEMBER LOANS

The greatest advantage of the FHLBS is the ability of member institutions to obtain funds when needed in the form of advances from their regional bank. This support of members by the system is a healthy change from the pre-FHLBS reliance of member institutions upon local funds. Now these same institutions are linked to the capital markets of the country through their regional banks and the FHLBS.

Three major controls are imposed upon advances (loans) made by regional banks to their members: statutory requirements, regulations promulgated by the Federal Home Loan Bank Board, and policies established by the regional banks.

By statute, member institutions are limited to borrowing not in excess of 50 percent of their total savings deposits. Regulations of the FHLBB, however, limit member institution borrowing to 25 percent of their total savings balances, with the exception that this latter limitation is inoperable when withdrawal demands of depositors must be met.

Advance to members may be on either a long-term (up to ten years) or short-term (up to twelve months) basis. Interest rates on advances are established with regard to market conditions and the type of loan—secured or unsecured; amortized or straight term. In recent years the overwhelming preference has been for secured, short-term advances.

At the end of 1977, FHLB members had advances outstanding from their regional banks totaling approximately $20.1 billion. Interest rates on short-term advances during 1977 averaged between 7.79 percent and 7.40 percent.

Examples of FHLBB action to bolster a sagging mortgage market took place in 1969 when the board, through its regional banks, offered advances to member institutions with five year maturities when this type of advance had not been used for over ten years and in 1971 when the banks revised their credit policies to offer a variety of plans.

In general the FHLBB lends funds heavily in times of heavy savings deposit outflows and receives repayment in times of savings deposit growth. In this manner the FHLBB can act to offset the imbalance in mortgage fund availability created by the deposit and withdrawal cycle.

MEMBERSHIP

As was pointed out in a previous chapter, membership in the FHLBS is both compulsory and voluntary. Federally chartered savings and loan associations are required by statute to become members of the system, whereas state chartered savings and loan associations, mutual savings banks, and life insurance companies may become members at their election, if approved for membership by the FHLBB.

Chart 14-3 shows the membership in the FHLBS at year-end 1977. Note that only two life insurance companies and 74 mutual savings banks were members at that time. At the end of 1977, the FHLB System had 4175 members—down from a total of 4792 in 1969, and 4281 in 1974. Savings and loan association members of the FHLBS account for 98.5 percent of all savings and loan association assets.

LIQUIDITY REQUIREMENTS

The Federal Home Loan Bank System was not established for nor was it meant to be a substitute for sound management by member institutions. The system was created to act as a "backstop" to support its members in times of monetary crisis and to keep an even flow of funds into the mortgage market. Thus, rules and regulations governing members' operations are established to insure that such institutions will first use their own abilities and resources to accomplish the stabilization and mortgage fund flow purposes of the FHLBS. The most important regulation so imposed upon member institutions, then, is the liquidity requirement. This requirement places a responsibility upon member associations to maintain from 4 percent to 10 percent of their savings accounts

CHART 14-3

Membership of the FHLB System at Year-End 1974

| Bank District | Total Number | Savings and Loan Associations | | Other State-Chartered | Mutual Savings Banks | Life Insurance Companies | Total Member-ship |
| | | Insured by FSLIC | | | | | |
		Federally Chartered	State-Chartered				
Boston	159	73	50	36	36	...	195
New York	356	117	237	2	7	...	363
Pittsburgh	348	145	165	38	2	...	350
Atlanta	695	468	226	1	...	...	695
Cincinnati	553	303	197	53	...	1	554
Indianapolis ...	226	139	86	1	2	1	229
Chicago	563	190	368	5	2	...	565
Des Moines	280	153	124	3	1	...	281
Little Rock	540	196	344	...	...	...	540
Topeka	225	103	121	1	...	...	225
San Francisco ..	197	84	113	...	...	...	197
Seattle	139	89	50	...	7	...	146
Total	4,281	2,060	2,081	140	57	2	4,340

Source: Federal Home Loan Bank Board.

plus those borrowings maturing in less than one year in liquid form, such as in cash, government securities, certificates of deposit or bankers acceptance.

Since January 1, 1972, an amount equal to 3 percent of savings and borrowings payable in less than one year has to be maintained in short-term liquid assets (cash, government securities with eighteen months or less maturities, or time deposits and bankers acceptances with six months or less maturities).

Failure to meet liquidity requirements results in a cash penalty based upon a formula involving the deficiency in liquidity and the cost of regional bank advances.

ADVICE AND COUNSEL

Two major advisory bodies have been established to assist the FHLBS and its members. The Federal Savings and Loan Advisory Council was established pursuant to the Federal Home Loan Bank Act and is composed of twenty-four members. The conference of federal home loan bank presidents is made up of the twelve regional bank presidents. These two bodies are an important and influential part of the FHLBS's development. They helpfully recommend and advise on many items of legislation, proposed rules and regulations, liquidity requirements of member institutions, and supervision of members.

RECENT TRENDS

Title III of the Emergency Home Finance Act of 1970 entitled the Federal Home Loan Mortgage Corporation Act provides for the establishment by the Federal Home Loan Bank of the Federal Home Loan Mortgage Corporation (FHLMC). This federally-chartered corporation, often called "Freddie Mac," is authorized to function as a secondary market for residential mortgages sold to it by:

1. Any federal home loan bank
2. The Federal Savings and Loan Insurance Corporation
3. Any member of a federal home loan bank
4. Any other financial institution, the deposits or account of which are insured by any agency of the United States, such as a national bank.

The board of directors of the corporation is composed of the members of the Federal Home Loan Bank Board, who serve without additional compensation. The chairman of the corporation is the chairman of the Federal Home Loan Bank Board.

Mortgage operations of the corporation extend to both FHA and VA loans as well as conventional loans, even though the main purpose for creating the Federal Home Loan Mortgage Corporation is to provide an outlet for conventional loans originated by savings and loan associations.

The operations of the FHLMC are discussed in detail in chapter 19 of this text.

The net effect of this new legislation and the regulations issued pursuant thereto will be an increase of primarily savings and loan association lending capacity due to their ability to dispose of conventional, and FHA and VA mortgage loans and receive funds from re-investment in similar securities.

It is well to note that federal home loan banks have also recently been given the authority to purchase FHA and VA loans for resale under the GNMA pooled security program. Since early 1970 several issues have been made. This authority is of further benefit to savings and loan associations in freeing up funds for re-lending.

Proposals suggested, of which three have been adopted, give a good indication of the FHLBB's trend toward providing more lending freedom to federally chartered savings and loan associations. The pending proposal and the three adopted proposals are as follows:

1. Graduated payment mortgage terms to tailor the loan to the borrower. The variation could be in the form of low initial payments with increases coming in stages during the life of the loan. This feature assists younger families whose economic situation should favorably change with time. For older families looking toward retirement, mortgage payments could be high in the early loan years with staged decreases in installment amounts.
2. Partially amortized income property mortgages. Many life insurance and savings bank permanent loan commitments call for 10- to 25-year loan maturities with the mortgage being amortized on a 25- to 30-year basis. This provides for relatively low payments with a balloon payment due at maturity or require refinancing. The FHLBB proposal would apply the same technique to federal savings and loan association investments in income property loans. (pending)
3. Another adopted proposal allows 80 percent loan-to-value apartment building

permanent loans to be made with 30-year maturities. Previous industry limitations were 75 percent loans with 25-year maturities.

4. Variable rate mortgages which provide for the coupon rate to be changed up or down periodically based upon a certain money market index.

Over the last few years the FHLBB has played an increasing role in streamlining and expanding the mortgage lending policies prevailing in the savings and loan industry. The intent of the board appears to be one of making savings and loan associations the most important factor in real estate financing in the United States.

FEDERAL SAVINGS AND LOAN INSURANCE CORPORATION

One of the earliest and most apparent results of the Great Depression was the skepticism which rapidly developed with regard to safety of deposits held by the nation's thrift institutions. Demonstrative of this nationwide feeling were tremendous withdrawal demands which caused many banks, savings and loan associations, and mutual savings banks to close their doors. Hence, Congress evidenced the pressing need to expeditiously develop a means of restoring public confidence in the banking system, thereby serving the dual purpose of continuing the nation's banking operations and putting the savings of individuals and businesses to work in the economy. Certainly, savings withdrawn from local banks and buried in back yards only added to and perpetuated the effects of the depression.

The results of Congressional attention to the problem of restoring faith in banking were twofold. The Federal Deposit Insurance Corporation (FDIC) was created in 1934 to insure accounts placed in commercial banks and mutual savings banks and later the same year the Federal Savings and Loan Insurance Corporation (FSLIC) was established under Title IV of the National Housing Act for the purpose of insuring savings accounts placed in savings and loan associations. Both the FDIC and the FSLIC were authorized to insure individual accounts up to $5,000 each. This maximum insurance was increased to $10,000 in 1950, to $15,000 in 1966 to $20,000 in 1969 and then in late 1974 to $40,000. (Public funds are insured up to $100,000.) While neither has been put to the test, both the FDIC and FSLIC appear actuarially sound and definitely have accomplished their purpose of restoring faith in the banking system.

INSURED INSTITUTIONS

Membership in FSLIC is composed of federal and state chartered savings and loan associations. The former are by law compulsory members while the latter may voluntarily seek membership if they meet the corporation's requirements of solvency and sound operations.

Chart 14-4 reflects that 4,035 savings and loan assocations had their accounts insured at year-end 1977, representing 98 percent of total association assets. Since 1966 the total number of insured associations has declined while the percentage of total association assets insured has increased.

CHART 14-4

FSLIC Membership and Member Assets

Year-End	Total Number of Insured Associations	Federally Chartered	State-Chartered	Assets of Insured Associations	
				Millions of Dollars	Per Cent of All Association Assets
1950	2,860	1,526	1,334	$ 13,691	81.0%
1955	3,544	1,683	1,861	34,198	90.8
1960	4,098	1,873	2,225	67,430	94.3
1965	4,508	2,011	2,497	124,576	96.1
1970	4,365	2,067	2,298	170,645	96.9
1971	4,271	2,049	2,222	199,984	97.1
1972	4,191	2,044	2,147	236,349	97.2
1973	4,163	2,040	2,123	264,797	97.4
1974	4,141	2,060	2,081	288,223	97.5

Source: Federal Home Loan Bank Board.

COST OF MEMBERSHIP

FSLIC operations are supported by member assessments. These assessments are of two types:

1. A *regular* premium, paid annually, equal to 0.083 percent of total savings accounts. Prior to the Rate Control Act of 1969 this premium was also payable against all creditor obligations as determined by the association's latest annual report.

2. A prepayment premium, also paid annually. This requirement, instituted in 1962, places an obligation on all member associations to make a prepayment on their regular premiums equal to 2 percent of the increase in savings deposits less a sum equal to required FHLB stock holdings.

The regular premiums constitute the FSLICs primary income, whereas the prepayment premium is credited to its secondary reserve and is not considered an income item.

An interesting event occurred in the mid-1960s. The "tight" money period of 1966 caused many savings and loan associations to experience a decrease in savings deposits that year. Therefore, they paid no prepayment premium. But the next year, most of them experienced an increase in savings up to 1965 levels and were assessed the prepayment premium on the increase. The net effect was no appreciable increase in savings from 1965 to 1967 coupled with the requirement to pay a premium on savings deposit increases which took place between 1966 and 1967. However, the deposit increases during 1966 and 1967 were not net increases. They were a recovery of previously experienced losses. This constituted a double payment on the 1965 increase and the 1967 increase, without creating any additional liability for the FSLIC. Thus, statutes were passed in 1968 and 1969 allowing a cash refund for double payments and providing that no prepayment premium would be assessed on future recaptured savings.

By law, regular premium payments are suspended whenever the FSLICs primary reserve reaches or exceeds 2 percent of all insured member savings accounts, but each association must pay a regular premium for at least twenty years.

Likewise, prepayment premiums are suspended when the FSLICs primary and secondary reserves equal 2 percent of all the insured member savings accounts. Once suspended, prepayment premiums do not commence again until the primary and secondary reserves fall to 1.6 percent of insured savings.

At year end 1969 the 2 percent suspension level was reached and it was announced that for 1970 the prepayment premium would be suspended and a portion of the secondary reserve would be credited toward payment of the regular premium. However, by 1972 the ratio of reserves dropped to 1.564 percent due to large savings inflows. Thus the cash premium and prepayment were again instituted. To eliminate this start-stop situation Congress in 1973 legislated an end to the prepayments to the secondary reserves. That legislation also provided that the regular premium is to be paid part in cash and part by a credit from the secondary reserve. When reserves drop to 1.25 percent the premiums must again be paid solely in cash. The secondary reserve will sometime in the future. On December 31, 1977, the primary reserve of the FSLIC totaled $3653 million and the secondary reserve was $1220 million, for a combined total of $4873 million or 1.29 percent of insured liability.

An additional premium up to 0.125 percent of an insured member's savings and creditor obligations may be assessed by the FSLIC with the total additional premium in any event not exceeding FSLIC losses and expenses for the year of assessment. The additional premium will probably not be used until the corporation exercises two other powers it has to bolster its assets: the authority to borrow up to $750 million from the United States Treasury, and the power to require member institutions to deposit with it one percent of their total savings accounts.

SUPERVISION

Every insured savings and loan association is subject to a thorough annual examination by the corporation or FSLIC-approved public regulatory authority at the insured institution's cost. New applicants are subject to an initial examination. Both tbe initial and annual examination of savings and loan associations have the following as their purposes:

1. The uncovering of unsafe and unwise financial management policies
2. The determining of compliance with governing laws and FSLIC and FHLBB rules and regulations
3. The determining of whether or not an association is adequately serving the needs of its local community.

Problems and deficiencies uncovered by examination must promptly be corrected by the association's management.

Supervision by the FSLIC extends also to the establishment of operational standards for insured associations. Such standards cover:

1. The issuance of demand securities
2. The volume of sales of originated mortgage loans
3. The compliance with FHLBB regulations
4. The amount of commissions earned on the sale of savings accounts
5. The determination of adjusted net worth
6. The disposition of repossessed property
7. The reserves of member associations.

HANDLING OF CLAIMS

As of December 31, 1977, the FSLIC had processed only 119 claims during its 45-year history protecting a total of 1,022,711 savers (see Chart 14-5).

Several methods are used by the FSLIC to protect individual savings accounts when an insured institution finds itself in financial trouble or in receivership. The major methods of action are as follows:

1. To take over the defaulting institution's assets, pay all creditors, and meet all depositors' withdrawal demands, at least to the extent of $40,000 per account.
2. To arrange for another insured association to take over some of the defaulting association's assets by means of a loan made by the FSLIC, and move to meet creditor and depositor claims within the established limitations.
3. To make a loan or monetary contribution directly to the association in default, thus enabling it to solve its own problems.

This latter method is used in about half of the default cases and has the advantage of accomplishment without notoriety, thus enabling the defaulting association to continue its operations without facing a run on savings or liquidation or both.

In combination with the above the FSLIC may elect for the defaulting association to go into receivership or may institute changes in management. The main emphasis is upon finding a quiet and quick solution to an insured association's problem.

CONCLUSION

Out of the Great Depression came two stabilizing forces which have had a pronounced effect upon savings and loan association operations and correspondingly the mortgage market. These forces, the FHLBB and the FSLIC, are constantly bringing about innovations in the savings and loan industry. In times

CHART 14-5

Summary of FSLIC Insurance Settlement Cases
(Cumulative through December 31, 1974)

Method	Number of Cases	Number of Savers Protected
Acquisition of assets	13	75,782
Acquisition of assets and contribution	17	114,330
Contribution	57	420,164
Contribution and loan	2	10,715
Contribution, loan and acquisition of assets	1	14,542
Loan	4	137,383
Loan and acquisition of assets	1	26,137
Receivership and acquisition of assets	3	40,107
Receivership	10	50,467
Total	108	889,627

Source: Federal Home Loan Bank Board.

of economic crises both the FHLBB and the FSLIC have taken such action as was necessary to keep money flowing into home mortgages through savings and loan associations. Their impact is mostly felt in the areas of rules, regulations, and standards for member institution operations and insurance of savings accounts.

Recent innovations, such as the FHLMC, evidence a trend toward putting savings and loan associations in a position of home mortgage dominance to the detriment of mortgage companies, mutual savings banks, and commercial banks. The FHLBB in recent years has eased branching requirements, thus expanding savings and loan association operations, and has proposed a negotiated rate certificate of deposit which may well draw funds from commercial banks. In addition the FHLBB is studying such new proposals as allowing savings and loan associations to make checking accounts available to their customers.

Future proposals and regulations promulgated by these regulatory agencies, in particular the FHLBB, should be carefully watched and their impact upon savings and loan association operations and the mortgage market in general should be thoroughly studied and analyzed.

QUESTIONS FOR THOUGHT AND DISCUSSION

1. What conditions prompted the establishment of the FHLBB?; the FSLIC?
2. How does the FHLBS acquire funds for operation?; the FSLIC?
3. How are the following conditions insured (or promoted) through FHLBS and/or FSLIC actions?:
    a. Member institution liquidity
    b. Safety of depositor accounts
    c. Availability of mortgage funds
    d. Nationwide distribution of mortgage capital
4. What are the conditions for membership in the FHLBS?; FSLIC?
5. If you were chairman of the FHLBB what actions would you propose be taken under the following circumstances: Savings and loan deposits are remaining steady with decreases indicated, the demand for mortgage money is heavy and increasing, and interest rates are rising rapidly?

15

FEDERAL HOUSING ADMINISTRATION

The Federal Housing Administration is another outgrowth of the depression years and like FSLIC, FHLBS, and FNMA has survived to play a continuing role in mortgage financing.

LEGISLATIVE HISTORY

Created by the National Housing Act of 1934, FHA was given the authority to insure mortgage loans made by private lenders on single family homes through creation of a mutual mortgage fund, with the purpose of:

1. *Providing* immediate relief for slumping house construction and sales.
2. *Encouraging* more private investment in mortgages during a period of heavy losses resulting from mortgage foreclosures.
3. *Stepping-up* and promoting more home ownership.
4. *Upgrading* the country's housing standards.
5. *Providing* a continuing and sound pattern for mortgage loan financing.

Many amendments to the National Housing Act have been passed over the years. Two, however, are of importance: the 1947 Act and the 1965 Act.

The 1947 amendment to the National Housing Act established the Housing and Home Finance Agency with FHA as an important part of that agency. The Housing Act of 1965 created the Department of Housing and Urban Development as a cabinet level agency to include FHA and related functions dedicated to the improvement and generation of housing and more orderly development of the nation's urban areas.

Over the years, various amendments to the National Housing Act have established a variety of housing programs which come under the direct purview of FHA. These programs are divided into four specific areas—non-subsidized mortgage insurance programs, subsidized mortgage insurance programs, public housing programs, and interstate land sales regulation—and are the responsibiity of an assistant secretary of HUD for housing (Federal Housing Commissioner) (see Chart 15-1). This assistant secretary is also the Federal Housing Commissioner and thus the head of FHA.

Of the four program areas, the subsidized and non-subsidized programs are the ones generally referred to as FHA insured loans. The public housing programs are discussed in a subsequent chapter; interstate land sales regulation is not germane to this text discussion.

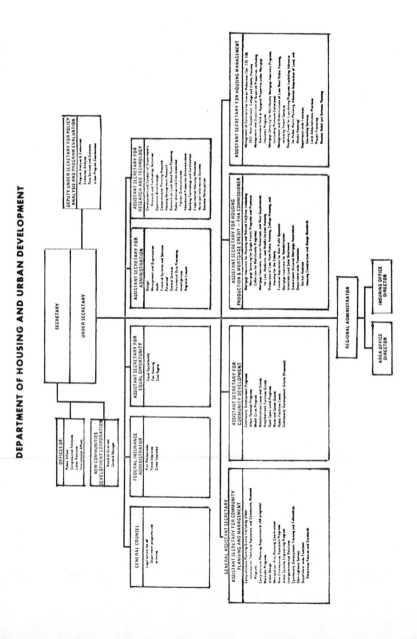

CHART 15-1

DEPARTMENT OF HOUSING AND URBAN DEVELOPMENT

MORTGAGE INSURANCE PROGRAMS

The subsidized and non-subsidized FHA mortgage insurance programs are designated and referred to by the section of the National Housing Act under which they were established. A brief discussion of these programs follows.

NON-SUBSIDIZED

Title I—Property improvement—Insurance for loans to repair or improve existing or proposed structures and for mobile home loans.

Title II Programs:

Section 203—Insurance of mortgages for construction or purchase of single family homes, including homes for disaster victims (203h), properties in outlying areas (203i) and seasonal homes (203m).

Section 207—Insurance of mortgages for construction or rehabilitation of multifamily rental projects and for construction or rehabilitation of mobile-home parks.

Section 213—Insurance for mortgages to finance cooperative housing projects.

Section 220—Urban Renewal Housing Mortgages—Insurance of mortgages for construction or rehabilitation of multifamily housing rental units in urban renewal areas.

Section 220—Urban Renewal Housing—Insurance on loans for repair or rehabilitation of single and multifamily housing projects in urban renewal areas.

Section 221(d)2—Insurance of mortgages for the construction, repair or purchase of single family homes for low to moderate income families and for families displaced by government action, such as urban renewal and eminent domain.

Section 222—Insurance of single family home mortgages for servicemen. Under this program the FHA mortgage insurance premium (MIP) is paid for by the Department of Defense or the Department of Transportation (Coast Guard).

Section 223(e)—Insurance for properties located in older declining urban areas where there is a need for adequate housing for low and moderate income families.

Section 223(f)—Insurance on loans for the purchase or refinancing of existing multifamily housing projects, whether conventionally financed or subject to federally insured mortgages at the time of application for mortgage insurance.

Section 231—Elderly Housing—Insurance of multifamily rental housing projects constructed or rehabilitated for occupancy by elderly or handicapped persons.

Section 232—Nursing Homes—Insurance of mortgages for construction or rehabilitation of nursing homes, including nursing home equipment.

Section 233—Experimental Housing—Insurance for mortgage financing obtained for the purpose of construction or rehabilitation of experimental multifamily rental housing projects through the use of new or untried materials or techniques.

Section 234—Condominiums—Insurance for mortgages to finance construction or rehabilitation of a condominium housing project or for the purchase of an individual unit in a condominium project.

Section 240—Insurance for homeowner loans obtained to purchase fee-simple title to property which is held under long-term ground leases and upon which the homeowners' houses are located.

Section 241—Supplemental Loans—Insurance for mortgages to finance the alteration, repair additions, and improvements to any multifamily housing project insured under any section of the National Housing Act and for the purchase of equipment to be used in the operations of nursing home or group practice facility.

Section 242—Hospitals—Insurance to finance construction or rehabilitation of hospitals up to a maximum of $50 million.

Section 245—Insurance for graduated payment mortgages.

Sections 809 and 810—Armed Services Housing—Insurance for mortgages to finance construction of single and multifamily housing units for civilian and military personnel on or near military defense, space agency, or Atomic Energy Commission installations.

Title X—Land Development—Insurance for loans to finance the development of land in proposed new community developments.

Title XI—Group Practice Facilities—Insurance for financing the construction or rehabilitation of facilities for the group practice of dentistry, medicine or optometry and including the purchase of major movable equipment.

SUBSIDIZED

Section 101—Rent supplemental payments to be made to private housing project owners on behalf of eligible lower income tenants.

Section 106(b)—Interest free loans to non-profit sponsors to cover 80 percent of planning and pre-construction expenses (seed money) for projects to be insured under Sections 234, 221 and 236.

Section 202—Elderly—Direct below market interest rate (BMIR) loans for construction of multifamily rental housing projects for the elderly or handicapped. Insurance under this section is being phased out in favor of Section 236.

Section 221—Insurance for mortgages on new or rehabilitated single family homes and multifamily rental units for low to moderate income or displaced families.

Section 221(d)3—Insurance for below market rate (BMIR) or market rate loans for construction or rehabilitation of multifamily rental housing units for families of low to moderate income. The BMIR insured loan program has been replaced by Section 236. Under the market rate program rent supplement payments are made by the Federal Government to project owners in order to reduce the tenants' rent cost.

Section 221(h)—Insurance of mortgages for the purchase and rehabilitation of single family homes for subsequent resale to low-income families.

Section 221(i)—Insurance on mortgages given with respect to the conversion of existing Section 221(d)3 BMIR multifamily rental projects to condominium ownership.

Section 235—Insurance for single family home mortgages for lower-income families with monthly FHA interest subsidy payment to the mortgagee effectively reducing the mortgagor's monthly payments.

Section 236—Insurance and subsidy for multifamily rental projects. This program is similar to the section 235 program.

Section 237—Insurance for special credit risk single family home mortgages to finance the acquisition of homes which would be eligible for insurance under Sections 203, 220, 221 and 235, if it were not for the proposed low-income family purchaser's poor credit standing. A requisite for this program is the establishment of a neighborhood or community counseling program for applicants under this section.

Section 243—Insurance for 7 percent interest rate mortgage loans made to moderate-income families.

FHA MORTGAGE INSURANCE

The FHA loan insurance program was established as a self-funded program. Under the National Housing Act of 1934 a mutual mortgage insurance fund was created to provide a pool of funds from which to pay insurance claims. In addition to monthly principal and interest payments each mortgagor on a FHA insured loan is required to prepay annually a mortgage insurance premium (MIP) of generally 0.5 percent of the principal balance outstanding at the time of payment. The MIP along with prepayment penalties and other applicable FHA fees are deposited into one of several funds from which claims of mortgagee's holding-insured mortgages are met.

The primary depository of premiums is the General Insurance Fund, created by the Housing and Urban Development Act of 1965. Monies deposited in this fund are used to pay the general expenses of operations in HUD which relate mortgages that are obligations of the General Insurance Fund.

The Mutual Mortgage Insurance Fund was established to receive premiums paid under the standard home loan programs (203 (b), 203 (h), and 203 (i)). Upon termination of an obligation against the Mutual Mortgage Insurance Fund by payment of any mortgage insured thereunder, a portion of premium paid by the mortgagor may be distributed to him.

Also, there is a Special Risk Insurance Fund for those loans which provide a greater than normal credit exposure, such as properties located in a deteriorating neighborhood or a poor mortgagor credit insured under Section 237, and a Cooperative Management Housing Insurance Fund for Section 213 insured loans.

When a claim is made, FHA has the option to satisfy it with cash or debentures. However, claims made under certain low to moderate income programs are paid in cash. Debentures issued by FHA mature after twenty years and bear interest rates usually well below the coupon rate of the mortgage under which an insurance claim is made. Thus the mortgagee in a debenture-backed situation is not fully protected against a loss and has to bear some financial burden. Since the Housing and Urban Development Act of 1965 the Secretary of HUD has had the option of paying insurance claims in cash or debentures. In recent years single family home loan claims have been met with cash.

Defaulted insured mortgages on single family homes are usually foreclosed and a claim is then presented to FHA by the mortgagee for losses incurred due to the mortgagor's default and claim settlement, foreclosure costs, attorney fees, and, of course, loan principal. Foreclosure expenses allowable by FHA, however, are fixed by statutes and can rarely be exceeded. Upon settlement of the mortgagee's claim the property, if acquired at the foreclosure sale by the mortgagee, is transferred to FHA. The mortgagee then receives an amount equal to the total losses allowed by FHA or, in the event that a third party purchased the property at foreclosure, the difference between total losses and the foreclosure sale proceeds.

Properties acquired by FHA through claim settlement are rehabilitated and sold through local real estate brokers.

Multifamily insured mortgages may be foreclosed on default and a claim made for losses incurred or they can be delivered to FHA for purchase at 99 percent of the principal value plus a portion of accrued and unpaid interest.

RATES, LOAN TERMS, MATURITIES

The Secretary of Housing and Urban Development is authorized by Congress to establish a maximum interest rate for loans insured by FHA. In late 1979, the maximum rate was 11.5 percent, an all time high, 2 percent greater than the 9.5 percent rate in 1974. With a fixed mortgage coupon rate, lenders and investors must purchase loans at discounts in order to obtain their required yield on investment. Thus, the fixing of a maximum rate has led to the universal practice of charging discounts or points to sellers of homes on which FHA mortgage insurance is obtained. Purchaser-mortgagors are prohibited by FHA from payment of any loan discounts, except in cases of refinancing and builder-mortgagors. Legislation has recently been proposed to allow for any rate of interest on an FHA insured mortgage, provided no discounts or points are assessed to either the home seller or purchaser.

Standard note and mortgage forms must be used on all FHA loans. These forms include all the loan provisions which FHA requires and which mortgagees have accepted such as limited late charges and prepayment penalties. Charts 15-2, 15-3, 15-4, and 15-5 are sample FHA note and mortgage forms for single and multifamily projects.

Loan maturities vary by program but are generally thirty years on home mortgages and forty years on multifamily mortgages.

REPRESENTATIVE PROGRAMS

Representative of the FHA home and multifamily programs are the Section 203(b), 245, 207 and Section 8 programs. They encompass both the subsidized and nonsubsidized areas and relate both the old and the new FHA-insured loan program theories.

SECTION 203(b)

The Section 203(b) home mortgage insurance program has been FHA's standard one-to-four family program for many years and is attributed with the distinct honor of having been the greatest single force in the development of the nation's subdivisions in the post-World War II years. Today it is still the most popular FHA program. In 1977 mortgages covering over 284,000 housing units were insured under Section 203, compared to mortgages covering approximately 321,000 housing units which were insured under all FHA Home Mortgage programs. (See Chart 15-6.)

Under this program insurance is given to finance the acquisition of one-to-four family homes which are proposed, under construction, or existing. Indebtedness existing on such property may be refinanced under Section 203(b).

CHART 15-2

FHA FORM NO. 9110
Revised September 1970

This form is used in connection with
mortgages insured under the one- to
four-family provisions of the National
Housing Act.

MORTGAGE NOTE

FHA CASE NO.

$, Florida,
                                                                     , 19

FOR VALUE RECEIVED, the undersigned promise(s) to pay to

                                              , a corporation organized and existing under
the laws of   , or order, the principal sum of
                                                                          Dollars
($), with interest from date at the rate of
per centum (%) per annum on the unpaid balance until paid. The said principal
and interest shall be payable at the office of
                              in   ,
or at such other place as the holder may designate, in writing, in monthly installments of
                                             Dollars ($),
commencing on the first day of   , 19   , and on the first day of each month thereafter until the principal and interest are fully paid, except that the final payment of the entire indebtedness evidenced hereby, if not sooner paid, shall be due and payable on the first day of

If default be made in the payment of any installment under this note, and if such default is not made
good prior to the due date of the next such installment, the entire principal sum and accrued interest
shall at once become due and payable without notice at the option of the holder of this note. Failure
to exercise this option shall not constitute a waiver of the right to exercise the same in the event of
any subsequent default. In the event of default in the payment of this note, and if the same is collected
by an attorney at law, the undersigned hereby agree(s) to pay all costs of collection, including a reasonable attorney's fee.

Presentment, protest, and notice are hereby waived,

CHART 15-3

STATE OF FLORIDA
FHA FORM NO 2110 M
Revised October 1972

> This form is used in connection with mortgages insured under the one- to four-family provisions of the National Housing Act

MORTGAGE

THIS MORTGAGE, dated the   day of   , A. D. 19 , by and, between
hereinafter called the mortgagor, and

    , a corporation organized and existing under the laws of
    , hereinafter called the mortgagee.

  WITNESSETH, that for divers good and valuable considerations, and also in consideration of the aggregate sum named in the promissory note hereinafter described, the said mortgagor does hereby grant, bargain, sell, alien, remise, release, convey, and confirm unto the said mortgagee all that certain piece, parcel, or tract of land of which the said mortgagor is now seized and possessed and in actual possession, situate in the county of
and State of Florida, described as follows

  Together with all structures and improvements now and hereafter on said land, and fixtures attached thereto, and all rents, issues, proceeds, and profits accruing and to accrue from said premises, all of which are included within the foregoing description and the habendum thereof; also all gas, steam, electric, water, and other heating, cooking, refrigerating, lighting, plumbing, ventilating, irrigating, and power systems, machines, appliances, fixtures, and appurtenances, which now are or may hereafter pertain to, or be used with, in, or on said premises, even though they be detached or detachable.

  TO HAVE AND TO HOLD the same, together with all and singular the tenements, hereditaments and appurtenances thereunto belonging or in anywise appertaining, and the reversion and reversions, remainder or remainders, rents, issues, and profits thereof, and also all the estate, right, title, interest, homestead, dower and right of dower, separate estate, possession, claim and demand whatsoever, as well in law as in equity, of the said mortgagor in and to the same, and every part thereof, with the appurtenances of the said mortgagor in and to the same, and every part and parcel thereof unto the said mortgagee in fee simple.

  And the mortgagor hereby covenants with the mortgagee that he is indefeasibly seized of said land in fee simple; that he has full power and lawful right to convey the same in fee simple as aforesaid; that it shall be lawful for the mortgagee, at all times peaceably and quietly to enter upon, hold, occupy, and enjoy said land, and every part thereof; that the land is and will remain free from all encumbrances; that said mortgagor will make such further assurances to prove the fee simple title to said land in said mortgagee as may be reasonably required, and that said mortgagor does hereby fully warrant the title to said land, and every part thereof, and will defend the same against the lawful claims of all persons whomsoever.

  PROVIDED ALWAYS, and these presents are executed and delivered upon the following conditions, to wit:

  The mortgagor agrees to pay the mortgagee, or order, the principal sum of
Dollars ($), as evidenced by a note of even date herewith, with interest from date at the rate of   per centum (%) per annum on the unpaid balance until paid. The said principal and interest shall be payable at the office of

or at such other place as the holder of the note may designate in writing, in monthly installments of
Dollars ($), commencing on the first day of   , 19 , and on the first day of each month thereafter until the principal and interest are fully paid, except that the final payment of principal and interest, if not sooner paid, shall be due and payable on the first day of
;

  And shall duly, promptly, and fully perform, discharge, execute, effect, complete, and comply with and abide by each and every the stipulations, agreements, conditions, and covenants of said promissory note and of this mortgage, then this mortgage and the estate hereby created shall cease and be null and void.

  And the mortgagor further covenants as follows:

  1. That he will pay the indebtedness, as hereinbefore provided. Privilege is reserved to pay the debt in whole, or in an amount equal to one or more monthly payments on the principal that are next due on the note, on the first day of any month prior to maturity; *Provided*, however, that written notice of an intention to exercise such privilege is given at least thirty (30) days prior to prepayment.

2. That, in order more fully to protect the security of this mortgage, the mortgagor, together with, and in addition to, the monthly payments under the terms of the note secured hereby, on the first day of each month until the said note is fully paid, will pay to the mortgagee the following sums:

    (a) An amount sufficient to provide the holder hereof with funds to pay the next mortgage insurance premium if this instrument and the note secured hereby are insured, or a monthly charge (in lieu of a mortgage insurance premium) if they are held by the Secretary of Housing and Urban Development as follows:

        (I) If and so long as said note of even date and this instrument are insured or are reinsured under the provisions of the National Housing Act, an amount sufficient to accumulate in the hands of the holder one (1) month prior to its due date the annual mortgage insurance premium, in order to provide such holder with funds to pay such premium to the Secretary of Housing and Urban Development pursuant to the National Housing Act, as amended, and applicable Regulations thereunder; or

        (II) If and so long as said note of even date and this instrument are held by the Secretary of Housing and Urban Development, a monthly charge (in lieu of a mortgage insurance premium) which shall be in an amount equal to one-twelfth (1/12) of one-half (1/2) per centum of the average outstanding balance due on the note computed without taking into account delinquencies or prepayments;

    (b) A sum equal to the ground rents, if any, next due, plus the premiums that will next become due and payable on policies of fire and other hazard insurance covering the mortgaged property, plus taxes and assessments next due on the mortgaged property (all as estimated by the mortgagee) less all sums already paid therefor divided by the number of months to elapse before one month prior to the date when such ground rents, premiums, taxes, and assessments will become delinquent, such sums to be held by mortgagee in trust to pay said ground rents, premiums, taxes, and special assessments; and

    (c) All payments mentioned in the two preceding subsections of this paragraph and all payments to be made under the note secured hereby shall be added together and the aggregate amount thereof shall be paid by the mortgagor each month in a single payment to be applied by the mortgagee to the following items in the order set forth:

        (I) premium charges under the contract of insurance with the Secretary of Housing and Urban Development, or monthly charge (in lieu of mortgage insurance premium), as the case may be;

        (II) ground rents, taxes, assessments, fire, and other hazard insurance premiums;

        (III) interest on the note secured hereby; and

        (IV) amortization of the principal of said note.

Any deficiency in the amount of such aggregate monthly payment shall, unless made good by the mortgagor prior to the due date of the next such payment, constitute an event of default under this mortgage. The mortgagee may collect a "late charge" not to exceed two cents (2c) for each dollar ($1) of each payment more than fifteen (15) days in arrears to cover the extra expense involved in handling delinquent payments.

3. That if the total of the payments made by the mortgagor under (b) of paragraph 2 preceding shall exceed the amount of the payments actually made by the mortgagee, for ground rents, taxes and assessments and insurance premiums, as the case may be, such excess at the option of the mortgagee, shall, be credited on subsequent payments to be made by the mortgagor, or refunded to the mortgagor. If, however, the monthly payments made by the mortgagor under (b) of paragraph 2 preceding shall not be sufficient to pay ground rents, taxes and assessments and insurance premiums, as the case may be, when the same shall become due and payable, then the mortgagor shall pay to the mortgagee any amount necessary to make up the deficiency, on or before the date when payment of such ground rents, taxes, assessments, or insurance premiums shall be due. If at any time the mortgagor shall tender to the mortgagee in accordance with the provisions of the note secured hereby, full payment of the entire indebtedness represented thereby, the mortgagee shall, in computing the amount of such indebtedness, credit to the account of the mortgagor all payments made under the provisions of (a) of paragraph 2 hereof which the mortgagee has not become obligated to pay to the Secretary of Housing and Urban Development and any balance remaining in the funds accumulated under the provisions of (b) of said paragraph 2. If there shall be a default under any of the provisions of this mortgage, resulting in a public sale of the premises covered hereby, or if the mortgagee acquires the property otherwise after default, the mortgagee shall apply, at the time of the commencement of such proceedings or at the time the property is otherwise acquired, the balance then remaining in the funds accumulated under (b) of paragraph 2 preceding as a credit against the amount of principal then remaining unpaid under said note and shall properly adjust any payments which shall have been made under (a) of said paragraph.

4. That he will pay all taxes, assessments, water rates, and other governmental or municipal charges, fines, or impositions, for which provision has not been made hereinbefore, and in default thereof the mortgagee may pay the same; and that he will promptly deliver the official receipts therefor to the mortgagee.

5. That he will permit, commit, or suffer no waste, impairment, or deterioration of said property or any part thereof; and in the event of the failure of the mortgagor to keep the buildings on said premises and those to be erected on said premises, or improvements thereon, in good repair, the mortgagee may make such repairs as in its discretion it may deem necessary for the proper preservation thereof, and the full amount of each and every such payment shall be immediately due and payable, and shall be secured by the lien of this mortgage.

6. That he will pay all and singular the costs, charges, and expenses, including reasonable lawyer's fees, and costs of abstracts of title, incurred or paid at any time by the mortgagee because of the failure on the part of the mortgagor promptly and fully to perform the agreements and covenants of said promissory note and this mortgage, and said costs, charges, and expenses shall be immediately due and payable and shall be secured by the lien of this mortgage.

7. That he will keep the improvements now existing or hereafter erected on the mortgaged property, insured as may be required from time to time by the mortgagee against loss by fire and other hazards, casualties, and contingencies in such amounts and for such periods as may be required by mortgagee, and will pay promptly, when due, any premiums on such insurance for payment of which provision has not been made hereinbefore. All insurance shall be carried in companies approved by mortgagee and the policies and renewals thereof shall be held by mortgagee and have attached thereto loss payable clauses in favor of and in form acceptable to the mortgagee. In event of loss he will give immediate notice by mail to mortgagee, and mortgagee may make proof of loss if not made promptly by mortgagor, and each insurance company concerned is hereby authorized and directed to make payment for such loss directly to mortgagee instead of to mortgagor and mortgagee jointly, and the insurance proceeds, or any part thereof, may be applied by mortgagee at its option either to the reduction of the indebtedness hereby secured or to the restoration or repair of the property damaged. In event of foreclosure of this mortgage or other transfer of title to the mortgaged property in extinguishment of the indebtedness secured hereby, all right, title, and interest of the mortgagor in and to any insurance policies then in force shall pass to the purchaser or grantee.

8. That if the premises, or any part thereof, be condemned under any power of eminent domain, or acquired for a public use, the damages, proceeds, and the consideration for such acquisition, to the extent of the full amount of indebtedness upon this Mortgage, and the Note secured hereby remaining unpaid, are hereby assigned by the Mortgagor to the Mortgagee and shall be paid forthwith to the Mortgagee to be applied by it on account of the indebtedness secured hereby, whether due or not.

9. That the mortgagee may, at any time pending a suit upon this mortgage, apply to the court having jurisdiction thereof for the appointment of a receiver, and such court shall forthwith appoint a receiver of the premises covered hereby all and singular, including all and singular the income, profits, issues, and revenues from whatever source derived, each and every of which, it being expressly understood, is hereby mortgaged as if specifically set forth and described in the granting and habendum clauses hereof, and such receiver shall have all the broad and effective functions and powers in anywise entrusted by a court to a receiver, and such appointment shall be made by such court as an admitted equity and a matter of absolute right to said mortgagee, and without reference to the adequacy or inadequacy of the value of the property mortgaged or to the solvency or insolvency of said mortgagor or the defendants, and that such rents, profits, income, issues, and revenues shall be applied by such receiver according to the lien of this mortgage and the practice of such court. In the event of any default on the part of the mortgagor hereunder, the mortgagor agrees to pay to the mortgagee on demand as a reasonable monthly rental for the premises an amount at least equivalent to one-twelfth (1/12) of the aggregate of the twelve monthly installments payable in the then current year plus the actual amount of the annual taxes, assessments, water rates, and insurance premiums for such year not covered by the aforesaid monthly payments.

10. That (a) in the event of any breach of this mortgage or default on the part of the mortgagor, or (b) in the event that any of said sums of money herein referred to be not promptly and fully paid without demand or notice, or (c) in the event that each and every the stipulations, agreements, conditions, and covenants of said note and this mortgage, are not duly, promptly, and fully performed; then in either or any such event, the said aggregate sum mentioned in said note then remaining unpaid, with interest accrued to that time, and all moneys secured hereby, shall become due and payable forthwith, or thereafter, at the option of said mortgagee, as fully and completely as if all of the said sums of money were originally stipulated to be paid on such day, anything in said note or in this mortgage to the contrary notwithstanding; and thereupon or thereafter, at the option of said mortgagee, without notice or demand, suit at law or in equity, may be prosecuted as if all moneys secured hereby had matured prior to its institution. The mortgagee may foreclose this mortgage, as to the amount so declared due and payable, and the said premises shall be sold to satisfy and pay the same together with costs, expenses, and allowances. In case of partial foreclosure of this mortgage, the mortgaged premises shall be sold subject to the continuing lien of this mortgage for the amount of the debt not then due and unpaid. In such case the provisions of this paragraph may again be availed of thereafter from time to time by the mortgagee.

11. That the mortgagor will give immediate notice by mail to the mortgagee of any conveyance, transfer, or change of ownership of the premises.

12. That no waiver of any covenant herein or of the obligation secured hereby shall at any time thereafter be held to be a waiver of the terms hereof or of the note secured hereby.

13. That if the mortgagor default in any of the covenants or agreements contained herein, or in said note, then the mortgagee may perform the same, and all expenditures (including reasonable attorney's fees) made by the mortgagee in so doing shall draw interest at the rate set forth in the note secured hereby, and shall be repayable immediately and without demand by the mortgagor to the mortgagee, and, together with interest and costs accruing thereon, shall be secured by this mortgage.

14. That the mailing of a written notice or demand addressed to the owner of record of the mortgaged premises, or directed to the said owner at the last address actually furnished to the mortgagee, or directed to said owner at said mortgaged premises, and mailed by the United States mails, shall be sufficient notice and demand in any case arising under this instrument and required by the provisions hereof or by law.

15. The mortgagor further covenants that should this mortgage and the note secured hereby not be eligible for insurance under the National Housing Act within   from the date hereof (written statement of any officer of the Department of Housing and Urban Development or authorized agent of the Secretary of Housing and Urban Development dated subsequent to the   time from the date of this mortgage, declining to insure said note and this mortgage, being deemed conclusive proof of such ineligibility), the mortgagee or the holder of the note may, at its option, declare all sums secured hereby immediately due and payable.

The covenants herein contained shall bind, and the benefits and advantages shall inure to, the respective heirs, executors, administrators, successors, and assigns of the parties hereto. Whenever used, the singular number shall include the plural, the plural the singular, and the use of any gender shall include all genders.

IN WITNESS WHEREOF, the said mortgagor has hereunto set his hand and seal the day and year first aforesaid.
Signed, sealed, and delivered in the presence of—

_____   _____ [SEAL]

_____   _____ [SEAL]

_____ [SEAL]

_____ [SEAL]

STATE OF FLORIDA
COUNTY OF   } ss:

Before me personally appeared   and
his wife, to me well known and known to me to be the individuals described in and who executed the foregoing instrument, and acknowledged before me that they executed the same for the purposes therein expressed.
WITNESS my hand and official seal this   day of   , 19

_____
Notary Public in and for the county and State aforesaid

My commission expires

STATE OF
COUNTY OF   } ss:

Before me personally appeared   , to me well known and known to me to be the individual described in and who executed the foregoing instrument, and acknowledged before me that he executed the same for the purposes therein expressed.
WITNESS my hand and official seal this   day of   , 19

_____
Notary Public in and for the county and State aforesaid

My commission expires

CHART 15-4

FHA FORM NO. 4116-D
(CORPORATE)
Revised December 1963

MORTGAGE NOTE

$, Illinois.
                                                                     , 19   .

FOR VALUE RECEIVED, The undersigned

                                                                     promise(s)

to pay to the order of   ,
a corporation organized and existing under the laws of   , the principal
sum of   Dollars
($), with interest from date at the rate of   per
centum (%) per annum on the unpaid balance until paid; the said principal and interest to be payable as follows:

Both principal and interest shall be payable at the office of
                              in   , or at such
other place as the holder may from time to time designate in writing.

Privilege is reserved to pay the debt in whole or in an amount equal to one or more monthly payments on principal next due, on the first day of any month prior to maturity upon at least thirty (30)
days' prior written notice to the holder. If this debt is paid in full while insured under the provisions
of the National Housing Act, as amended, all parties liable for payment thereof agree to be jointly and
severally bound to pay to the holder hereof such adjusted mortgage insurance premium as may be required by the applicable Regulations.

Notwithstanding any provision herein for a prepayment charge, such charge shall be applicable
only to the amount of prepayment in any one calendar year which is in excess of fifteen per centum
(15%) of the original principal sum of this Note.

If default be made in the payment of any installment under this Note, and if such default is not
made good prior to the due date of the next such installment, the entire principal sum and accrued interest shall at once become due and payable without notice, at the option of the holder of this Note.
Failure to exercise this option shall not constitute a waiver of the right to exercise the same in the
event of any subsequent default. In the event of default in the payment of this Note, and if the same is
collected by an attorney at law, the undersigned hereby agree(s) to pay all costs of collection, including a reasonable attorney's fee.

No default shall exist by reason of nonpayment of any required installment of principal so long as
the amount of optional additional prepayments of principal already made pursuant to the privilege of
prepayment set forth in this Note equals or exceeds the amount of such required installment of principal.

All parties to this Note, whether principal, surety, guarantor or endorser, hereby waive presentment for payment, demand, protest, notice of protest and notice of dishonor.

Signed and sealed this   day of   , 19   .

ATTEST:

_____   By _____

THIS IS TO CERTIFY, That this is the Note described in and secured by Mortgage of even date
herewith, in the same principal amount as herein stated and secured on real estate situated in the
                              of   , County of   ,
              , and State of Illinois.

Dated   , 19   .

_____
Notary Public

STATE OF ILLINOIS

LOAN NO.

Mortgage Note

TO

No. _____

Insured under   of the
National Housing Act and Regulations published thereunder

In effect on _____

To the extent of advances approved by the
Secretary of Housing and Urban Develop-
ment acting by and through the Federal
Housing Commissioner

By _____
(Authorized Agent)

Date _____

A total sum of $ _____ has been
approved for insurance hereunder by the
Secretary of Housing and Urban Development acting by and through the Federal
Housing Commissioner

By _____
(Authorized Agent)

Date _____

Reference is made to the Act and to the
Regulations thereunder covering assignments of the insurance protection on this
note.

43559-P Rev. 12/63   HUD-Wash., D. C.

CHART 15-5

FHA Form No. 4116-b
(Corporate)
(Revised August 1962)

MORTGAGE

THIS INDENTURE, made this   day of   , 19   ,
between

, a corporation
organized and existing under the laws of   , Mortgagor,
and   ,
a corporation organized and existing under the laws of   , Mortgagee.

WITNESSETH: That whereas the Mortgagor is justly indebted to the Mortgagee in the principal sum of
Dollars ($), evidenced by its
note of even date herewith, bearing interest from date on outstanding balances at   per
centum (%) per annum, said principal and interest being payable in monthly installments as provided in said note with a
final maturity of   , which note is identified as being secured hereby by a certificate thereon. Said
note and all of its terms are incorporated herein by reference and this conveyance shall secure any and all extensions
thereof, however evidenced.

Now, THEREFORE, the said Mortgagor, for the better securing of the payment of the said principal sum of money and interest
and the performance of the covenants and agreements herein contained, does by these presents CONVEY, MORTGAGE, and WARRANT
unto the Mortgagee, its successors or assigns, the following-described real estate situate, lying, and being in the
, in the County of   , and the State of Illinois, to wit:

TOGETHER with all and singular the tenements, hereditaments and appurtenances thereunto belonging, and the rents, issues, and profits thereof; and all apparatus and fixtures of every kind in, or that may be placed in, any building now or hereafter standing on said land, and also all the estate, right, title, and interest of the said Mortgagor in and to said premises; including but not limited to all gas and electric fixtures; all radiators, heaters, furnaces, heating equipment, steam and hot-water boilers, stoves, and ranges; all elevators and motors; all bathtubs, sinks, water closets, basins, pipes, faucets, and other plumbing fixtures; all mantels and cabinets; all refrigerating plants and refrigerators, whether mechanical or otherwise; all cooking apparatus; all furniture, shades, awnings, screens, blinds, and other furnishings; all of which apparatus, fixtures, and equipment, whether affixed to the realty or not, shall be considered real estate for the purposes hereof; and including all furnishings now or hereafter attached to or used in and about the building or buildings now erected or hereafter to be erected on the lands herein described which are necessary to the complete and comfortable use and occupancy of such building or buildings for the purposes for which they were or are to be erected, and all renewals or replacements thereof or articles in substitution therefor; together with all building materials and equipment now or hereafter delivered to said premises and intended to be installed therein;

To HAVE AND TO HOLD the above-described premises, with the appurtenances and fixtures, unto the said Mortgagee, its successors and assigns, forever, for the purposes and uses herein set forth.

AND SAID MORTGAGOR covenants and agrees:

1. That it will pay the note at the times and in the manner provided therein;

2. That it will not permit or suffer the use of any of the property for any purpose other than the use for which the same was intended at the time this Mortgage was executed;

3. That the Regulatory Agreement, if any, executed by the Mortgagor and the Federal Housing Commissioner, which is being recorded simultaneously herewith, is incorporated in and made a part of this Mortgage. Upon default under the Regulatory Agreement and upon the request of the Federal Housing Commissioner, the Mortgagee, at its option, may declare the whole of the indebtedness secured hereby to be due and payable;

4. That all rents, profits and income from the property covered by this Mortgage are hereby assigned to the Mortgagee for the purpose of discharging the debt hereby secured. Permission is hereby given to Mortgagor so long as no default exists hereunder, to collect such rents, profits and income for use in accordance with the provisions of the Regulatory Agreement;

5. That upon default hereunder Mortgagee shall be entitled to the appointment of a receiver by any court having jurisdiction, without notice, to take possession and protect the property described herein and operate same and collect the rents, profits and income therefrom;

6. That at the option of the Mortgagor the principal balance secured hereby may be reamortized on terms acceptable to the Federal Housing Commissioner if a partial prepayment results from an award in condemnation in accordance with provisions of paragraph 8 herein, or from an insurance payment made in accordance with provisions of paragraph 7 herein, where there is a resulting loss of project income;

7. That the Mortgagor will keep the improvements now existing or hereafter erected on the mortgaged property insured against loss by fire and such other hazards, casualties, and contingencies, as may be stipulated by the Federal Housing Commissioner upon the insurance of the mortgage and other hazards as may be required from time to time by the Mortgagee, and all such insurance shall be evidenced by standard Fire and Extended Coverage Insurance Policy or policies, in amounts not less than necessary to comply with the applicable Coinsurance Clause percentage, but in no event shall the amounts of coverage be less than eighty per centum (80%) of the Insurable Values or not less than the unpaid balance of the insured mortgage, whichever is the lesser, and in default thereof the Mortgagee shall have the right to effect insurance. Such policies shall be endorsed with standard Mortgagee clause with loss payable to the Mortgagee and the Federal Housing Commissioner as interest may appear, and shall be deposited with the Mortgagee;

That if the premises covered hereby, or any part thereof, shall be damaged by fire or other hazard against which insurance is held as hereinabove provided, the amounts paid by any insurance company in pursuance of the contract of insurance to the extent of the indebtedness then remaining unpaid, shall be paid to the Mortgagee, and, at its option, may be applied to the debt or released for the repairing or rebuilding of the premises;

8. That all awards of damages in connection with any condemnation for public use of or injury to any of said property are hereby assigned and shall be paid to Mortgagee, who may apply the same to payment of the installments last due under said note, and Mortgagee is hereby authorized, in the name of Mortgagor, to execute and deliver valid acquittances thereof and to appeal from any such award;

9. That it is lawfully seized and possessed of said real estate in fee simple, and has good right to convey same;

10. To keep said premises in good repair, and not to do, or permit to be done, upon said premises, anything that may impair the value thereof, or of the security intended to be effected by virtue of this instrument; to pay to the Mortgagee, as hereinafter provided, until said note is fully paid, a sum sufficient to pay all taxes and special assessments that heretofore or hereafter may be lawfully levied, assessed or imposed by any taxing body upon the said land, or upon the Mortgagor or Mortgagee on account of the ownership thereof to the extent that provision has not been made by the Mortgagor for the payment of such taxes and special assessments as hereinafter provided in subparagraph 17(b);

11. In case of the refusal or neglect of the Mortgagor to make such payments, or to satisfy any prior lien or encumbrance, or to keep said premises in good repair, the Mortgagee may pay such taxes, assessments, and insurance premiums, wher. due, and may make such repairs to the property herein mortgaged as in its discretion it may deem necessary for the proper preservation thereof, and any moneys so paid or expended together with any sums expended by the Mortgagee to keep the mortgage insurance in force, shall become so much additional indebtedness, secured by this mortgage, to be paid out of the proceeds of the sale of the mortgaged premises, if not otherwise paid by the Mortgagor and shall bear interest at the rate specified in the note from the date of the advance until paid, and shall be due and payable on demand;

12. It is expressly provided, however (all other provisions of this mortgage to the contrary notwithstanding), that the Mortgagee shall not be required nor shall it have the right to pay, discharge, or remove any tax, assessment, or tax lien upon or against the premises described herein or any part thereof or the improvements situated thereon, so long as the Mortgagor shall, in good faith, contest the same or the validity thereof by appropriate legal proceedings brought in a court of competent jurisdiction, which shall operate to prevent the collection of the tax, assessment, or lien so contested and the sale or forfeiture of the said premises or any part thereof to satisfy the same, but in the event of a tax contest, the Mortgagor shall deposit with the Mortgagee an amount estimated by the Mortgagee sufficient to satisfy all taxes, penalties, interest, and costs which may reasonably accrue during such contest;

13. That it will not voluntarily create or permit to be created against the property subject to this mortgage any lien or liens inferior or superior to the lien of this mortgage and further that it will keep and maintain the same free from the claim of all persons supplying labor or materials which will enter into the construction of any and all buildings now being erected or to be erected on said premises;

14. That the improvements about to be made upon the premises above described and all plans and specifications comply with all municipal ordinances and regulations made or promulgated by lawful authority, and that the same will upon completion comply with all such municipal ordinances and regulations and with the rules of the applicable fire rating or inspection organization, bureau, association, or office. In the event the Mortgagor shall at any time fail to comply with such rules, regulations, and ordinances which are now or may hereafter become applicable to the premises above described, after due notice and demand by the Mortgagee, thereupon the principa. sum and all arrears of interest and other charges provided for herein, shall at the option of the Mortgagee become due and payable;

15. The Mortgagor covenants and agrees that so long as this mortgage and the said note secured hereby are insured or held under the provisions of the National Housing Act, it will not execute or file for record any instrument which imposes a restriction upon the sale or occupancy of the mortgaged property on the basis of race, color or creed;

16. That the funds to be advanced herein are to be used in the construction of certain improvements on the lands herein described, in accordance with a building loan agreement between the Mortgagor and Mortgagee dated _____, 19 , which building loan agreement (except such part or parts thereof as may be inconsistent herewith) is incorporated herein by reference to the same extent and effect as if fully set forth and made a part of this mortgage; and if the constru_____ improvements to be made pursuant to said building loan agreement shall not be carried on with reasonable diligence, or shall be discontinued at any time for any reason other than strikes or lock outs, the Mortgagee, after due notice to the Mortgagor or any subsequent owner, is hereby invested with full and complete authority to enter upon the said premises, employ watchmen to protect such improvements from depredation or injury and to preserve and protect the personal property therein, and to continue any and all outstanding contracts for the erection and completion of said building or buildings, to make and enter into any contracts and obligations wherever necessary, either in its own name or in the name of the Mortgagor, and to pay and discharge all debts, obligations, and liabilities incurred thereby. All such sums so advanced by the Mortgagee (exclusive of advances of the principal of the indebtedness secured hereby) shall be added to the principal of the indebtedness secured hereby and shall be secured by this mortgage and shall be due and payable on demand with interest at the rate specified in the note, but no such advances shall be insured unless same are specifically approved by the Federal Housing Commissioner prior to the making thereof. The principal sum and other charges provided for herein shall, at the option of the Mortgagee or holder of this mortgage and the note securing the same, become due and payable on the failure of the Mortgagor to keep and perform any of the covenants, conditions, and agreements of said building loan agreement. This covenant shall be terminated upon the completion of the improvements to the satisfaction of the Mortgagee and the making of the final advance as provided in said building loan agreement;

17. That, together with, and in addition to, the monthly payments of interest or of principal and interest payable under the terms of the note secured hereby, the Mortgagor will pay to the Mortgagee, on the first day of each succeeding month after the date hereof, until the said note is fully paid, the following sums:

(a) An amount sufficient to provide the Mortgagee with funds to pay the next mortgage insurance premium if this instrument and the note secured hereby are insured, or a monthly service charge, if they are held by the Federal Housing Commissioner, as follows:

   (i) If and so long as said note of even date and this instrument are insured or are reinsured under the provisions of the National Housing Act, an amount sufficient to accumulate in the hands of the Mortgagee one (1) month prior to its due date the annual mortgage insurance premium, in order to provide such Mortgagee with funds to pay such premium to the Federal Housing Commissioner pursuant to the National Housing Act, as amended, and applicable Regulations thereunder; or

   (ii) Beginning with the first day of the month following an assignment of this instrument and the note secured hereby to the Commissioner, a monthly service charge which shall be an amount equal to one-twelfth of one-half per cent ($^1/_{12}$ of $^1/_2\%$) of the average outstanding principal balance due on the note computed for each successive year beginning with the first of the month following such assignment, without taking into account delinquencies or prepayments.

(b) A sum equal to the ground rents, if any, next due, plus the premiums that will next become due and payable on policies of fire and other property insurance covering the premises covered hereby, plus water rates, taxes and assessments next due on the premises covered hereby (all as estimated by the Mortgagee) less all sums already paid therefor divided by the number of months to elapse before one (1) month prior to the date when such ground rents, premiums, water rates, taxes and assessments will become delinquent, such sums to be held by Mortgagee to pay said ground rents, premiums, water rates, taxes, and special assessments.

(c) All payments mentioned in the two preceding subsections of this paragraph and all payments to be made under the note secured hereby shall be added together and the aggregate amount thereof shall be paid each month in a single payment to be applied by Mortgagee to the following items in the order set forth:
   (i) premium charges under the Contract of Insurance with the Federal Housing Commissioner or service charge;
   (ii) ground rents, taxes, special assessments, water rates, fire and other property insurance premiums;
   (iii) interest on the note secured hereby;
   (iv) amortization of the principal of said note.

18. Any excess funds accumulated under (b) of the preceding paragraph remaining after payment of the items therein mentioned shall be credited to subsequent monthly payments of the same nature required thereunder; but if any such item shall exceed the estimate therefor the Mortgagor shall without demand forthwith make good the deficiency. Failure to do so before the due date of such item shall be a default hereunder. In case of termination of the Contract of Mortgage Insurance by prepayment of the mortgage in full, or otherwise (except as hereinafter provided), accumulations under (a) of the preceding paragraph hereof not required to meet payments due under the Contract of Mortgage Insurance, shall be credited to the Mortgagor. If the property is sold under foreclosure or is otherwise acquired by the Mortgagee after default, any remaining balance of the accumulations under (b) of the preceding paragraph shall be credited to the principal of the mortgage as of the date of commencement of foreclosure proceedings or as of the date the property is otherwise acquired; and accumulations under (a) of the preceding paragraph shall be likewise credited unless required to pay sums due the Commissioner under the Contract of Mortgage Insurance;

19. IN THE EVENT of default in making any monthly payment provided for herein or in the note secured hereby for a period of thirty (30) days after the due date thereof, or in case of a breach of any other covenant or agreement herein stipulated, then the whole of said principal sum remaining unpaid together with accrued interest thereon, shall, at the election of the Mortgagee, without notice, become immediately due and payable, in which event the Mortgagee shall have the right immediately to foreclose this mortgage;

20. AND IN CASE OF FORECLOSURE of this mortgage by said Mortgagee in any court of law or equity, a reasonable sum shall be allowed for the solicitor's fees of the complainant, not to exceed in any case five per centum (5%) of the amount of the principal indebtedness found to be due, and for stenographers' fees of the complainant in such proceeding, and costs of minutes of foreclosure, master's fees, and all other costs of suit, and also for all outlays for documentary evidence and the cost of a complete abstract of title for the purpose of such foreclosure; and in case of any other suit, or legal proceeding, instituted by the Mortgagee to enforce the provisions of this mortgage or in case of any suit or legal proceeding wherein the Mortgagee shall be made a party thereto by reason of this mortgage, its costs and expenses, and the reasonable fees and charges of the attorneys or solicitors of the Mortgagee, so made parties, for services in such suit or proceedings, shall be a further lien and charge upon the said premises under this mortgage, and all such expenses shall become so much additional indebtedness secured hereby and be allowed in any decree foreclosing this mortgage;

21. AND THERE SHALL BE INCLUDED in any decree foreclosing this mortgage and be paid out of the proceeds of any sale made in pursuance of any such decree: (1) All the costs of such suit or suits, advertising, sale, and conveyance, including attorneys', solicitors', and stenographers' fees, outlays for documentary evidence and cost of said abstract and examination of title; (2) all the moneys advanced by the Mortgagee, if any, for any purpose authorized in the mortgage, with interest on such advances at the rate specified in the note, from the time such advances are made; (3) all the accrued interest remaining unpaid on the indebtedness hereby secured; (4) all the said principal money remaining unpaid. The over-plus of the proceeds of sale, if any, shall then be paid as the court may direct;

22. A RECONVEYANCE of said premises shall be made by the Mortgagee to the Mortgagor on full payment of the indebtedness aforesaid, the performance of the covenants and agreements herein made by the Mortgagor, and the payment of the reasonable fees of said Mortgagee.

23. IT IS EXPRESSLY AGREED that no extension of the time for payment of the debt hereby secured given by the Mortgagee to any successor in interest of the Mortgagor shall operate to release, in any manner, the original liability of the Mortgagor;

24. The Mortgagor hereby waives any and all rights of redemption from sale under any order or decree of foreclosure of this mortgage on its own behalf and on behalf of each and every person except decree or judgment creditors of the Mortgagor acquiring any interest in or title to the premises subsequent to the date of this mortgage;

25. THE COVENANTS HEREIN CONTAINED shall bind, and the benefits and advantages shall inure to, the successors and assigns of the respective parties hereto. Wherever used, the singular number shall include the plural, the plural the singular, and the use of any gender shall be applicable to all genders.

IN WITNESS WHEREOF, the Mortgagor has caused its corporate seal to be hereunto affixed and these presents to be signed by its   and attested by its
on the day and year first above written, pursuant to authority given by resolution duly passed by
of said corporation.

[CORPORATE SEAL]

By ....

ATTEST: ....

STATE OF ILLINOIS
COUNTY OF   } ss:

I,   , a Notary Public, in and for said County, in the
State aforesaid, do hereby certify that   and   ,
personally known to me to be the same persons whose names are respectively as President and Secretary of
                        , a corporation of the State of   , subscribed to the foregoing instrument,
appeared before me this day in person and severally acknowledged that they, being thereunto duly authorized, signed, sealed with the corporate seal, and delivered the said instrument as the free and voluntary act of said corporation and as their own free and voluntary act, for the uses and purposes therein set forth.

Given under my hand and notarial seal, this   day of   , 19   .

[SEAL]   ....
                                                                                    Notary Public.

My commission expires

STATE OF ILLINOIS

Loan No.

Mortgage

TO

Doc. No.

Filed for Record in the Recorder's Office
of   County, Illinois,
on the   day of
A.D. 19   , at   o'clock   m.,
and duly recorded in Book
of   , page

                                                  Clerk.

U.S. GOVERNMENT PRINTING OFFICE 196 —O—857814

CHART 15-6

Home and Multi Family Mortgages Insured—1974

MORTGAGES INSURED

MONTH AND YEAR	ALL HOME MORTGAGE PROGRAMS								
	TOTAL			PROPOSED			EXISTING		
	Cases	Units	Amount	Cases	Units	Amount	Cases	Units	Amount
Jan '74	16,459	17,365	$315,119,100	3,248	3,270	$72,588,125	13,211	14,095	$242,530,975
Feb	13,367	14,089	259,958,340	2,377	2,389	53,671,150	10,990	11,700	206,287,190
Mar	13,000	13,716	252,988,313	2,190	2,199	50,787,600	10,810	11,517	202,200,713
Apr 1/	15,858	16,611	303,856,550	2,293	2,302	51,966,000	13,565	14,309	251,890,550
May	17,272	18,060	334,102,038	2,239	2,255	51,774,700	15,033	15,805	282,327,338
Jun	15,835	16,583	305,497,960	1,988	1,992	46,762,150	13,847	14,591	258,735,810
Jul	18,695	19,523	366,471,057	2,535	2,549	61,437,750	16,160	16,974	305,033,307
Aug	16,827	17,623	335,879,309	2,539	2,554	62,177,100	14,288	15,069	273,702,209
Sep	16,832	17,556	340,277,998	2,567	2,585	64,283,400	14,265	14,971	275,994,598
Oct	18,809	19,693	392,738,704	3,212	3,234	83,597,450	15,597	16,459	309,141,254
Nov	16,355	17,096	352,565,454	2,732	2,751	72,594,800	13,623	14,345	279,970,654
Dec	16,541	17,251	374,249,875	2,925	2,941	80,315,480	13,616	14,310	293,934,395
Cal. '74	195,850	205,166	3,933,704,698	30,845	31,021	751,955,705	165,005	174,145	3,181,748,993
F.Y. '75	104,059	108,742	2,162,182,397	16,510	16,614	424,405,980	87,549	92,128	1,737,776,417

1/ Includes unknown number of cases processed in March but not reported until April.

MORTGAGES INSURED

MONTH AND YEAR	ALL PROJECT MORTGAGE PROGRAMS								
	TOTAL			PROPOSED			EXISTING 1/		
	No.	Units	Amount	No.	Units	Amount	No.	Units	Amount
Jan '74	60	6,200	$121,770,400	46	4,856	$89,005,700	14	1,344	$32,764,700
Feb	51	4,169	124,732,500	45	3,636	113,022,000	6	533	11,710,500
Mar	68	5,506	140,446,150	55	4,813	119,642,750	13	693	20,803,400
Apr	45	3,976	71,865,700	40	3,626	66,359,400	5	350	5,506,300
May	56	4,896	90,030,300	49	4,452	83,273,100	7	444	6,757,200
Jun	59	6,429	136,568,050	55	6,118	122,161,350	4	311	14,406,700
Jul	35	3,711	68,228,400	29	3,264	60,412,000	6	447	7,816,400
Aug	47	4,664	141,279,250	41	4,059	133,245,400	6	605	8,033,850
Sep	40	4,065	80,505,550	32	3,619	69,030,550	8	446	11,475,000
Oct	40	3,415	60,974,550	31	2,627	46,925,150	9	788	14,049,400
Nov	28	1,799	29,243,450	20	1,475	28,687,750	8	324	20,555,700
Dec	62	5,990	127,815,479	42	4,390	88,050,079	20	1,600	39,765,400
C.Y. '74	591	54,820	1,213,459,779	485	46,935	1,019,815,229	106	7,885	193,644,550
F.Y. '75	252	23,644	528,046,679	195	19,434	426,350,929	57	4,210	101,695,750

1/ A SUBSTANTIAL PROPORTION REPRESENTS REHABILITATION ACTIVITY.

RR: 301 (PROJECTS)

HUD-Wash., D. C.

Source: Department of Housing and Urban Development
Housing Production and Mortgage Credit—FHA
Management Information Systems Division
Multifamily Activities Branch 5/2/75

Source: HUD 1977 Statistical Yearbook

Mortgage insurance limits where the property is to be occupied by the borrower are as follows (higher limits prevail in Alaska, Guam, and Hawaii):

One family	$ 67,500
Two family	$ 76,000
Three family	$ 92,000
Four family	$107,000

Where FHA has approved the property prior to the beginning of construction or in those cases where construction of the property was completed more than one year from the date of the proposed mortgagor's application, the maximum mortgage allowable is computed as follows: 97 percent of the first $25,000 of FHA's estimate of property value plus closing costs, plus 95 percent of such value in excess of $25,000.

Thus, the maximum mortgage on a property estimated to be worth $40,000 and requiring $1,000 for loan closing would be $39,450. Under these circumstances, the borrower would require $1,550 cash to purchase the property, plus any additional closing costs not included in the $1,000 estimate.

In cases where construction was begun prior to FHA approval and was completed less than one year from the date of the mortgagor's loan application, the maximum loan is limited to 90 percent of FHA's estimate of property value and closing costs.

Veterans who generally have served on active duty in the United States Armed Forces for not less than ninety days and were released or discharged on any but a dishonorable basis are eligible for special maximum mortgages limits under the 203(b) program.

The maximum mortgage which FHA will insure for a veteran is computed s follows: 100 percent of the first $25,000 of FHA's estimate of property value plus closing costs (or $25,000 plus prepaid expenses, such as tax and insurance escrows, less $200, whichever is less), plus 95 percent of such value in excess of $25,000.

Where construction was commenced prior to FHA approval and was completed less than one year from the date of the veteran mortgagor's loan application the maximum loan is limited to 90 percent of the first $35,000 plus 85 percent of the amount over $35,000.

Mortgagors not intending to occupy a property may still purchase it under the Section 203(b) program, but are restricted to an 85 percent loan-to-value mortgage with the insurable amount limited to 85 percent of that specified for owner-occupants.

Mortgage loan maturities are generally thirty years, but may be reduced to three-fourths of the property's remaining economic life. The loan maturity may be increased to thirty-five years in cases where the property was constructed under FHA or VA inspections and the mortgagor's credit is insufficient to qualify him for a 30-year mortgage.

Property appraisals for FHA-insured loans are performed by appraisers approved or selected by FHA, but a certificate of reasonable value as issued by VA may be used to establish property value for FHA purposes.

The Section 203(b) program requires an insurance premium of 0.5 percent per annum. This premium is deposited in the Mutual Mortgage Insurance Fund. Mortgage interest rates are limited to the maximum rate established by the Secretary of HUD.

SECTION 245

One of the major deterrents to homeownership in recent years has been the rapid acceleration in the price of real estate and concurrent higher interest rate mortgages. Both of these factors have combined to limit the ability of the American public to afford that original home or to upgrade their housing.

In the 1977 Housing Act, Congress approved a new program under Section 245 of National Housing Act to temper the effects of inflation in real estate values and interest rates. Thus was born the Graduated Payment Mortgage or GPM, a plan that allows the purchase of a home with a slightly higher down payment than under a Section 203(b) loan, but with much lower initial monthly payments in the early years of the loan.

The philosophy behind the GPM is that by reducing the initial monthly mortgage payments, more families can qualify to purchase a home that is presently out of their financial reach. Then, as the mortgage payments increase in ensuing years, the theory is that the family, through upward job mobility of the wage earner(s) and/or by reason of inflation in income, will be able to afford them.

Under the GPM, additional money is borrowed in the early years of the mortgage, which money is used to reduce the monthly mortgage payments. These additional borrowings are added to the outstanding mortgage payments in the later loan years.

The homebuyer may select from one of five possible GPM repayment plans that best suit his/her needs. They are:

	Years of Increasing Payments	At Percent Each Year of
Plan 1	5	2.5
Plan 2	5	5
Plan 3	5	7.5
Plan 4	10	2
Plan 5	10	3

Plan 3 has become the most popular plan. An example of how that plan works is as follows:

Assume: Mortgage amount of $50,000
Interest rate of 9 percent
Term of 30 years

Monthly payment schedule as compared to a Section 203(b) loan would be as follows:

YEAR	SECTION 203(b) LOAN	GPM LOAN
1	$402.50	$303.94
2	402.50	326.74
3	402.50	351.24
4	402.50	377.59
5	402.50	405.96
6	402.50	436.35
7	402.50	436.35
Remaining Payments	402.50	436.35

Based on the above and using 25 percent of gross as standard for mortgage payment versus gross income, a family would require a $1,610 per month gross income to qualify for a $50,000 Section 203(b) loan, but would only need an income of $1,216 per month to obtain a GPM loan of the same amount.

The maximum insurable GPM loan amount cannot exceed the lesser of: (a) an amount which, when added to all deferred interest pursuant to the selected financing plan, shall not exceed 97 percent of the FHA-appraised value of the property. As to veterans, it shall not exceed 100 percent of the first $25,000 of property value and closing costs less $200, plus 95 percent of the remainder of the FHA-appraised value; (b) applicable Section 203(b) limits.

This maximum mortgage amount is computed using different factors for each of the five plans, then comparing the result to the maximum mortgage allowable amount under the 203(b) loan program and taking the lesser of the two.

For example, under Plan 3, the maximum mortgage allowed on a $60,000 sales price home would be computed as follows:

A. Sales Price/FHA Value	$60,000
B. Sales Price × 97 percent	58,200
C. Line B ÷ 1037.3747 (deferred interest factor(× 1000	56,103
D. Maximum Mortgage per 203(b) (3 percent first $25,000—5 percent of remainder)	57,500
E. Maximum GPM Amount (Lesser of line C or D)	56,100

In the above example, the additional down payment of $1,400 under the GPM provides an initial equity cushion against an early default in the loan when the principal amount of the loan is increasing instead of decreasing.

The standard Section 203(b) mortgage and note forms are used for this program, but with special wording and GPM payment schedule affixed to each instrument.

Presently, GPM mortgages are extremely popular, accounting for 25 percent of total FHA-insured loan volume. By 1983, it is estimated that one-half of all newly insured FHA loans will be GPMs.

SECTION 207

In essence the Section 207 program is the Section 203(b) plan applied to multifamily projects and is FHAs basic rental project insurance program. The program is used in the financing of construction or rehabilitation of rental housing of eight or more units.

Mortgagors under Section 207 may be private individuals or organizations or public bodies such as federal or state instrumentalities. Mortgages are insurable up to any FHA approved mortgage amount. The term of the mortgage loan can be for as long as and normally is forty years.

Insurable limits per family unit depends upon the type of structure to be constructed and may be increased by 45 percent in areas where cost levels so require. Present basic program unit limits are:

Elevator-type structures (Example: Medium or high rise apartment buildings)

Efficiency	$22,500
1-bedroom	$25,200
2-bedroom	$30,900
3-bedroom	$38,700
4 or more bedrooms	$43,758

Other types of strucures (Example: townhouse or garden apartment developments)

Efficiency	$19,500
1-bedroom	$21,600
2-bedroom	$25,800
3-bedroom	$31,800
4 or more bedrooms	$36,000

The maximum loan is generally limited to 85 to 90 percent of the FHA calculated replacement value. Thus, in a 24-unit townhouse apartment development with a mix of eight/3-bedroom, eight/1-bedroom and eight/2-bedroom apartment units, the maximum mortgage insurable by FHA would be:

$$8 \times \$21,600 = \$172,800$$
$$8 \times \$25,800 = \$206,400$$
$$8 \times \$31,800 = \$254,400$$
$$\text{Total} = \$633,600$$

The maximum replacement value under such circumstances and where an 85 percent loan is involved should be approximately $745,400.

In actuality, an 85 or 90 percent loan-to-value mortgage is not obtained. The replacement value as calculated by FHA does not include such project cost as loan discounts by FHA does not include such project cost as loan discounts over FHA's allowance, land cost in excess of that approved by FHA, and off-site costs. If a project was developed at the maximum value set forth above and an additional 2 percent loan discount was required plus $30,000 needed to bring utilities to the site, then the total project cost would be $788,072 ($745,400 plus $12,672 plus $30,000). On this basis the $633,600 mortgage would be only slightly more than 80 percent of project costs.

Other factors involved in FHA multifamily projects which present varying degrees of costs and consternation are listed below:

1. A **working capital** deposit of 2 percent of the mortgage amount must be placed with the mortgagee and held during the construction period to cover project costs not included in mortgage proceeds, such as rent-up expense.
2. Funds required to cover an FHA estimated **operating deficit** during the first months of project operation may be required to be deposited with the mortgagee prior to construction.
3. Cost certification by the contractor as to all project costs is required if the contractor has an identity of interest with the mortgagor, such as ownership of a part of the mortgagor entity or vice versa. In any event the mortgagor must certify to all project costs.
4. Contractors building Section 207 projects are required to provide assurance of project completion in the form of cash, letter of credit or bond in an amount equivalent to a percentage of the construction contract (normally 10 percent to 25 percent). In some states, 50 percent to 100 percent payment and performance bonds are required. Additionally contractors and sub-contractors must pay all labor on the job a "prevailing wage" which is usually equal to union scale.

The above problems, other difficulties, and the time required to process an application for multifamily project insurance prevented any great utilization of the Section 207 program by builders and developers until the scarce money period of the late Sixties. Since that time more and more builders have been drawn into the insured multifamily programs because of the availability of mortgage funds for FHA-insured projects. This trend could continue if there is no substantial long-term improvement in the money market.

Under the Section 207 program the mortgagor is not limited to the amount of return he receives on his investment as is the case in the subsidized programs. However, the mortgagor must execute a Regulatory Agreement (see Chart 15-7) with FHA which governs the operation of the project, and most importantly requires the approval of FHA before any increase in rents may be effected. Such rent increases may only cover increased operational costs and cannot provide additional profit to the mortgagor (see Paragraph No. 4 of the Regulatory Agreement).

The Section 207 program has been deemed one for luxury housing with the Section 221(d)4 multifamily program providing housing for low-to-moderate income families. The Section 207 and 221(d)4 programs are similar in all respects, except that the 221(d)4 program is calculated in a manner which produces 8 percent to 9 percent more mortgage funds than the Section 207 program when an identity of interest exists between mortgagor and contractor. Thus, in recent years, most multifamily FHA insured projects have utilized the Section 221(d)4 program.

The increased mortgage amount available under Section 221(d)4 is produced by the introduction into the replacement value calculation of a factor termed Builders and Sponsor Profit and Risk Allowance (BSPR). The BSPR is given in lieu of the builder's profit in profit-motivated projects (as opposed to non-profit sponsored projects) and is used to offset equity requirements. In essence, FHA recognizes that an equity will be created by project development and that it need not be put up in cash.

Both programs present an alternative to conventional income property financing, a method of finding mortgage funds when money is scarce, loan-to-value ratios in excess of normal conventional limits, and a way around lender participation in project income.

In 1977, 2884 units were financed under Section 207 and 70,809 units were financed under Section 221(d)4.

CHART 15-7

FHA FORM NO. 2466
Revised November 1969
(Previous Revision obsolete)

U. S. DEPARTMENT OF HOUSING AND URBAN DEVELOPMENT
FEDERAL HOUSING ADMINISTRATION

REGULATORY AGREEMENT FOR MULTI-FAMILY HOUSING PROJECTS
(Under Sections 207, 220, 221 (d)(4), 231 and 232, Except Nonprofits)

Project No.

Mortgagee

Amount of Mortgage Note   Date

Mortgage: Recorded: State   County   Date

                                   Book   Page

Originally endorsed for insurance under Section

This Agreement entered into this   day of   , 19   , between

whose address is

their successors, heirs, and assigns (jointly and severally, hereinafter referred to as Owners) and the undersigned Secretary of Housing and Urban Development and his successors (hereinafter referred to as Secretary).

In consideration of the endorsement for insurance by the Secretary of the above described note or in consideration of the the consent of the Secretary to the transfer of the mortgaged property or the sale and conveyance of the mortgaged property by the Secretary, and in order to comply with the requirements of the National Housing Act, as amended and the Regulations adopted by the Secretary pursuant thereto, Owners agree for themselves, their successors, heirs and assigns, that in connection with the mortgaged property and the project operated thereon and so long as the contract of mortgage insurance continues in effect, and during such further period of time as the Secretary shall be the owner, holder or reinsurer of the mortgage, or during any time the Secretary is obligated to insure a mortgage on the mortgaged property:

1. Owners, except as limited by paragraph 17 hereof, assume and agree to make promptly all payments due under the note and mortgage.

2. (a) Owners shall establish or continue to maintain a reserve fund for replacements by the allocation to such reserve fund in a separate account with the mortgagee or in a safe and responsible depository designated by the mortgagee, concurrently with the beginning of payments towards amortization of the principal of the mortgage insured or held by the Secretary of an amount equal to $ _____ per month unless a different date or amount is approved in writing by the Secretary.

   Such funds, whether in the form of a cash deposit or invested in obligations of, or fully guaranteed as to principal by, the United States of America shall at all times be under the control of the mortgagee. Disbursements from such fund, whether for the purpose of effecting replacement of structural elements, and mechanical equipment of the project or for any other purpose, may be made only after receiving the consent in writing of the Secretary. In the event of a default in the terms of the mortgage, pursuant to which the loan has been accelerated, the Secretary may apply or authorize the application of the balance in such fund to the amount due on the mortgage debt as accelerated.

   (b) Where Owners are acquiring a project already subject to an insured mortgage, the reserve fund for replacements to be established will be equal to the amount due to be in such fund under existing agreements or charter provisions at the time Owners acquire such project, and payments hereunder shall begin with the first payment due on the mortgage after acquisition, unless some other method of establishing and maintaining the fund is approved in writing by the Secretary.

3. Real property covered by the mortgage and this agreement is described in Schedule A attached hereto.

   (This paragraph 4 is not applicable to cases insured under Section 232.)

4. (a) Owners shall make dwelling accommodation and services of the project available to occupants at charges not exceeding those established in accordance with a rental schedule approved in writing by the Secretary. Accommodations shall not be rented for a period of less than thirty (30) days, or, unless the mortgage is insured under Section 231, for more than three years. Commercial facilities shall be rented for such use and

upon such terms as approved by the Secretary. Subleasing of dwelling accommodations, except for subleases of single dwelling accommodations by the tenant thereof,shall be prohibited without prior written approval of Owners and the Secretary and any lease shall so provide. Upon discovery of any unapproved sublease, Owners shall immediately demand cancellation and notify the Secretary thereof.

(b) Upon prior written approval by the Secretary, Owners may charge to and receive from any tenant such amounts as from time to time may be mutually agreed upon between the tenant and the Owner for any facilities and/or services which may be furnished by the Owner or others to such tenant upon his request, in addition to the facilities and services included in the approved rental schedule.

(c) The Secretary will at any time entertain a written request for a rent increase properly supported by substantiating evidence and within a reasonable time shall:

(i) Approve a rental schedule that is necessary to compensate for any net increase, occuring since the last approved rental schedule, in taxes (other than income taxes) and operating and maintenance cost over which Owners have no effective control, or

(ii) Deny the increase stating the reasons therefor.

5. (a) If the mortgage is originally a Secretary-held purchase money mortgage, or is originally endorsed for insurance under any Section other than Sections 231 or 232, Owners shall not in selecting tenants discriminate against any person or persons by reason of the fact that there are children in the family.

(b) If the mortgage is originally endorsed for insurance under Section 221 or 231, Owners shall in selecting tenants give to persons or families designated in the National Housing Act an absolute preference or priority of occupancy which shall be accomplished as follows:

(1) For a period of sixty (60) days from the date of original offering, unless a shorter period of time is approved in writing by the Secretary, all units shall be held for such preferred applicants, after which time any remaining unrented units may be rented to non-preferred applicants;

(2) Thereafter, and on a continuing basis, such preferred applicants shall be given preference over non-preferred applicants in their placement on a waiting list to be maintained by the Owners; and

(3) Through such further provisions agreed to in writing by the parties.

(c) Without the prior written approval of the Secretary not more than 25% of the number of units in a project insured under Section 231 shall be occupied by persons other than elderly persons as defined by the National Housing Act.

(d) All advertising or efforts to rent a project insured under Section 231 shall reflect a bona fide effort of the Owners to obtain occupancy by elderly persons as defined by the National Housing Act.

6. Owners shall not without the prior written approval of the Secretary:

(a) Convey, transfer, or encumber any of the mortgaged property, or permit the conveyance, transfer or encumbrance of such property.

(b) Assign, transfer, dispose of, or encumber any personal property of the project, including rents, or pay out any funds except from surplus cash, except for reasonable operating expenses and necessary repairs.

(c) Convey, assign, or transfer any beneficial interest in any trust holding title to the property, or the interest of any general partner in a partnership owning the property, or any right to manage or receive the rents and profits from the mortgaged property.

(d) Remodel, add to, reconstruct, or demolish any part of the mortgaged property or subtract from any real or personal property of the project.

(e) Make, or receive and retain, any distribution of assets or any income of any kind of the project except surplus cash and except on the following conditions:
(1) All distributions shall be made only as of and after the end of a semiannual or annual fiscal period, and only as permitted by the law of the applicable jurisdiction;

(2) No distribution shall be made from borrowed funds, prior to the completion of the project or when there is any default under this Agreement or under the note or mortgage;

(3) Any distribution or any funds of the project, which the party receiving such funds is not entitled to retain hereunder, shall be held in trust separate and apart from any other funds; and

(4) There shall have been compliance w th all outstanding notices of requirements for proper maintenance of the project.

(f) Engage, except for natural persons, in any other business or activity, including the operation of any other rental project, or incur any liability or obligation not in connection with the project.

(g) Require, as a condition of the occupancy or leasing of any unit in the project any consideration or deposit other than the prepayment of the first month's rent plus a security deposit in an amount not in excess of one month's rent to guarantee the performance of the covenants of the lease. Any funds collected as security deposits shall be kept separate and apart from all other funds of the project in a trust account the amount of which shall at all times equal or exceed the aggregate of all outstanding obligations under said account.

(h) Permit the use of the dwelling accommodations or nursing facilities of the project for any purpose except the use which was originally intended, or permit commercial use greater than that originally approved by the Secretary.

7. Owners shall maintain the mortgaged permises, accommodations and the grounds and equipment appurtenant thereto, in good repair and condition. In the event all or any of the buildings covered by the mortgage shall be destroyed or damaged by fire or other casualty, the money derived from any insurance on the property shall be applied in accordance with the terms of insured mortgage.

8. Owners shall not file any petition in bankruptcy or for a receiver or in insolvency or for reorganization or composition, or make any assignment for the benefit of creditors or to a trustee for creditors, or permit an adjudication in bankruptcy or the taking possession of the mortgaged property or any part thereof by a receiver or the seizure and sale of the mortgaged property or any part thereof under judicial process or pursuant to any power of sale, and fail to have such adverse actions set aside within forty-five (45) days.

9. (a) Any management contract entered into by Owners or any of them involving the project shall contain a provision that, in the event of default hereunder, it shall be subject to termination without penalty upon written re-request by the Secretary. Upon such request Owners shall immediately arrange to terminate the contract within a period of not more than thirty (30) days and shall make arrangements satisfactory to the Secretary for continuing proper management of the project.

(b) Payment for services, supplies, or materials shall not exceed the amount ordinarily paid for such services, supplies, or materials in the area where the services are rendered or the supplies or materials furnished.

(c) The mortgaged property, equipment, buildings, plans, offices, apparatus, devices, books, contracts, records, documents, and other papers relating thereto shall at all times be maintained in reasonable condition for proper audit and subject to examination and inspection at any reasonable time by the Secretary or his duly authorized agents. Owners shall keep copies of all written contracts or other instruments which affect the mortgaged property, all or any of which may be subject to inspection and examination by the Secretary or his duly authorized agents.

(d) The books and accounts of the operations of the mortgaged property and of the project shall be kept in accordance with the requirements of the Secretary.

(e) Within sixty (60) days following the end of each fiscal year the Secretary shall be furnished with a complete annual financial report based upon an examination of the books and records of mortgagor prepared in accordance with the requirements of the Secretary, certified to by an officer or responsible Owner and, when required by the Secretary, prepared and certified by a Certified Public Accountant, or other person acceptable to the Secretary.

(f) At request of the Secretary, his agents, employees, or attorneys, the Owners shall furnish monthly occupancy reports and shall give specific answer to questions upon which information is desired from time to time relative to the income, assets, liabilities, contracts, operation, and condition of the property and the status of the insured mortgage.

(g) All rents and other receipts of the project shall be deposited in the name of the project in a bank, whose deposits are insured by the F.D.I.C. Such funds shall be withdrawn only in accordance with the provisions of this Agreement for expenses of the project or for distributions of surplus cash as permitted by paragraph 6 (e) above. Any Owner receiving funds of the project other than by such distribution of surplus cash shall immediately deposit such funds in the project bank account and failing so to do in violation of this agreement shall hold such funds in trust. Any Owner receiving property of the project in violation of this Agreement shall immediately deliver such property to the project and failing so to do shall hold such property in trust. As such time as the Owners shall have lost control and/or possession of the project, all funds held in trust shall be delivered to the mortgagee to the extent that the mortgage indebtedness has not been satisfied.

(h) If the mortgage is insured under Section 232:

1. The Owners or lessees shall at all times maintain in full force and effect from the state or other licensing authority such license as may be required to operate the project as a nursing home and shall not lease all or part of the project except on terms approved by the Secretary.

2. The Owner shall suitably equip the project for nursing home operations.

3. The Owners shall execute a Security Agreement and Financing Statement (or other form of chattel lien) upon all items of equipment, except as the Secretary may exempt, which are not incorporated as security for the insured mortgage. The Security Agreement and Financing Statement shall constitute a first lien upon such equipment and shall run in favor of the mortgagee as additional security for the insured mortgage.

4. No litigation seeking the recovery of a sum on excess of $3,000 nor any action for specific performance or other equitable relief shall be instituted nor shall any claim for a sum in excess of $3,000 be settled or compromised by the Owners unless prior written consent thereto has been obtained from the Secretary. Such consent may be subject to such terms and conditions as the Secretary may prescribe.

(i) If mortgage is insured under Section 231, Owners or lessees shall at all times maintain in full force and effect from the state or other licensing authority such license as may be required to operate the project as housing for the elderly.

10. Owners will comply with the provisions of any Federal, State, or local law prohibiting discrimination in housing on the grounds of race, color, creed, or national origin, including Title VI of the Civil Rights Act of 1964 (Public Law 88-352, 78 Stat. 241), all requirements imposed by or pursuant to the Regulations of the Department of Housing and Urban Development (24 CFR, Subtitle A, Part 1) issued pursuant to that title, and regulations issued pursuant to Executive Order 11063.

11. Upon a violation of any of the above provisions of this Agreement by Owners, the Secretary may give written notice, thereof, to Owners, by registered or certified mail, addressed to the addresses stated in this Agreement, or such other addresses as may subsequently, upon appropriate written notice thereof to the Secretary, be designated by the Owners as their legal business address. If such violation is not corrected to the satisfaction of the Secretary within thirty (30) days after the date such notice is mailed or within such further time as the Secretary determines is necessary to correct the violation, without further notice the Secretary may declare a default under this Agreement effective on the date of such declaration of default and upon such default the Secretary may:

(a) (i) If the Secretary holds the note - declare the whole of said indebtedness immediately due and payable and then proceed with the foreclosure of the mortgage;

(ii) If said note is not held by the Secretary - notify the holder of the note of such default and request holder to declare a default under the note and mortgage, and holder after receiving such notice and request, but not otherwise, at its option, may declare the whole indebtedness due, and thereupon proceed with foreclosure of the mortgage, or assign the note and mortgage to the Secretary as provided in the Regulations;

(b) Collect all rents and charges in connection with the operation of the project and use such collections to pay the Owner's obligations under this Agreement and under the note and mortgage and the necessary expenses of preserving the property and operating the project;

(c) Take possession of the project, bring any action necessary to enforce any rights of the Owners growing out of the project operation, and operate the project in accordance with the terms of this Agreement until such time as the Secretary in his discretion determines that the Owners again in a position to operate the project in accordance with the terms of this Agreement and in compliance with the requirements of the note and mortgage;

(d) Apply to any court, State or Federal, for specific performance of this Agreement, for an injunction against any violation of the Agreement, for the appointment of a receiver to take over and operate the project in accordance with the terms of the Agreement, or for such other relief as may be appropriate, since the injury to the Secretary arising from a default under any of the terms of this Agreement would be irreparable and the amount of damage would be difficult to ascertain.

12. As security for the payment due under this Agreement to the reserve fund for replacements, and to secure the Secretary because of his liability under the endorsement of the note for insurance, and as security for the other obligations under this Agreement, the Owners respectively assign, pledge and mortgage to the Secretary their rights to the rents, profits, income and charges of whatsoever sort which they may receive or be entitled to receive from the operation of the mortgage property, subject, however, to any assignment of rents in the insured mortgage referred to herein. Until a default is declared under this Agreement, however, permission is granted to Owners to collect and retain under the provisions of this Agreement such rents, profit, income, and charges, but upon default this permission is terminated as to all rents due or collected thereafter.

13. As used in this Agreement the term:

(a) "Mortgage" includes "Deed of Trust", "Chattel Mortgage", and any other security for the note identified herein, and endorsed for insurance or held by the Secretary;

(b) "Mortgagee" refers to the holder of the mortgage identified herein, its successors and assigns;

(c) "Owners" refers to the persons named in the first paragraph hereof and designated as "Owners, their successors, heirs and assigned";

(d) "Mortgaged Property" includes all property, real, personal, or mixed, covered by the mortgage or mortgages securing the note endorsed for insurance or held by the Secretary;

(e) "Project" includes the mortgaged property and all its other assets of whatsoever nature or whatsoever situate, used in or owned by the business conducted on said mortgaged property, which business is providing housing and other activities as are incidental thereto;

(f) "Surplus Cash" means any cash remaining after:

    (1) the payment of:

        (i) All sums due or currently required to be paid under the terms of any mortgage or note insured or held by the Secretary;

        (ii) All amounts required to be deposited in the reserve fund for replacements,

        (iii) All obligation of the project other than the insured mortgage unless funds for payment are set aside or deferment of payment has been approved by the Secretary; and

    (2) the segregation of:

        (i) An amount equal to the aggregate of all special funds required to be maintained by the project;

        (ii) All tenant security deposits held;

(g) "Distribution" means any withdrawal or taking of cash or any assets of the project, including the segregation of cash or assets for subsequent withdrawal within the limitations of Paragraph 6 (e) hereof, and excluding payment for reasonable expenses incident to the operation and maintenance of the project.

(h) "Default" means a default declared by the Secretary when a violation of this Agreement is not corrected to his satisfaction within the time allowed by this Agreement or such further time as may be allowed by the Secretary after written notice;

(i) "Section" refers to Section of the National Housing Act, as amended.

14. This instrument shall bind, and the benefits shall inure to, the respective Owners, their heirs, legal representatives, executors, administrators, successors, in office or interest, and assigns, and to the Secretary and his successors so long as the contract of mortgage insurance continues in effect, and during such further time as the Secretary shall be the owner, holder, or reinsurer of the mortgage, or obligated to reinsure the mortgage.

15. Owners warrant that they have not, and will not, execute any other agreement with provisions contradictory of, or in opposition to, the provisions hereof, and that, in any event, the requirements of this Agreement are paramount and controlling as to the rights and obligations set forth and supersede any other requirements in conflict therewith.

16. The invalidity of any clause, part or provision of this Agreement shall not affect the validity or the remaining portions thereof.

17. The following Owners:

do not assume personal liability for payments due under the note and mortgage, or for the payments to the reserve for replacements, or for matters not under their control, provided that said Owners shall remain liable under this Agreement only with respect to the matters hereinafter stated; namely:

(a) for funds or property of the project coming into their hands which, by the provisions hereof, they are not entitled to retain: and

(b) for their own acts and deeds or acts and deeds of other which they have authorized in violation of the provisions hereof.

(To be executed with formalities for recording a deed to real estate)

SECTION 8

The Housing and Community Development Act of 1974 established the Section 8 Housing Assistance Payments (HAP) program for lower-income families. It replaced and modified the HUD's Section 23 leased housing program and became a substitute for the popular Section 236 program.

The Section 236 program, as well as its predecessor Section 221(d)3 program, as designed to provide low income housing by insuring or providing low interest rate loans to developers. By virtue of a low interest rate, the developer could offer units at lower than market rent. However, these programs created large projects totally occupied by tenants of like economic status. In many cases the projects rapidly deteriorated, some failed, and considerable losses were incurred by the government.

Under Section 23 and its successor, Section 8, the subsidy applies only to units in a structure developed for occupancy by primarily middle income tenants. Hence, low-income families normally constitute only a percentage of the total occupancy of a rental project. By mixing with higher income families, it is anticipated that the low-income families will have an incentive to upgrade themselves. At the same time these lower-income families are not segregated into a low-income project or burdened with that stigma.

The Section 8 program in essence utilizes existing, newly constructed and substantially rehabilitated housing units to enable families who otherwise would be unable to do so to live in decent housing.

Section 8 is not a construction or permanent financing program. Projects are constructed conventionally or under an FHA-insured multifamily program (such as Section 221(d)4 or Section 231). Section 8 provides a long-term commitment of housing assistance payments pursuant to a HUD contract. This rental support provides a solid basis for obtaining project financing.

Funds for Section 8 units are allocated to localities based upon factors such as need and conformance with approved local housing assistance plans. For example, if an adequate supply of existing housing is available in a locality, it will be given Section 8 funding priority over new or rehabilitated housing.

There are essentially two different Section 8 programs, one for existing housing and one for new or substantially rehabiliated housing.

A family seeking to occupy existing housing must first obtain from the Public Housing Authority (PHA) a Certificate of Family Participation. The family then seeks a suitable unit to rent within the PHA's jurisdiction. Once a decent, safe, and sanitary unit is found, the owner is found, the owner is agreeable, the gross rent reasonable and within HUD's limits, a PHA-approved lease may be signed. Upon execution of the lease, a Housing Assistance Payment (HAP) contract will be executed between PHA and the owner. Under the HAP, the owner receives a monthly rental payment directly from HUD equal to the difference between the rent payable to owner by the family and the gross rent for the unit. Generally, a family is required to pay between 15 and 25 percent of its gross income, depending upon its family income, number of dependents and medical expenses.

A review of the amount of rent payable by a family occupying an existing unit is made annually by PHA. As to families occupying new or substantially rehabilitated unit, a review is made at least annually by the owner. Reviews for elderly or handicapped families are made every two years.

For new and substantially rehabilitated housing, owners and developers submit development proposals to a local PHA in response to a HUD published invitation or they may apply directly to their state housing finance or development agency.

If a proposal is accepted by HUD, an agreement will be executed providing, among other things, for a HAP contract to be entered into upon successful project completion.

Up to 100 percent of the units in new and substantially rehabilitated projects may qualify for Section 8 assistance. However, preference is given to those projects in which 20 percent or fewer units receive Section 8 assistance. (This does not apply to 50 unit or less projects, nor to those projects designed specifically for occupancy by handicapped or elderly families.)

At least 30 percent of the qualifying units in a new or substantially rehabilitated project must be leased to "very low-income" families during the initial rent-up period of the project and the owner's best efforts must be used to maintain this ratio. A "very low-income" family is defined as one whose adjusted income (based on family size and other factors) does not exceed 50 percent of HUD's published medium income for the area. Lower-income families are those whose adjusted income does not exceed 80 percent of the median area income.

The contract rent plus utility allowance charged by an owner to a qualifying tenant cannot exceed HUD's established Fair Market Rent for the housing area in which the unit is located. Fair Market rents established by HUD are published in the FEDERAL REGISTER at least annually for each housing area by unit size and project structural type. (There is a separate schedule for existing units.) Under certain circumstances the established Fair Market rents may be exceeded by 10 to 20 percent.

The owner's contract rents for new and substantially rehabilitated units may be adjusted annually by applying an Automatic Annual Adjustment Factor as determined and published at least annually by HUD in the FEDERAL REGISTER.

Rents for existing units may be adjusted annually on the lease anniversary date upon PHA approval. However, the adjusted rent will have to be within the established Fair Market Rent limits.

For existing units the HAP contract runs concurrent with the lease term provided the lease is for not less than one year nor more than three. The maximum term for new or substantially rehabilitated housing is generally 20 years or 40 years in the case of projects owned by or financed by a loan or guaranty from a state or local housing agency.

As to units covered by Section 8 contracts but vacant, the owner may receive up to 80 percent of the contract rent for a period of 60 days. In the case of existing units, the vacancy must have occurred due to a violation of the lease by the eligible family.

Through December 31, 1977, reservation of Section 8 funds had been made for 982,439 units. Of that amount, 188,216 were under construction and 575,143 had been completed.

LENDER ACCEPTANCE AND ADVANTAGES

Lender acceptance of FHA-insured loans was relatively slow for the first decade of the program and did not gain momentum until World War II. Today FHA-insured loans are commonplace with acceptability geared to yield and a readily available second market with Federal National Mortgage Association.

The major value of FHA insurance is that loans are allowably made on more favorable loan-to-value ratios than are available on a conventional loan basis. In spite of the FHA insurance, however, lenders and investors require a higher yield on FHA loans than on 80 percent loan-to-value conventional loans. The reason for the higher yield is the loan-to-value ration on FHA loans. Even though FHA covers almost all the loss on a defaulted and foreclosed insured mortgage loan, the incidence of default remains greater on an FHA loan. In theory a family with 20 percent cash equity in its home has more to lose by giving up its property to foreclosure when economic conditions so warrant.

During the late 1960s and early 1970s FHA loans on the average were yielding approximately 0.25 percent more than 80 percent loan-to-value loans and about 0.25 percent less than high loan-to-value conventional loans.

An interesting phenomenon is that in the last few years FHA-insured mortgage loan yields have approached AAA corporate bond yields and for long periods of time have yielded 0.25 to 0.75 percent less than 80 percent conventional loans. If these yield comparisons can be maintained, there is an excellent possibility that more funds will be diverted into the mortgage market by those investors who have consistently purchased corporate bonds. The Government National Mortgage Association-backed mortgage security has certainly been a tremendous factor in the narrowing of the FHA loan corporate bond yield gap and in causing from time to time wide spreads between FHA loan yields and conventional loan yields.

CHANGING PATTERN OF FEDERAL INSURANCE

Over the past thirty years the impact and programs of FHA has greatly changed. In 1950, FHA major single family program, Section 203(b) accounted for 18 percent of all single family starts. In 1970, FHA accounted for 29 percent of all new

CHART 15-8
**New Privately-Owned Housing Units Started, by Type of Financing:
1969-1977**

(Units in thousands)

Year	Total	Federal Housing Administration			Veterans Adminis- tration	Total FHA or VA	Other	Percent of total private starts			
		Total	Homes	Projects				FHA	VA	Total FHA or VA	Other
1969	1,467	233	154	80	51	284	1,183	16	3	19	81
1970	1,434	421	234	188	61	482	952	29	4	34	66
1971	2,052	528	301	277	94	622	1,430	26	5	30	70
1972	2,357	371	198	173	104	475	1,882	16	4	21	80
1973	2,045	163	74	87	86	247	1,798	8	4	12	88
1974	1,338	94	57	37	73	167	1,171	7	5	12	88
1975	1,160	98	69	29	77	175	985	8	7	15	85
1976	1,538	144	81	64	100	245	1,293	9	6	16	84
1977	1,987	178	100	78	131	309	1,678	9	7	16	84

Source: Dept. of Commerce, Bureau of the Census, Construction Reports, Series C-20; Dept. of Housing and Urban Development; and Veterans Administration.

privately-owned housing units started, but by the mid-1970s this percentage had decreased to 8 percent (see Chart 15-8). Also, in 1950 the Section 203(b) program accounted for almost 100 percent of FHA's single family insurance activity. Due to the number of new FHA programs, Section 203(b) by the 1970s made up about 68 percent of FHA insurance for existing housing and about 30 percent for new construction.

The pattern of FHA insurance is changing to a variety of programs many of which are subsidized by the federal government. This changing pattern has led to much discussion about separating FHA in two entities. One to remain with HUD and handle the government financed subsidized programs, the other entity to become an independent agency, similar to FHMA, for unsubsidized programs.

Hence the future for FHA is quite uncertain and over the next decade FHA may evolve into quite a different operation than the present day FHA.

CONCLUSION

Statistics indicate that the wide range of FHA programs will play an increasing role in the production of housing units during the 1970s. Subsidized FHA programs will provide a major part of the housing impetus intent on bringing contemporary housing to families at all levels of the income spectrum. While government appropriated dollars are not needed for the nonsubsidized program, the federal budget will have to support the increasing requirements of subsidized units if the nation's housing goals are to be met.

Mortgage loans insured by FHA have traditionally been less favorable investments than low ratio conventional loans or AAA corporate bonds. In recent years this trend has changed. FHA loans and AAA corporate bonds are yielding about the same return and FHA loans are a more attractive investment than 90 to 95 percent loan to value conventional loans.

QUESTIONS FOR THOUGHT AND DISCUSSION

1. Is a private corporation approach to non-subsidized insured mortgage loans a better alternative to meeting the nation's housing problems, even if government support of a private mortgage insurance plan were required? Discuss.
2. Subsidized housing requires continuing government financial support in the form of subsidies. If project mortgages are for 40-year terms, then during each of those forty years the government will conceivably have to provide financial support. Is this a healthy situation or will the financial burden of increasing the number of subsidized units, and keeping present units occupied, place an unwieldy burden on the federal budget? Discuss.
3. What are some of the major FHA programs?
4. What is FHA's purpose and how is that purpose fulfilled?
5. How does the Section 8 program change FHA/HUD's method of approach to subsidized housing?
6. Is an FHA loan a safer investment than a 75 to 80 percent loan to value conventional loan? Why or why not? What about a 90 to 95 percent loan to value conventional loan?
7. Do low down payments and low interest rates affect a buyer's attitude toward care and maintenance of the property purchased? Discuss.

16

MORTGAGE LOANS FOR VETERANS

Near the end of World War II it became increasingly apparent to Congress that legislation was needed to assist returning war veterans in readjusting to private life. For many Americans the war meant that education had to be interrupted or postponed. Families were disrupted and personal income was decreased by reversion to military wages. Thus in 1944 the Servicemen's Readjustment Act, commonly referred to as the "GI Bill of Rights" was enacted by the representatives of a country grateful to those who had served in its armed forces.

BACKGROUND

The GI Bill of Rights contained several government loan guaranty and monetary contribution programs for World War II veterans. Paramount in this total package of benefits was a new mortgage loan program behind which was placed the full faith and credit of the federal government.

At first the mortgage guaranty program was helpful only with regard to homes costing $5,000 or less. Higher priced homes would require increasingly greater downpayments—a requirement only few veterans could meet. Hence, the following year brought about substantial changes in the program including the placement of full control over the mortgage guaranty function in the Veterans Administration instead of with the Comptroller-General.

Three major areas of authority are granted to the Veterans Administration with regard to mortgage loans:

1. To *partially guarantee* loans made to veterans by any person, firm, association, corporation, or governmental agency.
2. To *insure* loans made to veterans by a supervised lender (a lender subject to examination and supervision by a state or federal governmental agency).

3. To make *direct loans* to veterans in areas where mortgage credit is not generally available.

ELIGIBiLITY

Veterans entitled to mortgage loan benefits today under the GI Bill of Rights are:
1. Persons who were members of the United States armed forces during *World War II* (between September 10, 1940 and July 25, 1947) for either ninety days or longer were discharged or longer, or were discharged or released from active duty due to a service-incurred disability.
2. Persons who were members of the armed forces during the Korean Conflict (between June 27, 1950 and January 31, 1955) or the Viet Nam Conflict (between August 5, 1964 and May 7, 1975) serving anywhere in the world for either ninety days, or longer or were discharged or released from active duty due to a service-incurred disability.
3. Persons considered "cold war" veterans, who as members of the armed forces served 180 days or more on active duty during any of the following times: July 25, 1947 to June 27, 1950; January 31, 1955 to August 5, 1964; May 7, 1975 to present.
4. *Unremarried widows* of veterans who either died from service-incurred disability, are missing in action, or were captured or detained by a foreign government or power while performing in the line of duty. The veteran spouse must be missing in action or a prisoner for ninety days or more before eligibility commences.
5. American citizens who during World War II served as members of the armed forces of a government *allied* with the United States and who meet other requirements of the law, including residency in the United States at the time of seeking benefits.

Once eligibility or entitlement for benefits is established it remains available until used.

Prior to the Veterans Housing Act of 1970 (Public Law 91-506) signed into law by the President on October 23, 1970, "cold war" veterans were required to pay a 0.5 percent funding fee in connection with the use of their mortgage loan entitlement. The funding fee is no longer applicable.

Chart 16-1 is a copy of the VA form for eligibility determination.

BENEFIT REINSTATEMENT

In some cases it is necessary to reinstate a veteran's mortgage loan benefits. A veteran may lose or have to dispose of his home because of condemnation or eminent domain proceedings instituted by a governmental body, or a compelling reason (other than default) such as job relocation or fire or other hazard. If the home was purchased through use of GI Bill of Rights entitlement he may have the benefit guaranty, so lost, restored, particulary if the loan has been repaid in full, or the Veterans Administration has been released from liability for the loan, or if the Veterans Administration suffered a loss, that has been repaid.

The same restoration of benefits is available to any veteran who while on active military service must sell his home because of military transfer provided the prior VA insured or guaranteed mortgage loan is paid in full, and to any veteran whose loan is assumed by another veteran meeting the requirements of the GI Bill of Rights.

LENDERS

Lenders making VA insured or guaranteed loans are divided into two categories:

1. *Supervised* lenders are ones that are subject to examination and supervision by an agency of the federal or state government.
2. *Non-supervised* lenders are those not otherwise classed as supervised. Included in this category are FHA approved mortgages, such as mortgage companies.

Supervised lenders do not have to obtain prior approval from the Veterans Administration in order to make a VA-guaranteed loan. All they have to do is close and disburse the loan; then request the VA guaranty. Thus, the guaranty is automatic provided VA regulations have been adhered to.

Non-supervised lenders are required to seek prior VA loan approval. They file an application with VA for a loan guaranty commitment. Issuance of the guaranty commitment allows the lender to close the loan and then submit it to VA for guaranty. As a matter of practice many supervised lenders seek a prior commitment from VA in order to insure against the loan failing, and to be guaranteed in case of some technicality. Under recent Veterans legislation, non-supervised lenders meeting VA established guidelines may apply for and receive approval to close loans under the automatic guaranty provisions.

Lenders primarily involved in making VA loans include mutual savings banks, commercial banks, life insurance companies, and savings and loan associations.

Major holders of VA insured or guaranteed mortgage loans, according to the National Fact Book of Mutual Savings Banking for selected years, are here listed:

(IN MILLIONS)

End of Year	Mutual Savings Banks	Commercial Banks	Life Insurance Companies	Savings & Loan Assns.
1950	1,457	2,630	2,026	2,973
1960	8,986	2,859	6,901	7,222
1963	10,490	2,862	6,401	6,960
1966	11,471	2,599	6,201	6,157
1969	12,166	2,813	5,669	7,653
1972	12,622	3,203	4,700	13,500
1974	12,800	3,400	4,200	16,700
1975	12,070	3,003	3,484	19,442

Note the predominance of VA mortgage investments by mutual savings banks and Savings and Loan Associations and the decrease in VA mortgage holdings by life insurance companies.

PURPOSE

The Veterans Administration guarantees and insures loans for real estate and non-real estate purposes.

252

CHART 16-1

	VETERANS ADMINISTRATION	VETERANS ADMINISTRATION
	REQUEST FOR DETERMINATION OF ELIGIBILITY AND	ATTN: Loan Guaranty Division
	AVAILABLE LOAN GUARANTY ENTITLEMENT	TO

NOTE: Please read instructions on reverse before completing this form. If additional space is required, use reverse.

4. MILITARY SERVICE DATA—I request the Veterans Administration to determine my eligibility and the amount of entitlement based on the following period(s) of active military duty. (Start with latest period of service and list all periods of active duty since September 16, 1940.)

PERIOD OF ACTIVE SERVICE		NAME	SERVICE NUMBER	BRANCH OF SERVICE
DATE FROM	DATE TO			
4A				
4b				
4C				
4d				

9. Check only if this is a request for a DUPLICATE Certificate of Eligibility.

I certify that the statements herein are true to the best of my knowledge and belief.

FEDERAL STATUTES PROVIDE SEVERE PENALTIES FOR FRAUD, INTENTIONAL MISREPRESENTATION, CRIMINAL CONNIVANCE, OR CONSPIRACY PURPOSED TO INFLUENCE THE ISSUANCE OF ANY GUARANTY OR INSURANCE BY THE ADMINISTRATOR.

THIS SECTION FOR VA USE ONLY

VA FORM 26-1880 AUG 1974   DO NOT DETACH

IMPORTANT - You must complete Item 12, since the certificate of eligibility together with all discharge and separation papers will be mailed to the address shown in Item 12 immediately below. If they are to be sent to you, your current mailing address should be indicated, or if they are to be sent elsewhere, the name and address of such person or firm should be shown in Item 12.

The amount of loan guaranty entitlement available for use is endorsed on the reverse of the enclosed Certificate of Eligibility. This certificate must be returned to the VA at the time a loan application or loan report is submitted.

[PLEASE DELIVER THE ENCLOSED PAMPHLETS AND DISCHARGE OR SEPARATION PAPERS TO THE VETERAN PROMPTLY. THANK YOU]

26-1880

For mortgage loan purposes the real estate loans are the only ones that need to be considered. These loans are supported by VA for purposes such as the following:

1. The buying, constructing, alteration, repair, or improvement of a home or a farm residence.
2. The constructing, alteration, repairing, or improvement of a farm residence and/or its outbuildings and for farm business operations.
3. The building, alteration, repair or improvement of a building for business purposes, including the purchase of equipment and inventory.
4. The purchasing of a mobile home and/or mobile home lot. In all cases, the house or farm residence must be owned and occupied by the veteran as his home.

INSTRUCTIONS FOR VA FORM 26-1880

READ CAREFULLY BEFORE COMPLETING FORM.
USE TYPEWRITER OR PRINT CLEARLY.
COMPLETE ALL APPLICABLE ITEMS.

A. Use this form to request VA to determine your eligibility for Loan Guaranty benefits, and the amount of entitlement available.

B. To establish eligibility based on active military duty during World War II or the Korean conflict you must have been DISCHARGED OR RELEASED from active duty under conditions other than dishonorable (1) after active duty of 90 days or more any part of which was during the period September 16, 1940 to July 25, 1947, or during the period June 27, 1950 to January 31, 1955, or (2) by reason of a service-connected disability from a period of active duty, any part of which occurred during either of the above two wartime periods.

C. To establish eligibility based upon active duty after January 31, 1955, you must have been discharged or released from active duty under conditions other than dishonorable (1) from a period of continuous active duty of 181 days or more any part of which occurred after January 31, 1955, or (2) from active duty after such date for a service-connected disability. In the absence of a discharge or release, you must have served on continuous active duty at least 181 days in active duty status.

D. Unmarried surviving spouses of eligible veterans seeking determination of basic eligibility for VA Loan Guaranty benefits are NOT required to complete this form, but are required to complete VA Form 26-1817 for that purpose.

E. This request should be sent to the VA office serving the area in which the veteran resides.

F. <u>Proof of Military Service.</u> Attach to this request all your discharge or separation papers from active military duty since September 16, 1940, which show active duty dates and type of discharge. For those veterans separated after January 1, 1950, DD Form 214 must be submitted. You may submit either your original papers or legible copies thereof. In addition, if you are now on active duty submit a statement of service signed by the adjutant or personnel officer or commander of your unit or higher headquarters showing date of entry on your current active duty period and the duration of any time lost. Any VA Veterans Benefits Counselor in the nearest Veterans Administration Office or Center will assist you in securing necessary proof of military service.

G. Instructions on specific numbered blanks:

1. <u>Item 4.</u> List all periods of active duty covered by discharges or separation papers for the period September 16, 1940 - July 25, 1947, and the period June 27, 1950 to the present. When listing periods of service, start with your latest, or current, period of service on line 4A, and then work back to your earliest service. If you are now on active duty show as the first entry in item 4 the date you entered on your current active duty period, write the word "Present" in the column headed "Date To" and complete line 4A. Then list all prior periods of active duty covered by discharges or separaateion notices. If additional space is necessary, attach separate sheet.

2. <u>Item 7A.</u> Attach to this request the Certificate(s) of Eligibility previously issued to you. Certificates of Eligibility relating to World War II entitlement are not valid if you are eligible for loan benefits by virtue of active military duty during the period June 27, 1950 to date. Certificates of Eligibility relating to Korean conflict entitlement (PL 550) are not valid if you are eligible for loan benefits by virtue of active military duty after January 31, 1955. All of such certificates must be returned to the Veterans Administration.

3. <u>Item 12.</u> Print or type in Item 12 the name and address of the person or firm to whom you want the Certificate of Eligibility mailed.

GUARANTEED AND INSURED LOANS

As previously stated, veteran loans are either *guaranteed* or *insured*. The Veterans Administration contract with respect to guaranteed loans is to repay the lender for any loss experienced, within specific limitation.

A lender's loss on an insured loan is covered by the Veterans Administration up to the amount in the lender's insurance account or the unpaid balance of the loan, whichever is less.

GUARANTEED LOANS

Loans guaranteed by VA are the most popular and in the mortgage industry when the term "VA loan" is used it most often means a VA-guaranteed loan. The specific amount of VA guaranty varies as to the class of loan.

On home and farm home loans, the VA may guarantee up to 60 percent of the original mortgage amount or $25,000 whichever is less. (50 percent up to $30,000 as to disabled veterans.) Such loans may be for purchasing, constructing, improving, or repairing the home or farm home owned by the veteran and occupied by him as his residence.

The home and farm home guaranty is made only on the following conditions.

1. The proceeds must be used for payment of the purchase price (or cost of construction or repair) of the property concerned; the purchase price must not exceed the VAs determined reasonable value. As to this latter factor, the purchase prices of all loans must be reasonable as determined by the VA, not necessarily by a VA approved appraiser.
2. The payments set forth in the mortgage must bear a proper relation to the veteran's net income.
3. The home or farm home must be suitable for living purposes.
4. The veteran's credit must be satisfactory.
5. Any repairs, improvements, or alterations that are involved must improve or substantially protect the property.

Also included in this category and within these guaranty limits are loans to refinance existing mortgage loans or liens on homes occupied and owned by veterans, and loans to purchase individual residential units in condominium projects.

The above noted guaranty limits are maximums and must be reduced by any guaranty already used by the veterans. Hence, a veteran who has used a $10,000 guaranty to purchase a home can sell that home without release of liability and still have $15,000 of guaranty left to purchase another home.

In 1977, VA guaranteed $13.136 billion in loans, an increase of over 50 percent from the record $8.5 billion guaranteed in 1972 (see Chart 16-2).

INSURED LOANS

Only supervised lenders have the right and option to have loans made by them to veterans insured instead of guaranteed. In the normal course of operations all loans are guaranteed unless the lender makes a specific request for insurance. The VA mortgage loan insurance plan works like this: VA establishes an account in the particular lender's name and credits to that account 15 percent of each loan made or purchased by that lender. In the event of a default on an insured loan, VA will reimburse the lender up to the amount of the account so established or in an amount equal to the maximum dollar guaranty amount ($25,000 for home or farm homes; $17,500 for mobile home loans), whichever is less. If the veteran whose loan is insured has used up a portion of his entitlement, then the maximum claim payable shall be related to the unused benefit portion as opposed to the maximum entitlement.

LOAN TERMS AND CONDITIONS

Major terms and conditions under which VA loans are made as follows:

LOAN AMOUNT

There are no limitations placed upon the amount of mortgage loan that can be made to a veteran and still be insured or guaranteed (insured loans are limited to 6-2/3 times the amount of the veterans entitlement). However, the guaranty limits constitute a built-in maximum. For example, a VA-guaranteed home mortgage loan of $100,000 with no down payment is equivalent to a 75 percent loan-to-value ratio conventional loan due to the top $25,000 being guaranteed by the government. As mortgage loans are made in excess of $100,000 the lender's exposure increases over that which it normally and prudently accepts. Thus, a mortgage loan ceiling is built into the VA loan program equated to the VA's loan guaranty maximums.

DOWNPAYMENT

Neither the GI Bill of Rights nor VA regulations require any down payment to be made with regard to a mortgage loan. Thus the matter of down payment is a subject of negotiation between the veteran and the lender. As a matter of practice, most lenders will make no down payment loans to veterans up to a point determined by prudent judgment and market demands. For example, the Federal National Mortgage Association, a purchaser of large amounts of FHA and VA loans, sets a limit of $55,000 as to its purchases of VA, no down payment mortgage loans. (Up to $100,000 no-down VA loans are purchased by FNMA if special FNMA requirements are met.)

LOAN DISCOUNTS AND FEES

Due to the fixed interest rates on FHA and VA mortgage loans it has been the practice of lenders to charge a discount in order to obtain a "yield" (income on the mortgage investment) higher than the mortgage coupon or face interest rate. Such discounts are normally in the form of "points" (one point equals 1 percent of the mortgage amount) assessed against the seller or purchaser-mortgagor. According to VA regulations loan discounts or "points" cannot be collected from the veteran-purchaser-mortgagor, except in cases of a veteran refinancing or actually building his own home. Nothing prohibits the seller from paying "points" and in fact, the seller is the one who usually pays them.

Other discounts and fees, such as the one percent mortgage origination fee, are regulated by VA.

LOAN CLOSING COSTS

The VA regulates all closing costs, such as title and recording fees, appraisal fees, taxes and tax escrows and other such costs and prepaid items. Supervision of these charges and the payment of points are accomplished through review by VA of the seller and purchaser's loan closing statement.

Full disclosure of closing costs is now required by law for VA, FHA and conventional loans by reason of the Real Estate Settlement Procedures Act of 1974.

LOAN MATURITY AND SECURITY

Home and farm loans are limited to maximum maturities of thirty years and 32 days.

Loans for terms of five years or more must be amortized at least once annually.

CHART 16-2

HOME LOANS GUARANTEED OR INSURED BY VA

Calendar Year	Number of Loans	Initial Principal Loan Amount
1955	649,591	$7,156,567,679
1956	507,725	5,868,351,335
1957	306,735	3,760,837,710
1958	145,980	1,864,951,345
1959	213,019	2,786,752,514
1960	144,983	1,985,019,022
1961	134,327	1,831,528,214
1962	188,498	2,652,140,065
1963	210,964	3,045,048,763
1964	186,204	2,850,766,301
1965	163,409	2,650,442,507
1966	157,333	2,598,145,713
1967	200,846	3,404,110,077
1968	211,025	3,771,683,408
1969	213,938	4,073,410,256
1970	167,525	3,440,161,461
1971	283,981	6,082,960,394
1972	375,483	8,467,528,253
1973	321,521	7,521,962,197
1974	313,161	8,234,903,606
1975	301,000	8,902,000**
1976	330,000	10,439,000**

*Includes direct loans sold and guaranteed; and mobile home loans.
Source: Veterans Administration.
**Rounded figures.

Real estate loans (except those for repairs, improvements, or property alterations) must be secured by a first and best lien on the real estate. One exception is that the lien may be second only to a lien for assessment for common area maintenance and operation in condominium projects.

The repair, improvement, and property alteration loans may be unsecured if the mortgage amount is less than $1,000, provided the lender obtains a statement from the veteran that he has a vested estate (present ownership interest) in the property. Such mortgage loans for amounts in excess of $1,000, but less than 40 percent of the property's economic value must be secured by either a first or second lien. When for more than 40 percent of economic value, the security must be a first lien.

The rule of practicality applies with respect to non-realty loans.

INTEREST RATE AND PREPAYMENT

The maximum interest rate on VA loans is that established by the Veterans Administration. As a rule the VA maximum rate follows that established by the

Secretary of Housing and Urban Development.

All VA loans must provide for prepayment at any time without penalty.

INTENT TO OCCUPY

As with FHA, the VA mortgage loan program was established to promote home ownership, not real estate speculation. Thus all VA loans are conditioned upon the veteran certifying at the time of the mortgage loan application and at the loan closing that he intends to occupy the home as his residence.

STANDARD FORMS

The Veterans Administration has established standard note and mortgage forms for use in the making of VA loans. A sample note form is shown as Chart 16-3 and a sample mortgage form as Chart 16-4.

SPECIAL FHA PROGRAMS FOR VETERANS

All veterans who would qualify for a VA loan are eligible for loans under FHAs Section 203(b) program, except those veterans who will reside in an area for a limited time due to the character of their employment. This program covers single family dwelling more than one year old or constructed with FHA or VA inspections. A minimum downpayment of $200 including prepaid items is required on the first $25,000 of sales price, and 5 percent on any amount in excess of $25,000 up to a $67,500 maximum mortgage amount for a one-family home.

Veterans are also eligible for loans under FHA's Section 222 program. The essential difference between the Section 222 and Section 203(b) programs is that the veteran pays a higher down payment under Section 222 (minimum 3 percent down on the first $25,000 of sales price), but the FHA mortgage insurance premium of 0.5 percent is paid by the Department of Defense or Department of Transportation while the serviceman owns the property and remains on active duty. All in-service veterans applying for an FHA loan must use Section 222.

Certain World War I veterans and members of reserve and National Guard units with at least ninety days of active duty are not eligible for VA loans, but may be eligible for a FHA Sec. 203(b) veteran loan.

INTEREST COVERED

VA will insure or guarantee a loan on fee-simple realty, a leasehold estate with an original lease term (including renewals) of not less than fourteen years beyond the maturity of the proposed mortgage loans, or a life estate if the mortgage lien includes the reversionary interests.

APPRAISALS

In order to curb the purchasing of homes of inflated value, VA regulations require as a prerequisite to insurance or guaranty of a veteran's mortgage loan that the administrator establish the fact that the property is reasonably valued. After a VA-designated fee appraiser values a property, a "Certificate of Reasonable

CHART 16-3

VA Form 26-6308a (Home Loan)
Rev. January 1974. Use Optional.
Section 1810, Title 38 U.S.C.
Acceptable to Federal National
Mortgage Association.

FLORIDA

MORTGAGE NOTE

, Florida.

$, 19

FOR VALUE RECEIVED, the undersigned promise(s) to pay to

, a corporation organized and existing under the
laws of   , or order, the principal sum of
          Dollars ($), with interest from date at the rate of
per centum (%) per annum on the unpaid balance until paid. The said principal and interest shall be
payable at the office of
in   , or at such other place as the holder may designate, in writing
delivered or mailed to the debtor, in monthly installments of   Dollars
($), commencing on the first day of   , 19   , and continuing on the
first day of each month thereafter until this note is fully paid, except that, if not sooner paid, the final
payment of principal and interest shall be due and payable on the first day of   , 19   .

Privilege is reserved to prepay at any time, without premium or fee, the entire indebtedness or any part
thereof not less than the amount of one installment, or one hundred dollars ($100.00), whichever is less.
Prepayment in full shall be credited on the date received. Partial prepayment, other than on an installment
due date, need not be credited until the next following installment due date or thirty days after such
prepayment, whichever is earlier.

If any deficiency in the payment of any installment under this note is not made good prior to the due date of
the next such installment, the entire principal sum and accrued interest shall at once become due and payable
without notice at the option of the holder of this note. Failure to exercise this option shall not constitute a waiver
of the right to exercise the same in the event of any subsequent default. In the event of default in the payment of
this note, and if the same is collected by an attorney at law, the undersigned hereby agree(s) to pay all costs of
collection, including a reasonable attorney's fee.

This note is secured by Mortgage of even date executed by the undersigned on certain property described
therein and represents money actually used for the acquisition of said property or the improvements thereon.

Presentment, protest, and notice are hereby waived.

_____ [SEAL]

_____ [SEAL]

_____ [SEAL]

_____ [SEAL]

THIS IS TO CERTIFY that this is the note described in and secured by Mortgage of even date herewith and in
the same principal amount as herein stated and secured by real estate situated in the county of   ,
State of Florida.

Dated this   day of   , 19   .

_____
Notary Public.

CHART 16-4

VA FORM 26-8388 (HOME LOAN)
REV. JUNE 1974. USE OPTIONAL
SECTION 1810. TITLE 38. U.S.C.
ACCEPTABLE TO FEDERAL
NATIONAL MORTGAGE
ASSOCIATION

FLORIDA

SHORT FORM OF MORTGAGE

This Mortgage, dated the   day of   A. D. 19   , by and between

and

hereinafter called the Mortgagor, and

hereinafter called the Mortgagee,

WITNESSETH, that for valuable considerations, the said Mortgagor does hereby grant, bargain, sell and convey unto the said Mortgagee and his assigns, all that certain parcel of land of which the said

Mortgagor is now seized and possessed and in actual possession, situated in the County of

and State of Florida, described as follows:

Together with all structures and improvements now and hereafter on said land and the rents, issues and profits of the above described property (provided, however, that the Mortgagor shall be entitled to collect and retain the said rents, issues and profits until default hereunder); and all fixtures now or hereafter attached to or used in connection with the premises herein described and in addition thereto the following described household appliances, which are and shall be deemed to be, fixtures and a part of the realty, and are a portion of the security for the indebtedness herein mentioned.

TO HAVE AND TO HOLD the same, and every part thereof, with the appurtenances of the said Mortgagor in and to the same, and every part and parcel thereof, unto the said Mortgagee in fee simple.

The Mortgagor hereby covenants with the Mortgagee, that he is seized of said land in fee simple or such other estate, if any, as is stated herein; and that said Mortgagor does hereby fully warrant the title to said land, and every part thereof, and will defend the same against the lawful claims of all persons whomsoever.

PROVIDED ALWAYS, that if the Mortgagor should pay to the Mortgagee that certain promissory note of even date herewith, made by the Mortgagor and payable to the order of the Mortgagee in the

principal sum of   Dollars, payable in monthly install-

ments to principal and interest of $ starting on the   day of

19   , and if not sooner paid the final payment being due on the   day of

, or any extensions or renewals thereof and shall fully pay all other indebtedness or liability that may become due and owing hereunder and secured hereby, and shall faithfully and promptly comply with and perform each and every other covenant and provision herein on the part of the Mortgagor to be complied with and performed, and every other covenant and provision as contained in that blank or master form of mortgage, which is incorporated herein by reference as if set out herein in full, then these presents shall be void and released at the expense of the Mortgagor, otherwise to remain in full force and effect. The said blank or master form of mortgage was recorded on February 13, 1970, in the Official Records of the Clerk of the Circuit Court of the following counties in Florida in the Official Records Volume and at the page designated after the name of each county, to-wit: (except that it was recorded in Bradford, Brevard, Duval and Suwannee Counties on February 9, 1970, and in Dade County on February 10, 1970)

COUNTY	OFFICIAL RECORDS VOLUME	PAGE	COUNTY	OFFICIAL RECORDS VOLUME	PAGE
Alachua	620	195	Lake	398	193
Baker	10	79	Lee	578	125
Bay	295	679	Leon	399	286
Bradford	79	141	Levy	10	353
Brevard	1114	284	Liberty	13	430
Broward	4140	213	Madison	53	846
Calhoun	29	705	Manatee	442	574
Charlotte	328	964	Marion	415	556
Citrus	260	348	Martin	285	454
Clay	191	384	Monroe	447	20
Collier	342	791	Nassau	98	643
Columbia	256	622	Okaloosa	562	517
Dade	6754	279	Okeechobee	118	191
DeSoto	65	83	Orange	1917	203
Dixie	22	756	Osceola	198	390
Duval	3075	30	Palm Beach	1786	1448
Escambia	476	737	Pasco	482	601
Flagler	30	569	Pinellas	3268	593
Franklin	94	312	Polk	1270	68
Gadsden	121	74	Putnam	232	345
Gilchrist	33	244	St. Johns	164	300
Glades	46	273	St. Lucie	182	2689
Gulf	43	1	Santa Rosa	203	393
Hamilton	87	99	Sarasota	828	64
Hardee	96	237	Seminole	766	463.1
Hendry	124	191	Sumter	108	153
Hernando	205	0287	Suwannee	70	154
Highlands	349	481	Taylor	78	831
Hillsborough	2133	608	Union	14	249
Holmes	6	404	Volusia	1177	201
Indian River	341	467	Wakulla	22	591
Jackson	69	980	Walton	103	287
Jefferson	38	494	Washington	41	520
Lafayette	13	403			

(Documentary Stamps affixed to original note and cancelled.)

IN WITNESS WHEREOF, the said Mortgagor has hereunto set his hand and seal the day and year first aforesaid.

Signed, sealed and delivered in the presence of:

_____   _____ (SEAL)

_____ (SEAL)

_____   _____(SEAL)

_____ (SEAL)

STATE OF FLORIDA }
COUNTY OF   } ss:

_____

Space Below for Clerk's Use Only

On this   day of

19   , before me, a Notary Public in and for
the State of Florida at Large, personally appeared

known to me to be the person(s) whose name(s)

_____ subscribed to the within instrument,

and acknowledged that _____ executed the
same.

WITNESS my hand and official seal.

(SEAL)_____
          Notary Public
          State of Florida at Large

My Commission Expires_____

VA Form 26-8388
June 1974   DO NOT RECORD

Following is a copy of the provisions of that Blank or Master Form of Mortgage commencing with line immediately preceding paragraph 1 and including unnumbered paragraph following paragraph 18 thereof, recorded as set forth in Short Form of Mortgage attached.

The Mortgagor further covenants as follows:

1. That he will pay the indebtedness, as hereinbefore provided. Privilege is reserved to prepay at any time, without premium or fee, the entire indebtedness or any part thereof not less than the amount of one installment, or one hundred dollars ($100.00), whichever is less. Any prepayment made on other than an installment due date will not be credited until the next following installment due date.

2. In order more fully to protect the security of this mortgage, the Mortgagor, together with, and in addition to, the monthly payments under the terms of the note secured hereby, on the installment due date day of each month until the said note is fully paid, will pay to the Mortgagee as trustee (under the terms of this trust as hereinafter stated) the following sums:

(a) A sum equal to the ground rents, if any, next due, plus the premiums that will next become due and payable on policies of fire and other hazard insurance covering the mortgaged property, plus taxes and assessments next due on the mortgaged property (all as estimated by the Mortgagee and of which the Mortgagor is notified) less all sums already paid therefor divided by the number of months to elapse before one month prior to the date when such ground rents, premiums, taxes, and assessments will become delinquent, such sums to be held by Mortgagee in trust to pay said ground rents, premiums, taxes, and special assessments.

(b) The aggregate of the amounts payable pursuant to subparagraph (a) and those payable on the note secured hereby, shall be paid in a single payment each month, to be applied to the following items in the order stated:

(I) ground rents, taxes, assessments, fire, and other hazard insurance premiums;
(II) interest on the note secured hereby; and
(III) amortization of the principal of said note.

Any deficiency in the amount of such aggregate monthly payment shall, unless made good by the Mortgagor prior to the due date of the next such payment, constitute an event of default under this mortgage. At Mortgagee's option, Mortgagor will pay a "late charge" not exceeding four per centum (4%) of any installment when paid more than fifteen (15) days after the due date thereof to cover the extra expense involved in handling delinquent payments, but such "late charge" shall not be payable out of the proceeds of any sale made to satisfy the indebtedness secured hereby, unless such proceeds are sufficient to discharge the entire indebtedness and all proper costs and expenses secured hereby.

3. If the total of the payments made by the Mortgagor under (a) of paragraph 2 preceding shall exceed the amount of payments actually made by the Mortgagee, as trustee for ground rents, taxes and assessments, and insurance premiums, as the case may be, such excess shall be credited on subsequent payments to be made by the Mortgagor for such items or, at Mortgagee's option, as trustee shall be refunded to Mortgagor. If, however, such monthly payments shall not be sufficient to pay such items when the same shall become due and payable, then the Mortgagor shall pay to the Mortgagee as trustee any amount necessary to make up the deficiency. Such payment shall be made within thirty (30) days after written notice from the Mortgagee stating the amount of the deficiency, which notice may be given by mail. If at any time the Mortgagor shall tender to the Mortgagee in accordance with the provisions of the note secured hereby, full payment of the entire indebtedness represented thereby, the Mortgagee as trustee shall, in computing the amount of such indebtedness, credit to the account of the Mortgagor any credit balance remaining under the provisions of (a) of said paragraph 2. If there shall be a default under any of the provisions of this mortgage resulting in a public sale of the premises covered hereby, or if the Mortgagee acquires the property otherwise after default, the Mortgagee as trustee shall apply, at the time of the commencement of such proceedings or at the time the property is otherwise acquired, the amount then remaining to credit of Mortgagor under (a) of paragraph 2 preceding as a credit on the interest accrued and unpaid and the balance to the principal then remaining unpaid on said note.

4. He will pay all taxes, assessments, water rates, and other governmental or municipal charges, fines, or impositions, for which provision has not been made hereinbefore, and in default thereof the Mortgagee may pay the same; and that he will promptly deliver the official receipts therefor to the Mortgagee.

5. He will permit, commit, or suffer no waste, impairment, or deterioration of said property or any part thereof, except reasonable wear and tear; and in the event of the failure of the Mortgagor to keep the buildings on said premises and those to be erected on said premises, or improvements thereon, in good repair, the Mortgagee may make such repairs as in its discretion it may deem necessary for the proper preservation thereof, and the full amount of each and every such payment shall be due and payable thirty (30) days after demand, and shall be secured by the lien of this mortgage.

6. He will pay all and singular the costs, charges, and expenses, including reasonable lawyer's fees, and costs of abstracts of title, incurred or paid at any time by the Mortgagee because of the failure on the part of the Mortgagor promptly and fully to perform the agreements and covenants of said promissory note and this mortgage, and said costs, charges, and expenses shall be immediately due and payable and shall be secured by the lien of this mortgage.

7. He will continuously maintain hazard insurance, of such type or types and amounts as Mortgagee may from time to time require, on the improvements now or hereafter on said premises, and except when payment for all such premiums has theretofore been made under (a) of paragraph 2 hereof, he will pay promptly when due any premiums therefor. All insurance shall be carried in companies approved by Mortgagee and the policies and renewals thereof shall be held by Mortgagee and have attached thereto loss payable clauses in favor of and in form acceptable to the Mortgagee. In event of loss he will give immediate notice by mail to Mortgagee, and Mortgagee may make proof of loss if not made promptly by Mortgagor, and each insurance company concerned is hereby authorized and directed to make payment for such loss directly to Mortgagee instead of to Mortgagor and Mortgagee jointly, and the insurance proceeds, or any part thereof, may be applied by Mortgagee at its option either to the reduction of the indebtedness hereby secured or to the restoration or repair of the property damaged. In event of foreclosure of this mortgage, or other transfer of title to the mortgaged property in extinguishment of the indebtedness secured hereby, all right, title, and interest of the Mortgagor in and to any insurance policies then in force shall pass to the purchaser or grantee.

8. He will not execute or file of record any instrument which imposes a restriction upon the sale or occupancy of the property described herein on the basis of race, color, or creed.

9. If the premises, or any part thereof, be condemned under the power of eminent domain, or acquired for a public use, the damages awarded, the proceeds for the taking of, or the consideration for such acquisition, to the extent of the full amount of the remaining unpaid indebtedness secured by this mortgage, are hereby assigned to the Mortgagee, and his heirs or assigns, and shall be paid forthwith to said Mortgagee or his assignee to be applied on account of the last maturing installments of such indebtedness; provided, however, the Mortgagee or his assignee, may at his discretion pay direct to the Mortgagor, his heirs or assigns any part or all of such award; provided, that if the loan is guaranteed or insured, the consent of the guarantor or insurer is obtained in advance of said payment.

10. The Mortgagee may, at any time pending a suit upon this mortgage, apply to the court having jurisdiction thereof for the appointment of a receiver, and such court shall forthwith appoint a receiver of the premises covered hereby all and singular, including all and singular the income, profits, issues, and revenues from whatever source derived, each and every of which, it being expressly understood, is hereby mortgaged as if specifically set forth and described in the granting and habendum clauses hereof. Such appointment shall be made by such court as an admitted equity and a matter of absolute right to said Mortgagee, and without reference to the adequacy or inadequacy of the value of the property mortgaged or to the solvency or insolvency of said Mortgagor or the defendants. Such rents, profits, income, issues, and revenues shall be applied by such receiver according to the lien of this mortgage and the practice of such court. In the event of any default on the part of the Mortgagor hereunder, the Mortgagor agrees to pay to the Mortgagee on demand as a reasonable monthly rental for the premises an amount at least equivalent to one-twelfth (1/12) of the aggregate of the twelve monthly installments payable in the then current year plus the actual amount of the annual taxes, assessments, water rates, and insurance premiums for such year not covered by the aforesaid monthly payments.

11. In the event of any breach of this mortgage or default on the part of the Mortgagor, or in the event that any of said sums of money herein referred to be not promptly and fully paid according to the tenor hereof, or in the event that each and every the stipulations, agreements, conditions, and covenants of said note and this mortgage, are not duly, promptly, and fully performed or if the Mortgagor be adjudicated bankrupt or made defendant in a banruptcy or receivership proceedings; then in either or any such event, the said aggregate sum mentioned in said note then remaining unpaid, with interest accrued to that time, and all money secured hereby, shall become due and payable forthwith, or thereafter, at the option of said Mortgagee, as fully and completely as if all the said sums of money were originally stipulated to be paid on such day, anything in said note or in this mortgage to the contrary notwithstanding; and thereupon or thereafter, at the option of said Mortgagee, without notice or demand, suit at law or in equity, may be prosecuted as if all moneys secured hereby had matured prior to its institution. The Mortgagee may foreclose this mortgage, as to the amount so declared due and payable, and the said premises shall be sold to satisfy and pay the same together with costs, expenses, and allowances. In case of partial foreclosure of this mortgage, the mortgaged premises shall be sold subject to the continuing lien of this mortgage for the amount of the debt not then due and unpaid. In such case the provisions of this paragraph may again be availed of thereafter from time to time by the Mortgagee.

12. No waiver of any covenant herein or of the obligation secured hereby shall at any time thereafter be held to be a waiver of the terms hereof or of the note secured hereby.

13. The lien of this instrument shall remain in full force and effect during any postponement or extension of the time of payment of the indebtedness or any part thereof secured hereby.

14. This mortgage is given to secure the purchase money, or a part thereof, of the lands herein described and is executed and delivered contemporaneously with the deed therefor.

15. If the Mortgagor default in any of the covenants or agreements contained herein, or in said note, then the Mortgagee may perform the same, and all expenditures (including reasonable attorney's fees) made by the Mortgagee in so doing shall draw interest at the rate provided for in the principal indebtedness, and shall be repayable thirty (30) days after demand, and, together with interest and costs accrued thereon, shall be secured by this mortgage.

16. Upon the request of the Mortgagee the Mortgagor shall execute and deliver a supplemental note or notes for the sum or sums advanced by the Mortgagee for the alteration, modernization, improvement, maintenance, or repair of said premises, for taxes or assessments against the same and for any other purpose authorized hereunder. Said note or notes shall be secured hereby on a parity with and as fully as if the advance evidenced thereby were included in the note first described above. Said supplemental note or notes shall bear interest at the rate provided for in the principal indebtedness and shall be payable in approximately equal monthly payments for such period as may be agreed upon by the creditor and debtor. Failing to agree on the maturity, the whole of the sum or sums so advanced shall be due and payable thirty (30) days after demand by the creditor. In no event shall the maturity extend beyond the ultimate maturity of the note first described above.

17. The mailing of a written notice or demand addressed to the owner of record of the mortgaged premises, or directed to the said owner at the last address actually furnished to the Mortgagee, or if none, directed to said owner at said mortgaged premises, and mailed by the United States mails, postage prepaid, shall be sufficient notice and demand in any case arising under this instrument and required by the provisions hereof or by law.

18. Title 38 United States Code and the Regulations issued thereunder shall govern the rights, duties and liabilities of the parties hereto, and any provisions of this or other instruments executed in connection with said indebtedness which are inconsistent with said Title or Regulations are hereby amended and supplemented to conform thereto.

The covenants herein contained shall bind, and the benefits and advantages shall inure to, the respective heirs, executors, administrators, successors, and assigns of the parties hereto. Whenever used, the singular number shall include the plural, the plural the singular and the use of any gender shall include all genders and the term "Mortgagee" shall include any payee of the indebtedness hereby secured or any transferee thereof whether by operation of law or otherwise.

Value" is issued by VA establishing the value of the property for VA loan purposes.

Proposed subdivisions to be built under VA regulations and standards may be appraised prior to construction based upon proposed lot sizes and homes. A Master Certificate of Reasonable Value covering all proposed lots and homes is issued upon completion of such an appraisal.

TAX AND INSURANCE ESCROWS

Escrows for the purpose of payment of real estate taxes and hazard insurance premiums as they become due are not required by VA regulations, but many lenders customarily require such escrows be established and maintained.

REIMBURSEMENT ON DEFAULT

In the event of a veteran's default under a VA guaranteed loan, the lender must notify the appropriate VA regional office of such default. Usually the lender will foreclose the loan security and then submit its claim for losses.

A claim under the VAs loan guaranty may be discharged at the VAs option either by:

1. Paying the mortgagee a pro rate portion of the amount originally guaranteed with accompanying subrogation to the mortgagee's rights against the veteran-mortgagor
2. Paying the mortgagee the unpaid mortgage loan balance, plus all accrued interest, with an assignment of the loan and security required from the mortgagee to VA
3. Requiring the mortgagee to keep the foreclosed property with payment to the mortgagee of the difference between the determined value of the property and the mortgagee's loss.

As a practical matter the second option noted above is most frequently used. The latter option is used with properties which are in such a deteriorated condition that VA does not wish to recondition and dispose of them.

RELEASE OF LIABILITY

When a veteran sells his home to a person assuming an existing VA loan on the property, he normally wants to be released from any contingent liability with respect to the loan. The veteran may be released from such a liability by VA upon application. The release of liability by VA does not mean a release by the mortgagee, although the mortgagee usually follows VA's action.

DIRECT LOANS

In addition to its guaranteed and insured loan programs, the VA may make direct loans to veterans under certain circumstances. The direct loan program has as its purpose the supplying of mortgage funds to veterans living in rural, capital-scarce areas. Subject to reasonable value determinations, direct loans may be made by VA for any of the following purposes:

1. For the veteran to buy or construct a dwelling to be occupied by him as his home.
2. For the veteran to buy a farm on which there is a farm residence to be occupied by him as his home.
3. For the veteran to build a farm residence on land owned by him which is to be occupied by him as his home.
4. For the veteran to repair, alter, or improve a farm residence or other dwelling owned by him and occupied by him as his home.

PREREQUISITES

In order to qualify for a direct loan it must be shown that:

1. The veteran is a satisfactory credit risk.
2. The mortgage payments will bear a proper relation to the veteran's present and anticipated income and expenses.
3. The home or farm or farm home is located in an area where no private capital is available for the proposed mortgage loan, under terms of the

applicable VA guaranty program.
4. The veteran is unable to obtain a home or farm home loan from a private lender or from the Secretary of Agriculture under the Bankhead-Jones Farm Tenant Act or under the National Housing Act of 1949.

LOAN TERMS AND AMOUNTS

The maximum direct loan available to a veteran is generally $33,000. The interest rate, fees, and charges for direct loans are the same as those for guaranteed loans, except that the maximum maturity is twenty-five years (thirty years in exceptional cases).

BUILDER COMMITMENTS

In order to further assist in making mortgage funds available to veterans in rural areas and to stimulate house construction in those areas, the VA will reserve upon a builder's request funds for the making of direct loans to veterans purchasing homes from the builder. To qualify, the house construction must be in a "direct loan area." A direct loan area is defined as any rural area, small city, or town not in or near a large metropolitan area in which VA finds that private capital is not available for the VA loan program.

Builder commitments are made for three months, with time extensions available. VA charges the builder a 2 percent non-refundable fee for all funds reserved.

SALE OF DIRECT LOANS

VA may sell and private lenders may purchase VA-originated direct loans. The sale price is equal to the unpaid principal balance plus accrued interest. A regular VA guaranty is given to the lender purchasing the loan. If a direct loan is offered for sale and is purchased by a private lender within sixty days after the loan is closed by VA, the VA may pay to the purchasing lender all or a portion of the builder's paid commitment fee.

Recently VA has established a system of referring direct loan cases to a roster of private lenders located within a 100-mile radius of the subject property. It is anticipated that this referral program will bring more private capital and participation to the direct loan program.

Proceeds from the sale of direct loans are placed in a revolving fund to be used for future origination of direct loans.

MOBILE HOME LOANS

The Veterans Housing Act of 1970 established a VA program for the purchase by veterans of mobile homes and mobile home lots.

GUARANTY

The act and VA regulations issued pursuant thereto authorizes a 50 percent mobile home loan guaranty for any veteran who has not used any of his available $25,000 loan guaranty entitlement. However, use of the mobile home loan guaranty entitlement does not reduce the $25,000 home loan guaranty entitlement. But any veteran obtaining a guaranteed mobile home loan cannot use his $25,000 guaranty entitlement to purchase a conventionally constructed home until his mobile home loan is paid in full.

LOAN RATES

The VA is authorized to set a different interest rate for mobile home loans than that established for loans made to purchase conventionally constructed homes.

The interest rate charged to the veteran may be a combination of discount plus interest, provided the simple interest maxima are not exceeded.

Maximum interest rates under this program are subject to change and will vary in proportion to the established FHA/VA rate.

LOAN AMOUNTS AND TERMS

Maxima established for the mobile home loan program are:

a) No maximum loan amount is established for mobile home loans, but VA will guaranty or insure only 50 percent or $17,500, whichever is the less.

b) Maximum loan terms are as follows:

Mobile Home Only	Single-Wide	15 years and 32 days
	Double-Wide	20 years and 32 days
Mobile Home With	Single-Wide	15 years and 32 days
Undeveloped Lot	Double Wide	20 years and 32 days
Mobile Home With	Single-Wide	15 years and 32 days
Developed Lot	Double-Wide	20 years and 32 days
Developed Undeveloped		15 years and 32 days
Lot Only (Available		
only to veterans who		
already own mobile		
homes)		

Loans for the purchase of mobile home units and undeveloped lots may include an amount for preparation of the site as determined appropriate by VA.

In the case of a used mobile home, the maximum loan is limited to that shown above or the remaining physical life of the unit as determined by VA, whichever is less.

ADVANTAGES OF VA PROGRAM

In conclusion, the GI loan program affords veterans distinct advantages in financing the purchase or construction of homes:

1. Favorable interest rates, established by VA in accordance with market conditions.
2. Long term (up to thirty years) to repay the loan.
3. No monthly guaranty or mortgage insurance premiums on the loans as with FHA insured loans.
4. No down payments (except on larger loans).
5. An option to prepay the loans without penalty.
6. Mobile home financing for both the lot and the mobile home.
7. Other provisions of the VA regulations designed to assist veterans experiencing financial difficulties.

Lenders participating in the VA program obtain several substantial advantages:

1. Mortgage coupon rates equivalent to the maximum established FHA/VA rate plus any loan discounts obtained from the seller, coupled with virtually no risk due to the VA guaranty or insurance.
2. A VA Certificate of Guaranty, except in cases of fraud or misrepresentation.
3. Prompt cash settlements of guaranty claims filed after default.
4. Payments of interest on the mortgage loan amount during the foreclosure period.

QUESTIONS FOR THOUGHT AND DISCUSSION

1. a. What is the purpose of the GI Bill of Rights?
   b. The VA mortgage loan program?
2. Since VA loans can be obtained with no down payments, do you feel all veterans should buy homes instead of renting them? In other words, does the VA loan program make home ownership a far more attractive proposition than renting property?
3. What methods would you recommend for accomplishing the purposes of the direct loan program through private industry in order to terminate a federal government agency's involvement in direct lending?
4. Do you feel the government should encourage no down payment loans as it does through the VA loan program?
5. What is the purpose of the prepayment without penalty requirement of the VA?
6. What advantages do the VA-guaranteed loans have over the FHA-insured loan?

17

FEDERAL NATIONAL MORTGAGE ASSOCIATION

The national mortgage market is made up of lenders, generally those who originate mortgage loans by directly lending to borrowers, and investors, generally those who purchase mortgages originated by others. It has been shown that the same institution can be both lender and investor. Mutual savings banks, for example, originate mortgages in their local areas of operation and also purchase mortgages on a nationwide basis. Some institutions, such as pension funds, are solely mortgage investors whereas other groups—mortgage companies—are solely mortgage lenders.

SECONDARY MORTGAGE MARKET

For there to be a free flow of funds into the mortgage market it is necessary to have a strong secondary mortgage market operation or a flow of funds between purchasers and sellers of mortgages at times when money is available as well as times when it is not so readily available. Direct lenders of mortgage funds are more willing to place substantial funds in mortgage securities if they know they can readily liquidate their investments at current market rates by sale of mortgages on the secondary market to investors. This availability of purchasers for originated mortgages is particularly important to mortgage companies whose total operations are dependent upon their ability to continually and quickly liquidate their mortgage portfolios and use the proceeds to originate more mortgages for sale to investors. Thus, if the secondary market demand for mortgages falls, the amount of funds flowing into the primary mortgage market or available for the creation of new mortgages is proportionately curtailed.

The private secondary mortgage market has been subject over the years to the same economic pressures that are at work on the economy in general. Thus the support required of the private secondary mortgage market has been lacking at those times when it is needed most to provide liquidity to mortgage lenders and to channel funds into the mortgage market.

Hence it has been necessary for the federal government to take an active role in the nation's secondary mortgage market operations and to provide support and assistance to residential mortgage financing particularly during those critical times when private support of the secondary market is deteriorating.

Government assistance to the secondary market is provided through several media: the Federal Home Loan Bank Board, The Federal Home Loan Mortgage Corporation (FHLMC), Government National Mortgage Association (GNMA) and most importantly the Federal National Mortgage Association (FNMA), also called "Fannie Mae."

HISTORY OF FNMA

The Federal National Mortgage Association was established in 1938 as a subsidiary of the Reconstruction Finance Corporation (RFC) pursuant to Title III of the National Housing Act. Its primary function then was (and to a large extent still is), to purchase FHA-insured mortgages from private lenders, thereby assisting the secondary mortgage market in replenishing the supply of mortgage capital in the residential housing market for the making of additional mortgage loans. Mortgages so purchased by FNMA are held and then re-sold when money is plentiful.

FNMAs activities were expanded in 1948 to cover the purchase of VA guaranteed mortgages. In 1950, FNMA became a part of the Housing and Home Finance Agency and in 1954 was recharted under the provisions of Title III of the National Housing Act, as amended in that year.

Under the restructuring, FNMA was given three main areas of responsibility:
1. The support of the secondary mortgage market through private financing instead of the prior method of borrowing from the federal government in order to support its operations.
2. The special assistance functions.
3. The management and liquidation of its existing mortgage portfolio.

In 1968 a landmark was reached in FNMAs history. Legislative changes incorporated into the revolutionary National Housing Act of 1968 brought about a division of Fannie Mae into two corporate entities: the Government National Mortgage Association (GNMA), a government corporation contained in the Department of Housing and Urban Development (HUD) and the Federal National Mortgage Association, a government sponsored but privately owned corporation.

Fannie Mae retained its secondary mortgage market functions, while responsibility for the special assistance, management, and liquidation areas was transferred to GNMA.

Under the Emergency Home Finance Act of 1970, FNMA was authorized to purchase conventional loans. In 1972 FNMA began its conventional home loan purchase program and in 1974 expanded it to include loans on units in condominium and Planned Unit Development (PUD) projects.

PRESENT STATUS

The 1968 Housing Act provided that FNMA must obtain quasi-private status between May 1, 1970 and May 1, 1973 by individuals and corporations in the mortgage lending, real estate, and home building fields acquiring ownership of one-third of its outstanding capital stock.

In the summer of 1970, FNMA reached its goal of obtaining quasi-private status. Shortly after this achievement Fannie Mae's resulting private corporation status was enhanced by the listing of its shares on the New York Stock Exchange.

Fannie Mae operates today primarily as a private corporation seeking to profit from its activities, attentive to the demands of its shareholders. Additionally, FNMA pays income taxes on its earnings the same as any private, profit-oriented corporation or association.

The continuing public aspect of FNMA and its relationship with the executive branch of the federal government is exemplified by four provisions of the governing legislation:

1. The fifteen member board of directors of the corporation includes five members who are appointed by the President of the United States. The remaining ten are elected by FNMA's shareholders with at least one director representing the real estate industry, another the home building sector, and one the mortgage lending institutions and companies.
2. The Secretary of Housing and Urban Development must approve FNMA's borrowed capital, debit ratio, and stock dividend policies.
3. The Secretary of the Treasury has authority to purchase Fannie Mae debt obligations up to a maximum of $2.25 billion at any one time, in the event it is necessary to do so.
4. The Secretary of HUD has authority to require, to the extent that the corporation's income from business operations is not unreasonably endangered, that a portion of Fannie Mae's purchases of mortgages be directly related to accomplishment of the National Housing goal of providing adequate housing facilities for low-to-moderate income families.

Hence the best definition of FNMA's current status was given by the corporation itself when it termed itself "a private corporation with a public purpose."

OPERATIONS AND FINANCING ACTIVITIES

Fannie Mae is not a mortgage originator. It deals solely in existing mortgages. By using private capital it commits for, purchases, and sells conventional, government insured or guaranteed home mortgages, and government insured multifamily mortgages. In addition to these major activities, it provides funds for construction financing and engages in loan participation arrangements.

Funds to finance its operations, including income from its activities, come from several major sources:

1. Operating capital obtained from the sale of common stock. This is the primary source of funds for FNMAs operations. Its shares are sold through the New York Stock Exchange to lenders and other institutions who deal with it. Those doing business with FNMA are captive stock purchasers. They must purchase shares in order to sell loans to FNMA and must retain

shares of stock based upon the volume of mortgages serviced for FNMA.

2. Funds obtained by borrowing through the sale on the open market of notes, debentures, and other obligations. A special Internal Revenue Service ruling on December 31, 1970 held that while "FNMA debts are not obligations of the United States, they are lawful investments for all fiduciary, trust and public funds under the control of the federal government or federal officials." This ruling has helped to widen the market for FNMA debt obligations.

3. Commitment fees paid for mortgage loan purchase commitments issued by it.

4. Proceeds from sales of mortgage loans previously purchased. (As has been stated, Fannie Mae supports the secondary mortgage market by stepping up its purchase of mortgages during money-scarce times and selling mortgages to investors at times when money is plentiful. FNMA hopefully profits by selling mortgages for more than it originally paid for them.)

5. The differential between interest income on purchased mortgages and the cost of borrowings.

6. Income from non-mortgage type investments.

FNMA has additional financial backup in the form of a $600 million line of credit from a consortium of banks. It also obtains long term funds from the issuance of mortgage backed bonds guaranteed by GNMA and backed by pools of FHA/VA Mortgages.

SELLER-SERVICERS

Mortgagees dealing with Fannie Mae are termed "sellers." They include mortgage companies, commercial banks, savings and loan associations, mutual savings banks and other organizations that have applied for and been approved to sell loans to FNMA.

Generally, businesses that make or purchase mortgage loans as one of their main operations, that meet and maintain standards required by FNMA, and that are FHA-approved mortgages may qualify as "sellers." Enterprises qualifying as "sellers" must enter into a selling agreement with FNMA which requires the seller, with respect to each home mortgage offered for purchase, either to be qualified to service the mortgage for FNMA or to have use of the facilities of another institution, approved by FNMA, for servicing the mortgage. Businesses which are both approved sellers and loan servicers are termed "seller-servicers." Normally, those doing business with Fannie Mae are expected to be FNMA approved seller-servicers.

Servicers of FNMA-purchased home mortgages presently receive a fee of 0.375 percent of the principal balances on all mortgages purchased by FNMA. All servicers, however, must maintain a certain percentage of ownership of stock with respect to the aggregate principal balances of mortgages serviced by them. The exact stock retention percentage is determined from time to time by FNMA with the approval of the Secretary of Housing and Urban Development and is based primarily on current economic conditions. Such stock retention requirement cannot exceed by law 2 percent of the unpaid principal balances of loans serviced by sellers for FNMA or sold to FNMA.

FREE MARKET SYSTEM

The introduction in May 1968 of the Free Market System (FMS) of mortgage purchasers by FNMA greatly increased the effect of that association upon the secondary mortgage market.

Prior to this innovation, Fannie Mae would establish the price it was willing to pay for FHA/VA home mortgages. Any seller willing to accept Fannie Mae's announced price could do so. Many times Fannie Mae had the best price quote and, therefore, the seller would deal with it instead of selling to private institutions. Thus, in order to achieve its purposes of supporting the secondary market, of not attracting mortgages away from willing private purchasers, and of establishing a more competitive price determination, Fannie Mae created the Free Market System.

PROCEDURE

Under the FMS, Fannie Mae periodically (usually bi-weekly) holds pre-announced mortgage purchase auctions. The auction announcements state the date by which all offers must be tendered, the amount of funds that FNMA will make available for purchases, and competitive and non-competitive sellers' maximum allowable bids, if any.

Two separate auctions are held. One is for FHA and VA loan purchases, the other is for conventional loan purchases.

Bids are accepted for four month commitments only. Bidding is according to the loan yield at which the seller will deliver loans to FNMA.

Offers are submitted by sellers to Fannie Mae by telephone only. Offers of less than $10,000 are not accepted.

Sellers who do not engage in auction competition may submit a noncompetitive offer which will be accepted at the average yield of all accepted competitive offers made for the offering period.

Chart 17-1 is an offering announcement made by Fannie Mae on July 10, 1979, with regard to a FHA/VA auction to be held on July 23, 1979. The announcement also carries the results of the July 9, 1979, auction. In that auction FNMA accepted $19.4 million of the $36.5 million of offers received. The accepted yield range was 10.607 to 10.750 with a weighted average yield of 10.662. On July 9, 1979, the FHA/VA prevailing mortgage interest rate was 10 percent. To produce a yield of 10.662 percent to FNMA it is obvious that the loan must be sold at a discount. Fannie Mae computes yield on the basis of a 30-year maturity mortgage which is prepaid in twelve years. Using FNMA's yield table, a 10 percent loan sold to yield 10.662 must be priced at 95.69 percent of face value or sold at a discount of 4.31.

Chart 17-2 is FNMA's conventional loan announcement for the same period. At the July 10, 1979, conventional action, $27.5 million worth of offers out of $36.0 million were accepted by FNMA. Acceptable yields ranged from 11.497 to 11.631 for a weighted average yield of 11.538. If a seller at the auction bid 11.5 percent yield, its offer would have been accepted and the seller would be able to deliver loans at any coupon rate stated decimally in increments of either one-tenth of 1 percent (.01 percent), one-eighth of 1 percent (0.12 percent), or one-fourth of 1 percent (0.25 percent). An 11.5 percent interest rate mortgage would be deliverable at par. A loan bearing an interest rate in excess of 11.5 percent would also have to be delivered at

CHART 17-1

FEDERAL NATIONAL MORTGAGE ASSOCIATION

FNMA

NOTICE   FNMA No. FMS-FHA/VA 14-79
                                          July 10, 1979

TO: ALL FNMA FHA/VA SELLERS

SUBJECT: FREE MARKET SYSTEM/CONVERTIBLE STANDBY-FHA/VA
          NOTICE OF CURRENT FNMA COMMITMENT INFORMATION
          AND PROJECT REQUIREMENTS

The Federal National Mortgage Association announces that the next Free Market
System (FMS) Auction for commitments to purchase eligible FHA/VA home loans
will be as follows:

         Date of Auction: July 23, 1979
         Hours of Auction: 9 a.m. to 3 p.m., Washington, D.C. time
         Telephone Number: (202) 537-7970

The Offer(s) of a Seller for this Auction may not exceed the applicable maximums set
forth below:

Funds Available: NO LIMIT ESTABLISHED
Competitive Seller's Maximum Amount Per Offer: $3,000,000
Competitive Seller's Maximum No. of Offers: 5
Seller's Non-competitive Maximum: $ 250,000

This Auction will be conducted under the general rules which have been established for
FMS Auctions as stated in the FNMA Selling Contract, and Section 203 of the FNMA
FHA/VA Mortgage Selling Contract Supplement thereto.

Results of the FMS-FHA/VA Auction of   July 9, 1979   (*In Millions)

Type of Contract	Total Offers Eligible*	Total Offers Accepted*	Accepted Yield Range	Weighted Average Yield/ Price of Accepted Offers
4-months	36.5	19.4	10.607-10.750	10.662/95.69

Home Loan Convertible Standby Commitments may be obtained in accordance with
Section 203 of the FNMA FHA/VA Mortgage Selling Contract Supplement.

         -The current yield required is 11.650 , effective 10:00 a.m., 7/10/79
         -The previous yield required was 11.750 .
         -Convertible Standby Commitments issued:
            a) For the two-week period ending 7/9/79: $ 37,200,000
            b) Year to date volume is: $814,549,000
         -Seller's maximum Convertible Standby Commitment Activity per week
         (Monday through Friday) is limited to $ 2 million.

The current interest rate on Loans on the Security of Mortgages is 10.750, effective
10:00 a.m., Tuesday July 10, 1979.

CHART 17-2

FEDERAL NATIONAL MORTGAGE ASSOCIATION

FNMA

<u>NOTICE</u>

FNMA No. FMS-CHM 14-79
July 10, 1979

TO: ALL FNMA CONVENTIONAL SELLERS

SUBJECT: <u>FREE MARKET SYSTEM/CONVERTIBLE STANDBY-CONVENTIONAL</u>
NOTICE OF CURRENT FNMA COMMITMENT INFORMATION

The Federal National Mortgage Association announces that the next Free Market System (FMS) Auction for commitments to purchase eligible Conventional home loans will be as follows:

Date of Auction:	July 23, 1979
Hours of Auction:	9 a.m. to 3 p.m., Washington, D.C. time
Telephone Number:	(202) 537-7970

The Offer (s) of a Seller for this Auction may not exceed the applicable maximums set forth below:

Funds Available:	NO LIMIT ESTABLISHED
Competitive Seller's Maximum Amount Per Offer:	$3,000,000
Competitive Seller's Maximum No. of Offers:	5
Seller's Non-competitive Maximum:	$ 250,000

This Auction will be conducted under the general rules which have been established for FMS Auctions as stated in the FNMA Selling Contract, and Section 402 of the FNMA Conventional Home Mortgage Contract Supplement thereto.

Results of the FMS-CHM Auction of July 9, 1979   (* In Millions)

Type of Contract	Total Offers Eligible*	Total Offers Accepted*	Accepted Yield Range	Weighted Average Yield of Accepted Offers
4-months	36.0	27.5	11.497-11.631	11.538

Home Loan <u>Convertible Standby Commitments</u> may be obtained in accordance with Section 402 of the FNMA Conventional Home Mortgage Contract Supplement.

-The current yield required is <u>12.100</u>, effective 12:00 noon, 6/26/79
-The previous yield required was <u>12.000</u>.
-Convertible Standby Commitments issued:
    a)   For the two-week period ending 7/9/79: $45,042,000
    b)   Year to date volume is: $1,118,609,000
-Seller's maximum Convertible Standby Commitment activity per week (Monday through Friday) is limited to $ 2 million.

par as FNMA will not pay an over par premium for higher yielding loans, but will allow the seller of the loan to retain the excess interest as an additional servicing fee.

FEES AND CHARGES

With each competitive bid submitted under the FMS, the seller agrees to pay to FNMA an offering fee of 0.01 percent of the amount of funds requested. No fee is required for noncompetitive bids.

Acceptance by FNMA of a seller's offer obligated the seller to pay a non-refundable commitment fee of 1/2 of 1 percent. In addition to the commitment fee and at time of delivery of loans to FNMA, the seller must subscribe and pay for Fannie Mae stock equal to 1/4 of 1 percent of the unpaid principal balances of loans so delivered. The stock thus purchased must be retained in order to comply with FNMAs requirement that a seller hold stock equivalent to 1/4 of 1 percent of the unpaid balances of all loans serviced for FNMA. The stock subscription price for FNMA stock during 1974 and early 1975 was $18 per share.

Sellers are not required to deliver loans under commitments purchased. However, failure to deliver will result in the loss of the offering fee and the commitment fee. Such fees compensate FNMA for the risks it takes in agreeing to purchase loans at a fixed yield.

CONVERTIBLE STANDBY COMMITMENTS

FNMA will also purchase FHA/VA and conventional loans outside of the FMS auction pursuant to 12-month convertible standby commitments. As noted in Chart 17-1, the then current FHA/VA yield for a 12-month convertible standby commitment was 11.65 percent and for conventional loans, per Chart 17-2, it was 12.1 percent. Standby commitments were limited to $2 million per seller per week. The cost of these commitments is 0.01 percent commitment fee plus a 0.5 percent processing fee. At time of delivery an additional 0.5 percent fee must be paid.

Loans may be delivered under the standby at the standby yield any time during the life of the commitment. Any time subsequent to four months after issuance of the commitment but prior to expiration, it may be converted to the weighted average yield then prevailing under the FM's auction system. After conversion loans must be delivered in four months or prior to the original expiration date of the standby commitment, whichever date fist occurs. Upon conversion the 0.5 delivery fee becomes due and payable.

The purpose of the standby commitment is to provide the seller with insurance against future increases in yield requirements, a commitment term longer than that obtainable in the FMS auction and an opportunity to improve the standby yield by conversion. The yield requirements for the standby commitments are always higher than the current FMS auction weighted average yield due to the time risk taken by FNMA. Loans must be delivered under a standby within ninety days of their creation.

FHA MULTIFAMILY PROJECT FMS COMMITMENTS

FMS prices for the purchase of FHA-insured multifamily mortgages (mortgages insured under the provisions of the National Housing Act, other than home expiration date of the standby commitment, whichever date first in time occurs. Upon conversion a 1 percent fee becomes due and payable.

Commitments can be obtained by sellers for immediate purchase of mortgages by Fannie Mae or for future delivery (standby commitments).

Immediate purchase contracts are made at the FMS-announced yield with delivery of the loan mandatory within forty-five days. At time of delivery the property secured by the FHA-insured multifamily mortgage must be sufficiently occupied so that the income will cover all project expenses, carrying charges, and payments required by the mortgage. A purchase and marketing fee of 0.5 percent is charged for immediate purchase contracts.

For a loan to be delivered in the future a 24-month standby commitment is available. The prices for FHA-insured multifamily standby commitments are determined periodically by FNMA and are usually much lower (higher discount) than those curently available for FHA/VA loans under the FMS auction. The reason for the lower price and correspondingly higher yield is that they encourage the seller to seek a better price in the private investor sector while still providing a commitment which will enable the holder to obtain construction financing. The seller has the option at the time of delivery to sell the mortgage at the standby price or at the immediate purchase yield. A 1 percent commitment fee is paid for the standby commitment (0.75 percent in the case of a Section 223(b) mortgage) and a purchase and marketing fee of 0.5 percent is due at time of delivery only if the loan is delivered at the immediate purchase contract yield.

An extension of time beyond the 24-month commitment period is allowable at a cost of 0.0416 percent for each 30-day extension.

The majority of FHA insured multifamily projects are committed for under GNMA's special assistance programs (see Chapter 18). Therefore, FNMA's FHA-insured multifamily program is presently only used with regard to mortgages insured by FHA under Sections 213(j), 220(h), 232, 232(i), 223(f), 242, 234(d), or under Section 207 to finance mobile home facilities. FHA multifamily loans sold to FNMA are serviced by FNMA, not by the seller.

RESIDUAL BALANCES

If a balance remains under a FNMA FMS single family commitment, the seller is allowed to deliver one mortgage which exceeds the residual balance. The processing fee, commitment fee, and stock requirement are all applicable to the amount of increase occasioned by the additional loan delivery. The residual balances on several contracts may not be combined. On FMS single family standbys, loans up to 10 percent in excess of the commitment may be delivered.

BACK-TO-BACK COMMITMENTS

Many times builders want a guaranteed fixed price on permanent loans for houses under construction in order to better project sales prices and, accordingly, anticipated profit. They can get a firm price by arranging for a seller to obtain a FNMA free market system commitment for them. This is accomplished by the builder putting up the commitment fee and the seller purchasing the required stock. The seller then issues its commitment to the builder supported

CHART 17-3

PROJECT MORTGAGE REQUIREMENTS

FNMA NO. FMS FHA/VA 14-79   **REPORT DATE: 7-10-79**

MORTGAGE RATES	IMMEDIATE PURCHASE COMMITMENTS PRICE[1]	STANDBY COMMITMENTS PRICE[2]	PRICE[3]	COMMITMENTS PRICE[4]	CONSTRUCTION FINANCING CHARGE[5]	PARTICIPATIONS FINANCING CHARGE[6]
7%	69.75	68.89	64.81	64.17	3.22	3.34
7 1/2%	N/A	N/A	N/A	N/A	2.81	2.92
7 3/4%	75.39	74.47	70.11	69.42	2.60	2.72
8%	77.30	76.35	71.89	71.19	2.39	2.51
8 1/4%	79.21	78.25	73.69	72.98	2.19	2.31
8 1/2%	81.14	80.15	75.50	74.77	1.98	2.11
8 3/4%	83.07	82.06	77.31	76.57	1.77	1.89
9%	85.01	83.98	79.14	78.38	1.57	1.69
9 1/2%	88.92	87.85	82.81	82.02	1.16	1.28

(1) Price is based on a required yield of 10.900% for mortgages insured under Sections 220, 221(d)(3), 221(d)(4), 223(e), 233, and 236 of the National Housing Act.

(2) Price is based on a required yield of 11.050% for mortgages insured under Sections 207, 213, 213(j), 223(f), 231, 232, 232(i), 234(d), 242, and Titles X and XI, or insured under any of the foregoing sections or titles pursuant to Section 223(d).

(3) Price is based on a required yield of 11.800% for mortgages insured under Sections 220, 221(d)(3), 221(d)(4), 223(e), 233, and 236 of the National Housing Act.

(4) Price is based on a required yield of 11.925% for mortgages insured under Sections 207, 213, 213(j), 223(f), 231, 232, 232(i), 234, 242, and Titles X and XI, or insured under any of the foregoing sections or titles pursuant to Section 223(d).

(5) Financing charge is based on a required yield of 10.900% for mortgages insured under Sections 220, 221(d)(3), 221(d)(4), 223(e), 233, and 236 of the National Housing Act.

(6) Financing charge is based on a required yield of 11.050% for mortgages insured under Sections 207, 213, 231, 232, 232(i), 234(d), 242, and Title XI.

NOTE: SINCE THE ABOVE PRICES ARE BASED ON A 40 YEAR MORTGAGE WITH AN AVERAGE LIFE OF 20 YEARS, ADJUSTMENTS IN PRICE WILL BE MADE FOR MORTGAGES HAVING A DIFFERENT MORTGAGE TERM AND AVERAGE LIFE. SECTION 241 MORTGAGES ARE PRICED ACCORDING TO THE SECTION UNDER WHICH THE FIRST MORTGAGE IS INSURED.

by the FNMA takeout commitment. The seller's commitment to the builder will usually provide for a cash penalty in the event of nondelivery of the permanent loan. The penalty is imposed in order to insure a fee to the seller for arranging the commitment in the event that the builder decides to abandon all or part of the commitment by not delivering the previously agreed upon number of loans to the seller.

FNMA MORTGAGE PROGRAMS

In the above discussion of FNMA's Free Market System most of FNMA's mortgage programs were mentioned. However, many of the specific details relating to FNMA's major loan programs: the FHA/VA home mortgage program, its five conventional loan programs, and the FHA Sec. 245 program were not covered. These details are discussed below.

FHA/VA HOME MORTGAGE PROGRAMS

Under its FHA/VA home mortgage program, FNMA will buy mortgages up to the maximum allowed by Congress. Eligible FHA mortgages are those that do not exceed a mortgage amount of $67,500(higher amounts prevail in Alaska, Guam, and Hawaii) and are insured under any of the following sections 220; 221(d)(2); 222; 233; 234; 235; 237; 809; and 223(e). (These programs are further explained in Chapter 15—Federal Housing Administration.)

VA loans guaranteed pursuant to Section 1810, Chapter 37, of Title 38, U.S. Code are acceptable only if such guarantee is based upon the entire amount of the loan and the mortgage amount does not exceed $100,000. All VA loans purchased by FNMA must be guaranteed to the minimum extent of $5,000 or 25 percent of the original principal amount of the mortgage, whichever is the lesser. Acceptable loans must bear an original principal amount, after subtraction of the guaranteed portion, which is not in excess of 75 percent of the purchase price of the property or the reasonable value of the property as determined by VA, whichever is the lesser. VA loans in excess of $55,000 must be accompanied by an independent fee appraisal and meet other specific FNMA requirements.

Loans eligible for purchase are those with unpaid principal balances of $5000 or more with an unexpired term of mortgage no less than ten years. Loans insured or guaranteed for more than twelve months prior to delivery to FNMA may be rejected for purchase.

Units in an FHA-insured condominium or PUD project or VA guaranteed condominium or PUD unit loans are automatically eligible for FNMA's FHA/VA loan purchase program.

CONVENTIONAL HOME MORTGAGE PROGRAMS

For the first time in history, Congress took positive action through passage of the Emergency Home Finance Act of 1970 to provide, under Title II of that act, an increased flow of investment funds into the conventional mortgage market.

This legislation provided for both FNMA and the Federal Home Loan Mortgage Corporation (FHLMC) to adopt conventional mortgage loan purchase programs. In early 1972, FNMA announced its first program for the purchase of conventional home mortgages.

ELIGIBLE MORTGAGES

Mortgages submitted to FNMA for purchase under the conventional loan program must have either an unpaid principal balance not in excess of 80 percent of the value of the property secured or an unpaid principal balance of up to 95 percent of the value of the property under either of the following two circumstances:

1. On loan to values up to 90 percent the seller agrees to repurchase the mortgage upon demand by FNMA if the mortgage is in default and the unpaid principal balance is not below 80 percent of property value; or
2. The portion of unpaid principal balance in excess of 80 percent is guaranteed or insured by a private mortgage loan insurer approved by FNMA. (FNMA maintains a list of approved private mortgage insurers.)

Original loan maturity may not exceed thirty years and the remaining term of all loans submitted for purchase cannot be less than ten years. All loans, however, must be dated less than one year from the date of purchase by FNMA.

The size of the mortgage loan as to unpaid principal balance, must be at least $10,000. The maximum loan amount depends upon the loan to value ratio and the use of acceptable private mortgage insurance. On loan to values up to 80 percent, the maximum loan amount is $93,750 and no private mortgage insurance is required. On 80 percent to 90 percent loan-to-value mortgages, the maximum loan amount is $93,750. On loan to values between 90 percent and 95 percent, the maximum mortgage amount is 75,000. In Alaska and Hawaii the maximums are $112,500 for 95 percent loans and $140,625 for loans 90 percent loan to value and under.

APPRAISAL

Mortgages submitted under the conventional loan program must be accompanied by an appraisal report and supporting data compiled by an appraiser recommended by the seller and acceptable to FNMA.

UNDERWRITING

Sellers are responsible for underwriting all conventional mortgage loans sold to FNMA. Underwriting includes primarily the evaluation and approval of the borrower's credit and the property given as security, Fannie Mae uses a statistical spot check system to determine seller compliance with prudent underwriting standards.

STANDARD FORMS

Both FNMA and FHLMC publish standard note and mortgage forms for use in each state and the District of Columbia, Puerto Rico and the Virgin Islands. Mortgages submitted for purchase to FNMA must be on either FNMA or FHLMC standard forms. FHLMC forms are usually used since they are more universally accepted and provide a seller more options for sale of the loan. If FHLMC forms are used, the seller must notify the mortgagor that while FNMA owns the loan it will not enforce the FHLMC mortgage form provisions pertaining to pre-payment penalty or acceleration upon sale. (Sample FHLMC approved forms are contained in Chapter 19.)

All mortgages must be fully amortized over the loan term on a level payment basis, and must provide for tax and insurance (both hazard and any private loan insurance premiums) escrows.

FNMA will allow the mortgagor to prepay the loan prior to maturity without penalty.

OWNER OCCUPANCY

All loans sold to FNMA must contain the borrower's certification that he will occupy the property securing the loan as his principal residence.

SELLER—SERVICERS

The sellers and servicers of conventional loans sold to FNMA are determined and approved in the same way as sell/servicers for FNMA's FHA/VA loan programs. However, sellers must have their personnal qualified with FNMA to underwrite conventional loans. Servicers receive a fee of 0.375 percent on the unpaid principal balances of all loans serviced for Fannie Mae. When late charges are permissibly included in the loan documents, they may be charged to the mortgagor and retained by the servicer.

SECOND MORTGAGES AND REFINANCING

Under certain circumstances FNMA will purchase a conventional first mortgage loan, subject to an existing second mortgage. Second mortgage loans, however, are not eligible for purchase.

Refinancing of existing mortgages are eligible for purchase if the proceeds of the new loan are used for major improvements to the secured property and if normal financing conditions otherwise exist.

CONVENTIONAL CONDOMINIUM AND PUD MORTGAGE LOAN PROGRAM

In 1974, FNMA began its program for purchase of loans on units in condominium and PUD projects. In addition to compliance with all requirements of FNMAs conventional home mortgage program, loans on units in condominiums or PUD projects must meet specific additional requirements.

ELIGIBLE SELLERS

Sellers eligible under FNMA's other loan programs cannot sell condominium and PUD loans without first qualifying with FNMA. Sellers must qualify one or more of their full-time personnel as number 1 or number 2 underwriters. To qualify as a number 1 underwriter a minimum of three years experience in underwriting one-to-four family homes, residential lots, and units in a condominium or PUD project is required. To qualify as a number 2 underwriter a minimum of five years of full time experience in underwriting at least three of which should be in underwriting commercial or condominium or PUD program is required. All individual loans submitted must be underwritten by seller's number 1 approved underwriter, and all projects submitted for FNMA approval must be underwritten by the seller's number 2 underwriter.

APPRAISERS AND ATTORNEYS

The seller must recommend for FNMA approval appraisers and attorneys experienced respectively in condominium or PUD valuation and legal matters. Each loan submitted for purchase under FNMA's condominium and PUD program must contain an appraisal by such approved appraiser. Each project submitted for approval must have a project appraisal by an approved appraiser and legal documentation prepared or reviewed by an attorney designated by the seller and approved by FNMA.

MASTER PROJECT APPROVAL

The first step in condominium and PUD processing through FNMA is to obtain approval of the project itself. This is accomplished by submitting an application to FNMA which includes:
1. The master evaluation by an accepted appraiser,
2. An opinion of the lenders approved attorney,
3. A thorough market analysis and feasibility by the seller's approved underwriter, and
4. A proposed construction processing fee of $1500 or an existing construction fee of $10.00 per unit for each unit that is submitted for approval.

FNMA will issue its Master Project Approval. Such approval will allow the seller to purchase a FMS commitment and to deliver individual unit loans under the FMS commitment for purchase. Upon delivery of a condominium or PUD loan under a FMS commitment to FNMA for purchase an additional fee of 0.125 percent is to be paid.

ELIGIBLE MORTGAGES

Mortgages eligible for sale are similar to those eligible for sale under the conventional home mortgage program. However, condominium loans cannot exceed 90 percent loan-to-value even though PUD loans may be made up to 95 percent loan-to-value.

A special rider must be attached to the standard mortgage forms when used in conjunction with condominium and PUD loans. These loans are required to have a pre-payment penalty and an acceleration upon sale clause.

SPECIAL CONDOMINIUM AND PUD MORTGAGE LOAN APPROVALS

In 1978 FNMA announced a new program for less involved approval of condominium and PUD loans. In general, this new program covers units in projects which are at least three years old, successfully operating, and in which at least 90 perc of the units have been sold and conveyed.

Under this special program examination fees, market reports, and attorney's opinions are not required.

CONVENTIONAL TWO-TO-FOUR
FAMILY HOME MORTGAGE PROGRAM

Also in 1978, FNMA announced a program for two-to-four family home mortgage. This program moved FNMA into two new areas:
   a) Multiunit conventional lending and
   b) Non-owner occupied property.
The two-to-four family program is generally the same as FNMA's conventional home mortgage program except for occupancy requirements and mortgage amounts.

OCCUPANCY

The borrower on a two-to-four family property is not required to occupy the property. However, non-occupant owner loans are limited to 80 percent loan-to-value and 20-year terms.

MORTGAGE AMOUNTS

The maximum mortgage allowable on a two-to-four family home mortgage is subject to the per unit limits specified under FHA Section 207(c)(3). These limits are related to:
   a) Type of structure,
   b) Number of bedrooms per unit,
   c) Total number of units in the property,
   d) Location of the property, i.e., some areas are FNMA-designated "high cost areas."
Below are the range of mortgage amounts that were effective for FHA Section 207(c)(3) loans in August, 1976:

Number of Bedrooms Per Unit	Range of Amounts* Non-Elevator Structures Basic to Maximum	Elevator Structures Basic to Maximum
0	$19,500-$29,750	$22,500-$33,750
1	21,600- 32,400	25,200- 37,800
2	25,800- 38,700	30,900- 46,350
3	31,800- 47,700	38,700- 58,050
4	36,000- 54,000	43,758- 65,637

(The original principal amount of the mortgage must be a multiple of $50.)

---

* The above maximums may be exceeded by 75% in HVD designed high cost areas.

URBAN LOAN PROGRAMS

In response to requests from the Department of Housing and Urban Development, in 1978 FNMA adopted several programs to stimulate the flow of mortgage credit into the nation's urban areas, particularly inner-city areas.

Under their Urban Loan Participation Program, FNMA will purchase from approved sellers, a 60 to 90 percent participation interest in pools of conventional urban home mortgages on properties located in older residential areas. The criteria for purchase of mortgages under the urban loan participation program are similar to other FNMA conventional loan programs with the following major differences:

a) While the mortgages in the pool need not be originated by the seller, they must be owned by the seller.

b) Two-to-four family mortgages, as well as FNMA-approved condominium and PUD units, are eligible for purchase with mortgage amounts and loan-to-value ratios the same as for FNMA's standard programs.

c) The proceeds of the sale of the participation to FNMA must be re-invested in mortgages on residential or commercial urban properties.

Other urban programs include (a) the purchase of first mortgages financing the acquisition or refinance and rehabilitation of one-to-four family urban area properties, and (b) the making of a line of credit available to eligible institutions for re-investing in FHA, VA, and conventional loans loans on urban area residential or commercial properties.

Special purchase commitments are issued by FNMA for urban loans and provide for either a 4-month term plus a 2-month extension for mortgages on existing urban property, or a 6-month term plus a 6-month extension for mortgages on urban property that is proposed, under construction, or being substantially rehabiliatated. A convertible standby commitment for the purchase of FHA, VA, and conventional mortgages on urban properties is also made available by FNMA.

GRADUATED PAYMENT MORTGAGES

When the graduated payment mortgage (GPM) program was adopted by FHA in 1978, FNMA was the only source for secondary market sales of these loans. Since 1978, financial institutions as well as the GNMA security program have become sources for the purchase of GPM's. Nevertheless, FNMA played a major initial role in the introduction of the GPM and continues to be a purchaser of these loans.

GPM's are purchased by FNMA under the same commitment and delivery procedure used for FHA/VA loans. However, due to the negative amortization characteristic of these loans during the initial loan years, FNMA requires a premium discount on purchase over and above its FHA/VA loan pricing.

The premium discounts are by GPM plans and are as follows:

PLAN NUMBER	PRICE ADJUSTMENT
I	0.10 of 1 percent
II	0.20 of 1 percent
III	0.30 of 1 percent
IV	0.20 of 1 percent
V	0.30 of 1 percent

Graduated payment mortgages are discussed in detail in Chapters 1 and 15.

PRIOR APPROVALS

Some lenders wish to be assured that a permanent mortgage will be salable if originated. To facilitate this situation, FNMA has formulated a prior approval program. The prior approval procedure covers not only the individual buyer and property, but can also be used by sellers to gain prior FNMA approval of subdivisions, condominiums, and PUDs. By first obtaining a prior approval, the seller knows that the loan when originated will be fully salable to FNMA. FNMAs prior approval is not unlike obtaining an FHA or VA buyer and property approval as is done under normal FHA and VA loan processing.

CONSTRUCTION LOANS

Under its participation program FNMA will provide funds for loan advances during the construction period on a participation basis with the seller for certain eligible FHA multifamily housing projects where the long-term permanent financing is to be provided either by GNMA or FNMA. All loan advances under the program are disbursed and administered by the seller in accordance with FHA regulations and procedures.

ELIGIBLE PROJECTS

Projects eligible for construction loan participations include all major FHA insurance programs for which FNMA provides permanent loans, except Section 213 (j), 223 (d), and Title X.

FEES

FHA project loan mortgages include a fee equal to 2 percent of the mortgage amount, which fee is designated an "initial service charge." This fee is collected by the seller at the time of the project loan closing and is shared with FNMA as compensation to FNMA for its construction loan participation. Fannie Mae's share of the initial service charge is 1.5 percent on its participation; the seller will receive 0.5 percent on FNMA's participation plus 2 percent on its own share of the loan.

In addition FNMA collects a finance charge related to the interest rate on the insured mortgage. The finance charges in effect by FNMA on July 10, 1979, are noted on Chart 17-3. The finance charges are assessed in order to provide FNMA with a constant yield irrespective of the FHA-insured rate. As can be seen from Chart 17-3, there would be a 1.57 percent finance charge on a Section 221(d)(4) loan if the FHA-insured rate on the project mortgage in the construction loan participation is 9 percent. But if the rate on this same loan is 7 percent, a 3.22 finance charge would be made. The finance charge presumes a 24-month loan period. Hence, if the construction loan is for less than 24-months, the finance charge reduced by one-twenty-fourth for each month less than twenty-four. In the event that the project is not completed during a 24-month construction loan term, then an additional finance charge equal to one-twelfth of the original finance charge is assessed for each month in excess of 24 months until the project is completed and FNMA is repaid.

PARTICIPATION EXTENT

Fannie Mae's participation in the construction portion of a mortgage loan will not exceed 95 percent of the amount of each FHA insured advance, based upon the seller and FNMA being the only participants. In the event there are others willing and desirous of participating in the loan, the specific participation percentages are negotiated between the parties and must be prior approved by FNMA.

REQUIREMENTS

Primary requirements of the construction loan participation program are that no construction has commenced on the project, unless FHA has authorized the start of construction prior to the FHA initial closing, and that FHA has issued its firm commitment to insure the project loan and all construction advances.

The interest rate and loan maturity on construction loans are as established by FHA.

FLOOD INSURANCE

Flood insurance is required on all mortgages purchased by FNMA where the properties are located in areas designated by the Secretary of HUD as having special flood hazards. Mortgages on properties in those locales designated as hazard areas in jurisdictions which have not agreed to participate in the national flood insurance program will not be purchased by FNMA since HUD approved flood insurance is not available in those areas. Flood areas are shown on HUD Flood Insurance Boundary Maps or Insurance Rate Maps issued by HUDs Flood Insurance Administration. Acceptable flood insurance policies are those standard policies issued by members of the National Flood Insurers Association.

MORTGAGE SALE

As has been stated, FNMAs purpose is to purchase mortgages in times when funds for mortgage investment are scarce and to sell loans when funds are again in plentiful supply. However, only, in 1958 and 1963 was FNMA able to sell more loans than it purchased. Below is a list of mortgage loan purchases and sales by FNMA during the 10-year period 1969-78:

YEAR	TOTAL PURCHASES (rounded)	TOTAL SALES (rounded)
1969	$4.2 billion	None
1970	5.5 billion	$ 20 million
1971	4.0 billion	336 million
1972	3.9 billion	208 million
1973	6.3 billion	71 million
1974	7.0 billion	4 million
1975	4.3 billion	2 million
1976	3.6 billion	86 million
1977	4.8 billion	82 million
1978	12.3 billion	9 million

It can readily be seen that even though FNMA does buy and sell mortgages it in fact is primarily a long-term investor in mortgages for its portfolio has grown steadily in size as FNMA has purchased far more loans than it has sold.

Particularly, when there is an excess of funds in the mortgage market, FNMA does stand ready to sell loans. Sales are accomplished by FNMA in three ways:

1. Under its "over-the-counter" program FNMA announces the availability of mortgages for sale at posted prices. The method works best when mortgage rates are stable. When rates are rising, sales under this program drop sharply as investors wait yields higher than those posted by FNMA.

2. Negotiated sales on an individual basis is best when mortgage rates are rising.

3. From time to time FNMA will hold a sale auction of mortgages. However this method is feasible only when a large volume of loans are involved.

RECENT TRENDS

FNMA has dynamically moved into the conventional loan market in recent years. In 1976 and 1977, FNMA purchased more conventional home loans than FHA/VA loans, and in 1978, issued more conventional loan commitments than FHA/VA

CHART 17-4

Financial and Statistical Data
Dollars in millions

For the Year	1974	1973	1972	1971	1970
Commitments Issued:					
FNMA Direct:					
Home—Government insured or guaranteed	$ 4,333	$ 3,793	$ 3,047	$ 3,695	$ 4,914
—Conventional	1,051	2,332	319	—	—
Total home mortgage commitments	5,384	6,125	3,366	3,695	4,914
Project	5	41	79	1,440	2,676
Total FNMA direct commitments issued	5,389	6,166	3,445	5,135	7,590
Tandem Plans (a)	5,376	2,748	5,478	4,692	417
Total commitments issued	$10,765	$ 8,914	$ 8,923	$ 9,827	$ 8,007
Mortgages and Loans Purchased:					
Home—Government insured or guaranteed	$ 3,617	$ 3,231	$ 2,541	$ 2,742	$ 4,778
—Conventional	1,129	939	55	—	—
Total home mortgages purchased	4,746	4,170	2,596	2,742	4,778
Project	2,208	1,957	1,104	832	301
Participations in project construction loans	65	125	164	466	453
Total mortgages and loans purchased	$ 7,019	$ 6,252	$ 3,864	$ 4,040	$ 5,532
Debt Issued:					
Discount notes	$ 6,396	$ 4,124	$ 2,782	$ 4,474	$ 8,755
Debentures	6,600	6,061	4,314	8,350	6,300
Subordinated capital debentures	—	—	250	—	200
Convertible capital debentures	—	—	—	250	—
Mortgage backed bonds	—	278	—	—	1,000
Total debt issued	$12,996	$10,463	$ 7,346	$13,074	$16,255

(a)"Tandem plans" refers to various programs wherein the Federal National Mortgage Association has contracted with the Government National Mortgage Association (GNMA), an agency in the Department of Housing and Urban Development, in the issuance of commitments and the purchase of mortgages pursuant to certain Federal programs.

commitments (see Chart 17-4). This trend should continue as the new FNMA conventional loan programs gain acceptance.

It is also important to note FNMA initial involvement in inner-city financing, an involvement that has political overtones and may be a continued requirement for FNMA as the nation tries to find solutions for reactivating its blighted urban areas.

CONCLUSION

In 1978, Fannie Mae support of the secondary mortgage market through loan purchases totaled slightly more than $12.3 billion, representing a year of record loan purchase for FNMA. At the same time FNMA sold approximately $9 billion in mortgage loans. It also borrowed over $20 billion to support its purchase operations.

The volume of support given by FNMA to the mortgage market in future years will be governed by economic conditions in general, the amount of funds plowed into mortgage purchases by the thrift institutions, and the additional volume created by Fannie Mae's conventional loan programs. Nevertheless, Fannie Mae has proven its worth by giving valuable and considerable support to the secondary market in times of need. Its support of $7 billion in the money-short, economically disastrous year of 1974 and again with $12.3 billion in 1978 is proof of this contention.

QUESTIONS FOR THOUGHT AND DISCUSSION

1. What is the secondary market and what part does FNMA play in it?
2. How does FNMA conduct its business?
3. Do you feel FNMA should be totally public, totally private, or maintain its present status? Why?
4. What is the Free Market System and how does it operate?
5. Should FNMA as a private corporation be required by the government to increase its urban loan involvement?
6. Describe FNMA's construction loan participation program.

18

GOVERNMENT NATIONAL MORTGAGE ASSOCIATION

The Housing Act of 1968, which made FNMA a private corporation, established a new corporation known as the Government National Mortgage Association (GNMA). Ginnie Mae, the popular name given to GNMA, was invested with the purpose of carrying on the FNMA functions which could not economically be carried out in the private sector and thus were left with the Department of Housing and Urban Development (see Chart 18-1).

HISTORY

GNMA assumed responsibility for the remaining two functions of the 1954-68 FNMA and added one new function, as follows:

1. The special assistance function.
2. The management and liquidating of certain previously acquired mortgages, as well as the administration as trustee of Fannie Mae's old Participation Certificate program.
3. The mortgage backed security program (a new function).

Eligibility to deal with GNMA is extended to those companies and institutions which have met FNMA qualifications. Common procedure is for the seller to be jointly approved by FNMA/GNMA when application is made to either for seller approval. Through its regional offices Fannie Mae handles the day-to-day administrative functions for FNMA. Additional qualification is required of those participating in the mortgage backed security program.

SPECIAL ASSISTANCE FUNCTION

This function involves a number of programs under which Ginnie Mae

CHART 18-1

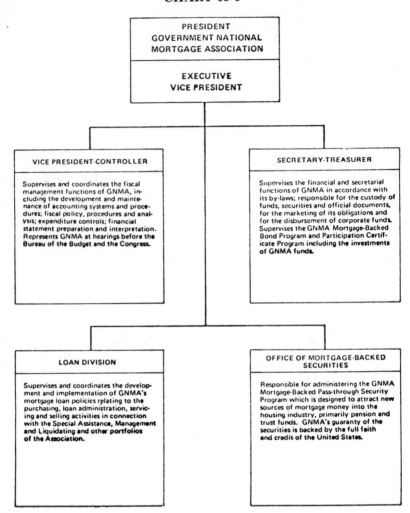

Source: Department of Housing and Urban Development, Washington, D.C.

purchases mortgage loans from private lenders. The specific programs are established from time to time by Congress or the President of the United States. By nature, all such programs involve mortgages which otherwise would not be readily salable, unless at deep discounts, due either to the unconventional nature of the risk involved or to the low coupon interest rates producing uncompetitive and thus unattractive yields.

Funds for GNMA's special assistance function are borrowed primarily from the treasury. Specific limitations on Ginnie Mae's borrowing are obtained from its portfolio liquidations, sales of beneficial interest certificates, sales of mortgage participations, and net earnings.

The special assistance function is generally geared to providing a market for selected residential property mortgage loans pending their private market acceptance. All programs are designed to provide acceptable housing to persons otherwise unable (for economic or geographic reasons) to obtain such housing under normal real estate financing programs. Directly providing a market for otherwise undesirable mortgage loans has the indirect effect of stimulating private development of housing.

Mortgage lenders are willing to finance buildings when they know they have a ready investor for the mortgages they originate.

Presently, Ginnie Mae has twenty-seven special assistance programs, some of which have been phased out and others which have been newly created.

Program Number	Description	Effective Date	Comment
1	Disaster Housing	Nov. 1, 1954	GNMA will purchase FHA/VA mortgages on properties in areas designated by the President of the United States as major disaster areas. The purpose of the program is to provide housing for families who are victims of disasters such as floods, earthquakes, tornadoes, and fires. As of late 1975, 283 disaster area housing programs have been established.
2	Properties in Guam	Nov. 4, 1954	Under this program FHA/VA mortgages secured on property located in Guam are eligible for GNMA purchases.
3	Urban Renewal	May 1, 1955	This program covers the purchase of FHA/VA mortgages on properties in urban renewal areas including home improvement mortgage loans and mortgages on displaced family occupied residences.
4	Properties in Alaska		Program terminated.
5	Military and Defense Housing		Program terminated.
6	Cooperative Housing Mortgages	Aug. 16, 1955	This program covers purchase of FHA Sec. 213 cooperative Housing Mortgages.
7	Armed Services Housing		Program Inactive since December, 1965.
8	Elderly Housing	Oct. 19, 1956	GNMA is authorized under this program to purchase FHA Sec. 231 insured mortgages on non-profit sponsored (mortgagor) elderly housing projects.
9	Low Cost Housing Mortgages		Program terminated.
10	Low and Moderate Priced Housing Mortgages		Program terminated.
11	Below Market Interest Rate (BMIR) Mortgages	Aug. 9, 1961	Under this program mortgages insured under FHA Secs. 21(d)3.21(h).221(i) and 21(j) and containing a below market interest rate are eligible for purchase.
12	Experimental Housing Mortgages	Aug. 9, 1961	This covers mortgages insured by FHA under Sec. 233 of the National Housing Act.
13	Restricted Indian Lands Mortgages	Nov. 21, 1962	GNMA may purchase under this program FHA/VA mortgages on properties covering housing for owners of property in Indian Lands.

14	Low and Moderate Cost Housing Mortgages	Nov. 29, 1966	This program allows GNMA to purchase FHA/VA mortgages on single family properties FHA loans purchased must be insured under either Sec. 203(h). 203(i), 220,221(d), or 222 of the National Housing Act. Further limitations of maximum loan values are placed upon mortgages eligible for purchase. For example, the original principal obligation on one family residences mortgages cannot exceed $18,000 or $21,000 in high cost areas with an increase of $3000 allowed where a 5 or more person family is purchasing a 4 or more bedroom home.
15	Rent Supplement Project Mortgages		Program terminated.
16	Rehabilitation Housing Sales Mortgages	Sept. 12, 1969	Under this program mortgages insured under Sections 235(j)(l) and 235(j)(4) are eligible for purchase. Such mortgages are created through a release from a project mortgage obtained to rehabilitate groups of houses, usually in low to moderate income areas.
17	Low and Moderate Cost Housing Mortgages	Nov. 26, 1969	This program covers GNMA purchase of FHA Sec. 221(d)(3) Rent Supplement and Sec. 236 (Interest Supplement mortgages). These mortgages cover properties for multifamily occupancy where the occupants or the mortgagee receives subsidies from the federal government which effectively reduce the unit rental to the occupant. This program utilizes the tandem plan later described.
18	Constructed or Rehabilitated Housing	Jan. 26, 1970	This program provides for Tandem Plan purchase of Sec. 235(i) and Sec. 237 FHA insured mortgages on single family residences. Sec. 235 provides for interest subsidies to cause a reduction in mortgages payment geared to the mortgagor's annual income. Sec. 237 is used where the normal Sec. 235 applicant has credit problems.
19	Operation Breakthrough	Jan. 18, 1971	Through this program support is given to Operation Breakthrough prototype projects developed throughout the country by private enterprise under the auspices of FHA. The Operation Breakthrough program is explained in Chapter 20.
20	Mortgages on Properties in Guam	Feb. 17, 1971	This GNMA special assistance program covers the purchase of FHA/VA mortgages on properties located on Guam and is designated for use in conjunction with the Tandem Plan. It in essence replaces Program No. 2.
21	Unsubsidized Multifamily Mortgages	Aug. 7, 1971	This program was adopted to provide such assistance as is necessary to maintain the FHA interest rate at 7 per cent per annum by holding discounts to an established maximum. Loans insured under FHA Sections 207, 213, 220, 221(d)3, 221(d),4, 231, 232, 233, 234(d), and 236, are eligible for benefits under this program.

			(Section 221(d)3 and Section 236 mortgage are also eligible for purchase under Program No. 17)
22	Unsubsidized Home Mortgages	Aug. 7, 1971	This program was adopted at the same time and for the same purpose as Program No. 21. It applies to newly constructed home mortgages insured under FHA Sections 203, 220, 221(d)(2), 222, 223, 234(c), 235(i), 235(j)(4), 237, 223(e), or 809, and to VA loans.
23	Unsubsidized Project Mortgages		Applicable to below market interest rate mortgages insured under 233(e), 207 (except mobile homes), 213, 220, 221(d)3 market rate, 221(d)4, 231, 232, and 234.
24	Unsubsidized Home Mortgages	Jan. 2, 1975	This program, created by the Emergency Home Purchase Act of 1974 provides for the purchase of FHA and VA loans at below market interest rates.
25	Section 8 Project Mortgages		This program provids for the purchase of mortgages on multifamily projects under contract for Section 8 Rental Assistance.
27	Multifamily Projects in Action Grant Cities		For purchase of multifamily project mortgages located in designated cities and insured under FHA Sec. 223(e), 207, 213, 220, 221(d)(3) Market Rate, 221(d)4, 231, and 234(d).
29	Multifamily Projects in Neighborhood Strategy Areas in Action Grant Cities		Same as Program 27 but multifamily project must be located in a designated or proposed neighborhood strategy area of concentrated community development activity in an Action Grant eligible city or county.
30	Unsubsidized Conventional Home Mortgages		Below market interest rate program for conventional single family home loans—GNMA/FNMA Conventional Home Mortgage Program.

A major benefit derived from the GNMA Special Assistance Program is the ability of lenders to deliver loans at or close to par (100 percent of face value of mortgage without discount). Many FHA-insured mortgages, such as those insured under Sec. 213, Sec. 221(d)3, Sec. 236 or others, would have to be sold to FNMA or another investor at heavy discounts, depending upon the market. The ability to deliver to GNMA allows the mortgagor to save the discount and may provide the lender with a lending opportunity that might otherwise fail. The discount savings is particularly helpful to nonprofit sponsors of FHA-insured multifamily programs who do not usually have the excess funds required to pay mortgage discounts.

There are, however, eight exceptions to the par purchase of mortgages by GNMA. The exceptions are Programs 18, 21, 22, 23, 24, 25, 27, and 29.

In mid-1971, with discounts on FHA and VA loans as high as ten points, the President of the United States decided to hold the prevailing FHA and VA rate at 7 percent rather than raise the interest rate and a reasonable discount floor, GNMA was authorized to support the price of FHA and VA mortgages at a price of 96 for new construction and 95 for existing structures. Program 21 provides the rules and regulations for the mortgage price support as set forth above for single family mortgage. Program 22 is a similar program for multifamily mortgages. Both programs still exist today with different price support than when originally created. These programs are designed for tandem plan use, which will be explained later.

Providing special assistance for unsubsidized mortgages was a revolutionary theory which greatly affected the cost of FHA and VA loans. By using government funds to hold the interest rate and discounts at a set level, GNMA through programs 21 and 22, supported mortgages at yields less than corporate AAA bonds and low ratio conventional loans—a historic first.

The Emergency Home Purchase Assistance Act of 1974, passed on October 18, 1974, again brought revolutionary changes to the GNMA special assistance programs. This act established a joint FNMA/GNMA loan purchase program for conventional loans designated the: GNMA/FNMA Conventional Home Mortgage Program. For the first time in history, a special assistance program was created for non-FHA/VA loans. The program further deviated from the previous norm by allowing 10 percent of all funds appropriated for this program to be used for the purchase of mortgages on existing homes.

Programs 25, 27, and 29 were adopted to stimulate multifamily project development. All three programs provide for below market interest rate loan without which the majority of such projects would be economically unfeasible. Program 25 is for FHA multifamily projects which provide Section 8 rental assistance payment for lower income occupants, whereas Programs 27 and 29 seek to create housing activity in designated inner city and urban areas.

Programs 21, 22, 23, 24, and 30 are significant of a trend that will most certainly continue into the future—government support of interest rates in order to constantly stimulate the sale and purchase or rental of housing for low to moderate income families, particularly in times of high interest rates and mortgage money shortages. Programs 25, 27, and 29 are also significant of the trend toward low interest rate subsidies by GNMA, but are in themselves indicative of GNMA's increasing activity in the area of low income family housing and urban area redevelopment.

Thus the special assistance programs which began as programs to supply a source of funds for otherwise unsalable mortgages have now become programs to subsidize mortgage loan interest rates for both FHA/VA and conventional home and multifamily mortgages.

Each special assistance program has its own special requirements. However, in general GNMA will issue its forward or immediate purchase contact to buy mortgages under a specific program. Only those mortgages delivered under programs 1, 2, 3, 12, and 13 are eligible for either one or the other type commitment. All others must utilize the forward commitments. The period of commitment issued by GNMA parallels the FNMA program where there is dual purchase authorization; otherwise the specific program requirements govern.

Fees and charges under the GNMA's programs are similar to those established by FNMA, but vary according to the specific program.

The total dollar volume of support by GNMA under its special assistance mortgage purchase programs during fiscal 1978 amounted to $1,117 million in purchases and $1.96 billion in commitments (see Chart 18-2).

TANDEM PLAN

Since Ginnie Mae's special assistance function is supported primarily by borrowings from the United States treasury, the volume of assistance can be increased if mortgages purchased by GNMA can be immediately resold. Additionally the volume can be accelerated by underutilization of dollar ceilings placed on its programs. For example, the total amount of mortgages committed for or outstanding at any one time under Program 17 is limited to $1 billion.

Thus, if a $5 million mortgage is purchased by GNMA and immediately resold for $4.8 million, then only $200,000 and not $5 million of the $1 billion allocation is used. It can easily be seen how this multiplication effect can enhance GNMAs support of the mortgage market.

It is this concept that gave birth to the tandem plan. The tandem plan is a two-step process whereby GNMA commits to purchase mortgages under its particular programs and then obtains a FNMA commitment to buy the same mortgages at FNMAs prevailing discount rate. The plan, however, is not limited

CHART 18-2

GNMA Mortgage
Commitments-Purchases-Sales
October 1, 1977 Through September 30, 1978
(dollars in thousands)

Commitments:	Units	Amount
Program 17	1,457	$ 44,254
Program 21*	. . .	2,833
Program 23A*	. . .	2,755
Program 23B*	. . .	116,860
Program 25	50,263	1,262,359
Program 27	18,974	529,237
	70,694	$1,958,298

Purchases:		
Program 17	4,308	$ 98,724
Program 21	3,142	65,735
Program 23	47,385	953,032
	54,835	$1,117,491

Sales:		
Single-Family	18,662	$ 602,789
Multifamily	12,447	220,310
Conventional	3,408	114,221
	34,517	$ 937,320

**note: No additional units committed for in fiscal year 1978.
Figures in amount column refer to increases in dollar amount of outstanding commitments.

to sales to FNMA alone. Government National Mortgage Association may tandem a mortgage with any investor and does so if the sale can be made at a price more favorable than that quoted by FNMA. In fact, in recent years, GNMA has sold primarily to non-FNMA purchasers. When the commitments are filled, GNMA ends up out of pocket for only the discount. Hence, more projects can be financed and the federal budget is less burdened. As originally adopted, only mortgages made with nonprofit mortgagors were eligible for purchase under the tandem plan, but GNMA regulations have since been revised to include any mortgages normally eligible for asisstance, including nonsubsidized ones. This change has favorably affected Section 236 and Section 221(d)3 Rent Supplement Programs as well as nonsubsidized multifamily and home loans.

Public auction sales of special assistance mortgages over recent years has produced prices above the prevailing mortgage market level and has been a successful means of disposing of tandem plan acquired loans. Most purchases at the public auction of FHA/VA mortgages have pooled their loans under GNMA-guaranteed mortgage backed securities.

Chart 18-2 reflects that GNMA sales activity in fiscal 1978 nearly equaled the purchase activity.

MANAGEMENT AND LIQUIDATION FUNCTION

When FNMA was partitioned in 1968, GNMA acquired the responsibility of management and liquidation of mortgage loans acquired for the government's account by FNMA between 1938 and 1954, including mortgages acquired after 1954 from authorized sources, such as residential mortgages purchased from federal instrumentalities.

By statutory enactment, Ginnie Mae's management and liquidation function is to be performed at a minimum cost to the federal government and carried out both in an orderly manner and with as little adverse effect upon the residential mortgage market as possible.

Part of the financing for the management and liquidation function is attracted from private sources pursuant to fiduciary powers vested in FNMA by the Housing Act of 1964. Mortgages in portfolio and other similar obligations obtained from the Farmers Home Administration, HEW, HUD, VA, the Small Business Administration, and the Export-Import Bank are pooled together as collateral for shares of beneficial interest sold under a trust indenture or straight mortgage participation. These beneficial interest shares and participations are sold to private investors under what is termed FNMA's Participating Certificates Trustee Program. In its corporate, nonfiduciary capacity, GNMA is authorized to guaranty payment of the participations so issued. As of September 30, 1978, $3.2 billion in participation sales certificates were outstanding compared to $9.6 which were originally issued.

Funds for the management and liquidation function are borrowed from the United States treasury and are supplemented by sales of beneficial interest shares and participations portfolio liquidations, net earnings, and sometimes by the sale of GNMA obligations to private investors.

The most important power given Ginnie Mae under its management and liquidation function is the authority to guarantee the timely payment of principal and interest on certificates issued against pools of federal government guaranteed mortgages. This authority, as granted under the Housing and Urban Development Act of 1968, has been expanded into Ginnie Mae's mortgage backed security program.

MORTGAGE BACKED SECURITY PROGRAM

Under its statutory authority, contained in Section 306(g) of the National Housing Act, Ginnie Mae may guarantee the timely payment of principal and interest each month by issuers to holders of securities backed by pools of mortgages insured or guaranteed by FHA, VA, or the Farmers Home Administration. The Ginnie Mae guaranty is backed by the full faith and credit of the federal government. Thus the securities so guaranteed are better in grade than AAA rated corporate bonds. In the event Ginnie Mae has to perform under its guaranty, it is permitted to borrow needed funds from the United States treasury. (See Chart 18-3: Mortgage backed security certificate and reverse-side assignment.)

ELIGIBLE ISSUERS

Under the guaranty program, mortgages are pooled and securities issued by an FHA-approved mortgagee. The issued securities are then usually sold to investors. It is possible for the issuer to purchase his own securities for subsequent resale or to hold for investment purposes. In addition to FHA mortgagee status, however, the issuer must generally maintain a net worth of $100,000 to $500,000 depending upon the size of the issue.

The issuer is usually a mortgage company or financial institution that originated the mortgages which are pooled as collateral for the mortgage backed security. Under the program the issuer is required to administer the pooled mortgage either by directly servicing them or by sub-contracting the servicing function to others.

While there can be only one issuer per single mortgage pool, two or more mortgagees may agree to form a pool of morrgages so long as one mortgagor is designated the issuer and bears full responsibility for formation and administration of the pool.

POOL FORMATION

An FHA mortgagee, upon deciding to become an issuer of securities guaranteed by GNMA and backed by a pool of government insured or guaranteed mortgages, makes application to GNMA for approval of the proposed issue. Upon approval, the issuer has one year to originate or otherwise acquire the mortgages that will constitute the pool. The pool of mortgages must be in a minimum amount of one million dollars and is required to have homogeneity with respect to interest rates and type of dwelling (one-to-four family or multifamily). Where possible the mortgage maturities should be similar. Mortgages constituting the pool must have been insured or guaranteed within twelve months (twenty-four months for multifamily projects) from the date of GNMAs guaranty commitment.

When the pool is formed the issuer delivers the documents supporting the mortgages to a "custodian," usually the trust department of a commercial bank.

CHART 18-3(Front)

Sample Mortgage Backed Certificate Guaranteed by Government National Mortgage Association

Source: Government National Mortgage Association.

CHART 18-3(Back)

[Note: this is reverse side of GNMA Mortgage Backed Certificate.]

ASSIGNMENT

I AM THE OWNER, OR THE DULY AUTHORIZED REPRESENTATIVE OF THE OWNER, OF THE WITHIN MORTGAGE BACKED CERTIFICATE AND FOR VALUE RECEIVED HEREBY ASSIGN THE SAME TO

_____
(ASSIGNEE)

AND AUTHORIZE THE TRANSFER THEREOF ON THE BOOKS OF THE ISSUER.

_____
(SIGNATURE OF ASSIGNOR)

PERSONALLY APPEARED BEFORE ME THE ABOVE NAMED PERSON, WHOSE IDENTITY IS WELL KNOWN OR PROVED TO ME, AND SIGNED THE ABOVE ASSIGNMENT, ACKNOWLEDGING IT TO BE HIS FREE ACT AND DEED. WITNESS MY HAND, OFFICIAL DESIGNATION, AND SEAL.

_____   _____
(SIGNATURE OF WITNESSING OFFICER)   (OFFICIAL DESIGNATION)

SEAL   DATED AT_____   _____, 19____.

ASSIGNMENT

I AM THE OWNER, OR THE DULY AUTHORIZED REPRESENTATIVE OF THE OWNER, OF THE WITHIN MORTGAGE BACKED CERTIFICATE AND FOR VALUE RECEIVED HEREBY ASSIGN THE SAME TO

_____
(ASSIGNEE)

AND AUTHORIZE THE TRANSFER THEREOF ON THE BOOKS OF THE ISSUER.

_____
(SIGNATURE OF ASSIGNOR)

PERSONALLY APPEARED BEFORE ME THE ABOVE NAMED PERSON, WHOSE IDENTITY IS WELL KNOWN OR PROVED TO ME, AND SIGNED THE ABOVE ASSIGNMENT, ACKNOWLEDGING IT TO BE HIS FREE ACT AND DEED. WITNESS MY HAND, OFFICIAL DESIGNATION, AND SEAL.

_____   _____
(SIGNATURE OF WITNESSING OFFICER)   (OFFICIAL DESIGNATION)

SEAL   DATED AT_____   _____, 19____.

INSTRUCTIONS

TO ASSIGN THIS MORTGAGE BACKED CERTIFICATE, THE OWNER, OR HIS DULY AUTHORIZED REPRESENTATIVE, SHALL APPEAR BEFORE AN OFFICER AUTHORIZED TO WITNESS ASSIGNMENTS, ESTABLISH HIS IDENTITY TO THE SATISFACTION OF SUCH OFFICER, AND IN HIS PRESENCE EXECUTE THE ASSIGNMENT, USING ONE OF THE ABOVE FORMS. THE WITNESSING OFFICER MUST THEN AFFIX HIS SIGNATURE, OFFICIAL DESIGNATION, AND SEAL, IF ANY, AND ADD THE PLACE AND DATE OF EXECUTION. OFFICERS AUTHORIZED TO WITNESS ASSIGNMENTS INCLUDE EXECUTIVE OFFICERS OF BANKS AND TRUST COMPANIES INCORPORATED IN THE UNITED STATES OR ITS ORGANIZED TERRITORIES, AND THEIR BRANCHES, DOMESTIC AND FOREIGN. IF ADDITIONAL ASSIGNMENTS ARE REQUIRED, A FORM SIMILAR TO THE ABOVE MAY BE WRITTEN OR TYPED HEREON. FULL INFORMATION REGARDING ASSIGNMENTS MAY BE OBTAINED FROM THE ISSUER.

IMPORTANT

THIS MORTGAGE BACKED CERTIFICATE SHOULD NOT BE ASSIGNED UNLESS ACCOMPANIED BY A CURRENT MONTHLY REMITTANCE ADVICE SETTING FORTH THE OUTSTANDING PRINCIPAL BALANCE OF THE CERTIFICATE. THE PRINCIPAL BALANCE ON THE REMITTANCE ADVICE MAY BE VERIFIED BY CONTACTING THE ISSUER NAMED THEREON.

Source: Government National Mortgage Association.

Under agreement with the issuer the custodian is charged with the safekeeping of the mortgage documents. Whenever any of the documents are required in order to institute foreclosure proceedings, because of payment in full or for any other appropriate reason, the custodian is authorized upon satisfactory evidence to release them as required.

If a default occurs, Ginnie Mae may demand that all documents be turned over too it or may continue the custodial arrangement at will.

After the custodian inspects the documents and certifies that all is in order, GNMA issues its guaranty of the securities. The securities are then sold to investors.

SECURITIES

The major type of security authorized for issuance is the pass-through. This security provides for the timely payment by the security issuer to each registered holder, such holder's pro-rata share of principal when collected plus interest on the unpaid principal balance of each security at a fixed rate, whether or not collected by the issuer.

Principal and interest to be paid the holders include all mortgage prepayments and all mortgage foreclosure proceeds, but are reduced by servicing fees, costs of foreclosure and other costs as approved by GNMA.

The minimum face amount of any single pass-through security is required to be $25,000. Face amounts over the $25,000 minimum must generally be in increments of $5,000.

Each security must be registered. With the nationwide acceptance of the GNMA program the securities are readily transferable in the same manner as major common stocks.

Securities are sold in the same manner as bonds. That is, they are priced according to interest rate. For example, a security issued against a pool of 8 percent interest rate mortgages will bear a coupon rate of 7.5 percent after loan servicing and GNMA fees are deducted. If the security is purchased at 95 percent of par value, it would yield 8.20 percent on a 30-year maturity—prepaid on 12-year basis. However, if the investor only requires a 7.5 percent yield, the security can be sold at par. Similarly, resale prices depend upon the condition of the market at the time of sale.

Compared to a bond yield, however, the GNMA backed security is slightly higher. Bond interest is paid semi-annually whereas interest on the mortgage security is paid monthly. Thus a compounding of mortgage backed security interest rates produces a yield higher than the equivalent bond rate. An example is an 8 percent mortgage security which yields 8 percent at par and 8.13 percent at par with interest compounded monthly. This is a 13-basis points difference over a corresponding 8 percent par bond.

On the other hand, bonds do not return principal in dribbles, but pay it at one time. Hence, the mortgage backed security presents a principal reinvestment problem that is not present with a bond.

BOND TYPE SECURITIES

The desirability of securities which pay periodic interest and have single maturities was recognized by Congress in the creation of the mortgage backed security program.

From time to time GNMA will guarantee, subject to United States treasury approval, securities issued in individual minimum face amounts of $25,000 provided the total issue equals or exceeds $100 million. If the total issue equals or exceeds $200 million then one or more maturity dates are permitted.

Issuers of the bond-type security, however, are limited to those whose assets are $50 million or more. Interest is paid semi-annually on these securities and principal is paid only at maturity.

Issuers of the bond-type security, however, are limited to those whose assets are $50 million or more.

Under this security program the issuer must establish a method of principal reinvestment in order to insure continued payment of the interest rate specified in the bond-type security.

During the period from sale of the first mortgage backed security on February 19, 1970, through mid-1973, the bond-type securities accounted for $2.6 billion of a total of $6.6 billion in securities issued and guaranteed by GNMA. The only issuers of the bond-type securities have been the Federal National Mortgage Association and the Federal Home Loan Mortgage Corporation.

FEES

Fees assessed by GNMA in connection with its guaranty of any issue of mortgage-backed securities and in addition to the $500 application fee are calculated and paid monthly on the principal balances of securities outstanding on the last day of each month.

On pass-through securities a servicing fee of 0.5 percent is allowed with the issuer-servicer paying GNMA a fee of .06 percent out of the 0.5 percent servicing fee. Hence, the maximum servicing fee to the issuer on a pass-through security is 0.440 percent or six and one-half basis points greater than the normal 0.375 percent servicing fee.

In addition to the GNMA fee the issuer may have to pay a fee to the custodian and to any broker used to market the securities issue. In lieu of a fee the custodian frequently requires all escrows for taxes, insurance, etc., be placed on deposit with it, thereby indirectly receiving compensation for services rendered.

TAX TREATMENT

In order to maintain the market for GNMA-guaranteed mortgage backed securities, an Internal Revenue Service ruling was obtained permitting the investment in such securities by pension funds, real estate investment trusts, savings and loan associations, cooperative banks, and mutual savings banks without any adverse effect upon the tax status enjoyed by them.

DEFAULT

In the event of an issuer's default, in payment or due to noncompliance with the guaranty agreement, GNMA may terminate the issuer's control and ownership in the pool of mortgages and accede to the issuer's position with respect to the pool. In addition, GNMA can go against the assets of the issuer as required to satisfy the rights of security holders if the issuer is guilty of misfeasance.

Default on a pass-through security will occur normally because of the issuer's failure or inability to make payment to the security holders of required interest whether or not collected and of all principal due them from collections on mortgages composing the pool or due to failure of the issuer to make collections or administer the pool under reasonably accepted loan servicing standards.

LOSSES

Security holders are protected from losses due to the nature of the security in which they have invested. Any normally incurred losses due to problems with the mortgages contained in the pool against which securities are issued are absorbed by the issuer.

VOLUME

As of mid-1978, over $59 billion of single family pass-throughs had been guaranteed by GNMA accounting for 95.5 percent of all GNMA pools issued (see Chart 18-4).

OTHER TYPES OF SECURITIES

There are four other types of securities available under the GNMA program. They are Serial Note, the Project Loan Security, the Construction Loan Interim Security, and Mobile Home Loan and the Graduated Payment Mortgage pass-through security.

SERIAL NOTE

The serial note concept of mortgage-backed security was developed to offer investors a wide selection of maturities within a pool of one-to-four family FHA/VA mortgages. This security was created to bring the mortgage backed securities as close to a bond as possible and thereby help attract investment funds from traditionally corporate and government bond investors. Serial notes are issued in units against pools of mortgages and each has a definite maturity. Each sequential unit of the issue is in an amount of $25,000 except for the last unit which may be less than $25,000. The first unit in the issue is set to mature when $25,000 in principal payments are collected from the pooled mortgages. The second unit then matures when the next $25,000 in principal is collected, etc. Payments are made in lump sums of $25,000 each to the note holders. Each single certificate (note) may represent more than one sequentially numbered unit.

All issues of serial notes must be in $5,000,000 grouping plus one odd unit of less than $25,000.

As of September 30, 1978, a total of about $129 million in serial note securities were outstanding (see Chart 18-4).

PROJECT LOAN SECURITIES

On December 21, 1970, Ginnie Mae announced standardized guidelines for its project loan mortgage-backed security program. Prior to the announcement, fees and arrangements for issuance of securities-backed, FHA-insured multifamily and project mortgages were negotiated between GNMA and the issuer.

Securities issued against pools of FHA-insured project mortgages provide for the timely payment of principal and interest monthly to investors, whether collected or not.

POOL FORMATION

The project loan pool can be composed of one or more mortgages. All mortgages in the pool must bear the same interest rate, but may have differing maturities. Two years are allowed from the time of the GNMA commitment to obtain the mortgages for the pool. When the last mortgage is put into the pool, GNMA's guaranty takes effect as to the then unpaid principal balances of all loans in the pool. Only mortgages which have been finally endorsed for insurance by FHA under Sections 207, 207M, 221, 232, 236, and 242 of the National Housing Act are eligible for inclusion in the pool, even though Ginnie Mae's commitment may be obtained prior to initial FHA endorsement (prior to construction).

FEES

The basic GNMA guaranty fee and the issuer's servicing fee on project loan securities always totals 0.25 percent. Hence, the coupon rate on a project loan security is always 0.25 percent below the underlying mortgages' coupon rates.

Below is the schedule of GNMA guaranty fees and issuer servicing fees for project loan securities:

POOL AMOUNT	SERVICE FEES	GUARANTY FEES
Up to $1,999,999.	15.0	10.0
$2,000,000 to $2,999,999.	12.0	13.0
$3,000,000 to $3,999,999.	10.0	15.0
$4,000,000 to $4,999,999.	7.0	18.0
$5,000,000 to $5,999,999.	6.0	19.0
$6,000,000 and Over	5.0	20.0

ADDITIONAL RISK COVERAGE

As a part of its guaranty, GNMA insures the issuer of a project loan security against loss occasioned by several risks:

a) In the event any loan in the pool defaults and is subsequently paid for by FHA in the form of debentures instead of cash, then GNMA will purchase the debentures (which are usually marketable only at 10-20 percent discounts) at par.

b) In the event an issuer assigns a mortgage in the pool to FHA in consequence of default three years after security issuance, then GNMA shall reimburse the issuer for the assignment fee.

c) In the event the issuer makes advances of interest due by cocasion of default three years after security issuance, GNMA shall reimburse the issuer for 85 percent of the interest advanced and not paid by FHA.

CONSTRUCTION LOAN SECURITIES

A major problem was resolved by the construction loan security to the benefit of the Project Loan Security Program. The guaranty given by Ginnie Mae on project loan securities is good only after final FHA endorsement of the loan. This means that the securities cannot be sold until after the project is complete and the guaranty given. But a mortgagee must know at the time he commits to make a construction loan that he will be paid upon completion of construction by delivery of the permanent loan to an investor at a specific price. Likewise, a builder has to know the cost of permanent financing at the commencement of the project.

Under the GNMA project loan security loan program the price that will be paid for the permanent loan is not known until the securities are marketed. Hence, if a 9 percent mortgage is selling for par at the time of initial FHA endorsement (closing of the construction loan), there is nothing to indicate that the same price will prevail at the time the securities are sold, which could be one to two years later. Certainly the mortgagee cannot risk an unfavorable price change nor does the builder want to face an open-end cost on permanent mortgage funds. For the protection of both parties the price must be certain at initial FHA endorsement.

Prior to the construction loan security the only solutions to this problem were to obtain a prior investor commitment on the permanent loan, which loan will be delivered in the form of a GNMA-guarantee mortgage backed security, or to obtain a standby commitment. In most instances the standby is very costly and a permanent investor frequently requires a participation in the construction loan. Neither case allows for the marketing of the mortgage-backed security issue to a number of investors, unless a rare multiparticipation permanent loan commitment is obtained.

The GNMA construction loan security was perfected to give the permanent lender an opportunity to invest at the construction stage and to allow the security issuer to have a firm price for the permanent security at time of construction.

In essence, the construction loan security is an interim security. The issuer and the purchaser of a project loan GNMA security agree at a price for the security at the time of initial FHA endorsement. Then during construction interim securities are issued in minimum denominations of $25,000 and multiplies of $5,000 thereafter as construction funds are disbursed, but not more often than once a month. Each interim security bears the GNMA guaranty and provides for payment of interest only at a rate equal to the interest rate on the underlying mortgage, less the guaranty and servicing fees computed in accordance with multifamily security guidelines. Upon completion of construction all the interim construction loan securities are exchanged for project loan GNMA mortgaged-backed security.

The response to this security program has suffered from the fact that the issuer during the construction loan period must bear 5 percent of any loss that may incur and must deposit funds with GNMA initially to support such a potential loss.

As of mid-1978, approximately $488.8 million in construction loan securities had been issued.

MOBILE HOME SECURITY

On June 16, 1972, the first GNMA Mortgage backed mobile home security in the amount of $500,000 was sold to the National Automobile Dealers Retirement Trust. A year later over $23.6 million in these securities had been sold and by mid-1978, $566.9 million in mobile home securities had been issued.

Because of the full faith and credit backing of the government of the United States, mobile home paper sold under the GNMA security program yields much less that the typical mobile home installment paper. Hence this GNMA program is designed to provide mobile home purchasers with lower downpayment and monthly payments and better quality mobile homes due to GNMA's requirements that FHA and/or VA minimum property standards be met on all loans pooled against the securities.

Loans eligible to be pooled against the security issuance are FHA-insured and VA-guaranteed loans. Mobile home securities differ from all others in that pools aggregating $500,000 may be issued and loans in the same pool may have different coupon interest rates provided that no loan exceeds the FHA/VA permissible rate.

Maturities may also differ, provided that 50 percent of the principal balance of the pool must be in loans with a term equal to the longest maturity loan in the pool and no loan may have a maturity that exceeds by more than 60 months the term of any other loan in the pool.

Even though non-homogeneous interest rates are permissible on loans included in mobile home security pools, the mobile home security must bear an interest rate in a multiple of 0.25 percent and comply with the following:

a) Be at least 3.0 percent but not more than 3.5 percent less than the lowest FHA-insured loan's face rate.

b) Be at least 2.75 percent but not more than 3.25 percent less than the lowest VA-insured loan's face rate.

Issuer loan servicing fees are allowed to be no less than 3.0 percent for FHA-insured mobile home loans and 2.75 percent for VA guaranteed loans.

The GNMA guaranty fee on mobile home securities is 0.30 percent per annum.

An example of the above follows:

Pool consists of: $200,000 in FHA mobile home loans at 12 percent interest and $100,000 at 11.5 percent interest

$100,000 in VA mobile home at 12 percent interest and $100,000 of loans at 11.25 percent interest

Computation GNMA security coupon rate:
Maximum rate range based on FHA Loans: 8-8.5 percent
Maximum rate range based on VA Loans: 8-8.5 percent
Rate based on minimum servicing fee and GNMA guaranty fee:

FHA: 11.50%	VA: 11.25%
less 3.00%	less 2.75%
less .30%	less .30%
8.20%	8 . 2 0 %

The GNMA security coupon based on FHA loans cannot be more than 8.20 percent due to the minimum servicing fee on the lowest coupon loans, nor less than 8 percent based on the maximum rate range. Hence, 8 percent is the only qualifying rate based on these criteria and the 0.25 percent multiple rule.

The GNMA security coupon based on VA loans cannot be more than 8.20 percent due to the minimum servicing fee on the lowest coupon loans nor less than 8 percent based on the maximum rate range. Hence, 8 percent is also the only qualifying rate based on the pool requirements.

Hence, 8 percent is the selected security rate. Said rate will allow the issuer to service loans in the pool at the following rates:

LOAN RATE	SERVICING RATE = LOAN RATE LESS GNMA FEE LESS SECURITY COUPON (8.30%)
FHA/VA 12 percent	3.7 percent
FHA 11.5 percent	3.2 percent
VA 11.25 percent	2.95 percent

GRADUATED PAYMENT SECURITY

GNMA began guaranteeing pools backed by graduated payment mortgages (GPMs) in April, 1979. Graduated payment securities (GPM-GNMAs) are similar to the GNMA securities pass-through single family security except that only graduated payment mortgages (GPMs) reaching a constant payment level after five years (GPM Plans I, II & III) are eligible for inclusion in GPM-GNMA pools.

As explained in Chapter 15, a GPM is a single family graduated payment mortgae insured by FHA under Section 245 of the National Housing Act. The program is designed to enable primarily young families to purchase homes beyond their present means via reduced mortgage payments during the initial loan years. The monthly mortgage payments are geared to increase gradually over a 5-year (GPM Plans I, II and III) to 10-year (GPM Plans IV and V) period, hopefully in concert with the purchaser's increased family income and earning capability. The most significant factor in a GPM and consequently a GPM-GNMA is the insufficiency of payments in the early mortgage years to cover the full interest owed on the mortgage loan. Hence, the monthly shortfall is added to the loan balance (security balance) in the form of deferred interest. This period is reached five years (GPM Plans I, II and III) to ten years (GPM Plans IV and V) after the loan is made.

The GNMA pass-through single family security pays interest at the security coupon rate plus principal amortization monthly from inception. The GPM-GNMA pays interest at less than the coupon rate for five years and virtually no principal amortization during that period of time. However, while the unpaid principal amount of the GNMA pass-through decreases, the unpaid principal amount of the GPM-GNMA increases for about five years. Under the GPM-GNMA, a portion of the investor's earnings are actually being reinvested for him at the GPM-GNMA security coupon rate. Hence, the yield on a GPM-GNMA must be computed differently than that of a GNMA pass-through because of this reinvestment or increasing principal factor. In actuality, the GPM-GNMA sells at a larger discount than the GNMA pass-through except when the GPM-GNMAs are traded at an above par price. In this latter case the GPM-GNMAs would likely trade at a premium price as compared to the GNMA pass-throughs.

The future looks bright for GPM-GNMAs and it is anticipated that in the early 1980s, one of every four new GNMA pools will likely be a GPM-GNMA.

CHART 18-4

Types of Loans Included in Mortgage-Backed Securities Guaranteed by GNMA 1978 vs. 1977

Dollar Volume	Twelve Months Ending 9/30/78	Twelve Months Ending 9/30/77
FHA Mobile Home Loans	$ 206,744,863	$ 126,490,512
VA Mobile Home Loans	38,043,341	4,686,886
FHA Project Loans	344,590,022	340,519,137
FHA Single-Family Loans	6,062,864,637	7,367,592,144
VA Single-Family Loans	8,423,509,617	9,067,044,610
FHA Construction Loans	118,388,100	112,806,900
Total	$ 15,194,140,580	$ 17,019,140,189

Number of Loans

FHA Mobile Home Loans	10,179	14,136
VA Mobile Home Loans	385	2,671
FHA Project Loans	88	90
FHA Single-Family Loans	237,363	167,650
VA Single-Family Loans	291,276	233,254
FHA Construction Loans	17	8
Total Loans	539,308	417,809

Distribution by Pool Type Since Inception of Program

Pool Type	No. Pools	Amount (000)	Percent of all Pools
Single-Family	23,359	$59,104,210	95.45%
Serial Notes	26	129,283	.20
Mobile Homes	657	566,887	.92
Project Loans	375	1,644,922	2.65
Construction Loans	85	488,825	.78
Total	24,502	$61,934,127	100.00%

CHART 18-5

**Who Owns
GNMA
Mortgage-
Backed
Securities?**

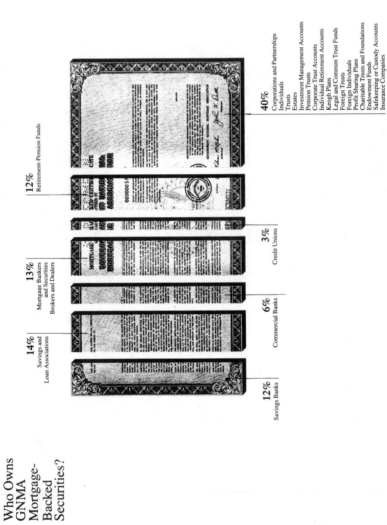

14%
Savings and
Loan Associations

13%
Mortgage Bankers
and Securities
Brokers and Dealers

12%
Retirement-Pension Funds

40%
Corporations and Partnerships
Individuals
Trusts
Estates
Investment Management Accounts
Pension Trusts
Corporate Trust Accounts
Individual Retirement Accounts
Keogh Plans
Legal and Common Trust Funds
Foreign Trusts
Foreign Individuals
Profit Sharing Plans
Charitable Trusts and Foundations
Endowment Funds
Safekeeping or Custody Accounts
Insurance Companies

3%
Credit Unions

6%
Commercial Banks

12%
Savings Banks

Source: GNMA ANNUAL REPORT

FUTURE PROSPECTS

Under its Special Assistance Program GNMA has already moved into the area of conventional loans. The next step will be for it to develop a mortgage backed security program for conventional loans. It is almost a certainty that such a program will in the future be available and will make funds more easily available for conventional loans. The problem to overcome is one of risk. GNMAs guaranty of pools of FHA and VA loans is in essence covered by government obligations already existing as to each FHA and VA loan. No such government guaranty is a part of conventional loans, hence to undertake such a security program GNMA will bear a risk far greater than under its present security programs. Nevertheless a solution to this problem will be found and the conventional security program will become a future reality.

ADVANTAGES

The major advantages to be derived by investing in a GNMA-guaranteed mortgage backed security as opposed to an investment in the mortgages themselves are:

1. The GNMA security is competitive in yield with high quality corporate bonds. In fact, the GNMA security is a safer investment than a corporate bond since it carries with it the full faith and credit of the United States government.
2. The investors in a mortgage backed security forego the necessity of inspecting the documentation involved in a block purchase of mortgages.
3. The pass-through security provides a regular return of principal and interest whether or not collected from the various mortgagors under the pooled mortgages.
4. The general public acceptance of the security makes it easily marketable

To date the Ginnie Mae guaranteed mortgage-backed security has been highly successful owing to its many advantages. More importantly, however, the program has accomplished its primary purpose of reaching new sources of mortgage capital such as private pension funds credit unions, bank trust funds, union funds, and other traditionally non-mortgage oriented institution. Over 50 percent of the securities sold and delivered since the inception of the GNMA security program have been purchased by these new mortgage money sources (see Chart 18-5).

It must be remembered that the GNMA programs, as well as those of FNMA, were created as backstops to the mortgage market, not as substitutes for private sector mortgage investments. The strength of the GNMA programs, in particular the mortgage-backed security, in the future will lie in the ability of these programs to supplement and not replace the functions of private industry.

QUESTIONS FOR THOUGHT AND DISCUSSION

1. What purpose is served by GNMA's special assistance functions?
2. How is the management and liquidation function of GNMA performed?
3. How does GNMA finance its special assistance and management and liquidation functions?

4. What is the tandem plan and why is it important?
5. a. Prices on standard FHA/VA mortgages fluctuate with the money market. If interest rates on these mortgages are held constant at a low point and interest rates in general rise, the result is a lower price (higher discount) on FHA and VA mortgages. Do you feel that the Secretary of Housing and Urban Development (the Administration) should raise interest rates in such circumstances to assist the mortgage market by keeping discounts low, or should interest rates be held at a low constant amount and a tandem plan imposed whereby GNMA would, with government funds, support the mortgage price below a certain point, as was done under Programs 18, 21, and 22?
   b. What are the pros and cons, in your estimation, of imposing such a tandem plan?
6. Discuss your opinion on whether or not the government should continue its trend of subsidizing interest rates home mortgages for low to moderate income families.
7. What is the GNMA mortgage backed security program and what was it designed to accomplish?
8. What are your recommendations, if any, for creation of a GNMA mortgage backed security that will more closely approximate the corporate bond?
9. How does the project loan mortgage-backed security program differ from the single family mortgage-backed security program and what problems are encountered with it?

19

FEDERAL HOME LOAN MORTGAGE CORPORATION

The Federal Home Loan Mortgage Corporation (FHLMC), sometimes referred to as "Freddie Mac" was established by enactment of Title III, The Emergency Home Finance Act of 1970 on July 24, 1970. Freddie Mac is a part of the Federal Home Loan Bank System and is owned exclusively by the twelve Federal Home Loan Banks. (Chapter 14 explains the operation of the Federal Home Loan Bank System). The corporation's board of directors consist of three members of the Federal Home Loan Bank Board. The chairman of the FHLBB is also chairman of FHLMC. Members of the Federal Home Loan Bank Board, hence the directors of FHLMC, are appointed by the President of the United States, for four year terms.

PURPOSE OF FHLMC

The purpose of FHLMC is similar to that of FNMA - the developing of a secondary market in residential mortgages. While FNMA deals with all mortgage lenders, FHLMC was created for the purpose of a secondary market primarily for savings and loan associations. By increasing the liquidity of savings and loan associations through creation of an outlet for their mortgage loans, ie FHLMC, more funds can be channeled through the savings and loan associations into the mortgage market. For example, by selling $1,000,000 in mortgage loans that it has originated to FHLMC, a saving and loan association can obtain $1,000,000 to use in originating new mortgage loans, hence increasing the housing finance availability to all Americans. As an analogy FHLMC is to the savings and loan industry what FNMA is to the mortgage banking industry.

CAPITAL FUNDS FOR FHLMC

The Federal Home Loan Mortgage Corporation was funded initially with $100 million obtained through the sale of 100,000 shares, par value $1000 each, non-voting common stock to the twelve Federal Home Loan Banks. Dividends may be declared on the stock, but as yet have not been. The law also provides for FHLMC to retire its stock at its issue price if such retirement will not reduce the reserves and surplus of FHLMC to less than $100 million. Additional funds are obtained by FHLMC through the sale of mortgage-backed securities guaranteed by GNMA, the sale of mortgage backed securities bearing its own guaranty and through the issuance of debt securities in capital markets. Since 1975, FHLMC has had a policy of selling its mortgages by means of its mortgage securities virtually as rapidly as it buys them. The corporation's principal mortgage security is its Participation Certificate (PC). In 1978, over $5.6 billion in PC's were sold. Therefore, FHLMC like FNMA acts as a conduit to channel capital market funds into the mortgage market. Chart 19-1 is a copy of FHLMC's balance sheet.

MORTGAGE LOAN OPERATIONS AND PROGRAMS

The mortgage loan operations of the Federal Home Loan Mortgage Corporation are handled on a regional basis. The regional offices of FHLMC are generally co-located with the District Banks of the Federal Home Loan Bank System.

FHLMC has three main loan purchase programs: FHA/VA loans; Conventional Whole Loans, and Conventional Mortgage participations.

FHA/VA LOANS

The FHA/VA loan program covers both single family and multifamily loans.

Single family loans are purchased by FHLMC on a Purchase Contract basis. Delivery under a Purchase Contract is on an immediate delivery (within sixty days) mandatory basis. A savings and loan association or other approved FHLMC Seller desiring to sell FHA/VA loans to FHLMC may do so at the then quoted purchase price. Such purchase price quotes may be obtained from any of the regional FHLMC offices. Contracts to purchase are made by mail or telephone. Once made, the savings and loan association must deliver the loans within sixty days at the quoted price or face the loss of the right to do business with FHLMC. There is no commitment fee charge for the purchase of FHA/VA loans.

Multifamily FHA insured loans are also purchased only on an immediate delivery purchase contract basis at the quoted FHLMC price. A purchase fee of 1/2 of 1 percent is assessed for multifamily loans. Delivery is not mandatory as it is with single family loans, but a 1 percent non-delivery fee is charged in the event that loan delivery does not take place.

CONVENTIONAL WHOLE LOANS

There are four major conventional FHLMC whole loan purchase programs:
1. Immediate delivery home loan purchases.

2. Forward commitment home loan purchases.

3. Immediate delivery multi family loan purchases.

4. Prior approval multi family loan purchases.

The Immediate delivery home loan purchase program is similar to the FHA/VA immediate purchase program and delivery is mandatory. Maximum loan amounts acceptable under the program are similar to FNMA's conventional loan program-$60,000, for loans in excess of ninety percent loan to value and $75,000, for loans of ninety percent loan to value or less. All loans over eighty percent loan to value must be insured by a FHLMC approved private mortgage insurance company. Coverage is required on the amount in excess of seventy-five percent of value and must remain in force until the mortgage is reduced to eighty percent of original value.

Townhouses, condominium units, and units in planned unit developments are acceptable under this program. However, such projects must be qualified with the FHLMC prior to any sale of loans. Project qualification is, however, much less detailed and onerous than under FNMA's condominium loan purchase program.

CHART 19-1
• FHLMC Statement of Condition

Item	December 31, 1977
ASSETS:	
FHA-insured and VA-guaranteed loans	$1,450,321,000
Participations in conventional loans	1,450,756,000
Conventional loans	365,892,000
Less: Loss reserves and unamortized discount	(81,090,000)
Total Mortgage Loans and Participations	$3,185,879,000
Cash and investments	121,367,000
Accrued interest	25,559,000
Claims against FHA and VA	1,201,000
Other assets	169,309,000
TOTAL ASSETS	$3,503,315,000
LIABILITIES:	
Notes and bonds	$3,109,692,000
Accrued interest	51,709,000
Accounts payable and other accrued expenses	24,344,000
Principal and interest due to Mortgage Participation Certificate investors	117,673,000
Commitment fees	2,258,000
Total Liabilities	$3,305,676,000
CAPITAL:	
Reserve for management fee and guarantees	$ 21,000,000
Capital stock	100,000,000
Retained earnings	76,639,000
Total Capital	$ 503,315,000
TOTAL LIABILITIES AND CAPITAL	$3,503,315,000

Source: Federal Home Loan Mortgage Corporation

Immediate purchase contracts are obtained on either a competitive or non-competitive basis.

A competitive offer is made in competition with other sellers. One seller may submit as many as five competitive offers at different yields in any one weekly auction, but they cannot be less than $100,000 each nor exceed an aggregate total of $3,000,000.

Non-competitive offers are submitted on a competitive auction day. Only one offer can be made but it may be divided into two purchase contracts, neither less than $100,000 and the total not in excess of $500,000.

A seller who successfully or unsuccessfully bid competitively in an immediately prior auction is not allowed to submit a non-competitive bid.

Competitive bids are accepted or rejected at FHLMC discretion based on the minimum yield they decide to accept. However, all acceptances are made within ten days of receipt of a sellers offer. Non-competitive offers are usually automatically accepted. Weekly auction results are published each Tuesday in the Wall Street Journal.

Six month and eight month forward commitment home loan purchase contracts are obtainable on a competitive or non-competitive basis to a maximum aggregate of $5,000,000.

For the first four months of the six month forward commitment delivery of mortgages is optional. At the end of the four months the commitment expires unless extended for the remaining two months, by Seller's submission to FHLMC of a Delivery Option Notification, in which event delivery becomes mandatory.

Delivery under the eight month commitment is completely optional.

A .75% fee is charged for the six month commitment and a 1.0% fee for the eight month commitment.

Due to the uncertainty of future interest rates, immediate delivery commitments are usually obtainable at lesser yields than six month commitments. Likewise the eight month commitment would be a higher yield than the immediate and six month commitments.

The *immediate delivery multi family purchase program* is mandatory within sixty days of offer acceptance by FHLMC. Offers to sell multi family conventional loans at FHLMC's required net yield may be in minimum amounts of $100,000 to a maximum $5,000,000 per contract. FHLMC's net required yield, as with home mortgages, is exclusive of servicing. To this net required yield must be added the fee that the seller will receive for servicing of the loan. The minimum servicing fee allowed on loans of $750,000 or less is .25. On loans over $750,000 it is .125. Hence, if FHLMC requires a net yield of 10% for a purchase of a multi family loan, a $1,000,000 would have to bear a 10.125% coupon to be sold at par. If the coupon is less than 10.125% it would have to be sold to FHLMC at a discount that would provide a 10.125% yield. If the coupon is greater than 10.125% FHLMC will still only purchase the loan at par, but the excess over 10.125% is retained by the Seller as an additional loan servicing fee. Similar net yield requirements apply to have mortgages sold to FHLMC.

Multifamily mortgages eligible for sale to FHLMC may have loan to values as high as 80% and original mortgage terms of up to 30 years (10 years minimum). At time of sale the multifamily project must have 80% occupancy or a higher percentage as is necessary to carry all expenses and mortgage debt. Maximum mortgage amounts per unit are established by FHLMC and cannot be exceeded.

CHART 19-2

NOTE

US $, Ohio

                                              City

                                                                                  , 19

FOR VALUE RECEIVED, the undersigned promise to pay
                                              , or order, the principal sum of
                                              Dollars, with interest
on the unpaid principal balance from the date of this Note, until paid, at the rate of
percent per annum. The principal and interest shall be payable at
                              , or such other place as the holder hereof may designate in
writing, in consecutive monthly installments of
Dollars (US $), on the   day of each month beginning
                         , 19   , until the entire indebtedness evidenced hereby is fully
paid, except that any remaining indebtedness, if not sooner paid, shall be due and payable on the
                    day of

If any monthly installment under this Note is not paid when due and remains unpaid after a date specified by a notice sent by certified mail to the undersigned at the address stated below, which date shall be not less than thirty days from the date such notice is mailed, the entire principal amount outstanding hereunder and accrued interest thereon shall at once become due and payable at the option of the holder hereof. Failure to exercise such option shall not constitute a waiver of the right to exercise such option if the undersigned is in default hereunder. In the event of any default in the payment of this Note and if suit is brought hereon, the holder hereof shall be entitled to collect in such proceeding all reasonable costs and expenses of suit.

The undersigned shall pay to the holder hereof a late charge of   percent of any monthly installment not received by the holder hereof within   days after the installment is due.

The undersigned shall have the right to prepay the principal amount outstanding in whole or in part, provided that the holder hereof may require that any partial prepayments shall be made on the date monthly installments are due and shall be in the amount of that part of one or more installments which would be applicable to principal. Any partial prepayment shall be applied against the principal amount outstanding and shall not extend or postpone the due date of any subsequent monthly installments or change the amount of such installments, unless the holder hereof shall otherwise agree in writing. If, within five years from the date of this Note, the undersigned makes any prepayments in any twelve month period beginning with the date of this Note or anniversary dates thereof ("loan year") with money lent to the undersigned by a lender other than the holder hereof, the undersigned shall pay the holder hereof (a) during each of the first three loan years percent of the amount by which the sum of prepayments made in any such loan year exceeds 20 percent of the original principal amount of this Note and (b) during the fourth and fifth loan years percent of the amount by which the sum of prepayments made in any such loan year exceeds 20 percent of the original principal amount of this Note.

Presentment, notice of dishonor, and protest are hereby waived by all makers, sureties, guarantors and endorsers hereof. This Note shall be the joint and several obligation of all makers, sureties, guarantors and endorsers, and shall be binding upon them and their heirs, personal representatives, successors and assigns.

The indebtedness evidenced by this Note is secured by a Mortgage, dated of even date herewith, and reference is made thereto for rights as to acceleration of the indebtedness evidenced by this Note.

Property Address

OHIO— FHLMC—1/72—1 to 4 family   *(Execute Original Only)*

Under the *prior approval multi-family loan purchase program*, FHLMC contracts with the loan Seller to purchase a conventional multi family mortgage on a specific project in advance of the closing of the mortgage. The minimum offer amount under this program is $250,000 and the maximum is $5,000,000. Once approved, all provisions of FHLMC's immediate delivery multi-family loan program applies. The benefit of the prior approval procedure is that the Seller can obtain FHLMC's commitment that the specific mortgage will be purchased. Under the immediate delivery program, FHLMC may accept or reject any loans offered for purchase.

A major factor in conventional loan purchases by FHLMC is the property valuation. All loans purchases must be accompanied by an appraisal made by a FHLMC approved appraiser on FHLMC appraisal forms.

Loans acceptable must be no more than one year old and have a minimum term of ten years and maximum term of thirty years. The property covered by the loan must be occupied by the mortgagor as his principal residence.

FHLMC allows junior financing to exist provided total financing on a property does not exceed 95 percent of value and the junior financing meets FHLMCs amortization requirements.

UNIFORM MORTGAGE DOCUMENTS

All loans submitted under the conventional whole loan programs need to be made on uniform documents approved by FHLMC. These uniform documents are similar from state to state and were developed after many hundreds of hours of involvement with thousands of participants, including lenders, attorneys, builders, politicians, and consumer representative. The FHLMC uniform documents are acceptable for use in selling loans to FNMA and GNMA. Charts 19-2 and 19-3 are sample uniform FHLMC single family note and mortgage documents, respectively.

ELIGIBLE SELLERS

FHLMC is allowed to purchase mortgage loans from members of the Federal Home Loan Bank System and other approved financial institutions, the deposits or accounts of which are insured by an agency of the United States. To be eligible, a seller must also be actively engaged in mortgage loan origination and servicing of mortgages owned by the seller, and must be in good standing with FHLMC. Over 80 percent of all loans purchased by FHLMC are acquired from Savings and Loan Associations.

Financial institutions, the deposits and accounts of which are insured by an agency of the United States, which have been approved by FHLMC as a seller, and are not members of the FHLB, the FSLIC or the FHLBS are classed as non-member sellers and must usually pay a 1/2 of 1 percent non-member fee on all commitments obtained from FHLMC.

CONVENTIONAL MORTGAGE PARTICIPATIONS

In its conventional mortgage loan participation program, FHLMC will purchase a percentage of each loan in a group of mortgages which are (a) all home mortgages,

CHART 19-3

OPEN-END MORTGAGE

THIS MORTGAGE is made this   day of   , 19   , between the Mortgagor,

(herein "Borrower"),

and the Mortgagee,   , a corporation organized and existing under the laws of   , whose address is

(herein "Lender").

WHEREAS, Borrower is indebted to Lender in the principal sum of

Dollars, which indebtedness is evidenced by Borrower's note of even date herewith (herein "Note"), providing for monthly installments of principal and interest, with the balance of the indebtedness, if not sooner paid, due and payable on   ;

To SECURE to Lender (a) the repayment of the indebtedness evidenced by the Note, with interest thereon, the payment of all other sums, with interest thereon, advanced in accordance herewith to protect the security of this Mortgage, and the performance of the covenants and agreements of Borrower herein contained, and (b) the repayment of any future advances, with interest thereon, made to Borrower by Lender pursuant to paragraph 21 hereof (herein "Future Advances"), Borrower does hereby mortgage, grant and convey to Lender the following described property located in the County of   , State of Ohio:

TOGETHER with all the improvements now or hereafter erected on the property, and all easements, rights, appurtenances, rents, royalties, mineral, oil and gas rights and profits, water, water rights, and water stock, and all fixtures now or hereafter attached to the property, all of which, including replacements and additions thereto, shall be deemed to be and remain a part of the property covered by this Mortgage; and all of the foregoing, together with said property (or the leasehold estate in the event this Mortgage is on a leasehold) are herein referred to as the "Property".

Borrower covenants that Borrower is lawfully seised of the estate hereby conveyed and has the right to mortgage, grant and convey the Property, that the Property is unencumbered, and that Borrower will warrant and defend generally the title to the Property against all claims and demands, subject to any easements and restrictions listed in a schedule of exceptions to coverage in any title insurance policy insuring Lender's interest in the Property.

UNIFORM COVENANTS. Borrower and Lender covenant and agree as follows:

1. Payment of Principal and Interest. Borrower shall promptly pay when due the principal of and interest on the indebtedness evidenced by the Note, prepayment and late charges as provided in the Note, and the principal of and interest on any Future Advances secured by this Mortgage.

2. Funds for Taxes and Insurance. Subject to Lender's option under paragraphs 4 and 5 hereof, Borrower shall pay to Lender on the day monthly installments of principal and interest are payable under the Note, until the Note is paid in full, a sum (herein "Funds") equal to one-twelfth of the yearly taxes and assessments which may attain priority over this Mortgage, and ground rents on the Property, if any, plus one-twelfth of yearly premium installments for hazard insurance, plus one-twelfth of yearly premium installments for mortgage insurance, or (b) all multifamily mortgages.

As to home mortgages, FHLMC buys participations in $100,000 increments respectively from 50 percent to 95 percent of the value of all loans in the group. For example, under an 85 percent participation arrangement, a group of underlying mortgages aggregating $117,647 in unpaid principal balances would be required.

Under the multifamily participation programs FHLMC's participation on each mortgage retained by the Seller must be sufficient to allow tht Seller to remit FHLMC's required net yield. All interest income over FHLMC's required net yield is retained by the Seller.

All participation commitments are on an immediate delivery mandatory basis, but at yields usually less than quoted for whole loans. Hence, the participation program allows the Seller the advantage of a better price for his loans due to the fact that the Seller is bearing a portion of the loan risk.

Loans eligible for purchase under the participation program must meet the same criteria as loans under the whole loan program.

An example of how a Seller may use the participation program is as follows:

Seller owns $1,000,000 of home mortgages all with a 10-1/2% coupon. FHLMC has announced its willingness to purchase home mortgage praticipations at 10% net yield.

Seller offers an 80% participation to FHLMC which is accepted.

Results: FHLMC receives a 10% yield on its 80% participation or $80,000 in the first year.

The Seller collects $105,000 on the $1,000,000 and remits the $80,000 required on FHLMC participation. Hence, the Seller keeps $25,000 as its return on what is now at $200,000 investment. The Seller's net yield on his participation has grown to 12.5% from the 10-1/2% he was previously receiving. Of course, the Seller has $800,000 that must be reinvested at a 10-1/2% yield in order to realize a net gain on the total $1,000,000 in this example.

PROGRAM SUMMARY

Charts 19-4 and 19-5 are summaries of the conventional whole loan and participation programs of the Federal Home Loan Mortgage Corporation.

WARRANTIES OF SELLERS

A seller of loans to FHLMC under any of its programs is required to warrant the validity of the mortgage as a first lien; proper recordation of the mortgage; compliance by the lender with state and federal laws particularly as regards truth-in-lending, usury and the Real Estate Settlement Procedures Act; absence of default of principal or interest payments; validity of title; title free and clear of liens and encumbrances prior to the first mortgage; and validity and existence of hazard and private mortgage insurance policies.

LOAN SERVICING

The servicing of loans sold to FHLMC is retained by the Seller. Servicing duties of the seller include collection and remittance of principal and interest payments, administration of escrow accounts, property inspections, collection of

CHART 19-4

The Mortgage Corporation
Federal Home Loan Mortgage Corporation

CONVENTIONAL HOME MORTGAGE SUMMARY

PROGRAM REQUIREMENTS	IMMEDIATE DELIVERY PROGRAM	FORWARD COMMITMENT PROGRAMS
Offer Procedure Competitive	Section 2.102 Phone (202) 789-2200 any Friday between 11:00 a.m. and 3:00 p.m. Washington, D.C. time and submit bid.	Section 2.103 Phone (202) 789-2200 between 11:00 a.m. and 3:00 p.m. Washington, D.C. time to submit bids: Six months program — 4th Friday any month; Eight months program — 2nd Friday any month.
Noncompetitive	Phone (202) 789-2200 any Wednesday between 11:00 a.m. and 3:00 p.m. Washington, D.C. time and submit offer at weighted average net yield as established by the previous Friday's immediate competitive bidding.	Same as procedure for forward commitment competitive offers, except Seller agrees to accept contract at the weighted average net yield which will be established by competitive bidding.
Commitment Fee	None	Section 2.103g Six months program — 0.75% Eight months program — 1.00% (% of contract commitment amount)
Delivery Period	Section 3.101c & 3.102c Mandatory within 60 days after Purchase Contract Date of Acceptance	Section 3.103c Six months program — Optional 1st 120 days. If delivery option (FHLMC Form 531) is exercised, mandatory after 120th day but prior to end of 6 months commitment period. Section 3.104c Eight months program — Optional entire commitment period.
Variance from contract amount	$10,000 more or less than purchase contract commitment amount (FHLMC's interest)	
Amount of Purchase Contract Competitive and Noncompetitive	Minimum $100,000; Maximum may be determined by contacting a Regional Office or by calling (202) 789-2200 during non-offer periods.	
Acceptance Procedure	FHLMC will execute a contract, in duplicate, accepting each successful offer and mail to Seller within five business days after receipt of offer. Seller must execute the contract to acknowledge receipt and return one copy of the acknowledged contract to the Applicable FHLMC Regional Office within 24 hours after receipt. Include commitment fee, when applicable.	
Purchase Amount Whole Loans Participations	100% of unpaid principal balance of loan. 95% maximum and 50% minimum of unpaid principal balance of each loan.	
Servicing Fee Whole Loans Participations	Section 2.203a & 2.203b ¾ of 1% minimum servicing spread required over FHLMC net yield requirement. Seller retains interest income over FHLMC net yield requirement.	
Delivery Requirements	See Section 3.501, or the Mortgage Corporation's single family packaging booklet.	
Nonmember Fee	Section 2.201 0.50% of FHLMC's interest in the mortgages purchased, to be deducted from amount due Seller at time of purchase.	

MORTGAGE REQUIREMENTS—ALL CONVENTIONAL HOME MORTGAGE PROGRAMS

Maximum Original Loan-to-Value Ratio **Home Purchase** 1 Family Dwelling 2 Family Dwelling 3-4 Family Dwelling **Refinance Loan** 1-2 Family Dwelling for purpose of improving subject property 1-4 Family Dwelling for any purpose	Section 3.201a 95% based on lower of purchase price or appraised value 90% based on lower of purchase price or appraised value 80% based on lower of purchase price or appraised value 90% based on appraised value at time of loan closing 80% based on appraised value at time of loan closing
Maximum Original Loan Amount LTV not in excess of 90% LTV in excess of 90%	Section 3.201a $75,000 ($112,500 in Alaska, Guam and Hawaii) $60,000 ($90,000 in Alaska, Guam and Hawaii)
Minimum Cash Down Payment or Equity LTV not in excess of 80% LTV in excess of 80% Refinance not in excess of 80% Refinance in excess of 80%	Section 3.201b 10% of purchase price must be cash or other equity. Remainder may be secondary financing. Difference between purchase price and mortgage must be cash or other equity. Secondary financing not permitted. 20% of appraised value must be borrower's equity. Difference between appraised value and mortgage must be borrower's equity.
Mortgage Insurance LTV not in excess of 80% LTV in excess of 80%	Section 3.201c Not required Required on mortgage amount in excess of 75% LTV
Amortization Constant Payment Flexible Payment	Section 3.201h Payments must commence within 62 days of final disbursement and fully amortize the mortgage by maturity through equal monthly payments. Same as constant payment except amortization of principal is not required during an initial period, not to exceed five years.
Original Mortgage Term	Section 3.201i Maximum 30 years Minimum 10 years
Origination Participation Mortgages Whole Loan Mortgages	Section 3.201j Loans must either be closed in Seller's name as lender or assigned and endorsed to Seller as holder in due course. Same as participations except chain of endorsements must be complete from lender to FHLMC.
Age of Mortgage	Section 3.201k Each loan must be closed prior to delivery to FHLMC.
Mortgage Instruments Participation Mortgages Whole Loan Mortgages	Section 1.407a & 1.407c Must be closed on FNMA/FHLMC Uniform Mortgage Instruments after January 1, 1976. Prior to that date, lender's mortgage instruments must be acceptable to FHLMC. Same as participations except prior to January 1, 1976, must be closed on FHLMC Mortgage Instruments.
Maximum Late Charge	Section 3.201d May not exceed 5% of monthly principal and interest payment nor be assessed prior to the 16th day payment is past due.
Prepayment Charges	Section 3.201e For loans purchased after December 31, 1979, any prepayment charge previously contracted for may NOT be enforced. See Sellers' Guide for complete prepayment charge details.

The section numbers in this summary refer to sections in the Sellers' Guide Conventional Mortgages. Please refer to the Sellers' Guide for complete and authoritative description of contractual rights and obligations.

Please call the Mortgage Corporation's Regional Office or Underwriting Office (as shown on the reverse) for additional information.

FHLMC 386 9/79

CHART 19-5

The Mortgage Corporation
Federal Home Loan Mortgage Corporation **CONVENTIONAL MULTIFAMILY MORTGAGE SUMMARY**

PROGRAM REQUIREMENTS	IMMEDIATE DELIVERY PROGRAMS	PRIOR APPROVAL PROGRAMS
Multifamily Security	Five or more units.	More than 12 units.
Offer Procedure	**Section 2.104** Phone (202) 789-2200 any Wednesday between 11:00 a.m. and 3:00 p.m. Washington, D.C. time and submit offer at required yield.	**Section 2.105** Sellers, specifically approved for this program, may submit application, required documentation and nonrefundable application fee of greater of $1,500 or 0.10% of original principal amount.
Commitment Fee	None	**Section 2.105i** 2.00% of amount of Purchase Contract. Refunded when mortgage meeting contract terms is funded.
Amount of Purchase Contract Minimum Maximum	**Section 4.101b & 4.102b** $100,000 $5,000,000	**Section 4.103c** $250,000 $5,000,000
No. of Contracts & Loans	**Section 4.101c & 4.102d** Seller may submit any number of contracts, but aggregate may not exceed $5,000,000 on one offer day. No more than 5 loans may be delivered under any one contract.	**Section 2.105c** Seller may submit any number of applications, but may not have more than $10,000,000 of applications pending at any one time. A request may include only one loan secured by a specific multifamily property.
Delivery	**Section 4.101e & 4.102g** Mandatory within 60 days after the Purchase Contract Date of Acceptance.	**Section 2.105h & k** Seller has 10 days to accept FHLMC's offer. If Seller accepts, delivery is mandatory within 60 days after the 10 day acceptance period.
Delivery Requirements	See Section 4.501	See Section 4.502
Acceptance Procedure	**Section 2.104g** FHLMC will execute a contract, in duplicate, accepting each successful offer and mail to Seller within 5 business days after receipt. Seller must execute the contract to acknowledge receipt and return one copy of the acknowledged contract to the FHLMC regional office within 24 hours after receipt.	**Section 2.105e through I** FHLMC will execute a contract, in duplicate, after review and mail both copies to Seller. If Seller wishes to accept, Seller must execute both copies and mail one copy to FHLMC within 10 days, including applicable commitment fee.
Delivery Variance Whole Loans Participation Repurchase	**Section 4.101e.** Aggregate outstanding principal balance must be within lesser of 10% or $100,000 of Purchase Contract amount. **Section 4.102g.** Must be such that FHLMC's retained interest in the mortgage(s) will be within the lesser of 10% or $100,000 of the retained interest amount stated in the Purchase Contract.	
Purchase Amount Whole Loans Participation Repurchase	**Section 4.101d.** 100% or such lesser amount as will equate mortgage note interest rate to the minimum gross yield. **Section 4.102.** 100% with simultaneous repurchase by Seller of from 15% to 50%, in increments of 5%, as stated in the Purchase Contract.	
Servicing Fee Whole Loans Participation Repurchase	**Section 4.101f.** 0.125% if original loan amount exceeds $750,000. 0.250% if original loan amount is $750,000 or less. **Section 4.102h.** Seller retains interest income over FHLMC Required Net Yield.	
Nonmember Fee	**Section 2.201.** 0.50% of FHLMC's interest in the mortgages purchased, to be deducted from amount due Seller at time of funding.	

MORTGAGE REQUIREMENTS — ALL CONVENTIONAL MULTIFAMILY MORTGAGE PROGRAMS (Section 4.201)

Origination	Loan must either be closed in Seller's name as lender, or assigned and endorsed to Seller as holder in due course. Chain of endorsements must be complete from lender to Federal Home Loan Mortgage Corporation. (Section 4.501b and 4.502b)
Maximum Original Loan Amount	$5,000,000
Maximum Loan to Value Ratio	80%
Age of Mortgage	Must be closed before FHLMC will purchase. Immediate delivery mortgages must be closed prior to initial delivery and prior approval mortgages must be closed prior to final delivery.
Original Mortgage Term	Minimum: 10 years Maximum: 30 years
Mortgage Instruments	Must be closed on FNMA/FHLMC Uniform Instruments (Multifamily) after January 1, 1976. Prior to that date, for whole loans, must be closed on FHLMC Mortgage Instruments and, for participation loans, may be closed on lender's instruments if acceptable to FHLMC.
Appraisal Forms FHLMC Form 71A FHLMC Form 71B FHLMC Form 72	May be used for all loans. Must be used for loans in excess of $750,000. May be used only for loans up to $750,000. May be used only for appraisal of properties with 12 or less units.
Occupancy	Required: 80% (or such higher percent as is necessary to pay all operating expenses and service the mortgage debt) at rents sufficient to support the appraisal.

Maximum Mortage Amount Per Unit	Living Unit # Bed Rooms	Nonelevator Building	Elevator Building	Amounts may be increased 25% in Alaska, Guam and Hawaii.
	0	$19,500	$22,500	
	1	21,600	25,200	
	2	25,800	30,900	
	3	31,800	38,700	
	4	36,000	43,758	

Prepayment Charges	10% first year, reduced by 1% each succeeding year down to a minimum of 1%; or one-half the mortgage note interest rate during the first 10 years, reduced to 1% in the eleventh year and thereafter. Not required if secured property contains 12 or less units.
Underwriting	The Mortgage Corporation expects to purchase investment quality mortgages and will review each multifamily loan to insure adherence to its underwriting requirements prior to making a purchase decision.

The section numbers in this summary refer to sections in the Sellers' Guide Conventional Mortgages. Please refer to the Sellers' Guide for complete and authoritative description of contractual rights and obligations.
Please call the Mortgage Corporation's Regional Office or Underwriting Office (as shown on the reverse) for additional information.
FHLMC Form 357 9/79

insurance claims, and if required the handling of foreclosures. The seller may contract with other eligible FHLMC sellers or FHA approved mortgagees for the loan servicing to be performed by them. A sub-servicing arrangement, however, does not relieve the seller of its obligations to FHLMC.

UNDERWRITING STANDARDS

Each whole loan or participation purchased by FHLMC must meet the underwriting standards established by FHLMC, generally a 25%/33% mortgage debt/total debts to income ratio. In addition to an appraisal by a FHLMC approved fee appraiser, the borrowers credit must meet specific guidelines and the property must measure up to established FHLMC criteria. As of early 1979, about 9 percent of whole loans and participations offered to FHLMC had been rejected due to failure to meet FHLMCs underwriting standards.

SALE PROGRAMS

As with FNMA and GNMA, FHLMC from time to time offers loans in its portfolio for sale to other investors. The sales may be in form of whole mortgage loans, mortgage backed bonds, or GNMA guaranteed mortgage backed securities.

OTHER PROGRAMS

During 1974 and 1975, several low interest rate loan purchase programs were approved by Congress for funding with U. S. Treasury monies. These programs were either exclusively administered through FHLMC or were participated in by FHLMC. With the evident need for government support of the mortgage market particularly in times of economic depressions, it is probable that more Treasury financed programs will be promulgated in the future and that FHLMC will be a major distributor of these funds.

Currently FHLMC is developing a program for purchase of Home Improvement Loans. This action on the part of FHLMC will increase the availability of funds for rehabilitation loans.

CHART 19-6
Federal Home Loan Mortgage Corporation Activity

(Millions of Dollars)

Year	Mortgage Transactions			Loan Portfolio (Year-End)	
	Purchases	Sales	Total	FHA-VA	Conventional
1970	$ 325	. . .	$ 325	$ 325	. . .
1971	778	$ 113	968	821	$ 147
1972	1,297	407	1,788	1,502	286
1.73	1,334	409	2,604	1,800	804
1974	2,190	53	4,586	1,961	2,625
1975	1,713	1,021	4,987	1,881	3,106
1976	1,129	1,396	4,269	1,675	2,594
1977	4,124	4,665	3,267	1,450	1,817

Note: Components may not add to totals due to rounding.
Source: Federal Home Loan Mortgage Corporation.

IMPACT

FHLMC's loan portfolio at year-end 1977 totaled $3.28 billion, comprised of $1.45 billion of FHA/VA loans and $1.82 billion of conventional loans. In 1977, FHLMC purchased a record $4.12 billion in loans and sold a record $4.67 billion. (See Chart 19-6)

CONCLUSION

Savings and loan associations are a major source of mortgage funds. By providing these associations and other financial institutions with an outlet for their mortgage loans, such as through FHLMC it is possible to enhance the market for mortgages and to provide a stable supply of funds for housing on the best terms possible.

QUESTIONS FOR THOUGHT AND DISCUSSION

1. What is the purpose of FHLMC?
2. What is the significance of bringing capital market funds into the mortgage market?
3. Contrast FNMAs and FHLMCs programs with regard to the purchase of
   a. FHA/VA loans,
   b. conventional loans.
4. What are the advantages of selling loans under a participation as opposed to selling whole loans?
5. What advantage does the purchaser gain by requiring that loans be made on uniform documents?

20

DIRECT GOVERNMENT INVOLVEMENT IN REAL ESTATE FINANCE

Federal government influence over housing and real estate finance is readily evident through its FHA insurance programs and the activities of FNMA, FHLMC and GNMA. These activities, however, are only part of a total involvement and commitment of the federal government to provide more and better housing for all citizens. Additionally, for years many states and cities throughout the country have conducted their own programs to provide housing for their residents. In recent years, existing government programs have been stepped up or supplemented, and new programs have been adopted. This is due in great part to an increasing awareness of the existence of many substandard housing units, of a pressing need to re-establish center city areas, and of the desire to industrialize the housing industry.

The purpose of this chapter is to explain the method of government involvement in providing housing, to emphasize the real estate finance aspect of such involvement, and to present briefly the various programs currently existing for government accomplishment of its housing goals. Some overlapping of subjects will be noted as many of the programs are directly related to the activities of FHA (Chapter 15).

PUBLIC HOUSING PROGRAMS

The major government subsidy program geared to meet the housing needs of the lower portion of the low-to-moderate income group is public housing.

Public housing has existed much longer than other FHA subsidy programs and has been sponsored and developed by local housing authorities (LHA) usually formed by cities, municipalities, or states in accordance with statutory state enabling acts. Subsidies required to bring LHA sponsored housing projects within the reach of low income families are furnished by local, state, and federal grants.

In the past LHA housing programs were designed, developed, constructed, and managed by the LHA with the private sector's involvement limited to architectural and building services contracted for on a competitive bid basis. This philosophy of almost total LHA control and development of public housing changed in the mid-1960s with the advent of the "turnkey" programs designed to produce public housing through the efforts of private enterprise in combination with government. A further change in public housing philosophy occurred in 1974 with the creation of the Section 8, Leased Housing Assistance Payment Program.

HISTORY

In Europe, socialized housing to meet the needs of families whose income was insufficient to pay market rents existed for many years before the concept was adopted for use in the United States.

Lavenberg House, built privately in New York City in 1927, was actually the first attempt in this country at housing for lower income families. Because its large and concentrated population included many immigrants and other persons unable to achieve a subsistance income during the depression years, it is no surprise that the nation's first housing authority was established in New York City. Founded in 1934, the New York City Housing Authority took two years to complete its first project, known as First Houses.

Congress, noting the need for low-rent housing, passed the Housing Act of 1937, Title I of which created the United States Housing Authority and vested in it the authority to provide funds to locally established housing authorities for development of public housing projects. The general purpose and policy of the 1937 housing act was to "assist the several states and their political subdivisions to alleviate present and recurring unemployment and to remedy the unsafe and unsanitary housing conditions and the acute shortage of decent, safe, and sanitary dwellings for families of low income."

Under authority contained in the 1937 law, a number of states passed legislation providing for the creation of LHAs in local areas throughout the state. Every state now has statutory provisions relating to establishment of local housing authorities.

The federal government's part in the public housing program was originally administered by the Department of Interior and is now handling through the Department of Housing and Urban Development under the direct charge of an Assistant Secretary for Renewal and Housing Management.

Today there are over 3,000 LHAs, each involved in one or more of four major types of public housing programs conventional, turnkey, leased housing and home ownership.

CONVENTIONAL

Under the conventional public housing program the LHA plans and implements projects with its own staff personnel, using private contractors and services only on a bid basis. The LHA handles the leasing of completed housing units and performs the property management functions. Normal procedure from commencement to completion of a project is as follows:

1. The LHA's staff plans the project and produces the site plans using sites selected in the local area. Local planning agencies are consulted on both the potential sites and the project plan. One site is finally chosen and the project is approved.
    a. If, as is the usual case, federal subsidies are arranged through the Department of Housing and Urban Development (HUD), then the LHA and HUD represented by its Regional Housing Assistance Office (HOA), enter into an Annual Contribution Contract which recites the amount of federal subsidy and contribution. Frequently the LHA will have obtained a "program reservation" from HUD, which is a subsidy allocation for a total number of units to be developed in one or more projects.
    b. When state or local subsidies are obtained, similar contracts are entered into between the LHA and the appropriate state or local agency.
3. With subsidy funds committed, the site is acquired, project plans and specifications are finalized, and the LHA issues its invitation for public bids for construction.
4. A contract is awarded to the successful bidder and preliminary conferences are held pursuant to commencement of construction.
5. Sometime prior to construction the LHA will have arranged for construction financing either by sale or short-term tax exempt notes or through a loan from HUD at a "going rate" of interest. Permanent financing is arranged by the sale of long-term tax exempt bonds. Debt service on the bonds is paid for by tenant rents and government subsidies under the annual contribution contract. The permanent financing can have a 40-year maturity and is guaranteed by the federal government.
6. Construction commences and is supervised by a LHA architect.
7. Prior to construction completion, the LHA staff qualifies families for occupancy of the project.
8. After construction the LHA staff will usually manage the project even though it is not uncommon for private property managers to be hired.

TURNKEY PROGRAM

During the mid-1960s private enterprise began to exert pressure on many LHAs to become more involved in the public housing program from planning to completion. The result of such pressure was the evolution around 1965 of the "turnkey" program which puts the site selection, architectural design, construction financing, and construction phases of project development into hands of private industry.

Three forms of turnkey are in common use: Conventional Turnkey, the Accelerated Turnkey Program (ATP), and Acquisition or Handshake Turnkey. In addition there are several new turnkey programs: Turnkey II, Turnkey III, and Turnkey IV. Also related to turnkey is the leased housing program.

Conventional Turnkey is the most common. First the LHA decides on the number of housing units it wants constructed in one project and advertises for local builder-seller proposals for construction of the proposed units. Then submitted bids are evaluated by both the LHA and HUD, including an appraisal of the proposed site and the obtaining of independent cost estimates. After

324

evaluation and approval of one of the proposals the LHA and the successful builder-seller meet to agree upon a price at which the LHA will purchase the completed project. The LHA must then seek HUD approval of the price and obtain an Annual Contribution Contract, after which local community project approval is also sought. After the necessary approvals and contract a formal agreement is entered into between the LHA and the builder-seller. Once executed, the agreement must be approved by HUD. The project is then constructed, the LHA handles the rentals and property management, and the project is purchased from the builder-seller by LHA upon completion.

Once a builder-seller's proposal has been accepted he may proceed under the **Accelerated Turnkey Program**. Under ATP the builder-seller does not await a "letter of intent" but proceeds with final project plans and specifications. (A letter of intent is the LHAs commitment to proceed with the project and to pay the builder-seller for the site and design work even if they cannot agree on a price for the improvements.) Thus many of the preliminary and time consuming steps of conventional turnkey are eliminated when ATP is used. Processing time under ATP can be cut in half but with a greater risk upon the builder-seller who stands to lose his costs of project planning and development in the event a contract of sale is not entered into with the LHA.

In some states, such as New York and New Jersey, statutory requirements impose an obligation upon private developers engaged in public construction projects to pay minimum wages and to be selected through competitive bid procedures. Many would-be builder-sellers under the turnkey program do not want to be faced with either situation. For that reason, they often are not interested in dealing with LHAs. Thus, in these areas LHAs attempted to widen the range of the builder-seller by introducing the **Acquisition or Handshake Turnkey Program**. This program provides for the purchase of completed units without any prior written agreement between the LHA and the builder-seller. The theory is that the purchase of a completed building is not, per se, public construction and therefore does not come within the purview of the troublesome statutes. Under acquisition or handshake turnkey the builder agrees informally with the LHA as to the proposed project and its sales price. Upon completion of the project the LHA tenders its offer to purchase at the previously agreed upon price and a sale is consummated. As with conventional turnkey and ATP, the LHA handles project rental and agreement.

TURNKEY ADVANTAGES

Several important advantages have been gained by the LHA, the builder-seller, and the public through the turnkey program. Some major advantages are:
1. Time savings of up to three years in producing needed public housing.
2. Cost savings of up to 15 percent of total project cost.
3. Flexibility in project design and location due to the number of private developers usually participating in the program.
4. No completion bond required of builder-sellers as is required of successful bidders under the conventional public housing program.

TURNKEY II

The turnkey program described above has been labeled "Turnkey I" since the advent in 1967 of "Turnkey II." Turnkey II simply carries Turnkey I a step further by encouraging private management to replace LHAs in operation of public housing projects. Since improper management and maintenance has been the cause for failure of several public housing projects throughout the country, Turnkey II is a concerted effort to bring quality, experienced, private management into an area which sorely needs professionals skilled in resolving the problems inherent in lower income housing developments. Standard property management is only a part of Turnkey II, for the real focal point is on providing social services so tenants of low income housing communities can better attune themselves to society. By their own ability tenants hopefully will remove themselves from the lists of those needing the benefits of government financial assistance.

LEASED HOUSING

Section 10-C and Section 23 of the National Housing Act of 1937, as amended by the National Housing Act of 1965, provide for the leasing of privately-owned housing units by LHAs for occupancy by eligible public housing families. The Section 10-C leasing program has rarely been utilized. It authorizes LHA's to lease entire buildings on a long term basis as an alternative to project development or purchase.

Section 23, previously the most popular program, authorizes the leasing of individual apartment units in existing buildings with the purpose of placing low-income families throughout a community instead of concentrating them in individual housing projects. Under the Section 23 program a low-income family can conceivably live in a middle-income community and hopefully become a part of it. The procedure under Section 23 is for the LHA to evidence a need for leased housing units, to gain program approval from the local community governing body and HUD, to enter into an annual contribution contract with HUD for a specified number of units, and then to seek out units to lease. Leases entered into between the LHA and the property owner usually run for terms of three to five years with renewal options and specifically provide for unit occupancy by low-income families. This program was stepped up by the provisions of the National Housing Act of 1970 which required 30 percent of all dwelling units for which annual contribution contracts are entered into to be units in private accommodations leased under the Section 23 authority.

In early 1973 the Section 23 program was subjected to a federal housing moratorium. After the moratorium was lifed in late 1973, the program was not further pursued by HUD. The philosophy of leased housing changed during 1973 and 1974. Instead of LHA's leasing units directly from landlords for subsequent reletting to low-income tenants, HUD developed a program of direct cash assistance. This new program was legislated in the Housing and Community Development Act of 1974, which established a new leased housing program designed Section 8 of the United States Housing Act of 1937 as renumbered.

Under the Section 8 program, a direct contractual arrangement is made between HUD and the owner of existing, new or rehabilitated housing units for the payment of the difference between the unit's fair market rent and the tenant's gross income.

Tenants eligible for Section 8 leased housing are required to pay 15 to 25 percent of their income toward rent with the balance of the fair market rent being subsidized by HUD and paid directly to the landlord. To be eligible, tenants must have incomes that do not exceed established area income limits.

All types of units and structures are eligible for assistance under the Section 8 program, including mobile homes. HUD has established project eligibility criteria under which projects designed to accommodate a substantial number of large families are favored.

Housing assistance payments under this program are normally given for twenty years, but may be made for as long as forty years where the project was financed by a state housing finance agency.

The 1974 Act provides for leased housing assistance for 400,000 new, rehabilitated and existing units.

HOME OWNERSHIP

The home ownership program, also known as "Turnkey III" was proposed in order to stimulate home ownership by low-income families occupying units in public housing projects. It was given further impetus in the late 1960s by HUDs proclamation of a new proposal for Home Ownership Opportunities through public housing programs. The Home Ownership Opportunities program embodies Turnkey III, as well as the Section 10-C and Section 23 programs. The mechanics of the program are initially the same as standard public housing in that the LHA sponsors or purchases a housing project which is then rented to low-income tenants. Then Turnkey III is introduced and the project converted to a cooperative, condominium, or single-family ownership development where the tenant-occupant can become a homeowner through a lease-purchase arrangement. The low-income tenant-purchaser continues to pay the same rental until such time as his individual unit is converted into ownership by him. The tenant-purchaser builds up sufficient "sweat equity" by repairing and maintaining his individual unit.

When the built-up "sweat equity" equals a normal down payment, financing is arranged for the tenant, usually with FHA Section 265 insurance, and conversion to homeownerhsip takes place. Obtaining sufficient "sweat equity" usually takes many years. "Sweat equity" may be supplemented by tenant family contributions in order to speed up the ownership opportunity. Equity credit may also be accumulated by an allocation of rent payments to that purpose by the LHA.

TURNKEY III

The pilot program for Turnkey III consisted of 200 homes built in North Gulfport, Mississippi during 1968-1969. Homeownership conversions in this project were financed under either the Section 235 or Section 221(d)2 FHA insurance programs.

The goal of encouraging homeownership by low-income families is a significant one and its attainment could well create a sense of achievement in families for whom homeownership has been a desired but not readily realized eventuality. At a very minimum, the movement of government toward helping low-income families help themselves is a very encouraging and progressive step.

TURNKEY IV

The homeownership program is further implemented by Turnkey IV which provides for tenant acquisition of property occupied under the Section 23 leasing program. The pilot program for Turnkey IV was conducted in 1969 in Los Angeles, California. Known as "Inner City Townhouses," the project was sponsored by a nonprofit group and consists of clustered two-story townhouse units built under FHAs Section 221(d)3 Rent Supplement Program. The Housing Authority of the City of Los Angeles through an annual contribution contract with HUD leased units from the nonprofit sponsor for occupancy by low-income families. Tenants then built up equity and purchased their units in a manner similar to the Turnkey III program.

Both Turnkey III and Turnkey IV will make it possible for families with incomes below the Section 235 insured loan limits to purchase a home.

PUBLIC HOUSING PROGRAMS SUMMARY

It is quite evident that revolutionary innovations have taken place in the public housing programs over the last ten years. Such innovations are indicative of the future of public housing and the government's attitude toward it. Summarized, the major trends have been these:

1. To allow private enterprise a greater participation in planning, development, construction, and management of low-income housing projects.
2. To provide for eventual tenant ownership of the units they occupy.
3. To integrate low-income families into middle-income housing projects and areas.
4. To include social programs in overall project management in order to assist low-income families in bettering themselves.
5. To combine the public housing programs with other federal housing programs, such as building an FHA-insured Section 22(d)4 Rent Supplement Project for lease to a LHA under the Section 23 program, with tenant homeownership potential, under FHA Sections 235 (265) or 221(d)2.

Today, however, new activity under the conventional, turnkey, and homeownership programs has ceased and leased housing is now concentrated in the Section 8 program (fully explained in Chapter 15). Thus, the future direction of public housing will undoubtedly be toward subsidy assistance instead of LHA and HUD project development.

STATE HOUSING ASSISTANCE PROGRAMS

There has been a recent trend toward the establishment of state agencies and state programs to assist in the financing of privately sponsored housing projects for low-to-middle income families. These state agencies and programs parallel the purposes of the Federal Housing Administration and its programs. (See Chart 20-1).

CHART 20-1

State Housing Assistance Agencies

State Agency	Year Established
Alaska Housing Finance Corp.	1971
Colorado Housing	1973
Connecticut Housing Finance Authority	1969
Delaware State Housing Authority	1968
Georgia Development Auth. for Housing Finance	1972
Hawaii Housing Authority	1970
Iadho Housing Agency	1972
Illinois Housing Development Authority	1967
Kentucky Housing Development Corporation	1972
Louisiana Authority for Housing	1972
Maine Housing Authority	1969
Maryland Community Development Administration	1972
Massachusetts Housing Finance Agency	1966
Michigan State Housing Development Authority	1966
Minnesota Housing Finance Agency	1971
Missouri Housing Development Commission	1969
New Jersey Housing Finance Agency	1967
New York State Housing Finance Agency	1960
North Carolina Housing Corporation	1969
Ohio Housing Development Board	1972
Pennsylvania Housing Agency	1971
Rhode Island Housing & Mortgage Finance Corp.	1973
South Carolina Housing Authority	1971
South Dakota Housing Development Authority	1973
Tennessee Housing Development Agency	1973
Utah Housing Finance Agency	1975
Vermont Home Mortgage Credit Agency	1968
Virginia Housing Development Authority	1972
West Virginia Housing Development Fund	1968
Wisconsin Housing Finance Authority	1972

In the early years of the decade of the 1970s, fifteen states had existing housing agencies, fourteen of which were created since 1966, and eight states were planning the establishment of agencies.

The first and best known state housing finance program is the one created in New York in 1960 by the Mitchell-Lama Law. Under the Mitchell-Lama program developers are able to obtain financing from the state for construction of low-to-middle income housing projects. The financing is arranged through the sale by the state of New York of federal income tax exempt bonds. Funds so obtained are lent to project sponsors for 0.5 percent more than the cost of the bond issue. The maximum mortgage loan available is 90 percent to 100 percent of project replacement value with up to a 50-year maturity. Benefits derived from the below-market interest rate mortgages are passed on to project tenants in the form of lower rent, thereby creating an indirect subsidy at no cost to the public. In addition to low interest rates, rental susidies may be produced through tax abatement by the municipality in which the project is located. In New York City, where real estate taxes are extremely high, tax abatements are likely to reduce the monthly rental by as much as $80 to $120.

State programs, such as those conducted under the Mitchell-Lama Law, can also be used in conjunction with federal subsidies in connection with state-produced subsidies, the amount of available federal subsidy funds can be significantly stretched. Subsidies are combined by the federal government making up the interest differential between the low cost state funds and one percent interest. For example, if a FHA Section 236 project mortgage is insured at a market interest rate of 7 percent per annum the government would subsidize the difference between an effective one percent per annum interest rate and the 7 percent rate, the cost of the subsidy in that instance equalling 6 percent per annum. But if the project is conducted under the Mitchell-Lama or similar state program the mortgage rate may be only 5 percent, reducing the government subsidy to 4 percent or by one-third, thus allowing the unused government subsidy to be employed elsewhere in the production of more housing.

As in the federal subsidy programs, project sponsors are limited to the specific percentage return of their equity investment.

The impact of state financing programs upon low-income housing is well demonstrated by the record of the New Jersey Housing Finance Agency (NJFHA), which during the first six years of its existence financed the construction of over 8,300 units in seventeen local New Jersey communities.

State programs and agencies that give attention to the housing needs of their citizens are importantly different from the vast majority of state programs. Agencies for the programs are conducted and primarily funded on a breakeven basis by obtaining monies from private investment sources and channelling them into mortgage financing. Operating expenses are covered by interest income and fees charged by the state to developers and project sponsors for use of mortgage funds.

It is not anticipated that state housing finance programs will supplant any of the federal insurance programs in the near future, but rather they will be of great assistance in providing the twenty-six million new and rehabilitated housing units that it is said this country will require between 1968 and 1978. In fact it is the opinion of many state and federal government officials that the housing programs of many states may be expanded in the near future to produce housing on a large-scale total community concept. Unlimited bonding authority and the investment attractiveness of federal tax-exempt bonds coupled with the provisions of Title VII of the Housing Act of 1970, which makes state housing agencies eligible for bond guaranties, interest loans, public service grants, and planning grants for new community development, are all the encouragement needed to prod state agencies into dynamically expanding their programs. Thus, state housing programs and agencies have become a real estate financing force and housing phenomenon of the 1970s.

NEW COMMUNITIES

The post-war population explosion has had its effect upon the growth of the nation's cities and towns. Most communities have been infected with what is known as urban sprawl—a hodge-podge of buildings which sprang up so rapidly that little thought was given to the location of housing units, social facilities, and industries with respect to each other.

In the early 1960s several large private developers began the development of "new towns" which would be self-contained to the extent of providing housing, shopping, social facilities, recreation, and employment in one planned area. Reston, Virginia and Columbia, Maryland are the most notable examples of the first new towns. Such developments were viewed as methods of putting an end to urban sprawl through large scale community planning, while at the same time providing housing to meet the nation's growing needs.

A number of problems existed with regard to the development of new towns and were evidenced from the experiences at Reston and Columbia. The primary problem concerned the ability of developers to acquire sufficient capital to undertake a large scale development. Since land acquisitions and development loans are rated high risks, it is difficult to obtain funds on a small scale, let alone for the development of thousands of acres. Additionally, such funds have historically been available only on a short-term basis.

CREATION

The federal government, recognizing the advantages of new communities and the problems concerning their development, incorporated into the Housing and Urban Development Act of 1968, Title IV, known as the New Communities Act. This act expanded the existing Title X land development loan authority of the Department of Housing and Urban Development. It authorized the secretary of that agency to guarantee obligations issued by private developers to help finance new community development projects. It also authorizes the secretary to make grants to state and local public bodies and agencies to supplement the federal assistance that is otherwise available for certain water, sewer, or open space projects if these projects are needed or desirable in connection with an approved new community development project. The amount of such grant may not exceed 20 percent of project costs. In addition, the projects must meet the requirements for regular grants under the applicable sections of the Housing Act of 1965.

PURPOSES

The New Communities Program is designed to provide a better living environment through quality self-contained community developments. As with most other recent government programs, it is anticipated that this one will also help to solve the tremendous housing supply problem facing the nation through use of private capital rather than government appropriations.

New towns developed under the new communities program are to provide a variety of housing units for a wide range of family income levels. Single-family residences, townhouses and apartments (high rise, low rise, and garden type), both on a rental and sale basis are preferably included in any planned development. Integrated with living units will be social facilities (churches and schools), recreational areas, shopping centers, and industry. In essence the program adopts the theory that a large scale town-size development can be planned and constructed to best serve all the needs of its residences. Schools and shopping can be strategically located to provide easy accessibility and can directly relate to population concentrations. Streets and roadways can be designed for minimum traffic in residential areas. Industry can be located next to labor markets, thereby providing job opportunities for the new town's inhabitants. New community dwellers can enjoy recreational facilities not usually available or as conveniently located in normal housing situations. These are but a few of the values that sponsors of the New Communities Act hope will be derived from the program.

The major impediment to such large scale development has been the need for an overabundance of capital for an extended period of time prior to and during the sale of housing units, the proceeds of which can be used to retire the land development debt. This impediment will hopefully be removed to some extent through government assistance. Nevertheless the problem of repayment through a well-planned and managed construction and sales program will still exist.

ELIGIBILITY AND LIMITATIONS

Because of the proposed scale of development, only those private developers with substantial financial and administrative ability are able to meet the eligibility requirements for the government guarantees. Developers applying for eligibility must evidence previous experience or demonstrate present ability in order to even be considered. An eligible developer must also produce a feasible site for development. While there are no specific location or size limitations, each proposed site must meet several tests to determine whether or not it will serve the purposes of the assistance program.

A guaranty limitation of $50 million is placed on any single new community development otherwise qualifying for assistance. The guaranty is further restricted to amounts not in excess of the lesser of 80 percent of HUD's estimate of the property after land development or 75 percent of HUD's estimate of land value plus 90 percent of development costs. It is the latter formula which is most frequently used.

Commonly included in land development costs are grading, utility installation, roadways, sidewalks, streets, storm drainage facilities, financing charges, and services of required professionals.

The guaranty does not extend to costs of housing units or buildings unless the buildings are used as a part of the land development, such as a structure housing sewer disposal equipment or a community building which is part of the community owned recreational facilities. Housing units are intended to be constructed either with conventional financing or through the use of any one or more of the various federal, state, and local housing programs.

THE GUARANTY

Any normal form of obligation issued by the developer is eligible for guaranty under the program. The guaranty places the full faith and credit of the federal government behind the debt obligation and the only recourse that holders of the obligations have is against the government guaranty. Thus the government in reality acts as a co-signer rather than a guarantor.

Only long-term obligations may be guaranteed. Maturities are approximately twenty years with a closed period (no pre-payment) of ten years. Usually beginning the eleventh year, an annual sinking fund computed as a percentage of the debt must be established. A pre-payment penalty is required on a declining basis after the tenth loan year.

The government's security for its guaranty is a first lien on the real property being developed.

COST OF THE GUARANTY

Fees required of the developer as payment for the government's guaranty are substantial:

Application Fee: $5,000
Commitment Fee: 0.5 percent of principal up to $30 million and 0.1 percent of the principal amount in excess thereof, payable at the time of the government's commitment to guaranty.
Guaranty Fee: 3 percent of the principal amount guaranteed payable at time of guaranty.
Annual Fee: 0.5 percent of the average outstanding principal balance due annually for the first seven years and thereafter at the rate of 1 percent per annum.

EXISTING NEW COMMUNITIES

The first debt issue guaranteed by the government under the new community program was an 8.5 percent 20-year debenture issue for $8 million to be used to acquire and develop the new town of Jonathan, Minnesota, near Minneapolis. Jonathan is proposed to house 50,000 people within the next twenty years.

Fourteen other new communities have now been approved including St. Charles, Maryland, near Washington, D.C., and Park Forest South, Illinois, in the Chicago metropolitan area.

RECENT DEVELOPMENTS

More emphasis upon the development of new towns and an expansion of that program was approved as part of the Housing and Urban Development Act of 1970. Title VII of that act is known as the Urban Growth and New Community Development Act of 1970. A new corporation called the Community Development Corporation was established by the 1970 act as a part of the Department of Housing and Urban Development.

The purpose of this new corporation is to "provide for the development of a national urban growth policy and to encourage the rational, orderly, efficient and economic growth and development of our states, metropolitan areas, cities, counties and towns."

Most importantly the new communities guaranty is extended to cover 100 percent of obligations of debt issued by public bodies, such as housing agencies for the acquisition and development of new towns. Other changes brought about by the Urban Growth and New Community Development Act are as follows:

1. The new Community Development Corporation (CDC) will guarantee the debt obligations issued for the development of new towns.
2. The CDC will be able to make grants to private and public developers to

cover costs of initial development planning.

3. The CDC will be able to make grants to public bodies only to supplement costs of installation of public facilities to serve new communities and to cover costs of the interest differential between market rates and that payable on tax exempt obligations.

4. The CDC will make loans to cover payments of interest due during the first fifteen years on guaranteed debt obligations. This authority will greatly assist developers in surviving the cash burden of carrying a new town project through the early stages when little or no income is being produced. Huge carrying costs have in the past been the greatest deterrent to and prime cause of failure of proposed new communities.

Establishment of the Community Development Corporation has answered several of the problems which existed in the original new communities act contained in the 1968 Housing Act. However, one significant problem remains, that of finding developers large enough, interested enough, and experienced enough to undertake the time and financial obligations of building new towns. Irrespective of the problems that it faces, the Community Development Corporation is a valid step toward combating urban sprawl and bringing about planned urban growth.

FARMERS HOME ADMINISTRATION

Title V of the Housing Act of 1949 created the Farmers Home Administration FmHA) for the primary purpose of providing funds for housing non-metropolitan rural America.

Originally, FmHA was created as a credit agency for lower-income farmers who were unable to obtain loans anywhere else. Today its mortgage credit program for non-farm rural and small town residents is by far its major operation.

FmHA is considered a direct lender even though its loans are sold on an insured basis to private investors. It is the FmHA county supervisor, rather than an approved mortgagee, who originates the loan and services it after sale to an investor.

FmHA HOUSING PROGRAMS

Farmers Home Administration has two major housing programs, Section 502 and guaranteed loans for singly family sales housing and Section 515 for multifamily rental housing.

Section 502 loans may be obtained for the purchase of.an existing structure or a newly constructed one or to construct, rehabilitate, or relocate a single family dwelling. Loans under Section 502 may include the cost of stove, refrigerator, washer and dryer if these items are normally sold with the house in the area concerned.

FmHA has no maximum mortgage limits, but requires houses to be modest in size, design and cost. It does not set income limits for families purchasing homes under Section 502 and these limits affect the mortgage amount.

Loans are restricted to those made to low and moderate income families with limited net worth who reside in rural areas of 10,000 population or less or reside in 10,000-20,000 population areas outside a metropolitan area and where there is a serious lack of mortgage credit.

Those families qualifying for Section 502 loans may receive 100 percent financing. Also available to low income families are loans with as low as 1 percent interest or 20 percent of family adjusted income, whichever is less. Mortgage maturity may not exceed thirty-three years.

Section 502 loans are direct loans to borrowers by FmHA. As an adjunct to this loan program, under the 1972 Rural Development Act, FmHA is authorized to guarantee up to 90 percent of any loss of principal and interest on loans made by private lenders to families residing in rural areas.

The guaranteed loan program is designed for above moderate income families and requires a down payment similar to FHA's 203(b) program to be made. Interest rates on guaranteed loans are not set by FmHA, but are negotiated between lender and borrower.

Section 515 is a direct mortgage loan program to promote the development of newly constructed or substantially rehabilitated rental or cooperative housing in rural areas.

Occupancy in Section 515 project is restricted to low and moderate income families, persons 62 years old or older, and the handicapped.

Interest credit assistance to a minimum of 1 percent interest is available for Section 515 loans under the project built with Section 8 rent subsidy assistance.

Interest rates for these loans are determined by FmHA and amortization and loan terms are forty years (fifty years for senior and handicapped citizen projects).

OTHER PROGRAMS

Other programs conducted by FmHA are:

1. Disaster Rural Housing Loans to repair or replace buildings damaged or destroyed by a natural disaster.
2. Home Improved Enlargement loans up to $3500 for the purpose of improving or enlarging existing buildings or completing one on which substantial construction work has already been done.
3. Farm Labor Housing Loans and Grants. Loans under this program are made at low interest rates to insure low enough rents to accommodate farm workers.
4. Rural Housing Site Loans made on a short term basis to public bodies and private nonprofit organizations to finance the purchase and development of adequate building sites.
5. Technical assistance for Self-Help Housing which involves the cooperative work of family groups which provide a major portion of the labor required in the construction of their homes. Financing for housing built under this program is furnished under Section 502 with interest credit included.
6. Home Repair Loans of up to $2500 ($3500 where the funds are used to finance repairs or improvements involving water supply, septic tank, or bathroom or kitchen plumbing facilities) are made at 1 percent interest for ten years for the purpose of making housing safer and healthier for its occupants.

NATIONAL CORPORATION FOR HOUSING PARTNERSHIPS

On December 11, 1968, the Committee on Urban Housing, better known as the Kaiser Committee for its chairman Edgar Kaiser, presented its findings and recommendations to its creator, the President of the United States, Lyndon B. Johnson. One of the main recommendations of the Kaiser Committee was incorporated into the Housing and Urban Development Act of 1968. Under Title IX of that innovative act, the President of the United States is given the authority to create one or more private corporations, similar to the Federal National Mortgage Association, to engage in activities directed at providing more housing for low-to-middle income families, again through the use of private funds.

Pursuant to the act, President Johnson created the National Corporation for Housing Partnerships (NCHP), incorporated in December 1968, to carry out the purposes stated in Title IX of the Housing Act of 1968, in particular "to encourage the widest possible participation by private enterprise in the provision of housing for low-to-moderate income families."

ORGANIZATION

NCHP is essentially only the administrative body for the larger and more important National Housing Partnership (NHP). The NCHP acts as a housing consultant, a participant in local housing ventures, and sometimes as a project developer. On the other hand the NHP is a vehicle for private investment in those housing ventures in which the NCHP is a moving force. For example, as the general partner of the NHP, the NCHP will work with local developers to establish housing projects to be financed under one of the federally assisted FHA multifamily housing programs (Section 236 and Section 8), under federally assisted public housing, under federally assisted sales housing (Section 235) under state housing authority programs, or even under a nonassisted housing program (Section 221(d)4. Local developers and investors may join with the NCHP as sponsors of proposed housing projects and the joint venture will be funded with equity capital invested by the local developers, local investors, and the NHP. In most instances the NHPs contribution is limited to 25 percent of the required equity funds. If local investors cannot be found, the NHP may invest additional funds.

The NCHP can furnish all the assistance necessary for locating sites; processing FHA and LHA assistance applications; engaging architectural, engineering, site planning, construction, legal, accounting, property management and other similar services; obtaining financing; and in general creating and completing the proposed project.

CAPITALIZATION

Financing for the corporation and partnership was arranged through an initial offering of $42 million, consisting of investment units of common stock in both the corporation and the partnership. The proceeds from each investment unit were split 5 percent to the NCHP and 95 percent to the NHP.

The investment units were marketed by the NCHP and investment bankers, the latter providing assistance for no compensation other than out-of-pocket expenses. All units were sold only to business organizations interested in giving their support to the creation of housing for low-to-middle income families. Individuals were not allowed to purchase any investment units.

It was anticipated that the $42 million would be able to eventually produce $2 billion in actual construction due to the financial leverage between equity and debt available on FHA and other assisted projects. During its first ten years of operation (1968-78) the NHP was responsible for the construction of $827 million in multifamily housing units containing 32,847 units (see Chart 20-2).

Purchasers of investment units are both shareholders in the NCHP and limited partners in the NHP. Thus, the purchasers (investors) receive a share of the income and depreciation generated by the local project ventures.

METHODS OF OPERATION

Three main plans have been adopted and used by the corporation and the partnership to accomplish their goal of creating low to moderate income housing. They are equity participation secured loan and equity participation and the joint venture.

EQUITY PARTICIPATION

Under this simplest plan, the NCHP agrees to assist the local developer in FHA processing. The NHP agrees to purchase a 25 percent equity position in the ownership of the project. This plan anticipates that the local developer has performed all the project ground work and needs assistance mainly in the areas of FHA processing and equity acquisition.

The project sponsor and owner will be a limited partnership with the local developer as general partner and local investors and the NHP as the limited partners.

THE SECURED LOAN AND EQUITY PARTICIPATION

This method provides local project sponsors with the "seed" money necessary to plan the project, including, if necessary, land acquisition. In addition the corporation makes available its staff and facilities to assist and guide the sponsors. Prior to commencement of construction, the partnership purchases an equity position in the ownership entity (priced to reflect the advantages given to the sponsors by the corporation through its seed money loan) and the loan made by the corporation is repaid, usually out of mortgage proceeds.

JOINT VENTURE

The full range of services and financial ability of the corporation is available when the corporation and a local project sponsor bind together in a joint venture to plan, develop, construct, and promote a housing project. The corporation shares all the risks of project development including the investment of time and seed money. For its participation the corporation receives an interest in the project ownership entity, usually a limited partnership. One-half of the corporation's interest is sold prior to construction to the NHP, and the other venture interests would be sold to local investors, with the original local sponsor retaining a general partnership interest.

Where necessary the corporation is authorized to proceed with the development of projects on its own. In such instances and prior to commencement of construction, 75 percent of the ownership interest would be sold to local investors and 25 percent sold to the partnership.

The majority of the NCHP's programs are designed to combine the local developer's expertise with the corporation's national exposure and staff experience in a venture to provide as much housing for low-to-middle income families as is possible in the shortest period of time.

HOUSING CAPITAL CORPORATION

In 1975, NHP launched a program designated to assist builders of single family for sale housing. This program resulted in the creation of a small business investment corporation called Housing Capital Corporation, Inc. (HCC). The purpose of HCC is to provide loan and equity funds to builders via the joint venture method.

At year-end 1978, HCC had committed a total of $21 million to ninety-four developments which have or will produce a total of 8840 homes.

CAPITAL HOMES, INC.

Carrying its support of single family housing a step further, NHP in 1976 organized Capital Homes, Inc. as a subsidiary of HCC.

Capital Homes, Inc. is engaged in the direct construction and sale of medium-priced housing in the Washington-Baltimore metropolitan area.

PROGRAMS UTILIZED

The NHP utilizes a cross section of housing programs to accomplish its goals. Some of the major programs utilized are:
1. The Section 8 Leased Housing Program utilizing financing by state housing finance agency, HUD/FHA, or conventional loan sources.
2. State Housing Finance agency Programs, both subsidized and non-subsidized.
3. HUD/FHA programs, particularly Section 221(d)4, 236, and 235.
4. Farmers Home Administration multifamily programs.
5. Sales housing of a single family and condominium nature with financing by: FHA, VA, FmHA, state housing finance agency, or conventional.

CHART 20-2
NHP'S INVESTMENT IN MULTIFAMILY HOUSING
AS OF DECEMBER 31, 1978

Major Program	Projects	Units	Develop- ment Cost	Original NHP Equity
Section 236	112	18,427	$399,991	$31,658
Section 221(d)(3)	20	1,731	32,338	2,725
Section 221(d)(4) and 220	14	2,233	51,768	5,339
Section 8	61	9,293	323,840	37,237
Other	4	915	13,568	1,354
FmHA	4	248	5,282	637
	215	**32,847**	**$826,787**	**$78,950**

QUESTIONS FOR THOUGHT AND DISCUSSION

1. What programs are now in existence which are designed to provide housing for low-to-middle income families primarily with the use of private capital?
2. Do you feel the nation's housing goals should be met, as much as possible, through private resources or should new programs be developed to channel more Government appropriated funds into housing? Why?
3. Is the public housing program, which encourages distribution of low-income families throughout middle-income family neighborhoods, a sound one from both a social and economic standpoint? Explain.
4. What housing programs are now being conducted by state housing agencies and how important are these agencies?
5. What is the FmHA and what is its function?
6. What services does the National Corporation for Housing Partnership perform and how does it assist in housing production?

21

PRIVATE MORTGAGE INSURANCE

Of the many recent developments that have taken place in the area of real estate finance, the phenomenal growth of private mortgage insurance companies must rank as one of the most significant. Over the last four decades FHA has been the primary source of mortgage insurance. However, the last ten years have seen FHA slowly preempted in the mortgage insurance field. In 1976, private insurers provided 44.6 percent of mortgage insurance; in 1977, this industry's total rose to 47.5 percent and in 1978 it reached 51.6 percent. Over $27 billion in policies on one-to-four family mortgage loans were written by private insurance companies in 1978, more than double the $13 billion written five years earlier in the boom year of 1973. These figures reflect that private mortgage insurance companies have firmly established themselves and should, in the future, continue as the new primary source of mortgage insurance.

HISTORY

Private mortgage insurance is not a new concept. It has been with us since the 1920s when several private mortgage insurance companies operated, free from any regulation. These companies, located primarily in New York, fell into bankruptcy in the 1930s due to inadequate reserve funds to meet real and potential claims that resulted for the collapse of real estate values during the Depression.

Today's private mortgage insurance companies trace their beginnings to the creation in 1957 of the Mortgage Guarantee Insurance Company of Milwaukee, Wisconsin, commonly referred to as MGIC. Since the creation of MGIC, thirteen other companies have been organized (see Chart 21-1). Nevertheless, MGIC has remained the leader of the industry in net premiums written. In 1978, $122.5 million of private mortgage insurance net premiums was written by MGIC. This represents about 40.6 percent of the $301 million 1978 industry total.

REGULATION

The private mortgage insurance industry today is far more highly regulated than its pre-Depression ancestor. Private mortgage insurers are governed by the laws of their state of incorporation and the laws of the states in which they conduct their business. Such laws set forth requirements for surplus, paid in capital, and contingency reserve in order to insure that the company can withstand times of real estate market depressions. Presently nineteen states have enacted mortgage guaranty insurance laws. The balance of the states have authorized mortgage insurance. In 1976, The National Association of Insurance Commissioners adopted a model state law for mortgage guaranty insurance. This model bill will facilitate the passage of such laws by the legislatures in those states not among the nineteen which have enacted mortgage insurance laws.

In addition to state laws, MIs are subject to FNMA and FHLMC financial and operation requirements. The requirements of FNMA and FHLMC parallel state insurance laws and regulations while also dealing with geographical diversity of insurance risk and conflicts of interest between lenders and MIs.

RESERVE REQUIREMENTS

Mortgage insurance companies are required to maintain three types of reserves to enable them to survive adverse economic conditions and to protect policyholders against catastrophic losses which may result from a severely depressed economy. These reserves are:

Unearned Premium Reserves—All premiums received for the term of a policy are placed in this reserve and are earned according to state law or regulation based upon a matching of premiums with losses and exposure.

Loss Reserves—This reserve is established for actual or potential losses on a case-by-case basis and for losses incurred but not reported.

Contingency Reserves—This special reserve is the largest in amount and includes half of each premium dollar earned. The funds put into his reserve cannot be removed for ten years unless (a) losses in a calendar year exceed 35 percent of earned premium, and (b) the state of domicile insurance commissioner concurs with the withdrawal.

Chart 21-2 is a comparison of the financial statistics of the fourteen MIs. As shown, industry reserves at the end of 1978 totaled $840.2 million, of which $542.9 million was in contingency reserves.

CHART 21-1
PRIVATE MORTGAGE INSURANCE COMPANIES

American Mortgage Insurance Co. (AMI)
5401 Six Forks Road
Raleigh, North Carolina 27609

Commercial Credit Mortgage Insurance Co. (CCMI)
300 St. Paul Place
Baltimore, Maryland 21202

Commonwealth Mortgage Assurance Co. (CMAC)
1523 Walnut Street
Philadelphia, Pennsylvania 19102

Foremost Guaranty Corporation (Foremost)
131 W. Wilson Street, Suite 1101
Madison, Wisconsin 53703

Home Guaranty Insurance Corporation (HGIC)
P.O. Box 13267
Richmond, Virginia 23225

Integon Mortgage Guaranty Corporation (Integon)
P.O. Box 3199
Winston-Salem, North Carolina 27102

Mortgage Guaranty Insurance Corporation (MGIC)
MGIC Plaza
P.O. Box 488
Milwaukee, Wisconsin 53201

PMI Mortgage Insurance Co. (PMI)
Bank of America Center, Suite 3580
555 California Street
San Francisco, California 94104

Republic Mortgage Insurance Co. (RMIC)
P.O. Box 2514
Winston-Salem, North Carolina 27102

Ticor Mortgage Insurance Company (Ticor)
6300 Wilshire Boulevard
Los Angeles, California 90048

Tiger Investors Mortgage Insurance Company (TIMI)
225 Franklin Street
Boston, Massachusetts 02102

United Guaranty Corporation (UGC)
826 N. Elm Street
Greensboro, North Carolina 27401

Verex Assurance, Inc. (Verex)
150 E. Gilman Street
Madison, Wisconsin 53707

Liberty Mortgage Insurance Corporation (LMI)
7840 Montgomery Road
Cincinnati, Ohio 45236

CHART 21-2

RELEVANT FINANCIAL COMPARISONS OF RESIDENTIAL MORTGAGE INSURERS
As Of December 31, 1978
($ In Millions)

	MGIC	VEREX	UGC	AMI	PMI	TICOR	TIMI	LMI	FORE-MOST	CCMI	RMIC	INTEGON	HMIC	CMAC	INDUSTRY TOTAL
I. YEAR FOUNDED	1956	1961	1962	1961	1972	1972	1968	1964	1972	1974	1972	1972	1972	1976	
II. ASSETS	$574.8	$118.8	$147.3	$85.3	$80.6	$98.5	$76.2	$17.9	$20.0	$12.4	$23.3	$6.1	$6.7	$10.7	$1,206.6
III. NET PREMIUMS WRITTEN 1978	122.5	31.4	30.3	20.9	22.6	20.9	19.0	3.6	4.4	1.3	6.3	.3	1.4	.5	301.4
IV. INSURANCE RESERVES:															
Loss Reserves	13.6	7.3	6.3	2.2	5.0	5.2	3.0	1.2	.6	.1	.5	.1	.1	NIL	45.2
Unearned Premium Reserves	121.3	25.7	28.7	17.8	13.8	10.0	12.0	2.5	3.2	.8	5.7	.6	1.6	.4	252.1
Contingency Reserves	203.1	55.9	58.1	39.2	21.0	21.7	40.5	9.9	3.6	.6	5.7	.7		.1	542.9
TOTAL	416.0	88.9	93.1	59.2	39.0	46.9	55.5	13.6	7.4	1.5	11.9	1.4	2.5	.5	840.2
V. POLICYHOLDERS' RESERVES:															
Unassigned Surplus	84.7	4.8	(3.2)	2.8	(13.3)	(8.2)	(20.5)	(5.2)	(1.7)	.7	(2.5)	(.5)	(.7)	(.1)	39.1
Contingency Reserve	283.1	55.9	58.1	39.2	21.0	23.7	40.5	9.9	3.6	.6	5.7	3.9	3.7	0.3	542.9
Paid In Surplus	54.8	18.5	38.3	14.1	50.5	54.5	36.0	6.9	11.0	5.0	12.0	3.9	1.2	2.0	318.3
Capital Paid-Up	1.8	3.4	8.0	3.0	3.0	2.0	2.3	1.2	3.0	5.0	1.4	1.2		.0	38.5
Other Surplus Items	.0	.0	10.0	3.0			.1				.0				13.0
TOTAL	426.4	82.0	111.2	62.1	61.2	72.0	59.1	12.8	15.9	11.3	16.6	5.3	5.0	10.3	951.8
VI. RATIOS:															
Loss Ratio -Earned	14.4	19.2	15.5	9.0	19.7	13.7	17.0	10.5	16.7	14.6	14.5	28.8	6.2	4.7	
Expense Ratio -Written	28.4	39.6	32.5	43.6	67.2	47.3	43.5	34.5	64.0	123.5	47.1	100.5	57.3	186.4	
Combined Ratio (S & P Basis)	42.8	58.8	48.0	53.4	86.9	61.0	60.5	45.0	80.7	138.1	61.6	129.3	63.5	191.1	
VII. CONCENTRATION OF BUSINESS: By Direct Premiums Written ($)															
1	TX 11.7	TX 9.6	CA 8.0	CA 9.4	TX 24.1	TX 26.0	CA 17.1	OK 13.2	TX 25.4	MD 30.6	NC 30.1	GA 82.3	VA 79.4	PA 67.6	
2	CA 6.9	CA 8.9	TX 6.0	NC 8.5	CA 18.0	CA 19.5	OH 7.2	TX 9.3	MI 16.6	VA 15.9	FL 16.6	MO 8.1	MD 9.5	CA 15.2	
3	MI 6.5	FL 6.0	NC 5.8	PA 6.7	IL 5.9	MD 4.4	CO 6.3	MD 9.2	PA 13.2	AR 9.0	TX 11.2	TX 3.3	SC 3.9	KY 7.0	
4	IL 4.9	MN 5.0	LA 5.0	FL 5.0	MA 5.0	CO 4.3	MA 6.2	IN 0.6	WI 9.6	CA 0.9	VA 0.3	OK 3.2	PA 2.8	DE 6.8	
5	PA 4.6	OH 4.9	WA 5.4	OK 5.8	MD 5.0	GA 4.2	TX 6.2	FL 8.4	NY 9.0	FL 7.3	MD 7.9	SC 1.0	DE 1.7	TX 2.0	
Total Top Five States	34.6	34.4	31.0	36.2	58.8	58.4	43.0	48.7	73.8	80.5	82.3	96.9	97.3	98.6	
VIII. INSURANCE IN FORCE ($ In Billions)	38.5	(A) 9.3	9.0	6.2	5.8	6.5	5.4	(B) 9.3	1.0	.3	.3	.1	.3	.1	64.1*
IX. RISK/CAPITAL RATIO	18.3/1	(A) 20.0/1	19.0/1	20.9/1	19.9/1	19.1/1	19.9/1	(B)20.0/1	13.9/1	5.3/1	17.9/1	4.6/1	12.0/1	1.8/1	

A. Insurance In Force and Risk to Capital Includes LMI.
B. Insurance In Force and Risk to Capital Includes Verex.
* Does not equal total of amounts shown because Verex and LMI are combined in amount and shown under both companies.

Source: Annual Statements.

REASONS FOR RECENT GROWTH

The recent growth of private mortgage insurance companies is the result of two major changes (1) in the regulations governing savings and loans, the Federal National Mortgage Association (FNMA), and the Federal Home Loan Mortgage Corportaion (FHLMC), and (2) of a basic characteristic of private mortgage insurers. These three factors are:

1. The Emergency Home Finance Act of 1970, which was the enabing legislation for FNMA to purchase conventional loans (theretofore FNMA was allowed to purchase only FHA/VA loans). The act provided that conventional loans in excess of 75 percent loan-to-value (now 80 percent) could be purchased by FNMA only if the seller retained a 10 percent participation or if the loan was insured by a FNMA-approved private mortgage insurer. FNMA's conventional program didn't go into effect until 1971. Today, almost all of the conventional loans purchased by FNMA are privately insured.

   This same act created the Federal Home Loan Mortgage Corporation (see Chapter 19) and authorized it to purchase conventional mortgage loans under the same terms and restrictions as FNMA.

   Purchases of conventional loans by these two entities were very slight at first, but has now accelerated to the point where it acts as a very important encouragement for the use of private mortgage insurance.

2. The amendments in early 1972 by the Federal Home Loan Bank Board to its regulations of savings and loan associations. Such amendments permitted federal savings and loan associations to make 95 percent loan-to-value mortgage loans up to $36,000 (now $67,500)on single family residences if the portion of the unpaid principal balance in excess of 75 percent (now 80 percent) of the property's value was insured by an approved private mortgage insurance company. This new regulation not only created a new opportunity for private mortgage insurers but produced an alternative to FHA financing. FHA insures a 97 percent loan-to-value mortgage up to $25,000. For a mortgage over $25,000 the loan-to-value that FHA will insure decreases rapidly from the 97 percent level. Hence, the 95 percent loan authority of savings and loans creates a very effective alternative to FHA financing particularly with mortgage loans in the $26,000 to $60,000 category. The cost of private mortgage insurance is also less than FHA by the fifth loan year. Private mortgage insurance companies charge 0.25 percent annual premium (plus an initial 0.80 percent not initially charged by FHA) while FHA charges 0.5 percent annually. The result, then, is a shift to using conventional financing with private mortgage insurance instead of the FHA program.

3. The basic characteristic of private mortgage insurers which distinguishes them from FHA—the ability to give a quick decision on an insurance application. With FHA it normally takes from one to two weeks to receive an insurance commitment. Private insurers, however, can respond within twenty-four hours of receipt of a complete loan file. Such notifications is usually given by telephone with a subsequent mail follow-up. Mortgage insurers (MI's) operate primarily on the lender's decision on the loan. In the event of a large number of claims emanating from one lender, closer scrutiny by the MI will result.

344

COVERAGES OFFERED

Private mortgage insurance insures lenders against loss when borrowers fail to meet their mortgage obligations. The insurance programs offered by these MI companies extend to residential mortgages, commercial mortgages, home improvement loans, lease guaranty, and mobile home credit. The bulk of the insurance written by MIs, however, is in the area of residential mortgages.

RESIDENTIAL MORTGAGE INSURANCE

Each MI has several insurance premium plans which vary according to term of coverage as well as extent of coverage. Four popular residential mortgage insurance programs are:
1. 25 percent coverage for 91-95 percent residential mortgage loans
2. 20 percent coverage for 81-90 percent residential mortgage loans
3. 20 percent coverage for 91-95 percent residential mortgage loans and
4. 20 percent coverage for 80 percent and under residential mortgage loans.
An example of how the insurance coverage works is as follows:

Property Value:	$30,000
Mortgage Loan Amount @ 95 percent of Value:	28,500
25 percent Insurance Coverage:	7,125

Accordingly, the risk taken by the lender is that, at a time of default, assuming no previous principal payments, the value of the property will not have fallen below $21,375 (the loan amount less the insurance coverage). Hence, taking the insurance into account, the lender is really in a 71.2 percent loan-to-value situation ($21,735 ÷ $30,000).

For loans going to FNMA or FHLMC, three special programs are available, as follows:
22 percent coverage for 91-95 percent residential mortgage loans
17 percent coverage for 86-90 percent residential mortgage loans
12 percent coverage for 81-85 percent residential mortgage loans

APPLYING FOR COVERAGE

To apply for coverage, a lender must first be approved by the private mortgage insurance company to whom an insurance application is to be made. The lender approval process involves an initial investigation of the lender and its underwriting procedures. Such investigation, if successful, results in the issuance of a Master Policy to that lender.

To obtain an insurance commitment on a specific loan, approved lenders then need only fill out and submit to the private insurer a simple 1-page application form (see Chart 21-4) supported by copies of the borrower's loan application, credit report, lender's appraisal, and a photograph of the property to be insured (if existing construction).

CHART 21-3

Annual Premium Plans

STANDARD COVERAGES			Renewal Premiums	
Coverage	LTV	1st Yr. Premium	Constant Yrs. 2-10	Decl. Bal. Yrs. 2-Term
30%	91-95%	1.25%**	.24%	.25%
	86-90%	.90%*	.24%	.25%
25%	91-95%	1.00%*	.24%	.25%
	86-90%	.65%	.24%	.25%
	81-85%	.50%	.24%	.25%
	80% and under	.35%	.24%	.25%
20%	91-95%	.75%	.24%	.25%
	86-90%	.50%	.24%	.25%
	81-85%	.35%	.24%	.25%
	80% and under	.25%	.24%	.25%
17%	81-85%	.30%	.24%	.25%
12%	80% and under	.14%	.13%	.14%
COVERAGE TO 75% EXPOSURE – Meets FNMA/FHLMC Requirements				
22%	91-95%	.80%	.24%	.25%
17%	86-90%	.40%	.24%	.25%
12%	81-85%	.15%	.14%	.15%
COVERAGE TO 80% EXPOSURE				
16%	91-95%	.625%	.24%	.25%
12%	86-90%	.25%	.24%	.25%

*Optional plan available at .50% each of 1st 3 years, .25% annual renewal thereafter.

**Optional plan available at .625% each 1st 3 years, .25% annual renewal thereafter.

NOTES

(1) The annual renewal premium under the Constant plan for years 11-term is .125% of the original loan amount.

(2) Five-year renewals are available as an option to the annual renewals in the 10 and 15 year programs. The five-year renewal rates are .50% of the principal balance.

(3) For seasoned loans on which, prior to application, (i) 12 or more monthly payments have been received, (ii) no contractual delinquencies exist; (iii) no payments have been received after the expiration of a "30 day grace period"; and (iv) company underwriting standards are met, the premium rate shall be determined by subtracting .25% from the initial premium rate. However, no annual plan may be reduced below a minimum of .25%, and no single premium may be reduced by an amount greater than that applicable to the annual premium plan in the same loan-to-value and coverage percentile grouping.

CHART 21-4

APPLICATION FOR MORTGAGE LOAN INSURANCE

LIBERTY MORTGAGE INSURANCE CORPORATION
A SUBSIDIARY OF AMERICAN FINANCIAL CORPORATION

P.O. BOX 3E16S   CINCINNATI, OHIO 45236   TELEPHONE (513) 793-4144
TOLL FREE 800-645-6610 — OHIO TOLL FREE 800-682-9219

1. LMI lender number _____

2. Lender name _____

3. Lender address _____
   Street   City   State   Zip

   Please confirm by telephone: _____ ☐Yes ☐No Area Code _____ No. _____ Contact: _____

4. Borrower name _____

5. Address of property _____
   to be insured   Street
                          City   State   Zip

6. Will property be occupied by borrower? ☐Yes ☐No
7. Appraised value of property _____ $ _____
8. Sales price or proposed cost _____ $ _____
9. Mortgage terms: $
   Amount of loan _____ $ _____
   Amount of collateral pledge _____ $ _____
   Net amount to be insured _____ $ _____
   Interest rate _____ %
   Term of mortgage _____ Yrs.
10. Purchaser's total equity consists of:
    Cash _____ $ _____
    Trade-in or lot value _____ $ _____
    Other _____ $ _____
                    Total $ _____
11. Age of borrower _____ Yrs.
12. Property:
    Location _____   ☐Urban   ☐Suburban   ☐Rural
    Age _____ Yrs.
    Number of living units _____   ☐One   ☐Two   ☐Three or Four
13. Monthly payment:
    Principal & interest _____ $ _____
    Tax accrual _____ $ _____
    Insurance accrual _____ $ _____
    LMI accrual _____ $ _____
               Total monthly payment $ _____

COVERAGE & PREMIUM PLAN DESIRED
Please see inside front cover for Coverage & Plan Code

LMI PREMIUM PLAN NUMBER: _____

☐ANNUAL PLAN   SINGLE PLAN FOR _____ YEARS

COVERAGE ☐20%   ☐25%

14. Gross monthly Income   Husband $ _____
                           Wife $ _____
                           Other $ _____

15. Loan Purpose   ☐Purchase   ☐Refinance
                   ☐Other _____

REQUIRED EXHIBITS

1. Copy of lender's loan application
2. Current credit report
3. Employment verification

4. Tax returns if self employed
5. Past payment record if refinance
6. Appraisal report including legal description and photo

Date _____ Lender's Authorized Representative _____

FOR LMI USE ONLY

CC	GVI	TD	PRI	EC	SC		D-%	H-%	T-%

ORIGINAL — MAIL TO LMI

LMI 3-3-74

Source: Liberty Mortgage Insurance Company, Cincinnatti, Ohio.

LOAN UNDERWRITING

There is a variance between private mortgage insurers as to what constitutes an insurable risk. In general, however, loan underwriting follows the following guidelines:

1. Income, employment, and credit rating of the borrower must be favorable in relation to the family's obligations. Normally, consideration is given to the wife's income.
2. The term of amortization (30-year maximum) is determined by the age of the borrower and the remaining economic life of the property and neighborhood.
3. Quality of the property to be insured is determined by the character of the neighborhood and by convenience, livability, and marketability. Also considered are the quality of construction materials and equipment since they will determine the economy of maintenance, utility, and repair expense.

INSURANCE PREMIUMS

There is little variance in the insurance premiums charge by the major private mortgage insurance companies. Chart 21-4 reflects rates and charges as approved by the Insurance Commissioner of the State of Wisconsin. Generally, coverage will be on an annual renewal basis continuing only until the loan is reduced, by amortization, to 75 percent of original value.

MORTGAGE LIMITS

Normally, a private mortgage insurer's loan limits are governed by those lenders and institutions it deals with. For example, lenders and institutions originating loans for sale to FHLMC, GNMA, and FNMA are governed by the established limits on mortgage loans that these agencies will purchase. On 95 percent loans FNMA, GNMA, and FHLMC have a limit of $75,000 and on 90 percent loans and less, a limit of $93,750 (for specific limits please refer to the individual chapters in this text on FNMA, GNMA, and FHLMC). When these constraints are not involved, then the more liberal limits of the individual private mortgage insurers governs. These limits usually provide for mortgage insurance up to $150,000.

MORTGAGE INTEREST RATES AND OTHER LENDER CHARGES

Unlike FHA, the private mortgage insurance companies do not regulate or attempt to regulate interest rates and charges. The interest rate, loan discount, origination, fees, closing costs, and other charges on mortgage loans covered by private mortgage insurance are matters of negotiation between lender and borrower.

SELLING INSURED PROPERTY

Insurance coverage automatically continues on assumption of a mortgage resulting from a transfer of real estate, so long as the original borrower is not released from primary liability by the lender. If the private mortgage insurer approves the new owner, then coverage may continue when the original borrower is released from liability by the lender.

CHART 21-5

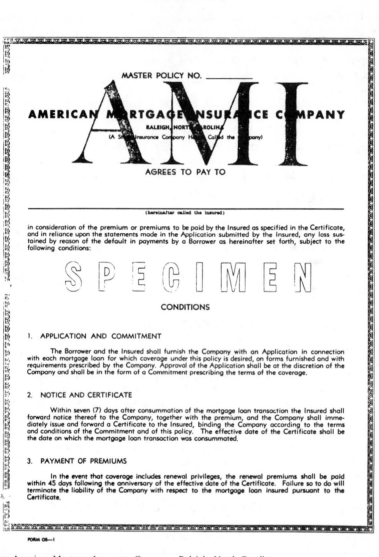

MASTER POLICY NO. _____

AMERICAN MORTGAGE INSURANCE COMPANY

RALEIGH, NORTH CAROLINA

(A State Insurance Company Herein Called the Company)

AGREES TO PAY TO

_____

(hereinafter called the Insured)

in consideration of the premium or premiums to be paid by the Insured as specified in the Certificate, and in reliance upon the statements made in the Application submitted by the Insured, any loss sustained by reason of the default in payments by a Borrower as hereinafter set forth, subject to the following conditions:

SPECIMEN

CONDITIONS

1. APPLICATION AND COMMITMENT

    The Borrower and the Insured shall furnish the Company with an Application in connection with each mortgage loan for which coverage under this policy is desired, on forms furnished and with requirements prescribed by the Company. Approval of the Application shall be at the discretion of the Company and shall be in the form of a Commitment prescribing the terms of the coverage.

2. NOTICE AND CERTIFICATE

    Within seven (7) days after consummation of the mortgage loan transaction the Insured shall forward notice thereof to the Company, together with the premium, and the Company shall immediately issue and forward a Certificate to the Insured, binding the Company according to the terms and conditions of the Commitment and of this policy. The effective date of the Certificate shall be the date on which the mortgage loan transaction was consummated.

3. PAYMENT OF PREMIUMS

    In the event that coverage includes renewal privileges, the renewal premiums shall be paid within 45 days following the anniversary of the effective date of the Certificate. Failure so to do will terminate the liability of the Company with respect to the mortgage loan insured pursuant to the Certificate.

FORM OS—1

Source: American Mortgage Insurance Company, Raleigh, North Carolina

INSURANCE CANCELLATION

Private mortgage insurance may be cancelled by surrendering the policy. In this event a short-rate refund is given to the party paying the premium.

POLICY CLAIMS

Within sixty days after finalization of a foreclosure, the lender may file a claim which includes the principal balance of the loan, accumulated interest, real estate taxes and hazard insurance premiums advanced, the expense of necessary property repairs and maintenance during foreclosure, disbursements in foreclosure, and reasonable attorney and trustee fees allowed by court, but not to exceed 3 percent of principal and interest.

The private mortgage insurer then has the option to either pay the claim in full and accept title to the property free and clear of all liens; or pay the lender a sum equal to 20 percent or 25 percent (depending upon the specific coverage) of the claim and relinquish all title to the property to the lender.

As example of a claim is as follows:

Principal balance due and owing:	$30,000.00
Accumulated interest from date of default to date of claim:	1,000.00
Subtotal	$31,000.00
Attorney and trustee fees (maximum of 3 percent of sub total):	$ 930.00
Property taxes and/or insurance premiums advanced:	800.00
Preservation of property (repair and maintenance during foreclosure):	300.00
Disbursements during foreclosure for filing fees, publication of notice, etc:	100.00
Total Claim	$33,130.00

OPEN-END PROVISION

Most private insurance policies contain an open-end provision giving the lender the right to increase the loan without the prior consent of the insurer. The additional premium due on the increased loan amount is then governed by the premium rate of the original loan.

SAMPLE POLICY

Chart 21-5 is a copy of a sample residential mortgage insurance policy as issued by American Mortgage Insurance Company, Raleigh, North Carolina.

4. TERMINATION BY COMPANY

The Company shall remain liable under this policy with respect to such Commitments or Certificates issued to the Insured, as long as the terms and conditions herein contained are fully complied with. However, the Company reserves the right to terminate this policy at any time, subject to its remaining liable on such Commitment and Certificates already issued to the Insured.

5. CANCELLATION BY INSURED

The Insured shall have the privilege of canceling the coverage pursuant to any Certificate by returning such Certificate to the Company. On receipt thereof, the Company shall refund to the Borrower or assigns such sum as may be determined to be due in accordance with the cancellation schedule set forth herein; providing, however, that no refund shall be paid in the event that a claim for loss has been filed.

6. RESTORATION OF DAMAGE

As a prerequisite for the payment of such loss as may be determined to be due herein, should there be physical loss or damage to the property from any cause, whether through accidental means or otherwise, the Insured shall cause the said property to be restored to its condition at the time of the issuance of the Certificate, reasonable wear and tear excepted.

7. OPEN-END PROVISION

The Insured may increase the mortgage loan balance by making an additional loan to the Borrower, provided that an Application is made therefor subject to approval by the Company. In the event of such approval, the prevailing premium therefor shall be paid to the Company, for the additional amount loaned to the Borrower, and the Company shall issue a Certificate insuring the additional amount.

8. COMPLETED CONSTRUCTION

In the event that the mortgage premises consists of improvements in the process of construction, the Company shall not be liable until such construction is completed.

9. NOTICE OF DEFAULT

Within 10 days after the Borrower is four (4) months in default, notice thereof shall be given to the Company by the Insured. Monthly reports indicating the default status of the Borrower's account shall be given to the Company thereafter until such time as appropriate proceedings are commenced, title has been vested in the Insured or the Borrower is less than four (4) months in default.

10. PROCEDURE ON DEFAULT

When the Borrower's account is four (4) or more months in default, the Company may direct that the Insured commence appropriate proceedings as herein defined, which shall be commenced, in any event, when the Borrower's account is nine (9) months in default. Such proceedings, when instituted, shall be diligently pursued, and should applicable laws permit the appointment of a receiver, application therefor shall be made by the Insured, with the recommendation that an agent of the Company be appointed to so act. The Company shall be furnished, within a reasonable time, copies of all notices and pleadings required in such proceedings, and with any pertinent information requested by the Company. The Insured shall also furnish to the Company, at least fifteen days prior to the foreclosure sale, if any, a statement indicating the amount anticipated to be due, at the time of the sale, to the Insured under the terms of this policy and shall be required to bid, at the sale, the amount due to the Insured under the terms of this policy. Acceptance by the Insured at any time of a voluntary conveyance from the Borrower of his interest in the mortgaged real estate or commencement by the Insured of appropriate proceedings on default of the Borrower, even though his account is less than four (4) months in default, shall not preclude the Insured from recovery for loss under this policy.

11. COMPUTATION OF LOSS

The amount of loss payable to the Insured shall be limited to the principal balance due pursuant to the mortgage agreement, accumulated interest computed through the date of the tender of conveyance, as hereinafter set forth (penalty interest excluded), real estate taxes and hazard insurance premiums necessarily advanced by the Insured, any expenses necessarily incurred by the Insured in the preservation of the mortgaged real estate, and all other necessary expenses of the appropriate proceedings, including court costs, and reasonable attorneys' fees not exceeding three (3%) per cent of the principal and interest due as herein set forth.

12. WHEN LOSS PAYABLE

Any loss due to the Insured shall be payable within 60 days after filing a claim for such loss on a form to be furnished by the Company. The claim for loss must be accompanied by a tender to the Company of conveyance of title to the mortgaged real estate together with satisfactory evidence that such title is good and merchantable in the Insured, free and clear of all liens and encumbrances. Failure to file a claim for loss within 60 days after completion of appropriate proceedings shall be deemed an election by the Insured to waive any right to claim payment under the terms of this policy.

13. OPTION TO PAY 20% OR 25% OF AMOUNT DUE

In lieu of conveyance of title to the mortgage premises and payment in accordance with Condition 11, the Company shall have the option of paying twenty per cent (20%) of such amount due to the Insured and have no c. to said real estate, such payment to be a full and final discharge of the Company's liability. By a Special Condition in the Certificate of Insurance issued evidencing the coverage on a particular loan transaction, the optional guaranty payment herein provided may be increased to twenty-five per cent (25%) of the amount due the insured.

14. WHERE NOTICE IS GIVEN

All notices, pleadings, claims, tenders, reports and other data required to be given by the Insured to the Company shall be mailed postpaid to the home office of the Company.

15. SUBROGATION AGAINST BORROWER

The Borrower shall not be liable to the Company for any loss paid to the Insured pursuant to this policy; provided, however, that the real estate shall consist of a single family dwelling occupied by the Borrower, otherwise, the Company reserves the right to make claim against the Borrower for any loss paid or deficiency suffered by the Company.

16. TO WHOM PROVISIONS APPLICABLE

The provisions of this policy shall inure to the benefit of and be binding upon the Company, and the Insured, and their successors and assigns.

17. SUIT

No suit or action on this policy for recovery of any claim shall be sustained in any court of law or equity unless all the conditions of this policy have been complied with, unless specifically waived by the Company in writing, and unless commenced within two (2) years after the loss can be determined.

18. CONFLICT WITH LAWS

Any provision of this policy which is in conflict with the laws of the jurisdiction in which this policy is effective is hereby amended to conform with the minimum requirements of such laws.

19. DEFINITIONS

Four (4) months of default is defined as the failure to pay the total aggregate amount of four (4) monthly payments due under the terms of the mortgage agreement. Similarly, nine (9) months of default is defined as the failure to pay the total aggregate amount of nine (9) monthly payments due under the terms of the mortgage agreement.

Mortgage agreement is defined to include a note, mortgage, bond, deed of trust, or other instrument used in connection with the Borrower's loan.

Appropriate proceedings are defined as any practical legal remedy permissible, under the laws of the jurisdiction in which the real estate is located, to vest title in the Insured, including, but not limited to, foreclosure by public or private sale.

The term Borrower, or Insured, when used herein, shall mean the single or plural, male or female, individual, partnership, or corporation, as the case may be.

IN WITNESS WHEREOF, The Company has caused its Corporate Seal to be hereto affixed and these presents to be signed by its duly authorized officers in facsimile to become effective as its original seal and signatures and binding on the Company by virtue of countersignature by its duly authorized agent.

AMERICAN MORTGAGE INSURANCE COMPANY

PRESIDENT

SECRETARY

DATE _____

AUTHORIZED REPRESENTATIVE

SHORT RATE CANCELLATION SCHEDULE
ANNUAL PREMIUM PLAN

SINGLE PREMIUM PLANS

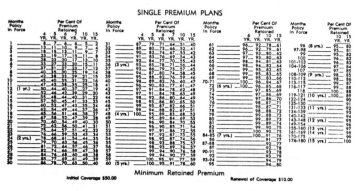

Initial Coverage $50.00 — Minimum Retained Premium — Renewal of Coverage $10.00

Source: American Mortgage Insurance Company, Raleigh, North Carolina

COMMERCIAL MORTGAGE INSURANCE

Commercial mortgage insurance protects lenders against borrowers who default on loans secured by income-producing properties such as apartment complexes, office properties, clinics, retail stores, service-type properties, warehouses, and light and medium manufacturing facilities. The insurance covers the top 20 percent of qualifying mortgage loans having loan-to-value ratios of 80 percent or less. Such coverage will reduce the risk on an 80 percent loan to 64 percent of value and on a 70 percent loan to 56 percent of value. As with residential loans, no restrictions are imposed on interest rates, service charges, or other loan terms.

Insurance premiums for commercial mortgage insurance are as follows:

Multifamily loan premiums:	0.1 percent of loan amount
5-year single premium, prepaid non-cancellable policy:	1.75 percent of loan amount
Installment premium:	First year—0.5 percent of loan amount plus 0.375 percent per annum on outstanding loan balance for four additional years. After five years annual renewals are available at 0.375 percent per annum on the outstanding loan balance.

Commercial and Industrial loan premiums:	0.1 percent of loan amount
5-year single premium prepaid, non-cancellable policy:	2.9 percent of loan amount
Installment premium:	First year—1.2 percent of loan amount plus 0.5 percent per annum on the outstanding loan balance for four additional years.

After five years annual renewals are available at 0.5 percent per annum on the outstanding loan balance.

HOME IMPROVEMENT LOAN INSURANCE

Home improvement loan insurance protects lenders against losses sustained on lons made to finance the alteration, repair, conversion, improvement, or modernization of real estate. Loans eligible for this type of coverage are generally limited to a maximum amount of $7,500 and term of ninety-six months.

Insurance coverage is for either 90 percent or 100 percent of losses incurred. The annual premium for 90 percent coverage is 0.5 percent of net loan balance and for 100 percent coverage it is 0.75 percent of net loan balance.

The private mortgage insurance home improvement program offers a reasonable, conventional substitute for FHA Title I insurance program by allowing the lender to obtain a higher loan yield, allowing a 50 percent higher than FHA insurable loan amount, and by allowing a one year longer loan term.

LEASE GUARANTY INSURANCE

Lease guaranty insurance protects the landlord against loss which may result from a commercial tenant's failure to make rental payments. This insurance of the landlord's rentals protects the lender from default occasioned by the landlord's lack of rental income. Hence, lease guaranty insurance assures a lender of a certain lease income stream requisite to meet mortgage loan debt service.

Where a tenant's credit is marginal or in an instance where a tenant has not been in business very long, lease insurance will serve to upgrade the tenant's risk level to that normally associated with national high credit rated tenants. It also allows the tenant to obtain space in a more favorable commercial location and usually allows the landlord to obtain better mortgage rates and terms.

Eligibility for insurance is extended to tenants engaged in retail, service, or light manufacturing businesses and to space in properties such as shopping centers, industrial parks, office buildings, retail stores, warehouses, and light manufacturing structures. In some instances ground leases may even be eligible for lease guaranty insurance.

Lease guaranty policies are written for a minimum of five years and a maximum of twenty years or the term of the lease being guaranteed, whichever is less.

Policies are written on a single premium basis with the premiums expressed as a percentage of the rent guaranteed for the policy period. After payment of a $100 commitment fee the following premium schedule would govern:

Premium as Percent of Total Policy Period (years)	Premium as Percentage of Total Guaranteed Rental
5	5.4 percent
6	5.4 percent
7	5.2 percent
8	4.8 percent
9	4.4 percent
10	4.0 percent
11	3.7 percent
12	3.4 percent
13	3.1 percent
14	2.9 percent
15 through 20	2.8 percent

A requirement of the private mortgage insurers is that the tenant must escrow with them three months rent at time of premium payment. If no default occurs, the full amount of funds escrowed are returned to the tenant with interest at 4 percent per annum. In some cases a 90-day deductible policy may be issued in lieu of an escrow.

MOBILE HOME CREDIT INSURANCE

Mobile home credit insurance is obtained by lenders in order to protect them against losses resulting from defaults on loans to finance the purchase of a mobile home and the resulting repossession.

Premiums for mobile home insurance are based on a single premium for the entire policy period. The premium is calculated on the basis of the net unpaid loan balance × the loan term × the premium rate of 0.75 percent.

CONVENTIONAL MORTGAGE-BACKED SECURITIES

Mortgage insurance companies are playing a key role in the evolution of conventional mortgage-backed securities.

In addition to the normal coverage of over 80 percent loan-to-value loans in the pool of mortgages constituting the collateral for the security, mortgage insurance is issued for the entire loss on any given claim (plus accrued interest and other expenses) subject to a limitation that losses cannot exceed 5 percent of the aggregate original principal balance of the pooled loans.

The mortgage-backed security is not a general obligation of the issuer. Thus, the investor must rely upon the quality of the loan collateral. By having the mortgage-backed security covered by the new blanket-type mortgage insurance policy, the collateral is in effect upgraded and in many cases is eligible for a rating that will increase its marketability.

Presently, the conventional mortgage-backed security is in a process of evolution with the only major issuers since inception in September, 1977, being large savings

CHART 21-6
Comparison of Private Mortgage Insurance vs.
FHA Section 203 and VA Guaranty
1976-78
(number of mortgages)

Year	MIC	FHA (203)(b)	VA
1976	452.023	230,371	328,612
1977 January	32,061	20,626	29,834
February	29,378	23,322	28,543
March	39,897	22,452	30,199
April	42,258	21,492	26,312
May	50,860	32,435	32,544
June	62,041	20,997	42,941
July	59,589	21,524	26,838
August	66,796	29,871	43,120
September	62,200	22,919	42,699
October	57,954	23,835	28,149
November	59,396	28,234	35,474
December	54,968	16,587	32,445
Total	617,398	284,294	399,098
1978 January	47,764	23,994	41,763
February	39,657	22,560	36,449
March	50,031	27,061	24,763
April	57,065	19,806	25,252
May	61,670	23,722*	30,142
June	68,963	21,565*	28,338

Source: Department of Housing and Urban Development, Division of Housing and Finance Analysis.
*Includes Sec. 245(GPMs)

and loan associations and commercial banks. As the security is perfected and its acceptance increases, a substantial new market for private mortgage insurers will have been created.

FUTURE OF PRIVATE MORTGAGE INSURERS

The main question that has been in the minds of lending institutions was "Can the private insurance industry withstand catastrophic loss?" This question was soundly answered in May, 1975 when the results of a comprehensive study of the private mortgage insurance industry conducted by Arthur D. Little, Inc., a research and consulting organization, was released.

The Little report found the private mortgage insurance industry to be strong enough to survive economic conditions comparable to those which led to the Great Depression.

Based on this proven stability of the MI companies, it can be said that private mortgage insurance has been universally accepted today by lending institutions. Its acceptability is also reinforced by the fact that more loans are being insured by MIs than by FHA and VA (see Chart 21-6). The trend in single family policies plus the accelerating interest in conventional mortgage-backed securities should provide a continued growth environment for MIs.

A definite trend away from the writing of commercial mortgage insurance, lease guaranty insurance and mobile home credit insurance has taken place in the industry. These product lines are being replaced by the mortgage-backed security insurance policy and by diversification into other insurance areas such as directors and officers liability insurance and municipal bond blanket guaranty policies. Hence, the future should reflecct a concentration by MIs on their main product line—single family mortgage insurance—and a diversification into related insurance fields.

QUESTIONS FOR THOUGHT AND DISCUSSION

1. What are the advantages of private mortgage insurance of conventional loans as compared to FHA mortgage insurance?
2. What is the initial insurance premium for 25 percent coverage of a 95 percent loan of $50,000 under an annual coverage policy? What is the renewal fee?
3. In what instances would a lender want to require commercial mortgage insurance?
4. What are the advantages to (a) landlord (b) tenant, and (c) lender of lease guaranty insurance?

GLOSSARY

The following terms are those most frequently used in real estate financing. The list is far from being inclusive and is presented only to assist the reader in a better understanding of the text.

Abstract—An historical summary of the conveyances, transfers, legal action and other facts relied on as evidence of title; a summary of the documents having a bearing on the continuity of ownership to a property.

Acceleration—The right of the mortgagee to demand, upon default of the mortgagor, the immediate repayment of the unpaid balance of the mortgage loan.

Acknowledgment—A formal declaration before a duly authorized officer by a person who has executed an instrument, such execution being his free act and deed.

Ad Valorum—According to the value; an assessment of taxes against property.

Agent—A person entrusted with authority received from the person he represents.

Allotment—The amount of money allocated for the purchase of mortgages within a specified time by a permanent investor, with whom a mortgage loan originator has an ongoing relationship, but does not have a specific contract in the form of a commitment. The allotment may indicate the investor requirements as to prices, the term of the loan, and/or underwriting standards.

Amenity—That which contributes satisfaction rather than direct monetary income to its owner or enhances and contributes to the value of the property. A recreational area within an apartment community is an amenity.

Amortization—The liquidation of the principal portion of a mortgage loan on an installment basis.

Appraisal—An estimation of the value of real property which represents the opinion of a party having knowledge of real estate prices and the market for real estate.

Assessed Value—A valuation of real or personal property by a public body for purposes of taxation.

Assessment—A local tax levied against property for a specific purpose, such as a sewer assessment.

Assignee—One to whom real property or an interest in real property is transferred, assigned, or set over.

Assignment of Mortgage—A legal document or instrument that evidences a transfer of ownership of a mortgage from one mortgagee to another.

Assignor—One who transfers, assigns, or sets over real property or an interest therein to another.

Assumption Agreement—An agreement by one party to pay an obligation originally incurred by another on terms contracted for by the original obligor.

Balloon Payment—The balance due on a Note at maturity that is in excess of one regular principal payment.

Basic Rent—The rent charged in a subsidized housing project and computed on the basis of a maximum subsidy.

Basket Provision—A provision contained in the regulatory acts governing investments by insurance companies and mutual savings banks which allows for a certain small percentage of total assets to be placed in otherwise unauthorized or illegal investments.

Beneficiary—(1) entitled to the benefit of a trust; (2) one who receives profit from an estate, the title of which is vested in a trustee; (3) the lender on the security of a note and deed of trust.

Bond—An obligation issued by a corporation or Government to pay a sum certain on a specific date with interest due, payable in installments during the term of the bond.

Borrower—One who receives funds in the form of a loan with the intention of repaying the loan in full.

Broker—One who, for a commission or fee, brings parties together and assists in negotiating contracts between them.

Buyer's Market—A market in which buyers can purchase property at lower prices and on more advantageous terms than those prevailing earlier; a market characterized by many properties available and few potential users demanding them at current prices.

Capitalization—Determining value by considering net income as a percentage that represents a reasonable return on total investment.

Cash Flow—The amount of cash derived over a certain measured period of time from the operation of income-producing property. The cash flow is used to pay expenses of operation, maintenance cost, debt service, and return on investment.

Chattel Mortgage—A mortgage on personal property as distinguished from a mortgage on real property. Under the Uniform Commercial Code a security interest in personal property replaces what was known as a chattel mortgage.

Closed Period—That portion of the term of a mortgage loan during which the loan cannot be prepaid.

Closing—The conclusion or consummation of a real estate transaction by exchange of a deed for consideration. (See Loan Closing)

Cognovit Note—A note or promissory obligation which contains a provision authorizing the holder of the note or obligation (the lender) to obtain judgment against the borrower upon a default, without giving prior notice to the borrower or allowing the borrower to present a defense. Without such a provision in the note or obligation, the lender would not receive judgment until he sued on the note and proved the default. The advantage of the cognovit provision is that the lender may obtain immediate judgment and thereby a lien against all of the borrower's real property. The lien remains until the borrower pays his indebtedness in full or has the judgment set aside. Otherwise thirty days or more may be required to obtain judgment on a defaulted note or obligation.

Collateral—Property, real or personal, pledged to secure payment of a debt.

Commitment—An undertaking by one party to perform in the future a particular transaction in a stated manner; a promise by a lender to make a loan on specific terms and conditions to a borrower; a promise by an investor to purchase mortgages from a loan originator.

Commitment Fee—The consideration paid for a binding agreement to lend on security of a mortgage or to purchase at a future date. Such consideration may be refunded upon completion of the committed transaction or retained as liquidated damages in the event of noncompliance or default.

Conditional Sale Contract—A contract for the sale of property stating that delivery is to be made to the buyer, title to remain vested in the seller until the conditions of the contract have been fulfilled.

Constant Payment—The periodic payment on a note of a fixed sum which is applied first to interest on the principal balance and then to reduction of principal. As the payments progress, the portion applied as interest decreases and the portion applied to reduce principal increases.

Constant Rate—The rate used to compute the constant payment.

Construction Loan—A loan made to finance the actual construction of buildings on land.

Construction Loan Agreement—A written agreement between the lender and the builder-borrower in which the specific terms and conditions of a construction loan are recited.

Contract—An agreement between two or more parties, either written or oral, to do or not to do a specific thing.

Contract of Sale—A contract between a purchaser and a seller of real property to convey a title after certain conditions have been met and payments have been made.

Conventional Loan—A mortgage loan made by a financial institution without benefit of FHA insurance or VA guaranty.

Conveyance—The transfer of a title to real property by conveyance from one person or class of persons to another.

Coupon Rate—The rate of interest specified on a mortgage or other security instrument.

Debenture—A form of bond or note issued without any specifically pledged security but backed by the general credit of the obligor. Also, a form of payment made by FHA to mortgage lenders in satisfaction of insurance claims.

Debt—A sum of money due by certain and express agreement.

Debt Service—The periodic payment made on mortgage loans, inclusive of interest and a portion of the principal sum borrowed.

Default—The nonperformance of a duty or obligation, whether arising under a contract or otherwise, such as the failure to make a payment called for by a note or mortgage.

Demand Mortgage—A mortgage which is payable on demand of the holder of the evidence of the debt.

Development Loan—A loan made for the purpose of bringing real property to a position whereby construction of buildings can be commenced. Development may include grading and installation of utilities and roadways.

Discount—The difference between the principal amount of a note or mortgage and the price at which such obligation is sold or originated when the latter price is less.

Dower—By operation of law, the interest that a wife has in property owned by her spouse.

Dwelling—Living quarters occupied or intended for occupancy by a household.

Earnest money—A sum of money offered in conjunction with an agreement to purchase rights in real property.

Eminent Domain—The inherent right of a sovereign power (government) to acquire private property for a necessary public use with or without the consent of the owner, by paying to the owner a reasonable consideration for the property so appropriated.

Encumbrance—A claim or lien upon title to real property, such as a mortgage.

Equity—The value which an owner has in real estate over and above the liens or claims against it.

Escalation—The right reserved by the lender by reason of the loan terms, to increase the amount of the payments and/or interest upon the happening of a certain event.

Escheat—The lapsing or reverting of land to the state.

Escrow—Funds that are set aside and held in trust by a third party for a particular use or application. (also see impounds)

Estate—The degree, quantity, nature, and extent of interest which a person has in a real property.

Estate for Years—An interest in real property which will expire after the passage of a fixed period of time. A lease for twenty years is an estate in real property which will terminate at the end of twenty years.

FHA Loan—A mortgage loan that is insured by the Federal Housing Administration.

Fee Simple—Absolute ownership of real property without limitation as to any restrictions or any particular class of heirs. An inheritable estate in land.

Financial Intermediary—A financial institution which acts as an intermediary between savers and borrowers by selling its own obligations for money and, in turn, lending the accumulated funds to borrowers (definition taken from Savings and Loan Fact Book).

Firm Commitment—A commitment by an investor to purchase a specific mortgage loan, or a commitment by FHA to insure or VA to guarantee specific mortgage loan.

Forfieture—Loss of money or anything of value due to failure to perform, for instance under an agreement to purchase.

Grantee—The person to whom title to real property is conveyed.

Grantor—The person conveying title to real property.

Gross Income—The total income from property before deduction of expenses or debt service.

Guaranty—A promise by one party to pay a debt or perform an obligation contracted for by another in the event that the original obligor fails to pay or perform as contracted.

Hazard Insurance—Those forms of insurance designed to reimburse the insured for specific physical damage to his property, such as damage due to fire or windstorm.

Home Loans—A mortgage loan for which the security is a residential structure housing one to four families.

Impounds—An escrow trust - type account established by lenders for the accumulation of funds to meet taxes on the property, FHA mortgage insurance premiums, private mortgage insurance premiums, and/or future insurance policy premiums required by them to protect their security. Impounds (escrows) are usually collected with the note payment each month.

Income Limits—Limits established on a family size basis to determine a family's eligibility for admission into a subsidized housing project. Different income limits are established for each subsizided housing program.

Income Property—Property which produces a money income to the owner.

Income Property Loan—A loan secured on income-producing property.

Institutional Lender—A mortgage lender that invests its own funds in mortgages and carries a majority of such loans in its own portfolio. Individuals that hold mortgage loans made with their own funds are not generally classified as institutional lenders.

Interest—Consideration in the form of money paid for the use of money, usually expressed as an annual percentage.

Interim Financing—Financing during the period of time from project commencement to closing of a permanent loan, usually in the form of a construction loan.

Land Acquisition Loan—A loan, the proceeds of which are used by the mortgagor to acquire title to real property in an unimproved or improved, but vacant, state.

Land Bank—The practice of purchasing and holding land for use in future development. Builder and developers purchase land in advance in order to have it available for use in a continuous building and development program.

Land Development Loan—(see Development Loan)

Land Loan—A loan for acquisition or development of real property (see Land Acquisition Loan and Development Loan).

Land Purchase Loan—(see Land Acquisition Loan)

Late Charge—An additional charge which a mortgagor is contractually required to pay as a penalty for failure to pay a mortgage loan installment by a specified date after the installment due date. FHA permits a 2 percent of monthly payment late charge, whereas 4 percent is allowed by VA.

Leverage—The ability to borrow more than your equity in property. The greater the ratio of amount borrowed to amount of equity, the greater the leverage.

Lien—A claim by one party against the property of another as a security for a debt or charge. The claim can be legally enforced by an action to have the property sold.

Liquidity—The cash position of an individual or business measured by cash on hand and securities quickly convertible into cash.

Loan—A sum of money lent for consideration, usually in the form of interest, to be repaid.

Loan Closing—The closing of a mortgage loan transaction as opposed to a real property purchase even though the loan closing and property transfer may be accomplished simultaneously.

Loan-to-Value Ratio—The relationship between the amount of mortgage loan and the appraised value of the security, expressed as a percentage.

M.A.I.—Member of the Appraisal Institute—The highest professional designation of a real estate appraiser.

Market Rent—The highest price charged by a landlord to his tenants for the use and occupancy of real property, based upon current prices for comparable property without regard to any subsidy.

Maturity—The date by which a mortgage loan must be paid in full.

Moratorium—The temporary suspension, usually by statue, of the enforcement of liability for debt.

Mortgagee—The lender of mortgage funds, and the receiver of security therefor in the form of a mortgage.

Mortgage Insurance Premium (MIP)—The price paid by a mortgagor annually to FHA for loan insurance given by FHA to the mortgagee.

Mortgage Investor—Generally one who purchases existing mortgage loans as opposed to originating them. Anyone who places funds in mortgages as a means of investment.

Mortgage Lender—Generally one who originates mortgage loans by directly lending to the borrower. Anyone who lends funds on the security of a mortgage.

Mortgage Portfolio—The aggregate of mortgage loans held by the lender.

Mortgagor—The borrower of a mortgage fund and giver of a mortgage on real property as security for the repayment of funds so borrowed.

Multifamily Mortgages—Mortgages secured on dwellings other than those containing one-to-four family units. Under FHA regulations multifamily loans cover a broad class of properties including nursing homes, hospitals, mobile home parks, and group practice facilities.

Net Income—That portion of gross income remaining after payment of all charges, expenses and costs.

Net Yield—That part of gross yield which remains after the deduction of all costs, such as servicing, and any reserves for losses.

Note—A signed obligation in writing acknowledging the existence of a debt and promising repayment.

Origination Fee—The fee charged by a mortgagee for processing a mortgage application leading to the closing of a mortgage transaction.

Permanent Loan—A long term mortgage loan.

Permanent Investor—One who invests in a long term mortgage loan.

Personal Property—Movable property of a nonrealty nature (also called chattels).

Points—The amount of discount on a mortgage loan expressed as a percentage.

Prepayment Penalty—A penalty due for the payment of a debt before it actually matures.

Price—A statistical expression for the consideration given for the purchase of a mortgage or group of mortgages and stated as a percentage of par or principal balance.

Principal—The amount of mortgage debt.

Quit Claim Deed—A deed to relinquish any interest in property which the grantor may have.

Real Property—Land and whatever is erected thereon, affixed thereto, or is growing upon the land.

Recourse—The right to claim against a prior owner of a property or note.

Reversion—The portion of an estate left with the grantor which entitles him to possession at the end of another estate.

Reversionary Interest—The grantor's interest in a reversion.

Risk Rating—A process by which various risk are evaluated, usually employing grids to develop precise and relative figures for the purpose of determining the overall soundness of a loan. The "risks" are normally divided as to (1) neighborhood; (2) property; (3) the mortgagor; and (4) the mortgage pattern.

Satisfaction—A written instrument that evidences the payment in full of a mortgage debt, and extinguishes the mortgage lein.

Security—That which is given or pledged to secure the fulfillment of an obligation or charge; the real property described in a mortgage instrument which is collateral for a mortgage debt.

Seed Money—Funds required to cover initial costs of planning a project.

Seller—An organized business enterprise which has as one of its principal purposes the making or purchasing of loans secured by real estate mortgages (FNMA term).

Servicing—The collection of payments of principal, interest, and escrows, such as hazard insurance premiums, real property taxes, FHA mortgage insurance premiums, as called for by a mortgage. Included in servicing is the payment of premiums and taxes when due, periodic inspection of mortgage property, loan analysis, delinquency follow-up, and foreclosure.

Single Family Mortgage—A mortgage on property intended for one family occupancy. The term is also used frequently to refer to one-to-four family dwelling mortgages (see Home Loan).

Special Assessments—Assessments levied for specific purposes such as providing streets, sewers, sidewalks, and the like, an assessment related to benefit derived by the taxed property.

Subordination—The act of a mortgagee acknowledging by written recorded instrument that the debt due him from a mortgagor shall be inferior to the debt due another mortgagee from the same mortgagor secured on the same property.

Subsidy—Direct or indirect grants of money by the government to reduce the cost of housing to the tenant or occupant.

Sweat Equity—Equity in property created by the performance of work or labor which acts to directly increase the value of the property.

Takeout Investor—An investor who agrees to make a long-term loan (permanent loan) that will be used to pay off a short-term loan, usually a construction loan.

Term—The period of time between the commencement date and termination date of a note, mortgage, or other contract.

Title—Evidence that the owner of real property is in lawful possession thereof or an instrument which so evidences real property ownership.

Title Insurance—Insurance written by a title company to protect a property owner against loss if title is imperfect.

Tract Loan—A loan made on the security of a tract of land or subdivision covering proposed construction of single family homes.

Usury—Charging more for the use of money than is allowed by law.

Utility—Ability of real estate to serve a useful purpose; usefulness of real property.

Variabile Rate Mortgage—A mortgage which permits an increase or decrease in interest rate coincident with the variation in a specified financial indicator, such as the prime rate.

Vendee—The party to whom property is sold.

Vendor—The seller.

VA Loan—A mortgage loan guaranteed by the Veterans Administration under the provisions of the Servicemen's Readjustment Act of 1944, as amended. It is sometimes referred to as a "G.I. Loan."

Waiver—The relinquishment of a right or refusal to accept a right.

Warehousing—The practice of obtaining funds on a short-term basis from banking institutions through the pledge of mortgage loans as collateral or the holding of long-term mortgages for the interim period between origination and sale to an investor.

Word of Grant—Words used in a deed or instrument to recite the conveyance of title to real property. An example of words of grant is: "Grantee hereby grants and conveys unto Grantor its heirs, successors and assigns the following described real property."

Zoning—Specification by city or county authorities of the type of use to which property may be put in specific areas.

BIBLIOGRAPHY

American Banker, Published daily by American Banker, New York, N. Y.

Apartment Construction News, published monthly by Gralla Publications, New York, N. Y.

Atteberry, William and Pearson, Karl and Litka, Michael, *Real Estate Law,* Grid, Inc., Columbus, Ohio, Second Edition 1978.

Bailey, Henry J. (editor), *Encyclopedia of Banking Làws,* Banking Law Journal, Boston, Mass., 1964.

The Banking Law Journal, *Encyclopedia of Banking Laws,* Boston, Mass., 1964.

Bartke, Richard, *Home Financing At The Crossroads: A Study Of The Federal Home Loan Mortgage Corporation,* Federal Home Loan Mortgage Corporation, Washington, D. C. 1972.

Best's Insurance Reports Life-Health, 73rd Edition, A.M. Best Company, Morristown, J.J., 1978

Black, Henry Campbell, *Black's Law Dictionary Fourth Edition,* West Publishing Company, St. Paul, Minn., 1951.

Bogen, Jules I. (Editor) *Financial Handbook* Fourth Edition, The Ronald Press Company, New York, N. Y., 1964.

Break, George F., et al, *Federal Credit Agencies,* prepared for The Commission on Money and Credit, Prentice-Hall, Inc. Englewood Cliffs, N.J., 1963.

Bryant, Willis R., *Mortgage Lending,* McGraw-Hill Book Co., New York, N. Y., 1962.

Clurman, David L., *The Business Condominium, A New Form Of Business Property Ownership,* John Wiley and Sons, New York.

Clurman, David L. and Hebard, Edna L., *Condominiums and Cooperatives,* John Wiley & Sons, Inc., New York, N. Y., 1970.

368

Colean, Miles L., *Mortgage Companies and Their Place in the Financial Structure, Commission on Money and Credit,* Prentice-Hall, Inc., Englewood Cliffs, New Jersey, 1962.

Committee on Banking and Currency, House of Representatives, *Basic Laws and Authorities on Housing and Urban Development,* Revised through January 31, 1970, U.S. Government Printing Office, Washington, D.C., 1970.

Conway, Lawrence V., *Mortgage Lending,* American Savings and Loan Institute Press, Chicago, Ill., 1960.

Cooperatives and Condominiums, Real Estate Law and Practice Transcript Series Number 4, Practicing Law Institute, New York, N. Y., 1969.

Delluszar, William I., *Mortgage Servicing,* Fourth Printing, Mortgage Bankers Association of America, 1964.

Farquhar, Norman J., *FHA Financing for Rental Housing, Section 236 a Hypothetical Case,* National Association of Home Builders, Washington, D. C., 1969.

Farquhar, Norman J. and Grossman, Robert W., *New Money How to Find It, Securing Pension Fund Investment in Mortgages,* National Association of Home Builders, Washington, D.C., 1969.

Farquhar, Norman J. and Preston, Paul F., *The New Mortgage Market,* National Association of Home Builders, Washington, D.C., April 1971.

Federal Aids to Financing, a loose leaf service, Prentice-Hall, Inc., Englewood Cliffs, N. J.

Federal Control of Banking, a loose leaf service, Prentice-Hall, Inc., Englewood Cliffs, N.J.

FHLMC Seller's Guide, Federal Home Loan Mortgage Corporation, Washington, D.C.

FNMA *Selling Agreement (Supplement),* Federal National Mortgage Association, Washington, D. C.

Glassner, Herman M. and Lore, Kurt W., *Real Estate Financing,* Practicing Law Institute, New York, N. Y., 1968.

Glenn, Garrard, *Mortgages (Deeds of Trust, and other Securities Devices as to Land)* Volumes I, II and III, The Michie Company, Charlottesville, Va., and Baker, Voorhis & Co., Inc., New York, N. Y., 1943.

Government National Mortgage Association Seller's Guide, Government National Mortgage Association, Washington, D. C.

Greenough, William C. and King, Francis P., *Pension Plans and Public Policy,* Columbia University Press, N.Y. 1976

A Guide To Fannie Mae, Federal National Mortgage Association, Washington, D. C., 1974.

Guide to Federal Law & Moderate-Income Housing and Community Development Programs, Second Edition, The National Urban Coalition, Washington, D. C., 1970.

Handbook of Member Trusts, National Association of Real Estate Investment Funds, 1973.

Housing Affairs Letter, published weekly by Housing Affairs, Washington, D. C.

HUD Challenge, published monthly by the U.S. Department of Housing and Urban Development, Washington, D. C.

Klaman, Saul B. *The Postwar Residential Mortgage Market,* Princeton University Press,

Princeton, N. J., 1961.

Kratovil, Robert, *Real Estate Law,* Prentice-Hall, Inc., Englewood Cliffs, N. J., 1964.

Life Insurance Association of America, *Life Insurance Companies as Financial Institutions,* prepared for The Commission on Money and Credit, Prentice-Hall, Inc. Englewood Cliffs, N. J., 1962.

Life Insurance Fact Book, published annually by the Institute of Life Insurance, New York, N. Y.

Maisel, Sherman J., *Financing Real Estate,* McGraw Hill Book Co., New York, N. Y., 1966.

McMichael, Stanley L. and O'Keefe, Paul T., *Leases, Percentage, Short and Long Term,* Fifth Edition, Prentice-Hall, Inc., Englewood Cliffs, N. J., 1959.

McMichael, Stanley L. and O'Keefe, Paul T., *How to Finance Real Estate,* Prentice-Hall, Inc., Englewood Cliffs, N. J., 1963.

The Mortgage and Real Estate Executives Report, published twice monthly by Warren, Gorham, and Lamont, Inc., Boston, Mass.

Mortgage Banker, published monthly by the Mortgage Bankers Association of America, Washington, D. C.

Mortgage Banking 1969, Trends, Financial Statements and Operating Ratios, Research Committee Trends Report No. 8, Mortgage Bankers Association, Washington, D. C.

Mutual Savings Banks, an excerpt from Comparative Regulations of Financial Institutions, issued by Subcommittee on Domestic Finance Committee on Banking and Currency, House of Representatives 88th Congress, November 22, 1963.

Mutual Savings Banking, published monthly by the National Association of Mutual Savings Banks, New York, N. Y.

National Fact Book of Mutual Savings Banking, National Association of Mutual Savings Banks, New York, N. Y., 1970.

The National League Journal of Insurance Savings Associations, published monthly by the National league of Insured Savings Associations, Washington, D. C.

Pearson, Karl G., *Real Estate; Principles and Practices,* Grid, Inc., Columbus, Ohio 1973.

Pease, Robert H. and Kerwood, Lewis O., *Mortgage Banking,* McGraw Hill Book Co., New York, N. Y., 1965.

Private Capital and Low-Income Housing, A case study of private investment in federally assisted Limited Dividend Housing under Sections 235 and 236, Development Forum 6, The National Urban Coalition, Washington, D. C.

Profitable Opportunities in Low and Middle Income Housing, Real Estate Law and Practice Course Handbook Series Number 30, Practicing Law Institute, New York, N. Y., 1970.
Real Estate Review, published quarterly by Warren, Gorham & Lamont, Inc., Boston, Mass.

Real Property, Probate and Trust Journal, published quarterly by the Section of Real Property, Probate and Trust Law, American Bar Association, Chicago, Ill.

Robinson, Roland I. (editor) *Financial Institutions,* Richard D. Irwin, Inc., Homewood, Ill., 1960.

Rohan, Patrick J. and Reskin, Melvin A., *Condominium Law and Practice,* Matthew Bender,

New York, N. Y., 1968.

Savings and Loan Fact Book, Published annually by the United States Savings and Loan League, Washington, D. C.

Sellers Guide, Conventional Home Loans, Federal Home Loan Mortgage Corporation, Washington, D. C.

Sellers Guide, FHA/VA, Federal Home Loan Mortgage Corporation, Washington, D. C.

Sherman, Malcolm C., *Mortgage And Real Estate Investment Guide,* updated semi-annually, Marshfield, Mass.

Tiffany, Herbert Thorndike, *The Law of Real Property,* Volumes 1-6, Callaghan & Co., Chicago, Ill., 1939.

Title News, published monthly by the American Title Association, Detroit, Mich.

Turnkey III, a case study of the Pilot Program of Home Ownership under Public Housing in North Gulfport, Mississippi, Nonprofit Housing Center, Urban American, Inc., Washington, D. C.

United States Code Annotated, Title 42, The Public Health and Welfare, West Publishing Co., St. Paul, Minn.

U. S. Congress-House, *Comparative Regulation Of Financial Institutions,* Banking and Currency, Subcommittee on Domestic Finance, November, 1973.

U. S. Department of Housing & Urban Development, *Government National Mortgage Association's Mortgage-Backed Securities Guide,* handbook GNMA 5500.1A, Washington, D. C. October 1970.

U. S. Department of Housing and Urban Development, *Homeownership for Lower Income Families (Section 235),* HUD Handbook FHA 4441.1, Washington, D. C., October 1968.

U. S. Department of Housing and Urban Development, *Low-Rent Housing Homeownership Programs Handbook,* HUD Handbook RHA 7495.1, Washington, D. C., January 1970.

U. S. Department of Housing and Urban Development, *Low-Rent Housing Turnkey Handbook,* HUD Handbook RHA 7420.1, Washington, D. C., June 1969.

U. S. Department of Housing and Urban Development, *Operation Breakthrough-Questions and Answers,* Washington, D. C., March 1971.

U. S. Department of Housing and Urban Development, *Rental Housing for Lower Income Families* (Section 236), HUD Handbook FHA 4442.1, Washington, D. C., October 1968.

Urban Land, published monthly by the Urban Land Institute, Washington, D. C.

Von Furstenburg, George, *Economics of Mortgages With Variable Interest Rates,* Federal Home Loan Mortgage Corporation, Washington, D. C. 1973.

Welfling, Weldon, *Mutual Savings Banks,* The Press of Case Western Reserve University, Cleveland, Ohio, 1968.

TABLE OF CHARTS

INDEX